fourth edition

Work Psychology

Understanding Human Behaviour in the Workplace

John Arnold

with Joanne Silvester,
Fiona Patterson, Ivan Robertson,
Cary Cooper & Bernard Burnes

FT Prentice Hall
FINANCIAL TIMES

An imprint of **Pearson Education**
Harlow, England • London • New York • Boston • San Francisco • Toronto • Sydney • Singapore • Hong Kong
Tokyo • Seoul • Taipei • New Delhi • Cape Town • Madrid • Mexico City • Amsterdam • Munich • Paris • Milan

Pearson Education Limited
Edinburgh Gate
Harlow
Essex CM20 2JE
England

and Associated Companies throughout the world

Visit us on the World Wide Web at:
www.pearsoned.co.uk

First published 1991
Second edition 1995
Third edition 1998
Fourth edition 2005

© Financial Times Professional Limited 1998
© Pearson Education Limited 1991, 1995, 2005

ISBN 0 273 65544 2

British Library Cataloguing-in-Publication Data
A catalogue record for this book is available from the British Library

Library of Congress Cataloging-in-Publication Data
Work psychology : understanding human behaviour in the workplace
   / John Arnold . . . [et al.].–4th ed.
        p. cm.
     Rev. ed. of: Work psychology / John Arnold. 3rd ed. 1998.
     Includes bibliographical references and index.
     ISBN 0–273–65544–2 (pbk.)
     1. Psychology, Industrial. 2. Work–Psychological aspects. I.
        Arnold, John, 1958- II.
   Arnold, John, 1958- Work psychology.

HF5548.8.A78 2004
158.7–dc22

                                                      2004046992

10 9 8 7 6 5 4 3 2 1
10 09 08 07 06 05

Typeset in 9.5/12pt Stone Serif by 3
Printed and bound by Mateu Cromo, Spain

*The publisher's policy is to use paper manufactured from sustainable
forests.*

CONTENTS

1 Work psychology: an initial orientation 2

Introduction • Basic psychology and work psychology • Five traditions in psychology • The origins of work psychology • Work psychology today • The changing world of work • Work psychology and changes in workplace technology • Work psychology and workplace diversity • Work psychology and specific groups in the workplace • Summary • *Test your learning* • *Suggested further reading*

2 Theory, research and practice in work psychology 50

Introduction • The nature of theory in work psychology • Theory and practice in work psychology • Research methods in work psychology • Research designs • Key principles in hypothesis testing using quantitative data • Some common statistical tests • Other phenomena in statistical testing • Analysing qualitative data • Summary • *Test your learning* • *Suggested further reading* • *Appendix: psychological associations in various countries*

Companion Website resources
Visit the Companion Website at **www.booksites.net/arnold_workpsych**

For students
Multiple choice questions to help test your learning
Links to relevant sites on the web
Online glossary to explain key terms

For lecturers
Complete, downloadable Instructor's Manual
PowerPoint slides of figures from the book to help with lecture preparation

Also: This website has a Syllabus and Profile Manager, online help, search functions, and email results functions.

LIST OF TABLES

LIST OF FIGURES

LIST OF CASE STUDIES

LIST OF EXERCISES

PREFACE

Work psychology is about people's behaviour, thoughts and emotions related to their work. It can be used to improve our understanding and management of people (including ourselves) at work. By work, we mean what people do to earn a living. However, much of the content of this book can also be applied to study, voluntary work and even leisure activities.

All too often, work organisations have sophisticated systems for assessing the costs and benefits of everything except their management of people. It is often said by senior managers that 'our greatest asset is our people', but sometimes the people do not feel that they are being treated as if they were valuable assets. People are complicated, and their views of themselves and their worlds differ. They do not necessarily do what others would like them to do. One reaction to all this is for managers to focus on things that don't talk back, such as profit and loss accounts or organisational strategy. Another is to adopt a highly controlling 'do as I say' approach to dealing with people at work. Either way, the thinking behind how people in the workplace function, and how they might be managed, tends to be rather careless or simplistic. Work psychologists seek to counter that tendency by carefully studying people's behaviour, thoughts and feelings regarding work. As well as developing knowledge and understanding for its own sake, this also leads to insights about motivation, leadership, training and development, selection, and many other people-related aspects of management. Work psychologists are also concerned about the ethical use of psychological theories and techniques, and their impact on the well-being and effectiveness of individuals, groups and organisations.

This book is designed to appeal to readers in many different countries, especially in Europe and Australasia. Judging by the feedback and sales figures for previous editions, we seem to have generally been successful in appealing to a range of people in a range of places. We have tried to make the book suitable both for people encountering the subject for the first time and for those who already have some familiarity with it. Specifically, and in no particular order, we intend that this book should be useful for:

- Undergraduate students in psychology, taking one or more modules with names such as work psychology, work and organisational psychology, organisational psychology, occupational psychology, and industrial-organisational psychology.

- Undergraduate students in business and management taking one or more modules that might have titles such as organisational behaviour, managing people or human resource management.

- Postgraduate (MSc, MBA, MA) and post-experience students in psychology or business/management taking one or more modules with any or all of the titles listed above.

- Students taking professional qualifications, particularly (in the United Kingdom) those of the Chartered Institute of Personnel and Development (CIPD).

- Students on undergraduate or postgraduate courses in other vocational subjects such as engineering, whose curriculum includes some elements to do with managing people at work.

We aim to give clear and straightforward – but not simplistic – accounts of many key areas of contemporary work psychology. More specifically, we try to achieve several objectives in order to make this book as useful as possible to its readers.

First, we seek to blend theory and practice. Both are important. Without good theory, practice is blind. Without good practice, theory is not being properly used. We therefore describe key theories and evaluate them where appropriate. We also discuss how the concepts described can find practical application. We provide case studies and exercises (many more than in previous editions) to which material in the book can readily be applied. These can be used as classroom exercises, or as assignments for individual students. Some guidance and suggestions about how to use these are included on the website for this book (see page xx).

Second, we try to present material at a level the reader should find intellectually stimulating, but not too difficult. It is all too easy to use a slick, glossy presentation at the expense of good content. There is always the temptation to resort to over-simple 'recipes for success' that insult the reader's intelligence. On the other hand, it is equally easy to lose the reader in unnecessarily complex debates. We hope that we avoid both these fates.

Third, we try to help the reader to gain maximum benefit from the book by providing several more aids to learning. Each chapter begins with clearly stated learning outcomes, and concludes with some short self-test questions and longer suggested assignments that reflect these outcomes. At the end of each chapter we provide a small number of suggestions for further reading. Throughout the text we specify key learning points that express succinctly the main message of the preceding two or three pages of text. We include a number of diagrams as well as text, in recognition that pictures can often express complex ideas in an economical and memorable way. At the end of the book there is a comprehensive glossary explaining in a concise way the meaning of lots of key words and phrases. There is also a very long list of references, to enable interested readers to find more material if they wish – for more advanced study for example.

Fourth, we have chosen topics that we judge to be the most useful to potential readers of this book. Some usually appear in organisational behaviour texts, whereas others are generally found in books of a more specifically psychological orientation. We believe we have found a helpful balance between these two overlapping but different worlds, so that there should be plenty of relevant material both for people who want to be psychologists and those who do not. The topics we cover in chapters or parts of chapters include individual differences, employee selection, assessing work performance, attitudes at work, training and development, teamwork and inter-group relations (including negotiation), behaviour modification, work motivation, stress in work and unemployment, technological change, managing diversity, leadership, careers, organisational change, the nature of work psychology as a discipline and profession, and how to design, conduct and understand research studies in work psychology.

Fifth, we provide up-to-date coverage of our material. There are currently exciting advances in many areas of work psychology, and we try to reflect these. At the same time, where the old stuff is best, we include it. There is nothing to be gained by discussing recent work purely because it is recent.

Sixth, we attempt to use material from many different parts of the world, and to point out cross-national and cross-cultural differences where these seem particularly important. Much of the best research and practice in work psychology originates from North America, but it is possible to go too far and assume that nowhere else has contributed anything. No doubt we have our own blinkers, but we try to include perspectives from places other than North America, especially the United Kingdom and other European countries. Nevertheless, the United States and Canada provide much valuable material. We therefore also make use of research and theory originating in those countries.

Developments from the Third Edition

Readers familiar with the third edition of this text, published in 1998, may find it helpful if we describe the changes we have made. These are quite substantial, though more evident in some parts of the book than others. Readers familiar with previous editions will readily recognise this book as a direct descendant of the others, but will also notice quite a few differences. The scale of the changes from the third edition and the expanded team of authors are among the reasons (or excuses!) why this edition has taken longer to produce than we would have liked. We apologise for this, not least because we know that some readers have been waiting a long time, and might justifiably have been losing patience with us.

The changes from the third edition are substantial mostly because quite a lot has happened in work psychology over the last few years, and we want to reflect this in our writing. Some of the old structure and material was creaking a bit, and reviewers commissioned by the publisher (plus users' comments made direct to us) helped us to see where re-thinks were required.

This edition also sees two new authors, Jo Silvester and Fiona Patterson, while Ivan Robertson and Cary Cooper have taken more of a back seat this time. Bernard Burnes has again contributed a chapter on organisational change and culture. John Arnold remains responsible for the book as a whole though, so any errors, omissions, etc. are primarily his responsibility. Jo and Fiona have brought some new perspectives and deep knowledge in the areas of individual differences, selection, assessment and training, and I (John Arnold) am grateful to them for joining the team. We are proud of this fourth edition. But your opinion is the one that matters!

Feedback from readers of the third, second and first editions clearly indicated that they appreciated the clarity of style and the combination of theoretical and practical considerations. They also very much valued the substantial list of references, many quite recent. Naturally, we have tried to preserve these features in this fourth edition. The style remains the same and the reference lists have been revised and updated. We are grateful for the feedback we have received from readers of the earlier editions, and wherever possible we have reflected it in this edition. We have again increased the extent to which cross-cultural issues are discussed, in recognition that, to a large extent, there is now a global economy.

So, apart from routine updating, adjustment and internationalising of material, what specifically is new about this fourth edition?

■ There are many more exercises and case studies (78, compared with 36 last time). After the first two, introductory, chapters, each chapter has an opening case study to illustrate some of the areas the chapter will cover, and a closing one that gives students a chance to use what they have learned in a practical way. Each of the chapters 3 to 15 also has several additional exercises, some of which are also based on case study material. Many of the case studies and exercises use real recent events in many different countries.

■ There is now a website associated with this book at http://www.booksites.net/arnold_workpsych. It is mainly for teaching staff, and contains some notes of guidance about the exercises, some multiple choice questions (and answers!) associated with each chapter, and some PowerPoint slides also associated with each chapter.

■ Chapter 1 has a major section on how the world of work is changing in terms of technology and labour force, and the implications of this for work psychology. This includes discussion of managing diversity, and specific consideration of the labour market issues faced by women, ethnic minorities, and people with a disability.

■ Chapter 2 includes more discussion of qualitative and interpretivist research, and also the link between theory and practice.

■ In Chapter 3 there is more coverage of new aspects of individual differences, such as emotional intelligence and practical intelligence.

■ The material on individual differences and selection now has more common threads and continuity - for example, competencies figure throughout.

■ There is now a separate chapter on assessing people at work (Chapter 6), and this includes more than previous editions on performance appraisal, as well as the psychological processes inherent in all evaluation. The competencies theme is also reflected in this chapter.

■ The coverage of training and learning at work now has a more organisational focus, and is structured around the 'training cycle'.

■ Stress and stress management have been combined into one chapter (Chapter 11), and it includes more consideration both of critiques and applications of stress research.

■ Chapter 12, on groups and teams, now includes more critical analysis of the teamwork phenomenon and its incidence in European workplaces.

■ Chapter 14, on careers, now includes much more discussion of career success, as well as elaboration on some of the material in Chapter 1 concerning the changing world of work.

Some of the content of the third edition has been dropped, radically cut back or moved around. This is normally because we believe that the material is too out of date, or not sufficiently central to readers' concerns. The old Chapter 1 on organisational structure and design has gone. So has the statistical examples chunk of what was Chapter 4, though this will appear on the website associated with this book. We consistently got the feedback that although many people thought it was very worthy to include worked statistical examples in the book, few people actually used them! However, we have retained and updated the conceptual material on the logic of statistical testing.

The old Chapter 5, on minorities at work, has also been dropped. This might seem like a retrograde step but we believe the opposite. In truth the material in that chapter was quite limited and, as one reviewer put it, had the air of being written by men who had suddenly noticed with surprise that not everyone in the workplace was like them! More attention to diversity in the workplace, and the specific concerns of minority groups, is now evident throughout the book, and these topics receive fairly detailed specific coverage in the latter half of the new Chapter 1. Another chapter that has disappeared is the one on person perception. Clearly this is an important phenomenon in work psychology, but we felt that giving it its own chapter looked too much like a social psychology text, and it would be better to discuss person perception where it was most relevant to the workplace. Accordingly, some of that material now appears in adjusted form in the chapters on assessment (Chapter 6) and groups and teams (Chapter 12). Finally, the old Chapter 19, on job redesign and new technology, has also been dropped. The updated job design material is now part of the motivation chapter (Chapter 9). It always had close connections with motivation, and says it feels quite at home. The 'new technology' content was, by now, not so new. It has been re-written and appears in Chapter 1 as part of our analysis of how the world of work is changing.

Overall, then, the fourth edition has 15 chapters compared with the 20 of the third edition. However, the average length of chapter is greater, and we hope that the coverage is more integrated than before. That is certainly our intention. Lecturers using the book may want to recommend parts of certain chapters, rather than whole chapters, to support a particular lecture topic, so it is worth having a close look at the contents pages to check what is where.

As before, we welcome feedback and dialogue about this book. Please direct it to John Arnold, The Business School, Loughborough University, Ashby Road, Loughborough LE11 3TU, UK (j.m.arnold@lboro.ac.uk). Thank you for reading this preface, and please now carry on into the rest of the book!

Acknowledgements

We thank Jacqueline Senior and Karen Mclaren at Pearson Education for their immense patience in waiting for the manuscript, and for doing anything they could to help it along without putting the authors under pressure, even when we deserved it. Special thanks to Tracey Preston for great work in tidying up the chapters, compiling the glossary and references into one big list, and assembling the final complete manuscript. John Arnold would also like to thank his parents Ann and Rev, and his wife Helen, for their love, wisdom and support.

ACKNOW-
LEDGEMENTS

We are grateful to the following for permission to reproduce copyright material:

The Daily Mail for an extract from 'Will Fatties Fit in?' published in *The Daily Mail*, May 2003; Guardian Services Limited for extracts from the articles 'War of Nerves' by Kate Hilpern published in *The Guardian*, 28 July 2003 © Kate Hilpern, 'Students face personality tests for University places' by Gaby Hinsliff and Martin Bright published in *The Observer*, 2 March 2003 © The Observer and 'How do you test someone's intelligence?' by Alok Jha published in *The Guardian*, 30 October 2003 © The Guardian; HSE for an extract from 'Minister welcomes practical help to tackle stress at work' HSE press release, 30 October 2003 © Crown Copyright Health and Safety Executive; People Management for an extract from 'Playing the game' by Rosie Blau published in *People Management*, 30 May 2002; Telegraph Group Limited for an extract from 'Hostility to Euro growing says survey' published in *The Daily Telegraph*, 23 November 2003 © Telegraph Group Limited 2003; and Jonathan Watts for the article 'Lion King and the politics of pain' by Jonathan Watts published in *The Guardian*, 1 September 2001 © Jonathan Watts.

We are grateful to the Financial Times Limited for permission to reprint the following material:

Criteria: Streamlining the selection process, FT.com, © *Financial Times*, 7 March 2003; How Shell finds the brightest sparks, FT.com, © *Financial Times*, 29 December 2003; People parameters: Employee performance management, FT.com, © *Financial Times*, 7 May 2003; Survey – Mastering People Management: Rewards that work, © *Financial Times*, 5 November 2001; Inside Track: Land Rover frees its creative assets, © *Financial Times*, 27 October 2000; Classified Section: Stress among the paper clips, © *Financial Times*, 6 March 2003; Inside Track: Executive search: Corporate Leadership, © *Financial Times*, 21 September 2001; Inside Track: Life, work and other uncertainties: Career Management, © *Financial Times*, 30 April 2001; Inside Track: From dead-end job to bright career: Human Resources, © *Financial Times*, 3 September 2001; Companies & Finance International: Shake-up plan gives fillip to TPSA shares, © *Financial Times*, 19 November 2001; Inside Track: Take-off delayed by squabbles in the cockpit, © *Financial Times*, 16 November 2001.

Credits for figures and tables appear in situ.

Every effort has been made by the publisher to obtain permission from the appropriate source to reproduce material which appears in this book. In some instances we have been unable to trace the owners of copyright material, and we would appreciate any information that would enable us to do so.

GUIDED TOUR

The **full colour design** and **photographs** that open each chapter make for a more stimulating read. Have fun guessing why each image was selected to represent its chapter!

Chapter opening case studies set a real-life context to which the theory can be related.

Opening Case Study   **Stress Among the Paper Clips**

The unkind stereotype harboured by many UK private sector workers about their public sector colleagues is that they are a lazy bunch. The vision is of a working day spent unbending paper clips, until the office clock hits ten to five and it is time to go home.

That is not an environment where stress should be a problem. The private sector likes to believe it has something of a monopoly here, thanks to volatile stock markets, unpredictable sales patterns and big redundancy programmes triggered by restructurings.

A survey published late last year by the Chartered Institute of Personnel and Development, a body representing personnel managers, therefore made surprising reading. This showed that public sector employees felt significantly more stressed and undervalued than people who work for companies.

Researchers who polled 1000 workers for the CIPD found only 21 per cent of those employed in the private sector reported being 'very or extremely stressed'. In contrast, the figure was 28 per cent for central government employees, a category ranging from civil service chiefs working in Whitehall (central London) to staff at employment advice centres in towns and cities throughout the United Kingdom. It rose to 30 per cent for local government, a category that included teachers, taking another step up to 38 per cent for the National Health Service (NHS).

In the hard-bitten world of commerce, with its dictatorial bosses and boardroom coups, just 21 per cent of staff thought their organisations cared about their opinions. But the total fell to 16 per cent for the NHS and local government and slumped to 7 per cent for central government.

Similarly, only 12 per cent of central government respondents 'strongly agreed' that their organisation cared about their well-being. This rose to 18 per cent for the NHS and 20 per cent for local government, with the private sector just a whisker ahead, again with 21 per cent.

'The message for central government, which trails in every category, is stark,' says Mike Emmott, employment relations adviser at the CIPD. 'It is worse managed than every other sector and has a massive amount of work to do to catch up.' By now, you should not be surprised to learn that central government workers came bottom for job satisfaction too, with an average of 6.1 out of 10. Mr Emmott says this reflects 'ambiguity about what the job is because of the political element'.

Owen Tudor, a health and safety expert at the Trades Union Congress, believes stress has risen sharply in the public sector as a result of Labour's triumphant return to government in 1997. He says: 'It has become a much tougher place to work, because the current government wants to do so much more but until recently has not provided the extra resources needed.'

Key learning points emphasise the crucial building blocks of the subject whilst the **glossary** at the end of the book is useful for revision purposes.

motivated bias). A score based on the average of all items will almost certainly be more reliable than a score derived from a single item (see Fig. 6.3).

Key Learning Point

Multiple items will help to improve the reliability of rating scales.

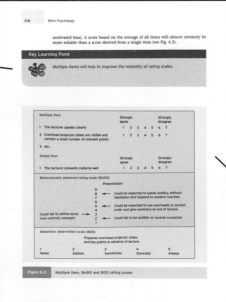

Figure 6.3   Multiple item, BARS and BOS rating scales

Where possible ideas are illustrated by **figures** and **tables** to appeal to all learning styles.

Regular **exercises** throughout the chapters enable students to apply their knowledge and own experience to what they have learned.

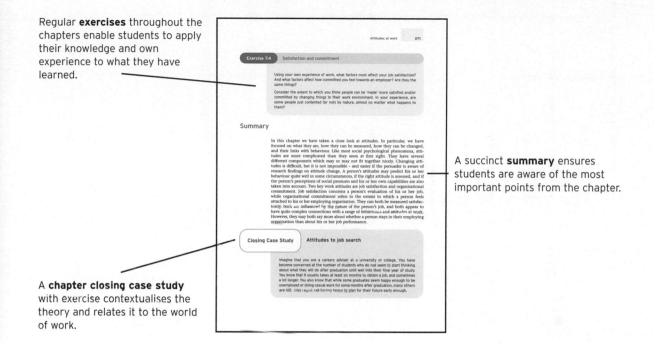

Attitudes at work   271

Exercise 7.4   Satisfaction and commitment

Using your own experience of work, what factors most affect your job satisfaction? And what factors affect how committed you feel towards an employer? Are they the same things?

Consider the extent to which you think people can be 'made' more satisfied and/or committed by changing things in their work environment. In your experience, are some people just contented (or not) by nature, almost no matter what happens to them?

Summary

In this chapter we have taken a close look at attitudes. In particular, we have focused on what they are, how they can be measured, how they can be changed, and their links with behaviour. Like most social psychological phenomena, attitudes are more complicated than they seem at first sight. They have several different components which may or may not fit together nicely. Changing attitudes is difficult, but it is not impossible – and easier if the persuader is aware of research findings on attitude change. A person's attitudes may predict his or her behaviour quite well in some circumstances, if the right attitude is assessed, and if the person's perceptions of social pressures and his or her own capabilities are also taken into account. Two key work attitudes are job satisfaction and organisational commitment. Job satisfaction concerns a person's evaluation of his or her job, while organisational commitment refers to the extent to which a person feels attached to his or her employing organisation. They can both be measured satisfactorily, both are influenced by the nature of the person's job, and both appear to have quite complex connections with a range of behaviours and attitudes at work. However, they may both say more about whether a person stays in their employing organisation than about his or her job performance.

A succinct **summary** ensures students are aware of the most important points from the chapter.

Closing Case Study   Attitudes to job search

Imagine that you are a careers adviser at a university or college. You have become concerned at the number of students who do not seem to start thinking about what they will do after graduation until well into their final year of study. You know that it usually takes at least six months to obtain a job, and sometimes a lot longer. You also know that while some graduates seem happy enough to be unemployed or doing casual work for some months after graduation, many others are not. They regret not having begun to plan for their future early enough.

A **chapter closing case study** with exercise contextualises the theory and relates it to the world of work.

Relevant websites and extensive and up-to-date **further reading** offer opportunities to take your studies further.

t-answer tions and **ested nments** test understanding llow you to track progress.

272   Work Psychology

You decide that you should try to change students' approach to planning for their future career. You decide to compose a handout of not more than 200 words which will be distributed to students during their penultimate year of study.

Suggested exercise

Using the information in this chapter, compose a handout of not more than 200 words designed to persuade students to start their career planning earlier. Let someone else read your handout. Ask them to tell you whether or not they find it persuasive, and why. Justify your wording of the handout to that person.

Test your learning

Short-answer questions

1 Define three aspects of an attitude.
2 Why are attitudes useful for a person?
3 Compare and contrast Likert and Thurstone attitude scaling.
4 List the features of the communicator of a persuasive message which affect the success of that message.
5 List the features of a persuasive message which affect the success of that message.
6 Draw a diagram to show the theory of planned behaviour, and define its key concepts.
7 Briefly describe three general phenomena that can influence job satisfaction.
8 Define organisational commitment and its component parts.

Suggested assignments

1 In what circumstances do attitudes determine behaviours at work?
2 Examine how much is known about what factors determine *either* job satisfaction or organisational commitment.
3 To what extent does the research evidence about organisational commitment suggest that managers in organisations should care about how committed their staff are?

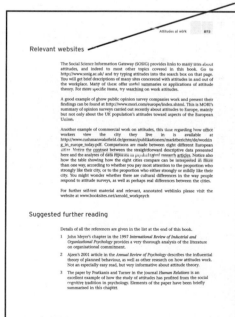

Attitudes at work   273

Relevant websites

The Social Science Information Gateway (SOSIG) provides links to many sites about attitudes, and indeed to most other topics covered in this book. Go to http://www.sosig.ac.uk/ and try typing attitudes into the search box on that page. You will get brief descriptions of many sites concerned with attitudes in and out of the workplace. Many of these offer useful summaries or applications of attitude theory. For more specific items, try searching on work attitudes.

A good example of ghow public opinion survey companies work and present their findings can be found at http://www.mori.com/europe/index.shtml. This is MORI's summary of opinion surveys carried out recently about attitudes to Europe, mainly but not only about the UK population's attitudes toward aspects of the European Union.

Another example of commercial work on attitudes, this time regarding how office workers view the city they live in is available at http://www.cushmanwakefield.de/german/publikationen/marktberichte/de/workin g_in_europe_today.pdf. Comparisons are made between eight different European cities. Notice the contrast between the straightforward descriptive data presented here and the analyses of data reported in psychological research articles. Notice also how the table showing how the eight cities compare can be interpreted in more than one way, according to whether you pay most attention to the proportion who strongly like their city, or to the proportion who either strongly or mildly like their city. You might wonder whether there are cultural differences in the way people respond to attitude surveys, as well as perhaps real differences between the cities.

For further self-test material and relevant, annotated weblinks please visit the website at www.booksites.net/arnold_workpsych

Suggested further reading

Details of all the references are given in the list at the end of this book.

1 John Meyer's chapter in the 1997 *International Review of Industrial and Organizational Psychology* provides a very thorough analysis of the literature on organisational commitment.

2 Ajzen's 2001 article in the *Annual Review of Psychology* describes the influential theory of planned behaviour, as well as other research on how attitudes work. Not an especially easy read, but very informative about attitude theory.

3 The paper by Pratkanis and Turner in the journal *Human Relations* is an excellent example of how the study of attitudes has profited from the social cognitive tradition in psychology. Elements of the paper have been briefly summarised in this chapter.

Visit the companion website at **www.booksites.net/arnold_workpsych** to find valuable teaching and learning material. See page viii for full contents.

CHAPTER 1

Work psychology: an initial orientation

LEARNING OUTCOMES

After studying this chapter, you should be able to:

1 describe five areas of basic psychology;

2 examine the relationship between basic psychology and work psychology;

3 describe the key features of each of the following traditions in psychology:

psychoanalytic

trait

behaviourist

phenomenological

social cognitive;

4 identify the main similarities and differences between the traditions;

5 specify how each tradition contributes to work psychology;

6 specify the topics covered by work psychologists;

7 describe the employers of, and roles adopted by, work psychologists;

8 specify ethical issues in work psychology;

9 describe the main sources of information about work psychology research and practice;

10 outline five important recent changes in the world of work;

11 identify how work psychologists are seeking to reflect those changes.

Introduction

In this chapter we aim to help the reader gain a broad understanding of the nature of work psychology and the context within which it operates before tackling more specific topics later in the book. We start with a brief description of the discipline of psychology as a whole. We discuss the links between what we call basic and applied psychology, with work psychology positioned as one branch of applied psychology. Then we provide a brief analysis of images of the person offered by five traditions within basic psychology. These are psychoanalytic, trait, phenomenological, behaviourist and social cognitive. Each of these traditions has influenced work psychology, even though in some respects they contradict each other. The nature of their contribution is briefly outlined and the portions of this book that examine those contributions in more detail are identified. We then briefly recount some history of work psychology before moving to coverage of work psychology today. Here we give an account of the different labels sometimes given to work psychology, the topics it covers, what work psychologists do, and ethical issues that arise in practice. We also alert readers to the best sources of good knowledge about work psychology (apart from this book of course!).

In the latter part of this chapter we examine how the world of work is changing, particularly in terms of the technology and the nature of the working population. We identify some key issues that are thrown up by these changes, and point out some of the ways in which people in work psychology and related disciplines have tried to (i) investigate the impact of those changes and (ii) reflect those changes in the way they go about their own work. We discuss some of the contributions of work psychology to understanding how new technology and working patterns affect individuals and organisations. We also take a close look at the role of work psychology in understanding the nature of diversity in the workforce, and in particular the fate of minority groups at work.

Basic psychology and work psychology

Psychology has been defined in various ways. Perhaps the simplest yet most informative definition is that provided long ago by Miller (1966): 'the science of mental life'. Mental life refers to three phenomena: behaviours, thoughts and emotions. Most psychologists these days would agree that psychology involves all three.

The notion that psychology is a science is perhaps rather more controversial. Science involves the systematic collection of data under controlled conditions, so that theory and practice can be based on verifiable evidence rather than on the psychologist's intuition. The aims are to describe, explain and predict behaviours, thoughts and emotions (*see* Chapter 2 for more on psychological theory). Not everyone agrees that it is appropriate to study behaviours, thoughts and emotions in a scientific manner. Some argue that human behaviour is too complex for that, and anyway people's behaviour changes in important ways when they are being observed or experimented upon (*see also* Chapter 2). Nevertheless, most psychologists do favour a scientific approach. As a result, most courses and training in psychology place considerable emphasis on practical classes and the statistical analysis of data – somewhat to the surprise of some students.

The discipline of psychology can be divided into several subdisciplines, each with its own distinctive focus. Collectively they can be termed *basic psychology*. There are several ways of splitting psychology. Perhaps the most helpful of these is as follows:

- *Physiological psychology* concerns the relationship between mind and body. For example, physiological psychologists might investigate the electrical activity in the brain associated with particular behaviours, thoughts and emotions, or they might be interested in the bodily changes associated with feeling stressed at work.

- *Cognitive psychology* focuses on our cognitive functioning; that is, our thought processes. This includes topics such as how well we remember information under various conditions, and how we weigh up information when making decisions.

- *Developmental psychology* concerns the ways in which people grow and change psychologically. This includes issues such as how and when children become able to understand particular concepts, and how they learn language. Also, developmental psychology is beginning to pay more attention to change and growth throughout adult life.

- *Social psychology* concerns how our behaviours, thoughts and emotions affect, and are affected by, other people. Topics include how groups of people make decisions, and the extent to which a person's attitudes towards particular groups of people influence his or her behaviour towards them.

- *Personality psychology* focuses on people's characteristic tendency to behave, think and feel in certain ways. It is concerned with issues such as how people differ from each other psychologically, and how those differences can be measured. It also increasingly recognises that situations as well as personality influence a person's behaviour, thoughts and emotions. Hence some attention is also paid to defining how *situations* differ from each other.

Work psychology is defined in terms of its context of application (*see* Fig. 1.1), and is not in itself one of the subdisciplines of psychology defined above. It is an area of applied psychology. Work psychologists use concepts, theories and techniques derived from all areas of basic psychology. The same is true of psychologists working in other applied contexts such as education and health. Clinical psychology involves the investigation and treatment of psychological difficulties and handicaps.

As shown in Fig. 1.1, areas of applied psychology use ideas and information from basic psychology. Conversely, they can also contribute ideas and information to the development of basic psychology. Sometimes theory from basic psychology can directly contribute to the solution of real-world problems, and conversely those problems can also stimulate developments in basic psychology. But more often, applied psychology rather than basic psychology offers theories and techniques directly applicable to practical problems in real-life situations. In fact, it

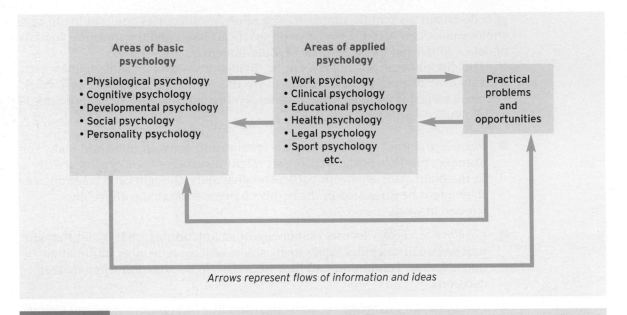

Arrows represent flows of information and ideas

| Figure 1.1 | The relationship between areas of psychology |

Key Learning Point

The five areas of basic psychology all contribute ideas and techniques to work psychology.

might be argued that some applied psychologists are more interested in solving practical problems than in theory and ideas from basic psychology. Thus there may be a danger that the areas of applied psychology will fail to reflect advances in basic psychology. It might also be the case that some more theoretically inclined psychologists fail to take sufficient account of work in applied psychology, or of current real-world issues. The development of psychology as a profession that can be put to good use depends upon the information flows shown in Fig. 1.1.

The relationship between basic and applied psychology has been the subject of several articles published over the last decade. For example, Schönpflug (1993) argued that applied psychology has not benefited much from basic psychology. Applied psychologists are interested in solving problems, while basic psychologists are driven by a love of knowledge for its own sake. It seems that work psychology has only a small foothold within the discipline of psychology as a whole, if psychology textbooks are anything to go by. Raley *et al.* (2003) analysed no less than 60 psychology textbooks. They found that only half of them contained *any* material that could be classified as work psychology, and even then it averaged only about 5 pages out of 600! This seems strange given the reasonable popularity of work psychology among undergraduate students.

Whatever the strength of these diverse and sometimes contradictory viewpoints, it can be said that work psychology, as one branch of applied psychology, does have its own theories and techniques. The following chapters will demonstrate this. Some draw upon basic psychology a lot, others less so.

It would be dishonest to pretend that psychology is a well-integrated discipline with generally accepted principles. Underlying it are several competing and quite different concepts of the person. These are most apparent in personality psychology – not surprisingly since personality psychology is the subdiscipline most concerned with the essence of human individuality. These competing conceptions of humanity will now be briefly examined. The interested reader can find much fuller coverage of each in texts such as Ewen (2003) and Schultz and Schultz (2001). Table 1.1 summarises some of the differences and similarities between the five traditions reviewed in the next section.

Key Learning Point

Psychology is a discipline that includes many different views of what a person is. Some of these views contradict each other.

| Table 1.1 | **Key characteristics of five theoretical traditions in psychology** |

	Behaviour	Emotion	Thinking/ reasoning	Self-actualisation	The un-conscious	Biologic-ally based needs/ drives	Personal change	Self-determi-nation
Psychoan-alytic (Freud)	O	✓	✗	✗	✓	✓	✗	✗
Trait	✓		✓	✗	✗	✓	✗	
Phenom-enological (Rogers)	O	✓	O	✓	O	O	✓	✓
Behav-iourist (Skinner)	✓	✗	✗	✗	✗	✗	✓	✗
Social cognitive	✓	O	✓	O	O	✗	O	✓

✓ = Emphasised   O = Acknowledged but not emphasised   ✗ = De-emphasised or considered unimportant

Five traditions in psychology

The psychoanalytic tradition

This approach, also sometimes known as *psychodynamic*, was developed by Sigmund Freud (1856–1939). Freud is probably the best-known psychologist who ever lived. He developed a completely new approach to human nature which has had a great influence on many areas of pure and applied social science, literature and the arts. Perhaps in reaction to the stilted Viennese society in which he spent much of his life, Freud proposed that our psychological functioning is governed by instinctive forces (especially sex and aggression), many of which exert their effect outside our consciousness. He developed his ideas in a series of famous published works (e.g. Freud, 1960).

Freud identified three facets of the psyche:

1   The *id*: the source of instinctual energy. Prominent among those instincts are sex and aggression. The id operates on the *pleasure principle*: it wants gratification and it wants it now. It has no inhibitions, and cannot distinguish between reality and fantasy.

2   The *ego*: this seeks to channel the id impulses so that they are expressed in socially acceptable ways at socially acceptable times. It operates on the *reality principle*. It can tolerate delay, and it can distinguish between reality and fantasy. But it cannot eliminate or block the id impulses, only steer them in certain directions.

3   The *superego*: the conscience – the source of morality. It develops during childhood and represents the internalised standards of the child's parents. It defines ideal standards and operates on the principle of *perfection*.

According to Freud, these parts of the psyche are in inevitable and perpetual conflict. Much of the conflict is unconscious. Indeed, Freud's concept of the psyche has often been likened to an iceberg, of which two-thirds is under water (unconscious) and one-third above water (conscious). When conflicts get out of hand we experience anxiety, though often we cannot say *why* we feel anxious.

Because anxiety is unpleasant, people try to avoid it. One way to do this is to distort reality and push unwelcome facts out of consciousness. Freud proposed a number of *defence mechanisms* that accomplish this. For example, *projection* occurs when we see in other people what we do not like in ourselves. It is easier to cope with righteous indignation about somebody else's faults than to come to terms with our own. *Denial* is when we pretend things are not as they really are.

Defence mechanisms consume energy, and impair realism. They therefore detract from a person's capacity to live a full life. When asked what a psychologically healthy person should be able to do, Freud replied 'love and work'. Even many people who have little time for his general approach regard this as a valid point.

For Freud, the key to understanding a person is to uncover unconscious conflicts. Most of these have their origins in childhood and are very difficult to change.

They are revealed most clearly when the person's guard is down – for example, in dreams or in apparently accidental slips of the tongue ('Freudian slips') where the person expresses what he or she *really* feels. Freud believed that virtually no behaviour is truly accidental, but that people can rarely account for it accurately. Some psychologists working from other perspectives in psychology would agree that people cannot report accurately the causes of their own behaviour (Nisbet and Wilson, 1977). If correct, this would make a mockery of current work psychology, much of which is based on self-reports (e.g. using questionnaires, *see* Chapter 2) which are taken more or less at face value.

Key Learning Point

The psychoanalytic tradition places a high emphasis on unconscious psychological conflicts which can reduce personal effectiveness at work.

Some psychologists who initially followed Freud subsequently broke away from him, though they remained within the psychoanalytic school of thought. Their biggest quarrels with Freud were that the drives he proposed were too few and too negative, and that the ego was more powerful than he gave it credit for. They tended to place greater emphasis than Freud on social behaviour, and believed that strivings for ideals reflect something more noble than rationalisation of instincts. Perhaps the best known of these post-Freudian psychoanalytic psychologists is Carl Jung. He extended the concept of the unconscious to include the *collective unconscious* as well as the personal unconscious. Jung saw the collective unconscious as an inherited foundation of personality. It contains images that have never been in consciousness such as God, the wise old person and the young hero. Jung (1933) also examined the ways in which different people relate to the world. He distinguished between *introversion* (a tendency to reflect on one's own experiences) and *extroversion* (a preference for social contact). He identified *sensing, intuition, feeling* and *thinking* as other ways of experiencing the world. Some of these concepts have been taken up in trait-based approaches to personality (*see* next section).

Within psychology as a whole, the psychoanalytic school of thought lost its earlier domination around the 1950s, and has never regained it. Critics complain that it is highly interpretative, incapable of being proved or disproved, and therefore unscientific. They argue that Freud was a product of his time (but aren't we all?), and was over-influenced by its hang-ups about sex. Many also claim that he does not account for women's psychological functioning nearly as well as men's.

Nevertheless, the psychoanalytic approach is far from dead. Freudian terms and concepts (e.g. defence mechanisms) have found their way into common parlance, and some psychologists have used psychoanalytic concepts in the world of work. Much work of this kind seeks to demonstrate that individual and collective behaviour in business is not driven by straightforward pursuit of profit but by the conflicts, defence mechanisms and personal concerns of the people involved. For example, Schneider and Dunbar (1992) analysed media coverage of hostile takeover bids, where one business makes an unwelcome attempt to take over another one. They identified several different themes in media accounts of these events (e.g. growth, control, dominance and synergy) and related these to developmental themes identified by psychoanalytic psychologists, including dependency, control, mastery and intimacy. Also, Vince (2002) applies psychoanalytic ideas to the ways in which major organisational change was understood and managed in a large company.

Key Learning Point

 The psychoanalytic tradition tries to explain why behaviour at work can often seem irrational, hostile or self-defeating.

The trait tradition

This approach is essentially concerned with measuring a person's psychological characteristics. These characteristics, which include intellectual functioning, are generally assumed to be quite stable. That is, a person's personality is unlikely to change much, especially during adulthood (McCrae and Costa, 1990). Some theorists have developed personality types, or 'pigeon-holes', in which any individual can be placed. One good example dates back to ancient Greek times when Hippocrates wrote of four types: phlegmatic (calm); choleric (quick-tempered); sanguine (cheerful, optimistic); and melancholic (sad, depressed).

These days psychologists more often think in terms of traits than types. A trait is an underlying dimension along which people differ one from another. Hence rather than putting people into a pigeon-hole, trait theorists place them on a continuum, or rather a number of continua. Trait psychologists such as Eysenck (1967) and Cattell (1965) did pioneering work by identifying specific traits through much careful experimental and statistical investigation. Some of this work is covered in more detail in Chapter 3. Favoured assessment devices of trait psychology are personality questionnaires, which consist of a number of questions about people's behaviour, thoughts and emotions. The better questionnaires are painstakingly developed to ensure that the questions are clear and responses to them are stable over short and medium time periods (*see also* Chapters 3 and 4). Of course, ideally one would collect information about a person's actual behaviour rather than *reports* of their behaviour. Indeed, Cattell among others did just this. However, normally that would be too time consuming. Personality questionnaires are the best alternative.

Most trait psychologists argue that the same traits are relevant to everyone, though for any individual some traits (usually those on which they have extreme scores) will be more evident than others in his or her behaviour. However, some trait psychologists have taken a rather more flexible approach. Allport (1937) long ago argued that for any given person, certain traits may be *cardinal* (that is, pervasive across all situations), *primary* (evident in many situations), or *secondary* (evident only in certain quite restricted situations). So if we wanted to predict a person's behaviour, it would be important to identify his or her cardinal traits. These traits would be different for different people.

In recent years there has been a growing consensus among trait theorists that there are five fundamental dimensions of personality – the so-called 'Big Five' or five factor model (FFM) (Digman, 1990; *see also* Chapter 3). Interestingly, there is perhaps more agreement on the *number* of traits than in *what* the traits are, but probably the following is about right:

1   extroversion, e.g. sociability, assertiveness;

2   emotionality, e.g. anxiety, insecurity;

3   agreeableness, e.g. conforming, helpful to others;

4   conscientiousness, e.g. persistent, organised;

5   openness to experience, e.g. curiosity, aesthetic appreciation.

Key Learning Point

Recent research by trait theorists suggests that there are five fundamental personality dimensions.

Most advocates of the trait approach argue that traits are at least partly genetically determined, which is one reason why they are stable. Research comparing the personalities of identical and non-identical twins tends to support this conclusion, though it is very difficult to separate the effects of environment from those of genes. About one-quarter of the variation in personality seems to be due to genetic factors (Bouchard and McGue, 1990). This of course means that three-quarters of the variation is due to other factors.

Trait theory carries the danger of circularity. Advocates of behaviourism (see section after next) such as Skinner have always been keen to point this out. How do we know somebody scores high on a particular personality trait? Because they behave in a certain way. Why does the person behave in that way? Because they score high on that personality trait. Behaviour is therefore taken as a sign of certain traits, which is all very well so long as the underlying traits not only exist but also determine behaviour. But there is also plenty of evidence that situations, as well as personality, influence behaviour (see Cervone and Mischel, 2002). In situations where social rules are strict and widely understood, personality will influence behaviour less than in unstructured situations that lack clearly defined codes of behaviour. For example, in selection interviews usually the candidate must answer questions fully, and avoid interrupting the interviewer. Thus the demands of this situation dictate the candidate's behaviour to a considerable extent. This makes it difficult for the interviewer to make inferences about the candidate's personality.

In spite of such caveats, the trait tradition has had a great influence in work psychology. This is particularly evident in selection (*see* Chapter 5) and vocational guidance (*see* Chapter 14), where the aim is to match individuals to work they will enjoy and in which they will work effectively. Salgado (2003), among others, has produced some evidence that people's scores on personality tests based on the FFM do indeed say something about their work performance.

Large sums of money are spent on the development and use of personality tests such as the 16PF (published by ASE, 1994; see also Cattell and Cattell, 1995) and

The trait tradition emphasises the importance of stable and measurable psychological differences between people which are frequently reflected in their work behaviour.

the Occupational Personality Questionnaires (SHL, 1984). The latter was developed by the British consultancy firm Saville and Holdsworth with the backing of many large organisations. Such ventures testify to the continuing prominence of the trait approach in work psychology.

The phenomenological tradition

Phenomenology concentrates on how people experience the world around them. It emphasises our capacity to construct our own meaning from our experiences (Spinelli, 1989). With roots in philosophy as well as psychology, phenomenologists assert that our experience of the world is made up of an interaction between its 'raw matter' (i.e. objects) and our mental faculties. Thus, for example, a piece of music exists in the sense that it consists of a series of sounds, but has meaning only when we place our own interpretation on it.

Phenomenologists argue that what appears to be objectively defined reality is in fact merely a widely agreed *interpretation* of an event. They also assert that many interpretations of events are highly individual and not widely agreed. Thus phenomenology places a high value on the integrity and sense-making of individuals. That general sentiment underlies many somewhat different perspectives that can loosely be called phenomenological. Several of these perspectives also portray the person as striving for personal growth or *self-actualisation*; that is, fulfilment of his or her potential. This optimistic variant of phenomenological theory is often called *humanism*.

A good example of humanism is provided by Carl Rogers (e.g. Rogers, 1970). He argued that if we are to fulfil our potential, we must be *open to our experience*. That is, we must recognise our true thoughts and feelings, even if they are unpalatable. Unfortunately we are often not sufficiently open to our experience. We may suppress experiences that are inconsistent with our self-concept, or that we feel are in some sense morally wrong. Rogers has argued that often we readily experience only those aspects of self that our parents approved of when we were children. Parents define *conditions of worth* – in effect, they signal to children that they will be valued and loved only if they are a certain sort of person.

For Rogers, the antidote to conditions of worth is *unconditional positive regard* (UPR). In order to become a fully functioning person, we need others to accept us as we are, 'warts and all'. This does not mean that anything goes. Rogers argues for a separation of person and behaviour, so that it is all right (indeed desirable) to say to somebody 'that was not a sensible thing to do', and if necessary punish him or her for it. But it is not all right to say 'you are not a sensible person', because that signals disapproval of the person, not just his or her behaviour. Only when people realise that their inherent worth will be accepted whatever their actions can they feel psychologically safe enough to become open to their experience. Further, since Rogers believes that people are fundamentally trustworthy, he has argued that they will not take advantage of UPR to get away with murder. Instead, UPR encourages more responsible behaviour.

Key Learning Point

The phenomenological tradition puts high emphasis on personal experience and the inherent potential of people to develop and act responsibly.

Humanism has been criticised for being naive. Certainly in the authors' experience some business/management students do not find it convincing. Social workers and others in the caring professions are, however, much more sympathetic, and so are psychology students. As far as work psychology is concerned, the basic point that people's *interpretations* of events are crucial has been heeded to some extent. Many questionnaire-based measures of people's experiences at work (for example, their supervision) have been developed (*see* Cook *et al.*, 1981). On the other hand, people's responses on such questionnaires are often taken as approximations of an objective reality rather than as a product of the individual's interpretative faculties, which rather contradicts the humanist position.

Phenomenological approaches find expression in some theories of work motivation and the design of jobs (*see* Chapter 9). The idea that people strive to express and develop themselves at work is quite a popular one, though by no means universally held. Trends in management towards empowerment of employees and total quality management (TQM) are based on the assumption that people can and will use their skills to help their organisation, not sabotage it. Phenomenology has also contributed to career development (Chapter 14). Many counsellors make extensive use of Rogers' ideas when working with clients on career decisions and other work-related issues. They work on the assumption that showing a client unconditional positive regard will allow him or her to bring true career interests and ambitions into consciousness. By and large, though, phenomenological approaches are not currently dominant in work psychology. Chapter 2 includes some further discussion of this.

The behaviourist tradition

In its more extreme forms, behaviourism makes no inferences whatever about what is going on inside the organism. It is concerned only with observable behaviour and the conditions (situations) that elicit particular behaviours. A person, and his or her personality, is a set of behaviours; nothing more and nothing less. There is no need to invoke invisible concepts such as traits or defence mechanisms when what we are really interested in – behaviour – can be observed directly. A leading advocate of this position was B. F. Skinner (1904–1990) (*see*, for example, Skinner, 1971). He and other learning theorists argued that our behaviour is environmentally controlled. He used the concept of *reinforcer* to refer to any favourable outcome of behaviour. Such an outcome reinforces that behaviour, i.e. makes it more likely to occur again in a similar situation. *Punishment* is where a behaviour is followed by an unpleasant outcome. A more detailed description of this and some other related concepts can be found in Chapter 8.

Behaviourists therefore argue that the behaviour a person performs (which is his or her personality) is behaviour that has been reinforced in the past. If a child is consistently reinforced for being polite, he or she will behave in a polite manner. Abnormal behaviour is the result of abnormal reinforcement. If a child's parents pay attention to him or her only when he or she misbehaves, the child may learn to misbehave because parental attention is a reinforcer. Behaviour problems can also rise from *conflicts*. One is an *approach–avoidance conflict*. This occurs when a particular behaviour is associated with both reinforcement and punishment. For example, a person may find that volunteering to take on extra tasks at work is reinforced by a pay rise, but also punished by the disapproval of workmates.

The behaviourist approach to personality implies that behaviour (and therefore personality) can be changed if reinforcement changes. The introduction of a reward for arriving at work on time is likely to lead to greater frequency of staff arriving on time. This change in behaviour would *not* mean that staff had changed their position on a personality trait of punctuality or conscientiousness. Behaviourists do not believe in traits. The change would simply be the result of reinforcement.

Of course, when we ask *why* a particular outcome reinforces a particular behaviour, it becomes difficult to avoid reference to a person's internal states. We might say a person liked or wanted that outcome, and then we would probably enter a debate about *why* they liked or wanted it. Some behavioural psychologists have acknowledged the necessity of taking internal states into account, and have suggested that biologically based drives or needs are the bases for reinforcement (Hull, 1952). Skinner's reliance solely on observable behaviour may perhaps have been viable for the rats and pigeons with which he performed many of his experiments. Most psychologists these days agree that it is insufficient for human beings, though there are also some claims that Skinner made more allowance for cognitive processes than he was given credit for (Malone and Cruchon, 2001).

One interesting and controversial implication of Skinner's version of behaviourism is that we do not plan for the future, even though we talk about plans. Our behaviour is governed by what has happened to us in the past, not what might happen in the future. Although all this might sound very negative and demeaning of people, Skinner did show a real concern for the future of humanity and the planet. He also believed there were ways of organising society that could protect both human welfare and the environment, as illustrated in his novel *Walden Two* (Skinner, 1948).

Key Learning Point

Behaviourism focuses on what people do, and how rewards and punishments influence that.

A major development of behaviourist theory is *social learning* (e.g. Bandura, 1977b). This differs from traditional learning theory in a number of ways, and is one basis of the social cognitive tradition described in the next section. Briefly, advocates of social learning theory stress our capacity to learn from the reinforcements and punishments experienced by other people as well as ourselves. Other people may *model* certain behaviours, and we notice the reinforcements that follow for them. They also point out that we do not necessarily *immediately* do something that will obtain reinforcement. We may choose to delay that behaviour if we would prefer to be reinforced at some other time. In short, social learning ideas portray people as much more self-controlled and thinking than traditional behaviourist theory.

Concepts from learning and social learning have been used quite a lot in work psychology. They appear quite frequently throughout this book. In training (*see* Chapter 10), rewards can be used to reinforce the desired behaviours when trainees perform them. Trainees can also learn appropriate behaviours if they are performed (modelled) for them by a competent performer. More generally, in *organisational behaviour modification*, rewards are used to reinforce behaviours such as arriving for work on time or taking appropriate safety precautions (*see* Chapter 8). Some organisations make extensive use of *mentoring* in their career development (*see* Chapter 14), based partly on the social learning idea that the experienced mentor will model desirable behaviours that the less experienced young employee will learn. Some motivation theories (Chapter 9) draw upon social learning theory. Social learning has in recent years developed further into what is now termed social cognition (*see* next section).

The social cognitive tradition

From around the mid-1970s, psychology has become increasingly influenced by a fusion of ideas chiefly from social psychology and cognitive psychology but also from behaviourism and to a lesser extent phenomenology. *Social cognition* focuses on how our thought processes are used to interpret social interaction and other social–psychological phenomena such as the self. There is also a recognition that our thought processes reflect the social world in which we live, as well as formal logic. As noted in the previous section, one major root of the social cognitive tradition is social learning. Advocates of social cognition see the person as motivated to understand both self and the social world in order to establish a sense of order and predictability. The existence of other people (whether or not they are actually physically present) affects the nature of thought processes.

Bandura (1986) among others has argued that although the person is partly a product of his or her environment (including reinforcement history), the person can also influence that environment. This is the principle of *reciprocal determinism*. It can apply to groups of people and whole societies as well as to individuals. For example, we can administer our own rewards and punishments rather than relying on the environment to do it. Thus I might decide that I will allow myself a cup of coffee when I have finished re-writing this section, and not before. The coffee becomes a self-administered reward for my work. In the process of observational learning, we notice the behaviour of other people and the reinforcement that follows, but we do not necessarily copy them even if the reinforcement is positive.

Two important traditions in work psychology concern how jobs can be fitted to people and how people can be fitted to jobs.

The FMJ and FJM traditions essentially concern the relationship between individuals and their work. The other root of work psychology can be loosely labelled *human relations* (HR). It is concerned with the complex interplay between individuals, groups, organisations and work. It therefore emphasises social factors at work much more than FMJ and FJM. The importance of human relations was highlighted in some famous research now known as the *Hawthorne studies*. These were conducted in the 1920s at a large factory of the Western Electric Company at Hawthorne, near Chicago, USA. The studies were reported most fully in Roethlisberger and Dickson (1939). Originally, they were designed to assess the effect of level of illumination on productivity. One group of workers (the experimental group) was subjected to changes in illumination, while another (the control group) was not. The productivity of both groups increased slowly during this investigation; only when illumination was at a small fraction of its original level did the productivity of the experimental group begin to decline. These strange results suggested that other factors apart from illumination were determining productivity.

This work was followed up with what became known as the *relay assembly test room study*. A small group of female assembly workers was taken from the large department, and stationed in a separate room so that working conditions could be controlled effectively. Over a period of more than a year, changes were made in the length of the working day and working week, the length and timing of rest pauses, and other aspects of the work context. Productivity increased after every change, and the gains were maintained even after all conditions returned to their original levels.

Why did these results occur? Clearly, factors other than those deliberately manipulated by the researchers were responsible. For example, the researchers had allowed the workers certain privileges at work, and had taken a close interest in the group. Hence some factor probably to do with feeling special, or guessing what the researchers were investigating, seemed to be influencing the workers' behaviour. The problem of people's behaviour being affected by the knowledge that they are being researched has come to be called the *Hawthorne effect*. The more general lessons here are: (i) it is difficult to experiment with people without altering some conditions other than those intended, and (ii) people's behaviour is substantially affected by *their interpretation* of what is happening around them (Adair, 1984).

These conclusions were extended by a study of a group of male workers who wired up equipment in the bank wiring room. A researcher sat in the corner and observed the group's activities. At first this generated considerable suspicion, but apparently after a time the men more or less forgot about the researcher's presence. Once this happened, certain phenomena became apparent. First, there were social *norms*; that is, shared ideas about how things should be. Most importantly, there was a norm about what constituted an appropriate level of production. This was high enough to keep management off the men's backs, but less than they were capable of. Workers who either consistently exceeded the productivity norm or fell short of it were subjected to social pressure to conform. Another norm concerned supervisors' behaviour. Supervisors were expected to be friendly and informal with the men: one who was more formal and officious was strongly disapproved of. Finally, there were two informal groups in the room, with some rivalry between them.

The bank wiring room showed clearly how social relationships between workers were important determinants of work behaviour. These relationships were often more influential than either official company policy or monetary rewards.

Key Learning Point

The human relations tradition in work psychology emphasises individuals' experiences and interpretations at work.

Highhouse (1999) has argued that one outcome of the Hawthorne studies was a huge increase in the use of personal counselling in American workplaces during the middle part of the twentieth century. This included Hawthorne itself, where in 1941 55 counsellors served 21 000 workers. The idea was that counsellors were available to every member of the workforce, and indeed would often circulate amongst them. They would help employees solve personal problems, which in turn was thought to lead to an increase in their productivity. However, Highhouse also notes that personal counselling had virtually disappeared from workplaces by the 1960s. He identified several reasons for this. Some of them reflect continuing and general problems for work psychologists almost half a century later:

■ It was difficult to demonstrate the contribution of counsellors to company profitability.

■ Senior managers thought that counsellors were on the side of the workers.

■ Trade union officials thought that counsellors were trying to win workers' loyalty to their employer.

■ Counsellors were loaded with administrative work.

■ Managers and supervisors were increasingly trained in human relations and could do (or thought they could do) any counselling required.

There has been much criticism of the experimental methods used by the Hawthorne researchers and considerable debate about the exact reasons for their findings. However, subsequent research by other social scientists confirmed and extended the general message that human relations matter. For example, Trist and Bamforth (1951), working in British coalmines, showed that if technology is introduced that disrupts existing social groups and relationships, then there are serious consequences for productivity, industrial relations and employee psychological well-being. Their work gave birth to the *socio-technical systems* approach to work design (*see also* Chapter 9).

Work psychology today

What is work psychology?

One source of confusion is that work psychology has a lot of different names. In the United Kingdom and the United States, the old-established term (still some-times used) is *industrial psychology*. The newer label in the United States is *industrial/organisational psychology* (or I/O psychology for short). In the United Kingdom, it is often called *occupational psychology*, but this term is uncommon in most other countries. Throughout Europe, increasing use is made of *the psychology of work and organisation* and *work and organisational psychology* to describe the area. Just to confuse things further, some specific parts of the field are given labels such as *vocational psychology*, *managerial psychology* and *personnel psychology*. Meanwhile, there are also some bigger areas of study to which psychology contributes greatly. These include *organisational behaviour* and *human resource management*.

Our advice for the confused reader is: don't panic! The differences between these labels do mean something to some people who work in the field, but should not unduly worry most of us. The main distinction mirrors that made in the earlier section between individually orientated versus group- or organisation-orientated topics. In the United Kingdom, the label 'occupational psychology' is most commonly applied to the first, and 'organisational psychology' to the second (Blackler, 1982). But many psychologists in the workplace regularly cross this rather artificial boundary. We use the term *work psychology* because of its simplicity, and because to us it encompasses both the individual and organisational levels of analysis.

A reading of this chapter so far should have given the reader a reasonable idea of what work psychology is. In order to be more specific, we now list eight areas in which work psychologists operate as teachers, researchers and consultants. This list is adapted from the British Psychological Society website (http://www.bps.org.uk).

1 *Personnel selection and assessment*: for all types of job by a variety of methods, including tests and interviews.

2 *Training*: identification of training needs and the design, delivery and evaluation of training.

3 *Performance appraisal and career development*: identification of key aspects of job performance; design of systems for accurate performance assessment and development; training in the use of appraisal and development interventions such as personal development plans.

4 *Organisational development and change*: analysis of systems and relationships, leadership and negotiation skills; analysis and change of organisational culture and/or climate.

5 *Human–machine interaction*: analysis and design of work equipment and environments to fit human physical and cognitive capabilities.

6   *Counselling and personal development*: techniques of listening and counselling regarding work and career-related issues; assessment and analysis of people's career interests and aspirations.

7   *Design of environments and work – health and safety*: the assessment of existing and preferred features of the environment such as light levels, workspace positioning, and sources of danger, risk or stress.

8   *Employee relations and motivation*: allocation and design of jobs that are as motivating and satisfying as possible; team-building; negotiating and bargaining; techniques for analysing and improving inter-group relations.

These are content areas of work psychology. It is also expected that qualified work psychologists will not only know about these areas, but also possess the skills in several of the areas to conduct problem diagnoses, research, consultancy and assessment, and deliver training.

Key Learning Point

Work psychology concerns all aspects of human behaviour, thoughts, feelings and experiences concerning work.

The qualifications and roles of work psychologists

How can one tell whether somebody who claims to be a work psychologist is in fact appropriately qualified? In the United Kingdom, the British Psychological Society (BPS) oversees the professional practice of psychologists. To become a Chartered Psychologist (C. Psychol.) a person must possess not only an approved degree in psychology (or the equivalent), but also several years of appropriate specialist postgraduate training and/or work experience. It is also possible to be a Chartered *Occupational* Psychologist, though some people who could become one prefer to stick with the generic C. Psychol. To be a Chartered Occupational Psychologist, a person must be eligible for membership of the Division of Occupational Psychology of the BPS. In turn, this requires demonstrable *practical expertise* and experience in several of the areas listed above – *knowledge* is not enough. Certain tests of ability and personality can be administered only by Chartered Psychologists or (in some cases) by people who have been awarded a Certificate of Competence in Occupational Testing after training from a Chartered Psychologist.

Chartered Psychologists and Chartered Occupational Psychologists in the United Kingdom are bound by BPS ethical guidelines and disciplinary procedures. Information on all of these matters, including lists of Chartered Psychologists, can be obtained from the BPS. The Directory of Chartered Psychologists is also available for consultation in many UK public libraries.

The ethical code of conduct produced by the BPS (British Psychological Society, 2000) covers a range of topics. They include the ways in which work psychologists are allowed to advertise their services, guidelines for the use of non-sexist language, and guidelines on conduct in professional practice and in psychological research. Regarding the last of these, psychologists are required to consider the following:

■ *Consent*: those who participate in the research should normally be made aware beforehand of all aspects of it that might reasonably be expected to influence their willingness to participate.

■ *Deception*: deception of those who participate in the research should be avoided wherever possible. If deception is necessary for the effective conduct of the research, it should not be the cause of significant distress when participants are debriefed afterwards.

■ *Debriefing*: after participation, the participants should be given any information and other support necessary to complete their understanding of the research, and to avoid any sense of unease their participation might have engendered.

■ *Withdrawal from the investigation*: the psychologist should tell participants of their right to withdraw from the research at any time.

■ *Confidentiality*: subject to the requirements of legislation, including (in the United Kingdom) the Data Protection Act, information obtained about a participant is confidential unless agreed otherwise in advance. This is in some ways especially important in work psychology where, for example, a senior member of an organisation may put pressure on the researcher to reveal what a junior member has said.

■ *Protection of participants*: the investigator must protect participants from physical and mental harm during the investigation. The risk of harm should normally be no greater than the participant's normal lifestyle.

Key Learning Point

Work psychologists are required to demonstrate their academic and practical competence, and also to adhere to ethical principles. This is partly to protect the rights and well-being of people who pay for their services and/or participate in their research.

Whatever country they live in, work psychologists can be teachers, researchers and consultants. Many are found in academic institutions, where they tend to engage in all three activities, especially of course the first two. Shimmin and Wallis (1994), among others, have noted that work psychologists in academia are now much more often employed in departments of business and management than in departments of psychology. This reflects both a tendency for work psychology to be used primarily to achieve management goals, and a mixing of psychology with other disciplines in a subject that has come to be called organisational behaviour (OB) (indeed, this book is recommended reading on many OB courses). Other work psychologists operate as independent consultants, advising organisations and individuals who seek their services on a fee-paying basis. There are also some specialist firms of psychologists and/or management consultants. Some psychologists are employed full-time by such firms. Others work for them on an occasional basis as independent associates. Still other psychologists are employed by larger organisations to give specialist advice, in effect acting as internal consultants. In the UK, the Civil Service, the armed forces, and the postal and telecommunications industries have been prominent in this regard. As noted earlier, however, large organisations now employ fewer psychologists than was once the case.

Another issue concerns the influence of work psychologists on organisations which purchase their services. Many tend to see themselves as technical experts (Blackler and Brown, 1986), able to advise on the detail of specific procedures – for example, psychometric tests, assertiveness training, ergonomics and so on. On the other hand, human resource managers are attempting to play an increasingly central and strategic role in their organisations. If work psychologists are to influence organisational functioning, they need to move away from a technical specialist role toward that of a general business consultant (Anderson and Prutton, 1993). They must understand the organisational impact of their techniques, be able to work on 'macro' issues such as organisational change and human resource planning, and be able to demonstrate the likely financial impact of their recommendations. They must be able to speak the language of business, and to communicate with a wide range of people. They need to be open to new ideas and techniques, including those originating outside psychology (Offerrmann and Gowing, 1990). They need to recognise the politics of doing work psychology – that is, the power relationships between individuals and organisations involved in it. Regarding research, this means being able to 'sell' a research proposal so that practical benefits for the potential sponsoring organisation are apparent (and exceed the costs), to be prepared to negotiate and renegotiate on how the research will be conducted, and to develop and maintain contacts within the organisation. All of this must be done without contravening the ethical guidelines described earlier. Some would, however, argue that ethical and practical issues go deeper than this. Who, exactly, is the psychologist working for? Consider, for example, the British Psychological Society's stance:

> Chartered Occupational Psychologists are concerned with the performance of people at work and in training, with developing an understanding of how organizations function and how individuals and groups behave at work. Their aim is to increase effectiveness, efficiency and satisfaction ... Occupational Psychologists are the best qualified group to advise on human resource strategies and solutions.

This is quite an ambitious description of the scope and expertise of work psychologists. It attempts to position them at a strategic level in organisations, and implicitly as working partners with senior managers. It may be significant that 'satisfaction' (a human welfare concept) is outnumbered by 'effectiveness' and 'efficiency' (concepts related to profitability), as well as being listed after them. Alternative, more radical aims such as increasing workers' collective power are not mentioned. This is *not* to argue that psychologists' intentions and effects are malign, only that their agendas are most heavily influenced by concerns that might be described as managerial.

Reading about work psychology

Where can one find out about advances in work psychology? Some can be found in books. General texts such as this give a necessarily brief account of major developments. Other specialist books are devoted to particular topics and sometimes even to particular theories. For example, Warr (1987) brought together much evidence from diverse sources to explain psychological well-being in employment and unemployment. He also developed an analogy with the impact of vitamins on *physical* health in order to improve our understanding of environmental influences on *mental* health.

Many new theoretical developments, and also tests of established theories, can be found in certain academic journals. Leading journals of work psychology include *Journal of Occupational and Organizational Psychology* (published in the UK), *Journal of Applied Psychology* (USA), *Journal of Organizational Behavior* (USA/UK), *Applied Psychology: An International Review* (The International Association of Applied Psychology), *Organizational Behavior and Human Decision Processes* (USA), *Personnel Psychology* (USA), *Human Relations* (UK/USA) and *Journal of Vocational Behavior* (USA). There are also other prestigious journals which include work psychology along with other disciplines applied to work behaviour. These include *Academy of Management Journal* (USA), *Academy of Management Review* (USA), *Administrative Science Quarterly* (USA), and *Journal of Management Studies* (UK). Some other journals concentrate more on the concerns of practitioners; that is, people who earn their living by supplying work psychology to organisations. These include *The Industrial–Organizational Psychologist* (USA) and *Selection and Development Review* (UK).

This is of course a long list of journals, and plenty more could be added to it. But there are subtle differences among journals in content and approach, which soon become evident to the observant reader. This makes information search easier if one has carefully defined the topic one wishes to explore. Also, computerised literature searches can be accomplished through most academic libraries using databases such as PsychInfo, Social Science Citation Index, and ABI-Inform. Many journals and academic or professional bodies have World Wide Web sites which are useful sources of information about current research and other activities. Electronic searches help to make the quest for knowledge much quicker and less tedious. Most of the journals listed above publish reports of carefully designed evaluations of theories or psychological techniques. They also publish review articles summarising the current position and perhaps proposing new directions.

Sometimes people feel that when they read about psychology (including work psychology) what they get is common sense dressed up with jargon. Indeed, one of the better jokes about psychologists is that they tell you what you already know, in words that you do not understand. Like most good jokes, it has a grain of truth – but only a grain. To see why, let us look a little more at the notion of common sense.

Common sense is sometimes expressed in proverbs such as 'look before you leap'. Yes, one says, that is common sense – after all, it would be stupid to proceed with something without checking first to see if it was wise. But the reader may already have called to mind another proverb: 'He who hesitates is lost'. Well, yes, that is common sense too. After all, in this life we must take our chances when they come, otherwise they will pass us by. This example illustrates an important characteristic of common sense: it can be contradictory. Interestingly, one research study found that students sometimes endorsed pairs of contradictory proverbs of this kind as both having high 'truth value' (Halvor Teigen, 1986). And so they should. Both *are* true – sometimes, and in some circumstances. Psychologists are in the business of working out when, and in what circumstances. Even so, psychologists' claims about common sense can sometimes undermine their credibility. Kluger and Tikochinsky (2001) suggest that, over the years, psychologists have often too readily claimed that their research findings on specific topics contradict common sense, only to find later that they have over-generalised from the results of their study.

Key Learning Point

Work psychology seeks to go beyond 'common-sense' views of work behaviour, thoughts and feelings.

Because most research, training and consultancy in organisations are paid for by senior managers, it is likely that the agenda will be driven by their perspectives and priorities. Obtaining the informed consent of people at lower levels of the organisation does not really get round that reality. An alternative is to work only on behalf of individuals or groups and communities with low power and resources. Decisions such as this have obvious links with the psychologist's own values and political stance, and equally obvious consequences for the level of financial rewards he or she enjoys. Most work psychologists take the view that usually organisations are sufficiently unitarist (that is, united in objectives and values) to permit all constituencies within them to gain from the psychologist's interventions, or at least not lose. Some might argue that this is a convenient assumption, as opposed to a carefully considered and justified position, and that ensuring that a person or group is not harmed by the work psychologist's activities is not the same as actively working for their interests.

Key Learning Point

Many work psychologists wish to influence top managers. But they may be seen as technicians, not strategists. Also, it is important for the work psychologist to consider his/her impact on all parties, not just senior managers.

The changing world of work

Workplace trends

It is probably true to say that nobody has ever lived at a time when they felt that not very much was happening or changing in their world. However, there is quite a lot of consensus that the last part of the twentieth century saw some quite radical changes in the nature of work, and that these are continuing in the early part of the twenty-first century (Sparrow, 2003). Many of these changes arise from a combination of technological advances and economic trends, which themselves go hand in hand to some extent. Improved communication and information technologies mean that, for example, it is now much easier than it used to be to work away from a physical location yet still keep in touch with what is going on. This means that some individuals can work at, or from, home, and employing organisations can save money by shutting down and selling off surplus office space. The same technologies make it easier for producers of goods and services to reach potential markets in other parts of the world, and for individual consumers to find suppliers of the goods and services they seek, even if those suppliers are far away. So, for example, some companies now provide customer services from call centres in countries far away from their main markets. This can bring some problems, such as when the call centre staff perhaps do not know enough about the culture and people of the country or countries they are dealing with, but nevertheless moves of this kind are happening and may well continue (Batt, 2000). For some time, many companies have been reducing their workforces, partly by outsourcing functions such as catering, premises security, and sometimes human resources, IT and other functions too (*see also* Chapter 14). In some companies (though by no means all), only staff who are core to the company's business have full-time employment contracts with the company. Others come and go, often employed short term via an agency or as independent contractors.

A longer-term trend is the relocation of manufacturing operations from developed countries to developing ones where wages are lower. This means the export of some jobs (predominantly, but not only, relatively low-skilled work) from rich countries to poorer ones. In order to find ways of competing, governments and companies in Northern and Western Europe, Japan, Australasia and North America are emphasising both cost-cutting and the need to stay ahead of the game in advanced skills and knowledge – areas in which less developed lands at present find it hard to compete, though with the increasing internationalisation of higher education, this may not always remain the case. Again in order to cut costs and improve performance, some Western governments have privatised some public services and industries. This means they are no longer funded by taxpayers, and they have to perform well enough to survive in their markets. These changes have led to what is sometimes referred to as the intensification of work in the developed countries (Delbridge *et al.*, 1992). Intensification refers to increasing work hours and pressure, the need for lifelong learning, the ability and willingness to change the type of work one does, perhaps several times in one career. Some people who during the middle-to-late part of the twentieth century were able to jog along in seemingly secure jobs without much need to change or work very hard, now find themselves in a far less comfortable position (*see also* Chapter 14, on careers).

In many developed countries there are also changes in the working population brought about by demographic patterns. For example, for some years there have been trends toward smaller families which means that now there are relatively small numbers of people starting work and in early career than there were in some earlier times (Central Statistical Office, 1996). Hence the average age of the working population is increasing. Life expectancy is also on the rise in most of the developed countries. This may necessitate increases in the retirement age and changes in pension provision in order to ensure that economies produce enough wealth to remain competitive while also sustaining social care. One of the authors of this book well remembers his parents telling him in the 1970s how lucky he was to be growing up in an era of plenty. They both took early retirement in the late 1980s, so he now has the dubious pleasure of telling them how lucky they are to be senior citizens who are able to enjoy a lengthy and financially comfortable retirement, because it probably will not be as good for him as it has been for them!

Other changes to working populations arise from changing views about the rights and roles of various groups within societies. Often these views are backed up with legislation to try to ensure that those rights are upheld. During nearly all of the twentieth century many countries saw sustained moves towards equality of provision and treatment for men and women. Many would argue that there is still a long way to go on that score, but it is equally clear that big changes have occurred, at least in terms of what people are doing with their lives. For example, in the United Kingdom in 1971, women constituted 37 per cent of the labour force, while a quarter of a century later this figure had risen to 45 per cent, and 75 per cent of women were economically active (Ellison, 1995). This change has several inter-related causes, including many women's wish to be employed, changing expectations about the roles of women in society, the introduction of legislation to promote equal opportunities, maternity leave, etc., a wish for higher material standards of living for households, and a realisation in many organisations that competitiveness depends on having the right people in the right jobs, whatever their gender (Cassell, 2000). Less optimistically, there is still a clear tendency for women to be segregated in certain kinds of work (e.g. caring, teaching, secretarial), and for their work to be paid less than work typically done by men (Labour Force Survey, 1998). This suggests that although progress has been made, there is still some way to go, even to conform to legislation, let alone to transform social attitudes. At the same time, there is also concern that the role of home-maker (whether a woman or a man) should be recognised as valuable, and definitely not an easy ride. There is perhaps a danger that admiration for people who can make a success of dual-career family life makes home-makers feel like second class citizens.

But gender is not the only basis for potential discrimination. Most developed countries have quite ethnically diverse populations. There are numerous statistics and specific incidents that show clearly how people with ethnic minority affiliations tend to get a raw deal in the labour market. Legislation to promote equality of opportunity has been introduced of course, and strong cases have been made for the value to organisations of having a diverse workforce (Kandola and Fullerton, 1994). These measures have arguably reduced bias against people with ethnic minority affiliations, but they have not eliminated it. The issues underlying this are complex, and include not just overt prejudice, but also more subtle phenomena of social perception of individuals and groups (*see also* Chapter 12).

Another potential basis for discrimination is disability, and again many countries now have legislation to protect and promote the rights of people with a disability to live a full life, including in employment where possible. Attitudes towards people with a disability have moved away somewhat from a so-called medical model of illness and lifelong child-like dependence (Oliver, 1990). This attitude was illustrated by the saying 'does he take sugar?' which was allegedly a frequent question asked by a well-meaning but insensitive tea-maker to an able-bodied person accompanying a person with a disability, even though that person was well able to answer for him- or herself. Indeed, it became the title of a long-running UK radio programme about issues to do with disability. In recent years there has been a shift towards recognising that people with a disability are, in many respects, just as able to do worthwhile work as anybody else, and sometimes more so. UK legislation now puts an onus on workplaces and educational institutions to take on and then cater properly for people with a disability, even though this may mean some additional cost and inconvenience in providing appropriate equipment and adjustments to physical layout. Again, though, much depends on how individuals (especially those who have power in a workplace) perceive people with a disability.

Key Learning Point

The world of work is changing rapidly because of technological advances, global competition, and societal demographic and cultural trends. Work psychology can examine the human consequences of these changes, and in many areas is already doing so.

Workplace trends and work psychology

Work psychology formed and rapidly developed as a discipline and profession before most of the economic and technological trends described above became apparent, and before some of the population and cultural changes described above had gained full momentum. Also, we have already noted in this chapter that work psychology tends to adopt a managerialist perspective – that is, it tends to ask whether the techniques being used to manage people at work, and/or their implementation, are effective in enhancing productivity and/or satisfaction. There is little investigation of the wider power relations and control mechanisms of the workplace, or asking whether these should change. Some argue that all this is readily apparent in the way that work psychologists carry out and report their research, even when that research concerns the changes in the workplace noted above (Legge, 2003). It is probably true that work psychology has some historical baggage arising from its development in workplaces which were:

- predominantly male;
- predominantly large organisations;
- concerned with manufacturing more than service provision;

- relatively ethnically homogeneous, and located in rich countries (especially the United States);

- populated by people with full-time permanent employment contracts;

- characterised by clear and stable structures and practices.

Nevertheless, there is no doubt that many work psychologists have been keen to investigate the consequences of some of the workplace changes described above. This is shown by the number of articles on (for example) advanced manufacturing technology, virtual working, work–life balance, agency workers, the psychological contract and women in management, among other topics. Much of this work explicitly investigates how the world is changing and the consequences of that. However, the changing nature of the workplace implies wide and deep changes of emphasis across most areas of work psychology. In Table 1.2 we note some of the world of work changes and suggest some consequences for what are, or should be, hot topics within work psychology. Note that some similar issues are addressed in other chapters in the context of specific topics (*see* especially Figure 14.1).

Work psychology and changes in workplace technology

One of the best-known examples of how technology has changed work is call centres. These have been defined by Holman (2003, p. 116), drawing on Health and Safety Executive (1999), as a work environment in which the main business is mediated by computer and telephone-based technologies that enable the efficient distribution of incoming calls (or allocation of outgoing calls) to available staff, and permit the use of display-screen information when customer–employee calls are in progress. Worries have been expressed that call centre work is alienating because it is designed to minimise costs and skill requirements (i.e. so-called Taylorism, *see* Chapter 9). Often the workers have to stick to a script and a call time limit, and their adherence to both is monitored closely. This does indeed make for stressful and unfulfilling work (Holman *et al.*, 2002). However, it is also clear that call centres are not necessarily designed in this way. It is possible to give workers more freedom about how they interact with customers, and occasionally even the order in which customers are dealt with. This freedom can make interactions more like relationships than encounters (Gutek, 1995). Although customer resistance to this can occur when they perceive that a sales pitch is masquerading as a relationship, on the whole people (both customers and call centre workers) seem to prefer being treated as individuals than in a standardised way. It also seems to be possible to use monitoring systems in ways that support the development of call centre workers, rather than as a disciplinary device to catch workers who deviate from the script and/or deal with calls too slowly (Aiello and Kolb, 1995).

Thus it seems that, in call centres, the technology does not have inevitable consequences. It does not necessarily deskill and dehumanise people who work there. This should not surprise us, because exactly the same conclusion was drawn by work psychologists investigating the impact of changes in manufacturing technology (especially computer-controlled machine tools) in the 1970s and 1980s

Table 1.2	World of work changes and their implications for work psychology

World of work changes	Implications for work psychology (i.e. topics of increasing importance)
Ageing working population	Learning, performance, satisfaction and engagement with work of older people
Increasing labour market participation and equality for historically disadvantaged groups, including ethnic minorities and people with a disability	Further development of fair selection procedures; the work experiences of members of disadvantaged groups; impact of diversity on workplaces and organisational performance; diversity policies; inter-group relations at work
Increasing workloads for people in work	Stress and pressure at work; burnout and mental health; balance between work and other aspects of life; effects of workload on thinking and behaviour
More people working remotely (e.g. at home) using information and communication technologies (ICT)	Selection of people suited to home working; supervision and leadership of people not physically present; impact of isolation on work performance and satisfaction; effective virtual communication and teamwork; recruitment and selection via the internet
Pressures on organisations both to cut costs and to use knowledge well	Impact of these competing pressures (including new technology) on the design of jobs; organisational learning and knowledge management; stress and pressure at work; innovation and creativity; organisational change
Downsized, delayered and outsourced organisations	Fewer and more ambiguous organisational career paths; individual coping with change and uncertainty; relations between 'core' and 'peripheral' workers; working life in small organisations; entrepreneurship
(Slow) increase in women's participation in traditionally male-dominated high-status work	The experience of being a woman in a man's world; gender stereotypes; women's career success, rewards and costs relative to men's; 'feminine' ways of working
Reduction in availability of manual work; growth of low-skill service sector jobs; growing divide between those with marketable skills and qualifications and those without	The psychological and societal impact of income and wealth differences; the experience and consequences of unemployment and underemployment
Increasing internationalisation of organisations and markets	Cross-cultural comparisons of workplaces; working abroad; interpersonal and intercultural influence; the appropriateness of selection, etc. procedures across cultures

(Wall *et al.*, 1987). How new technology affects jobs, well-being and individual and organisational performance depends not just on how clever the technology is, but also on the motives of those who introduce it, the processes by which it is introduced, and how well it fits with existing social systems in the workplace (Blackler and Brown, 1986; Burnes, 1989). Table 1.3 summarises three ways of introducing new technology identified by Blackler and Brown (1986). The muddle-through approach seems to be the most common, then and probably now as well. The task and technology approach is often thought of as rational and efficient, and in some circumstances may work well. However, although messy and unpredictable, the organisation and end-user approach is most likely to produce good results because it makes use of the knowledge of system operators and has the best chance of securing their commitment (because they have been consulted).

It is notable that more recent work on what is now termed advanced manufacturing technology (AMT) has largely reinforced the conclusions drawn one or two decades earlier (Chase and Karwowski, 2003). In particular, it is noted that new technology usually increases the importance of the operator rather than decreasing it. This is because the technology is expensive and does complex and costly things. If an operator is not properly trained in how to work and/or monitor the technology, or is not sufficiently vigilant, expensive errors or accidents are more likely to occur. A key factor is whether operators are trusted not only with monitoring the machinery, but also with doing some of the trouble-shooting and problem-solving rather than simply calling in an 'expert' to do it. The former pattern seems to foster a lot more job satisfaction and better performance than the latter. It also fits better with the socio-technical systems principle of dealing with variance as close to its source as possible (Cherns, 1976). Chase and Karwowski, (2003, p. 66) conclude:

> One of the ironies of AMT is that human and organizational factors become more, not less, important. . . . Of course, AMT may be implemented and used in such a way that it reduces the skill of the operators and reduces role breadth and job control. It would appear that not only will this increase the level of employee stress, but it will not permit the efficient use of AMT. Rather, the full benefits of AMT may only be realised when accompanied by appropriate job designs that include wide job roles and high levels of operator control.

Key Learning Point

Recent research on new technology at work reinforces earlier conclusions that the introduction of new technology does not inevitably de-skill jobs. However, the impact of new technology on organisational success is often less positive than anticipated because the technology is not well-suited to the psychological characteristics of individuals, nor to the patterns of social interaction in the workplace.

Some similar ideas about the importance of individual and social/cultural factors also emerge from the literature on knowledge management (KM), which has been defined by Bassi (1997) as 'the process of creating, capturing, and using knowledge to enhance organizational performance'. Given the emphasis in

| Table 1.3 | Three ways of introducing new technology into work organisations |

Phase	Muddle-through approach	Task and technology approach	Organisation and end-user approach
1 Initial awareness	Vague awareness that new technologies are available	Staff viewed as costly resource to be reduced if possible. Concern with operating costs, flexibility and operational control. Mainly top management involved	Staff viewed as costly resource which should be better utilised. Concern with operating costs, quality, flexibility, and organisational integration. Initial involvement from any part of organisation, then with top management
2 Feasibility analysis	Fascination with the technology. Short-term returns sought. Expectation that technology can be introduced into existing organisational systems	Mainly management project team but includes technical experts and is approved by top management. Search for most modern equipment. Priority given to technical and operational matters, which are reviewed in light of new technology. Precise objectives formulated	Diverse and representative project team, approved by top management. Search for ways to use and involve staff better. Priority given to system potential, rather than machine capability. General objectives formulated
3 System design	Reliance on technical experts. Technology seen as controlled by inherent laws. Technology to economise on staff	Tasks broken down into their constituent parts. Engineers and technical consultants seek technically neat final design. Consideration of ergonomic issues and staffing levels	Ways sought to enrich jobs and improve team working. Variety of experts and representatives seek designs which are compatible with individuals and groups. Consideration of ergonomic issues, staffing levels and likely social and psychological impact of systems
4 System implementation	Unexpected problems with system bugs, staff motivation, industrial relations. Unexpected need for staff training	Minor modifications only are expected. One-off skill training for operators. Union negotiates over conditions of employment. Operational responsibility passes to line management	Continuing staff and organisation development expected. Union negotiates over conditions of employment, staffing levels, training, grading, etc. Continuing review of system operation

Source: Adapted from Blackler and Brown (1986, pp. 298–9).

advanced economies on the importance of competitiveness through superior knowledge, it is not surprising that KM has attracted a lot of attention from managers. The basic idea of KM is to capture the local and tacit (i.e. unspoken, unformalised) knowledge held within an organisation, to express it in formal terms and to share it with other members of the organisation. Information technology is usually seen as a key to this endeavour, because it allows the storage, presentation and dissemination of a lot of information to a lot of people (Scarbrough, 2003). But of course it is not as simple as that. In spite of incentives or even requirements to do so, people in organisations are often reluctant to share their knowledge with all and sundry. They may see it as undermining their value to the organisation. It may run counter to organisational culture, custom and practice, which might emphasise the sharing of information in small groups of people who do similar tasks, or who have special friendships with each other (McKinlay, 2000). This is another reminder that psychological and social factors often over-ride the impact of an IT system. Some organisations, including Shell, have tried to get round this by encouraging what are called communities of practice. These are informal groups of people who share their learning and experience in order to learn from each other. This is likely to work well if it builds upon existing patterns of interaction between people, but less so if it forces together people who have not hitherto had much to do with each other. Of course, it might be very helpful if they did share information more, but in workplaces governed by short-term performance goals, talking to people who may or may not tell you something useful is not necessarily seen as a priority.

One of the consequences of ICTs is that more people are able to engage in telework, which usually means working at home or some other remote location, and communicating and conducting other work activities by means of electronic equipment. There are many potential benefits of teleworking for both individuals and employing organisations (Cascio, 2000). These include cost reduction and improved productivity for organisations, and better co-ordination between work and non-work lives, less commuting and greater autonomy for individuals. There may also be wider benefits, such as more community cohesion and less pollution. But there are also dangers, including less opportunity for supervision, social isolation, and possible difficulties in keeping work and non-work separate. Perhaps the acid test is whether a person experiences more or fewer interruptions at home than they would in a 'normal' workplace. Estimates vary, but it seems likely that in North America and Northern Europe (where take-up of telecommuting seems greatest), perhaps 5 per cent of the labour force spend all or a substantial part of their work time teleworking (e.g. European Commission, 1998).

Lamond *et al*. (2003) provide a review of the literature of teleworking. Among the points they make is that certain personality types may be better suited for teleworking than others. For example, conscientious individuals (i.e. those who are inclined to take a well-organised and diligent approach to their work) may be at an even bigger advantage when teleworking than when in a more traditional workplace. But Lamond *et al*. also repeatedly make the point that much depends on the exact nature of the job. Not all teleworking is the same. What might be termed 'telejobs' differ in terms of:

- location – at home or elsewhere; same place or nomadic;
- the amount and sophistication of IT usage required;

- how much knowledge is required to do the work;
- how much communication is required within the organisation;
- how much communication is required outside the organisation.

So, for example, it is sometimes suggested that teleworkers will be more difficult to socialise into organisational ways of doing things and of looking at the world. But if a lot of communication is required within the organisation – especially real-time communication such as phone, video-conferencing or even messaging – then probably socialisation of teleworkers will be less of a problem, because there are plenty of opportunities for the newcomer to learn how the old hands see things. Daniels (2000) has used Warr's (1987) 'vitamin model' of what makes a good job (*see also* Chapter 9) and concluded that one desirable element, opportunity to participate in decision-making, is likely to be in shorter supply for teleworkers than others. Another one, variety, may also be reduced, though perhaps less so for nomadic teleworkers than other types of teleworker. Tasks with low knowledge requirements may offer less autonomy and control for teleworkers than for others because of the opportunities for electronic surveillance.

Key Learning Point

Only a minority of people engage in teleworking, and only a minority of companies have made a major move to e-business. The consequences of these changes, when made, are quite profound and complicated. Again, much depends on how managers decide to let technology change the nature of jobs.

Another technology-driven influence on the nature of work is the advent of e-business. Wright and Dyer (2001) distinguish between four aspects of e-business. First is e-commerce, which is links between businesses and customers, i.e. online marketing and selling. The customers can be individuals or other organisations. Second is the use of intranet to improve within-company integration and communication. The third aspect is supply-chain management, which involves relationships with suppliers and increasing speed of order delivery. Finally there is what they term 'integrated e-business', which is doing all of these. The more a company is into e-business, the more likely it is that some employees and contractors will have to work with sophisticated ICT, and the more likely they will get a chance to work at flexible times and locations. However, work by Clegg (2003) suggests that most companies have so far made only modest moves towards operating as e-businesses. Communication with potential customers via the Internet is quite well advanced, but in the United Kingdom at least, it seems that fewer are conducting transactions electronically, and the value of those transactions is still a small proportion of total business.

Work psychology and workplace diversity

Ever since major Civil Rights legislation was enacted in the United States, the United Kingdom and many other European countries in the 1960s and 1970s, considerable attention has been devoted in work psychology to fairness in selection and other organisational procedures, especially regarding women and ethnic minorities. Work psychologists are seen (or at least, see themselves!) as having a lot to offer in the systematic evaluation of techniques (such as selection interviews) and instruments (such as psychometric tests), including how to make them free from bias. Chapters 3, 4 and 5 have more on these topics. Managers in organisations were said to be motivated to implement equal opportunities by (i) support for the ethical principle of fairness (Kandola and Fullerton, 1994) and (ii) fear of prosecution (Werner and Bolino, 1997).

From around the late 1980s onwards, however, the thinking and language began to change somewhat. The term 'managing diversity' became popular, and it still is (Cassell, 2000). Managing diversity is said to include, but also go beyond, a narrow (though important) focus on making sure that no group is disadvantaged. It signals the enthusiastic acceptance of the value to organisations of workforces that are diverse in terms of gender, ethnicity, nationality, age and (dis)ability, and also sexual orientation, social class, personality and values (Jackson and Joshi, 2001). The motivation for this is still partly ethical and partly to avoid prosecution. But now it is also argued that diversity is good for business, and that it makes for good publicity for the organisation. The business case for managing diversity has been strengthened by persistent shortages of skilled labour, particularly in the United States, which mean that organisations cannot afford to neglect any subsection of the population in their search for competent staff. Furthermore, members of the labour forces in most developed countries are nowadays quite diverse – for example, compared with a quarter of a century ago there is a much more even split between men and women, and the proportion of people from ethnic minorities is considerably higher (International Labour Organisation, 1998). They also tend to be more open about their differing attributes. For example, it is now much more acceptable to be known as gay or lesbian than it would have been a quarter of a century ago. For many readers of this book, that period is more than a lifetime. But for us older lags, and for society in general, we can assure you it is not a very long time! This is a relatively quick and big change.

The business case for diversity is not based only on the need to recruit and retain the most talented people. It is also argued that a diverse labour force helps organisations to (i) devise marketing and sales campaigns that appeal to diverse markets; (ii) be flexible in responding to environmental change, and (iii) be creative and innovative because of the variety of perspectives offered by organisational members. The validity of this last argument has been tested by researchers of groups and teams at work (*see* Chapter 12 for much more on groups and teams). On the whole it seems that management teams with diverse membership do perform better than others, at least on tasks that require the generation and evaluation of ideas (Jackson and Joshi, 2001). However, this does depend quite a lot on the ways in which conflicts within the team arise and are handled. Incidentally, in some of this research, the definition of diversity includes variables such as departmental membership, educational qualifications and prior career experience as well as some of those mentioned earlier. This suggests that the aspects of difference between people that matter may well vary a lot between contexts (Jackson and Joshi, 2001). In one workplace (for example a hospital serving a highly multi-ethnic local population) it might be ethnicity, and in another (e.g. the research laboratory of a pharmaceutical company) it might be whether one's qualifications are in pharmacy, biochemistry or medicine.

Key Learning Point

Effective management of diversity requires attention to many kinds of difference between people, not just the obvious ones such as gender and ethnic origin.

Jackson and Joshi point out that a lot depends on historical context too. They give the example of the United States, where in the 1940s and 1950s black youngsters tended to value a white identity higher than a black one. But in the 1960s civil rights movements began to emphasise that being black was nothing to be ashamed of. The pop song 'Young, gifted and black' exemplifies this endeavour. It was first a hit in the 1960s and has been performed by many artists including Aretha Franklin and Elton John. The campaign was successful in changing the preferred identity of young black people, and not only in the United States. People of that generation are now in leading and established positions in their workplaces. Their identities are likely to influence their attitudes to managing diversity. This example also points to another aspect of diversity. It is not just a person's racial or national background that matters, but also how they see themselves – i.e. their ethnic identity.

Lau and Murnighan (1998) have pointed out that how differences are distributed also matters. For example, suppose a six-person team consists of three middle-aged white male senior managers without university degrees who have all been production managers, and three young black female women managers with PhDs who have all been marketing managers. In this case, the many differences all stack up together and find expression in the same people. Lau and Murnighan refer to this as a 'faultline'. If, for example, seniority had been mixed up a bit so that one of the men was a middle manager and one of the women was a senior manager, then perhaps the dynamics of the group would have changed significantly. Although the group would be equally diverse, the distribution of the differences would have been different, and the 'faultline' less deep and wide.

Most writers acknowledge that there are problems in making the business case for managing diversity. It is difficult to demonstrate a clear impact on profitability for example (Cassell, 2000). One study found a tendency for companies with conspicuous diversity initiatives to fare better than others on the stock market (Wright *et al.*, 1995), but Richard and Johnson (1999) have argued that in general the connection between diversity and organisational financial performance has not been proven. Cassell (2000) suggests that an emphasis on more local financial criteria such as cost savings through decreased staff turnover and decreased litigation may appeal to many managers, though in fact evidence suggests that on the whole turnover is (or at least, has been) higher in more diverse workplaces than less diverse ones (Jackson *et al.*, 1991).

It should be fairly apparent by now that work psychology has quite a lot to offer to theory and practice in managing diversity. Fair procedures and techniques for employee selection and performance in diverse teams have already been mentioned. More fundamentally, problems in managing diversity often stem from perceptions of dissimilarity between individuals and/or groups. On the whole, people tend to feel more attracted to people who are similar to themselves than to those who are dissimilar. They also tend to be more generous towards them, and happier to co-operate with them. These and other findings about interpersonal perception and inter-group relations are well-established ones within psychology. The identification of these tendencies, and the analysis of the circumstances in which they occur and their consequences for behaviour, have wide implications for many aspects of working life, including motivation (*see* Chapter 9), leadership (*see* Chapter 13), career development (*see* Chapter 14) and performance appraisal (*see* Chapter 6), as well as selection (Chapters 4 and 5).

Following on from this, work psychology should also offer the tools to evaluate the impact of attempts to manage diversity. Ellis and Sonnenfeld (1994) identified the following common forms of diversity management in organisations:

- Multicultural workshops designed to improve understanding and communication among members of different groups.

- Support groups, mentoring and networks for minority and/or disadvantaged groups.

- Advisory councils reporting to top management.

- Rewarding managers for their development of members of minority and/or disadvantaged groups.

- Fast-track developmental programmes and special training opportunities for minority and/or disadvantaged groups.

On the whole it looks as if interventions that aim solely to increase awareness of other groups and their perspectives do not make much difference (*see also* Chapter 12). Pettigrew (1998) suggests that contact between groups can improve relations, but only if the nature of the contact: (i) encourages *learning* about the other group as opposed to just co-existing; (ii) requires behaving differently towards the other group; (iii) creates positive emotions associated with the other group; and (iv) enables new insights about one's own group. This last point is interesting and important, because arguably empathy with members of other groups is possible only if one can appreciate that the world-views of group(s) to which one belongs are just one way of looking at things rather than the absolute truth. Situations that meet these four criteria can sometimes be engineered in workplaces, and sometimes they occur naturally. Probably their key features are that they require members of different groups to work co-operatively towards a common goal, that goal-achievement is a real possibility, and that nobody is allowed to opt out of the endeavour.

Of course, there are significant dangers in attempts to manage diversity. It is supposed to value all types of people equally and highly, but there can be a backlash from white males who may feel vilified for nothing they have personally done wrong. There is also some evidence that attempts to increase contact and understanding can sometimes backfire, and make stereotypes more entrenched (Nemetz and Christensen, 1996). Also, it is important not to equate being a minority group with being disadvantaged in all respects. For example, there is evidence that Asian Americans achieve more in education and earn more than European Americans, though on the other hand the average boost to earnings provided by education is less for Asian Americans that European Americans, which shows the complexity of the phenomena involved (Friedman and Krackhardt, 1997). Perhaps the biggest danger, though, is of treating individuals as if they were identikit members of one or more groups. Even if different groups (for example men and women) are different on average, this does not mean that all men are the same. Nor are they different from all women in the same way.

Work psychology and specific groups in the workplace

Much of the material in the previous sections applies to most or all groups of people within the workplace. So please bear in mind that this section should be read in conjunction with the material above about diversity in general. In this section we make some additional points about three specific elements of diversity: gender, ethnicity and disability. They have been selected because at present they are the aspects of diversity that most often feature in legislation, and they affect large numbers of people. There are of course other important elements of diversity. For example, differences in, and potential discrimination on the basis of, age, religion and sexual orientation are real concerns for many people and workplaces. Another aspect of diversity is nationality. This is associated with ethnicity of course, but not always the same. Hofstede (2001) and Trompenaars (1993), among others, have found systematic cultural differences between people from different countries. Cross-national differences crop up quite a lot in this book, most notably in Chapters 9 (motivation), 12 (groups and teams), 13 (leadership) and 14 (careers). For all three group differences discussed below, it is noticeable that:

- their position in the labour market (e.g. ability to get jobs, the types of jobs they get, how successful they are in their occupation) is improving somewhat;

- their position still does not match that of the majority group (in this case, white able-bodied males);

- this appears not to be entirely attributable to possibly legitimate factors such as differences in qualifications and experience;

- the disadvantage has not been entirely eradicated by legislation;

- it is probably due partly to subtle or not-so-subtle prejudice and/or discrimination;

- in some instances, people's sense of identity (i.e. how they see themselves) may matter as much as their objective group membership.

Chapter 14, on careers, explores some of the factors that affect the extent and nature of career success that people experience. It is highly relevant to this section, particularly regarding the career success experienced by women.

Key Learning Point

Women, ethnic minorities and people with a disability are all seeing moves towards better recognition in the labour market, but still do not enjoy equality, and legislation to protect them is not always fully effective.

Women

Women make up about 41 per cent of the European workforce, and across Europe in 1996, 38 per cent of working women were providing the only or main income for their household (Vinnicombe, 2000). Over 80 per cent of UK women are in some form of employment. However, women are still disproportionately found in low-prestige jobs, and at the lower end of the status hierarchy in higher-prestige jobs such as management and professions. In the United Kingdom, Vinnicombe (2000) reports that 33 per cent of people in management-type jobs are women, and this is steadily increasing. International comparisons are tricky here because of differences in the way terms such as 'manager' and 'professional' are defined. However, some comparison figures are Switzerland 28 per cent, Norway 32 per cent, Finland 25 per cent, the United States and Australia 43 per cent. Only about 4 per cent of UK management jobs at the highest (director) level are held by women, and although this figure is also increasing, it is still too low, from the points of view of both fairness and the effective deployment of national human resources. In the United States, about 10 per cent of top management jobs are held by women, and this appears to be slowly rising (Catalyst, 1996).

Women's earnings are lower than men's too, in spite of equal pay for equal work legislation. In the United Kingdom, average earnings for women are between 70 and 80 per cent of those for men, depending on occupation. The pay gaps are bigger than that in some other European countries, and smaller in yet others, but the gap is always present. They cannot be entirely explained away by women being in less skilled employment than men. Even if they could, it is necessary to ask why women (whose educational achievements are on average higher than men's) are in less highly skilled and/or highly paid employment than men. According to the UK government's Labour Force Survey 1998, the mean salary for UK male managers (mean age 43) was £37 325, while for women (mean age 37) it was £31 622.

There are some good arguments why women, on average, may have certain attributes that are valuable in twenty-first century workplaces (Fondas, 1997) to a greater extent than men. Some of these are mentioned in Chapter 14. As a general statement, women's more communal as opposed to individualistic orientation should be well suited to teamwork, and to workplaces where relationships and social networks are said to be more important than rules and procedures. Women's apparent advantage in (and often more experience of) multi-tasking and flexibility should also prove an advantage over men, who are often thought to be more single-task focused and less able to switch between tasks at short notice. But while people may pay lip service to these attributes, it could be argued that while men are in most of the positions of power, they will not really be valued as highly as masculine single-minded, individual, aggressive task-focused achievement. Also, some aspects of the way people approach their work are influenced by their sense of identity, and there are plenty of men who see themselves in some quite stereotypically feminine ways, e.g. nurturing, relationship-orientated (Bem, 1981). So it might be a mistake to focus purely on a person's biological sex (i.e. their genes) or their gender (i.e. whether they live as a man or a woman). As an aside, sex and gender are usually consistent with each other, but in some cases not.

In any case, it is important not to become too obsessed with alleged psychological differences between men and women. As we note in Chapter 3, most differences in ability and personality are really quite small, or even non-existent. In Chapters 4–6 we discuss, among other things, ways of assessing people for selection and appraisal that avoid biases that may stem from assessors' beliefs about how men and women differ. In Chapter 13, on leadership, we comment briefly on how men and women leaders might be perceived as different, and the consequences of that.

One consistent finding from research is that when both a woman and her male partner are in employment, it is the woman who does most of the housework and (if relevant) childcare (Barnett and Shen, 1997), particularly the elements that are most time-pressured such as getting the children ready for school. This is one reason why, among UK managers, Nicholson and West (1988) found that 71 per cent of women were unmarried or married but childless, while only 18 per cent of men were in one of those two positions. One might think also that men and women experience different kinds of stress at work, and/or cope with it differently. One possible trend that seems plausible is that women might experience more interference of home life with work, but this depends on how much men and women think they should be working in the first place. In fact, although some studies have shown differences, others have failed to find them (Nelson and Burke, 2000). One of the more persistent findings, though still not universal, is that women cope with stress by expressing their feelings about it, and seeking social support, while men treat it as a problem to be solved, usually through individual effort (Ptacek *et al.*, 1994). Nelson and Burke (2000) suggest that a half-way position of problem-solving through discussion with supportive colleagues and friends might suit both men and women.

There are nevertheless some sources of stress that clearly are more relevant to women than to men. Women are more likely to experience sexual harassment than men, and according to some figures depressingly likely (Burke and McKeen, 1992). Women are more likely than men to suffer from anxiety and depression, and this is sometimes attributable to stresses at work. On the other hand, men are more likely to suffer from more life-threatening stress-related illnesses such as heart problems (see Chapter 11 for more on stress).

Much of the literature on supporting women at work concerns childcare. This reflects the reality that women do most of the childcare, even if they have a male partner. Cooper and Lewis (1993) provided a thorough analysis of the problems faced by dual-career couples and how they can be solved. Provision such as work-place crèches, career breaks, extended maternity (or paternity) leave, flexible work hours and family leave are among the initiatives taken by some employers. In the United Kingdom, during the 1990s the Opportunity 2000 programme involved a number of large employers in developing ways of improving the support for women at work, and Europe-wide, the same was true for the New Opportunities for Women (NOW) project. It remains the case, though, that there is still some poten-tial stigma, friction with colleagues, and loss of career prospects associated with taking advantage of such provision (Judiesch and Lyness, 1999; Bagilhole, 2002 – *see also* Chapter 14). These potential losses apply to men too.

More generally, it has been noted that countries with the most supportive gov-ernment and organisational policies for women in employment appear not to have a higher proportion of women in top jobs – if anything rather the reverse (Vinnicombe, 2000). Various explanations have been put forward for this. One is that employers are wary of employing women because of the high costs incurred if they take advantage of the support employers are obliged to offer. Another expla-nation, and it's a controversial one, is offered by Hakim (2002), who argues that a minority of women are primarily homemakers and another minority at the other extreme are primarily career-orientated. The majority are somewhere in between. The proportions of women in each group in developed countries (about 20–60–20) seems not to have changed over at least 20 years, according to Hakim. The middle group is highly responsive to policies regarding women and work, and will engage more or less in the labour market accordingly. But on the whole they do not aspire to top jobs, nor necessarily to full-time work – just some work. Hakim argues that women are not, on the whole, blocked from their preferences, but instead they exercise them and by and large feel much less discontented than some academics and other observers think they ought to.

Key Learning Point

Although it is clear that women are still paid less and have lower-status jobs than men, arguments rage about whether women are oppressed, or whether they are free to make choices never previously available to them.

Finally, Travers and Pemberton (2000) among others, discuss the role of social networking in women's working lives. It is widely acknowledged that who you know is important in career development, and some would say much more important than what you know (*see* Chapter 14). A problem for women in male-dominated environments is the difficulty of being part of social networks where up-to-date information is informally shared about what is going on, what jobs are coming up, etc. Sometimes it is difficult for men to appreciate just how left out women can be in a male-dominated environment, even without the men realising it is happening. One might argue that it would do a lot of men good to be on the other side of this, for example by regularly picking the children up from school, or going to an aerobics class – both settings usually inhabited mainly by women. It seems that people tend to network with people like themselves. Furthermore, men network a lot with colleagues in the same organisation or close to it, and in an instrumental task-focused way, whereas women are more inclined to network with other women, perhaps in other organisations, and use these contacts for mutual support rather than, for example, getting known by the people (men!) at the top (Vinnicombe and Colwill, 1996). It may also be the case that women tend to have relatively small networks of people they know quite well, whereas men have larger numbers of contacts, each of whom they know only slightly. Most of the research suggests that the latter is better for 'getting on', but it might also be suggested that the former is better for quality of life. Nevertheless, it is important not to generalise too readily. Travers and Pemberton (2000) report a survey they conducted which found significant, though not huge, differences between women from different countries regarding how they viewed networking. American women seemed to see it in quite instrumental masculine terms, British women in terms of their development, and Spanish women on socialising and enjoying the company and support of other women.

Ethnic minorities

Many anecdotal reports, 'fly on the wall' television programmes and research studies indicate clearly that people from ethnic minorities in any given country are at a disadvantage relative to members of the majority when it comes to getting jobs and other opportunities. It is often tempting to think that things are better than they used to be, but one wonders. In 2003 a journalist joined a UK police force posing as a trainee and recorded some (not all) other white trainees expressing some extremely negative views of people from ethnic minorities. Senior police officers were very dismayed and promised to continue their attempt to rid the force of racism, but clearly there was much still to be done.

Some would argue that the police trainees were simply expressing what other people secretly think. Others claim that even though we may believe we are not prejudiced against other ethnic groups, given the right cues we show that we are. Particularly if led to believe that favouring ethnic majority over minority people is normal and accepted practice, many people do the same, perhaps without even realising it (Stewart and Perlow, 2001). Huffcutt and Roth (1998) examined the existing research using meta-analysis and discovered that, across a large number of research studies, the mean rating given to black candidates in employment interviews was about one-quarter of a standard deviation lower than to whites (*see* Chapter 2 for explanations of meta-analysis and standard deviation). The difference was not huge, but it was easily big enough to have a major effect on the working lives of a lot of people. Greenhaus *et al.* (1990) found that black managers (in the United States) felt less accepted than white managers, and on average their work performance was rated lower than that of white managers by their supervisors.

Given the evidence described in the previous paragraph, perhaps it is not surprising that members of ethnic minorities seem less likely to enter high-prestige occupations than members of the majority, and even if they get there, they often do not progress as far. This is in spite of legislation in many countries to ensure equal rights. Cokley *et al.* (2004) summarise statistical evidence from the US Census Bureau which shows that white men's earnings are 25 per cent or more higher than the salaries of black and Hispanic men. They also note that the higher the proportion of black people in an occupation, the lower its salary. Durr and Logan (1997) found that black managers often inhabited small and specialist job markets, often in jobs to do with their minority status, such as 'Affirmative Action Officer'. In the United Kingdom, Bhavnani and Coyle (2000) draw figures from the Labour Force Survey showing that members of ethnic minorities were slightly less likely to be employed in the private sector than white British, and indeed less likely to be employed at all. They were slightly more likely to work in the public sector, or be self-employed. These and other figures suggest a small but significant disadvantage for minorities in the United Kingdom.

People from ethnic minorities cope in different ways with working in white-dominated environments. Cross developed and later refined a theory to try to describe and explain how black people's identities develop in different ways (Cross, 1995). Some remain what Cross called 'pre-encounter'. These are people who feel more white than black. Then there are those who encounter a jolting experience that makes their ethnic identity salient, usually because the experience is unpleasant. Some of those who take on a black identity by this or other means may be described as 'immersed' because they are very focused on their black identity, which is good, in contrast to being white, which is bad. Some people move on from there and are able to accept their black identity without feeling hostile towards white people. They become either 'black nationalists' or 'multiculturalists'. Both accept their identity as black. The former are focused on being black to the exclusion of most other aspects of identity, while the latter are more engaged with dimensions such as gender as well as being black. It is likely that people's identity status will be a major determinant of how easy or difficult they find it to function in a white-dominated organisation. Perhaps the 'immersed' in particular will be inclined to leave or never join in the first place, and this in turn might lead white people to believe there is less of a culture gap than there actually is (Cokley *et al.*, 2004). Cross's theory is a good example of how it is important to look beyond factual information such as skin colour in defining groups. The identity dynamics of being black in a white-dominated society perhaps say more about likely job satisfaction and relations between groups than the fact that a person is black. Of course, the same could be true in reverse. Members of ethnic majorities also construct identities, the content and process of which have implications for how they think of themselves and others.

Key Learning Point

Members of ethnic minorities tend to be at a disadvantage in the labour market relative to the majority. This is mostly due to aspects of person perception and identity that lead majority and minority groups to hold certain opinions about themselves and each other, sometimes without realising it.

The kinds of social networks that people build up are also probably partly a consequence of their identities, as well as the opportunities that they are given.

People in minorities tend to form networks that consist of other members of minorities, and members of the majority also stick together. Usually, members of the majority hold most of the powerful positions, and the people who get to know them also tend to be from the majority. To the extent that decisions such as who gets which job are made on the basis of the decision-maker knowing the people concerned, then these social networks will become self-perpetuating (Ibarra, 1995). One way round this is to institute mentoring or other schemes where members of the (powerful) majority take some responsibility for the development of one or members of a minority. There is more about the roles of social networks and mentoring (among other things) in Chapter 14, on careers.

People with a disability

Barnes (1991) defines disability as 'the loss of opportunities to take part in the normal life of the community on an equal level with others due to physical and social barriers'. This definition highlights the social element of disability – it is not simply a physical phenomenon, but also a social one. How disability and disabled people are viewed by society as a whole affects the opportunities available to people with disabilities (McHugh, 1991). It is clear that, although the lot of people with a disability in the workplace is improving, they are still at a disadvantage compared with people with no disability. The introduction in many countries of laws protecting and enhancing the rights of people with a disability has reduced the gap, but not eliminated it. It seems that the image of disabled people as ill, dependent on others, childlike and asexual does persist, even though much of the medical and other provision for people with a disability has moved away from treating people in that way (Oliver, 1990). Yet many of the technological advances outlined earlier make it easier for people with a disability to work productively, because they compensate for any limitations people may have in physical co-ordination and mobility. But much of the provision required to make workplaces usable for people with a disability is hardly rocket science, which is one reason why the UK Disability Discrimination Act, which came into force in 1996, insists that employers make 'reasonable accommodations' where the working arrangements and/or physical features of the workplace put people with a disability at a significant disadvantage. Even so, the UK Labour Force Survey in Spring 2001 recorded 41 per cent of disabled people as being economically active, compared with 85 per cent of people without a disability. Of course, some of this difference may be due to fewer disabled than non-disabled people looking for work, but that is not the whole story because the UK unemployment rate (which includes only those seeking work) is approaching twice as high for disabled people than non-disabled ones.

As is the case with other equal opportunity and diversity issues, legislation does not in itself over-ride human perceptions, beliefs and prejudices about people with a disability. So it is likely to remain difficult for disabled people to rise to the top of their professions. Numerous studies in the 1980s confirmed that disabled people tend to be concentrated in lower-status occupations and if they did get into higher-status occupations, they tended to be at junior levels within them (Walker, 1982). There is little evidence that much has changed in terms of disabled people's achievements, but there is much more concern than there used to be with identifying ways in which disabled people can be supported in achieving independence. Furthermore, this is increasingly being done by finding out the experiences of disabled people themselves, rather than simply implementing what able-bodied people think would be good for them (Hendey and Pascall, 2001).

Key Learning Point

The talents of people with a disability are being increasingly recognised in employment and education, and this is supported by laws upholding their rights in many countries. But there is still some disadvantage relative to people without a disability.

The persistent difficulties of disabled people in the labour market are not only due to real limitations in their capabilities, nor to unreasonable employers. It also seems clear that gender, ethnicity and social class play their parts, through the ways in which children with a disability are socialised. In fact, in some respects, these factors may be more important than disability in shaping what a disabled person expects of him- or herself. Shah *et al.* (2004a) for example have shown that, among a group of disabled professionals who had achieved considerable career success, those raised in middle class professional households recalled rarely being allowed to use their disability as an excuse for failure. Education is also a key factor. Some people with a disability are educated in separate schools whereas others are in mainstream schools. Which of these two forms of schooling is more successful has been debated at length over many years (e.g. Jenkinson, 1997), and it is likely that much depends on the personal resources of the young person in dealing with whichever environment they are in. As a generalisation, it seems that mainstream schools offer a relatively challenging curriculum, but sometimes not much social support, while segregated schools tend to be the other way round (Shah *et al.*, 2004b).

Summary

Modern psychology can be divided into several subdisciplines which reflect different facets of human psychological functioning. Cutting across these divisions are competing theoretical traditions in psychology. These are the psychoanalytic, trait, behaviourist, phenomenological and social cognitive traditions. None of them can be described as correct, though the social cognitive tradition is the most recent, and makes most use of other traditions. The traditions make some contradictory assumptions about the fundamental nature of the person. Their differences and similarities are summarised in Table 1.1. Each tradition finds some expression in work psychology. The differences between them emphasise that any apparent coherence of work psychology is due to the fact that it always takes place in the work setting. It does not possess a generally agreed view of human nature.

Work psychology concerns both the interaction between an individual and his or her work, and the relationships between people in the work setting. This includes personnel selection and assessment, training, performance appraisal, career development, organisational change and development, human–machine interaction, counselling, the design of work environments, and employee relations and motivation, among other things. Work psychologists act as researchers, teachers and consultants in these areas. In the United Kingdom, the British Psychological Society oversees the professional qualifications and conduct of work psychologists. Many other countries have equivalent bodies.

We also believe it is important to examine the context in which work psychology is operating. Changes have been occurring over the past two decades or so which mean that many work organisations are more pressured than they were, with flatter structures, fewer employees and more varied terms and conditions. Employees may well be required to be flexible to suit employers' needs, but there is also often a chance for them to work flexibly to suit their own needs. It is clear that new technology in the workplace does not have inevitable consequences – its effects on people, jobs and organisations depend a lot on how it is introduced and subsequently used. The changing mix of people in the labour force in terms of their gender, ethnic affiliation, (dis)ability, religion, nationality, age, sexual orientation and other factors presents both challenges and opportunities for work psychology. So does the increasing awareness of diversity issues, independent of the changing nature of the workforce. Work psychology needs to ensure that it moves well beyond its roots in large manufacturing organisations with predominantly white male workforces and stable structures. It should be analysing and answering questions such as 'how do different groups at work relate to each other?', 'how can fairness be achieved at work?', 'how can the potential value of a diverse workforce be made a reality?' and 'how can small organisations with limited resources make use of what work psychology can offer?'

Test your learning

Short-answer questions

1   What are the areas of basic psychology, and what kind of issues does each area address?

2   Draw a diagram to show the relationship between basic psychology and work psychology.

3   In psychoanalytic psychology, what are (i) the id, (ii) the ego, (iii) the superego and (iv) defence mechanisms?

4   What is a trait? Briefly describe two key features of the trait approach to personality.

5   In behaviourism, what is reinforcement? Why do behaviourist psychologists think that personality can be changed?

6   In phenomenological psychology, what are (i) conditions of worth, (ii) unconditional positive regard and (iii) self-actualisation?

7 Why is the self an important concept in the social cognitive tradition?

8 What were the key lessons learned by work psychologists from the Hawthorne studies?

9 Name and briefly describe eight areas of work undertaken by work psychologists.

10 If you were a manager considering buying the services of a work psychologist, what would you want to know about the psychologist's qualifications and experiences?

11 How would you evaluate whether the research undertaken by a work psychologist was ethical?

12 Specify five ways in which workplaces tend to be different now from 30 years ago.

13 Choose one of these, and comment on what work psychology can contribute to understanding its impact.

14 Suggest three ways in which work psychology should be able to help in the management of diversity.

15 Choose one way in which people at work differ from each other, and specify three insights from work psychology about this difference.

Suggested assignments

1 Compare and contrast any two approaches to personality.

2 Select any two traditions in personality. Imagine two managers. One believes one tradition is correct; the other supports the other tradition. Examine the probable impact of their beliefs on the way they deal with other people at work.

3 Examine whether the ethical codes of practice governing work psychologists adequately reflect all the ethical issues that can arise in work psychology research and practice.

4 In what ways has technology changed the way people work over the past 20 years or so? What lessons can be learned about how this technology *should* be introduced and deployed?

5 How can work psychology help to ensure that people of different genders and ethnic affiliations work effectively together?

Relevant websites

One of a number of websites devoted to supporting people who experience disadvantage in the workplace is http://www.eurosur.org/wide/home.htm. This is a

European network for women, with a particular interest in training and development.

The UK's Commission for Racial Equality (CRE) has a broad mission to support equality in all aspects of life. However, the CRE is taking increasing interest in workplace issues, and you can find out about current activities at their 'Working with Business' pages: http://www.cre.gov.uk/gdpract/wwb.html.

Professional psychology associations offer considerable information about the theory and practice of psychology, including work psychology. Three good ones are The International Association for Applied Psychology (IAAP) at http://www.iaapsy.org, The European Association of Work and Organisational Psychology (EAWOP) at http://www.eawop.org/, and the British Psychological Society at http://www/bps.org.uk/index.cfm. Some briefing sheets about various aspects of work psychology can be found at the website of the Institute of Work Psychology, University of Sheffield, UK at http://www2.shef.ac.uk/~iwp/publications/index.html#whatis.

For further self-test material and relevant, annotated weblinks please visit the website at http://www.booksites.net/arnold_workpsych.

Suggested further reading

1   The chapters by Sylvia Shimmin/Peter van Strien and Charles de Wolf in the second edition of Volume 1 of the *Handbook of Work and Organization Psychology* give helpful perspectives on how the field of work psychology has evolved and how it looks today, particularly from European and North American perspectives.

2   The sixth edition of Robert Ewen's book *An Introduction to Theories of Personality* provides a thorough but readable account of different traditions in psychology, particularly concerning how each tradition has construed the nature of the person and personality. Although Ewen majors on the psychoanalytic tradition, his coverage of the other traditions is clear and informative.

3   The 2003 book edited by David Holman and colleagues called *The New Workplace*, published by Wiley, offers a really good detailed look at the human side of nearly every technology-driven workplace change that has happened over the last two decades.

4   Binna Kandola and Johanna Fullerton's book titled *Managing the Mosaic: Diversity in action* provides a down-to-earth but not over-simple account of some of the practical issues in managing a diverse workforce, and is written by two of the UK's leading consultants in this area.

CHAPTER 2

Theory, research and practice in work psychology

LEARNING OUTCOMES

After studying this chapter, you should be able to:

1 describe the main elements of a psychological theory, and explain the links between those elements;

2 distinguish between two opposing philosophies in the conduct of psychological research;

3 describe the various methods of data collection used in research by work psychologists;

4 describe the key features, advantages and disadvantages of four research designs used by work psychologists;

5 define the null and alternative hypotheses in psychological research;

6 explain the concept of statistical significance;

7 explain the concepts of power and effect size in statistical testing;

8 define in words the circumstances in which the following statistical techniques would be used:

t-test,

analysis of variance,

chi-square,

correlation,

multiple regression,

meta-analysis;

9 describe how qualitative data can be analysed using content analysis and discourse analysis.

Introduction

In this chapter we build on the previous one by looking more closely at how theories in work psychology can be developed, evaluated and used. We start with an examination of the nature of theory and we provide a concrete example to show the factors that a good theory needs to take into account. Then we turn to the relationship between theory and practice. We argue that good practice requires good theory, and we discuss the problem that all too often theory-orientated and practice-orientated work psychologists find it difficult to communicate with each other. Then we take a look at the ways in which work psychologists conduct research, from the point of view of the overall strategy (research design) and also specific techniques (research methods). We consider how work psychologists' assumptions about the nature of knowledge and theory influence how they go about their research work, the kinds of data they obtain, and how they interpret their data. Finally, we explain how statistical and qualitative techniques for analysing data can be utilised in order to draw conclusions about what the data mean. Many complex issues are involved in the appropriate use and interpretation of research data, and psychologists sometimes ignore them (Judd *et al.*, 1995). This chapter attempts, in a straightforward way, to help the reader avoid some of the more common pitfalls.

The nature of theory in work psychology

A theory in psychology can be defined as an organised collection of ideas that serves to describe, explain or predict what a person will do, think or feel. To be successful, it needs to specify the following five elements (*see also* Fig. 2.1):

1   The particular behaviours, thoughts or emotions in question. These should have significance for human affairs.

2   Any differences between people in the degree to which they characteristically exhibit the behaviours, thoughts or emotions in question.

3   Any situational factors that might influence whether or when the behaviours, thoughts or emotions in question occur.

4   Any consequences of the interaction between 2 and 3 for the behaviours, thoughts or emotions.

5   Any ways in which the occurrence of particular behaviours, thoughts or emotions might feed back to produce change in 2 and 3.

To take an example, let us suppose that a psychologist wishes to develop a theory to explain and predict the occurrence of arriving late for work. Relevant individual characteristics might include a person's job satisfaction and the extent to which he or she tends to be well organised. Relevant past experiences might include punishments for being late. Situational features might include the distance

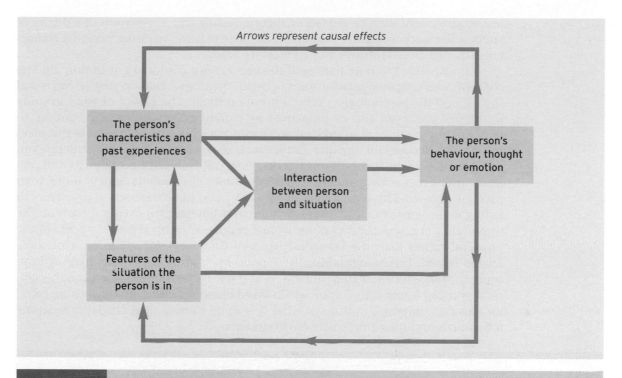

| Figure 2.1 | **A simplified structure of psychological theory** |

from home to work, the simplicity or complexity of travel between home and work, and the expectations of the person's workmates. They may also include factors that change day by day such as the weather. These might all directly affect the person's actual incidence of arriving late for work. But so might the *interaction* between person and situation. For example, a well-organised person may have no difficulty making complex travel arrangements between home and work. For such a person, complexity of travel arrangements might *not* have much effect on time of arrival at work. A poorly organised person may be able to cope with straightforward travel arrangements but not complex ones. For that person, the complexity of travel to work could make a big difference to punctuality. This is an example of an *interaction effect* – the travel between work and home affects the lateness of some people but not others.

Just to make things more complicated, it is likely that person and situation influence each other. This can occur in at least three ways. Two of these will have happened before the specific events of interest to the psychologist. First, people's characteristics can affect the types of situation they expose themselves to. In this example, a badly organised person might not think carefully about travel to work when deciding where to live. Second, people may be able to change features of their situation, or features of their situation may change them. Third, a person's behaviour right now may lead him or her to change ('I'm late again; I must become a better organised person') or may cause a change in his or her situation (in an extreme case, being dismissed for being late once too often).

Naturally, it is possible to suggest many other personal characteristics and situational features that could influence lateness for work. The choice of which to investigate might itself be guided by theory. Testing and application of a theory of lateness for work would also require sound methods for assessing personal characteristics, situational features and lateness for work.

It is important to note that good theories are not conjured out of thin air. The concepts and proposed relationships between them are based on past research and theory, and the psychologist's reflections upon them. The choice of what to study in the first place can also be influenced by current events and public opinion. In fact, a frequent criticism of psychology (including work psychology) is that it takes insufficient account of broader factors such as social class, power structures in society and economic conditions (Pfeffer, 1991). Sociologists, economists and political scientists, among others, focus on those phenomena much more than psychologists do. This leaves work psychology open to accusations of (i) naivety in failing to recognise the 'real' causes of human behaviour; (ii) over-emphasis on the importance of characteristics of individual people; and (iii) acting as agents of the powerful rather than the powerless (*see also* Chapter 1 for an account of some related issues). Psychologists usually respond by arguing that individuals *do* have some control over what they think, feel and do. Each of us is more than the sum total of social forces acting upon us. To avoid bland generalisations, or those based on naïve or simplistic notions of what it is to be human, it is crucial to examine individuals and their immediate environments.

Key Learning Point

The conventional view of good theory in work psychology is that the theory should be precise in specifying the behaviour, thoughts or feelings it is designed to predict, and the individual and situational characteristics which influence them.

The point was made in Chapter 1 that psychology is not a united or unified discipline. The multiplicity of views certainly extends to what research and theory are about and how research should be conducted. The most fundamental polarity has been described nicely by, among others, Easterby-Smith *et al.* (2002, Chapter 3) as positivism versus social constructionism. Each of these positions has distinct and very different philosophical roots. Easterby-Smith and colleagues stress that in practice nowadays much research includes a bit of both, and that they represent two extremes.

Positivism assumes that the social world exists objectively and should therefore be measured using objective methods rather than subjective ones such as intuition. This usually implies quantitative (i.e. numerical) data. Science is seen as advancing by making hypotheses about laws and causes of human behaviour and then testing those hypotheses, preferably by simplifying the problem of interest as much as possible. It is also assumed that the researcher can investigate without influencing what is being investigated: that is, his or her presence and actions are assumed not to alter how people would naturally behave, think or feel.

The other extreme is labelled social constructionism by Easterby-Smith *et al*. It might also be termed phenomenological (*see* Chapter 1). This viewpoint suggests that reality is not objective. Instead, the meaning of events, concepts and objectives is constructed and interpreted by people, through their thought processes and social interactions. Research conducted on the basis of this philosophy will aim 'to understand and explain why people have different experiences, rather than search for external causes and fundamental laws to explain their behaviour' (Easterby-Smith *et al.*, 2002, p. 30). So instead of measuring how often certain behaviours occur, the aim of research is to examine the different ways in which people interpret and explain their experience. The data produced by such research tend to be harder to obtain and to summarise than those produced by positivist research, but also richer in meaning, detail and explanation.

Many topics in work psychology can be investigated from both perspectives and all points in between. To continue the example of arriving late for work, a positivist research project (which was the sort implied in the example given earlier) would assess the frequency of this behaviour and try to link it with objective factors such as distance from work as well as perhaps more subjective factors such as job satisfaction. The assumption would be that such factors may *cause* lateness for work, irrespective of the sense individuals might make of their situation. On the other hand, social constructionist research on lateness at work would focus much more on how individuals thought and felt about being late for work, and how they explained their own behaviour in this area. The general theoretical framework outlined in Fig. 2.1 would still have some relevance, but aspects of the person and situation to be examined would be treated as part of people's ways of understanding and/or explaining their own behaviour rather than as objectively verifiable forces causing it. Ways of understanding and explaining might be researched by asking people about them directly, or alternatively by observing their behaviour and making inferences from the observations.

Work psychology research published in academic journals such as those listed in Chapter 1 is mostly positivist. This probably reflects psychology's attempts to position itself as a science subject, with consequences for the ways in which work psychologists are trained, as well as the kinds of people it attracts in the first place. Some psychologists (e.g. Johnson and Cassell, 2001) have, however, criticised the highly positivist and quantitative orientation of work psychology. They argue strongly that phenomenological studies have many advantages over positivist ones, and deserve a more prominent place in work psychology.

Key Learning Point

There is an important philosophical disagreement in psychology between positivism and phenomenology. The former emphasises objectively verifiable causes of behaviour, thoughts and emotions; the latter focuses more on people's subjective explanations and accounts.

Theory and practice in work psychology

Some might argue that theory has little to offer practice. There are various reasons for advancing that argument. Theories in a particular area may not be very good, in the sense that they do not adequately or accurately specify the phenomena portrayed in Fig. 2.1. A psychologist may find that a particular technique seems to work well, and not be concerned about theoretical reasons why it works. Work psychology is predominantly problem centred. There is no single dominant theoretical perspective, and (again as noted earlier) work psychology has sometimes been somewhat isolated from theoretical developments in mainstream psychology. Sparrow (1999), for example, criticised work psychologists for ignoring theoretical developments in social psychology in their study of people at work. But the present authors firmly believe that a good theory is essential to *good* practice. It is incorrect to say, as people sometimes do, that an idea is good in theory but not in practice. A good theory does a good job of describing, explaining and predicting behaviour, thoughts or emotions which have important outcomes. Basing practice on good theory *is* better than basing it on superstition, guesswork or an inferior theory. As the distinguished social psychologist Kurt Lewin (1945) long ago argued, there is nothing so practical as a good theory.

In an excellent article, Gary Johns (Johns, 1993) analysed why techniques advocated by work psychologists (e.g. in personnel selection or job design) are not always adopted in organisations, even if they seem to be based on good research and have potential to save (or make) money. He argued that work psychologists often neglect the political and social contexts of organisations. Yet these considerations loom larger in managers' minds than the finer points of a psychologist's arguments concerning the technical merit of, for example, a particular personality test. Managers are likely to respond to such factors as how rival companies do things, what legislation requires and what their bosses are likely to find readily acceptable. Evidence for the effectiveness of a psychological theory or technique is often derived from quite complex, abstract research, where the social and political context in which the research was carried out is either not adequately reported or non-existent. Johns (2001) develops the theme of the importance of context and applies this analysis to a recently published article. The sorts of contextual variables he has in mind include an organisation's recent history, the state of the labour market (e.g. how much unemployment there is) and cultural influences on what constitutes appropriate behaviour at work.

Johns (1993) argued that if work psychologists want to influence management practice, they should also be prepared to publicly name organisations that adopt good practice, since permission to do so is usually granted, and managers are more impressed by information about named organisations than unnamed ones. Work psychologists should also actively seek to publish their work in managers' journals as well as academic ones. This can, however, often be a challenge for research-orientated academic work psychologists on two counts. First, they are not accustomed to writing for manager audiences. Second, the reward system in academia rarely gives them sufficient encouragement to do so.

In recent years work psychologists and their professional bodies have become increasingly concerned about an apparent lack of communication between those who produce new knowledge (researchers) and those who might put it to use in real workplaces (consultants and managers). It seems that researchers often believe that consultants and managers fail to make proper use of existing knowledge, preferring instead to follow their 'gut feeling' or established practice. Managers and consultants commonly think that researchers fail to produce information that is relevant to their day-to-day concerns, and even if they do, they fail to communicate it well.

Anderson *et al.* (2001b) distinguish between two ways of doing research in work psychology: scientific enquiry and problem-solving. These are shown in Fig. 2.2. It can be seen that the latter involves much more engagement than the former with people in the workplace(s) being researched. However, Anderson *et al.* also argue for the importance of conducting problem-solving research rigorously using careful methods and relevant theory rather than just chatting to a few people or 'getting the feel of things'.

Rynes *et al.* (1999) have examined how research projects can have an impact on practice within work organisations. They found that the amount of time spent by the researcher on site and whether the organisation contracted the research (as opposed to simply helping a work psychologist conduct his or her research) both appeared to influence whether the research findings were implemented. Both of these factors are consistent with a 'problem-solving' rather than 'scientific enquiry' approach to research. Yet the most common form of work psychology research is the use of questionnaires designed on the basis of the researcher's knowledge and interests and completed by employees with minimal researcher involvement in the organisation. We should not be surprised if this research has little practical impact.

Key Learning Point

If work psychology is to have a substantial influence on organisational and public policy, work psychologists must get involved in the organisations they research, and address the political acceptability as well as the technical merit of their recommendations.

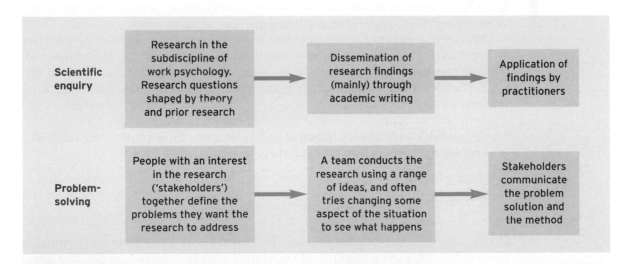

Figure 2.2	**Two ways of doing research in work psychology**
	Source: adapted from Anderson *et al.* (2001b)

Researchers often complain that managers and consultants are far more keen on management fads (i.e. the latest popular ideas about how to do management) than on the findings of rigorous research. Academics tended at one time to be very dismissive of so-called fads such as business process re-engineering (BPR), total quality management (TQM) and emotional intelligence (EI), because they were not based on good research showing their validity. More recently, though, academics have become more interested in understanding how management fads start, are sustained and then fade away. There is now more acknowledgement that fads do meet some needs and concerns of managers, that they are sometimes broadly consistent with research findings, and that even when they have gone out of fashion, they may well leave a lasting mark on management practices (Jackson, 2001).

In other words, the task for researchers is not to moan about fads, but to understand them. Many would add that the existence of management fads may partly be a consequence of researchers' failure to produce and communicate findings that are perceived to be useful. One possible reason for this is that theories most favoured by academics are in fact not very easy to apply. However, Miner (2003) has found that theories perceived to be valid by senior academics in organisational behaviour and strategic management also tended to be seen as usefully applicable in work organisations. This suggests that, at least to some extent, academics do indeed see good theory as linking with good practice. Miner sees this as a positive trend, and one that is considerably more evident now than when he conducted a rather similar study 20 years earlier.

Finally in this section, we should note that the effective application of theory and research is rarely straightforward. It depends on many broader factors such as policy priorities, values and demographics. Two examples can illustrate this well. First, Gardner (2003) points out that the finding that it is difficult to change intelligence as measured by psychometric tests (*see* Chapter 3) could mean that (i) it is not worth trying or (ii) we need to try extra-hard and devote lots of resources to the effort. The choice depends on many factors, including what we think intelligence test scores say about an individual's behaviour and quality of life, and what value we ascribe to those potential consequences of intelligence.

The second example arises from the work of one of the authors (Arnold). He and colleagues conducted research for the UK Government's Department of Health, investigating why people did or did not want to work for the UK's National Health Service (NHS) as nurses, radiographers or physiotherapists. Two of the findings were as follows:

1   People who were already qualified in one of those three professions and had chosen to leave the NHS were unlikely to return.

2   After allowing for factors such as whether someone is already qualified, and their perceptions of NHS work, older people were less inclined to work for the NHS than younger people.

On the face of it, two implications for the Department of Health in its attempts to raise NHS staffing levels might be: do not target already-qualified people, and target younger people more than older ones. However, it is possible to draw quite different conclusions. On the first point, it can be argued that already-qualified people are quite easy to find (for example via professional associations) and do not require extensive training, so even a low success rate in attracting them back to the NHS might be a worthwhile investment. On the second point, given that the general population of the United Kingdom (like most countries) is ageing, it would be unwise to stop trying to recruit older people. Instead extra efforts and new strategies should be devised to attract older people.

Key Learning Point

A schematic summary of some key points of this section is shown in Fig. 2.3. The formulation, conduct, output and utilisation of research in work psychology are all part of a complex process.

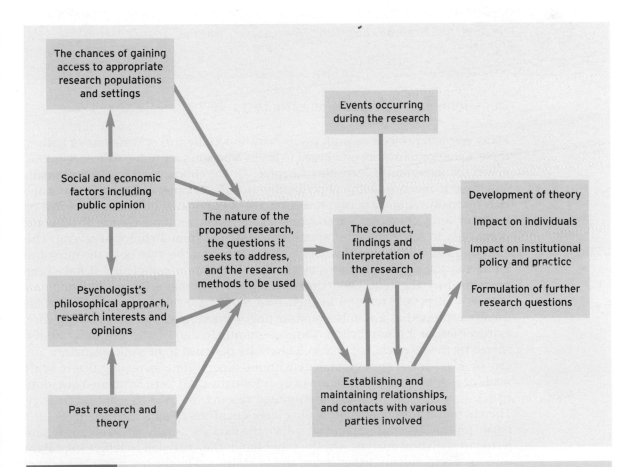

Figure 2.3   The research process in work psychology

Research methods in work psychology

Work psychologists use a variety of techniques in their research on human behaviour, thoughts and emotions in the workplace. In considering these techniques, it is helpful to distinguish between research *designs* and research *methods*. The former concern the overall research strategy employed. This strategy depends on the researcher's beliefs about scientific investigation as well as the nature of the phenomena being researched. Research methods are the specific ways in which information is gathered within the overall research strategy. Drawing on Bryman (2001), a number of designs and methods can be identified. There is more than one way of carrying out each design and each method. The designs are discussed later in this chapter. First, it is necessary to make a few points about each of the research methods.

Key Learning Point

Research design refers to the overall strategy in conducting research, whereas research methods are the procedures by which information is collected.

Questionnaires and psychometric tests

Many research projects in work psychology, especially surveys, use one or both of these. Questionnaires are often used to assess a person's attitudes, values, opinions, beliefs or experiences (*see also* Chapter 7). Psychometric tests are normally employed to measure ability or personality (*see also* Chapter 4). Questionnaires and tests normally require a person to answer a series of written questions presented on paper or on a computer screen. Answers are often multiple-choice; that is, the person has to select the most appropriate response from a choice of several. This kind of questionnaire is often referred to as *structured*, because both the questions asked and the response options available to the person completing it have been predefined by the researcher. Unstructured questionnaires, where questions are broader and people respond in their own words, are much rarer. Responses are usually expressed as a number representing, for example, a person's intelligence, extroversion or job satisfaction. Some questionnaires and tests need to be administered by the researcher in person. Others are designed to be self-explanatory and can be filled in by the respondent without supervision. Increasing use is being made of web-based administration of questionnaires and tests. Structured questionnaires are easily the most commonly used research method in work psychology. They have the advantage of providing large quantities of data with relatively little hassle for researcher or respondents. Also, the data are usually relatively easily subjected to statistical analysis. On the other hand, they may fail to reflect important aspects of respondents' experiences, and be (mis)used by the researcher as a way of getting quick and easy information rather than truly engaging with people in the setting being researched (see also the previous section of this chapter).

Interviews

A work psychologist may conduct one or more interviews, normally with an individual, but sometimes with a group of people. Group interviews are often designed to encourage discussion among interviewees about one or more topics, and are often referred to as focus groups (Millward, 2000). The work psychologist asks questions and records responses, either by making notes or using a tape recorder. The questions may be specified in advance, in which case it is a *structured interview*. On the other hand, the interviewer may define only the general topic he or she wishes to investigate and permit respondents to talk about whatever they wish within that topic. This is an *unstructured interview*.

Interview data, and some forms of archival data (see below), are particularly open to alternative forms of analysis. Content analysis usually involves assigning interviewee responses to one or more categories or types, according to what the interviewee said when asked a particular question. This is probably the most common way of analysing interview data in work psychology. Discourse analysis and conversation analysis involve a closer look at sequences of interviewee statements, often including information about the length of pauses, voice intonation and perhaps (if video-taped) other aspects of non-verbal behaviour. The aim here would usually be to show how the interviewee is seeking to present him- or herself in certain ways, and/or to construct plausible accounts. The researcher might also be interested in how the normal rules of conversation are reflected (or not) in the interviewee's talk. An example of how interview data can be analysed appears later in this chapter.

Psychophysiological and psychophysical measures

Psychophysiological and psychophysical measures involve assessing a person's neurological, biological, physical or physiological state or performance. So, for example, in a study of work stress, blood samples may be taken to gauge the concentration of fatty acids in a person's bloodstream. Research on visual perception may use a device called a tachistoscope to present a person with a visual image (such as a written word) for a very short time in order to study how long a stimulus needs to be present if it is to be consciously recognised. Other types of measures (see Barrett and Sowden, 2000) include muscle activity, eye movements, and electrical activity in the brain (electroencephalogram, EEG). These methods of data collection are less common in work psychology than in some other areas of psychology.

Observation

A work psychologist may observe people's behaviour by stationing himself or herself as unobtrusively as possible, and recording the frequency, source and timing of behaviour. This can be termed *structured observation*. Alternatively, the work psychologist may participate in the events he or she is studying. For example, King (1992) investigated innovations on a hospital ward while also working as a nursing assistant. This is *participant observation*. Where people are being observed in their workplace, they are normally informed, or asked about it in advance. Their awareness may itself affect their behaviour (*see* Chapter 1), but that is usually preferable to the alternatives of secrecy or even deception. Observation may also include observing the consequences of behaviour; for example, a person's work productivity. Silverman (2001, Chapter 3) emphasises that observation is not simply seeing and hearing what is 'out there'. The researcher's observations will inevitably be influenced by his or her theoretical orientation and the focus of his or her research. This is not bad in itself, but needs to be acknowledged. Observation without some focus or goals will in any case lead to an unmanageable amount of uninterpretable data. Clearly, a strength of observation is that it allows the researcher to form impressions of what is said and done in a workplace at first hand. It also allows access to everyday mundane events, not just 'big' events, and not just the kind of summary of a person's opinions and perceptions that is usually obtained from questionnaires and interviews. One possible disadvantage of observation is that if people know they are being observed, they may behave, think or feel differently from how they otherwise would.

Diaries

People may be asked to keep a diary of key events and/or their behaviour, thoughts and feelings. It is normally necessary to give people a fair amount of structure to help them to focus their written comments, and to stay in contact with them as an encouragement to keep up the diary-filling. For example, in a study of the impact of achieving goals on people's sense of emotional well-being, Harris *et al.* (2003) obtained diary data from 22 call centre workers twice a day for 12 days. Most of these data consisted of workers' responses to questions about their goals and their mood – in effect, a questionnaire in diary form. Respondents were emailed each day to remind them to complete their diary. One important advantage of the diary method is the ability to track the detailed and fast-moving developments of people's day-to-day lives. One disadvantage is that, almost inevitably, some people on some occasions will forget to complete their diary, or simply not bother.

Archival sources

As Bryman (2001, Chapter 10) has pointed out, archival sources are a potentially rich but sometimes neglected form of data. This is, strictly speaking, a source of data rather than a method of collecting it. Archival information is anything that already exists in organised form before the work psychologist's investigation. Examples include absenteeism data, company accounts, productivity records, human resource policy documents, accident statistics and many others. Data from archival sources are most often used either to provide a context for a particular research project, or to investigate the impact of an event on the functioning of an organisation. Archival sources often yield quantitative data such as how much a workgroup has produced or how many people were promoted in a particular year. But archival methods can also produce qualitative data, which may be the main focus of a particular research study. For example, in research on media coverage of a particular topic, newspaper stories often *are* the data. A researcher may wish to examine what kinds of narrative structure are present in the articles, what purposes they are designed to achieve and so on. For example, Delgado (2003) analyses press coverage in the United States of the soccer match between the United States and Iran in the 1998 World Cup, and discusses how political and ideological issues, as well as sporting ones, affected how the match was reported.

Research methods and philosophical stances

We noted earlier that there is a broad distinction between two kinds of research in work psychology (Easterby-Smith *et al.*, 2002). One (easily the most common in published work psychology research) is based on the proposition that the data collected reflect (albeit imperfectly) an objective reality. This research is sometimes referred to as positivist research. The other kind is based on the assumption that most or all of what work psychologists study is best seen as *socially constructed* – that is, it reflects subjective experience that is made sense of by individuals and groups through their own thought processes and social interactions.

In work psychology, most of the first kind of research uses questionnaires and tests because these tend to produce the most 'ready-made' quantitative data, and because the researchers believe that they will yield data that approximate to an objectively verifiable reality. There is also some use of psychophysical and psychophysiological methods – these are quite rare in most areas of work psychology, but where they are used, they are almost always in research of the positivist kind. The other methods listed above may also be used in that kind of research, but tend not to be. Qualitative researchers tend to use interviews, observations and/or archival material, and possibly unstructured questionnaires and recorded naturally occurring conversations.

The same method may be viewed in different ways by researchers from the two traditions. For example, a positivist researcher who uses interview data will aim to obtain facts about the interviewee's behaviour, thoughts or emotions. If there is some other information that appears to contradict what the interviewee said, or if researchers analysing the interview data do not agree on what an interviewee's response means, the validity of the data is seen as being open to question. Qualitative researchers, on the other hand, are more likely to treat the interviewee's talk as reflecting his or her authentic experiences, or as something mutually constructed in conversation with the interviewer. Either way, the existence of other information which contradicts what the interviewee said (possibly even other information from the interviewee him or herself) may be seen as interesting or as inconsequential, but not usually as a problem (*see* Silverman, 2001, Chapter 4).

Key Learning Point

A work psychologist's research data can be obtained using questionnaires, psychometric tests, interviews, observation of behaviour, measurement of bodily activity and existing data banks.

Research designs

The survey design

The key distinguishing feature of a survey is that it does not intervene in naturally occurring events, nor does it control them. It simply takes a snapshot of what is happening, usually by asking people about it. The aim is usually to gather quantitative information about certain phenomena (for example, events, attitudes) from a large number of people. On occasions this will be done simply to ascertain the frequency of occurrence of a certain event, such as feeling anxious at work. But more commonly, a survey will attempt to discover the relationships of variables with each other – for example, whether anxiety at work tends to be accompanied by low job satisfaction.

The survey design could involve use of any of the methods described above. However, it most commonly involves questionnaires. Questionnaires cannot be just thrown together (as they are in some popular magazines) if they are to do a proper job. Consistent with the positivist research philosophy, they must be carefully devised so that they unambiguously measure what they are supposed to measure – i.e. so that they are *valid* (*see* Chapter 4). It is important to ask the right people to participate in the survey. Ideally, the respondents should be a *random sample* of all those people to whom the survey is relevant. This means that everyone to whom the survey was relevant would have an equal chance of participating in it. In practice, of course, this is rarely the case.

But to whom is a survey relevant? Let us suppose that a psychologist wanted to examine whether doing work where the pace of work is not under one's own control (e.g. on an assembly line) makes people feel negative about their work (*see* Cox, 1978, Chapter 7). If a work psychologist sent questionnaires only to people doing work of controlled pace, there would be no basis for comparison with anybody else. One way round this might be to include some questions asking people what effect they think the paced nature of their work has on them. For some work psychologists, especially those who prefer phenomenology to positivism, how people make sense of such things is important in its own right. But for most, this would not be sufficient. They would insist that comparison was necessary with people whose work was *not* paced. The trouble is, these people may be different in a number of ways from those whose work *is* paced. Any one (or more) of these differences could explain differences between the groups in work attitudes.

This leads to another point: exactly what information should be collected in the survey? Continuing our example, the work psychologist might ask about any number of things. Age, sex, work experience, educational attainment, abilities required by work, job status, supervision, friendships at work, wage levels and working conditions are just a few. If the paced and non-paced groups differed on one or more of these, it would be difficult to tell what was responsible for any difference between the groups in job satisfaction. Also we could not be certain whether paced work led to (low) job satisfaction, or low job satisfaction led to paced work. The latter might occur if managers allocated the jobs with controlled pace to those employees who expressed dissatisfaction. Another possible interpretation would be that some third factor, for example prior work experience, determined *both* a person's job satisfaction *and* the kind of work he or she did. Unless we knew about his or her prior experience, we could not tell.

Thus the survey has both advantages and disadvantages (*see* Bryman, 2001). It can be used with people directly involved in the issues to be investigated. It can investigate their experiences in their day-to-day setting. It is normally fairly easy to conduct, and makes relatively low demands on people's time. These are advantages. On the other hand, the survey does not involve any manipulation of the variables being investigated. This makes it very difficult to establish cause and effect. The survey takes the world as it is. The world is complicated, and unless the survey takes all relevant factors into account, it may lead the psychologist to draw incorrect conclusions. Various sophisticated statistical techniques can reduce this danger, but not eliminate it.

Key Learning Point

Surveys are relatively easy to conduct and they investigate the real world in which people work. However, it is often difficult to be sure about causes and effects.

Longitudinal surveys can help to clarify what causes what. In a longitudinal survey, data are gathered on more than one occasion. This contrasts with *cross-sectional* surveys, where data are collected on one occasion only. Longitudinal data can help to tease out possible causal connections. Conditions pertaining at time 1 may cause those at time 2 but not, presumably, vice versa. Again, though, there remains the danger of key information not being collected. Also, even if event A happens before event B, that does not necessarily mean that A *causes* B.

Sometimes survey research involves collection of information from sources other than the people concerned (for example, archival data from the personnel records of a company). But often *all* the data consist of people's *self-reports* of their behaviour, thoughts and/or emotions. These may not be accurate or complete, and in any case the questions asked of respondents may not reflect what matters most to them. Data that are entirely self-reported are also subject to a problem called *common method variance*, which is where the relationship between variables is artificially high simply because all of the data are obtained by the same method.

Finally, survey information can be collected using interviews (*see* previous section). Market researchers and social researchers often conduct them. The interview is in effect often used as a talking questionnaire. However, it can also be employed to explore issues with respondents in more depth than a questionnaire allows. Conducting research interviews is a skilled business. From a positivist point of view, care must be taken to gain the trust of the respondent, to explore issues to the extent required, and to avoid accidentally influencing the respondent's answers. All these are in order to maximise the accuracy of the data and reflect the true state of affairs. Of course, work psychologists who are not sympathetic to positivist research would say that there is no absolute truth out there to find, and that while establishing a good relationship with the interviewee might be ethically desirable, it inevitably influences what is said in the interview.

The experimental design

The claim of psychology to be a science rests partly on its extensive use of experiments. One key advantage of an experiment is that it allows the psychologist *control* over what happens. This in turn permits inference about causes and effects. On the other hand, there are some disadvantages too. These are discussed below, but first let us examine a concrete example.

The most controlled environment is the psychologist's laboratory. To return to our earlier example concerning paced work, the psychologist might set up a conveyor belt in the laboratory. He or she would probably choose a task typical of conveyor belt work – perhaps checking that boxes of chocolates have been properly packed. The boxes travel along the conveyor belt at a set speed, and the worker has to remove any faultily packed ones. People might be asked to work on this task for a period of several weeks, and to indicate their job satisfaction at various points during that period.

All of this would, of course, cost a lot of money. A large research grant would be required. The psychologist would probably also take the opportunity to record other things apart from job satisfaction, such as work performance (proportion of incorrectly packed boxes identified) and perhaps some physiological measures of stress (e.g. heart rate, blood cholesterol levels).

But this would not be enough on its own. It would also be necessary to include a *control group* as well as the *experimental group* already described. People in the control group should as far as possible do the same job as the experimental group, except that their task would not be machine-paced. Hence, the control group would perhaps be given piles of boxes of chocolates, and instructed to check them. Data on job satisfaction, etc. would be collected from members of the control group in the same way and at the same times as from the experimental group.

The work psychologist would try to ensure that the conditions experienced by the experimental and control groups differed *only* in whether or not their task was machine-paced. The two groups have the same task. They perform it in the same laboratory (though the groups may not see each other or even be aware of each other's existence). They can be paid the same amount with the same pay rules, and be supervised in the same way, though the difference between paced and non-paced work may make these last two similarities difficult to achieve in practice. The groups can be given the same opportunities (or lack of them) for interaction with other workers. It would not be easy to ensure that the two groups did the same *amount* of work. The control group could be told that they had to check the same number of boxes per day or week as the experimental group. This would introduce some degree of pacing, though not nearly as much as a conveyor belt running at a constant speed.

Two key terms in experimental jargon are as follows. The *independent variable* is what the psychologist manipulates in order to examine its effect on the *dependent variable*. In this example, therefore, the independent variable is whether or not the work is machine-paced, and the dependent variable is job satisfaction. More complex experiments often have more than one independent variable, and more than one dependent variable.

Another important point concerns the people who undertake the work for the sake of the experiment (who used to be called the *subjects* but are now more often *participants*). Ideally, they would be typical of people who do that kind of work. If so, this would increase the confidence with which experimental results could be applied to the 'real world'. An attempt to recruit such people to the experiment could be made by advertising in local newspapers. This might not be successful, however. Since most researchers work in higher education, they would be tempted to recruit students because they are easy to find – and they usually need the money that is often paid for participation in experiments! But because students are unlikely to work at conveyor belts for much of their career, their reactions in the experiment might not be typical of those who do. Whoever participates in the experiment, individuals would normally be *assigned at random* to either the experimental group or the control group. This random assignment helps to ensure that the people in the two groups do not differ in systematic ways.

It should now be clear that the laboratory experiment allows the psychologist to make unambiguous inferences about the effects on job satisfaction of machine-paced work. Or does it? The psychologist's control necessarily makes it an artificial situation because the real world is rarely so neat and tidy. Unless the psychologist indulges in a huge (and unethical) deception, the experimental participants will know that they are not in a real job, and that the experiment will last only a few weeks. This could crucially affect their reactions to the work. So could the guesses they make about what the psychologist is investigating. These guesses will be influenced by unintentional cues from the experimenter via (for example) tone of voice and body posture. Such cues are termed *demand characteristics*. Every experiment has them.

Key Learning Point

Laboratory experiments allow the work psychologist to control and manipulate the situation in order to establish whether there are causal relationships between variables. But it is often not clear whether the same relationships would occur in real-life situations.

The artificiality of the laboratory experiment is seen by some as a fatal flaw. Sometimes it is possible to conduct a *field experiment* instead. For a work psychologist this would take place in a real work setting, probably with the people who worked there. It would gain over the laboratory experiment in realism, but almost certainly lose in control. Even if managers and union officials at a factory were prepared to allow the psychologist to create an experimental and control group on the factory floor, they would probably not allow random assignment of subjects to groups. Also, they probably could not arrange things such as identical supervision and identical opportunities to interact with co-workers even if they wanted to.

Occasionally, it is possible for psychologists to conduct a field experiment using events that are occurring anyway. This is sometimes called a *natural experiment*. For example, a chocolate factory may be changing some, but not all, of its chocolate inspection from self-paced work to conveyor belts (*see* Kemp *et al.*, 1983, for a rather similar situation). The psychologist could use this profitably, especially if he or she was able to obtain data on job satisfaction, etc. both before and after the change was made. Here again, though, the gain in realism is balanced by a loss of control and the consequent presence of confounding factors. For example, the people working at the factory might have some choice of which form of work they undertook. This immediately violates the principle of random allocation to groups. On the other hand, one might argue that if this is the way the world works, there is nothing to be gained by trying to arrange conditions that do not reflect it.

Key Learning Point

It is occasionally possible to conduct experiments in real-world settings, though usually the work psychologist has less control over the situation than in laboratory experiments.

Qualitative design

Both surveys and experiments normally express data using numbers (i.e. quantitatively). They allow the people participating in the research little chance to express their opinions in their own words, since the work psychologist investigates a limited number of variables of his or her own choice, selected in advance. Hence surveys and experiments do not obtain a detailed picture of any individual's world. They both involve the psychologist in a fairly detached, quasi-scientific role, and tend to reflect the positivist research philosophy described earlier.

Qualitative research often (though not always) involves a much greater emphasis on seeing the world from the point of view of the people who participate in it (Johnson and Cassell, 2001). That is, it tends to reflect the phenomenological research philosophy described earlier. This normally means collecting detailed information using observation and/or unstructured interviews from a fairly small number of individuals or organisations – perhaps only one. This information is intended to paint a picture rather than measure a limited number of specific phenomena. It is therefore normally in the form of words or images, not numbers. Drawing on Gubrium and Holstein (1997), Silverman (2001, pp. 38–9) has identified four kinds of qualitative research:

- *Naturalism*: the emphasis is on observing what goes on in real-life settings. This tends to produce rich descriptions of behaviour and events, but little insight into how those things are understood by the people involved.

- *Ethnomethodology*: focuses on a close analysis of interactions between people and how these maintain and reflect social order. This can show how social groups and cultures work, but runs the risk of neglecting the role of broader contextual factors such as economic conditions.

- *Emotionalism*: here the primary interest is in establishing a close rapport with the people being researched, and finding out about their experiences and feelings. This differs from the previous two categories in giving priority to people's personal opinions, rather than the researcher's frame of reference, but runs the risk of over-emphasising emotion.

■ *Postmodernism*: rejects the notion that there is an objective truth, focusing instead on how people portray themselves and their contexts in order to achieve personal goals and/or affirm their sense of identity.

Rather than testing a prespecified theory, a work psychologist who conducts qualitative research may well begin the research with some loose theoretical ideas, and then develop and perhaps later test theory in the light of the data obtained during the course of the research. Data collection should also be influenced by developing theoretical ideas as the research proceeds. This process has been termed *grounded theory* by Glaser and Strauss (1967).

Returning to our earlier example, a work psychologist engaging in qualitative research would most likely be interested in how people working on paced and/or unpaced inspection of boxes of chocolates made sense of their situation, and how they coped with it. The psychologist might work on the task as a participant observer, and might also interview individuals or groups about it.

Key Learning Point

Qualitative research often involves an attempt to describe and analyse how individuals make sense of the situations they are in. The focus may be on behaviour, social interaction, personal experience or self presentation.

Qualitative research usually produces a large amount of data, which requires some editing and interpretation by the researcher. It is time consuming and difficult to carry out. Even obtaining the necessary access to people in their workplace can prove impossible. It leaves researchers vulnerable to the accusation that they have simply discovered in the data what they expected to find. Because this research is usually conducted with relatively small numbers of people, it is often not clear whether the findings would be repeated with a bigger, different sample. These are some of the reasons why there are relatively few articles reporting qualitative research in leading work psychology journals. On the other hand, many qualitative researchers reject positivist criteria for evaluating research (such as generalisability and objectivity). They point out that qualitative work has the advantages outlined in the second paragraph of this section. It is becoming more popular as dissatisfaction with the shortcomings of surveys and experiments slowly grows. Some journals (for example the *Journal of Occupational and Organizational Psychology*) explicitly state an editorial policy encouraging qualitative research.

Action research design

Lewin (1946) coined the term *action research* to describe research where the researcher and the people being researched participate jointly in it. Action research is intended both to solve immediate problems for the people collaborating with the researcher, and to add to general knowledge about the topic being researched. It involves not only diagnosing and investigating a particular problem, but also making changes in a work organisation on the basis of research findings, and evaluating the impact of those changes. Increasingly, it also involves the development of an organisation's capacity to solve problems without external help in the future (Eden and Chisholm, 1993).

Action research can involve any of the research methods described earlier but, like qualitative research, is most likely to use interviews and participant observation (*see* Meyer, 2001). Much more than other research designs, it focuses on a specific problem in an organisation and what to do about it. It abandons the detachment of survey and experimental designs. Like qualitative research, it seeks to examine how people participating in the research see things, and it usually covers fairly long periods of time. Unlike most qualitative research, it involves attempting to solve a problem, and monitoring the success of that attempt.

From the point of view of the researcher, action research can be exciting, difficult and unpredictable. Because of its problem orientation, it requires close involvement with an organisation. This in turn requires careful negotiation and renegotiation of the researcher's role in the organisation, particularly concerning who in the organisation (if anyone) the researcher is 'working for'. Also, people in the organisation may reject the researcher's recommendations for dealing with a problem. This creates obvious difficulties for the evaluation of attempts to deal with the problem, though the researcher may be permitted to evaluate the success of any alternative strategy produced by organisation members. In action research, therefore, the process of conducting the research can become as much a focus of interest as the problem it was originally designed to address.

Key Learning Point

In action research, the psychologist and the people involved in the situation being researched work together to define the aims of the research and solve practical problems.

Key principles in hypothesis testing using quantitative data

Much research in work psychology, particularly in the positivist tradition, examines one or both of the following questions:

- Do two or more groups of people *differ* from each other?

- Do two or more variables *covary* (that is, go together) within a particular group of people?

Work psychologists ask these questions because the answers to them enhance our understanding of human behaviour in the workplace. For example, the first question is central to the issue described earlier in this chapter concerning the effect of machine-paced work on job satisfaction. If a psychologist conducted an experiment something like that described earlier, he or she would obtain job satisfaction data from each individual within the experimental group (which experienced machine-paced work) and the control group (which experienced self-paced work).

Clearly, to establish the effect of machine-pacing on job satisfaction, it is necessary to compare the job satisfaction scores of the two groups. This could be done using a statistical technique called a *t*-test, which is described later in this chapter.

To move on to the second question, a psychologist might conduct a survey in order to establish whether or not people's age is associated with the amount of job satisfaction they experience. It would be possible to divide people into age-groups (e.g. 20–29; 30–39, etc.) and compare pairs of groups using a *t*-test. But this would lose information about people's ages – for example, 29-year-olds would be lumped together with 20-year-olds. Also, the age-groupings would be arbitrarily defined. It would be better to see whether age and job satisfaction go together by means of a *correlation*. This essentially plots each person's age against their job satisfaction on a graph, and assesses the extent to which as age increases, job satisfaction either increases or decreases. Correlation is discussed further below.

Key Learning Point

Work psychologists use statistics to assess whether two or more groups of people differ psychologically in some way, or whether two or more aspects of people's psychological functioning tend to go together.

Psychologists often test *hypotheses* in their research. An important concept here is the *null hypothesis* (H_o). Essentially, this is the hypothesis that there is 'nothing going on'. Thus, if a psychologist is investigating whether two or more groups differ in their job satisfaction, the null hypothesis would be that they do not. If the psychologist is investigating whether age and job satisfaction tend to go together, the null hypothesis would be that they do not. That is, knowing someone's age would tell you nothing about their level of job satisfaction, and vice versa.

In each case, we can also make an *alternative* or *experimental hypothesis* (H_1). This can either be directional or non-directional. For example, a directional alternative hypothesis would specify whether people doing machine-paced work would experience higher or lower job satisfaction than those doing self-paced work, or whether job satisfaction increases or decreases as age increases. Non-directional hypotheses would be less specific. They would simply state that there was a difference between groups in levels of job satisfaction (but not which group was higher) or that age and job satisfaction do go together (but not whether older people are more satisfied or less satisfied).

Hypotheses refer to the *population(s)* from which the sample(s) of people who participate in research are drawn. They do *not* refer to those samples alone. In essence, then, when doing research, a psychologist is asking: 'given the data I have obtained from my research sample, is the null hypothesis or the alternative hypothesis more likely to be true for the population as a whole?' Note that 'population' does not mean everyone in the whole world, or even in a particular country. It should refer to those people to whom the psychologist wishes to generalise the results. This might be 'production line workers in Denmark' or 'people currently employed in the Netherlands'.

Interestingly, researchers are sometimes not very specific concerning what population they wish to draw conclusions about. Also, they sometimes use *samples of convenience* – that is, people they can get hold of easily. Ideally, from a statistical point of view, those who participate in the research should be a *random sample* of the population of interest (*see* 'The survey design' section earlier in this chapter). Surveys may involve questionnaires being sent to a *random sample* of people from a given population, but of course not everybody replies. One inevitably wonders whether responders differ in important ways from non-responders. Responders may, for example, be more conscientious/conforming, or simply have more time on their hands.

Therefore, rather than attempting to obtain a random sample, it is more common for researchers to try to show that their inevitably non-random sample is reasonably *representative* (for example in age, sex, type of employment, location) of the population as a whole. Put another way, the proportions of people of each age, sex, and so on, among those participating in the research should not differ much from those in the wider population. But it is still possible that participants differ from non-participants in other respects, including those of interest in the research. So, for example, it may be that people high on the conscientiousness dimension of personality are more likely to respond than others. This obviously matters if, for example, the research concerns overall levels of conscientiousness in the population.

Statistical analysis of data in work psychology most often involves assessment of *the probability of accepting the alternative hypothesis when the null hypothesis is in fact true for the population*. The lower this probability, the more confident the psychologist can be that the alternative hypothesis can be accepted, and the null hypothesis can be rejected. This probability is also called *statistical significance* – a crucial concept in psychology. Typically, psychologists are not prepared to accept the alternative hypothesis (thus rejecting the null hypothesis) unless there is only a probability of 0.05 or less that the null hypothesis is true given the data the psychologist has collected. Erroneously rejecting the null hypothesis is sometimes called *type I error*.

Key Learning Point

The concept of statistical significance refers to the probability of the null hypothesis being true, given the data obtained.

The psychologist is therefore saying 'I must be at least 95 per cent sure that I can reject the null hypothesis before I am prepared actually to do so'. This might be considered pretty conservative – perhaps *too* conservative. After all, how many of us wait until we are 95 per cent certain of something before we act on the basis of it in our day-to-day lives? There is also the other side of the coin, less often considered by psychologists: the probability of accepting the null hypothesis when the alternative hypothesis is in fact true. Erroneously accepting the null hypothesis is sometimes called *type II error*.

If the psychologist finds that, on the basis of his or her data, there is less than a 0.05 (i.e. 1 in 20) chance of mistakenly rejecting the null hypothesis, he or she will usually declare that the result is *statistically significant at the 0.05 level*. If the probability is less than 0.01 (i.e. 2 in 100), the result is *statistically significant at the 0.01 level*. A similar rule applies for a probability of 0.001 (1 in 1000). These are, of course, arbitrary cut-off points. Basically, the lower the probability, the more confident the psychologist is in rejecting the null hypothesis. Notice also that the lower the probability, the more 'highly statistically significant' the result is said to be.

But how do psychologists calculate statistical significance given their research data? They use one or more techniques referred to collectively as *statistical tests* of the data. We now examine some of these in general terms. There are some worked examples on the website associated with this book. Doing worked examples is an excellent way of understanding the principles of statistical testing. However, there are several commercially available software packages for conducting statistical analyses, and normally these are used. The most commonly used is called SPSS – the Statistical Package for Social Sciences.

Some common statistical tests

The *t*-test

Suppose for a moment that a psychologist is interested in seeing whether production managers are more or less numerate than accountants. He or she administers a test of numeracy to (say) 20 of each and obtains a mean score of 25 for the production managers and 30 for the accountants. Clearly, the accountants score higher on average, but what other information is required before deciding whether to accept or reject the null hypothesis that the populations of production managers and accountants do not differ in their numeracy?

First, we need to consider whether the difference between sample means is large relative to the overall range of scores. After all, if scores in the sample ranged from 10 to 50, a difference of 5 between the two means might not mean very much. But, if scores ranged only from (say) 20 to 35 that difference of 5 might seem quite large in comparison.

The most commonly used numerical measure of the spread of scores is the *standard deviation*. The bigger the standard deviation, the more variable the individual scores are. The standard deviation is a function of the differences between each individual score and the overall mean score, and of the sample size. Hence if all scores were exactly the mean, the standard deviation would be zero because there would be no differences between individual scores and the mean. Apart from this exceptional case, we can normally expect about 68 per cent of all individual scores to be within one standard deviation either side of the mean. About 96 per cent of scores are within two standard deviations of the mean.

Sample size is also important in evaluating the significance of a difference between two means. Suppose for a moment that the null hypothesis was in fact true. If a psychologist repeatedly took samples of 20 production managers and 20 accountants, he or she would *on average* expect their mean scores to be equal. But of course in small samples, it takes only one or two exceptional scores to make quite a big difference between the two group means. Thus, although on average the mean scores for the samples should be equal, in some samples there could be quite big differences. If the psychologist repeatedly took bigger samples (say 100 production managers and accountants), then the influence of a few extreme scores would be more diluted. If the null hypothesis was in fact true, we would again expect the difference between the two group means to be zero, but this time there would be less variation from that figure between samples.

So, to evaluate the statistical significance of a difference between two mean scores in a research study, we need to consider not only the magnitude of that difference, but also the *standard deviation* and the *sample size*. For any given difference between means, the smaller the standard deviation, and the larger the sample size, the more likely it is that the psychologist could reject the null hypothesis.

Typically, in order to assess whether two mean scores show a statistically significant difference, psychologists use a *t*-test. This statistical procedure takes into account the factors noted above. A *t* score of more than about 2 or less than about -2 generally indicates a statistically significant difference between means, but the exact value required for significance depends on the sample size. Most statistics textbooks include tables that show the minimum values (sometimes called *critical values*) of *t* required to achieve statistical significance at the 0.05, 0.01 and 0.001 levels for any given sample size.

Key Learning Point

The t-test assesses the significance of a difference between two group mean scores, taking into account the sample sizes and the amount of variation in scores within each group.

Of course, the *t*-test requires that the data are *quantitative*. That is, the data should reflect scores on a dimension along which people vary, not different types, or pigeon-holes, into which they fall. Strictly, the data should also be such that a difference of a given number of units between two scores should reflect the same amount of difference no matter what the absolute level of the scores. So, a score of 100 should be the same amount more than 90 as 20 is more than 10. This may seem straightforward, but with many self-report measures (e.g. job satisfaction) we cannot strictly be sure whether it is the case. Further, scores should approximate to a *normal distribution* (*see* Fig. 2.4). This is a technical term for a bell-shaped distribution of scores, which peaks at the mean, and drops off at equal rates on either side of it, with that rate being linked to the standard deviation. Fortunately, the *t*-test is not usually invalidated if the data do not approximate a normal distribution (Sawilowsky and Blair, 1992). In the jargon, it is a *robust* test. This is just as well, because the research data obtained by psychologists are often very unlike the normal distribution (Micceri, 1989).

A somewhat different version of the *t*-test can be employed if we wish to see whether the means of two sets of scores from the *same* people differ significantly.

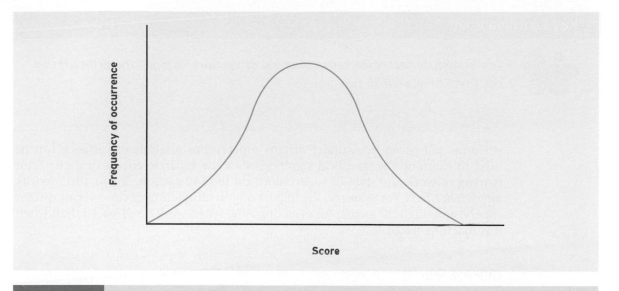

| Figure 2.4 | The normal distribution |

So, for example, we might be interested in assessing people's performance at a task before and after training. The formula is somewhat different, but most of the principles for this *t*-test for non-independent samples are the same as those for the independent samples *t*-test described above.

Analysis of variance

What happens when the scores of more than two groups are to be compared? In this situation, another very common statistical test is performed – it is called *analysis of variance*. Essentially, it is an extension of the *t*-test procedure. The resulting statistic is called *F*, and the principles concerning statistical significance are applied to *F* in the same way as to *t* (see above). The same limitations to the use of *t* also apply to *F*. *F* can also be used instead of *t* to compare just two means. Indeed, $F = t^2$ in this instance.

F reflects the ratio of variation in scores between groups to variation in scores within groups. The greater the former relative to the latter, the higher the *F* value, and the more likely it is that the population means differ (i.e. there is a low probability of obtaining our results if the null hypothesis is in fact true for the population). If a statistically significant *F* value is obtained, we can reject the null hypothesis that the population means are identical. If we wish, we can then use a modified form of the *t*-test to identify which particular pair or pairs of groups differ significantly from each other.

Data from more complex research designs can be analysed using analysis of variance. Suppose, for example, the psychologist was interested in the effects of both machine-paced work *and* style of supervision on job satisfaction. He or she runs an experiment with four groups of people. One group does machine-paced work under close supervision. Another does the same work under distant supervision. The third does self-paced work under close supervision, and the fourth performs self-paced work under distant supervision. Analysis of variance can be used to examine the statistical significance of the separate effects of each factor (pacing of work and style of supervision) on job satisfaction. It can also identify *interaction effects*. For example, the impact on job satisfaction of close versus distant supervision might be greater (or even opposite) when work is self-paced than when it is machine-paced.

Chi-square

As indicated earlier, data are sometimes qualitative rather than quantitative. Suppose, for example, that a psychologist wishes to examine whether production managers and marketing managers differ in their views of 'human nature' at work. The psychologist devises a way of assessing whether each of 50 production managers and 50 marketing managers believes in 'theory X' (people have to be controlled and forced to work), 'theory Y' (people are essentially responsible and trustworthy) or 'social' (people are most concerned with social relationships at work) (*see* Chapter 9). Each manager is classed as believing in one of these three views of human nature.

The psychologist cannot use *t* or *F* because the data are *categorical*, not quantitative. Believing in one view of human nature is not 'more' or 'less' than believing in another – it is simply different. Hence although the psychologist might arbitrarily give managers a score of 1 if they believe in theory X, 2 for theory Y and 3 for social, the numbers are not a scale. Believing in theory Y is not 'more' or 'less' than believing in theory X. The psychologist is therefore interested in determining whether there is a statistically significant difference in the frequency with which members of the two groups of managers endorse each view of human nature. The statistical test employed in this instance is known as chi-square (χ^2). The more the groups differ, the higher the chi-square figure for the data, and the less likely it is that the null hypothesis is true. As with *t* and *F*, critical values of chi-square at various levels of statistical significance can be checked in tables in most statistics texts. Unlike *t* and *F*, these critical values do not depend directly on sample size. Instead, they depend on the number of rows and columns in the data when tabulated. In the above example, the table would contain six cells altogether: 2 (types of manager) $\times$ 3 (views of human nature). The figure in each cell would be the number of managers falling into that category. The chi-square procedure compares the observed numbers with those that would be expected if the proportion subscribing to each view of human nature was the same for each type of manager. A worked example of chi-square appears on the website for this book.

The statistical technique called chi-square is used to test differences between groups in the frequency with which group members fall into defined categories.

Correlation

The second question posed at the start of this section concerned whether two or more variables tend to go together. Correlation is most commonly used in survey research. Thus, for example, a psychologist might wish to find out whether job satisfaction and intention to leave one's job are connected. Alternatively, he or she might be interested in seeing whether self-esteem and salary are connected. In these cases, the variables are on continuous scales, as for *t*-tests, but unlike *t*-tests the psychologist is not looking to compare mean scores. Instead, he or she wishes to find out whether the two variables correlate (co-relate).

There are several different but similar statistical tests of correlation, each of which produces a *correlation coefficient*. The most common of these is Pearson's product–moment correlation coefficient, or *r* for short. Correlation coefficients cannot exceed a value of 1, and cannot be lower than −1. A Pearson's *r* of 1 would mean that when scores on the two variables of interest were plotted on a graph, a straight line could be drawn that would go through all of the plotted points (*see* Fig. 2.5a). This line would rise from left to right, indicating that as variable *A* increased, so did variable *B*. This line would not need to be at any particular angle, nor would it necessarily go through the origin. An *r* of −1 would also mean that a straight line could be drawn through all of the plotted points, but this time it would slope the other way, so that as *A* increased, *B* decreased (*see* Fig. 2.5b). An *r* of 0 would mean not only that it was impossible to draw a straight line through all of the data points, but also that there was no tendency whatever for scores on either of the two variables to rise or fall with scores on the other one (*see* Fig. 2.5c).

The reader may already have grasped that an *r* of 0 is a statistical representation of the null hypothesis, that there is no linear relationship between the variables. The psychologist therefore typically asks 'Does the correlation coefficient I have obtained with my sample differ sufficiently from 0 for me to reject the null hypothesis?' Just as with other statistics, for any given sample size we can look in statistical tables to find the critical value of *r* required to achieve particular levels of statistical significance. Thus, for example, with a sample size of 20, the critical value of *r* for significance at the 0.05 level is ± 0.444. Corresponding values at the 0.01 and 0.001 levels are 0.590 and 0.708. A worked example of Pearson's *r* appears on the website for this book.

Another form of correlation is the *Spearman rank correlation (rho, ρ)*. This is used when the data do not reflect absolute scores, but only a rank order. This would mean that we know, for example, that score *x* is greater than score *y*, but not by how much. The formula for calculating rho looks different from that for *r*, but in fact it boils down to the same thing. Rho can also be useful when the data deviate a great deal from the normal distribution (*see* Fig. 2.4) and when there are a few scores hugely different from the others.

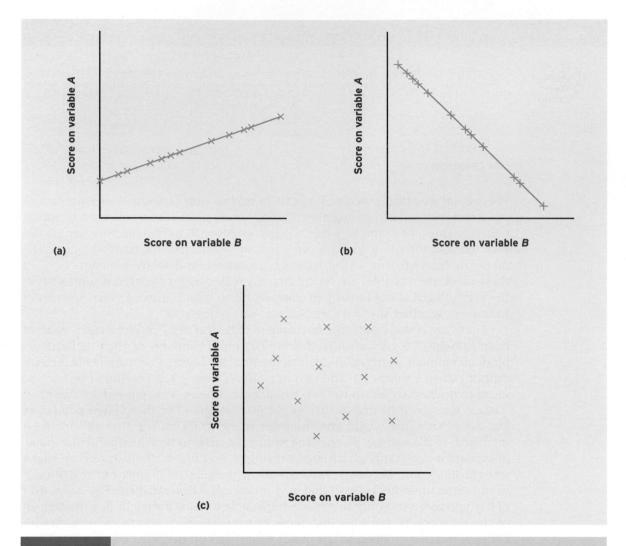

(a)

(b)

(c)

Score on variable *A*

Score on variable *B*

<table>
<tr><td>**Figure 2.5**</td><td>**Correlation: (a) a correlation of 1; (b) a correlation of −1; (c) a correlation of 0 (each X represents data collected from one person)**</td></tr>
</table>

Key Learning Point

The statistical technique called correlation tests the extent to which scores on two variables tend to go together (i.e. covary).

Whatever the exact correlation technique, it is important to remember the old maxim *correlation does not imply causality* (see also the earlier section on survey design). Often, a psychologist would like to infer that the reason why two variables are correlated is that one causes the other. This may seem plausible, but it is hard to be sure. Suppose that a psychologist finds a highly significant positive correlation between self-esteem and salary. If both are measured at the same time, there is no basis on which to decide whether self-esteem causes salary or salary causes self-esteem. It is fairly easy to think of possible explanations for either causal direction. It is also possible that some other variable(s) (e.g. social status, educational attainment) cause both self-esteem and salary, but unless we have measured them, we can only speculate.

As noted earlier in this chapter, obtaining data over time (a *longitudinal study*) can help, in so far as it may uncover whether scores on one variable at time 1 predict scores on the other at time 2. But even then, the fact that phenomenon A happens before B does not necessarily mean that A *causes* B.

Multiple regression

Just as analysis of variance is an extension of the *t*-test for more than two groups, so multiple regression is an extension of correlation for more than two variables. Suppose a psychologist wishes to assess the correlation with self-esteem of each of salary, educational attainment and social status. He or she might well find that the latter three variables are all correlated with each other, and also with self-esteem. In this case, the psychologist might wonder which one(s) really matter in predicting self-esteem.

Multiple regression is a statistical technique that allows the social scientist to assess the *relative* importance of each of salary, educational attainment and social status as predictors of self-esteem. It involves estimation of the correlation of each of the three with self-esteem *independent of the other two* (the technique can of course be extended to larger numbers of variables). In this way the researcher can end up with an equation that specifies the weighting to be given to each predictor variable in predicting self-esteem, as well as an overall indication of just how predictable self-esteem is using all of the predictor variables. But note: just because variables are designated 'predictors' in multiple regression analyses, it does not mean that they are necessarily 'causes' of the variable to be predicted.

Multiple regression is a much-used technique in work psychology. It is quite complex. Its intricacies are beyond the scope of this book, but the interested reader can find out more by consulting Licht (1997) or Cohen *et al.* (2003).

Other phenomena in statistical testing

Effect size

The reader may have wondered whether statistical significance is necessarily the same as significance for practical purposes. At least one behavioural science statistics text (Rosenthal and Rosnow, 1984) repeatedly reminds its readers that statistical significance depends on the size of the effect (e.g. the difference in means between two groups relative to the standard deviation; or the value of *r* for two variables) *multiplied by* the size of the study. Thus, when research uses large samples, quite small effect sizes can lead us to reject the null hypothesis – probably correctly, of course, *but* if the effect is so small, albeit detectable, are we going to worry about it? For example, a psychologist might find that, in a large sample, marketing managers score on average 58 out of 100 on a numeracy test whereas production managers score on average 59.5 out of 100, and that this difference is highly statistically significant. So what? How much does this tell us about, for example, the relative effectiveness of marketing and production managers? Clearly although production managers do slightly better, there are many marketing managers who score higher than many production managers. One way of addressing this issue is to assess the relationship between numeracy and work performance, focusing particularly on the extra work performance one could expect given a specified increase in numeracy, and then translating this into practical benefits (*see* Chapter 4 concerning utility analysis).

However, it is also useful to consider effect size in more abstract terms. We can think of it as *the degree to which the null hypothesis is false*. For *t*, we can consider the difference between group means as a proportion of the standard deviation of scores (*d*) to be a measure of effect size. For *r*, we can use the proportion of variance in scores common to both variables. This is r^2. Thus, a correlation of 0.60 indicates that $0.60 \times 0.60 = 0.36$, or 36 per cent of the variance in one variable is 'accounted for' by scores in the other. With large samples, it is often possible for a correlation of only 0.2 or less to be statistically significant. In this case, the variables share just 4 per cent of variance. This sounds small, but Rosenthal and Rosnow (1984, pp. 207–11) have demonstrated that it can nevertheless reflect practical outcomes of real importance. For example, if one form of treatment for depression is 4 per cent better than another, over a whole nation that could amount to a lot more happy people.

Key Learning Point

Effect size goes beyond statistical significance by assessing the magnitude of the relationship obtained, rather than how confident one can be that the relationship is not zero.

For *F*, one often-used indicator of effect size is called *eta* (η). It reflects the proportion of total score variation that is accounted for by group membership. Like r^2, eta can be considered an indicator of the proportion of total variance accounted for.

There is nothing mysterious about indices of effect size. They are often quite simply derived, and are sometimes even routinely calculated on the way to a test of statistical significance. Examples appear on http://www.booksites.net/arnold_workpsych.

Statistical power

Statistical power refers to the probability of rejecting the null hypothesis when it is indeed false and therefore should be rejected. It is, in other words, the probability of avoiding making a type II error. Like all probability estimates, it can vary from 0 to 1. The level of power operating in any particular research study depends on the level of statistical significance the psychologist wishes to work at, the size of the sample, and the size of the effect under examination. The chief practical lesson to be learned is that small sample sizes have very low power – that is, a high probability of missing a relationship that does exist in the population from which the sample is drawn.

Cohen (1977) has produced tables that specify the sample sizes required to achieve certain levels of power for particular statistical tests at specified significance levels and effect sizes. These tables are a useful guide for researchers wondering how many participants they need for their study.

These observations about statistical power are very important. Often in research, one investigator reports a statistically significant finding with a moderate to large sample size. Then another researcher attempts to replicate the result with a smaller sample, fails to find a statistically significant effect, and declares that the original finding must have been a fluke. But close examination shows that the *effect size* in the second study is as large as the first – it is just that the smaller sample prevents statistical significance being achieved.

Key Learning Point

There is a high probability that small-scale studies will fail to find effects which exist in the population of interest.

Meta-analysis

Some published research articles report a *meta-analysis* of findings from a number of studies. This type of article is quite common, especially in topic areas where a lot of research has been conducted. The aim of meta-analysis is to provide an overview and summary of what general conclusions can be drawn from a body of research. Using concepts such as effect size and statistical power (see the previous section of this chapter), a researcher conducting a meta-analysis extracts (and if necessary adjusts) measures of association (usually correlation) between variables of interest from each relevant research study, and weights them according to the sample size. Other information may well also be recorded – for example whether the people studied were managers or blue-collar workers, how variables of interest (e.g. job satisfaction) were measured, and whether the study was an experiment or a survey. Then the person conducting the meta-analysis is in a position to make some general statements about the extent to which two or more variables are statistically associated with each other, and whether the strength of the association depends partly on factors such as the measures used and the populations studied.

Meta-analysis has been criticised by some as being something of a blunt instrument that cannot capture important details of how particular research studies were carried out. Others have defended meta-analysis. Rosenthal and DiMatteo (2000) have reviewed these arguments and conclude that many of the criticisms are invalid. An example of meta-analysis is provided by Lee *et al.* (2000). They examined the relationships between occupational commitment (the extent to which a person feels a sense of belonging and loyalty to the type of work they do) and other variables, including organisational commitment and job involvement (*see* Chapter 7 for more about work-related attitudes such as these). Lee and colleagues aggregated the results of 77 different studies, with a total sample size of nearly 16 000 people, so their conclusions were based on a great deal of data.

Analysing qualitative data

Just as there are many techniques for analysing numerical data, so the same is also true for qualitative data. Just as statisticians sometimes disagree about which statistical techniques are appropriate in which circumstances, so qualitative researchers sometimes disagree about the best ways to analyse qualitative data. But statistical arguments are usually about technical issues, whereas disagreements over how to analyse qualitative data are more often to do with the researcher's philosophical and theoretical position. Much qualitative data analysis is conducted by hand, but here too there are computer packages available to help locate and code data according to categories nominated by the researcher. The exotically named NUDIST is probably the most used.

Table 2.1 shows an extract from a research interview conducted by the first author of this book. The interview was one of 80 conducted by the author and colleagues as part of an investigation of how lawyers and architects see their work, and in particular how they, as professionals, view management and being managed. In this extract, the interviewer (I) and respondent (R – a lawyer working for a large firm of solicitors) discuss how the respondent's work is evaluated.

First of all notice that this is not a highly structured interview. To some extent the interviewer follows up what the respondent says, for example when he asks 'But it doesn't sound like you feel that way about your PDR?' A highly structured interview would not include such a specific question based on what the interviewee just said, since all or virtually all of the questions would be specified in advance. However, the interview was semi-structured rather than unstructured because there was a list of topic areas to be covered, but also scope to adjust the depth in which each was covered. Second, notice how the interviewer to some extent adopts what Silverman (2001) terms an 'emotionalist' position. This is evident in the question mentioned a few sentences back. Also, in his first question of this extract he is clearly interested in the respondent's opinion as well as trying to elicit what might be thought of as factual information about the way the respondent's work performance was evaluated. On the other hand, the interviewer also wants to use the interview to go beyond the interviewee's own experiences. This is demonstrated by his observation 'There's a couple of indications that it might not be for everybody'. That could be seen as an attempt to gain a more general picture

Table 2.1	An excerpt from a research interview

A lawyer discusses assessment of work performance

Note: I = Interview, R = Respondent

I: How is your performance evaluated here and what do you think of that?

R: They have an annual PDR, which is Personal Development Review. You are given a form to complete a short time before and then you meet with whoever's undertaking it generally – the partner that you report to – and you sit in a room and discuss it.

I: And is that a fruitful discussion or is it going through the motions?

R: For me it was fruitful because I think the . . . The difficulty I have with these is that more senior people can see the benefit and the relevance of them. When you get down to the secretaries, they view it very, very much as a . . . almost as a disciplinary matter. It's their annual kicking from the boss because they haven't been up to standard.

I: But it doesn't sound like you feel that about your PDR?

R: No. I think it's the only true way of finding out your own standing and seriously expressing ambitions and what you have to achieve to reach those.

I: And is it sufficiently candid and open to achieve that?

R: It was for me, yes.

I: There's a couple of indications that it might not be for everybody. Is that...? Or am I reading too much into that?

R: No, you're right. There are some people who I've been told on the quiet have reached as far as they will go, but having spoken to those individuals – not directly about their PDRs, but you know, just generally – I don't think they've actually been told that clearly.

I: Okay.

R: I think that's more a function of whoever's actually doing the PDR because I had two very forthright speakers who will tell you exactly whereas others are a little bit more political.

I: Okay. There would have been a time when having your performance assessed and working in a managed system was a bit of an insult for a professional person, but it sounds like that comes with the territory now.

R: It does. I've only had them since I've been here. It was a new concept to me. And yes, I was very nervous before it. But unless you do get some form of independent view, I don't think you're the best judge of your own performance.

of performance assessment in that firm. But it could also arguably be an extension of the emotionalist position because the interviewer is seeking to access indirectly the experiences of other people in the firm.

How might these data be analysed? What general statements can be made, and conclusions drawn, on the basis of data such as these? This depends heavily both on the research questions being asked (together with the theoretical and/or practical basis for considering those questions important), and on the philosophical assumptions of the researcher. Excellent coverage of the range of methods available for analysing qualitative data (including interviews) can be found in Symon and Cassell (1998).

One way of analysing this transcript would in effect involve turning qualitative data into quantitative data. The researcher could attempt to assess how positively the interviewee felt about the firm's methods for assessing the work performance of employees, perhaps on a numerical scale. Another researcher could be asked to do the same, partly in order to check that the scoring of the interviewee's opinion about the performance assessment showed inter-rater reliability.

While such a scoring procedure might be useful, it would of course be a huge waste of information if that was all that was done with these data. Another approach would be to conduct a *content analysis* of what the interviewee says. Bryman (2001, p. 180) defines content analysis as 'an approach to the analysis of documents and texts that seeks to quantify content in terms of predetermined categories and in a systematic and replicable manner'. So in this case, the researcher might have prepared the content categories shown in Table 2.2 based on prior theory and research.

Table 2.2	Example of content analysis categories
Respondent's name:	
Content category	**Coding option (tick as applicable)**
1. Frequency of assessment	Less frequently than annual Annual More frequently than annual
2. Prior preparation	Thinking only Some written None specified
3. Who does the assessment?	Boss Other more senior person(s) Peer(s) Other

The researcher would study the interview transcript and decide, for each content category, which response option(s) were evident in what the interviewee said. Probably another researcher would do the same, in order to establish inter-rater reliability. Notice that agreement between raters is normally considered a sign that their 'scoring' of the interview is getting at objective truth, though it might also be argued that such agreement simply means the two raters share similar perceptions (sometimes referred to as *inter-subjective agreement*).

Sometimes the categories for a content analysis are specified in advance of the data being gathered. This is consistent with the idea that the categories are 'systematic' and 'predetermined' (see the definition above). However, it is usually very difficult to anticipate the kind of responses interviewees will offer. Categories are therefore defined in some studies by the researchers doing an initial reading of interview transcripts and then devising content categories that reflect as much as possible the things the interviewees chose to focus on. At its best, this can achieve a good balance between deductive reasoning (that is, deducing what types of response are important on the basis of prior theory and research) and inductive reasoning (that is, starting with the data and trying to develop theory on the basis of it). At its worst, it can mean considerable confusion as the researcher abandons his or her prior thinking yet also proves unable to do much with the data provided.

Content categories tend to be quite specific. It is also possible to code interview (and other textual) data more broadly, using a technique that is sometimes called template analysis (King, 1998). The categories are often devised on the basis of an initial look at the data. Some themes that might be recorded in this example are:

- description of personal experience of the performance assessment system;

- differences in perception between staff at different levels;

- belief that PDRs have value;

- variation in PDR process and outcome according to who conducts it;

- existence of 'off the record' communications about people's performance.

These themes would probably do better than content analysis at capturing the meaning of what was said in the interview. On the other hand the themes, in themselves, might miss some of the more precise points made.

It might also be said that thematic analysis still does not get at the complex and dynamic nature of what is going on in talk and text. Some researchers might use *discourse analysis* (Potter, 1997) to try to access this. Researchers have used several different approaches to discourse analysis. They have in common a desire to analyse in detail the versions of reality offered by a person, and their purposes in presenting themselves and their worlds in the way they do. Often this endeavour requires quite a lot of interpretation. It rests partly on subtle elements of what is said, and indeed what is not said. Some versions of discourse analysis use features such as voice intonation and the existence and length of pauses, as well as what is actually said. Researchers who use discourse analysis frequently (though not always) take the view that reality is entirely defined by people through their talk, interaction and thought. These researchers can therefore be described as social constructionist rather than positivist.

An analysis of the discourse in Table 2.1 might lead to the following conclusions about what the interviewee is trying to do: through expressing appreciation of the PDR, he is showing himself to be a loyal company man who is valued by the firm, and who is concerned to perform well and advance his career. His depiction of himself as initially nervous about the PDR could be taken to indicate an attempt to show how the firm's benevolence had convinced a sceptic about the integrity of the performance assessment system, to the benefit of both parties. His points about how secretaries experience PDR might serve to emphasise the difference in status between them and him, yet also show his good-hearted concern for their situation. Being the recipient of 'on the quiet' information about the performance of others could be offered as a sign that he is well-placed in informal company social networks.

This is, of course, quite speculative and focused more on the motives and purposes that could lie behind what was said than on the content of what was said. This analysis, then, entirely avoids the kinds of conclusions that might be reached by positivist or realist researchers, particularly if a number of interviewees and not just this one come up with the same point. These conclusions might be that the PDR is experienced as disciplinary by secretaries but as developmental by lawyers, and that nevertheless PDRs still on occasions fail to deliver open and honest feedback. Instead, the discourse analyst draws conclusions about the broad nature of the realities offered by interviewees and about their reasons for presenting those realities in the way they do.

Summary

Research designs used by work psychologists include surveys, experiments, qualitative research and action research. These designs vary in the amount of control exerted by the work psychologist, the degree of difficulty in carrying out the research, the role of theory and the nature of the data obtained. Perhaps most importantly, work psychologists using different designs often have different philosophical positions about the nature of knowledge and the existence (or not) of an objective reality. Research designs can be distinguished from methods of data collection. Methods include questionnaires, tests, interviews, observation, psychophysiological measures and archival sources. The characteristics of research published in leading journals of work psychology have been summarised by Schaubroeck and Kuehn (1992, p. 107):

> a majority of published studies were conducted in the field, although laboratory work comprises nearly one-third of the research. Half of the published research was experimental ... most studies minimized common method factors by using diverse data sources. On the down side, a majority of field studies were cross-sectional in nature, there was very little cross-validation of findings, 'hard' data such as physiological measures and archival records were used infrequently ... Researchers appeared to invest in particular design strengths and compromise on others.

Statistical techniques are available to help draw appropriate conclusions from quantitative data. Collectively, these techniques are intended to address two general situations. Firstly, where two or more groups of people are being compared (*t*-test; analysis of variance; chi-square), and secondly where two or more variables are being examined to see whether they tend to go together (correlation; multiple regression). The concept of statistical significance is important in interpreting the results produced by statistical tests. So is the notion of effect size. Techniques for analysing qualitative data such as interview transcripts vary in the extent to which they divide the data into small chunks and assign the data to categories. But they have in common the purpose of establishing meaning rather than causal connections between variables.

Test your learning

Short-answer questions

1   Briefly describe a psychological study of your own invention and specify a null hypothesis and an alternative hypothesis suitable for that study.

2   Explain the concepts of statistical significance, statistical power and effect size.

3   Explain (in one sentence) the type of data and research question to which each of the following techniques can be applied:

   t-test

   Correlation

   Chi-square

   Content analysis

4   Imagine that you are trying to develop a theory to explain successful performance in telephone sales work. For each box in Fig. 2.1, suggest at least two possible factors.

5   List three important differences between positivist research and social constructionist research.

6   List five methods by which work psychologists obtain research information.

7   Write a short paragraph on the differences between experimental and survey research in work psychology.

8   What is action research?

Suggested assignments

1   Choose any issue in work psychology that interests you. Examine how different research designs might be used to tackle that issue. Is any one design better than the others?

2   'It is not worth distinguishing between research designs and research methods in work psychology because the choice of design dictates the choice of method.' Discuss.

3   Find an article in an academic work psychology journal. Check that it reports research in which some kind(s) of data were collected. Report on the research philosophy, design, methods and data analysis techniques used, and discuss (i) whether these were appropriate given the research hypotheses or questions specified, *and* (ii) whether you think the research hypotheses/questions were appropriate.

Relevant websites

The publisher Sage produces many books on research methods in psychology and the social sciences more generally. There are both general books about a range of methods, and specific books about one or a small number of similar methods. Check out the following address for their latest offerings: http://www.sagepub.com/subject.aspx?scode 1=L00&sc=1&sname1=Research+Methods+%26+Evaluation&scode2=L40

To do with the results of research more than method, the American Psychological Association (APA) publicises recent research in various fields of psychology. To see recent research on psychology in the workplace, go to http://www.significant difference.org/workplace.html.

A neat article discussing the possible dangers in the workplace of applying so-called 'pop' psychology (i.e. ideas that people can relate to, but which have not necessarily been tested or thought through) can be found at http://performance-appraisals.org/Bacalsappraisalarticles/articles/poppsych.htm.

For further self-test material and relevant, annotated weblinks please visit the website at http://www.booksites.net/arnold_workspych.

Suggested further reading

Note: full references for all four pieces of suggested reading are given in the list at the end of this book.

1   The book by Sylvia Shimmin and Don Wallis, *Fifty Years of Occupational Psychology in Britain*, provides a well-written description of how work psychology has evolved in the United Kingdom and the topics it focuses on. Although the historical details are of course specific to the UK context, much of the content of this book can be generalised to other countries.

2 Although about management rather than work psychology, the 2002 book by Mark Easterby-Smith, Richard Thorpe and Andy Lowe, *Management Research: An introduction*, gives a clear and practical guide to key issues in formulating and doing research.

3 Alan Bryman's book, *Social Research Methods*, is in many respects a rather more advanced and detailed version of Easterby-Smith *et al.*, with slightly greater emphasis on conceptual as well as practical issues.

4 The book by Adamantios Diamantopoulos and Bodo Schlegelmilch, *Taking the Fear out of Data Analysis*, is a gentle and entertaining introduction for those who feel they are not particularly numerate but want to understand how to apply basic statistics appropriately. The examples used are not confined to psychology.

Appendix: psychological associations in various countries

Albania	**Association of Albanian Psychologists** Rruge e Kavajes, P 63/1, N.7 Tirana, Albania
Argentina	**Association Argentina de Ciencias del Comportamiento** Presidente Peron 1292, 5700 San Luis, Argentina
Australia	**The Australian Psychological Society Ltd** PO Box 38, Flinders Lane PO, Melbourne, Victoria 8009, Australia
Austria	**Fed of Austrian Association of Psychologists** University of Graz, Department of Psychology, Universitatplatz 2, Austria
Bangladesh	**Department of Psychology** University of Dhaka, Dhaka – 1000, Bangladesh
Barbados	**Psychological Association of Barbados** PO Box 931, National House, Rocbank Street, Bridgetown, Barbados
Belgium	**Department of Psychology** Vrije Universiteit Brussel, Pleinlaan 2, B-1050 Brussels, Belgium
Brazil	**Sociedade Brasileira de Psicologia** R. Florencio de Abreu, 681, sala 1105, 14015-060 Ribeirao Preto SP, Brazil
Bulgaria	**Bulgarian Psychological Society** Druzhestvo na Psycholosite v Balgaria, 14 Lulin Planina Street, Sofia 1606, Bulgaria

Canada	**Canadian Psychological Association** 151 Slater Street, Suite 205, Ottawa, Ontario, Canada K1P 5H3
Chile	**Colegio Psicologos de Chile A.G.** Av. Gral. Bustamante No. 250 Depto. H. 3oPiso, Providencia, Santiago, Chile
Colombia	**Colombian National Committee of Psychology** Apartado 88754, Bogota, Colombia
Croatia	**Croatian Psychological Association** Ivana Lucica 3, 1000 Zagreb, Croatia
Cuba	**Society of Cuban Psychologists** Faculty of Psychology, University of Habana, Calle San Rafael No 1168, Ciudad de La Habana, Cuba
Czech Republic	**Czech–Moravian Psychological Society** Kladenska 48, CZ 16000, Prague 6, Czech Republic
Denmark	**Danish Psychologists' Association** Stockholmsgade 27, Copenhagen, DK-2100, Denmark
Egypt	**Egyptian Association for Psychological Studies** Faculty of Education, Ain-Shams University, Heliopolis, Code No 11757 Cairo, Egypt
Estonia	**Union of Estonian Psychologists** Dept of Psychology, University of Tartu, Tiigi 78, Tartu 50410, Estonia
Ethiopia	**Ethiopian Psychologists' Association** PO Box 55239, Addis Ababa, Ethiopia

European Federation of Psychology Students' Associations
EFPSA
www.efpsa.org

Finland	**Suomen Psykologinen Seura** Liisankatu 16A, FIN-00170, Helsinki, Finland
France	**Société Française de Psychologie** 28-32 rue Serpente F-75006, Paris, France
Germany	**Federation of German Psychological Associations** Geschäftsstelle des BDP, Heilsbachstrasse. 22-24, D-53123 Bonn, Germany

Greece	**Hellenic Psychological Society** Department of Psychology, School of Philosophy, University of Athens, Panepistemiopolis, Athens 15784, Greece
Guam	**Guam Psychological Association** PO Box 12061, Tamuning 96931, Guam
Hong Kong	**Hong Kong Psychological Society** Department of Psychology, Chinese University of Hong Kong, Shatin, Hong Kong
Hungary	**Hungarian Psychological Association** Budapest, Tcrezkrt 13, H-1536 Budapest, PO Box 220, Hungary
Iceland	**Icelandic Psychological Society** Lágmúli 7, IS-108 Reykjavik, Iceland
India	**Indian Psychological Association** Department of Psychology, Zakir Hussain College, J.L Nehru Marq, New Delhi 110 002, India
Indonesia	**Indonesian Psychologists Association** IPA/HIMPSI, Kebayoran Centre Block A/16, Kebayoran Baru, Jakarta 12240, Indonesia
Iran	**Iranian Association of Psychology** Faculty of Psychology and Education, Teheran University, Martyr Chamran Highway, Al-Ahmad Ave, Opposite Nasr. St, Teheran, Iran
Iraq	**Iraqi Educational and Psychological Association** c/o Al-Mistansiriyah University, PO Box 46017, Codeno 12506, Baghdad, Iraq
Ireland	**Psychological Society of Ireland** CX House, 2A Corn Exchange Place, Poolbeg Street, Dublin 2, Ireland
Israel	**Israel Psychological Association** PO Box 11497, Tel Aviv 61114, Israel
Italy	**Società Italiana di Psicologia** via Tagliamento 76, 00198 Roma, Italy
Japan	**Japanese Psychological Association** 5-23-13-7F, Hongo, Bunkyo-ku, Tokyo 113-0033, Japan

Jordan	**Jordanian Psychological Association** PO Box 1339, Jubeiha 11941, Amman, Jordan
Kenya	**Kenya Psychological Association** PO Box 42905, Nairobi, Kenya
Korea (South)	**Korean Psychological Association** Room 917, Sung Jie Heights Officetel, 702-13 Yeoksam-Dong Kangnam-Ku, Seoul 135-080, South Korea
Latvia	**Latvian Association of Professional Psychologists** Humanitatian Institute, Brivilaas Str. 32, LV-1051, Riga, Latvia
Liechtenstein	**Berufsverein der Psychologen Innen** Und Psychologinnen Liechtenstein, Meierhofstrasse 100, FL- 9495 Triesen, Liechtenstein
Lithuania	**Lithuanian Psychological Association** Didlaukio Street 47, Vilnius 2057, Lithuania
Luxembourg	**Association Luxembourgeoise des Psychologues** Service Medico-Psycho-Pedagogique, 3 Place Norbert Metz, L-4239 Esch-sur-Alzette, Luxembourg
Malta	**Malta Union of Professional Psychologists** PO Box 341, Valletta, Malta
Mexico	**Sociedad Mexicana de Psicologia A.C.** Indiana no. 260, int. 608, Col. Napoles, Deleg, Benito Juaraz, DF CP 03710, Mexico
Morocco	**Association Marocaine des Etudes Psychologiques** Faculté des Lettres et des Sciences Hum, Université Mohammed V, Rabat, Morocco
Namibia	**Psychological Association of Namibia** PO Box 9500, Windhoek 9000, Namibia
Nepal	**Nepalese Psychological Association** Post Box 3213 GPO, Kathmandu, Nepal
New Zealand	**New Zealand Psychological Society** PO Box 4092, Wellington, New Zealand
Nicaragua	**Association Nicaraguense de Psicologos** PO Box C-142, Managua, Nicaragua

Nigeria	**Nigerian Psychological Association** Department of General and Applied Psychology, University of Jos, PMB 2084 Jos, Nigeria
Norway	**Norwegian Psychological Association** PO Box 8733, Youngstorget, 0028 Oslo, Norway
Pakistan	**Pakistan Psychological Association** 101, 102, Latif Plaza, 103 Ferozepur Road, Lahore, Pakistan
People's Republic of China	**Chinese Psychological Society** Institute of Psychology, Chinese Academy of Sciences, Beijing 100101, China
Peru	**Peru Psychological Association** Jr. Portugueze 165-13, Lima–25 (Rimac), Peru
Philippines	**Psychological Association of the Philippines** Philippines Social Science Centre, Commonwealth Avenue, Diliman, Quezon 1101, Philippines
Poland	**Polish Psychological Association** ul. Stawki 5/7, PL-00-183 Warszwawa, Poland
Portugal	**Associacao dos Psicologos Portugueses, APPORT** University of Lisbon, Faculty of Psychology Ed, Alameda da Universidade, Lisbon 1600, Portugal
Puerto Rico	**Association de Psicologos de Puerto Rico** PO Box 363435, San Juan 00936-3435, Puerto Rico
Republic of Armenia	**Union of Psychologists of Armenia** Yerevan Abovyan Pedagogical Institute, Yerevan, Armenia
Republic of Georgia	**Georgian Psychological Association** D. Uznadze Institute of Psychology, 22 Lashvili Street, Tbilis 380009, Georgia
Republic of Panama	**Panamanian Association of Psychologists** Apartado 9832-0116, World Trade Centre, Panama City, Panama
Republic of Yemen	**Yemen Psychological Association** PO Box 6181, Khormaksek-Aden, Yemen
Romania	**Romanian Psychologists Association** Bd. Luliu Maniu nr. 1-3, Corp A., et 5, Bucharest, Romania

Russia	**Russian Psychological Society** Institute of Psychology, Russian Academy of Sciences, Yaroslavskaya St. 13, Moscow 129366, Russia
Saudi Arabia	**Saudi Educational & Psychological Association** PO Box 2458, Riyadh 11451, Saudi Arabia
Serbia	**Psychological Association of Serbia** Djustina 7/111 YU-11000 Beograd, Serbia
Singapore	**Singapore Psychological Society** Newtown Post Office, PO Box 192, Singapore 912207
Slovenia	**Slovenian Psychological Association** Prushnikova 74, SI-1210 Ljubljana-Sentvid, Slovenia
South Africa	**Psychological Association of South Africa** PO Box 66083, Broadway, 2020, South Africa
Spain	**Colegio Oficial de Psicologos** C/Conde de Penalver, No. 45-50, Madrid 28006, Spain
Sweden	**Swedish Psychological Association** Box 3287, 10365 Stockholm, Sweden
Switzerland	**Swiss Psychological Society** Department de Psychologie, 2 rue Faucingny, 1700 Fribourg, Switzerland
Thailand	**The Thai Psychological Association** Faculty of Psychology, Chulalongkorn University, 16th Floor, Witthyakit Bldg, Phayathai Road, Pathumwan, Bangkok 10330, Thailand
The Netherlands	**Nederlands Instituut van Psychologen** Postbus 9921, 1006 AP Amsterdam, Netherlands
Turkey	**Turkish Psychologists Association** Mesrutiyet Caddesi 22/12, Kizilay/Ankara 06640, Turkey
Uganda	**Uganda National Psychological Association** Department of Psychology, Makerere University, PO Box 7062, Kampala, Uganda
Ukraine	**Ukrainian Psychological Society** Ukranian Science-Method Centre for Applied Psychology & Social Work, Shevchenko blvd. 27-A Office 305, Kiev 01032, Ukraine

United Kingdom   **The British Psychological Society**
St Andrews House, 48 Princess Road East, Leicester LE1 7DR, UK

United States   **American Psychological Association**
750 First St NE, Washington, DC 20002-4242, USA

Uruguay   **Sociedad de Psicologia del Uruguay**
Colonia 1342, Esc. 19 y 20, C.P. 11100 Montevideo, Uruguay

Venezuela   **Venezuelan Federation of Psychologists**
Av La Guaira con, Av Naiguata, Macaracuay, Caracas, Venezuela

Vietnam   **Psycho-Pedagogical Association of Vietnam**
7 Nguyen Canh Chan Street, Hanoi, Vietnam

Zimbabwe   **Zimbabwe Psychological Association**
5 Exe Road, Vainona, Harare, Zimbabwe

CHAPTER 3

Individual differences

After studying this chapter, you should be able to:

1 describe the approach to the testing of human intelligence adopted by Binet and Simon;

2 explain the difference between Spearman's 'g' factor and Thurstone's 'primary mental abilities' approach to intelligence testing;

3 outline contemporary theories of human intelligence and intelligence testing;

4 compare conventional approaches with emotional and practical intelligence;

5 describe trait-based theories of personality and personality assessment;

6 define the 'Big Five' personality constructs;

7 name three personality questionnaires available in the United Kingdom;

8 describe socio-cognitive approaches to understanding behaviour at work.

Students Face Personality Tests for University Places

British universities are to introduce personality tests and City-style recruitment techniques to identify bright students from poorer backgrounds under government plans to overhaul admissions. The UK Government's Minister for Education will publish plans this month for an access regulator to ensure teenagers win places on merit following controversy over whether universities are unfairly rejecting privately educated pupils.

To reassure middle-class parents, the regulator is likely to monitor not only 'ivory towers' discrimination against poor children but also clumsy positive discrimination that is unfair to wealthy pupils. Ministers want universities to adopt methods such as psychometric testing, the psychological questionnaires widely used in City recruitment which explore personality traits and ability to learn, and US-style aptitude tests as fairer ways of assessing teenagers. They fear too many academics rely on old-fashioned interviews favouring confident teenagers coached in the 'right' answers. Whitehall sources say dons will have to show they use efficient 'professional' selection techniques as well as A-level results. 'Why do the most competitive businesses in the UK not just accept everyone on the basis of their CV? It's because there is an understanding that there are various different qualities that matter,' said one source at the Department for Education and Skills. 'Universities should be measuring aptitude and potential. Exams are a very important way of measuring that but not the only way.'

Source: The Observer, *2 March 2003*

Introduction

The case study demonstrates that there is a growing usage of measures of intelligence and personality assessments in order to predict academic success and job performance in many different settings. So, what do intelligence tests actually measure? In this chapter we explore various theories of intelligence and personality and provide a brief historical overview of the research literature in these areas. Traditionally, studies of intelligence and of personality have been treated separately but more contemporary theories of individual differences have begun to integrate these approaches in order to explain behaviour. Although there are many approaches to conceptualising and understanding human individual differences, only one kind of approach (which represents individual differences as measurable, structural concepts) has been widely influential in work psychology research and practice. This approach, which has been applied to both cognitive abilities and personality, is the trait-factor analytic approach. The basis of trait theory is that there are cross-situational generalities in behaviour. In other words, personality traits explain why people behave in similar ways in different circumstances.

In their attempts to explain personality, psychologists have tended to empha-sise the role of either internal (person) factors or external (situational) factors. It is important to understand that debate about the relative importance of people and situations in determining behaviour is a long-standing issue within psychology. Many of the approaches described below focus on the structure and measurement of individual differences; they do not emphasise the role of situational factors in determining behaviour. It would be a mistake, however, to conclude that the approaches described do not recognise the potential for situations to influence how people behave.

Recent theoretical and research work has developed an important, more soph-isticated concept than the idea that both people and situations are important. This is the idea that people and situations interact with each other to determine behav-iour. An influential current theory which adopts an interactionist perspective is the social cognitive (previously referred to as social learning) theory of Bandura (1977a, 1986). The impact of this theory can be seen in various fields of work psychology, and will be discussed later in this chapter (*see also* Chapters 1 and 8).

Key Learning Point

Personal and situational factors interact to determine behaviour.

Traditional models of cognitive ability

Some people are better at processing information than others. We are constantly exposed to evidence that, when it comes to cognitive (thinking) ability, there are significant variations among people. It is equally clear that some of these differ-ences are the result of differences in opportunities to learn (i.e. they are situationally or environmentally determined). Psychologists have expended a great deal of time and effort trying to understand and measure differences in cognitive ability. One approach to the issues involved has a long history and is particularly relevant to personnel selection and assessment. The core of this approach involves the use of carefully designed tests to assess people's levels of cognitive ability. Such tests need to be administered under standardised conditions and require people to attempt to answer written questions, all of which have been evolved through a highly technical process of trialling and analysis (*see* Table 3.1 for illustrative ques-tions). Because of the need for standardisation in administration and test content, this approach cannot assess people on their capacity to conduct everyday, real-life tasks. This is seen by some psychologists as a serious weakness. Also, note that cog-nitive ability is often tested within a maximal performance paradigm (i.e. the very best you can do within a set time frame) .

In the early years of the twentieth century, two French psychologists, Alfred Binet and Theodore Simon, developed what is generally accepted as the first satis-factory test of human intelligence. At the turn of the nineteenth century, France, in common with other industrialised nations, had introduced compulsory education.

Most of the children entering the schools seemed well able to benefit from the regular schools. Some were perhaps in need of special help, but could be dealt with by the regular system. A third group, however, was retarded to the point of being unable to benefit from the regular system. It was not always easy to identify the children in need of special treatment, and the test developed by Binet and Simon was intended to help in identifying these children by assessing their intellectual capabilities.

The approach adopted by Binet and Simon is still the basis for contemporary intelligence tests. In essence, Binet and Simon considered that intelligence could be measured by assessing a person's ability to answer a carefully selected collection of questions. Although the questions in modern tests (*see* Table 3.1) sometimes differ from those used by Binet and Simon, the principle of sampling behaviour on a carefully selected set of tasks is still at the basis of most tests. Clearly, by sampling behaviour one runs the risk of drawing false conclusions about a person – perhaps because of the particular questions asked, the circumstances in which the test is taken, or various other reasons. Binet and Simon certainly recognised that test scores alone were not enough and they proposed that, before any decision about a child was taken, other types of assessment should also be made.

Since the pioneering work of Binet and Simon, psychologists have carried out a considerable amount of work in their attempts to measure intelligence and to understand its structure. Much of this work makes use of statistical methods, developed to aid research into human intelligence. These statistical methods (the principal ones are correlation and factor analysis) are now used in many disciplines. Factor analysis, because of its important influence on theoretical work in intelligence, is outlined at the appropriate point in this chapter.

In some ways, of course, this view of intelligence seems a long way from the kind of thinking we have to do in our day-to-day lives. As we will see later in this chapter, some psychologists have tried to capture notions of 'practical intelligence' (e.g. Sternberg and Wagner, 1986; Scribner, 1986). Table 3.2 illustrates some points of comparison between practical thought and traditional intelligence tests.

Structural models of intelligence

Human beings are capable of showing considerable ability in a wide range of pursuits. For some (e.g. a bookmaker's clerk), considerable numerical skill is required; for others (e.g. a journalist), the ability to use words correctly and fluently is important; while yet others (e.g. an architect) need the ability to visualise objects in three dimensions. It would be possible to suggest many further occupational areas and associated abilities. The important point, however, is that it may be superficial to consider intelligence as a single or unitary attribute that can be represented by an overall measure.

Table 3.3 shows a typical correlation matrix derived by intercorrelating the results of a group of people in a collection of tests (see Chapter 2 for a brief explanation of correlation). Notice that although some of the correlations are smaller than others, none of them is negative. In other words people who do well in one test, do well (or at least not very badly) in the others. The results in Table 3.3 are typical of those obtained when people are tested on a wide range of intellectual tasks. Results such as this led Spearman (1927) to propose the so-called two-factor

Table 3.1	Some questions from an intelligence test

Q7   Mountain is to molehill as valley is to ...
 1   2   3   4   5
 hollow   chasm   hill   plain   mound

Q8   The third member of this series is omitted. What is it?
 0.1, 0.7, ... , 34.3, 240.1

Q9   Which one of the five words on the right bears a similar relation to each of the two words on the left?
                        1   2   3   4   5
 Class; shape   Rank   Grade   Analyse   Size   Form

Q10   Here are five classes. Write down the number of the class which contains two, and two only, of the other four classes:
 1   2   3   4   5
 Terriers   Mammals   'Scotties'   Dogs   Canines

Q11   Sniff is to handkerchief as shiver is to ...
 1   2   3   4   5
 blow   fire   catarrh   burn   sneeze

Q12   How many members of the following series are missing?
 1, 2, 5, 6, 7, 11, 12, ... , 20, 21, 22, 23

Q13   Which one of the five words on the right bears a similar relation to each of the two words on the left?
                        1   2   3   4   5
 Stream; tolerate   Brook   Contribute   Bear   Support   Pour

Q14   Working from the left, divide the fourth whole number by the fifth fraction:
 8, 6, 5/7, 3, 9, 2/9, 3/8, 1, 17/31, 4/9

theory of the structure of intelligence. This suggested that an underlying factor of general intelligence ('g') was helpful in performance in all areas of human ability. The existence of such a factor would explain why there is a persistent positive correlation between such a wide range of tests of human intellectual ability. Spearman explained the fact that performance in different types of test varied by proposing that, as well as 'g', there was a series of test-specific factors ('s').

Other researchers, notably Thurstone (1938), opposed Spearman's view. The view of Thurstone was that intelligence is made up of a loosely related set of 'primary abilities' and that the relationships between the various aspects of human performance could be explained more effectively by these underlying primary abilities than by a general factor or 'g'. Thurstone proposed 12 or so 'primary mental abilities', including:

Table 3.2	Practical thought and intelligence testing

Practical thought	Traditional intelligence tests
Problem formulation	Usually the problem is stated in a clear unambiguous fashion and there is no call to reconstruct or explore its nature or relevance
Flexibility in devising solutions, i.e. the 'sample' problem is solved in different ways, each suited to the occasion. For example, a waiter uses many strategies to remember a round of drinks	Familiar and generally inflexible algorithms are used to tackle all problems of a certain type
Incorporation of the environment into the problem. Expert problem solvers take account of the environment in work settings or items in the environment to help with the problem	The environment is standardised and irrelevant to problem-solving
Least effort strategies are used	Probably similar
Use of setting-specific knowledge	The construction of tests tries to ensure that general intellectual processes, rather than setting-specific knowledge, determine success

- *verbal comprehension* (v): important in reading, comprehension and verbal reasoning;

- *space or visualisation* (s): concerned with the perception and visualisation of objects in space;

- *number* (n): the speed and accuracy of straightforward arithmetic calculation.

Investigations of the structure of human abilities usually involve the use of a statistical technique known as factor analysis. Factor analysis is a mathematical technique that can be used to analyse a correlation matrix. It shows how each of the tests used to produce the original correlation matrix can be divided up and allocated to a smaller collection of underlying factors. Table 3.4 shows a correlation matrix. To simplify things, the actual correlation coefficients have not been given, merely an indication of where the correlations have high values.

Table 3.3	Correlations between some intellectual tests

	Maths	English	Geography	IQ
Maths test				
English test	+0.51			
Geography test	+0.52	+0.34		
IQ test	+0.55	+0.50	+0.48	

Source: adapted from Satterly (1979)

Key Learning Point

Statistical methods such as correlation and factor analysis have been useful in exploring the structure of human intelligence.

Table 3.4	Sizes of correlations in a correlation matrix

	A			B		
	1	2	3	4	5	6
1 Verbal reasoning	✗					
2 Vocabulary		✗				
3 Spelling	High positive		✗			
4 Spatial reasoning				✗		
5 Drawing accuracy	Moderate positive				✗	
6 Geometry				High positive		✗

Table 3.4 shows that the correlations between the tests in group A (1–3) are high, as are the correlations between the tests in group B (4–6). The correlations of tests from group A with tests from group B are only moderate. What this pattern of correlations suggests is:

- the tests in group A all have something in common (probably a 'verbal' factor);

- the tests in group B also have something in common (probably a 'spatial' factor).

Notice also that all of the tests are correlated positively with each other (the correlations in the bottom-left shaded area, although lower, are still positive). These positive correlations between all of the tests suggest:

- the existence of some factor common to all tests (presumably 'g').

Table 3.5 shows how a factor analysis for this matrix might appear. The factor analysis provides a numerical statement of the factors underlying the correlation matrix, and the loading of each test on each factor indicates the extent to which the test involves this factor. The first test (verbal reasoning), for example, loads heavily on factor I ('g'), less heavily on factor II (verbal) and not at all on factor III (spatial).

Table 3.5	The results of a factor analysis		
	Factors		
	I (g)	II (verbal)	III (spatial)
Verbal reasoning	0.6	0.5	
Vocabulary	0.7	0.4	
Spelling	0.8	0.3	
Spatial reasoning	0.4		0.6
Drawing accuracy	0.5		0.5
Geometry	0.5		0.7

A hierarchy of abilities

The factor analysis in Table 3.5 produces both a general intelligence factor (which would offer support for Spearman) and some specific factors (supporting Thurstone). Some of the differences between the theories of Spearman and his followers and Thurstone and his were due to the use of different techniques of factor analysis, the use of different samples for investigation and so on. In fact, a reconciliation of the two theories is not as difficult as it might at first seem.

The 'compromise' theory was proposed by Burt (1940) and elaborated by Vernon (1969). The hierarchical organisation of mental abilities that they proposed incorporates both general and specific factors (*see* Fig. 3.1). At the top of the hierarchy is 'g', the broad general ability factor that is involved in all intellectual performance. But intellectual performance is not explained by 'g' alone. Differences of intermediate generality are also important, between verbal–numerical–education (v : ed), for example, and practical–mechanical–spatial–physical (k : m) factors. In turn, the major group factors may be subdivided into increasingly less general minor and specific factors. In general, psychologists in the United Kingdom have adopted this hierarchical view of mental abilities. American psychologists have been inclined to adopt a view more in line with Thurstone's original ideas and have continued to search for related specific abilities. Guilford (1967), for instance, developed a 'structure of the intellect' model that classifies abilities by operation, product and content (*see* Fig. 3.2). Guilford argued and attempted to demonstrate that it should be possible to produce tests that are independent (i.e. not intercorrelated) for each cell in the cube shown in Fig. 3.2 (i.e. 120 separate abilities in all). Despite the general acceptance of Vernon's theory, the distinction between 's' and 'g' has been retained in many theories of human mental ability. Cattell (1987) put forward the view that an initial general ability, referred to as fluid 'g' or 'g_f' is utilised in specific experience and 'crystallises' into more specific skills. Cattell refers to this as crystallised intelligence (g_c) (*see* Jensen, 1992).

Key Learning Point

Various different models for the structure of intelligence have been proposed. Vernon's hierarchical model has been widely accepted as a solution that combines the key features of the major competing models.

Intelligence testing using traditional models

So far we have managed to discuss the underlying structure of intelligence without directly confronting the problem of what intelligence actually is! The defining of intelligence presents problems for psychologists, and to this day there is no universally accepted definition. Many psychologists will settle for the definition first proposed by Boring (1923, p. 35): 'Intelligence is what intelligence tests measure'. In fact, this definition is not as meaningless as it seems at first sight. Tests of general intelligence are designed to examine the ability of people to carry out certain mental operations. Refer back to Table 3.1 for examples of intelligence test questions. Don't

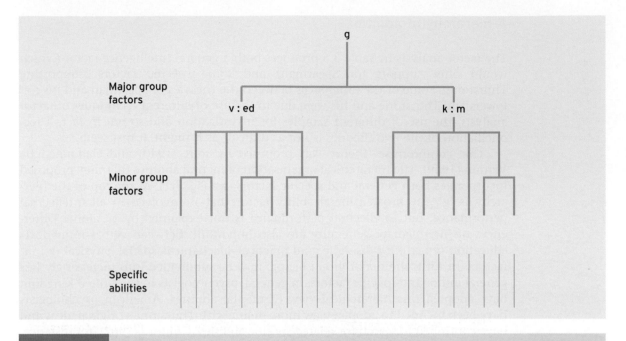

g

Major group
factors

v : ed

k : m

Minor group
factors

Specific
abilities

Figure 3.1   **The hierarchical structure of human abilities**

worry if you find them difficult – they are! The various tests of general intelligence ('g') are all interrelated and people obtain similar scores in different tests. Thus, 'g' is a quality that can be measured reliably and with some precision; but as Eysenck and Kamin (1981, p. 25) pointed out, 'we cannot at this stage say that "g" is the same as the term as understood by the man in the street'. Eysenck, however, clearly considerd that what intelligence tests measure is pretty close to what most people think of as intelligence. Others, such as Kamin (Eysenck and Kamin, 1981), held a different view and argue that IQ tests do not provide a good measure of what most people regard as intelligence. Both of these authors were eminent psychologists but held quite different views about our current ability to measure intelligence. They did not disagree that the available tests measure something with reasonable accuracy – they disagreed fundamentally about *what* such tests do measure.

Regardless of whether the available tests measure what we think of as intelligence or some other qualities, tests of intelligence and specific abilities have been used with some success in personnel selection (*see* Chapters 4 and 5). Many tests of specific abilities (mechanical, verbal, numerical, etc.) and of 'g' can be used to provide quite good predictions of people's competence in certain jobs. Tests have been criticised on various grounds. One criticism is based on the argument that intelligence tests do not measure pure underlying intelligence, but a mixture of it and of taught or acquired knowledge. Vernon (1956, p. 157) distinguished between intelligence and attainments in the following way:

the former refers to the more general qualities of thinking – comprehension, level of concept developing, reasoning and grasping relations – qualities which seem to be

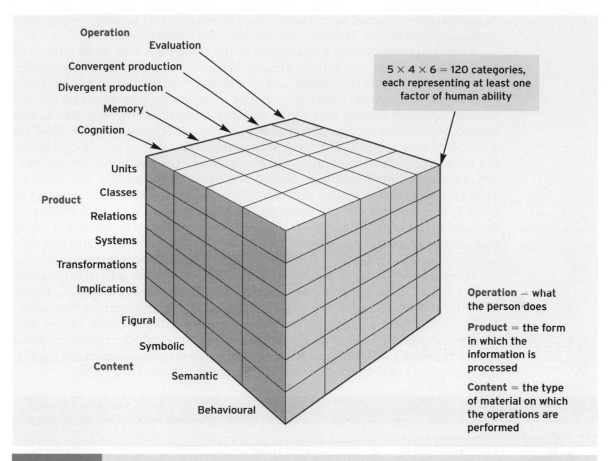

Operation – what the person does

Product = the form in which the information is processed

Content = the type of material on which the operations are performed

5 × 4 × 6 = 120 categories, each representing at least one factor of human ability

Figure 3.2	**Guilford's structure of the intellect model** *Source:* reproduced by permission of the McGraw Hill Companies from *The Nature of Human Intelligence* by J.P. Guilford (1967)

acquired largely in the course of normal development without specific tuition; whereas the latter refers more to knowledge and skills which are directly trained.

Unfortunately, it is one thing to make such a distinction in writing but quite another to put it into practice by developing tests that are 'pure' tests of one or other factor. Proponents of intelligence tests believe that this can be done; others consider that it has not been done properly and is probably impossible.

In the personnel selection context, tests are also criticised because they are biased in favour of certain ethnic or cultural groups. Consider Vernon's description of intelligence given above – as qualities that seem to be acquired largely in the course of normal development. What is the 'normal environment' in which this 'normal development' takes place? White middle-class family groups, some critics would say! The argument of cultural bias asserts that the intellectual development that takes place naturally is dependent on the specific environmental and cultural background in which a person develops, so that perfectly bright and intelligent people from certain socio-economic or ethnic backgrounds will fail to develop the normal qualities assessed in the tests. The consequence will be that, despite their underlying intelligence, the tests will label them as unintelligent.

A rational and unbiased examination of the advantages and disadvantages of psychological tests in the light of criticisms such as the ones raised above is of value to both the science of psychology and to society. The criticism that intelligence tests are biased against certain ethnic groups is, at least in part, based on the frequently replicated finding that ethnic minority groups (mostly black Americans) produce lower scores on cognitive tests than whites (*see* Schmitt and Noe, 1986, for a review of evidence). Despite these subgroup differences, the prevailing view of the scientific community is that it is not unfair to use such tests for selection decision-making. In essence this conclusion is based on the finding that although there are consistent differences between subgroups in mean scores, the accuracy of prediction of the tests (i.e. the prediction of future levels of work performance) is the same for different ethnic groups. Most of the evidence on the fairness or otherwise of cognitive testing in selection is from studies in the United States and such data may need to be interpreted differently in the European context.

There is a wide range of different tests available to measure general intelligence (i.e. Spearman's 'g' factor) and various specific abilities (mechanical, spatial, numerical, etc.) and several publishers of psychological tests are operating in the United Kingdom. Evidence concerning the value of cognitive tests and the fairness of such tests is discussed in Chapter 5. A widely used test of 'g' which requires minimal special experience or training is Raven's progressive matrices – which measure 'g' through a series of abstract diagrammatic problems (Raven *et al.*, 1996).

Key Learning Point

There are consistent differences in the general mental ability test scores obtained by different subgroups.

Exercise 3.1   How do you test someone's intelligence?

An article in *The Guardian* newspaper in October 2003 reported as follows:

There are endless methods, each one claiming to have an edge over the others. Earlier this week *The Observer* told the story of how Andrew Nierman was named the world's smartest person by the New York-based International High IQ society, after he answered correctly 22 out of 25 questions in the Haselbauer-Dickheiser Test for Exceptional Intelligence. Each question in the test is a puzzle and the more questions you answer, the more intelligent you are. Mensa, the UK's high IQ society, prefers to use the Cattell test developed by psychologists in the early 20th century. It avoids using questions that require previous knowledge and tries to measure how quickly and clearly someone thinks. But is it better than the Haselbauer-Dickheiser test?

'We would say so,' says a spokesperson for Mensa. 'Because it's measuring your speed of thought, which is very important in IQ testing.'

Munder Adahami, a researcher at the Centre for the Advancement of Thinking, King's College London, says that both tests have flaws. 'The problem with IQ tests is that they can be taught,' he says. 'You improve by 10 points by having some practice on them.' In addition, he says, someone's cultural background has an impact on how they interpret, and perform on the test. Adahami uses the Jean Piaget technique. 'Intelligence is neither a fixed or inherited quality nor is it something you acquire by experience alone. There's some dynamic interaction between the two.' It is that interaction the Jean Piaget test tries to tease out. The test does not require any previous knowledge and can eliminate the problems associated with cultural references. But perhaps the biggest problem in measuring intelligence is actually defining what intelligence is. Many argue, for example, that there is a central processor somewhere in the brain governing our ability to interpret the world around us. Others say this function is spread across different parts of the brain. Working out who is right or wrong is enough to test anyone's head.

Consider the arguments presented above. What conclusions can you draw? Why do you think this debate has arisen? What advice would you give about how intelligence is best measured?

More recent models of intelligence

Unlike previous structural models of intelligence, systems models expand the concepts underlying intelligence to include concepts other than cognitive abilities. Three contemporary approaches are briefly reviewed. Several 'new' approaches to intelligence theory have become fairly widespread in both their acceptance and application. Two prominent approaches are Gardner's Theory of Multiple Intelligences (Gardner, 1983) and the Triarchic Theory of Intelligence (Sternberg, 1985). An emerging approach is that of emotional intelligence (see Goleman, 1995; Bar-On, 2000; and Mayer *et al.*, 2001).

Gardener's Multiple Intelligences (MI)

Drawing on studies of giftedness and brain injury deficits, Howard Gardner (1983) proposed a theory of multiple intelligences (MI), arguing that there is more than a single, general factor of intelligence. His theory has attracted a great deal of attention, particularly in the media, and the theory has some intuitive appeal. Gardner proposes seven different types of intelligence as follows:

1 *linguistic* – a mastery of language, the ability to effectively manipulate language to express oneself;

2 *spatial* – ability to manipulate and create mental images in order to solve problems;

3 *musical* – capability to recognise and compose musical pitches, tones, and rhythms;

4 *logical-mathematical* – ability to detect patterns, reason deductively and think logically;

5 *bodily kinaesthetic* – ability to use one's mental abilities to co-ordinate one's own bodily movements;

6 *interpersonal* – ability to understand and discern the feelings and intentions of others

7 *intrapersonal* – ability to understand one's own feelings and motivations).

Each of these seven intelligences is derived from Gardner's subjective classification of human abilities based on a set of scientific criteria such as neuropsychological evidence (e.g. speech and language functions appear to reside in the left cerebral hemisphere in the brain), support from experimental psychology and from psychometric findings. For example, there is evidence that some individuals may perform very poorly on IQ tests, yet demonstrate exceptional talent in certain domains such as music. Gardner claims that although the seven intelligences are anatomically separated from each other, they rarely operate independently. In other words, the intelligences are hypothesised to operate concurrently thereby complementing one another as individuals develop skills or solve problems. For example, the theory suggests that a dancer can perform well only if he/she has, (1) strong musical intelligence to understand the rhythm of the music, (2) interpersonal intelligence to understand how she can inspire her audience, and (3) bodily-kinaesthetic intelligence to provide her with the dexterity and co-ordination to complete the movements successfully.

Although many educationalists have used Gardner's theory in schools, MI theory has been criticised by many academics. Criticisms include the observation that MI theory is subjective, and is incompatible with 'g', and with environmental influences. Gardner (1995) has vehemently defended MI theory by referring to various laboratory and field studies for support, arguing that researchers should be interested in understanding intellectual processes that are not explained by 'g'. Matthews *et al.* (2003a) argue that there are some potentially serious omissions in MI theory. For example, among the primary mental abilities associated with intelligence such as word fluency, inductive reasoning, memory and perceptual speed cannot be classified in his system. They also argue that MI theory has some limitations:

> for example, assuming bodily kinaesthetic intelligence is a distinct domain, do we take it that one should also distinguish tennis intelligence, athletic intelligence, football intelligence, dance intelligence, and golf intelligence? If not, one might assume that an individual who turns out to be highly proficient at football might equally have turned that talent to performing in a classical ballet production. (p. 121).

Sternberg's Triarchic Theory of Intelligence

Robert Sternberg is best known for his studies of human intelligence. His Triarchic Theory (Sternberg, 1985, called *Beyond IQ: A triarchic theory of human intelligence*) builds on Spearman's 'g' and underlying information processing components of intelligence. The theory consists of three parts (also known as subtheories) used to describe and measure intelligence. The three facets (or subtheories) are: *Analytical* (componential), *Creative* (experiential) and *Practical* (contextual). Each is defined as follows:

■ *Analytical (componential) subtheory:* analytical intelligence refers to academic problem-solving, such as solving puzzles, and reflects how an individual relates to his or her internal world. Sternberg suggests that analytical intelligence (problem-solving skills) is based on the joint operations of 'metacomponents' and 'performance' components and 'knowledge acquisition' components of intelligence. *Metacomponents* control, monitor and evaluate cognitive processing. These are the executive functions to help organise strategies for performance and knowledge acquisition. In other words, metacomponents decide what to do and the performance components actually do it. *Performance* components are the basic operations that execute the strategies governed by the metacomponents. They are the cognitive processes that enable us to encode information, hold information in short-term memory, perform mental operations and recall information from long-term memory. *Knowledge acquisition* components are the processes used in gaining and storing (memorising) new knowledge (i.e. the capacity for learning).

■ *Creative (experiential) subtheory:* creative intelligence involves insights, synthesis and the ability to react to novel situations and stimuli. Sternberg suggests that this experiential aspect of intelligence reflects how an individual associates his or her internal world to the external world. Creative intelligence comprises the ability to think creatively and the ability to adapt creatively and effectively to new situations.

■ *Practical (contextual) subtheory:* practical intelligence involves the ability to understand and deal with everyday tasks. It is referred to as 'real-world intelligence'. This contextual facet of intelligence reflects how the individual relates to the external world. People with this type of intelligence can adapt to, or shape their environment. Sternberg and Wagner's test of Practical Managerial Intelligence includes measures of the ability to write effective memos, to motivate people, knowing when to delegate and so on. In contrast to structural models of intelligence, measures of practical intelligence go beyond mental skills and include assessment of attitudes and emotional factors (Sternberg and colleagues, 2000). In this way, one of Sternberg's most important contributions to intelligence theory has been the redefinition of intelligence to incorporate practical knowledge. Sternberg's discoveries and theories have influenced cognitive science, and have resulted in the re-thinking of conventional methods of evaluating an individual's intelligence.

Emotional intelligence

Over the past few years there has been an explosion of interest in the concept of emotional intelligence (EI), in both the media and in the academic literature. Since Daniel Goleman's book *Emotional Intelligence* was published in 1995, many researchers have initiated studies of EI, believing that a gap in knowledge has been identified. Not surprisingly, this has led to heated debate among researchers and practitioners, who are keen to define EI and understand how EI differs from established theories of intelligence, or how it is best measured. For practitioners, a key question is whether EI provides incremental validity in predicting job performance over and above measures of cognitive ability (*see* Chapters 5 and 6 for a discussion of validity in assessment).

To date there have been three main conceptualisations of EI appearing in the research literature, proposed by Goleman, Bar-On, and Mayer and Salovey (e.g. Bar-On, 2000; Goleman, 1995, 1998; Mayer and Salovey, 1997). Each approach has been put forward in an attempt to better understand EI and although there is some obvious commonality, there exists some significant divergence of thought. Each is briefly reviewed in turn. For a thorough review of the emotional intelligence literature see Matthews *et al.* (2003a).

Goleman defined EI to be 'abilities such as being able to motivate oneself and persist in the face of frustrations; to control impulse and delay gratification; to regulate one's moods and keep distress from swamping the ability to think; to empathize and to hope' (Goleman, 1995, p. 34). Goleman's conceptualisation has been criticised on the basis that the definition is overinclusive and that it is 'old wine in new bottles'. In other words, some have argued that EI is a repackaging of previous literature on personality and intelligence and nothing 'new' has been identified (Chapman, 2000). Matthews *et al.* (2003a) suggest that Goleman's conceptualisation of EI rests on aspects of what psychologists today would describe as cognition, motivation, personality, emotions, neurobiology and intelligence. However, Goleman has insisted that EI is an ability, although there is limited empirical evidence to support some of his claims. In later publications, Goleman (1998, 2001) suggests how his EI theory represents a framework of an individual's potential for mastering the skills in four key domains, of self-awareness, self-management, social awareness and relationship management. Unlike other conceptualisations of EI, Goleman's framework (2001) specifically refers to behaviours in the workplace and is based on content analyses of competencies in several organisations. He defines an emotional 'competence' as 'a learned capability based on emotional intelligence that results in outstanding performance at work'. In this way, each EI domain is viewed as a competency. For example, in considering the EI domain of self-awareness, this provides the underlying basis of the extent to which an individual is accurate (competent) in his or her self-assessment of personal strengths and limitations.

Equally influential in this area is the work of Reuven Bar-On (1997, 2000). He defines EI as 'an array of non-cognitive capabilities, competencies and skills that influence one's ability to succeed in coping with environmental demands and pressures' (1997, p. 14). He has produced the first commercially available measure of EI, based on a self-assessment instrument called the *Emotional Quotient Inventory* (EQi; similar to the concept of IQ). Bar-On (2000) currently defines his model in terms of an array of traits and abilities related to emotional and social knowledge that influence our ability to effectively cope with environmental demands. In this way, he views EI as a model of psychological well-being and adaptation. His model includes five domains including the ability to (1) be aware of, to understand and to express oneself (intrapersonal intelligence); (2) be aware of, to understand and relate to others (interpersonal intelligence); (3) deal with strong emotions and control one's impulses (stress management); and (4) adapt to change and to solve problems of a personal or social nature (adaptability). Bar-On has reported several validation studies of the EQi and there is reasonable evidence that predicts academic success and presence of some clinical disorders. However, one of the main criticisms regards whether the EQi captures any construct that is unique and is not already captured in existing personality measures (see Mayer *et al.*, 2000). Further research is clearly warranted in this area to explore whether the EQi is measuring personal qualities beyond personality as it is currently understood.

The research of Jack Mayer and Peter Salovey (1997) has perhaps been the most influential in this area and they were first to publish their accounts of EI in scientific peer-reviewed journal articles. Unlike other approaches, Mayer and Salovey and colleagues describe EI as extending traditional models of intelligence. They define EI as 'a concept of intelligence that processes and benefits from emotions. From this perspective, EI is composed of mental abilities, skills or capacities' (Mayer *et al.*, 2000). They suggest that traditional measures of intelligence fail to measure individual differences in the ability to perceive, process and effectively manage emotions and emotional information. In this way, the Mayer and Salovey approach defines EI as the ability to perceive emotions, to access and generate emotions to assist thought, to understand emotions and emotional knowledge, and to reflectively regulate emotions to promote emotional and intellectual growth (Mayer and Salovey, 1997). For measurement purposes Mayer *et al.* (1999) have produced a Multi-factor Emotional Intelligence Scale (MEIS) to assess facets of EI, comprising 12 subscales. To date, the evidence on the validity of the measure is mixed (see Roberts *et al.*, 2001) and much further investigation is needed to explore the potential utility of the model. Unlike other approaches, this model attempts to measure EI as a distinct concept beyond personality. Further evidence will undoubtedly unfold over the coming years.

In exploring the commonality and differences between the three approaches, Bar-On has tried to develop a general measure of social and emotional intelligence associated with psychological well-being and adaptation. Mayer and Salovey attempt to establish the validity of a new form of intelligence, whereas Goleman's approach is specific to the organisations based on social and emotional competencies. In a recent meta-analysis examining the validity of EI, Van Rooy and Viswesvaran (in press) found EI to show evidence of predictive validity for job performance. However, when compared with IQ or general mental ability in the workplace, the results showed IQ to be a better predictor of job and academic performance than EI. Alternatively, Emmerling and Goleman (2003) attempt to explain this finding by suggesting that when it comes to assessing whether a person will become a top performer in a job role, EI may be a more powerful predictor than general mental ability. In this way, some argue that EI is something unique over and above general mental ability. In this respect, some practitioners believe that EI is a useful concept in assisting decisions about promotion to leadership positions, for example.

There is clearly more research that needs to be conducted to answer many questions about EI. There is no doubt that the debate associated with EI has begun to challenge previous assumptions of what leads to success in organisations. EI emphasises the role of social and emotional intelligence as distinct to the role of cognitive abilities associated with traditional theories of intelligence. The research evidence is only just unfolding so we predict there will be much more debate in this area in the near future before we arrive at some clear conclusions.

However, one final more fundamental point is also relevant. The work reviewed in this section treats EI as if it was a 'thing' – that is, as if it was a definable entity that exists independently of the minds of the people who try to define and measure it. This is very much in line with the positivist approach to psychology (*see* Chapter 2) which is dominant in work psychology. An alternative approach would be to adopt an interpretivist perspective. This would see EI as a phenomenon constructed by those who are interested in it, with arguments about its definition and measurement reflecting personal preference rather than a search for objective truth (Fineman, 2003). This perspective encourages us to be more interested in questions such as why the notion of EI has come to prominence at this time, why it is defined in the ways it is, and how different groups of people (e.g. academics, consultants, managers) are seeking to use it (Chapman, 2000). This alternative perspective can be applied to many different phenomena in work psychology, not just EI.

Key Learning Point

Emotional intelligence is seen by many as an exciting concept because it encompasses thought, emotion and interpersonal awareness more effectively than earlier models of intelligence.

Trait views of personality

Psychoanalytic theories of human personality such as Freud's are often criticised by other psychologists for their lack of scientific rigour, lack of satisfactory definition of key concepts and the fact that the theories either do not generate testable predictions about human behaviour or, when predictions are made, that they do not work out in practice (*see* Chapter 1 for an introduction to alternative views of personality). One of the strongest critics of these theories is Eysenck (e.g. Eysenck and Wilson, 1973), who developed an alternative approach to personality based on the rigorous application of scientific methods and statistical analysis. Eysenck, working in the United Kingdom, and the British-born psychologist Cattell, working in the United States, pursued an approach that attempts to uncover the underlying personality traits which they believe can be used to explain human behaviour in a variety of different situations.

Trait theories perhaps come closest to describing the structure of personality in a way that matches our everyday use of the term. Trait theories use words such as shy, outgoing, tense and extroverted to describe the basic factors of human personality. These basic elements – traits – represent predispositions to behave in certain ways, in a variety of different situations. In the United Kingdom the main exponent of the approach was Hans Eysenck (1970, 1981; Eysenck and Eysenck, 1985).

Trait theorists such as Eysenck (1970) and Cattell *et al.* (1970) used the technique of factor analysis in attempts to identify the underlying structure of human personality. Eysenck argues that personality is best understood in terms of a hierarchical organisation (*see* Fig. 3.3). The underlying building blocks for personality can be represented by a small number of basic dimensions (types) that have been identified from the factor analysis of large numbers of personality questionnaires asking people how they behave and feel in various situations. Two major dimensions emerging consistently from factor analytic studies conducted by Eysenck and others were *extroversion* and *neuroticism*. Extroverts are lively, sociable, excitable people and neurotics are characterised by high levels of anxiety and tension. Two important points should be borne in mind in relation to these dimensions. The first is that they are continuous dimensions and most people are not extreme in either extroversion or neuroticism. The second point is that the dimensions are independent; in other words, someone's position on one dimension bears no relationship to his or her position on the other.

As well as providing empirical evidence concerning basic human personality factors, Eysenck's work provides a theory concerning the origins and development of personality. This involves the impact of both inherited, neurological differences and environmental influences due to the processes of conditioning and socialisation. The main measuring instruments associated with Eysenck's theory are the Eysenck Personality Inventory (EPI) (Eysenck and Eysenck, 1964), a self-report questionnaire that measures the factors extroversion and neuroticism, and the Eysenck Personality Questionnaire (EPQ) (Eysenck and Eysenck, 1975) which measures extroversion and introversion, together with a third factor – psychoticism. The EPQ is now incorporated into the Eysenck Personality Scales (Eysenck and Eysenck, 1991).

Working in the United States, Cattell, using similar statistical techniques to those of Eysenck, also pursued a trait approach to personality. One notable difference between the two theorists is the number of stable factors that they feel need to be used to describe and measure personality structure. Although neither Cattell nor Eysenck based theories entirely on data from self-report questionnaires, some of the differences between them become apparent when the questionnaires used by each of them are compared. The EPI uses two dimensions (extroversion–introversion and neuroticism), and Eysenck recognises the existence of a third important factor – psychoticism. Cattell's main personality questionnaire (the 16PF) includes16 personality factors. To some extent the differences are due to the different statistical procedures that the researchers employ. The latest version of the 16PF available for use in the UK is the 16PF5. UK norms for this version are available (Russell and Karol, 1994; Smith, 1994).

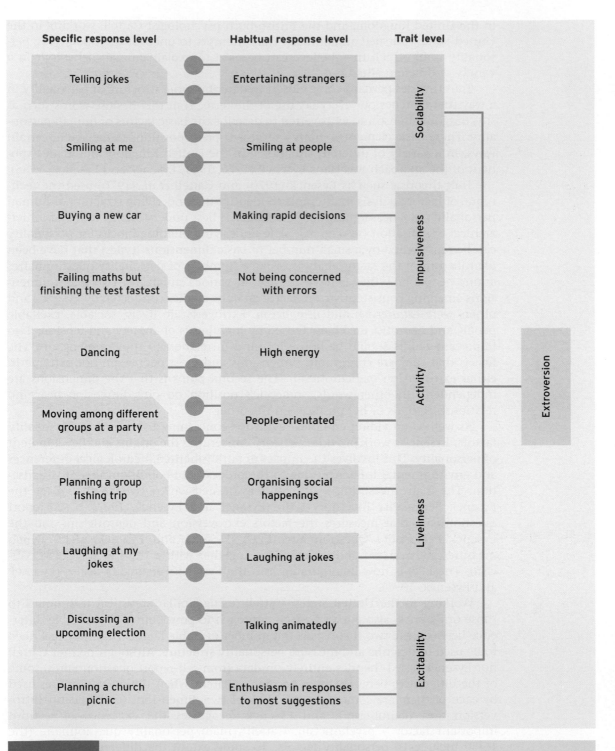

Figure 3.3   **The hierarchical organisation of personality**
Source: From Eysenck, *The Biological Basis of Personality* (1967). Courtesy of
Charles C. Thomas Publisher, Ltd, Springfield, Illinois

Research exploring the similarities and differences between the models of Eysenck, Cattell and other trait-orientated theorists has produced some fairly consistent evidence of the existence of five (the so-called 'Big Five') major personality factors. A series of studies has administered the leading personality questionnaires to large groups of people. With the aid of factor-analytic techniques, the investigators have sought to identify the minimum number of underlying personality dimensions that will account for the range of responses produced in people's answers to the questionnaires. A fairly high degree of consensus has emerged and investigators have agreed that a five-factor structure represents an adequate way of describing the basic dimensions of personality (Digman and Takemoto-Chock, 1981; McCrae and Costa, 1990; Costa and McCrae, 1992). This fivefold structure involves the following:

1 *Extroversion* – warmth, gregrariousness, assertiveness, activity, excitement-seeking, positive emotions.

2 *Neuroticism* – anxiety, angry hostility, depression, self-consciousness, impulsiveness, vulnerability.

3 *Conscientiousness* – competence, order, dutifulness, achievement striving, self-discipline, deliberation.

4 *Agreeableness* – trust, straightforwardness, altruism, compliance, modesty, tender-mindedness.

5 *Openness to experience* – fantasy, aesthetic, feelings, actions, ideas, values.

Extroversion and neuroticism have already been described. Conscientiousness, as the label suggests, concerns an individual's predisposition to be well organised and to focus on targets, goals and deadlines. Agreeableness concerns the extent to which someone is good natured, eager to co-operate with others and concerned to avoid conflict. Openness to experience is related to a person's tendency to be influenced by new experiences.

Key Learning Point

The 'Big Five' has become a universal template for understanding the structure of human personality.

Substantial evidence exists that the 'Big Five' structure is consistent across various national groups. For example, McCrae and Costa (1997) reported results comparing six diverse samples (German, Portuguese, Hebrew, Chinese, Korean and Japanese) showing substantial similarity in a 'Big Five' structure with a large American sample. This and other evidence suggests very strongly that the Big Five structure is a useful general framework although, as McCrae and Costa acknowledge, this may be limited to modern, literate, industrialised cultures. It also seems that the 'openness to experience' dimension is less well defined than the others.

At first glance, the emergence of the Big Five may seem to suggest that perhaps the Eysenck scales focus on a more limited set of factors than is useful whereas Cattell's 16PF uses too many. It is certainly true that several attempts to replicate Cattell's 16 factors have not been very successful (*see*, for example, Kline and Barrett, 1983) and have generally suggested that a smaller number of factors fits the data more efficiently.

The identification of the Big Five personality factors is a marked development in the trait-factor analytic approach. It is important to realise, though, that the establishment of the Big Five does not mean that other conceptualisations of personality become redundant (Hough and Oswald, 2000). The Big Five provide a useful view of the minimum factors that must be included in any description of human personality. In many circumstances it may make sense to use a more detailed set of dimensions. Hough and Ones (2001), for example, make an important distinction between the use of personality variables for description and their use for predicting job performance. In other words, while the Big Five may be a useful framework for describing the minimum dimensions of personality, they may not be as valuable for other purposes, such as predicting job performance. Evidence that Hough (1992) presents shows different patterns of criterion-related validity for at least nine different personality constructs. The role of personality in personnel selection decision making is discussed further in the next two chapters. For the moment it is sufficient to recognise that the Big Five provide a level of description for personality that is not always the most relevant.

Exercise 3.2   Assessing the propensity to innovate at work

A long-standing problem for HR managers has been how to select and develop innovative individuals effectively. Getting the right raw material in the first place is a critical issue. The propensity to innovate is often listed as a key competency in person specifications, but there has been little available to assess it in a reliable way. Traditional measures of creative thinking have been of the kinds that ask 'How many uses for a paper clip can you think of?' in say, three minutes. Such measures may indicate some level of conceptual thinking, but are of limited use in identifying individuals who are innovative in the workplace. Organisations are interested in the successful introduction of new products and processes in a competitive marketplace to generate revenue. This necessarily involves influencing others in the organisation to adopt the ideas suggested. Some organisations use trait-based personality questionnaires to assess the propensity to innovate.

Previous literature has been confused as to whether the propensity to innovate is predicted by an individual's level of intelligence or whether it is more concerned with personality. Early research suggested that innovative potential was an aspect of general intelligence. However, many authors have demonstrated that aspects of intelligence may be a necessary, but not a sufficient, condition for innovation to occur. Later research focused on the propensity to innovate as an aspect of personality. More recently, researchers have noted that motivation and job-specific knowledge are key components in predicting the propensity to innovate at work. Although there has been a vast amount of work examining these characteristics, this has lacked an integrative model with which to understand how all these aspects inter-relate.

1   Create a list of the person level variables that might influence the propensity to innovate at work. How do you think these variables inter-relate?

2   Suggest how these person variables might be best measured. What further research could be conducted to learn more about innovation at work?

Personality tests

Although several studies have shown that the factors measured by many personality tests can be related to the Big Five, the tests themselves provide scores on a variety of personality dimensions. For example, as already mentioned, the EPQ assesses three personality factors (extroversion, neuroticism and psychoticism). Table 3.6 gives some information on the better-known personality questionnaires available in the United Kingdom.

As with all kinds of psychological measures, personality tests need to satisfy various well-established psychometric criteria before they can be considered to be acceptable measuring instruments. These criteria are concerned with assessing the extent to which the test measures what it is intended to measure (the issue of validity) and the precision or consistency of measurement that the test achieves (reliability). The British Psychological Society has produced a detailed review of all of the most widely used personality tests in the United Kingdom (Bartram, 1995). This review gives a thorough technical evaluation of each test. These concepts are discussed in relation to personnel selection and psychometric testing in Chapter 5.

As a light-hearted illustration, Table 3.7 provides descriptions of the 16PF scales together with examples of historical or literary figures who are supposed to exemplify the person qualities described. You may want to think of some other famous individuals who display such qualities!

Work competencies

One helpful and increasingly widely used way of describing the qualities needed by candidates is the identification of the *work competencies* required by effective performers. In this approach, rather than describing the attributes required by candidates with the aid of established psychological frameworks, such as personality dimensions or subcomponents of cognitive ability, a direct description of the competencies needed for the job is attempted (*see* Chapters 4 and 5 for more on competencies).

This approach represents a fusion of the common-sense approach adopted by human resource practitioners in organisations, who have long described candidate requirements in terms of skills, and the work of psychologists (*see* earlier in this chapter), attempting to capture the essence of 'practical intelligence'. Sternberg and Wagner (1986) have provided a useful exploration of the distinction between conventional psychological thinking about intelligence and this approach. They

Table 3.6	Personality questionnaires

Instrument	Personality characteristics measured
Eysenck Personality Questionnaire (EPQ; Eysenck and Eysenck, 1964)	Extroversion, neuroticism (or emotional stability), psychoticism
The Sixteen PF (16PF; Cattell *et al.*, 1970). Several versions of short/long forms are available and measure second-order personality factors, etc., in addition to the 16 factors mentioned here	Sixteen personality factors, e.g. submissiveness (mild, humble, easily led, docile, accommodating); self-assurance (placid, serene, secure, complacent); tender-mindedness (sensitive, clinging, over-protected)
The Occupational Personality Questionnaire (OPQ; SHL, 1990)	Thirty personality dimensions are measured in the most detailed version of the OPQ (the concept model). Other versions/models of the questionnaires are available. Illustrative personality dimensions are: ■ caring (considerate to others, helps those in need, sympathetic, tolerant) ■ emotional control (restrained in showing emotions, keeps feelings back, avoids outbursts) ■ forward planning (prepares well in advance, enjoys target-setting, forecasts trends, plans projects)
The revised NEO Personality Inventory (NEO PI-R, Costa and McCrae, 1992)	The Big Five personality factors, plus facet scores for six subscales within each of the Big Five domains

argue that 'tacit knowledge' – that is, knowledge that is usually not openly expressed or stated – is of crucial importance in the skilful performance of work tasks. In some interesting studies they have shown that measures of tacit knowledge provide good predictions of people's performance on real-work tasks. They also show that scores on their tests of tacit knowledge are not strongly correlated with scores on traditional tests of mental ability, suggesting that tacit knowledge is distinct from intelligence, as defined in earlier sections of this chapter. A final important feature of their work is the finding that individual differences in tacit knowledge are general, rather than specific, in nature. In much the same way that Spearman found high intercorrelations between different tests of mental ability and hypothesised a general intelligence, 'g' factor, Sternberg and Wagner, for

Table 3.7	The personality traits assessed by the 16PF with examples of famous individuals exemplifying the traits			

Factor	Trait descriptions		Famous individuals	
	High	Low	High	Low
A	Outgoing Warm-hearted	Reserved Detached	Falstaff	Greta Garbo
C	Unemotional Calm	Emotional Changeable	Washington	Hamlet
E	Assertive Dominant	Humble Co-operative	Genghis Khan	Jesus
F	Cheerful Lively	Sober Taciturn	Groucho Marx	Clint Eastwood
G	Conscientious Persistent	Expedient Undisciplined	Mother Theresa	Casanova
H	Venturesome Socially bold	Shy Retiring	Columbus	Sylvia Plath
I	Tough-minded Self-reliant	Tender-minded Sensitive	James Bond	Robert Burns
L	Suspicious Sceptical	Trusting Accepting	De Gaulle	Polyanna
M	Imaginative Bohemian	Practical Conventional	Van Gogh	Henry Ford
N	Shrewd Discreet	Forthright Straightforward	Machiavelli	Joan of Arc
O	Guilt prone Worrying	Resilient Self-assured	Dostoevsky	Stalin
Q1	Radical Experimental	Conservative Traditional	Karl Marx	Queen Victoria
Q2	Self-sufficient Resourceful	Group-dependent Affiliative	Copernicus	Marilyn Monroe
Q3	Controlled Compulsive	Undisciplined Lax	Margaret Thatcher	Mick Jagger
Q4	Tense Driven	Relaxed Tranquil	Macbeth	Buddha

Note: Dimension B (intelligence) is omitted.
Sources from Conn and Rieke (1994), Matthews and Deary (1998)

similar reasons, suggested that tacit knowledge may also be a general, rather than specific, psychological construct.

With these findings and ideas in mind, it is interesting to look at the work that has been conducted by various investigators, studying the competencies required by people in particular jobs, or families of jobs. For example, investigators looking at managerial work have repeatedly found the need for job holders to display similar sorts of competencies, even though the specific jobs were different. Indeed, several researchers have suggested generic sets of competencies applicable to managerial work as a whole. Table 3.8 gives examples of two such competency frameworks, proposed by Dulewicz (1989) and Klemp and McClelland (1986). The similarities between the frameworks themselves are obvious. Looking at this work, it is tempting to propose that such competencies may well be predicted very accurately by scores on traditional cognitive ability tests plus scores on measures of tacit knowledge.

Key Learning Point

The knowledge, skills and abilities required for jobs may be described in terms of key competencies.

Socio-cognitive approaches to individual differences

In an interesting critique of developmental psychology, Bell (1979) commented that 'parents too are thinking beings'. Bell was referring to the fact that developmental researchers at that time were typically focusing on how parents and children behaved with little consideration of the thought processes behind such action. Developmental research had reduced parents and children to little more than unthinking reactants to their environment. Bell's paper helped to prompt a change of focus within the developmental field, where research began to explore how parents made sense of their child's behaviour, and how these interpretations in turn influenced decisions about how to respond.

The beginnings of this approach were evident in the debate about whether individual differences or situations dictate people's behaviour. To most of us it is clear, from everyday experience, that our behaviour is not completely at the mercy of situational influences. There is some cross-situational consistency in how we behave from one setting to another, particularly in terms of key features of our psychological make-up, such as extroversion, agreeableness and anxiety. On the other hand most people will behave quite differently at a lively party and at a very important formal business event. The relative influence of person and situation variables has been a topic of some controversy. Some people have argued very strongly for the predominance of situational influences, suggesting that stable individual differences in psychological make-up have a relatively small role to play (e.g. Mischel, 1968). Despite these historical differences of opinion, it is clear that modern psychology allows for the influence of both person and situation variables

Table 3.8	Competency frameworks

Klemp and McClelland	Dulewicz
The intellectual competencies ■ Planning/causal thinking ■ Diagnostic information seeking ■ Conceptualisation/synthetic thinking *The influence competencies* ■ Concern for influence (the need for power) ■ Directive influence (personalised power) ■ Collaborative influence (socialised power) ■ Symbolic influence *Additional competency* ■ Self-confidence	*Intellectual* ■ Strategic perspective ■ Analysis and judgement ■ Planning and organising *Interpersonal* ■ Managing staff ■ Persuasiveness ■ Assertiveness and decisiveness ■ Interpersonal sensitivity ■ Oral communication *Adaptability* ■ Adaptability and resilience *Results orientation* ■ Energy and initiative ■ Achievement motivation ■ Business sense

Sources: Klemp and McClelland (1986), Dulewicz (1989)

(*see* Pervin, 1989). Eysenck, whose theory of personality was dealt with earlier, has captured the essential futility of trying to identify a single cause by writing, 'Altogether I feel that the debate is an unreal one. You cannot contrast persons and situations in any meaningful sense ... No physicist would put such a silly question as: which is more important in melting a substance – the situation (heat of the flame) or the nature of the substance?' (quoted by Pervin, 1980, p. 271).

Situations presumably influence our behaviour because we think about how we should respond to them. If we look at much selection research, we could argue that work psychologists are equally guilty of ignoring the thought processes that underlie behaviour. Most selection research has sought to determine *how* predictive various selection methods are, rather than *why* these methods predict. For example, we know that personality traits predict work performance, but we know much less about how personality traits influence behaviour. Moreover, it is highly unlikely that there is a direct relationship between personality traits and behaviour (Skarlicki *et al.*, 1999). After all, individuals will appraise the situation that they find themselves in and decide how they should best respond. There is increasing recognition that cognition plays a central role in work performance (e.g. Hodgkinson, 2003). Most of this research has focused on senior managers, particularly how CEOs' and senior executives' explanations for key organisational events, such as company performance, can influence strategic decisions (Sparrow and Hodgkinson, 2002). However, more relevant to selection research is recent research concerned with the role that relatively stable individual differences in cognitive style can play in job performance.

A number of cognitive-based personality characteristics have been proposed over the years, including: example, proactive personality, personal initiative, self-efficacy, attributional style, locus of control (e.g. Bandura, 1982; Frese *et al.*, 1997; Silvester *et al.*, 2003). Interestingly, all of these appear to relate to motivation – a construct that has been notoriously difficult to pin down in terms of a personality trait explanation. Kanfer and Ackerman's (2002) recent work on motivational traits acknowledges the importance of cognition in motivation (*see also* Chapter 9). This raises the intriguing possibility that the impact of personality traits on work performance will be mediated by individual differences in cognitive style. Certain evidence for this can be found in work examining the relationship between attributional style and the performance of sales personnel. For example, Corr and Gray (1996) found that male insurance sales agents who attributed positive outcomes such as making a sale to internal, stable and global causes (such as their own personality) were more successful than individuals who externalised the cause to more unstable causes (e.g. luck, or being in a good mood that day). Silvester *et al.* (2003) also found that individuals who perceived themselves to have more control over sales outcomes (both successful and unsuccessful) were rated more successful by their managers. They argue that, even in the case of failure, individuals who attribute the outcome to more internal controllable causes (e.g. using the wrong sales strategy) will be more likely to maintain a higher level of motivation and effort than sales staff who typically put the failure down to external uncontrollable causes (e.g. the customer had seen a cheaper version elsewhere). Clearly there is tremendous potential for selection researchers to explore the role of individual differences in sense-making and cognition, both in selection contexts and work performance more generally.

Key Learning Point

Stable individual differences in cognitive style represent another potential source of variance in job behaviour.

Summary

Individual differences in personality and cognitive ability have been the subject of much psychological research. Although there are many different theoretical frameworks (*see* Chapter 1), the trait-factor analytic approach is most important in work psychology. Factor-analytic research has uncovered stable, underlying structures for both cognitive ability (a general factor and specific abilities) and personality (five major factors). Measures have been developed for cognitive ability and personality. To be of value in work psychology, such measures need to be both reliable and valid (*see* Chapter 4). There is recent research exploring the concept of emotional intelligence and whether it might offer something new about our understanding of behaviour at work. There is also increasing recognition that while intellect and personality influence work behaviour, they do not determine it. A number of other inter-related factors, such as a person's thought process, learned patterns of social interaction and features of the situation, also influence work behaviour.

Closing Case Study

A Socio-cognitive Approach to Individual Differences in Empathic Ability among Trainee Doctors

Empathy and help giving behaviour are central to a broad range of jobs including customer service, education, nursing and healthcare roles. They are also, arguably, core to those aspects of managerial roles that involve understanding employee behaviour and responding more appropriately to needs. In a recent research project, Silvester and Patterson (2003) investigated a socio-cognitive model of individual differences in empathic ability among trainee doctors. This model predicted that the way in which doctors explained patient outcomes would impact upon their willingness to help. More specifically, it argued that doctors who typically believed that they could influence outcomes for their patients would be perceived by patients as empathic because they communicated with the patient in an open way. Doctors who perceived themselves to have less control over patient outcomes would seek to reassert control by using a more doctor-centred communication style, involving more closed questions, a focus on the specific presenting medical condition, and little opportunity for the patient to discuss personal topics or matters that he or she considered important. In contrast, a doctor who perceived him- or herself to have higher levels of control over patient outcomes would be more willing to allow the patient control over the interaction, encourage discussion of more personal topics and be more sensitive to patient needs.

One hundred doctors participated in a patient exercise where they were asked to role-play a hospital doctor responsible for admitting a patient who was played by a trained medical actor. The patients followed a script, which required them to offer a series of cues indicating that they would like to discuss particular issues and ensured consistency across interactions. Each doctor was rated, in terms of the level of empathy they displayed, by an assessor (senior medical professional) and the patient. The interactions were tape-recorded, transcribed and then content analysed using the coding categories below: ▶

- Number of open questions ('How is everything at home?').

- Number of closed questions ('Did you have any tests for phlegm?').

- Number of missed patient cues (Patient: 'My husband has helped with the cooking'. Doctor: 'Right'. Patient: 'So I haven't really noticed that I haven't been eating'. Doctor: 'Yes'. Patient: 'Anyway, thank you doctor, I'll go back to . . .').

- Personal topics discussed ('It must be quite frightening for you at the moment?').

- Medical procedure discussed.

- Interruptions of patient by doctor (Patient: 'I was told to be here at . . .' Doctor: 'About that . . .').

- Doctor accepting responsibility ('I'm sorry we didn't get off to a good start').

- Statements of action taking by doctor ('I'll make sure I tell the consultant that you have requested this').

- Positive comments ('It's probably nothing serious').

- Summary statements ('So basically what we're saying is that you're a smoker, you've had a different cough to normal and you're producing brown plegm').

The research findings supported the hypotheses. Specifically, doctors who attributed positive patient outcomes to causes that were more internal, stable and controllable (by the doctor) were more likely to use an open communication style (more personal topics, fewer missed cues) and less likely to use a controlling communication style (more interruptions, summary statements and closed questions), and open communication style was significantly associated with assessor ratings of empathy.

In summary, a doctor's attributional style impacts upon empathy ratings via its influence upon communication behaviour. Doctors who perceive themselves to have more control over patient outcomes appear more willing to allow patients to control the direction of verbal interactions.

Suggested exercise

Reflect on the times you have been to see your family doctor. What did the doctor do to make you think that he or she was empathic?

Empathy can be an important performance criterion for many job roles. Suggest some other jobs where empathy might be important. To what extent do you think empathy can be trained?

Test your learning

Short-answer questions

1 Give examples of how cognitive ability can be assessed.

2 Are a person's scores on tests of different cognitive abilities likely to be similar? Explain your answer.

3 Outline the role that factor analysis has played in identifying the structure of intelligence.

4 What are Gardner's multiple intelligences?

5 What are the 'Big Five' personality factors?

6 What is emotional intelligence?

7 Suggest three general reasons why a person's scores on personality and intelligence tests might influence his or her work performance.

8 Now suggest three reasons why those test scores might have only a limited impact on work performance.

Sugggested assignments

1 Critically evaluate the trait-factor analytic approach to cognitive ability.

2 Discuss the extent to which the 'Big Five' provide a comprehensive picture of human personality.

3 What evidence is there that emotional intelligence is distinct from traditional conceptualisations of personality and intelligence?

Relevant websites

A directory of just some of the many consultancy firms that offer psychometric testing products and services in the workplace can be found at http://directory.google.com/Top/Regional/Europe/United_Kingdom/Business_and_Economy/Human_Resources/Psychometric_Profiling/.

A very useful site for learning about psychometric testing from the points of view of both the tester and the person being tested is provided by the British Psychological Society at http://www.psychtesting.org.uk/.

If you are interested in intelligence testing, Indiana University, USA, hosts a site with material you may find helpful. It is not specifically about the workplace, but much here is relevant to the workplace. Find it at http://www.indiana.edu/~intell/.

For further self-test material and relevant, annotated weblinks please visit the website at http://www.booksites.net/arnold_workpsych.

Suggested further reading

1   Paul Kline's book *Handbook of Psychological Testing* (2nd edition, Routledge, London, 1999) provides a good overview of the theoretical underpinnings of personality and intelligence and how it translates into measurement. Also see *The New Psychometrics: Science, Psychology and Measurement* (Routledge, London, 2000) by Paul Kline.

2   Matthews, Deary and Whiteman's book on *Personality Traits* (details are given in the list at the end of the book) provides an excellent overview of the research literature in personality and provides a summary of evidence relevant to work psychology.

3   Matthews, Zeidner and Roberts' book called *Emotional Intelligence: Science and Myth* (details are given in the list at the end of the book) provides an in-depth analysis of the evidence on emotional intelligence.

CHAPTER 4

The foundations of personnel selection: analysing jobs, competencies and selection effectiveness

LEARNING OUTCOMES

After studying this chapter, you should be able to:

1 outline the personnel selection design and validation process;

2 name and describe four different job analysis techniques;

3 define competencies and competency models in organisations;

4 describe the outputs from competency analysis and how they are used as assessment criteria;

5 describe the relative advantages and disadvantages of different job analysis techniques;

6 in the context of personnel selection, define reliability and five different types of validity: faith validity, face validity; content validity; construct validity; and criterion-related validity;

7 outline the criterion problem and the practical difficulties associated with conducting validation studies in organisations;

8 describe the roles that validity, selection ratio and other factors play in determining financial utility.

Opening Case Study

Streamlining the Selection Process

Over the past two decades, the UK Government has refined the process it uses to recruit new staff to a level that equals and often exceeds comparable processes in the private sector. The process is regarded as both detailed and thorough. It aims to define job specifications very precisely and provide a straightforward assessment of a candidate's suitability. It is also rated highly by recruitment professionals.

'In many parts of the public sector the mechanisms used for recruitment are very advanced and some of the stereotypes of the public sector are misplaced. Over the last 15 years, successive governments have been seeking to improve the way recruitment is carried out', says Hamish Davidson, chairman of Veredus Executive Resourcing.

Gill Lucas, head of public sector recruitment at KMPG, says that this approach has helped the public sector to meet its obligations to provide equal opportunity employment: 'The public sector recruitment process has evolved over time to ensure positions are defined in terms of the skills and competencies needed to do the job. They look carefully at what is needed and are rigorous at matching CVs to positions.'

Jeremy Ebster, head of public sector recruitment at Penna Consulting also praises the public sector's approach to recruitment: 'The sector follows very good practices and in many ways leads the way in recruitment. Selectors are properly trained and they take the process more seriously. The process ensures consistency across the public sector.'

But he has some reservations: 'It is well-suited to the larger government departments. But it falls down in some of the smaller ones where greater flexibility is needed.'

There are several reasons why the public sector has devised a well-structured approach to recruitment. The inevitable political pressures - to ensure that personnel selection is fair and comprehensive - top the list. But the dual pressures of advancing technology and a changing economic environment also play a part. Structural changes in the way that public services are to be delivered, based on a switch to e-government, are forcing the public sector to compete with the private sector for many of the same skills.

The UK Government has set ambitious targets for public service reform. Where appropriate, services will be provided by private sector partners. One of the keys to success is to recruit people who can work in partnership with external services suppliers. This means more outsourcing so people with good procurement skills are needed - people who fully understand which services can be put out and which ones must be kept internal. Inevitably, this means expanding recruitment policy to include additional skills and more diverse backgrounds.

Source: adapted from an article at FT.com, 7 March 2003

FT

Introduction

The research and practice of work psychology have important contributions to make in many areas of organisational life. Personnel selection and assessment probably constitute the area where the biggest and most consistent contribution has been made (see Patterson, 2001, for a review of recent developments in work psychology). In fact, the contribution of psychology to this area of activity is distinctive and complements the work of other professional groups, such as human resources personnel in organisations. Whereas others may have interests in administrative or managerial issues, such as the collection and storage of information about the competencies of employees, the focus of attention for psychologists has always been the assessment process itself. The opening case study shows the complexity of the task, with issues such as job analysis, matching person to job, enhancing equal opportunity and diversity, employee flexibility and sector-specific skills all being prominent.

Research and development work has concentrated on the production and evaluation of technically sound assessment procedures. Given the centrality of psychological measurement to psychological science in general, psychologists are recognised as experts in the design and validation of selection processes. This chapter and the two following it focus on different aspects of selection and related processes. In this chapter we examine some building blocks of good selection, namely the careful analysis of jobs, and competencies, and ways of checking on the effectiveness of any selection process. Then in Chapter 5 we examine some specific selection techniques in more detail, and in doing so we apply some of the concepts introduced in this chapter. In Chapter 6 we take a closer look at the psychology of how people's performance in selection tasks and everyday work can be assessed.

Two main principles underlie the roles that personnel selection and assessment procedures play in organisational settings. The first principle is that there are individual differences between people (e.g. differences in aptitudes, skills and other personal qualities). This simple principle leads to the very important conclusion that people are not equally suited to all jobs, and suggests that procedures for matching people and jobs could have important organisational benefits. The second principle is that future behaviour is, at least partly, predictable. The goal of selection and assessment activities is to match people to jobs and ensure the best possible levels of future job performance; the belief that *future job performance* can be estimated is an important facet of the second principle mentioned above. The essential function of personnel selection and assessment procedures (e.g. interviews, psychometric tests) is to provide means of estimating the likely future job performance of candidates.

Over several decades, work psychology research has had a significant influence on the way people are recruited into jobs, through rigorous development and evaluation of personnel selection procedures. Since the early part of the twentieth century a great deal of research has concentrated on the development and evaluation of personnel selection procedures. Much of this work will be considered in the next chapter. The present chapter is *not* concerned with a detailed analysis of alternative personnel selection methods. Instead, it focuses on those aspects of psychological theory and practice that underlie the successful application of personnel selection procedures. The main topics covered in this chapter are related to the two principles given above. First, since personnel selection has traditionally involved the matching of people to the requirements of jobs, job analysis is covered (individual differences between people were discussed in Chapter 3). The second part of the chapter concentrates on topics concerned with the development of procedures for predicting future job performance; specifically, validation studies and associated issues regarding the practicalities of conducting research in organisations.

The design and validation process

Figure 4.1 provides an outline of the main elements involved in designing and implementing a personnel selection procedure. The process begins with a job analysis to define a job description, a person specification and a competency model, where appropriate. This information is used to identify the selection and assessment criteria and may also be used for advertising the job role. In deciding to apply for a job, prospective candidates will engage in *self-selection* where they can make an informed judgement about whether the particular role suits their skills and abilities. The job analysis information is used to decide which selection instruments to use to access applicant behaviour related to the selection criteria. Once the selection decisions are made and the accepted applicants enter the organisation (assuming they accept the organisation's offer), information on the work performance of job holders related to the original competency model is then used to examine the validity of the selection instruments (i.e. whether high and low scores on the selection instruments are associated with good and poor work performance respectively).

Key Learning Point

Personnel selection is one of the most prominent topic areas in work and organisational psychology, and research findings have had a major impact on recruitment practice.

Organisations have become increasingly aware that it is important to evaluate candidates' reactions to the selection process, particularly in relation to fairness. Since many organisations spend a great deal of time and resource in selection procedures, the financial costs and benefits of selection may also be evaluated. The information collected at selection is also invaluable at helping to design training and development plans and activities for individuals entering the organisation.

A thorough job analysis is the foundation of an effective selection process and is used to guide choice of selection method, for example. The outputs from a job analysis should detail the tasks and responsibilities in the target job and also provide information about the particular behavioural characteristics required of the job holder. The analysis may suggest, for example, that certain personality and

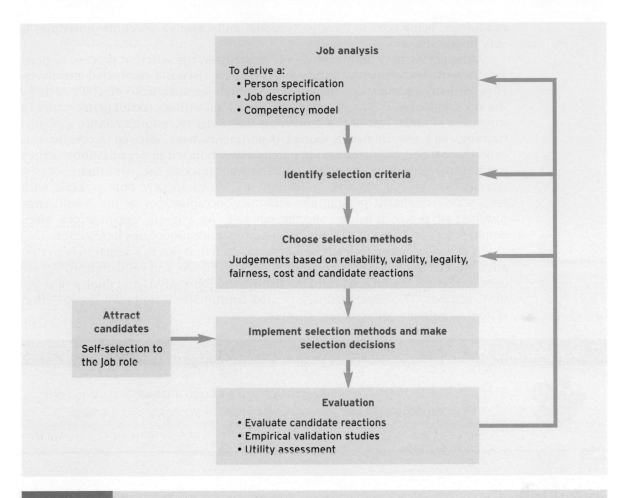

Figure 4.1   **The personnel selection, design and validation process**

dispositional characteristics are desirable, together with specific previous work experience, technical qualifications, and levels of intelligence and specific abilities.

The next stage in the process is to identify selection instruments (e.g. psychometric tests, work simulation exercises, interviews, application forms) that can be used to examine whether candidates display the required characteristics or not. These instruments are then used to assess candidates and selection decisions are taken. Conducting empirical validation studies monitors the quality of the selection process. Here, the psychologist is focusing on how useful (and accurate) the selection procedure was in identifying 'the right person for the job'. In addition, it is important to assess the candidates' reaction to the process too. Poorly run selection processes are likely to result in candidates having a negative first impression of the organisation. As a consequence, the best candidates for the job could decide to work for another (possibly competing) organisation. Historically selection has tended to be a 'buyers' market'. Recently, there has been a recognition in some organisations that selection is a 'two-way' process where in order to attract the best candidates, being seen to have professional and effective selection procedures is very important.

Although we have outlined the core elements in the selection process, in practice there are two elements in the process that are often not conducted effectively. First, in many organisations there is no thorough job analysis to precisely identify the key knowledge, skills and behaviours associated with successful performance in the target job role. Part of the problem is that these techniques require specialist training, and few human resources departments have internal access to this expertise. Second, validation studies are rarely conducted in organisations as they can be time-consuming and costly. It often means tracking the performance of new recruits over several months. Validation studies are usually only possible with large-scale recruitment programmes and many organisations do not recruit large numbers of people into one specific job role. As a result, organisations often employ work psychologists to advise on best practice procedures in selection.

In overview, research clearly demonstrates that best practice selection is an iterative process. In other words, the results from evaluation and validation studies are used to reassess the original thinking behind the job analysis and choice of selection methods. Therefore, feedback is used continually to improve the selection system to enhance accuracy and fairness.

Key Learning Point

Best practice personnel selection involves thorough job analysis and using feedback from validation studies to continually improve accuracy and fairness.

Job analysis

Job analysis procedures are designed to produce systematic information about jobs, including the nature of the work performed, responsibilities, equipment used, the working conditions and the position of the job within the organisation. The outputs from a job analysis are often used to generate a job description and/or a person specification for the job role. It is worth noting that satisfactory job analyses are prerequisites for many decisions and activities that have a crucial influence on the lives of employees within the organisation, including the design and validation of selection procedures, training and career development schemes, job design or redesign, job evaluation and safety. There is a wide range of techniques and procedures available. Algera and Greuter (1998) and Robertson and Smith (2001) provide detailed critical examinations of the principal techniques that will be introduced in this chapter.

Although not always clear cut, there is an important distinction between *job-orientated* and *worker-orientated* job analysis procedures. As the term suggests, job-orientated (or task-orientated) procedures focus on the work itself, producing a description in terms of the equipment used, the end results or purposes of the job, resources and materials utilised. In contrast, worker-orientated (or person-orien-

tated) analyses concentrate on describing the psychological or behavioural requirements of the job, such as communicating, decision-making and reasoning (see
Sandberg, 2000, for a detailed review). There has been little research reported on
task-orientated job analysis over the past decade (see Robertson and Smith, 2001)
and the majority of authors have tended to focus on use of future-orientated job
analysis for newly created job roles, focusing on the knowledge, skills and abilities
associated with the job role now, and in the future. The reason for this is because
many organisations are, or have been involved in business process re-engineering
where downsizing and re-organising job roles is commonplace. In this way, many
jobs are now 'newly created job roles' (NCJs) where there are no pre-existing job
descriptions nor indeed, current job holders.

Simultaneously, there has been a shift in the research literature towards considering models of work performance more generally, that distinguishes between *task
performance* (focusing on specific responsibilities in the job) and *contextual performance* (for example organisational citizenship behaviours such as courtesy, pro-social
behaviour and being altruistic towards others at work; *see* Viswesvaran and Ones,
2000, and *also* Chapter 9). Each of these might imply using different selection criteria and related techniques to assess them. In general, there still tends to be more
emphasis on the discrete task-orientated analyses rather than considering the contextual aspects in job analysis research and practice. Traditional job analysis
approaches in personnel selection are aimed at 'fitting the person to the job'. With
recent changes in the nature of work and employee work patterns, this approach is
becoming less relevant.

Key Learning Point

*Job analysis procedures are generally either worker-orientated or job-orien-
tated, and much research now focuses on the future requirements of the job
role.*

Competencies and competency analysis

Traditionally, job analyses have aimed to identify the tasks and responsibilities
associated with a job role. In practice, it is sometimes difficult to translate the information into describing observable behaviours that underpin the tasks and
responsibilities. As a result, *competency analysis* has become very popular in organisations to help define the person-focused assessment criteria. A *competency* can be
defined as the specific characteristics and behaviour patterns a job holder is
required to demonstrate in order to perform the relevant job tasks with competence. Many organisations now use competency analysis to identify the required
knowledge, skills and behaviours that are essential to perform a specific job role.
The main aim of competency analysis is to derive a *competency model* for the target
role. A competency model comprises a comprehensive list of all the relevant competencies associated with a given job role. For more detailed discussions see
Sparrow and Hodgkinson (2002) and Shippman *et al.* (2000).

In general, job analysis is an umbrella term for many different analyses and involves analysing job tasks, whereas competency analysis focuses on the required behaviours for a job role. To illustrate the use of competency analysis, imagine you are examining the person-focused requirements for the job of a sales assistant, in a large retailing company. A key competency of a sales assistant might be called 'customer service'. The observable behaviours (or behavioural indicators) that underlie this competency could be:

■ actively listens to customers and attempts to understand their needs;

■ proactively seeks feedback and involvement of customers in decision-making processes;

■ ensures that customers feel at ease and in control of a sales interaction.

Note that these are all positively associated with job performance. Many competency models also detail the negative behavioural indicators, i.e. what job holders are expected to avoid doing. Competency analysis is used to build a competency model for each job role, where a model may define several competencies with associated behavioural indicators. In practice, a specific job may have between 6 and 12 competencies in a competency model, although there is wide variation between organisations depending on the target job role.

Competencies can be used as assessment criteria which have a whole variety of different applications including selection, performance appraisal, management development, careers counselling and so on (see also Chapter 6). One of the key advantages in using competencies as assessment criteria is that competencies can become a 'common language' shared by employees in the organisation to describe the desired (and undesirable) behaviours during performance appraisal and career development activities. In this way, the competency analysis outputs can directly inform the design of the assessment criteria in selection. For example, if demonstrating positive communication skills is a key job requirement for sales assistants, the researcher could design a competency-based interview question for selection purposes as 'Describe a time when you have encountered an angry customer and had to use your communications skills to deal with the situation. What did you do and what was the outcome?' An applicant's response could then be assessed on pre-defined behavioural criteria derived from the competency model. Exercise 4.1 provides further opportunities to explore the use of competencies and behavioural indicators in defining assessment criteria.

Exercise 4.1   Competency analysis and defining behavioural indicators

A key competency for the job of retail sales assistant is *team involvement*. An initial job analysis indicates that a sales assistant is required to use a collaborative style and value the contribution of others in the work group. Some example behavioural indicators are illustrated below.

Example positive behavioural indicators:

■ Accepts and promotes new ways of working.

■ Treats other team members as equals and recognises people as individuals.

■ Demonstrates a co-operative interaction style and views success in terms of the team rather than individual outcomes.

■ Seeks to understand other people in the team and values their contribution.

Example negative behavioural indicators:

■ Demonstrates a competitive interaction style, and focuses on individual successes.

■ Criticises individual differences in style.

■ Treats group members differently according to status.

■ Is openly critical of others' suggestions and actions.

1   Imagine the role of a sales assistant in a large retailing organisation. Describe additional behavioural indicators associated with team involvement (both positive and negative) in this context.

2   Describe other competencies that might be associated with the job role of sales assistant. For each, suggest some example positive and negative behavioural indicators.

Although the use of competencies and competency modelling has become commonplace in organisations, there is considerable confusion about what competencies are and how this differs from other job analysis outputs. As we have seen, competency models define the relevant behaviours or behaviour patterns. However, in many organisations competency models for a job role have been developed but appropriate psychological techniques have not been used to identify precisely the requirements in behavioural terms. In other words, many have failed to specify the observable behaviours involved, which can be targeted for measurement purposes in selection, and other contexts. Further, in some organisations a generic *competency framework* has been developed, comprising a set of core competencies relevant to many job roles in that organisation. The competency framework approach is used by many organisations, for application in a range of activities including selection. Although this approach is appealing for ease of interpretation, thorough application is patchy, and generic competency frameworks often lack sufficient behavioural specificity for many job roles. In other words, the behavioural indicators in a competency model should be directly relevant to the job role and the context within which the employee operates. By adopting a tailor-made approach, the assessment criteria can be more accurately defined which in turn may optimise their use at selection.

In a job analysis of the role of General Practitioner (GP) doctors, Patterson *et al.* (2000) suggest that organisations too often rely on 'off-the-shelf' competency models and the more specific the competency analysis is to the target job, the more useful (and potentially more accurate) the behavioural indicators are as assessment

Key Learning Point

Competency models define the key behaviours associated with performance in the target job role.

criteria. In Table 4.1 we provide an example of three competencies in a competency model for a GP. In the example, each competency heading is defined by a series of behavioural indicators. Note that the behavioural indicators (assessment criteria) associated with GP communication skills share some similarities with those of the retail sales assistant, but the content is qualitatively (and significantly) different.

It is important to note that competency models are not static documents. It was noted earlier that best practice personnel selection is characterised by a continuous improvement cycle. Over time, as the needs of the organisation evolve (possibly in response to a range of external influences such as changes in legislation or customer demand), the job requirements and competencies required for a specific role may also change. For example, for GP doctors there have been significant changes in the role where familiarity with information technology, financial acumen and legal awareness are now core requirements for the job. The evidence suggests that competency models and outputs from job analyses should be regularly reviewed, and especially after a selection programme has been implemented to evaluate the original assessment criteria. Further, there are now legal reasons for ensuring accurate selection procedures are used and it is essential for compliance with current employment law. Organisations could be asked to demonstrate that they have used fair and accurate selection processes.

Job analysis data

Sources of job analysis data may be divided into four categories: written material, job holders' reports, colleagues' reports and direct observation.

Written material and existing documentation

Until the 1990s, many organisations held written job descriptions available for many job roles, which provided the researcher with useful information, particularly for more 'blue-collar' job roles. Unfortunately, in many organisations existing job descriptions are rarely up to date, comprehensive or detailed enough. With the rapid pace of organisational change caused by the introduction of technology for example (*see* Chapter 1), there has been a dramatic change in the nature of various job roles and work patterns in general. The introduction of highly technical equipment has made many jobs more complex. For other employees, in many manufacturing job roles for example, their role has become more like equipment monitors where they follow procedures, rather than having cognitively demanding

Table 4.1	Three competencies from a competency model for general practitioners	
Competency	**Definition**	**Example positive behavioural indicators**
(1) Empathy and sensitivity	Patient is treated with sensitivity and personal understanding, asks patient about feelings. GP is empathetic, in control but not dominating, and creates atmosphere of trust and confidence. Focuses on the positive rather than negative, works to involve the patient, shows interest in the individual, gives reassurance and checks patient needs are satisfied	■ Generates an atmosphere where the patient feels safe ■ Patient is taken seriously, treated confidentially ■ Picks up on patient's emotions and feelings ■ Encourages patient, gives reassurances ■ Use of 'I understand what you're saying' ■ Focuses on the positive ■ Is sensitive to feelings ■ Treats individuals as people ■ Checks patient needs are satisfied ■ Demonstrates a caring attitude
(2) Communication skills	Active listening to patients, understands and interprets body language. Able to use different questioning styles and probe for information to lead to root cause. Matches patient language, uses analogy to explain, engages in social conversation, confident style. Clarity in both verbal and written communication	■ Demonstrates active listening skills ■ Is not patronising ■ Confident in approach ■ Able to form relationships with people and build rapport easily ■ Uses analogy to explain problems/complex issues ■ Re-states information for understanding ■ Open body language and direct eye contact ■ Matches patient's language ■ Allows patients time to talk ■ Engages in social conversation ■ Refers to the patient by name
(3) Clinical expertise	Able to apply and trust their judgement (and others') in diagnosing problems. Fully investigates problem before prescribing, able to anticipate rather than just react and to maintain knowledge of current practice. Does not allow patient to develop a dependency	■ Trust in your clinical judgement ■ Clinical competence ■ Provides anticipatory care ■ Guards against dependency ■ Has courage to make decisions ■ Seeks to update clinical skills ■ Gives clear decision and diagnosis ■ Prescribes and checks medication ■ Provides clear explanation of facts and systems ■ Gets to the root of the problem ■ Encourages patient compliance

tasks. In this way, the assessment criteria for use in selection procedures must reflect these changes, and must be updated regularly.

In some organisations, rather than having precise job descriptions, job holders may have 'performance contracts' that detail the broad objectives and responsibilities for the job, to be fulfilled within a prescribed time frame. Where this approach is used for appraising job performance, expectations are documented and an employee is assessed on the extent to which he or she has met the specified objectives. In general, published analyses of jobs may provide useful leads but are of limited value, since jobs analysed elsewhere are likely to be similar but not identical to the one under consideration. An accountant's, secretary's or production manager's job will vary considerably from one organisation to another, perhaps in ways that are crucial. Other written material such as production data, organisation charts, training manuals, job aids and so on may also provide useful additional information.

Job holders' reports

Interviews in which job holders are asked, through careful questioning, to give a description of their main tasks and how they carry them out, provide extremely useful information, and such interviews are usually an essential element in any job analysis. On the other hand, it is difficult to be sure that all of the important aspects of the job have been covered by the interview and that the information provided by the job holder is not too subjective, biased (owing to faulty memory, perhaps) or even deliberately untrue. Therefore, it is usual that several job holders are interviewed to get a consistent picture of the target job role. However, this can be problematic for newly created jobs, as there may not exist job holders to describe the tasks and responsibilities in the required depth. In this case it is likely that senior personnel would be consulted to describe the key responsibilities and performance indicators for the target job role, using a future-orientated approach.

Where there are existing job holders, reports may be obtained by asking them to complete a diary or activity record. Since this is done on a regular basis as the job is being carried out, it avoids problems associated with faulty memory and so forth. The advantage here is that the psychologist can gain an insight into the temporal components to the job, and the information can offer a useful level of detail on the job activities. Work diaries, however, are a difficult and time-consuming procedure, for both the job holder and the analyst. The diaries have to be constructed in such a way as to provide the appropriate level of detail. For example, Exercise 4.2 illustrates a hypothetical work diary for a finance manager working in a large manufacturing company. The diary is a record of daily events and is only structured through time spent on different tasks. In this example, the information gathered is limited as it lacks specificity and the information can be difficult to translate into behavioural indicators, to be used perhaps as assessment criteria in the selection process.

Exercise 4.2 Excerpt from an unstructured work diary

8.00–8.20	Examined e-mail and related correspondence.
8.20–8.30	Met with secretary to plan priorities and responses to correspondence. Organised diary of events and had to reschedule two meetings.
8.30–10.00	Attended strategy meeting with the Executive. Presented a 15 minute summary of the new product launch and projected impact report. Responded to technical questions about calculation of the key performance indicators and profit margin.
10.00–12	Analysed data tables of departmental expenditure for 1st quarter and sketched out a draft report to go to senior management for the forthcoming business process re-engineering review. Involved calculating spend versus income and forecasting total year spend, both for staff salaries and associated costs. Highlighted key figures in the report and illustrated in graphical format.
12–12.20	Grabbed sandwich!
12.20	Made telephone call to key supplier to negotiate pricing of materials for product launch.
12.30–1.30	Chaired a team meeting with my staff. Presented news update and business figures. Discussed implications of re-structure of job roles.

1 Examine the extract from the work diary shown above and create a list of behaviours that appear to be associated with successful performance in this Finance Manager's job role. (*Hint*: you may find it useful to highlight particular words that refer to behaviours, e.g. 'prioritise', or 'negotiate'.)

2 Having created your list, comment on how the information you have can be used. Suggest ways in which the work diary could be improved to provide additional information in order to design relevant assessment criteria.

Flanagan (1954) developed a procedure known as the *critical incident technique* (CIT). In brief, using this technique involves asking the interviewee to recall specific incidents of job behaviour that are characteristic of either highly effective or highly ineffective performance in the job. A critical incident is defined as 'any observable human activity that is sufficiently complete in itself to permit inferences and predictions to be made about the person performing the act'. By describing the behaviours and characteristics that led to the incident, the analyst can get an excellent insight into the relevant job behaviour(s) that are important. Not only will this information enable the analyst to differentiate between good and poor job holders, it can provide some contextual information that might be helpful in designing the actual selection methods, such as work sample tests. CIT is a versatile technique since it can be conducted either during interviews with individuals or with groups of job holders. A group-based CIT can be very useful to get initial 'cross-validation' of information, where job holders might have experienced or witnessed similar incidents (see Patterson *et al.*, 2000).

McCormick *et al.* (1972) produced the *position analysis questionnaire* (PAQ), which is an example of a structured questionnaire approach to job analysis. The elements in the questionnaire are worker-orientated in that they focus on generalised aspects of human behaviour and are not closely tied to the technology of specific jobs. The PAQ consists of nearly two hundred items organised into six broad categories including (1) information input, (2) mediation processes (i.e. the mental processes of reasoning, decision-making, etc.), (3) work output, (4) interpersonal activities (i.e. relationships with others), (5) work situation and job context, (6) miscellaneous aspects. One problem with the PAQ is that it requires a fairly high level of reading ability on the part of respondents. Nevertheless, the PAQ is a well-researched and valuable means of analysing jobs as a standardised and well-established technique.

Key Learning Point

Generic job analysis questionnaires are available. They can be used to analyse a wide variety of jobs.

McCormick and others carried out the original development work for the PAQ in the United States, and there has also been development of British job analysis questionnaires such as that by Banks and colleagues (Banks *et al.*, 1983; Banks, 1988) who produced the *job components inventory* (JCI). This inventory focuses on both job and worker facets, and the outputs from the analysis include quantified profiles of the absolute and relative skills required for the job under investigation. Another British questionnaire is the work profiling system (WPS; produced by UK occupational psychology consultants SHL), which consists of a set of over eight hundred items. A subset of about two hundred items is usually used for any particular job, depending somewhat on its level of complexity.

A self-contained technique for analysis, which is job rather than worker-orientated, has been described by Fine and Wiley (1974). Known as *functional job analysis* (FJA), this approach makes use of a standardised language to describe what job holders do and provides a means of examining the complexity and the orientation of the job. Orientation here is described as the extent to which the job is directed towards 'data', 'people' or 'things', and, as a result of analysis, can be expressed in percentage terms. The basic unit of analysis in FJA is the task – that is, an action or action sequence organised over time and designed to contribute to a specific end result or objective. Using a very similar definition of the task, Annett and others (Annett *et al.*, 1971; Shepherd, 1976) have developed a means of analysis known as *hierarchical task analysis* (HTA). A more recent development is the use of flexible, large-scale, computer-driven databases that contain information about not just the work behaviours but also the associated worker attributes including information on the personality, behavioural and situational variables (see Hough and Oswald, 2000).

A procedure for collecting job analysis information that still remains popular involves the use of Kelly's (1955) *repertory grid technique*. This approach provides systematic worker-orientated data. It has an advantage over other means of obtaining worker-orientated data such as PAQ in that it does not limit the responses of the job holder by providing a prestructured set of categories. Repertory grid technique is based on Kelly's Personal Construct Theory as a method to elicit an individual's personal construct system. Kelly describes a personal construct as 'a reference axis, a basic dimension of appraisal, often unverbalised, frequently unsymbolised'. Metaphorically, the theory suggests that individuals view the world through their own personal 'spectacles', and hold a set of 'mental models' and beliefs about how the world works. Repertory grid technique involves a highly structured interviewing process to elicit an individual's mental model of the world. The theory assumes that behind any act of judgement (conscious or unconscious) lies an *implicit theory* about the domain of events within which the individual is making judgements. In addition, it is assumed that these implicit theories are unique but that similar constructs may occur between individuals. For job analysis purposes, repertory grid technique is often used to interview job holders about the knowledge, skills and abilities involved in the target role and provides a rich source of qualitative data (Fransella and Bannister, 1977). It is more powerful than many other techniques in that job holders may describe constructs that they have never verbalised before. In practice, repertory grid technique is most useful as a starting point in a job analysis, to help explore the breadth of the job domain (particularly if it is not well known). In this way, the technique avoids predetermining the domain of questioning, unlike structured work profiling questionnaires.

Colleagues' reports

In addition to gleaning information directly from job holders, it can be useful to obtain data from direct reports, peers and supervisors. For example, when collecting critical incident data, the views of a job holder, a direct report and a supervisor on the nature of such critical incidents might provide for interesting comparisons. It might also be useful to gain information from customers or the *user group* of the intended job holders. For example, in a job analysis of GPs (Patterson *et al.*, 2000), job analysis information was collected not just from the GPs themselves, but also from patients. An important part of this study was to compare the patient perceptions alongside doctor perceptions of the job role. In this way, the user group perspective can be reflected in the assessment criteria in both selection and performance management applications.

Direct observation

In any job analysis some direct observation of the job being carried out is invariably helpful. It is, of course, possible that the presence of the researcher may alter the job holder's behaviour, and as with the approaches described earlier the data obtained cannot be perfect. Yet data derived from observation, perhaps even from participant observation, where the analyst does all or some of the job, can provide insights that no other method can. Observation is most useful for jobs where there is a manual or visible component such as a factory line worker, as the tasks conducted can be viewed clearly by the observer. For managerial jobs however, where there are extended periods of time spent working on a computer or on the telephone, observation may not add a great deal of useful information for the job analysis.

A variety of different techniques for job analysis have been introduced and it is often useful to conduct an analysis using a variety of methods rather than just one. On this basis, as well as being useful for personnel selection, the outputs may be helpful in other applications, such as training and development or job evaluation.

Key Learning Point

Job analyses are usually best developed by using as many different approaches and means of data collection as possible and pooling the results.

When deciding which approach (or approaches) to adopt in conducting a job analysis in practice, Table 4.2 provides a checklist of questions or criteria that you may wish to consider when deciding which methods to use in a given setting.

Using job analysis information

The job analysis information is used in a number of ways. A job description can be prepared from the job analysis data to give an outline of the key responsibilities. It

Table 4.2	A checklist of considerations for conducting a job analysis

- Is my purpose to conduct a task-orientated or worker-orientated analysis (i.e. precise tasks and responsibilities or primarily psychological factors)?

- What level of expertise is required for the analyst?

- What is the level of job proximity in using this technique (direct observation versus remote analysis of self-report on a questionnaire)? How will this influence the quality of data I collect?

- What type of data does this technique provide and how will this be analysed?

- How can I best validate my initial findings?

- What is the capacity of using this technique to generate usable outcomes?

- What is the cost (both in terms of time and resource) of using this technique?

- Are there issues regarding employee sensitivity and access to job holders that need to be addressed?

can be useful in the initial stages of the selection procedure to give candidates some understanding of the job, and can also be used within the organisation to provide information for training, job evaluation and other purposes. The job analysis also provides information that might be used when recruitment advertisements and so forth are prepared to attract candidates for the job.

A personnel specification represents the demands of the job translated into human terms. It involves listing the essential criteria that candidates must satisfy and also those criteria that would exclude candidates from consideration. As described earlier, job analysis information may also be used to define a competency model for the job role. However, moving from a job analysis to a clear specification of the psychological qualities thought to be required by a successful job holder is a difficult process. Various procedures have been suggested and used to make this step but it is important to remember that none of them is entirely objective and that some inferences are required. It is also worth noting that the inferential steps needed and the nature of these inferences are different, depending on whether one is designing a sign- or sample-based selection procedure. Wernimont and Campbell (1968) made this important distinction between what they described as *signs* and *samples* of behaviour. Consider, for example, how a candidate for a sales position may react to being asked to complete a personality questionnaire, containing questions such as 'Do you often wish that your life was more exciting?' Consider also how the same candidate may react to being required to conduct a role-play exercise and expected to persuade a client to make a purchase. The relevance of the role-play exercise and its potential to provide the selection decision-makers with a realistic *sample* of the candidate's behaviour is obvious. Although it may not be so obvious to the candidate, the results of the personality test may also provide important *signs* relating to certain job-relevant psychological characteristics. For example, success in sales jobs may be more likely when someone is extroverted, emotionally stable and agreeable.

Job analysis data may be used in two broadly different ways in the design of selection procedures depending on whether the selection procedure will be used to assess samples or signs of behaviour.

Key Learning Point

Job analysis information may be used to design sign- or sample-based personnel selection procedures.

The more traditional use of job analysis involves moving from the analysis to make inferences about the kind of psychological characteristics (signs) needed for successful job performance. By contrast, the sample approach involves focusing on the job tasks and designing selection procedures that provide representative samples of the actual behaviour needed for successful jobs. With increased prevalence of newly created job roles, traditional job analysis techniques may be less relevant as current job holders may not exist. In this way, the challenge of psychologists is to find new ways of conducting future-oriented job analysis techniques (see Hough and Oswald, 2000). Exercise 4.3 presents a case study based on a real example of the issues that psychologists face in conducting job analysis in organisations today.

| Exercise 4.3 | Using job analysis procedures in organisations |

Background

Specs-R-Us are a well-established UK-based opticians company, specialising in eye-sight testing and the sale of related eyewear. There are 350 stores throughout the country. The company has been the market leader for several years but has recently experienced tough competition from other optical sales providers coming into the market. The competition is fierce and is primarily based on cost and 'express delivery' of spectacles and eyewear. Spec-R-Us has been a trusted brand over the years and has established a reputation for expertise in optometry and quality service delivery. In each store there is usually one optometrist, who conducts the eye examinations and produces a prescription for the customer. Depending on the size of the store, the optometrist is supported by several optical assistants. The optical assistants' role is to conduct initial eye screening tests and to advise on choice of frames and lenses, based on the customer's prescription. Historically, Specs-R-Us optical assistants have tended to treat people coming into the stores as 'patients' with a prescription, and there has been little or no emphasis on generating sales and selling goods with a higher profit margin.

The job analysis issue

Given increased competition in the market, Specs-R-Us have been losing revenue to other organisations that are generating higher profit through increased sales. In response, the Executive has decided to restructure the organisation and create a new job role called sales advisers. This represents a major cultural change in the organisation, where sales performance is now a core requirement of the job role. The new sales adviser's role is designed specifically to increase revenue based on sales in store. These advisers will work alongside the optical assistants, where the optical assistants will conduct the 'technical' elements such as pre-screening eye tests before customers see the optometrist. Once customers have their prescription, the sales advisers will focus on guiding customers on choice of frames and lenses. For sales advisers, a key performance indicator is based on sales revenue, and they will be encouraged to sell goods that carry a high profit margin such as 'designer frames and lenses'.

Your task

In light of these changes, you have been asked by the Executive to conduct two job analyses, one for the role of optical assistants and the other for sales advisers. Prepare an outline of the process you would conduct for the job analysis for each role. In your response:

1 explain why it is important for Specs-R-Us to conduct the job analyses, in terms that the Executive in the organisation could understand;

2 describe how the information could be used in the organisation;

3 outline the various techniques you might employ to conduct the analyses;

4 outline any potential difficulties in accessing the data.

Validation processes

The key stage in the personnel selection process occurs when the selection decision is taken and a candidate is either offered a position within the organisation, or turned away. At this point various pieces of evidence concerning the current or past performance of candidates (e.g. behaviour at an interview, psychological test scores or references), usually referred to as predictors, are used to decide whether or not a candidate is suitable for the job in question. Although job analysis may suggest that certain candidate characteristics might be desirable, alone it cannot *prove* that candidates with these characteristics will do better than others on the job. This evaluation of the accuracy of the selection methods is obtained by assessing the criterion-related validity of the predictors.

Criterion-related validity

Criterion-related validity refers to the strength of the relationship between the predictor (e.g. psychological test scores or interview ratings) and the criterion (e.g. subsequent work behaviour indicated by measures such as output figures or supervisor's ratings). Criterion-related validity is high if candidates who obtain high predictor scores obtain high criterion scores *and* candidates who obtain low scores on a predictor also obtain low criterion scores. Figure 4.2 shows a scatter plot of some hypothetical data obtained by using two predictors:

1 a job knowledge test score; and

2 a cognitive ability test score;

and one criterion:

3 average number of units produced per day.

Inspection of the scatter plot in Fig. 4.2b shows that the criterion-related validity of the cognitive ability test appears to be quite good. Participants' scores in this test correspond closely with the number of units produced. Although the predictor and criterion scores are obviously closely related, it is worth noting that the correspondence is not perfect. For perfect correspondence all of the points would lie exactly on the diagonal line drawn in on Fig. 4.2b. For the job knowledge test

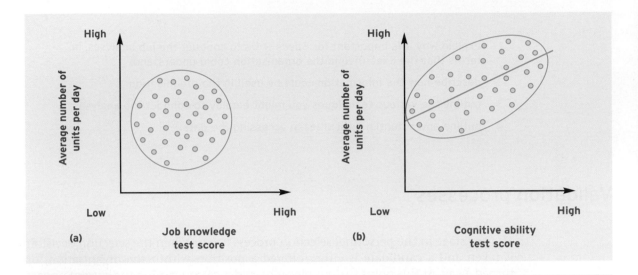

Figure 4.2	Some hypothetical predictor and criterion scores: (a) job knowledge test; (b) cognitive ability test

there is no correspondence at all and, as Fig. 4.2a clearly shows, the points are distributed more or less in a circle and high scores on one variable can be associated with either high or low scores on the other variable.

The strength of the relationship between predictor scores and criterion scores is usually expressed as a correlation coefficient (referred to as a validity coefficient). *See also* Chapter 2 for an explanation of correlation. Perfect correlation between two variables will produce a correlation of one. No correlation at all, as in Fig. 4.2a, will produce a coefficient of zero.

Key Learning Point

The criterion-related validity of a selection procedure is normally indicated by the magnitude of the validity coefficient (the correlation between the predictor and criterion scores).

When the correlation between two variables is high it is possible to predict the score of one when supplied with the score on the other. Consider, for example, Fig. 4.3, where the predictor–criterion relationship is perfect (i.e. a validity (correlation) coefficient of +1.0). In the case of a new candidate, it would be possible to obtain his or her score on predictor A and thus predict a score on the criterion. For example, if the organisation wished to select staff who would produce an average of at least 75 units per day, what should be done?

As Fig. 4.3 shows, if only people who obtained a score of above 80 on predictor A were offered jobs by the organisation, all future employees would be likely to produce 75 units (or more) per day. Unfortunately, in practice selection can rarely

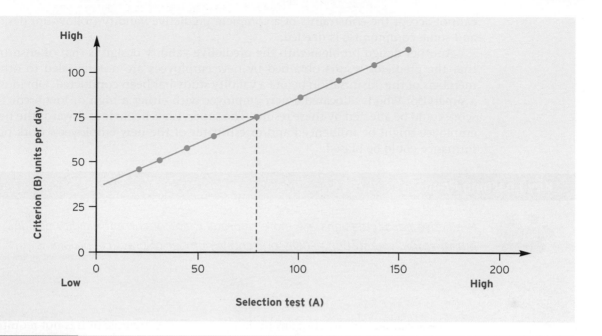

Figure 4.3   **Prediction of criterion scores from selection test scores**

be conducted in such an idealised and clear-cut fashion and there are several practical problems that must be considered.

Research (e.g. Muchinsky, 1986; Smith and George, 1992; Salgado *et al.*, 2001) has shown that it is most unusual in practical situations to obtain validity coefficients much in excess of +0.5, let alone the coefficient of +1.0 that will allow perfect prediction. Nevertheless, validity coefficients of considerably less than +1.0 can provide a basis for improved personnel selection. Theoretically the ideal way to collect criterion-related validity data is to use a predictive (or follow-up) design. This design involves collecting predictor information (e.g. interview ratings, test scores) for candidates and then following up the candidates (e.g. during their first year of employment) to gather criterion data on their work performance. An alternative design for conducting criterion-related validity studies is the *concurrent* design. In the concurrent design, predictor data are obtained from existing employees on whom criterion data are already available.

Ideally, in a study of predictive validity the predictor scores should not be used to take selection decisions until after a validation study has been conducted. In other words, until the relationship between predictor and criterion is firmly established, candidates should be offered employment regardless of their performance on the predictors. Often this is a difficult step for an organisation to take in practice. If job analysis and other information (in the absence of validity data) suggest that the use of certain predictors should improve their selection decisions, in many organisations managers would not be willing to permit candidates with low scores on these predictors to enter employment. Sometimes it is possible to convince them not to use the results of potential predictors and to continue to use their existing methods while a validation study is carried out. Often, however, they cannot accept the constraints of a complete predictive validity (follow-up) design and some compromise is needed.

Another design problem with the predictive validity design is that of ensuring that the predictor results obtained by new employees are not revealed to other members of the organisation before a validity study has been conducted. Obviously a supervisor who is allocated a new employee with either a high or low predictor score could be affected by these results. The supervisor's behaviour towards the new employee might be influenced and/or estimates of the new employee's work performance could be biased.

Key Learning Point

Predictive validity designs are more rigorous than concurrent validity designs but their implementation usually presents a number of practical problems.

One advantage of the concurrent design is that the organisation is not required to collect predictor data from candidates (for employment) without making use of the data for selection decisions. Predictor data are collected from existing employees only. A second advantage of the concurrent design is that there is no time delay between the collection of predictor and criterion data. Existing employees' predictor scores are correlated with their criterion performance. The criterion data are likely to be available already, or at least can be collected quickly. There is certainly no need to wait for the lengthy follow-up period involved with the predictive design. Figure 4.4 compares the two designs in a hypothetical situation and indicates the considerable differences in time scales and data collection effort that can occur.

Because of these advantages the concurrent design is attractive to many organisations. However, there are disadvantages. The workers presently employed by an organisation provide a population that may be very different from the population of job applicants. Current job holders have already survived existing company selection procedures and represent a pre-selected group of people who have been with the organisation for some time. No data are available on people who were not hired by the company, or on those who were hired but have subsequently left. Thus the concurrent sample is incomplete and not representative of the potential workforce. If, as a result of a concurrent validity study, a link between, say, scores in an arithmetic test and job performance is established, it is difficult to be sure if the people tested come to the job with such skills or whether arithmetic skills are acquired as a result of training and job experience. Such problems make it hard to be certain about the actual predictive value of results derived from a concurrent validity study.

Validation studies can become very complex in practical terms since organisations rarely use one single predictor to make selection decisions and applicants are likely to be judged on multiple assessment criteria. Given the multifaceted nature of job analysis information, recruiters are likely to design multiple selection tools to assess these criteria. Therefore, recruiters must decide whether a job applicant

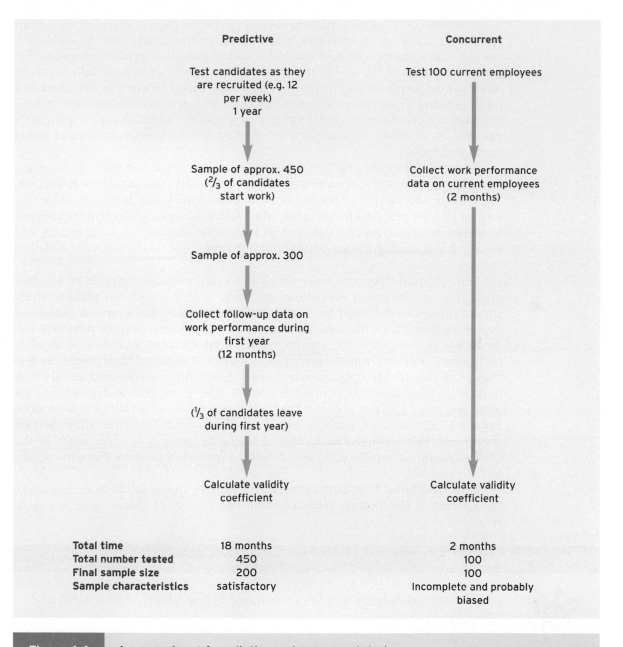

Figure 4.4   A comparison of predictive and concurrent designs

must score highly on all assessment criteria (non-compensatory) or whether high scores on some criteria can make up for low scores on another (compensatory). In practice, recruiters might assign different weightings to various assessment criteria, depending on the nature of the job role. For example, in the sales assistant job role, it might be decided that customer service skills is the most important criterion and applicants who do not achieve a certain score will not be considered further.

Most selection systems combine several predictors (selection tools), such as an applicant's score on an interview and on a cognitive ability test. In validation studies, a key question is how much does adding another predictor increase the predictive power of the selection process. This is known as *incremental validity*. In other words, recruiters might want to know how much accuracy is improved as a result of using a psychometric test (rather than relying solely on interview scores). Information on the incremental validity of a specific selection tool is extremely valuable as it allows organisations to conduct a cost–benefit analysis of using additional tools.

Another significant practical difficulty in today's organisations is in accessing an adequate sample size in order to perform certain statistical analyses on the data. The design and sample of the study need to be sufficiently robust to allow the analyst to draw firm conclusions about the validity of various selection techniques. Most organisations are not involved in large-scale recruitment programmes and usually it is sizeable graduate recruitment initiatives that are the focus of validation studies.

One important point to make about any validity study, regardless of whether predictive or concurrent procedures are used, is that the initial validity study should always be followed by a 'cross-validation' study on a second sample of people to cross-check the results obtained. For studies that involve relatively few predictors this requirement is perhaps not essential and represents a 'counsel of perfection'. However, when a study has investigated many possible predictors and those with the strongest predictor–criterion relationship are to be used for selection purposes, cross-validation is more important. The more potential predictors are used, the more likely it becomes that random or chance variations will produce apparent relationships between some of these predictors and the criterion measure(s). Relationships due to chance would be unlikely to occur again in the cross-validation sample – only 'real' relationships would produce the same results in both samples.

Some additional important points about validity appear in the next chapter, in the context of interpreting evidence about the validity of specific selection techniques.

Key Learning Point

Cross-validation is necessary to be confident of the results from a validation study, unless the sample is very large.

Other types of validity

Criterion-related validity is the most important type of validity as far as selection is concerned, but there are other important types of validity as well. The first two are not 'real' forms of validity, in the sense that they refer to appearance rather than substance.

Faith validity

Sometimes organisations might believe that a selection method (e.g. a psychometric ability test) is valid because a reputable company sells it, and it is packaged in a very expensive-looking way. However, Cook (1996) suggests that money spent on 'gloss' could mean less money has been spent on research and development of the instrument. He suggests that organisations must be wary of blindly accepting the validity of an instrument without thorough inspection of all supporting data and documentation.

Face validity

A selection test or procedure displays face validity if it 'looks right'. For example, requiring an applicant for a carpenter's job to make a 'T-joint' from two pieces of wood would show face validity. On the other hand asking the applicant to carry out a test of general intelligence would probably have much less face validity for the candidate, since the link between that test and job performance would probably be less obvious to the candidate. One key advantage of face validity is the positive impact it has upon user acceptability.

Content validity

Content validity is established on a logical basis rather than by calculating validity coefficients or following other technical statistical procedures. A predictor shows content validity when it covers a representative sample of the behaviour domain being measured. For example, a content valid test of car-driving ability would be expected to cover all of the essential activities that a competent driver should be able to carry out. A test that did not include an emergency stop and a reversing exercise would be lacking in content validity.

Construct validity

This involves identifying the psychological characteristics (or constructs) such as intelligence, emotional stability or manual dexterity that underlie successful performance of the task (such as a test or performance on the job) in question. Since construct validity involves relationships between predictors and characteristics that are not directly observable, it can be assessed only by indirect means. Often this is achieved by correlating a well-established measure of a construct with a new measure. A poor relationship would suggest that the new measure may lack construct validity. Exploring the construct validity of any psychological instrument is an important facet of understanding what the instrument actually measures. As material in Chapter 5 shows, the construct validity of several frequently used personnel selection methods is not well understood.

Exercise 4.4 gives an opportunity to reflect upon your own experiences of selection processes, particularly in relation to your perceptions of the validity of the process.

Exercise 4.4   The validity of selection processes

In this exercise you are asked to reflect upon your own experience(s) of selection and recruitment processes. Think about a job in which you have been employed (whether full-time or part-time) and consider the following issues:

1   What are the key responsibilities of the role?

2   Describe the elements of the recruitment process. Did the selection procedures display face validity and content validity at each stage?

3   In general, what is your impression of the accuracy of the selection process?

4   What recommendation would you make to improve the likely validity of this selection process?

Reliability

Any measuring instrument (whether predictor or criterion) used in a selection procedure must be both valid and reliable. The reliability of a selection instrument is an extremely important characteristic and refers to the extent to which it measures consistently under varying conditions. If the same candidate produces very different scores when he or she takes a test on two different occasions, the reliability of the test must be questioned. In technical terms, if a selection tool has high reliability it has 'relative freedom from unsystematic errors of measurement'. An example of unsystematic error could be the conditions under which the test is administered.

If we want to assess the reliability for an ability test we could calculate the *test re-test reliability* (where participants are administered the same test on two separate occasions with a significant time lag between administrations). If the test had high reliability we would expect a strong positive correlation between scores at time 1 and time 2 administrations. In this way, the researcher can account for unsystematic error due to differences in conditions during administration of the test.

Another form of reliability is *parallel forms*, where test developers might design two tests to be equivalent, including items of similar content and equal difficulty. For example, often organisations involved in graduate recruitment use similar psychometric ability tests. In order to prevent practice effects, test publishers produce parallel forms of the same ability test. In designing parallel forms of the same test, the test developers assess the external reliability between scales, where high reliability is characterised by a strong positive correlation between participant scores on both tests.

Test re-rest and parallel forms can both be described as *external* forms of reliability, because scores on the measure in question are compared with a reference point, even if that is scores on the same measure at a different time.

The *internal* reliability of a scale can be assessed by a variety of different statistical methods and formulae (see Smith and Robertson, 1993; Kline, 1998, for relevant formulae and further technical information). The common feature is that internal reliability always concerns the extent to which different parts of the same measure produce results consistent with each other. The type of scale and its content determines the specific approach to assessing internal reliability. Common approaches to assessing the internal reliability of scales include Cronbach's coefficient alpha, and the 'split half' method (where the researcher can examine the association between scores on two halves of a test, for example).

Key Learning Point

To be effective, personnel selection methods must be both valid and reliable.

Financial utility

Like many organisational practices, personnel selection procedures cost money to implement. Using selection procedures with good predictive validity is always important but, unfortunately, procedures with good predictive validity alone do not guarantee that a selection procedure will be cost-effective. Two important factors determining cost-effectiveness (usually referred to as utility) are:

1   selection ratio, i.e. $\dfrac{\text{number of jobs}}{\text{number of candidates}}$;

2   the financial benefit of improved job performance.

Let us now examine in a little more detail the role that validity, selection ratio and the other factors play in determining utility. Figure 4.5a shows the situation for a validity coefficient of 0.1. The shaded areas (B and C) identify people who will be hired by the organisation. Notice, however, that although all of these people achieve the minimum score on the predictor, only a proportion of them (B) also show satisfactory work performance. Similarly, although all of the people in the unshaded areas (A and D) fail to achieve the cut-off score on the predictor, some of them are capable of satisfactory work performance (those in area A). Areas B and D represent correct selection decisions; area D contains people who have been justifiably rejected, known as true negatives. Area C contains the false positives; that is, people who would be hired but produce unsatisfactory work performance. Area A contains the false negatives; that is, people who would not be hired but are capable of satisfactory work performance. Areas A and C represent errors in the selection process. Note that unless the validity coefficient is 1.0 there will *always* be errors of selection.

As Fig. 4.5b shows, when validity increases (0.5), the proportions in areas A and C decrease and the proportion of correct decisions (areas B and D) increases. Thus, as validity increases, the quality of selection decisions also increases.

If validity was perfect, error-free selection could be achieved and the relative performance of candidates on the selection method would be reproduced in their

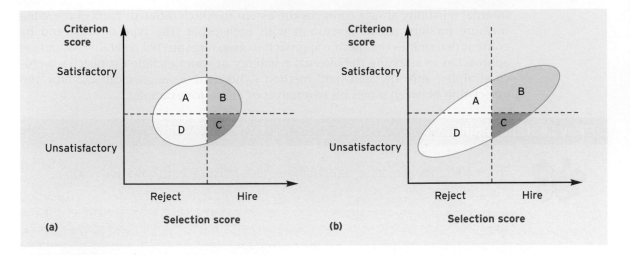

| Figure 4.5 | The effect of different validity coefficients on the proportion hired: (a) validity coefficient = 0.1; (b) validity coefficient = 0.5 |

work performance. Thus, a group of candidates with selection scores in the top 10 per cent would deliver work performance scores at the same level (remember that in perfect selection, work performance is perfectly correlated with selection score).

If the assumption that candidates' scores are normally distributed is made, then it is possible to use statistical tables to calculate the average standard score (*z*-score) of any group of candidates (e.g. the top 10 per cent). With *perfect selection*, the average *z*-score of the selected candidates would also be their average work performance score:

Average selection score (z_s) = average work performance score (z_w)

Of course, in reality, selection is never perfect and the predictive accuracy of the selection score is proportional to the magnitude of the validity coefficient. The work performance that can be expected of selected candidates will be dependent on the accuracy of selection:

(z_s)(validity coefficient) = z_w

The next step in the process is to consider how much value can be assigned to different levels of work performance. Several investigators have tackled this problem, and although there is no accepted solution (*see* Boudreau, 1989), a very conservative rule of thumb is to assign a value of 40 per cent of salary to each standard deviation of performance. Once this step has been made, it is a simple matter to derive an estimate of the financial gain that can be expected from different selection situations. Since *z*-scores are already expressed in standard score units, the estimate of z_w gives a direct estimate of financial gain. The cost of the procedure needs to be subtracted and account taken of the expected tenure of recruits and the number of people selected. The final equation is:

$(z_s)(r)(T)(N) =$ financial benefit

where: z_s =   average z-score of selected group
         r =   validity coefficient for the selection procedure
         T =   number of years recruits will stay
         N =   number of recruits taken in one year

This equation has many potential uses. It could be used, for instance, to calculate the gain to be derived from changing from one selection method to another. To make the relevant calculations it is often necessary to make some estimates of the various terms in the equation. For example, if a company was considering the use of assessment centres to replace a procedure that involved only unstructured interviews, it would be necessary to make estimates of the likely validity for the new procedure. Given the wealth of research on most selection methods such estimates can be made with reasonable confidence. Similarly, the equation could be used to estimate the gain that could be derived from the attraction of a bigger field of candidates (e.g. by extensive advertising). The financial gain derived from the improved selection ratio (see below) may then be set against the cost of the advertising campaign.

Key Learning Point

Utility calculations can be used to address a variety of problems and assist organisations in determining recruitment advertising strategies, etc., as well as indicating the direct benefits to be derived from selection procedures.

Clearly, when the selection ratio is greater than 1 (i.e. there are more available jobs than applicants), the use of any selection procedure is likely to be of relatively little benefit. In this situation the organisation may be forced to accept anyone who applies for a job. In practice, even with a selection ratio of more than 1, it may still be sensible for an organisation to apply stringent selection criteria and leave jobs empty rather than hire totally unsuitable employees. When the selection ratio is less than 1 (i.e. more applicants than jobs), the organisation can gain obvious benefits from using selection. Consider the situation for two different selection ratios. If the selection ratio is 0.7 (i.e. seven jobs for every ten applicants), the organisation can afford to refuse jobs to people with the lowest 30 per cent of scores on the predictor. If, however, the selection ratio is 0.4, the bottom 60 per cent of applicants can be rejected and the group of applicants selected will have a much higher score. In turn, as the material presented above shows, this will translate into financial gain.

Other factors

Studies where selection utility has been estimated have shown very clearly that, even with modest validity coefficients, striking financial gains may be made.

The cost-effectiveness of a personnel selection procedure is not dependent on validity alone.

Schmidt *et al.* (1984), for example, showed that gains of over US$1 million per annum could be expected if cognitive ability tests were used to select the large numbers of US Park Rangers recruited each year. Schmidt *et al.* (1979) showed that even more dramatic gains could be obtained if the *computer programmer aptitude test* (Hughes and McNamara, 1959) was used to select computer programmers in the United States. With a selection ratio of 0.5 (i.e. two applicants per job), gains of between US$13 and 37 million could be expected!

Summary

Selection processes are designed on the assumption that there are job-relevant, individual differences between people, which can be assessed. Assessment in organisational settings is a common activity, which can have a useful impact on individual and organisational success and well-being. The cornerstone of effective selection processes is the job analysis, which defines the assessment criteria that form the basis for many human resource activities in organisations and it is particularly important in personnel selection. More recently, organisations have used competency analysis to define the key behaviours that underpin successful performance in the target job role. A range of approaches to job analysis is available, including qualitative and quantitative techniques. Job analysis information may be used to develop (sign- or sample-based) selection procedures.

Given significant changes in the nature of work and work patterns in recent years, many jobs do not have specific, prescribed job descriptions. This presents a variety of challenges for the job analyst, particularly in deciding which job analysis techniques to employ. As a result, many analysts are trying to use more future-oriented approaches. Since the reliability and validity of such procedures determine the quality of personnel entering the organisation it is crucial that selection procedures provide valid assessments of future work behaviour. Several different (e.g. predictive or concurrent) validation processes are available for assessing validity.

Closing Case Study

A New Selection System in Applied Medicine

Background

The UK Government's Department of Health (DoH) is interested in improving the selection and recruitment practices in applied medicine. A recent government report suggested that 'Reform must take account of . . . weak selection and appointment procedures: these are not standardized and are frequently not informed by core competencies'. In addition, in many specialties there is an increased drop-out rate in recent years during early career training, which is proving costly.

This presents an opportunity to develop a robust selection system for three secondary care specialties (Psychiatry, Dermatology and Obstetrics & Gynaecology). Selection is targeted at doctors at the Senior House Officer grade, who apply in training in each specialty. They are already qualified as doctors, but usually have relatively limited specific knowledge of the specialty. The DoH believes that by using a validated approach, this is likely to ensure selection of properly informed and skilled doctors. The current selection process for each specialty is inconsistent and is usually decided at local level. Usually, a prospective candidate in each specialty submits a full CV (résumé) and is asked to attend a panel interview (a 1-hour interview with a panel of senior local staff). The DoH has asked you to design a new selection system for each specialty.

The DoH is concerned about the current process for a number of reasons. First, there is limited consistency in the selection process, both within and across specialties. The DoH has chosen these three specialties as a 'test bed' to learn more about best practice selection. Second, clear assessment criteria have yet to be established for use in both selection and in performance management activities. With funding pressures, rising numbers on waiting lists and increased legal responsibilities, the roles of these doctors (for each specialty) have expanded in recent years. Third, given recent media coverage and government enquiries, the DoH is concerned about delivering standardised selection and recruitment processes that account for issues relating to equal opportunities.

Your task

You have been asked by the DoH to provide recommendations that will help to begin the development of a new national selection system for doctors wanting to enter each of these specialties in the UK. Produce a 2-page report that provides recommendations for:

1. a systematic approach to assessing the competencies required in each specialty; and

2. how the validity and reliability of the new system should be examined once it is in operation.

Test your learning

Short-answer questions

1   Outline three job analysis techniques and describe the relative advantages and disadvantages of each.

2   For what purposes can job analysis outputs be used in organisations?

3   Draw a diagram of the personnel selection design and validation system.

4   What are competencies and competency analysis? Describe how they are used in organisations and for what purposes.

5   What are behavioural indicators in competency models and how are they used?

6   Describe the criteria you would use to make the decisions about which job analysis technique to use in practice.

7   Describe a predictive validity study for a selection process and explain the associated practical problems they present in organisations.

8   What are the differences between face, content and construct validity, and how is each type of validity assessed?

9   What are the main items of information needed in order to calculate the financial utility of a selection procedure?

Suggested assignments

1   Given recent changes in the nature of work and the increasing number of newly created job roles in organisations, discuss the relative effectiveness of job analysis techniques and suggest how psychologists might improve them.

2   You have been asked to design a job analysis process for the role of politician. Describe the techniques you might use and how this will inform the selection process.

3   Outline the key stages in the selection process. Discuss the practical problems associated with validating selection procedures in organisations.

Relevant websites

There is a lot of useful information about job analysis at http://www.job-analysis.net/. This is a site for human resources managers and consultants, but also offers quite a lot of general information about what job analysis is, how it can be done, and how to do it legally.

An easy-to-read analysis of the competencies that are needed to survive in 21st century global workplaces can be found at http://content.monster.com.sg/management/5808/. See whether you think that the notion of competency that lies behind this aticle is the same as what work psychologists regard as a competency.

For further self-test material and relevant, annotated weblinks please visit the website at http://www.booksites.net/arnold_workpsych.

Suggested further reading

1   For more depth on the issues raised in this chapter, consult a comprehensive text on personnel selection, such as *Personnel Selection: A theoretical approach* by Schmitt and Chan, 1998 (full reference in the list at the end of this book).

2   A very detailed treatment of validity and reliability is given in Anastasi's book, *Psychological Testing*, or Kline's *Handbook of Psychological Testing* (full references in the list at the end of the book).

CHAPTER 5

Personnel selection and assessment methods: what works?

LEARNING OUTCOMES

After studying this chapter, you should be able to:

1 list seven personnel selection methods and describe three in more detail;

2 state six major evaluative standards for personnel selection procedures;

3 name the chief sources of distortion in validation studies;

4 explain the contribution of meta-analysis to personnel selection research;

5 specify advantages and disadvantages of several selection methods, including: interviews; psychometric tests; work-sample tests and assessment centres;

6 specify which selection methods tend to be (i) most valid and (ii) most acceptable to applicants;

7 explain how some selection techniques could lead to bias and unfairness to some subgroups;

8 explain some of the issues associated with the increasing use of technology in personnel selection.

Opening Case Study | War of Nerves

When Anne Owen turned up for an interview for a job in telesales earlier this year, the recruiter's line of questioning wasn't quite what she'd expected. 'I was asked if I'd ever done a bungee jump' says the 23 year old. 'When I replied that I hadn't, I was told that I "probably wasn't right for the job then" and was bundled out of the room'. Anne is not alone. According to new research from the website Totaljobs.com, far from coming away celebrating their new dream job, candidates are just as likely to leave an interview feeling insulted and misled.

'Despite the amount of time and money invested by the human resources community to make the recruitment process as professional as possible, the majority of British job seekers still feel they get a raw deal at interviews,' explains Keith Robinson, chief operations director for Totaljobs.com. More than a quarter of the women said they were quizzed about their marital status and whether they planned to have children. Despite the fact that 76% of UK businesses say that 'opportunities to employ disabled people have not yet arisen', 20% of candidates have been asked personal questions about their disabilities and health that they felt were inappropriate. Older workers speak of negative experiences, too, with a number of respondents having reported sitting through interviews while seeing their age written or circled at the top of their CV. Having revealed her age as 45, one job-seeker was told the company 'did not want a coffin dodger'. Forty-one per cent of job-seeking candidates feel they have been totally misled by a job description, the research also found. People spoke of finding at interview stage that the reality of the job was less challenging and interesting, as well as lower status, than the profile had led them to believe. A further risk to businesses is losing customers. Almost two-thirds of job seekers are more likely to shun offending companies' products and services after a negative recruitment experience, according to Totaljobs.com. The biggest gamble of all for companies with bad practice at interview stage is the fact that potential employees have increasing rights. According to recent research by the Work Foundation, UK organisations could be leaving themselves open to discrimination pay-outs of millions of pounds from job seekers. Under the Data Protection Act, job applicants have the right to see a copy of notes made about them at interview. For a fee of up to £10, people can ask to see these documents and what's more, they don't have to provide a reason. So even if you think you may have been treated unfairly, you can investigate. Careless remarks on someone's appearance, family background or race could lead the recruiter straight to the law courts.

Source: The Guardian, 2003

Introduction

Over the past two decades work psychologists have had a major influence on the way selection processes are designed and implemented across many organisations. Although there are a variety of personnel selection methods available to use in organisational settings, research shows that not all of the methods are equally useful or appropriate in some selection processes. This chapter describes the main personnel selection procedures that are used frequently in organisations and examines their relative accuracy at determining who is the 'best person for the job'. The 'war of nerves' article illustrates that although we now know a great deal about the accuracy of different selection techniques, psychologists need to address how the various methods are implemented in practice. There is a growing need to understand issues regarding fairness and how adverse candidate reactions could lead to the law courts. Some of these issues are addressed in this chapter. After examining the evidence concerning the validity of each of the main methods, this chapter also explores the extent to which the various methods are used and shows how the costs and benefits derived from selection procedures may be expressed in financial terms.

Overview of personnel selection methods

Table 5.1 shows the major personnel selection methods that are available for use and also gives a brief explanation of what the methods involve. Most of the methods are well known, and many readers will have first-hand experience of some of them.

When using predictors such as interviews, psychological tests or work-sample tests, the specific areas to be investigated in the interview or the particular tests to be used should be derived from job analysis data (*see* Chapter 4). The information from the job analysis provides a basis for deciding which factors (e.g. numerical ability, communication skills) might be important for job success. Biographical data are often developed in a different way. When candidates apply for a job with an organisation it is likely that they will complete an application form and other documents in which they are expected to provide certain verifiable biographical information concerning factors such as age, previous employment, personal history and education. The basic procedure for using biographical data is to collect information on a number of candidates and correlate it with subsequent performance. Items of information that predict subsequent performance can then be identified. Items of information chosen on this basis do not necessarily have any obvious link with the job; it has merely been demonstrated, on a statistical basis, that they predict future performance.

In most practical situations it is not sensible to base selection decisions on the use of one predictor only (such as the results of one test) or even on one type of predictor. When several different predictors are used together, the basic aim should be to ensure that the various predictors complement rather than duplicate each other. One successful method of selection that makes use of many different predictors is

Table 5.1	Personnel selection methods

1   Interviews

Many involve more than one interviewer. When several interviewers are involved, the term *panel interview* is used. The most important features of an interview are the extent to which a preplanned structure is followed and the proportion of questions that are directly related to the job.

2   Psychometric tests

This category includes tests of cognitive ability (such as general intelligence, verbal ability, numerical ability) and self-report measures of personality.

3   References

Usually obtained from current or previous employers, often in the final stages of the selection process. The information requested may be specific or general and open-ended.

4   Biodata

Specifications of biographical information about a candidate's life history. Some biodata inventories may contain many (e.g. 150+) questions and ask objective questions, such as professional qualifications held, and more subjective ones, such as preferences for different job features.

5   Work-sample tests

Such tests literally use samples of the job in question (e.g. the contents of an in-tray for an executive position or specific kinds of typing for a secretarial post). The applicant is given instructions and then a specific amount of time to complete the tasks.

6   Handwriting analysis (graphology)

Inferences are made about candidates' characteristics by examining specific features of their handwriting (e.g. slant, letter shapes). Obviously, a reasonably lengthy sample of the candidate's normal writing is required.

7   Assessment centres

This procedure involves a combination of several of the previously mentioned techniques (e.g. psychometric tests, interviews, work samples). Candidates are usually dealt with in groups and some of the techniques used require the candidates to interact (e.g. simulated group decision-making exercises).

the 'assessment centre'. Assessment centres make use of many different predictors, including interviews, psychological tests, in-basket exercises and group discussions. They extend for a period of, say, two to three days, although they may be as short as a day or as long as a week. Candidates are usually assessed by trained assessors, who are often senior managers in the organisation. A typical assessment centre would involve groups of 12 candidates being assessed by six assessors (*see also* Chapter 6). Assessment centres are used frequently to evaluate people who already work within an organisation. The information gained from the assessment centre is then used to help take decisions concerning promotion and career development in general.

Key Learning Point

In most situations it is best to use a combination of several personnel selection techniques to ensure fairness and accuracy.

How well do selection methods work?

Before it is feasible to consider how well selection methods work it is necessary to be clear about what it means for a selection method to work. The previous chapter introduced the concept of criterion-related validity and demonstrated how this could be evaluated by means of validation procedures. Obviously, criterion-related validity is an essential requirement for a selection method but other features are also important. Table 5.2 lists a number of other features of personnel selection methods that are also important. A comprehensive evaluation of any selection method would require a thorough examination of the method in relation to each of the features given in Table 5.2. In the interests of clarity and simplicity, the evaluation of selection methods that follows is concentrated almost exclusively on criterion-related validity.

Key Learning Point

One of the key evaluative standards for personnel selection methods is criterion-related validity.

Estimating the validity of personnel selection procedures

As the previous chapter explained, predictive or concurrent validation processes may be used to estimate the criterion-related validity of a selection procedure. Most of the selection procedures mentioned so far in this chapter have been examined in this way and investigators have conducted validation studies on many selection procedures in many industries. Any single validation study is unlikely to provide a definitive answer on the validity of a selection method. This is because any particular study can be conducted on only a sample of relevant people and, of course, has to be conducted in a specific organisation, at a particular time, using particular

Table 5.2	Major evaluative standards for personnel selection procedures

1   Discrimination
The measurement procedures involved should provide for clear discrimination between candidates. If candidates all obtain similar assessments (i.e. scores, if a numerical system is used), selection decisions cannot be made.

2   Validity and reliability
The technical qualities of the measurement procedures must be adequate (*see* Chapter 4).

3   Legality and fairness
The measures must not discriminate *unfairly* against members of any specific subgroup of the population (e.g. ethnic minorities).

4   Administrative convenience/practicality
The procedures should be acceptable within the organisation and capable of being implemented effectively within the organisation's administrative structure. Those administering the procedures may need appropriate training.

5   Cost and development time
Given the selection decisions (e.g. number of jobs, number of candidates, type of jobs) involved, the costs involved and the time taken to develop adequate procedures need to be balanced with the potential benefits. This is essentially a question of utility.

6   Applicant reactions
Applicant reactions have important consequences for an organisation. If the best candidates reject the job offer, then the utility of the selection system is reduced. The best candidates may decide to work for competitor organisations and speak negatively about their treatment. In addition, dissatisfied candidates at selection are more likely to take legal action.

measures. There may be specific factors, to do with the sample of people used, the measures, the timing of the study and so on, which influence the study and bias the results in some way. It is obvious, then, that to estimate the validity of a particular selection procedure, more than one study is needed, so that any bias due to specific features of any particular study will not have an unduly large influence. But how many studies are required and how can we summarise and aggregate the results of several studies in order to draw conclusions? Various statistical techniques have been developed to resolve the problem and an outline is given below. The techniques described below are discussed within the context of personnel selection but have applications in many areas of work psychology.

An example will help to illustrate the way in which the results of validation studies may be cumulated and summarised. A researcher may, for example, be interested in the extent to which a particular individual difference characteristic, such as intelligence, achievement motivation or verbal ability (call this factor X) is predictive of managerial performance. As already noted, any individual study, using a particular sample of managers, will not give a definitive result for the validity of factor X. Consider for a moment why this is so. In other words consider what things might cause the results of any specific study to be less than perfectly accurate. Table 5.3 provides a list of these features, with a brief explanation of how they may influence the accuracy of the result obtained from any study. If you need a reminder of the meaning of the word 'correlation', refer back to Chapter 2. As Table 5.3 makes clear, some of the problems are caused by sampling error (item 1) and imperfect reliability in the selection method, imperfect reliability in the criterion measure (item 2) and range restriction in the selection method scores (item 3). Consider these sources of error in relation to our example of the predictive validity of factor X. The sources of error are usually referred to as artefacts since they are not part of the natural relationship under investigation, but are a consequence of the particular investigative procedures used in the study. If the researcher in our example was able to identify ten studies of the predictive validity of factor X, each study would be inaccurate due to the artefacts. Sampling error would be present because in each study the sample involved would not be perfectly representative of the population. Studies with larger samples would of course be less prone to sampling error.

Table 5.3	Major sources of distortion in validation studies

1   Sampling error
The small samples (e.g. 50–150) used in many validation studies mean that the results obtained may be unduly influenced by the effects of small numbers of people within the sample whose results are unusual. As sample size increases, these irregularities usually balance each other out and a more reliable result is obtained.

2   Poor measurement precision
The measurement of psychological qualities at both the predictor (i.e. selection method) and criterion (i.e. job performance) stage of the validation process is subject to unsystematic error. This error (unreliability) in the scores obtained will reduce the maximum possible observed correlation between predictor and criterion: the error is unsystematic and random, thus this element of the predictor or criterion score will not correlate systematically with anything. This means that as reliability decreases, the maximum possible correlation between predictor and criterion will decrease.

3   Restricted range of scores
The sample of people used in a validation study may not provide the full theoretically possible range of scores on the predictor and/or criterion measures. A restricted range of scores has a straightforward statistical effect on limiting the size of the linear correlation between two variables. So, like unreliability, range restriction in a sample serves to reduce the magnitude of the observed correlation coefficient.

Exercise 5.1   The importance of sample characteristics

To get a clearer idea of the importance of sampling error, think about how confident you would be that a random sample of six people from your family gave a good estimate of the average height of human beings. Then consider what you would need to do – and how large the sample would need to be – to get a good estimate.

As far as unreliability and range restriction are concerned, these artefacts will adversely affect observed validity coefficients. Test reliability may be calculated and expressed in a numerical form, with zero indicating total unreliability (i.e. in a totally unreliable test someone's score on a second administration could not be predicted with any accuracy whatever from his or her score on the first). To illustrate the impact of even modest deviations from reliability (0.8 is taken as the ideal, acceptable lower limit), Table 5.4 shows how the confidence interval for estimating an individual's true score on the test gets wider and wider as test reliability decreases.

Key Learning Point

Studies with larger sample sizes are less prone to sampling error and more likely to give reliable results.

Even with good reliability (0.8), two apparently quite different observed scores such as 94 and 112 could, because of a lack of measurement precision, have identical true scores. When data from unreliable tests are used to calculate correlation coefficients, the effect is clear. An unreliable test (or any set of scores) contains a

Table 5.4   The impact of different reliabilities on an estimated true score

	Reliability		
	0.9	0.8	0.6
Observed score	100	100	100
Probable (95 per cent confidence) range for candidate's true score	91–109	87–113	81–119

large amount of random error. Obviously these random factors will not vary systematically (i.e. correlate) with any other factors; hence, as the reliability of a measure decreases, the opportunity for the measure to correlate with any other variable also decreases. Indeed, in technical terms the reliability of a measure sets a precise limit on the possible magnitude of its correlation with any other variable: the square root of the reliability is the maximum possible level of correlation (see Moser and Schuler, 1989). Similarly, the availability of only a restricted range of scores will set an artificially low ceiling on the magnitude of any observed correlation. Consider what may happen, for example, in a predictive validity study when the candidates who score badly on the selection tests are not offered employment. If these low-scoring candidates were offered jobs they would be expected to perform badly. This link between people with low selection test scores producing low job performance scores is an important element in producing high validity coefficients. When these low scorers are excluded from the sample, the resulting validity coefficient can be based only on high and average scorers, where differences in job performance will be much less extreme. The resulting validity coefficient will thus be limited in magnitude. If the degree of range restriction in a study is known, then it is a simple matter to make a statistical correction for this range restriction (see Smith and Robertson, 1993, for the relevant formula).

Key Learning Point

Restriction of range in scores will artificially limit the magnitude of validity coefficients and give misleadingly low results.

The statistical procedures of meta-analysis (Hunter and Schmidt, 1990; Hermelin and Robertson, 2001) involve methods for estimating the amount of sampling error in a set of studies and hence calculating a more accurate estimate of the validity coefficient in question. As explained in Chapter 2, meta-anlysis is a statistical procedure for cumulating the results from many separate studies in order to obtain a more stable indication of the effect under investigation. More complex meta-analysis formulae also allow the estimation of validity coefficients corrected for unreliability and range restriction (Hunter and Schmidt, 1990). Notice that removing the effect of sampling error does not change the magnitude of the validity coefficient; it changes the estimated variance in observed coefficients and hence narrows the confidence interval around the mean coefficient. As expected from the discussion of these artefacts, correcting for unreliability and range restriction will increase the magnitude of the mean validity coefficients. The development and use of meta-analytic procedures have had a considerable impact on personnel selection research and have enabled investigators to get a much clearer picture of the validity of personnel selection methods.

Meta-analysis techniques have been applied to the available research evidence on the validity of all major personnel selection procedures. In a recent discussion of these issues, Hermelin and Robertson (2001) demonstrated that around 50 per cent of variance in the meta-analytic coefficients was explained by the correctable experimental artefacts of sampling error, direct range restriction in the predictor variable and criterion unreliability. Therefore, when interpreting results from meta-analysitc studies, note that statistical corrections are likely to have been applied so that the 'operational' or 'true' validity coefficients are reported.

Key Learning Point

Meta-analysis has been used extensively to derive estimates of the validity of personnel selection procedures.

Perhaps the most useful meta-analysis reported in recent years is by Schmidt and Hunter (1998), who based their results on 85 years worth of research in personnel selection. This study separated the results for training criteria and for overall job performance criteria. The results showed that the predictive validity for each method is broadly similar in predicting both training criteria and overall job performance. The significant research evidence on each of the techniques listed in Table 5.5 is discussed below. Also included is an estimate of the extent of usage and likely applicant reaction to each technique. Note that there are international differences in the extent of usage for various techniques. For example, assessment centres are used more frequently in the United Kingdom than in the United States.

Interviews

Interviews have long been the most popular form of personnel selection (e.g. Robertson and Makin, 1986). They are used by nearly every organisation for selecting employees at all levels. However, despite this popularity, interviews have been criticised for being subjective, unreliable and vulnerable to bias. This was probably fair criticism a number of years ago, when interviews were often little more than an informal chat between an interviewer and a prospective employee. The opening case study suggests that plenty of problems still exist. However, we now know considerably more about how selection decisions are reached, and potential sources of error and bias, so there is the potential to do much better. Interviews can be structured, and interviewers trained, in ways that considerably enhance their validity (Eder and Harris, 1999). Therefore an important point to remember is that the employment interview can represent an extremely important and valid means of selecting employees provided it is structured to ensure that (a) interviewer questions are based on a job analysis, (b) questions are consistent across interviewers and interviewees, and (c) the interviewers use a consistent set of criteria to evaluate interviewee responses. In fact, a recent meta-analysis by Huffcutt *et al.* (2001) found that criterion-related validities for interviews compared favourably with other forms of personnel selection such as cognitive ability tests.

Table 5.5	A summary of studies on the validity of selection procedures		
Selection method	Evidence for criterion-related validity	Applicant reactions	Extent of use
Structured interviews	High	Moderate to positive	High
Cognitive ability	High	Negative to moderate	Moderate
Personality tests	Moderate	Negative to moderate	Moderate
Biodata	Can be high	Moderate	Moderate
Work sample tests	High	Positive	Low
Assessment centres	Can be high	Positive	Moderate
Handwriting	Low	Negative to moderate	Low
References	Low	Positive	High

Key Learning Point

Situational interviews and competency-based structured interviews produce good criterion-related validity.

However, while there is considerable evidence to support the use of structured interviews in selection, there is much less agreement as to *why* selection interviews predict work performance. The two most common forms of structured interview used in selection are: behavioural interviewing (e.g. Janz, 1989) and situational interviewing (e.g. Maurer *et al.*, 1999). Also known as Behavioural Pattern Description Interviews (BPDIs), behavioural interviewing involves asking interviewees to describe previous behaviour in past situations that are job-relevant. This type of interviewing is based upon the central premise that past behaviour predicts future behaviour. In essence, interviewers are looking for evidence that an individual has demonstrated behaviour that would suggest he or she is capable of similar behaviour in a job situation. This type of interviewing forms the foundation of much of the competency-based interviewing that is popular today. For example, an interviewer may ask an interviewee: 'Can you please describe a time when you have been able to persuade someone to do something that they had initially been unsure about?' This could provide an opportunity to demonstrate behavioural indicators for a competency concerned with persuasion and negotiating skills. In both competency and BPDI interviews, interviewers use a behaviourally anchored rating scale to rate interviewee responses, thereby ensuring consistency across interviews.

In contrast, situational interviews are based on goal-setting theory. These interviews present interviewees with hypothetical job-related situations and ask them to indicate how they would respond. They are based on the assumption that intention to behave predicts future behaviour. For example, imagine you are applying for a place on a graduate recruitment programme with a national retail organisation. During the interview you are asked what you would do if you were the acting manager for a supermarket who arrived one morning to discover that nearly 25 per cent of your staff had called in sick because of a 'flu epidemic. How would you respond? Of course there are a number of different possible responses. However, the interviewer will compare your response with those provided by a group of experts who have been asked to indicate the type of responses they would expect from good, average and poor performers in this role. Again, interviewers will use a behaviourally anchored rating scale (BARS) to rate your response and compare it with those provided by other employees. Table 5.6 provides an illustration of a situational interview question and a scoring key using behavioural indicators.

A key problem with situational interviewing, however, is that it takes no account of different levels of experience. For example, there may be recent graduates with no relevant previous experience who are competing alongside other applicants with several years' experience. One might therefore expect the experienced applicants to have a better understanding of what is required in terms of a 'good' answer. Individuals with little experience yet great potential to learn may be disadvantaged. A further potential problem, which besets both behavioural and situational interviewing, is the criticism that what interviewees *say* in selection interviews may bear very little relation to what they actually *do* once in the job.

While no personnel selection will demonstrate absolute comparability between what is assessed during selection and subsequent work behaviour, interviews are particularly vulnerable to criticism. One reason for this is that interviewers are often worried about being deceived by assessees engaging in impression management (*see* Chapter 6). That is, individuals once appointed may demonstrate altogether different patterns of behaviour once in the job. It assumes that the task of the interviewer is to 'peel away' layers of impression management in order to uncover the 'true' person underneath. However, this may be an overly simplistic notion. Indeed, certain researchers have argued that personality is itself socially

| Table 5.6 | Example situational interview question and response anchors to assess initiative |

'You are the new personnel officer in a large car manufacturing plant and the boiler is not working properly. The temperature has dropped below the legal minimum and the shop floor workers are threatening to walk out at any minute. The Trade Union representative is demanding an urgent meeting with the managing director. The managing director is playing golf with the chairman today. Production is way behind schedule for the week and the costs of stopping the line could be enormous. What would you do in this situation?'

Behavioural indicators and score points (Poor, Satisfactory, Excellent)

Poor
Stop the line immediately.
Send the workers home.
Call the managing director on her mobile phone to ask advice.
Tell the Union representative that the meeting will have to wait.

Satisfactory
Ask the employees to stop work immediately.
Call all employees together including the Union representative for a public meeting.
Arrange for the technicians to repair the boiler on emergency call-out.
Text the managing director asking her to get in touch when she finishes playing golf with the chairman.

Excellent
Ask the employees to continue working on the line, arrange for portable heaters to be installed immediately. Ask catering to provide free hot drinks for all employees.
Meet the Union representative to discuss your actions and arrange a time later that day to review the situation.
Log the incident and actions you took and leave a note on the managing director's desk to discuss when she comes into the office.

Note: The indicators reflect an excellent, average and poor response reflective of initiative, and previously agreed by the personnel department in the car manufacturing company. Note that what constitute poor, satisfactory or excellent responses may be quite highly organisation-specific.

constructed, and that there is no 'true' persona hiding beneath layers of presentation waiting to be discovered. As such, individuals proactively adapt to different situations and people according to needs.

It could also be argued that this ability to understand different contexts and adapt one's behaviour to meet their varying needs is an exceptionally useful skill, one that can be useful in helping an individual to navigate their work environment successfully (Rosenfeld et al., 2002). However, recent research suggests that the way in which individuals choose to present themselves during interviews (their impression management) may reflect cognitive personality characteristics associated with motivation. For example, Silvester et al., (2002) found that more successful applicants demonstrated an attributional style also found in higher performers at work (Silvester et al., 2003). Individuals who explained past behaviour in terms of causes that were more controllable to themselves were rated more favourably by interviewers (e.g. 'I didn't do well in the exam because I left my revision until too late'). Interestingly, the interviewer's own attributional style was also important, suggesting an interaction effect between what the interviewer and interviewee consider important in terms of impression management during employment interviews. A summary of lessons learned from the voluminous research on selection interviews appears in Table 5.7.

Psychometric tests

In the 1980s, Cronbach described psychometric tests as providing 'a standardized sample of behaviour which can be described by a numerical scale or category system'. In other words, psychometric tests offer a quantitative assessment of some psychological attribute, such as verbal reasoning ability. For personnel selection purposes psychometric tests may be divided into two categories: cognitive ability tests (e.g. general intelligence, spatial ability, numerical ability) and personality tests (*see* Chapter 3 for more information on specific tests). The research for both categories of tests can be considered in relation to their validity for selection purposes in organisations.

Cognitive ability tests in selection

There has been an explosive increase in usage of cognitive ability tests in the past 20–30 years in organisations for selection purposes. For many practitioners con-

Table 5.7	Tips for best practice structured interview design

- Base questions on a thorough job analysis
- Ask exactly the same questions of each candidate, limit prompting, use follow-up questions but limit elaboration
- Use relevant questions and design them as either situational, competency-based, biographical or knowledge questions
- Use longer interviews or larger number of questions, control the input of ancillary information (e.g. CV (résumé), references)
- Do not allow questions from the candidate until after the interview (when the data have been collected)
- Rate each answer using multiple rating scales
- Use detailed anchored rating scales and take detailed notes
- Use multiple interviewers where possible
- Use the same interviewer(s) across all candidates and provide extensive interviewer training to enhance reliability
- Use statistical rather then clinical prediction

ducting large-scale recruitment programmes, ability tests are relatively cost-effective selection tools. Unlike most other selection techniques, to purchase and administer psychometric tests in many countries you have to demonstrate a specific level of competence in administration, scoring tests and interpreting test scores.

In the 1970s, particularly in the United States, cognitive ability testing became increasingly unpopular and it was common for people to argue that such tests had no useful role in personnel selection. The recent meta-analytic work and the evidence for validity generalisation (i.e. the generalisation of validity across job families) caused work psychologists to revise these views. In general, cognitive ability tests have been shown to be the single best predictor of job performance (e.g. Robertson and Smith, 2001; Schmidt and Hunter, 1998) with validity coefficients generally shown to be 0.55. Recent meta-analysis studies have consistently demonstrated that cognitive ability accurately predicts future job performance across almost all occupational areas.

In this respect, many researchers argue that cognitive ability tests are perhaps the best and most applicable predictor in personnel selection since all jobs require some cognitive ability to learn the job and perform effectively. Ones and Viswesvaran (2003) suggest that the predictive validity of cognitive ability tests tends to be higher for high-complexity jobs (0.58) than for low complexity jobs (0.23). A high-complexity job (such as a professor in work psychology) involves more dense processing of information than a lower-complexity job (such as a train driver).

In addition to tests developed to assess general cognitive ability ('g') (*see* Chapter 3), sometimes referred to as general mental ability (GMA), there are tests tailored to assess specific abilities such as mechanical comprehension, or spatial ability. Such tests measure 'g' to some extent, but also have a specific ability component. Some researchers argue that tests of specific abilities could be more predictive for specific jobs. For example, spatial ability might be more important in mechanical engineering jobs. However, Ones and Viswesvaran (2003) suggest that the predictive validity of specific abilities stems from their assessment of a general information processing ability (i.e. the general cognitive ability). Thus, if the general cognitive ability is held constant, most of the predictive power of specific ability tests disappears. On the other hand, in considering the practical application of tests in organisations, specific ability tests may have more face validity and generate positive candidate reactions in a selection context.

Bertua *et al.*, (in press) report a meta-analysis on the validity of tests of general mental ability (GMA) and specific cognitive abilities for predicting job performance and training success in the UK. The analyses were based on a data set of 283 independent samples with job performance as the criterion, and 223 with training success as the criterion. The results showed that GMA and specific ability tests are valid predictors of job performance and training success, with validity coefficients in the region of 0.5–0.6. As anticipated, occupational groups with greater job complexity demonstrated higher validities between cognitive tests and job performance and training success. Similarly, Salgado and colleagues (2003) examined the validity of GMA and other specific cognitive abilities, including verbal, numerical, spatial-mechanical, perceptual and memory across 10 European countries (with N ranging from 946 to 16 065). The analyses demonstrated similar results showing tests of GMA and specific cognitive ability to be very good predictors of job performance and training success across Europe.

With these problems in mind the rational approach to the development of biodata has been utilised. This approach reflects attempts to develop a theoretical rationale for the predictive validity of biodata. Using the rational approach involves clear hypotheses about specific job-relevant constructs such as ability to work in a team, which may be tapped by specific biodata items (e.g. membership of clubs and societies). Only items with a potential rational connection with the criterion will then be tried out, even in the pre-validation version of the biodata questionnaire. This approach is clearly much more appealing from the explanatory point of view, although evidence to date suggests that it has slightly poorer validity than the empirical approach. Gains in fairness and understanding may, however, outweigh this loss of validity. Stokes and Reddy (1992), after reviewing the evidence, suggest that a combination of approaches might produce the best and most interpretable results.

References

Reference reports are widely used methods for obtaining information on candidates, although it seems likely that in many situations potential employers take up references only when they are about to make a job offer. This high level of usage is not, however, matched by a comparable amount of research on references. In general, the validity evidence for reference reports is not particularly good (see Salgado *et al.*, 2001, for a review). One reason for the poor validity of references may be that they are not reliable and referees do not give consistent views on candidates. Further, there has been no analysis of whether reference reports add any incremental validity over cognitive ability tests, for example. Given their high level of usage, further research into references would seem to be important.

Other methods

Other potential selection methods not mentioned so far in this chapter include graphology (handwriting analysis), astrology and polygraphy (the use of the so-called lie detector test). In brief, none of these procedures is used to any great extent in the United Kingdom, although some continental European companies make extensive use of graphology (see Ryan *et al.*, 1999). As far as validity is concerned there is relatively little research available on the use of these methods for personnel selection but the clear balance of available evidence is that none of the methods shows any useful criterion-related validity. Summaries of the evidence on graphology and polygraphy may be found in the review paper by Salgado *et al.* (2001).

Key Learning Point

There is no evidence for the criterion-related validity of graphology in selection procedures.

The impact of selection procedures on applicants

Fairness

There has been relatively little work in personnel selection which has looked at the issues involved from the perspective of candidates, until recently. The main area of work concerns the extent to which selection procedures are fair to different subgroups (such as ethnic minorities or women) of the population. A large amount of research material focused on this issue has been produced. A variety of terms such as bias, adverse impact, fairness and differential validity are used in the literature on this issue and a clear grasp of the meanings and definitions of some of these terms is crucial to an understanding of the research results.

First, it needs to be made clear that a test is not unfair or biased simply because members of different subgroups obtain different average scores on the tests. Men and women have different mean scores for height; this does not mean that rulers are unfair measuring instruments. However, it would be unfair to use height as a selection criterion for a job, if the job could be done by people of any height, since it is important for selection criteria to be job-related. Normally, of course, the extent to which a selection method is related to job performance can be estimated by validation research, and it is clear therefore that fairness and validity are closely related.

Unfortunately, it is possible for tests to appear to be valid and yet be biased against some subgroups. This may happen if the relationship between the test score and job performance is not the same for the two subgroups. For example, it is possible to imagine that the link between job performance and certain personality or ability factors could be different for two subgroups of the population. A validity study based on a mixed sample of people would produce results that were somewhat incorrect for both subgroups; if the results were used to develop a selection procedure the predictions of candidates' work performance would be in error. Of course, the situation would be even worse if the validity study was based on only one subgroup but was then used to select members of another. Unfair direct discrimination is where the selection process treats an individual less favourably because of their gender or ethnic group, for example. Indirect discrimination is usually unintended and difficult to prove. It occurs when an employer applies a requirement for applicants (e.g. score on a test) which one group (defined by gender/race) finds it considerably harder to comply with, i.e. a larger proportion of one group cannot meet this requirement. This is known as *adverse impact*.

Key Learning Point

Indirect discrimination occurs when an employer applies a requirement for applicants (e.g. score on a test) which one group (defined by gender or race) finds it considerably harder to comply with.

This description of possible unfairness leads to the definition of test bias that is accepted by most work psychologists: 'A test is biased for members of a subgroup of the population if, in the prediction of a criterion for which the test was designed, consistent non-zero errors of prediction are made for members of the subgroup' (Cleary, 1968, p. 115). When, triggered by civil rights movements in the United States, fairness first became an issue in personnel selection research, it was felt that many selection procedures, including tests, were unfair. This was because of consistent differences in mean scores between different subgroups of the population (*see* Schmitt, 1989). As the discussion above makes clear, subgroup equality in mean scores is not the same as fairness. A procedure is biased or unfair when it shows different validity for different groups.

In using a selection test, the test designers would need to ensure that the difficulty level of items (percentage of applicants getting the item right) is not significantly different across different ethinic groups sitting the test. If differences are found, then there is said to be *differential item functioning*. There are sophisticated statistical procedures that can be applied to assess differential item functioning for tests. In general, the research evidence suggests that for professionally developed selection tests there is no evidence of differential item functioning across ethnic groups. The fact that the scientific research provides little evidence of differential validity for well-established selection procedures does not imply that all selection methods are unbiased, nor does it imply that unfair discrimination does not take place. It is clear, for example, that, despite the 1976 Race Relations Act, unfair discrimination still takes place in the United Kingdom. Robertson and Smith (2001) note that cognitive ablity testing is the method that has created the most frequent probelms with adverse impact in selection processes (*also see* Ones and Viswesvaran, 1998; Bobko *et al.*, 1999).

Applicant reactions

As the opening case study to this chapter illustrates, applicant reactions to a selection system are crucially important. In recent years, there has been more emphasis placed on applicants' decision-making where selection is now viewed as a two-way process. Attracting applicants to apply for a job is the first important step. If offered the job, an applicant with a negative reaction is likely to refuse a job offer (and the best applicants could work for a competing organisation). In an extreme case, an applicant who has a negative reaction to a selection procedure could make a legal challenge on the basis of unfair discrimination. Also, the war of nerves case study shows that applicants who have negative experiences with an organisation's selection system could boycott the organisation's products and encourage their friends and acquaintances to do the same.

Adverse reactions from candidates can lead to a legal challenge. The Head of Equality and Employment in the TUC (Trades Union Congress) in the United Kingdom, Sarah Veale, says

> There is nothing intrinsically wrong with tests but there is an over-reliance on them to the exclusion of other means of assessment. Lots of employers are not very good – they're quite sloppy, particularly smaller businesses. We have complaints from unions about employers relying on tests, using them to justify not taking somebody

Exercise 5.4 Adverse impact in selection

A large organisation was found to have discriminated against ethnic minority applicants after an employment tribunal. Following a re-structuring of the organisation, 100 new middle management posts were created. Approximately 30 per cent of employees are of ethnic minority origin, and currently, 3 per cent of management are of ethnic origin. The personnel department decided to use a structured interview and two cognitive ability tests (a measure of verbal reasoning and a measure of numerical reasoning).

600 employees applied for management posts, of whom 30 per cent were of ethnic origin. However, only 10 per cent of the job offers were made to ethnic candidates. The tribunal ruled that the tests were inappropriate in terms of the time allowed, the level of difficulty, the skills tested and the content covered. There was evidence of adverse impact and unlawful discrimination. The organisation conceded there was unintentional and indirect discriminatory impact on ethnic minority candidates and suggested compensation.

Respond to the following questions regarding this case study.

1 What's the difference between fair and unfair selection testing?

2 How can unfair discrimination be recognised?

3 What needs to be considered in evaluating the test?

on, and they worry the real reason was potentially discriminatory (*Financial Times*, FT.com, 19 June 2003).

Research has tended to explain the different factors that affect applicant reactions using theories of organisational justice (*see also* Chapter 9). Distributive justice focuses on perceived fairness regarding equity (where the selection outcome is consistent with the applicant's expectation) and equality (the extent to which applicants have the same opportunities in the selection process). Procedural justice refers to the formal characteristics of the selection process such as information and feedback offered, job-relatedness of the procedures and methods, and recruiter effectiveness. For a thorough review of these theories see Anderson *et al.* (2001a) and Gilliland (1993). Anderson *et al.* (2001a) suggest that four main factors seem to account for positive or negative applicant reactions where selection methods are: (1) based on a thorough job analysis and appear more job relevant; (2) less personally intrusive; (3) do not contravene procedural or distributive justice expectations; and (4) allow applicants to meet in person with the recruiters. Other literature suggests that applicants prefer multiple opportunities to demonstrate their skills and that the selection system is administered consistently for all applicants.

Of course, perceptions of injustice can depend partly on whether the person is successful in the selection process. For example, Elkins and Phillips (2000) explored the perceptions of fairness for a biodata measure and found that the most

Organisational justice theories are useful for understanding applicant reactions to selection methods.

important determinant of fairness perceptions was the selection decision. Robertson and Smith (2001) suggest that if the selection decision is in the candidate's favour, then the procedure is likely to be viewed as fair. However, 'if the decision goes against the candidate, it is unlikely to be viewed as fair ... it seems that the concepts of fairness and self-interest are closely entwined!' (p. 452).

The use of technology in selection

The rapid advances that have been made in the world of technology and telecommunications have presented selection practitioners and researchers with new opportunities and challenges. In an edition of the *International Journal of Selection and Assessment* devoted to technology and selection, a range of potentially important issues were raised (Viswesvaran, 2003). Not the least of these was how to balance the tremendous potential of technology to increasing the pool of potential applicants to an organisation, with the possibility that technology itself may influence the decisions that are reached (Anderson, 2003). Let us take the example of Internet-based application forms. There has been a dramatic increase in the number of organisations advertising via the Internet and expecting applicants to complete and submit on-line application forms (Bartram, 2000). The advantages for the organisation included the ability to create interactive application forms, to provide additional information to potential applicants by sign-posting other relevant web pages, and importantly, to request information from applicants in a standard format that can be processed and assessed by computer technology. For example, it is now possible for the first stage of a selection process involving analysis of biodata to be completed by computer without any member of the organisation gaining sight of the application form.

Some applicants may approve of on-line application forms, which could be perceived as easier and faster to complete and submit on line. Others may experience technical difficulties that may lead to negative applicant reactions. There are other potential problems that researchers, who are trailing in the wake of advances that have been made in practice, need to address. For example, Internet-based forms are often cited as a way of improving international recruitment in global organisations. However, we do not know as yet whether cultural differences and familiarity with technology will impact upon the way in which applicants present themselves in these applications. Certainly, by restricting application to Internet-based procedures, those with reduced access to computer technology, or who are less familiar with it, will be at a disadvantage. This may well include older workers and could be discriminatory under the new legislation being brought in within the United Kingdom.

In his review of applicants and recruiter reactions to the use of technology on selection, Anderson (2003) identifies three main themes to consider including (i) applicant reactions, (ii) equivalence (e.g. is an applicant's score on a selection test administered on-line equivalent to the same test administered using paper and pencil?) and (iii) adverse impact. For some selection methods there has already been extensive research (e.g. cognitive ability testing via computer), but for others there is very little evidence yet available (for a detailed review of this literature *see* Lievens and Harris, 2003). The concept of equivalence is a critical question since there is increasing usage of the Internet for use in recruitment in general. Research investigating the equivalence across different selection methods has produced mixed results. For computer-based testing the findings are generally positive, but for Internet-based tests there is a significant lack of literature available.

Key Learning Point

Applicant reactions, equivalence and adverse impact are key themes in investigating the use of technology in selection.

One important area where there is certain to be further development is in the area of interactive testing. At the moment test publishers are working on questionnaires that are able to make interim assessments of the ability level of respondents and alter the difficulty of subsequent questions accordingly. Similarly, a number of organisations such as the police are already using interactive computer technology to present intelligent training scenarios. For example, police officers undergoing firearms training are presented with realistic large-screen video scenarios depicting armed criminals. Using guns fitted with lasers and a light-sensitive screen, their decision to shoot and their shooting accuracy can be monitored and the endings of the scenarios changed accordingly. The potential for interactive work sample assessments is only beginning to be uncovered and there will undoubtedly be interesting developments ahead.

There is certain evidence that technology can change the way in which individuals are perceived. Although the telephone might be considered relatively old technology, there is surprisingly little research that has considered how interacting by phone might influence the way we perceive others. For example, recent research investigating the comparability of selection decisions made by interviewers in face-to-face and telephone interviews suggests that telephone ratings are harsher than face-to-face ratings (Silvester *et al.*, 2000). However, it is also suggested that ratings in telephone interviews may be more valid because there is a tendency for interviewers to focus on task-relevant information when visual information is absent. In a more recent study (Silvester and Anderson, 2003) interviewers tended to focus on information presented by applicants in telephone interviews that described more personal and unique aspects of themselves and may have made it easier for interviewers to discriminate more easily among interviewees whom they could not see. In summary, there is a great deal of further research needed to explore the various ways in which technology can influence the personnel selection process from both the organisation's and applicant's perspective.

Exercise 5.5   Applicants' reactions to on-line application forms in graduate recruitment

A study was conducted by Price and Patterson (2003) to examine applicant reactions to the use of on-line application forms as opposed to paper and pencil application forms. A small number of structured interviews were used to elicit applicant reactions to the use of on-line application forms in graduate recruitment. The results showed positive and negative applicant reactions. The negative applicant reactions are themed under the factors presented below. Each factor is listed with a corresponding quotation for the graduates.

Factor	Quotation from participant
Dehumanisation	'[A paper-based form allows you to] put more of yourself into it … on-line is more cold.'
Feedback	'Everyone else had e-mail acknowledgement, but I didn't. I rang up but they never got back to me.'
Technical issues	'I spent hours typing information, and the page expired. It hadn't saved properly and I lost it all. I ended up in tears absolutely frustrated and didn't apply in the end.'
Attitude	'Using an on-line application form means they have got more scope to make themselves look bad. It puts me off the company if I have technical problems.'
Motivation	'I got that sick of the technical problems that I just wanted to finish it and send it off.'
Fairness	'It feels like I haven't done justice to myself in the space provided.'
Satisfaction	'On-line application forms have the potential to be better and quicker, but they are more frustrating, and I think they've got a long way to go on the design issues.'

Your Task

Consider the applicants' reactions to on-line application forms for graduates. List the possible advantages of using on-line application forms for recruiters and applicants. To what extent do you think these outweigh the possible advantages? What advice and practical recommendations would you offer organisations involved in on-line recruitment?

Summary

A variety of personnel selection procedures is available for use in organisational settings. Research over the past three decades has provided a much clearer picture of the criterion-related validity of these procedures. Some of the methods, such as cognitive ability tests, seem to have broad applicability across a range of situations. As well as examining the validity of personnel selection procedures, research has also concentrated on the impact of the procedures on candidates. One area that has been reasonably well researched involves an examination of the fairness (to different subgroups) of the various techniques. Preliminary research suggests that the assessment experience itself may have an impact on candidates' psychological characteristics. Developments in utility theory have enabled the estimation of the financial benefit that may be gained through improved personnel selection. Further research is required to assess the impact of the use of technology for both organisations and applicants in personnel selection procedures.

Closing Case Study   How Shell Finds the Brightest Sparks

Tension is mounting in half a dozen basement rooms at a hotel in southern Portugal as a long day's exertion wears into late evening. Young men and women tap agitatedly at laptop computers; others stand at whiteboards calculating million-dollar sums with felt-tip pens. Small groups huddle in intense discussion.

For five days, 40 engineering, financial, legal and other specialists from 10 European countries have been racing against the clock to devise a five-year business plan for drilling, refining and marketing the offshore oil resources of a small country in the Indian Ocean. The next day they will make a pitch to three hard-nosed shareholders for $40m in investment funds.

'Stress levels are at a maximum,' says an aide to the team. 'They're eating their way through crisps and biscuits like there's no tomorrow.'

In this deviation from the caffeine and tobacco that traditionally fuel late-night business sessions lies a clue to the unusual nature of the whole enterprise. Gourami, the nation under intense scrutiny, cannot be found on any map. And the strategy for developing its energy resources is being drawn up not by hard-bitten corporate executives but by final-year university students with no business experience.

The next morning three senior managers from Shell, the Anglo-Dutch energy group, will hear the students put forward proposals to buy out the Gourami operations of a rival oil company, sharply cut staff levels in some local divisions and invest heavily in new refining techniques. But the real issue is not successful policies for a non-existent developing country but the competitiveness of Shell's recruitment policy.

▶

'Gourami is the fictional setting for a business challenge we have developed over the past 10 years as an important tool in the war to recruit the undergraduates with the strongest potential,' says Navjot Singh, global marketing manager of Shell's recruitment division. 'The course has been extremely successful in providing us with a constant stream of talented individuals.'

The Gourami business challenge was originally designed as a technical case study but has since grown to incorporate the commercial, human resources and legal aspects of running a global energy company. 'The main aim is to give undergraduates a taste of what it's like to work for an oil group and to see for themselves how they would cope at the sharp end of an international business,' says Mr Singh.

Forty final-year students from disciplines ranging from chemical engineering to marketing are brought together, supposedly in the small Islamic state of Gourami but in fact, in the latest European version of the challenge, in a large hotel in the Algarve. They are given five days to prepare a strategic 2005–2010 business plan for Shell's operations in this imaginary nation, which comes complete with a detailed political, geological and social history.

The students are divided into five teams, each responsible for a specific project. These can involve the management of offshore oil and gas discoveries, making strategic decisions about refineries and planning how to market and supply products.

Each individual project has to be co-ordinated into a coherent, long-term strategy. At the culmination of the challenge, each team has to convince three tough-minded senior Shell managers playing the role of shareholders to put up the money to fund their schemes.

'It is a very tough challenge that really puts students in touch with the reality of how a company makes things happen,' says Paul van Ditzhuyzen, a former vice-president of Shell Latin America who has been with the group for 30 years and regularly acts the part of a shareholder. 'They are working to professional standards under great pressure to draw up plans that are economically justified, politically sensible and socially responsible.'

A Gourami challenge is held each year in Europe, the US and one other location. The students participating in Portugal were selected from about 700 candidates who applied after the event was canvassed at a number of universities across Europe. From each group of students selected to participate, about 90 per cent go on to apply for a job with Shell and about half are successful.

In the Gourami challenge, students are faced with ethical dilemmas, political sensitivities and engineering problems designed to give them a taste of Shell's corporate culture and the group's business principles.

Sarah Nouwen, a Dutch law student from the University of Utrecht, says the experience gave her unexpected insights into the social and ethical issues involved in running a business. 'One of my specialities is human rights and I tended to see big business in a purely negative light. The Gourami challenge has enabled me to see the conflict between shareholders and stakeholders from both sides,' she says.

The experience of working in teams with colleagues from different disciplines and backgrounds was the most rewarding aspect of the chellange for most of the participants.

'Hard science students can be dismissive of what they see as "fluffy" disciplines like human resources management and vice-versa,' says Claire Gould, a mechanical engineering undergraduate at Imperial College in London. 'Dealing with the "real-life" challenges of Gourami made us all aware of the value of other skills and aptitudes and the need to work as a team.'

Her experience in the make-believe realm of Gourami has also given a new focus to her real-world ambitions.

'I've decided I want to work on an oil rig,' she says. 'I just haven't worked out how to tell my mum yet.'

Source: FT.com, 29 December 2003

Suggested exercise

Shell is not quite using the Gourami exercise as a selection tool. But if it did, how well do you think it would work in choosing the most appropriate graduates, and why? Use the contents of this chapter to justify your answer.

Test your learning

Short-answer questions

1   What selection methods are used in assessment centres?

2   How does sampling error distort validation studies?

3   What is adverse impact in personnel selection?

4   What stages are involved in developing a situational interview?

5   What problems may apply to designing and implementing work-sample tests?

6   What are unique features of biodata?

7   What are the advantages and disadvantages of on-line application forms for (a) applicants, (b) organisations?

Suggested assignments

1   Critically review the validity evidence for contemporary personnel selection procedures.

2   Discuss the advantages and disadvantages of using technology for personnel selection and assessment.

3   The closing case study provides a structured question.

Relevant websites

A neat summary of what assessment centres are about can be found on the website of the Polisth HR consultancy firm Solution. Check out http://www. solution.pl/ecase1_assessment.html. Note the interesting claim about the efficacy of assessment centres in identifying the right person for the job.

The UK-based consultancy SHL offers some advice about how to manage various selection techniques effectively and ethically. Go to http://www.shl.com/SHL/en-int/Thought_Leadership/Best_Practices_Guides/. You will need to register, but this is free.

The Recruitment and Employment Federation offers quite a practical site about how to select, and how to get selected. Find it at http://www. rec.uk.com/home.htm.

For further self-test material and relevant, annotated weblinks please visit the website at http://www.booksites.net/arnold_workpsych.

Suggested further reading

1   A special issue of the *Journal of Occupational and Organizational Psychology* (vol. 74, no. 4, 2001) includes the review article by Robertson and Smith on selection methods (full reference in the list at the end of this book).

2   A special issue of the *International Journal of Selection and Assessment* (2003) edited by Viswesvaran includes several articles on the impact of technology in selection and assessment.

3   The textbook on *Personnel Selection* by Schmitt and Chan, 1998 (full reference at the end of this book) provides more detail on all of the main topics covered in this chapter.

4   Schmidt and Hunter's (1998) review article explores the validity and utility of selection methods over 85 years of research (full reference at the end of this book).

CHAPTER 6

Assessing people at work

LEARNING OUTCOMES

After studying this chapter, you should be able to:

1 identify how interpersonal assessment can be biased and suggest ways in which this might be overcome;

2 name and define the four principles of effective assessment processes;

3 describe two methods of rating behaviour and explain how they work;

4 explain how assessment centres are constructed and why they can predict work performance;

5 define convergent and discriminant validity in respect to assessment centre functioning;

6 describe how the assessment of performance during selection processes can differ from assessment of an employee during performance appraisal;

7 define multi-source feedback and how it works;

8 suggest ways in which assessment processes might cope with changing job roles;

9 understand the limitations of current assessment processes in relation to cross-cultural assessment of people.

> **Opening Case Study**   **Fit for What?**
>
> In May 2003, the *Daily Mail* (a UK newspaper) published a story about a fitness organisation titled 'Will fatties fit in?' They reported that senior executives in this organisation had sent a memo around to managers reminding them that staff should not request uniforms over a size 16 (the average dress size for a woman in the United Kingdom). One of the reasons given was that larger uniforms added considerable cost to the organisation's merchandising budget. Apparently the memo also commented that 'as we are a health club and are promoting weight loss, please consider the impact of having larger employees. We are not asking you to have a discriminatory recruitment policy, but we would subtly like to make you aware of the situation'. However, one member of a club owned by the organisation commented that the club seemed to be staffed by 'identikit blondes'.
>
> **Do you think that the fitness organisation was right to assess prospective employees on the basis of how they looked? What assumptions were senior managers of this organisation making in their decision to warn managers of the 'impact of larger employees'?**

Introduction

Most work psychologists would probably agree that much of what they do is concerned with observing and assessing behaviour in order to judge whether someone is suitable for a particular job (selection), or whether a person is performing his or her job well (performance appraisal). So far we have concentrated for the most part on how individual differences such as intelligence and personality influence work performance, and how different methods (e.g. psychometric tests) can be used to assess these differences when selecting people for work. However, another equally important way in which we assess competence in others involves us making a judgement about that person based simply upon our *observation* of how he or she behaves. As Andrew Carnegie, a famous American entrepreneur, once commented: 'As I grow older I pay less attention to what men say . . . I just watch what they do'.

Informal assessment is an ongoing feature of organisational life. Colleagues frequently judge each other in terms of performance or contribution to projects. Employees may draw conclusions about their manager's competence, or seek to understand a customer's motives. But while informal assessment is undoubtedly important, the focus of this chapter is on interpersonal assessments in more formal contexts. These include assessments by managers when judging the competence or potential of their employees during appraisal, and recruiters' assessments of applicants during selection. Clearly these assessments have important consequences. They can impact upon decisions whether to promote an individual, provide additional support, or to punish someone for poor performance. Similarly, assessment during selection impacts upon an individual's ability to obtain work, or secure positions in areas that they are particularly interested in. Yet interpersonal assessment has been criticised for lacking the rigour of other methods such as psychometric tests. It can also be highly subjective and vulnerable to bias, and therefore increase the possibility of unfair discrimination against particular groups. In this chapter we will explore how we make assessment decisions about other people, the factors that can influence these decisions, and strategies for making such assessment more reliable, valid and fair. As interpersonal assessment is a common feature of both recruitment and performance management systems, we will draw upon examples from both of these to illustrate the importance of this type of assessment for employees and the organisations they work for.

Judging people

A great deal of social psychological research has been devoted to investigating how we make judgements about other people. We know from this research that people are generally subjective and often biased in these judgements and that people often draw invalid conclusions about the intentions underlying actions of others. This subjectivity and bias are largely consequences of cognitive shortcuts taken by our brain in an effort to cope with a very complex world. We rely on these shortcuts or cognitive heuristics to help us make sense of our surroundings without devoting too much conscious effort or cognitive capacity to processing less important information. In short, we rely upon automatic processing of cognitive schemata and stereotypes that are developed as a consequence of past experiences and stored in our long-term memory (LTM) to guide decisions about new situations and people (Klimoski and Donahue, 2001). For example, a manager may draw upon previous experience of managing poorly performing employees when he or she encounters a new poor performer. However, automatic triggering of a 'poor performer schema' associated with lack of important skills may not be appropriate in this new situation. If he or she relies upon automatic processing of the previous 'poor performer' schema, the manager may deal inappropriately with this new employee whose poor performance might, for example, be caused by low organisational commitment. Another example involving stereotypes can be found in our acceptance of patterns of behaviour from newcomers to an organisation that would not be acceptable from people who had been there longer. For example, we might think it appropriate for newcomers to be unsure and ask lots of questions, but similar behaviour from a long-term employee might surprise us and lead to a conscious effort to explain why they are behaving that way.

Although shortcuts make our lives easier by reducing the amount of cognitive effort required to negotiate the work environment, they can lead to problems when it comes to assessing people at or for work. For example, stereotypes that we hold concerning a particular group of people can prejudice our expectations regarding their suitability for a particular job. If we were selecting people for nursing positions, it is possible (although we might be wrong!) that rugby players would not leap to mind as the most suitable of candidates (rugby is a very physical ball game played mostly by big men). Indeed, our stereotype of what rugby players are like might lead us to assume that they are unsuitable for the role. However, we have no *evidence* upon which to base this assumption. This relates to an important component of assessing people at or for work: that decisions should be based on evidence.

In the next sections we consider the types of evidence we should look for, how to look for it, and how people (managers, interviewers, assessors) can identify and use this evidence more effectively. In order to be consistent, and because we are focusing on interpersonal assessment in both appraisal and selection contexts, we will use ASSESSOR to refer to the person doing the assessing and ASSESSEE as the person being assessed.

Key Learning Point

When assessing people at or for work, decisions should be based on evidence, not assumptions or stereotypes.

Social psychologists have identified a number of biases that come into play when we judge others, which are particularly relevant to organisational assessment situations. They include: halo and horns, primacy and recency effects, stereotypes, attribution biases, the 'like me' effect, and contact history. Each of these has implications for assessment. For example, the first of these, 'halo and horns', relates to an assessor's tendency to make a favourable (halo) or unfavourable (horns) general evaluation of a person based upon an initial judgement or prior information. This can happen when an assessor reads a reference letter before an interview describing an applicant as highly conscientious. This can create a positive expectation on the part of the assessor and lead them to attend more closely to information during the interview that confirms this initial impression than to information that disconfirms it. It is therefore important to design assessment systems in a way that minimises the potential impact of such a bias. One simple way to do this in a selection context is to ensure that assessors are not given information about an applicant prior to meeting that can lead the assessor to pre-judge the outcome. Of course, this type of strategy is not possible in performance appraisal situations, where managers have on-going relations with their employees, and we will consider the implications of this later in the chapter.

Primacy and recency effects concern the tendency for information presented early or late in a sequence to dominate our memory and judgement. For example, interviewers are most likely to remember the applicants they interviewed first or last in a group. Similarly, a manager who overhears an employee dealing inappropriately with a customer just before an appraisal meeting might find it difficult to ignore the incident, despite the employee having demonstrated consistently good performance over the past year. Stereotyping is another type of bias that derives from our tendency to simplify the characteristics of groups and attribute them to all group members. We generally hold preset images of other people based on their category memberships. These categories are fundamental tools for perceiving others, because they assist assessors by conveying immediate meaning based on category label (Taylor and Ilgen, 1981). Everyone relies on stereotypes, although they may not be aware of it. We have already mentioned rugby players – you may like to consider what stereotypes you hold about stamp collectors, Star Trek enthusiasts or academics. Clearly stereotypes are dangerous because they are too simple. Not all rugby players are the same as one another, neither are nurses. Interestingly, however, we also stereotype roles. For example, it is often assumed that salespeople need to be extrovert and gregarious, but can you think of a sales role where such personality characteristics might not be appropriate? One possibility might be a role that involves selling funeral services – sensitivity and tact are likely to be far more important qualities here than sociability.

Stereotypes are important because they impact upon our judgement of a person's competence or suitability for a particular role. Consequently, while categorisation and stereotyping offer speedy and adaptive means for understanding others, these benefits come with two important costs: accuracy (is this person really the best for this role?) and fairness (are all applicants being treated fairly?). They therefore impact upon the validity of an assessment process and the potential for unfair discrimination. Fortunately, we know that simply holding people accountable for assessment decisions can make them more careful and less likely to engage in automatic stereotypic thinking (Pendry and Macrae, 1996). For example, asking assessors to record their observations and explain their decisions leads them to engage in more controlled processing of information. Just as well, the cynic might say, as this type of information can be used to inform litigation proceedings when selection processes are challenged on the basis of fairness.

Various attribution biases occur when people explain their own and other people's behaviour. For example, we are more likely to see our own behaviour as being caused by situational factors, such as the behaviour of others or by the context we find ourselves in, than internal dispositions such as personality. Known as the fundamental attributional error, one perceptual explanation for the bias has been that we are more aware of situational factors that influence our behaviour than observers. During assessment, this can mean that assessors are more likely to attribute an assessee's behaviour to personality than circumstances (Herriot, 1989b). For example, managers may be more likely to attribute poor employee behaviour to their lack of motivation rather than the manager's own failure to provide development opportunities. In addition the 'ultimate attribution bias' describes our tendency to attribute good performance by members of our own group (in-group) to internal causes such as ability and effort, but similar performance by out-group members to luck. It has been suggested that this bias could partly explain instances of discrimination (Silvester and Chapman, 1996). For example, whereas a white male manager might attribute good performance by a white male employee (perceived as an in-group member) to ability, he might be more likely to attribute similar performance by a black female employee (perceived as an out-group member) to the ease of the task or help by colleagues.

The 'like me' or 'similarity' effect is caused by our tendency to be attracted to people whom we perceive to be like ourselves. While not entirely understood, social psychologists have long recognised that we are more likely to choose friends and partners who resemble ourselves. At work this phenomenon can often emerge in selection and promotion situations, particularly when there are no clear selection criteria, where interviewers tend to favour applicants whom they perceive to be more like themselves (Graves and Powell, 1988). The term 'organisational cloning' has been used to describe instances where managers' tendency to recruit others like themselves has resulted in departments and even organisations that are made up of highly similar individuals. A final source of bias in assessment derives from the degree of contact that an individual has had with the person he or she is assessing. The longer the assessor has known the assessee, the more likely the assessor is to rely on automatic processing. In this instance the assessor is also likely to be more accurate in their judgements, possibly because of the much larger repertoire of observed behaviour by the assessee, which they have been able to draw upon.

Exercise 6.1   Interviewer sense-making and subjectivity

The following extract comes from an interview with a manager responsible for interviewing individuals who had applied for graduate training positions in a UK distribution company. The interview was part of a study of what interviewers were looking for in 'good applicants' (Silvester, 1996) and illustrates how the interviewer has tried to make sense of an applicant's behaviour. Peter Herriot (1989a) reminds us that the employment interview is a 'social episode' and that we all bring our expectations, stereotypes and bias that can influence the judgements we make about other people. Read the example and then try to answer the questions that follow:

> One of the over-riding impressions I got of this year's graduates was that the women were very much to the fore. I interviewed at least three girls who left all but one of the men I interviewed standing. They were very good: independent, free-thinking, could develop an argument, had some real get up and go, real warmth of personality . . . It's difficult for a man in many respects. I mean when a bloke comes over to you as being good, it's because he's got ability. If a girl comes over to you as being good, you wonder if it's because she's attractive and pleasant and so it's hard to be objective. I mean one girl came in and flashed a yard of thigh to me and I thought "oh my god, this is going to be a difficult interview". But at the end of the day she was a very pleasant character, and the only reason that she did that was, not because she wanted to portray herself as female, but because she was a fairly outlandish person.'

1   What stereotypes do you think this manager holds that may influence his judgement of different applicants?

2   How might the person responsible for the overall selection process encourage assessors to be consistent and fair?

3   What sort of information do you think this interviewer should be focusing on?

The example in Exercise 6.1 demonstrates the potential for bias within organisations. Although all selection and assessment systems need to discriminate, they must do this fairly by identifying the person who demonstrates the best competence for the job (selection), or by recognising and rewarding individuals who demonstrate the best performance on the job (appraisal). Unfair discrimination exists when assessment decisions are made on the basis of information that is not relevant to performance on the job, for example, a person's race or gender, or because an assessor likes or dislikes a person. Strictly speaking, it is not illegal (in the United Kingdom) to discriminate against individuals on the basis of size (see the opening study), but you may want to consider whether you consider it fair and the implications of doing so for the organisation.

Key Learning Point

We tend to like people similar to ourselves, and make positive assessments of their work behaviour.

The factors that contribute to unfair discrimination have been explored most extensively for women and individuals from different ethnic groups. For example, Virginia Schein (e.g. 1975) coined the phrase 'think manager–think male' when she and her colleagues found identified commonly held biases that led assessors (male and female) to associate characteristics they perceived to be indicative of good managers with more stereotypically male than female characteristics. Whereas managers in general and males were seen to be more 'assertive', women were more likely to be perceived as accommodating. More recent work has found that female MBA students in the West are less likely to hold such stereotypes, but male managers and women and male managers from other countries still demonstrate the 'think manager–think male' bias (Schein *et al.*, 1996). There are widely held assumptions that men and women differ in the way they act as leaders. It has been argued, for example, that there should be more women at Board level within organisations because they demonstrate a more transformational leadership style. Yet evidence that these differences exist is far from convincing (Eagly *et al.*, 1992). Work psychologists therefore need to identify and challenge assumed differences between members of different groups that are based upon stereotypes.

How can we improve the assessment process?

Given that individuals are inherently subjective and biased in the judgements they make about others, the next question must surely be 'how can we improve the assessment process?' As we have seen in earlier chapters, one strategy has been to move away from interpersonal assessment in recruitment contexts by using psychometric tests to select people for work. This is based on the argument that these tools are more objective and reliable. However, while methods such as the employment interview have historically received a bad press, we have seen in Chapter 5 that recent meta-analytic research has shown that structured interviews compare favourably to other selection methods. In fact, we now have a much greater understanding of how interpersonal assessment processes (e.g. interviews, assessment centres and performance appraisal) can be improved: broadly, this involves four key principles of standardisation and structure, job-related, evidence-based and trained assessors.

Standardisation and structure

All assessment procedures should be structured in a way that ensures consistency across individuals and different assessment situations. For example, interviewers should ask the same or similar questions of all applicants in an employment interview (see Chapter 5). They should also ask the same questions as each other. In an appraisal context, a manager should apply the same criteria for judging all employees. Having a structure improves reliability in much the same way that asking different applicants to answer the same questions contributes to the reliability of a psychometric questionnaire. Structure also contributes to fairness by treating all people in the same way. This means that informal assessments, where assessors claim to be able to 'get to the real person' over a drink in the bar or over dinner during an assessment centre, are not appropriate. These unstructured meetings will vary from person to person and assessors are far more likely to base judgements on likeability rather than how well a person will perform the job.

Job-related

The next important principle is to ensure that the assessment criteria are associated with performance in the job or task for which an individual is being assessed. Although this may seem obvious, assessors can easily be distracted and influenced by information that, although interesting, is not relevant to job performance. For example, an interviewer might be very impressed by the fact that an applicant has won a golf championship (particularly if the interviewer also plays golf), but if playing golf cannot be shown to relate to skills required in the job (let us say air traffic control), it should not influence the interviewer's decision. After all, being interesting is unlikely to relate to the extent to which an individual can maintain their vigilance over a long period of time. We have seen in Chapter 4 that the starting point for developing an assessment procedure is usually a job analysis. This identifies behaviour predictive of job performance that can form the focus of any future assessment process.

However, related to this is another important feature of effective assessment processes. Identifying important behaviours means that not only is it possible to communicate this to assessors, thereby improving the validity of assessment processes, but also to the applicants or role incumbents themselves. Providing applicants with a realistic understanding of what they will need to do in the job enables them to make an informed decision as to whether they really want that role. Similarly, employees need to understand what they are expected to do in order to demonstrate good performance.

Evidence-based

In many ways the third principle, that assessment should be evidence-based, relates to the second. The process of identifying the behavioural indicators of good and poor performance also identifies the evidence that assessors need to look for when assessing an individual's level of competence. In most cases assessors will obtain this evidence in one of three ways: by directly observing the behaviour of individuals on the job (appraisal), by observing individuals performing work-sample exercises such as those in assessment centres, or by listening to individuals describe past behaviour in similar situations (interviews). Basing assessment decisions upon evidence that has been shown to relate to performance levels ensures that the process has predictive validity and enhances fairness and objectivity (Sandberg, 2000).

Trained assessors

Finally, the rigour of an assessment process depends upon the skill and expertise of the assessor. Yet as we have seen, individuals are not always objective observers. Furthermore, identifying, recording and assessing examples of relevant behaviour is difficult and requires training. In the case of performance appraisal, this means teaching managers (and employees) what behaviours are expected from a good performer and therefore what behaviour they should be looking for. A manager should also be able to identify these behaviours reliably across different staff, and be aware of the biases and distortions that increase the level of subjectivity in their own judgements. Trained assessors have been shown to be more accountable than untrained assessors, more aware of the dangers of stereotyping and categorisation and more likely to engage in effortful assessment (Klimoski and Inks, 1990). Training of assessors is therefore an essential component of ensuring that processes are reliable, valid and predictive.

Key Learning Point

Assessment processes should demonstrate structure, be job-relevant, evidence-based and include training for assessors.

Assessing performance

The main questions when assessing performance are 'what do you assess?' and 'how do you measure it?' The first of these questions has been addressed in Chapter 5 and is associated with conducting a job analysis, developing a competency model, and identifying behavioural indicators. The second question (how do we measure it?) deserves more attention here. There are three important components: (a) observing behaviour, (b) recording behaviour, and (c) rating behaviour. All three should be considered in the design of assessment systems and as a part of assessor training.

Observing behaviour

In judging another person, an assessor should be looking for evidence that the person is competent in key areas of the job. This may involve sampling relevant behaviours (e.g. punctuality at meetings, or involvement of others in decision-making) and then using these to decide whether he or she is competent. Assessors can also obtain relevant information by observing an individual performing the job or a work-sample task directly. They can also ask assessees to provide evidence of their competence by describing how they have behaved in past job-relevant situations. This latter approach is a key aspect of behavioural or competency-based interviews, and contrasts with situational interviews where assessees are asked how they might behave in job-relevant situations.

Clearly the needs of different assessment contexts will drive the strategy that assessors use for gathering evidence. For example, in selection interviews, asking applicants to describe past behaviour allows assessors to gather evidence of competence from a broader range of situations than it would be possible to simulate. However, managers may also adopt such strategies during appraisal by asking employees to reflect upon and describe their own performance over the past year. An important reason for this is that managers simply cannot observe all of an employee's behaviour. Indeed, many managers may supervise individuals who work in a different location. For example, managers of teleworkers (who work from home via a computer link) may never get the opportunity directly to observe the people whom they manage. In these cases, assessees may be asked to describe examples of past behaviour that are relevant to specific competencies or different areas of the job (e.g. 'can you give me an example of when you were able to demonstrate initiative?'). This type of evidence has been referred to as 'samples' of behaviour. Of course there are potential reliability issues here. How does one know whether the assessee is being honest? Are their descriptions overly positive or too modest? While issues of accuracy and reliability are important, it is also important to recognise that any attempt to evaluate behaviour will be subject to a variety of sources of error. Despite this, managers' ratings are the most frequently used criterion for assessing work performance in work psychology research (Arvey and Murphy, 1998). As we will see later in the chapter, one way to compensate for bias is to combine performance ratings provided by different sources such as self, manager, peer and subordinate. This type of rating is known as multi-source feedback (MSF).

Observing people is such a common phenomenon that we frequently assume it to be a relatively easy and straightforward process. However, being able to concentrate on an individual's performance, identify relevant behaviour and filter out potentially irrelevant information is a difficult skill. This is especially so, given our tendency to describe people in terms of personality characteristics (e.g. 'good fun', 'sociable', 'hard working', 'disciplined', 'lazy' or 'potential high flier') rather than behaviours. General, personality descriptors help us to simplify the world. Without realising it, we observe individuals, watch them respond to different situations and generalise patterns of behaviour into assumptions about personality characteristics. To assess individuals in a reliable and consistent way takes effort, knowledge of what evidence one is looking for and skill.

One of the authors was employed as a care-worker in a secure unit for adolescent offenders after completing her undergraduate studies. The experience was interesting and challenging, and provided an opportunity to work alongside clinical psychologists trained in techniques of behavioural observation. The role involved observing and assessing the behaviour of different boys. The purpose of this was to recognise and reward appropriate behaviour, and identify inappropriate behaviour (e.g. swearing or threatening others) that could be targeted for change using behaviour modification strategies. Key to this process was being able to describe the specific behaviours that needed changing. One example of this involved a 15-year-old boy called Stephen, who would run up smiling to anyone who came onto the secure unit. Despite his apparent enthusiasm, a number of careworkers found him threatening. We were taught by the clinical psychologist to recognise that having an initial 'feeling' about a person is simply a response to something that the person is doing. After all, none of us (unless we have telepathic powers) can get inside someone's head and discover their thoughts, feelings or intentions. We use behaviours as clues to inform our judgements. In this case, Stephen was behaving in a way that led us to feel wary and a little in danger, but the important task was to work out what Stephen was *doing* that led us to feel that way. With the psychologist's help we were able to work out that, although Stephen would run up enthusiastically with a smile on his face, he would then stand face-to-face very close to the person. The invasion of body space and confrontational position contrasted with his smile. However, by identifying what was inappropriate it was possible to explain and then reward Stephen for changing his behaviour.

Key Learning Point

Assessors must be able to identify and describe specific behaviours in order to give feedback effectively to individuals.

Although this example comes from a clinical context, there are important parallels to be drawn when assessing people at or for work. For example, managers and assessors must be able to identify and describe specific behaviours rather than rely on generalisations. This is particularly important in the case of performance appraisal when managers feed back assessments to individual workers. Using non-behaviour terms such as 'not very motivated' or 'needs to demonstrate more enthusiasm' are not specific enough. They are also potentially threatening to staff ('what do you mean – not very motivated?'); after all, it is a lot easier to change how one behaves than it is to change one's personality. Managers who feed back negative information to employees in terms of personality descriptors rather than behavioural descriptors risk upsetting and de-motivating their staff.

Exercise 6.2   Specifying behaviours

The following exercise is aimed at helping you to focus on behaviours rather than personality descriptors when making judgements about other people. It presents a series of 'non-behaviours' and then asks the respondent (manager, assessor, you) to identify the behaviours that might be associated with each of the listed non-behaviours. Importantly there are no right answers. Many different types of behaviour could legitimately be associated with an assessor's judgement that a person is 'conscientious'. However, in this exercise, 'wrong' answers are those that are not behavioural descriptors. It helps to visualise people you know who you might describe in terms of the following 'non-behaviours' and then identify the behaviour that they engage in that might lead you to draw such an inference about their character.

Non-Behaviour	Behaviour
1. Hard-working	*'She stayed late on three occasions this week to finish a report'*
2. Motivated	*'He called around all the European offices to find out whether there was anyone who could help with the project'*
3. Laid-back	
4. High-flier	
5. Uncaring	
6. [Your own example]	
7. [Your own example]	

Recording behaviour

Once a manager or assessor has observed behaviour, it should be recorded. This provides a check on consistency and reliability, and whether assessors focus on the same behaviours. Recording evidence also means that detailed information can be discussed later, as in the case of the 'wash-up' session at the end of an assessment centre, when assessors get together to make final decisions about candidates. It also means that selection and assessment methods are more resistant to legal challenge, in that an organisation can provide evidence of how decisions have been made and that they have not discriminated unfairly against a specific group or individual. For a manager it is important to record evidence that an individual has performed well or poorly over the course of an appraisal period. This will aid decision-making and make appraisal less vulnerable to recency bias when managers rely on memory to recall evidence. Similarly, when interviewing an applicant or observing an individual in an assessment centre exercise, assessors should write down evidence as it occurs so that they have a detailed recollection of the whole period. An example of an assessment centre rating form for a group exercise is given in Fig. 6.1.

Rating behaviour

Rating behaviour is probably the most difficult aspect of assessing behaviour. Essentially it involves using recorded observations to judge how an individual compares with other members of his or her group. The ability to compare individuals is important for a number of reasons. It means that organisations can rank order

	Evidence of positive behavioural indicator	Evidence of negative behavioural indicator
Communication skills	'Candidate allowed time for colleague to give their view, then summarised and reflected back the views of the group.'	'Candidate interrupted colleague on two occasions.'
Customer focus		
Motivating others		
Teamworking		

Figure 6.1   **Example of a behaviour recording sheet at an assessment centre**

applicants in terms of their suitability for a job. It also means that managers can reliably compare the performance of the different people who work for them. In certain instances, this is used when making decisions about performance-related pay. For work psychologists, the ability to rate work performance on a quantitative scale is the basis for research investigating the criterion-related validity of different selection methods. However, there are also ways of rating performance that do not rely on observation of individuals, but assess performance in terms of output or other criteria such as absenteeism, number of mistakes or wastage. For example, an insurance salesperson may be assessed in terms of the number of new contracts secured – not *how* they are secured. Similarly, roles that are highly dependent upon cognitive skills may be unsuitable for assessment of behaviour based on observation. For example, it would be difficult to assess the performance of authors simply by watching them write. Here, performance is best assessed in terms of the quality of the output. For most roles, however, the following methods are relevant.

Figure 6.2 shows a variety of different graphical rating scales that can be used to elicit performance appraisal data. Such scales vary in the extent to which they provide a satisfactory basis for performance appraisal. Like many forms of psychological measurement, the key issues revolve around the problems of reliability and validity. Such scales should provide a clear indication of the meaning that can be assigned to each point on the scale (validity) so that both the rater and anyone else who needs to interpret the rating on the scale can make a valid inference. Clearly with a scale such as Fig. 6.2a, clear and unambiguous interpretation is impossible, since the scale provides so little information. It is also important that the scale can be used consistently, either by different raters, or by the same rater on different occasions. Again a scale such as that in Fig. 6.2b poses problems, since so much subjective judgement is needed that the judgements may well change from rater to rater or from trial to trial. Although a scale such as that in Fig. 6.2c probably provides a better basis for validity and reliability, such graphical rating scales still contain many possible sources of error including the following:

- *Leniency*. This relates to a characteristic of the person doing the rating. Some people appear to be 'easy' raters and tend to provide a greater proportion of high scores (positive leniency). At the other extreme are harsh or severe raters (negative leniency). Leniency can often be observed when the results of two or more assessors are compared. There is also a potential for motivated leniency, which occurs when for political reasons a rater is motivated to favour one assessee over another. Can you think of a time when this might occur?

- *Halo*. The halo error involves a tendency to let our assessment of an individual on one trait influence our evaluation of that person on other specific traits. In other words, if we believe that someone is outstandingly good in one important area of performance, we might rate him or her high in all areas, regardless of true performance. This error can explain some of the problems of assessment centres that we will encounter later in the chapter.

- *Central tendency error*. Many raters are very reluctant to provide ratings at the extremes of the scale that they are using and tend to produce ratings that group around the mid-point of the scale. This may not necessarily be because the 'true' distribution of ratings should be like this, but because the rater is inhibited about assigning very high or low ratings.

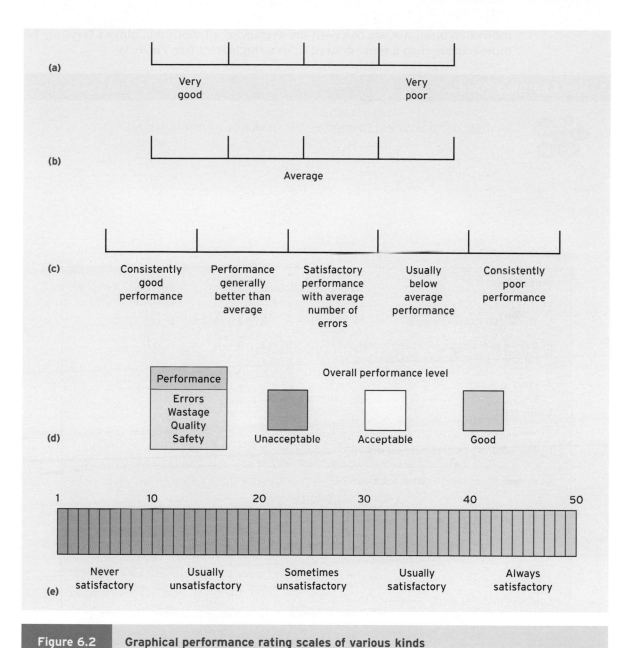

Figure 6.2 **Graphical performance rating scales of various kinds**

One straightforward way of helping to minimise the error in any type of rating scale is to use multiple questions (items) for each of the qualities (competencies, skills, etc.) being rated. Any individual item is open to some degree of misinterpretation by the rater. A set of items, all of which are relevant to the construct being rated, will help to reduce overall error. This is because the misinterpretations and errors related to each item will probably be random in their effect and will therefore balance each other out (although an exception to this will be the case of motivated bias). A score based on the average of all items will almost certainly be more reliable than a score derived from a single item (see Fig. 6.3).

Key Learning Point

Multiple items will help to improve the reliability of rating scales.

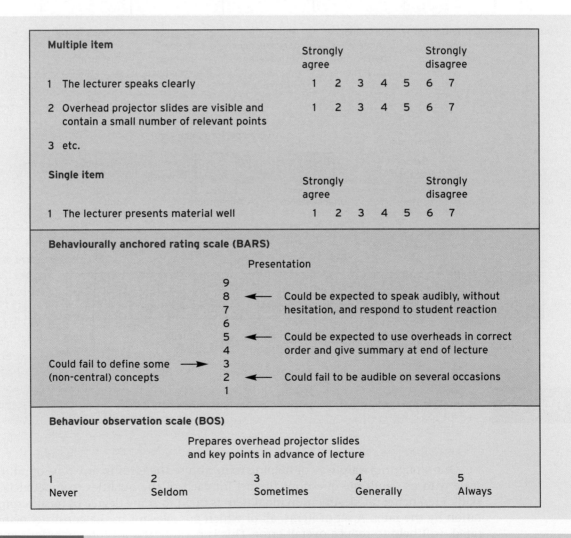

Figure 6.3   Multiple item, BARS and BOS rating scales

Behaviourally anchored scales

One problem with many unsatisfactory rating scales is that the 'anchors' that define the points on the scale are broad, generalised descriptions such as 'average', 'good' or 'excellent', This makes it impossible to be sure that the terms are interpreted in the same way by everyone who uses the scales. One promising means of providing unambiguous anchor points on a scale is to use *behaviourally anchored rating scales* (BARS), see Fig. 6.3. BARS use anchors that describe specific behaviour, which is critical in determining levels of job performance (Smith and Kendall, 1963). BARS are developed using a four-step procedure:

1   With the aid of a group of 'experts' (these are people who understand the role in detail, e.g. employees, supervisors or senior managers) define the factors needed for successful job performance.

2   Use a second group of 'experts' to provide examples of specific behaviour associated with high, average or low performance on the factors.

3   A third group takes the examples from step 2 and independently matches them with the factors from step 1. This 'retranslation' acts as a cross-check on the two previous steps. Examples that are not assigned correctly to the aspect for which they were written do not provide unambiguous behavioural anchors for that aspect of job performance and should not be used.

4   The final step involves using more 'experts' to assign scale values to the surviving items, which then serve as the behavioural anchors for the scale.

The research evidence concerning BARS suggests that they produce results that are slightly better than well-constructed graphic rating scales. These results lead some people to question whether the effort involved is worth the trouble. Two points are worth bearing in mind here. First, a well-constructed graphic scale may require an amount of effort equal to that involved in constructing a BARS. Second, with planning, it is possible to combine the process of eliciting information required to compile a BARS with undertaking a job analysis, minimising both cost and effort. Other more recent scale development procedures include *behaviour observation scales* (BOS) (e.g. Weirsma and Latham, 1986). BOS development procedures will also ensure the development of reasonably sound scales. In essence BOS, like BARS, are based on critical examples of behaviour. With BOS the rater assesses the ratee in terms of the frequency of occurrence of the relevant behaviour (see Fig. 6.3). Some research has shown that there is a preference among users for BOS in the case of appraisal. BOS are seen as better for providing feedback, determining training needs, setting goals and overall ease of use (see Latham *et al.*, 1993). Somewhat disappointingly, however, no procedures have been able to produce scales immune to rating errors.

Observing, recording and rating behaviour involves skill and requires practice.

Assessment in practice

In this section we will consider how assessment procedures operate in practice. We will start by considering assessment centres (ACs) as an example of assessment in a selection context, then discuss performance appraisal (PA) to illustrate the importance of assessment as an ongoing feature of organisational life.

Assessment centres

Assessment centres (ACs) are a very popular method of selecting and assessing people, particularly for management-level positions (Shackleton and Newell, 1997). They are an assessment process, not a place, and typically involve multiple assessments of individuals using different methods, and multiple observers called assessors. The assessment methods can include: work sample exercises (e.g. group exercise, presentation, in-tray exercise, role play), interviews (competency and/or situational) and psychometric tests (aptitude, personality, knowledge-based). ACs profile an applicant's ability across a range of competencies and job-related contexts and last from half a day to three days. The appeal of ACs lies in their generally good levels of criterion-related validity and face validity (Hough and Oswald, 2000, see also Chapter 5). Recent meta-analytic studies of selection methods show the average validity of AC studies to be approximately 0.37 for predicting overall job performance (see Robertson and Smith, 2001; Ones and Viswesvaran, 2003). In the context of this chapter the AC represents an important situation involving interpersonal assessment. We therefore focus on how assessors observe, record and rate candidates' behaviour in work-related contexts.

During an assessment centre an applicant would typically take part in a variety of exercises related to different aspects of the job they are applying for and be observed by different assessors for these exercises. According to a definition agreed by the 17th International Congress on the Assessment Centre Method in 1989 there are certain criteria that an assessment process must fulfil in order to be defined as an AC. These include: (1) explicit dimensions (also referred to as competencies) derived from a job analysis which define the key knowledge skills and abilities required by a candidate in order to perform the role they are being assessed for; (2) multiple techniques (methods) to provide information relevant to the dimensions to be assessed and the context in which those dimensions are to be demonstrated (e.g. different aspects of the role); (3) multiple, trained assessors to observe and evaluate each candidate; and (4) a systematic procedure to record and rate specific behaviours as they occur. Independent assessor ratings and reports are then pooled to form an overall rating for each candidate at what is often referred to as the 'wash-up' session.

The design of an AC reflects the need to assess the extent to which applicants can demonstrate these competencies. Consequently a series of exercises and assessment tools are developed that: (1) are able to elicit the required behaviours; (2) reflect the actual content of the role; (3) assess applicants' performance in a variety of job-related situations; and (4) allow for different assessors to assess these competencies over different exercises. One of the best ways to understand what happens in an AC is to look at the final candidate rating sheet that lists the scores for each of the competencies and exercises for a particular applicant. An example is provided in Fig. 6.4.

From this rating sheet we can see how an AC is structured such that different competencies (listed along the top row) are assessed on different exercises (listed

	Communication skills	Intellectual skills	Business awareness	Leading & motivating	Resilience & drive	Customer focus	Overall exercise ratings
Competency interview		3	2	1	2	3	
Presentation	4	3				4	
In-tray	4		2	2	3	4	
Group exercise	3		1	1	1		
Psychometrics		2					
Overall competency ratings							Overall AC rating

Figure 6.4   Assessment centre competency-exercise matrix

down the left-hand column). For example, the communication skills competency is assessed in the presentation exercise, the in-tray exercise and the group exercise. It is not assessed during the competency interview, nor by the psychometric questionnaire. Exercises are usually designed to assess a range (but not all) of the competencies. This allows exercises to be targeted on specific areas of the job and avoids overloading assessors with too many sets of behavioural criteria to assess (Sackett and Tuzinski, 2001). In this case assessors are using a 1–4 rating scale for competencies, where '1' means that the assessor has observed and recorded little evidence of positive behavioural indicators and considerable evidence of negative behavioural indicators on the part of the candidate during a particular exercise. A '4' means that the assessor has observed and recorded considerable evidence of positive behavioural indicators and little evidence of negative behavioural indicators. As you can see, this particular candidate has performed well on the 'Communication skills' and 'Customer focus' competencies, but less well on 'Business awareness' and 'Leading and motivating'. Overall, the candidate also seems to have done better on the presentation and in-tray exercise, but less well in the group exercise.

The rating sheet also has spaces for assessors to rate the candidate on their overall performance in each exercise and for each competency. While not strictly necessary, this does provide additional information during the wash-up session and helps to alert assessors to the potential problems with convergent and discriminant validity that are described in the next section.

Exercise 6.3   **Deciding on overall assessment scores**

Imagine that you are one of the assessors involved in rating the candidate whose scores are displayed in Fig. 6.4 (the meanings of ratings 1 and 4 are explained in the text shortly before this exercise). How might you go about awarding overall competency or exercise scores? It is not always appropriate to calculate a mean score. This is a good example of how human judgement is an integral part of assessment processes. Consider what information you might bring to bear when trying to make these decisions.

However, although ACs are popular, they have also been described as an enigma because work psychologists are still uncertain as to how they really work. Indeed, Sackett and Tuzinski (2001) point out that there is a growing body of research that suggests that traditional assumptions that dimensions (competencies) are central to how ACs work are unfounded. For example, it has generally been assumed that assessors look for evidence that assessees can or cannot demonstrate competence in each of the dimensions across the varying work-related situations in different exercises. Unfortunately, most research has found that assessor ratings for exercises rather than dimensions demonstrate most consistency (e.g. Robertson *et al.*, 1987; Reilly *et al.*, 1990). This relates to the problem of convergent validity versus discriminant validity.

For example, if dimensions are of central importance in assessor decision-making, one would expect relatively high correlations between different assessors' ratings of an assessee for the same competence (say communication skills) across different exercises. This would mean that the applicant demonstrates good communication skills in a presentation, in a group exercise and in an in-tray exercise. However, they may not score highly for all competencies within a particular exercise. Cross-situational consistency across exercises rather than within exercises indicates that the AC has discriminant validity. However, researchers have found that in most ACs assessors are more likely to provide similar ratings for an individual across different dimensions within the same exercise, rather than for the same competency across different exercises (Robertson and Smith, 2001). This represents convergent validity and suggests that exercises, not dimensions, are the important construct behind assessee ratings. Sackett and Dreher (1982) have therefore argued that evidence is lacking for the position that the constructs measured by ACs are those intended by their designers.

This poses several challenges to work psychologists (Lievens and Klimoski, 2001). Are ACs measuring what they are supposed to measure? If not, does it matter as long as they predict? What other mechanisms might contribute to the validity of ACs? Howard (1997) suggests that the lack of discriminant validity is not a threat, but that it represents an artefact of within-exercise coding. She suggests that because assessors are observing a range of different behavioural indicators for several dimensions, their judgements are not independent. This reflects the argument that the tasks that assessors have to undertake when observing and rating an assessee's behaviour are complex and demanding and that in general it is easier to provide an overall evaluation of effectiveness in a particular exercise. There may also be good reasons why performance on the same dimension can differ between exercises. For example, a person may be much more effective at communicating on a one-to-one basis than presenting information in a public speaking context, yet communication skills might be assessed in both contexts. Consequently, further training for assessors would be unlikely to overcome this.

ACs are generally assumed to have good predictive validity because assessment is based upon direct observation of job-relevant behaviours (Gaugler *et al.*, 1987). This enables assessors to predict how assessees will behave in the job by observing them engaging in job-relevant behaviour. Another explanation for why ACs work is that incremental validity is achieved by using multiple methods that assess separate and distinct aspects of performance. Therefore an AC is a better predictor because each exercise adds something to the predictive power of the process. However, Klimoski and Brickner (1987) identified five different explanations for why the ratings that individuals receive in ACs might relate to later work performance that have nothing to do with the effectiveness of the methods or the assessors. These include effects relating to: (1) contamination, (2) subtle contamination, (3) self-efficacy, (4) performance consistency and (5) intellectual functioning.

The contamination argument suggests that AC ratings might directly influence future decisions to promote an individual, because managers get to learn about and rely upon these ratings rather than their own observations of an individual in the job, when judging promotability. The subtle contamination argument proposes that AC assessors may rate assessees in terms of the qualities they think an individual needs to get on in the organisation, rather than the competencies needed for job performance. Third, Klimoski and Brickner argue that if an assessee performs well in the AC, his or her self-efficacy may improve, and this in turn may lead to better performance in the job. Fourth, despite the expectations that assessors have no prior knowledge of the assessee, there are still occasions when assessors do have information (such as biographical material or knowledge of candidates from other sources) that leads them to rate candidates in a particular way. Finally, assessors may be making an implicit assessment of the individual's intellectual aptitude rather than a judgement based upon specific behaviour during the AC exercises. Indeed, recent research evidence suggests that mental ability may be the most important contributor to assessor ratings (Goldstein *et al.*, 1998). Clearly, there is a need for further investigation of the mechanisms by which selection judgements are made and how these relate to work performance and ratings, although with such high face validity it is unlikely that AC popularity will wane in the short term.

Exercise 6.4   Assessing and selecting politicians

Arguably, work psychologists have been involved in defining most occupational roles. However, one area where their involvement has been noticeably missing is in the area of political selection. Indeed there are differences – in the United Kingdom Members of Parliament (MPs) are elected by the public, not selected by managers.

In a recent British project, the Conservative Party wished to develop a competency model for prospective parliamentary candidates. These are people who are members of the party and would like to try to be elected as an MP for a local area (constituency). As part of this process individuals apply to the party and are assessed to determine whether they were considered suitable candidates. The problem that the Conservative Party faced was a failure to get more women and ethnic minority candidates accepted as parliamentary candidates. They decided to use techniques from work psychology to identify the key skills and abilities required by an MP and develop an assessment centre to ensure that individuals were assessed rigorously, fairly and reliably by trained assessors.

From what you have read so far, how do you think a work psychologist would go about defining and assessing the competencies needed to be an effective MP?

Key Learning Point

Research suggests that assessment centres have quite good criterion-related validity, but this may not always be for the reasons originally expected.

Performance appraisal

So far we have discussed assessment processes in terms of people applying for work. However, formal assessment of people who are already in work usually involves performance appraisal (PA) and represents an important component of performance management. Performance appraisal information can be used for a variety of purposes, including decisions about promotion and salary increases, career development, counselling and training. Managers' ratings collected as a part of PA are also frequently used in the validation of selection procedures. Ideally, PA will inform and motivate an individual to perform more effectively (Fletcher, 2001). However, there is also evidence that employees can become demotivated and demonstrate reduced performance following PA (Kluger and DeNisi, 1996). It is therefore important to understand the factors that contribute to effective PA.

Traditionally, PA has involved a manager observing and rating an employee's performance, and then feeding this back to him or her in a review meeting. The purpose of this process has been to determine whether he or she is performing at an expected level, if not why not, to compare views, and to determine appropriate strategies for ensuring high levels of future performance. These strategies might include further training for the employee, goal setting, reprimand, or even a change to a different job setting. Appraisal systems can also be designed such that rewards will depend upon appraisal judgements (e.g. performance-related pay). Therefore, effective and fair PA, like assessment in selection contexts, depends upon rigorous, valid and reliable methods for assessing an individual's performance. However, there are several important differences between assessment in PA and selection contexts, and it is worth reviewing these in order to understand the unique aspects of assessment for appraisal.

Unlike selection, where assessors have often never met the people they are assessing and may never meet them again, in PA managers have on-going relationships with their subordinates. Furthermore, managers' own performance will usually depend partly upon the performance of those who work for them. Therefore assessment decisions during appraisal have potentially long-term repercussions both for the manager and the subordinate. However, the fact that managers will have known various employees for differing amounts of time and have varying opportunities to observe their work introduces inconsistencies into the assessment process that are more likely to be controlled for during selection. For example, one employee may have joined the team nine months ago, while another could have been a team member for five years. Managers often build up expectations of long-serving employees that can influence their assessment of behaviour in either a positive or negative way. As managers have had more opportunity to observe the performance of longer-serving employees in different management contexts, their ratings may be more valid. However, there is also evidence that managers develop schemata to explain the performance of particular individuals and that these are developed relatively early on in a relationship (Barnes-Farrell, 2001). Consequently, a manager may reach the conclusion that a particular employee is not very effective shortly after joining a team. The development of a schema to this effect is likely to mean that the manager will focus on information that confirms rather than disconfirms his or her belief. Thus, an employee may be disadvantaged in the long term if a manager develops an erroneous expectation regarding their ability early on.

Managers can also have different quality relationships with subordinates, which may or may not relate to the length of time they have worked together. The quality of the relationship can influence decisions, although this might not always be to the advantage of a well-liked employee. For example, a manager may be reluctant to provide a glowing reference for an employee whom they are dependent upon and do not want to lose. Managers who dislike poorly performing employees have also been known to provide relatively positive references for individuals they would quite like to lose. This is a good illustration of the political angle of assessment in organisational contexts, and should alert work psychologists to the potential pitfalls of assuming that all assessment can be rendered objective and reliable (Murphy and Cleveland, 1995).

Another difference between assessment in selection and appraisal is that in the latter managers' assessment of performance generally takes place over a longer period (possibly a year between appraisal meetings). Managers also have varying opportunities to observe different subordinates. Whereas some subordinates may work very closely with the manager, others may see him or her once every month. The advent of teleworking has meant that some managers may never observe their employees face-to-face, but interact (if at all) by telephone, email or video-link. We have relatively little information about how technology can impact upon appraisal decisions, but as we saw in Chapter 5, there is some evidence to suggest that ratings may well differ from those made in face-to-face situations. Finally, managers can vary in the extent to which they understand or have experience of a job that subordinates are performing, leading to assumptions about performance that are not always valid. All of these factors can introduce inconsistencies into the assessment process that are usually controlled for in the selection context. However, another important difference between assessment in PA and selection is that in the former, managers usually feed back their assessments to their subordinates in face-to-face situations. Therefore, feeding back to employees is also a skill that most managers need to develop through training and practice if they are to avoid worsening employee performance. Consequently, assessing performance in the workplace presents a unique challenge for work psychologists.

So, what do we know about how assessment processes in PA can be improved? Certainly, our understanding of the sources of difficulty for assessors (in this case managers) can be used to train assessors to be aware of potential bias and make an effort to avoid it. Similarly, PA systems can be designed to try to alleviate some of these problems (Fletcher, 2001). For example, it may be more effective (if potentially unpopular) to conduct review meetings more regularly. It is also important to ensure consistency by asking managers to rate employees using an agreed set of behavioural and performance criteria. Employees can reflect on their own performance against these criteria and managers and employees should identify behavioural evidence to support their ratings. Therefore, much of what we have already discussed about observing, recording and rating performance in assessment contexts is relevant here.

However, another method of increasing the accuracy of ratings that has become increasingly popular in PA is to use more than one rater. The arguments to support this approach derive from the principles associated with the use of multiple items. It is argued that errors and bias are more likely to balance out with multiple items and the resulting average ratings will be more accurate.

Multi-source feedback systems

London and Tornow (1998) argue that moves towards flatter organisational structures have posed particular problems for managers undertaking PA. Managers today

Key Learning Point

Assessment for performance appraisal differs from assessment for selection because assessors (managers) have on-going relationships with the people they are assessing.

often have a much greater span of control. As a consequence, they are often responsible for reviewing the performance of many more employees spread over more diverse job areas. This makes the task of PA much more difficult. Perhaps as a consequence there has been a tremendous increase in the popularity of multi-source feedback (MSF) systems over recent years. MSF involves an individual receiving feedback on his or her performance from several different sources. These might include manager, subordinates, peers and even customers. These ratings are usually collected using questionnaire surveys and the findings are collated to provide what is argued to be a more conclusive picture of an individual's perform-ance (London and Smither, 1995). One popular MSF system of appraisal is 360-degree feedback.

An important assumption underlying the use of MSF is that multiple individ-uals have more opportunity to observe an individual's behaviour across different job contexts than a single manager. For example, an employee might be especially attentive to a customer when she knows that her manager is watching, but by sur-veying a sample of customers, it is possible to overcome this potential bias. MSF is therefore assumed to provide a more rigorous and complete assessment of an indi-vidual's performance. In addition, the incorporation of self-assessment using what is essentially a psychometric instrument means that it is possible to statistically compare the ratings provided by different sources. This may be to the employee's advantage, particularly if the ratings provided by customers are much higher than those provided by a manager who underestimates the employee's potential. It can also provide useful information when there is a discrepancy between an employee's rating and the rating that he or she receives from another source. It has been suggested that this discrepancy can form an important source of feedback to an individual who has an unrealistic impression of his or her ability. However, the existence of a discrepancy highlights a potentially difficult question for MSF systems: whose perception should be believed? Historically, MSF was used as a developmental rather than a review tool. As such, any discrepancies in ratings were useful as information to discuss with the individual and identify developmental needs. However, when MSF is used as part of PA, discrepancies can become prob-lematic when determining potential rewards and future expectations (Fletcher *et al.*, 1998).

In general, the popularity of MSF among organisational users has out-paced research aimed at investigating mechanisms underpinning its effectiveness. However, there are a number of key questions that researchers have focused upon: How comparable are the ratings provided from different sources – for example, are self-assessments more lenient than managers' ratings? Do raters from different sources use different types of information when assessing an indi-vidual? How valid are the judgements made by raters from different groups?

What are the consequences of discrepancies in assessments? Should raters remain anonymous? Perhaps most importantly, does MSF result in better performance than traditional PA methods? Evidence for the latter is definitely mixed. For example, Walker and Smither (1999) found that managers who discussed MSF feedback with those who had provided it showed significantly greater improvement over five years compared with managers who did not. Similarly, Smither *et al.* (1995) found that self-ratings became closer to colleague ratings over time. However, Fletcher (1998) found that in many cases organisations introducing 360-degree feedback for PA had dropped it within two years. There is therefore still a need for research demonstrating the ability of MSF to add value to traditional PA systems. Interestingly, at present not all MSF systems incorporate training for all raters. Yet, we know that raters should be sufficiently expert and well trained to give accurate ratings (e.g. Smither *et al.*, 1988). Perhaps the psychometric rigour of survey methodology has meant that the more important components of interpersonal performance assessment have been overlooked. No doubt there will be considerably more research in this area over the coming years.

Key Learning Point

MSF involves multiple ratings of an individual's performance from different sources, including: manager, subordinate, colleague, self and customer.

Debates in practice

Assessing for change

One of the difficulties currently facing work psychologists and HR professionals is the fact that traditional selection and assessment systems are based upon the concept of person–job fit. This assumes that people possess relatively stable individual differences (e.g. personality traits and cognitive ability) and by matching these with the knowledge, skills and abilites required by a role (the person specification) we ensure higher levels of performance. However, the concept of person–job fit has received considerable criticism in recent years (see Anderson and Herriot, 1997). First, psychologists have pointed out that many individual differences associated with job performance are not static. While personality and intelligence are comparatively stable over time and contexts, other characteristics such as skills, knowledge, interests and work styles vary considerably. Moreover, the dominance of psychometric approaches to predicting job performance has meant that focus has shifted away from acknowledging that individuals can change and that this development is important to performance. Perhaps more damaging to the idea of person–job fit, and a major challenge to current assessment systems, is the fact that roles themselves change. Indeed, it has been argued that change is in fact a ubiquitous and, paradoxically, stable feature of organisational life. Consequently, evidence collected to validate selection and assessment systems may quickly become out of date if the role, and presumably the competencies required to perform that role, change.

There are no easy or immediately obvious solutions to this challenge. One possibility is to continue with the traditional person–job fit process, but to recognise that assessment criteria need to be reviewed on an on-going basis, possibly every couple of years. The down-side to this for organisations is expense – a tremendous effort needs to be directed at continually re-evaluating roles and adapting assessment systems. Another proposed solution is that individuals should be assessed on the basis of person–organisation fit rather than person-job fit. Person–organisation fit is really an extension of the idea of person–job fit, but in this case it is argued that organisations themselves have 'personalities' and that higher performance will ensue by recruiting individuals who fit the organisation rather than the job. The idea that organisations possess 'personalities' is not new. Psychologists such as Holland (1997) and Schneider (1987) have pointed out that there is a tendency for individuals with similar personalities to be recruited by particular organisations and that this leads organisations to appear different from one another. Schneider suggested that this happens when individuals are attracted to organisations that appear similar to themselves, when individuals within those organisations recruit individuals like themselves, and when individuals within the organisation who feel they are dissimilar, or do not fit, voluntarily leave the organisation. Schneider describes this as the A-S-A model: Attraction–Selection–Attrition.

More recently, Kristof (1996) has refocused attention upon the importance of person–environment fit in selection models. She identifies two different types of fit: 'complementary fit' and 'supplementary fit'. The former is based on the idea that a person may provide something (e.g. skills or knowledge) that is needed by the organisation but not currently available in it. Hence the person fits the organisation's needs, though he or she might feel a little isolated and different from the others. Supplementary fit is where a person's attributes match those of the people already in the organisation, which means he or she may well feel at home, but perhaps does not add much to overall organisational capability. Perhaps the ideal is a supplementary fit between person and organisation for values and culture, and a complementary fit for skills and knowledge. Organisational characteristics such as values and culture are seen as being quite resistant to change, and it is assumed that a match between these organisational and individual characteristics will lead to improved performance in much the same way as person–job fit. Consequently, organisations and researchers have been exploring methods for selecting and assessing individuals for person–organisation fit. Unfortunately, we seem to be some way off being able to define and therefore develop methods for assessing individual differences in values and organisational differences in culture and climate. There is also relatively little research evidence as yet to support the assertion that improved person–organisational fit leads to improved performance. No doubt this is an area likely to receive much research interest over the coming years.

Impression management and cross-cultural assessment

In this chapter we have generally focused on what assessors do rather than what assessees do. Indeed, most research is concerned with how assessors make sense of

Key Learning Point

Many of the assessment techniques devised by work psychologists assume that neither people nor their work environments change very much.

targets and the assessee is typically viewed as a passive participant in this process. Yet we know that assessees are not passive. They seek to make an impression on the assessor. One only has to think of how we prepare for interviews or appraisals to know that an assessee generally believes that he or she has at least some ability to influence the outcome. Moreover, PA systems often encourage assessees to take a more active role by reflecting on and presenting their own assessments of their performance. However, it is worth reiterating its importance within assessment, particularly as most research ignores the assessee's proactive attempts to make sense of and respond to his or her environment (Silvester *et al.*, 2003).

Key Learning Point

Assessees actively seek to influence the judgements that assessors make of them by engaging in impression management.

However, the efforts of an assessee to influence the way in which he or she is perceived by others is particularly relevant to situations involving cross-cultural assessment. The fact that organisations are becoming increasingly global poses a growing challenge for valid and reliable assessment of employees. Central to this difficulty is the question of how organisations can be sensitive to cultural differences in the behaviour of individuals from different cultures while simultaneously applying consistent assessment criteria throughout the whole company. Take the example of a multinational organisation that has a head office in Chicago and divisions in Europe, South East Asia, Africa, the Middle East and South America. Because it is important that the organisation has middle managers who are able to work in a variety of international locations, and because they must participate in multinational projects involving members from different countries, the senior managers may decide to develop a single competency model. This, and the associated behavioural criteria are then used to assess applicants applying for these roles in an assessment centre. However, these assessment centres can potentially involve assessors from Japan, who are assessing applicants from Nigeria, Greece, Brazil, Kuwait and Australia. We have relatively little understanding as yet of the cross-cultural factors that can influence assessment decisions in such contexts.

We do know, however, that there are cultural differences in the way people behave. For example Fahr *et al.* (1991) found differences between the way that employees in Taiwan and the United States typically explained their success at work. Whereas in the United States employees were more likely to take personal responsibility for success, in Taiwan employees generally demonstrated a 'modesty bias' attributing success more to the actions of their managers or colleagues. This difference has been explained in terms of the cultural norms that operate within collectivist cultures and individualistic cultures. Such cultural differences are important to the extent that they influence judgements of people. For example, an assessor from an individualistic culture might interpret the behaviour of an individual from a collectivist culture as being indicative of a lower drive for success. One from a collectivist culture might judge an applicant from an individualistic culture as insufficiently team-orientated and potentially disruptive. Moreover, an interpersonal style that focuses on challenging others may be highly valued in one culture as an indicator of leadership potential. However, in another culture, leadership potential might be more typically associated with an inclusive approach that focuses on teamwork. This is problematic when individuals from different cultures are being assessed together. Individuals from certain cultures might also be assessed more favourably, because their behaviour fits more closely with the prevailing notions of what behaviour pattern is preferred. Consequently, multi-national organisations keen to have assessment systems that can be used globally (thereby making it easier to share information and compare performance) might develop organisational competency models that are used throughout the company. However, behavioural indicators are likely to reflect the behavioural norms within the culture or country where they were developed. Again, we have no simple solutions to this problem as yet. It may well be that decisions regarding which behavioural indicators are deemed to be most important will reflect the winners in an ultimate power-play among organisations seeking to influence global outcomes. For work psychologists, however, the important challenge is to identify those behaviours that are consistently associated with performance across different national and international contexts.

Summary

This chapter is primarily concerned with the interpersonal judgements we make about people when assessing their suitability for work, or their performance at work. It includes discussion of how, even in formal assessment contexts, these judgements can be subjective and biased. As such they can lead to unfair discrimination against particular groups of employees. However, psychological research has identified a number of ways of improving the objectivity, rigour and predictive validity of assessment decisions and this chapter discusses the support for different strategies. Finally, we compare how the process of interpersonal assessment differs during selection and appraisal, and how decisions can be improved using such methods as multi-source feedback and assessment centres.

Closing Case Study

Hi-tech-Hard-edge Performance Management

Welcome to the world of employee performance management, a new breed of software that claims to improve employees' performance, productivity and satisfaction. It closely tracks the performance of individual workers using such targets as sales achieved, queries resolved, tasks completed, new skills learned and so on.

Such systems let employees track their progress online, and some show them how customers and colleagues rate them in anonymous surveys. The feedback can work both ways, with employees saying what they think of managers.

Companies get a better view of how people are performing and what they think, while staff get a better idea of how close they are to meeting targets, earning bonuses and maybe getting promoted. It is a bold vision, but it can work. Morse, the European IT services company, uses specialist software to track its consultants' skills and achievements, and to allocate them to customer projects. Tom Leonard, Morse's commercial manager, says the system helped to raise average consultant utilisation rates from 38 per cent in 2001 to 72 per cent earlier this year, contributing to an increase in profitability. It also helped Morse cut staff turnover and identify where it needed new skills, he says.

'It's now far easier to do staff appraisals, because we have clearly measured objectives that have been defined and tracked. When you have woolly, subjective measures, people lose focus on what they are trying to achieve,' says Mr Leonard.

This won't work for everyone, as some tasks and responsibilities are hard to measure objectively. The technology works best for the likes of salespeople, staff who bill for their time, and workers performing repetitive and measurable tasks.

Even when tasks are measured, unfortunate side effects can be produced. Microsoft used an employee performance management system to improve corporate customer service levels and increase engineers' productivity after it began centralising its European product-support operations in 2001. As part of this, it began to record how long individual engineers took to solve problems to help calculate bonuses. Microsoft says it saw a noticeable rise in the division's customer-satisfaction levels since the system was installed.

Yet earlier this year, the division started abandoning individual performance monitoring, in favour of team monitoring. Part of the problem was that when engineers accepted complex jobs that took longer than average to solve, they appeared less productive than their colleagues, and the system marked them down.

'Some people didn't want to take on complex cases,' admits Guido Häring, general manager of Microsoft's European global technical support centre. 'We found that if you manage performance at too granular a level, you drive the wrong behaviours. Goal setting can sometimes get in the way of company objectives.'

Employee performance management software is difficult to install, and often requires tweaking soon after installation. Moreover, it can create cultural disruption 'When we first introduced the system, there was a lot of scepticism and hostility. People don't necessarily understand why it's being introduced, so the way you educate your staff is key,' warns Mr Leonard.

Perhaps the greatest risk is that it will encourage weak, lazy or just inexperienced managers to abdicate their personal responsibility for managing people. That in turn will lead to worse, not better, employee performance and morale. 'If the system is perceived as a replacement for the manager–employee relationship, it will cause resentment and alienation, detracting from performance management rather than facilitating it,' says Jonathon Hogg, a senior consultant at PA Consulting.

Some employees baulk at being monitored by a computer. Individual-focused management techniques sometimes clash with cultural traditions that support collective mechanisms such as unions and workers' councils. 'There is resistance in parts of Europe, especially in France. This is still quite a new technology, and it's more acceptable in the US and in the UK than it is in the rest of Europe,' said one industry insider.

Source: Adapted from an article at FT.com, 7 May 2003

Suggested exercises

1   In what respects, If any, do you think the performance management systems described in this article are an advance on performance appraisal/feedback meetings? Why?

2   How can performance appraisal/management procedures be designed to minimise accidental side effects such as encouraging people to take on only the easy tasks?

Test your learning

Short-answer questions

1   Name and describe five sources of bias in interpersonal assessment.

2   What are the four principles of effective assessment?

3   Why is it important to train assessors?

4   How would you create a behaviourally anchored rating scale?

5 Why should managers avoid using non-behaviours to feed back to employees?

6 Define an assessment centre.

7 What has been referred to as the enigma of assessment centres?

8 What are the key differences between assessment for selection and assessment of performance in an appraisal context?

9 What is person–organisation fit and why is it important for assessment?

10 What are the main difficulties when assessing behaviour in cross-cultural contexts?

Suggested assigments

1 How can we make interpersonal assessment more objective and reliable?

2 Compare and contrast the validity and utility of interpersonal assessment decisions based upon observation of behaviour compared with those derived from psychometric questionnaires.

3 Assessment centres demonstrate good levels of criterion-related validity, but researchers are not sure why. Describe how an assessment centre works and the arguments that have been proposed to explain the effectiveness of assessment centres.

4 Multi-source feedback (MSF) has been proposed as an improvement on traditional appraisal systems. Why is this so, and what evidence is there to support such a view?

5 If interpersonal assessment is vulnerable to bias and subjectivity, why do organisations continue to use it?

6 Discuss how a multinational organisation might address the issue of consistency in the assessment of applicants from different cultures.

Relevant websites

An interesting and provocative site developed by the American consultant Robert Bacal can be found at http://performance-appraisals.org/. It contains a lot of information and opinion about how to do and how not to do performance appraisal.

HRGopher is a service which finds information about a range of topics in human resource management and related fields, and makes it available on the web. Try http://www.hrgopher.com/category/290.php?session=s4212ghzbqpet1gmssmq for material related to this chapter.

The Center for Creative Leadership, based in the USA but with international operations, is another consultancy firm which offers a range of products and services to

do with assessing people at work. An overview of these can be found at http://www.ccl.org/products/.

For further self-test material and relevant, annotated weblinks please visit the website at http://www.booksites.net/arnold_workpsych.

Suggested further reading

1 *How People Evaluate Others in Organizations* edited by Manuel London, published by Lawrence Erlbaum Press in 2001, is a detailed review of some of the most recent research concerned with assessing people at or for work that expands on many of the themes of this chapter.

2 Paul Rosenfeld, Robert Giacalone and Catherine Riordan have produced an interesting and thorough text called *Impression Management: Building and enhancing reputations at work* (full details in reference list at the end of this book) which discusses issues of impression management in more detail. This is part of the Psychology@Work series edited by Clive Fletcher and published by Thomson Learning.

CHAPTER 7

Attitudes at work

After studying this chapter, you should be able to:

1 briefly describe two ways in which attitudes have been divided into three components;

2 specify two functions of attitudes for the person who holds them;

3 describe Thurstone and Likert scaling in attitude measurement;

4 describe the factors that affect the success of attempts to change attitudes;

5 explain why attitudes and behaviour are not always consistent;

6 describe three features of attitudes that increase the probability that they will influence behaviour;

7 describe the theory of planned behaviour;

8 define job satisfaction and identify three general propositions about what affects it;

9 describe one research study that has suggested that a person's job satisfaction is not simply a function of the nature of his or her work;

10 define organisational commitment and its component parts;

11 specify the factors that appear to strengthen a person's organisational commitment.

Opening Case Study   **Attitudes to the Euro**

Managers in the UK are becoming more hostile to the euro because of the poor performance of the currency and the absence of 'proper debate', it was shown in a survey published yesterday.

The Institute of Managers poll, covering 228 of its members, showed 61 pc would vote against joining the euro in an immediate referendum compared with 43 pc in a survey 18 months ago.

Only 29 pc are in favour of joining, down from 47 pc. Half believe UK entry is inevitable in the next decade.

Mary Chapman, institute director general, said the research showed 'an increasingly hostile attitude to the currency'.

Source: The Daily Telegraph, *23 November 2000*

Introduction

This brief news report is typical of many that describe the results of an attitude survey. Such surveys are a common feature of twenty-first century life. The report of this one makes some implicit assumptions and claims that are common. First, it assumes that attitudes are not neutral. They include an element of emotion and/or evaluation – in this case hostility. Second, attitudes are linked to behaviour. In this case the behaviour is how the respondent would vote in a referendum. Third, there is an implication that attitudes can be changed by events. Fourth, it is assumed that the view expressed by a person in an attitude survey reflects something more long-term than a momentary opinion.

It is well over half a century since attitude surveys become a standard tool for managers to check on what employees thought of their work and their workplace (Schneider *et al.*, 1996). The design, analysis and reporting of attitude surveys have been prominent activities of work and organisational psychologists ever since. Over the same period, more theoretically minded academic social psychologists have developed some sophisticated analyses of the nature of attitudes, how they change, and how they predict behaviour (or fail to). In this chapter we first provide a discussion of what an attitude is, with particular reference to the work situation. Second, we briefly describe the ways in which attitudes can be measured. Then attention turns to the question of what factors affect the formation and change of attitudes at work. Attitude change might not be very important if it is not reflected in behaviour change, so the connection between attitudes and behaviour is then examined. Finally, we look at two important work attitudes: job satisfaction and organisational commitment. In each case we describe their nature, measurement, causes and consequences, and make links back to material earlier in the chapter.

What is an attitude?

Attitudes were defined by Secord and Backman (1969) as 'certain regularities of an individual's feelings, thoughts and predispositions to act toward some aspect of his [sic] environment'. Feelings represent the *affective component* of an attitude, thoughts the *cognitive component* and predispositions to act the *behavioural component*. Attitudes are evaluative; that is, they reflect a person's tendency to feel, think or behave in a positive or negative manner towards the object of the attitude. Evaluative dimensions of attitudes include good–bad, harmful–beneficial, pleasant–unpleasant and likeable–dislikeable (Ajzen, 2001). Attitudes can be held about the physical world around us (e.g. modern architecture), about hypothetical constructs (e.g. democracy) and about other people (e.g. the boss, mother-in-law, the Prime Minister). The general point is that attitudes refer to a particular *target* – e.g. person, group of people, object or concept. This is one way in which attitudes differ from personality, since personality reflects a person's predispositions across a range of situations. A person's attitudes at work can concern their job tasks, pay, supervision, employing organisation, colleagues, customers or physical work environment. They can even refer to quite specific things such as the quality of pencils one's employer provides.

Everyone holds attitudes, not least because it seems that we usually attach an evaluation to our perceptions of people and things around us (Ajzen and Fishbein, 2000). However, some people hold more attitudes more strongly than others. This is because the strength of the tendency to evaluate is partly an individual difference variable (Jarvis and Petty, 1996).

The affective component of an attitude is reflected in a person's physiological responses (e.g. blood pressure) and/or in what the person says about how he or she feels about the object of the attitude. The cognitive component refers to a person's perception of the object of the attitude, and/or what the person says he or she believes about that object. The behavioural component is reflected by a person's observable behaviour toward the object of the attitude and/or what he or she says about that behaviour. In practice, the term 'attitude' is usually taken to mean the cognitive and/or affective components. Behaviour is most often construed as an outcome of attitudes (*see* below, 'Attitudes and behaviour').

Key Learning Point

 Attitudes are a person's predisposition to think, feel or behave in certain ways towards certain defined targets.

Is it worth making distinctions between the three components of attitude? This is disputed (*see* Cacioppo *et al.*, 1989), but the answer seems to be yes. Breckler (1984) has shown that although our feelings, beliefs and behaviours towards an object do tend to be consistent with each other, they are not so highly consistent that they can be thought of as the same thing. Hence, for example, it is possible for a person to feel positive about his or her job (affective component) but to believe that the job has few attractive elements (cognitive component). Thus, a person can simultaneously hold two different attitudes to his or her job. Which attitude is expressed, and which one will influence behaviour on any given occasion, may therefore depend on whether the person is concentrating on emotions or on beliefs at that time (Millar and Tesser, 1989). On the whole, it seems that when beliefs and emotions conflict, the latter usually have more impact on a person's behaviour, though this partly depends on a person's personality (Haddock and Zanna, 2000).

It is also important to distinguish attitudes from other related concepts. George and Jones (1997) analyse the relationships between attitudes, values and moods. Values are a person's beliefs about what is good or desirable in life. They are long-term guides for a person's choices and experiences. Moods, on the other hand, are 'generalized affective states that are not explicitly linked to particular events or circumstances which may have originally induced the mood' (George and Jones, 1997, p. 400). Values, attitudes and moods differ in terms of (i) whether they concern the past, present, or future; (ii) their stability over time; and (iii) whether they are general or specific. These differences are summarised in Table 7.1. In the long run, attitudes can change values. For example, being dissatisfied with one's job for a long time may change a person's beliefs about the importance of work in life. A consideration of values and moods also helps to explain why attitudes do not always predict behaviour at work. A person may have negative attitudes towards his or her job and colleagues but still help out others at work because he or she places a high value on being responsible and co-operative. An example (Finegan, 2000) of how values can predict a person's attitude towards their employing organisation is given later in this chapter. The link (or lack of it) between attitudes and behaviour is also discussed further later in this chapter.

Exercise 7.1   Attitudes to this book

Consider your attitude (if any) to this book. How positively or negatively do you *feel* about it? (affective component). How positive or negative are your *thoughts* about it? (cognitive component). How positively or negatively do you *behave* towards it? (e.g. how often do you read it and for how long?) (behavioural component). In each case, describe what your feelings, thoughts and behaviours are.

Consider whether the extent to which you use this book is influenced by your values, attitudes and moods. What other factors affect your behaviour towards the book?

Pratkanis and Turner (1994) and Cialdini and Trost (1998) among others have analysed attitudes from a social-cognitive perspective (*see* Chapter 1), and asked the important question of why we have attitudes – in other words, what purposes do they serve? There seem to be three general answers to this:

Table 7.1	Values, attitudes and moods		
	Values	**Attitudes**	**Moods**
Time perspective	Future (how things should be)	Past (my past experience of a target)	Present (how I feel right now)
Dynamism	Stable (little change over long periods)	Evolving (slow or steady change)	Fluctuating (substantial change over short periods)
Focus	General (guides approach to life)	Specific (directed towards a specific target)	General (how I feel about everything right now)

Source: Adapted from J. M. George and G. R. Jones (1997) 'Experiencing work: values, attitudes and moods', **Human Relations**, vol. 50, pp. 393–416. Adapted with permission

Key Learning Point

Attitudes are related to, but distinguishable from, values, moods and personality.

1   Attitudes can help us to make sense of our environment and act effectively within it, so, for example, our attitudes can be a 'filter' through which we recall certain events but not others, and interpret events of unclear meaning. For example, people who are dissatisfied with their job are more likely than others to believe that ambiguous events are sure to end in disaster. Also, knowing our own attitudes and those of others helps us to categorise people into groups.

2   Attitudes can help us to define and maintain our sense of self-identity (who we are) and self-esteem (a sense of personal value). It seems to be important to most people to have a clear sense of who they are, and to feel reasonably positive about it. Also, knowing our own attitudes and those of others helps us to categorise people into groups.

3   Attitudes can help us maintain good relations with other people, particularly those who have the power to reward or punish us. By holding and expressing attitudes similar to another person, we can often make ourselves more

attractive to him or her, and more able to understand and empathise with him or her.

Pratkanis and Turner (1994) have argued that an attitude is stored in memory as a 'cognitive representation', which consists of three components:

1 An object label and rules for applying it. For example, if one is concerned about attitudes to colleagues, it is necessary to be clear about who counts as a colleague.

2 An evaluative summary of that object, i.e. whether it is broadly 'good' or 'bad'.

3 A knowledge structure supporting the evaluative summary. This can be simple or complex, and may include technical knowledge about the domain, arguments for or against a given proposition, or a listing of the advantages and disadvantages of a target.

Key Learning Point

Attitudes are cognitive representations which help us to structure our social world and our place within it.

As an example of some research on attitudes, let us take an article by Furnham *et al.* (1994). They used their academic contacts in 41 countries to obtain a total sample of more than 12 000 young people, who completed a questionnaire concerning their attitudes to work and economic issues. Furnham *et al.* assessed, among other things, the following attitudes, each of which was measured with several statements and a Likert response scale (*see* next section) asking the respondent to what extent he or she agreed or disagreed with each statement.

■ *Work ethic* – Example statement: 'I like hard work'.

■ *Competitiveness* – Example statement: 'I feel that winning is important in both work and games'.

■ *Money beliefs* – Example statement: 'I firmly believe money can solve all my problems'.

They found quite marked differences between countries in the extent to which young people held these attitudes. Work ethic was higher in America than in Europe or the East and Asia. The reverse was true for competitiveness. Money beliefs were highest in the East and Asia, lower in America, and lower again in Europe. At the level of individual countries, those with high economic growth tended to score higher on both competitiveness and money beliefs. However, it is not clear whether the attitudes caused the economic growth, were caused by it, both, or neither. This illustrates one of the problems of the survey method, as discussed in Chapter 2.

How are attitudes measured?

Attitudes are almost always assessed using self-report questionnaires. In other words, attitude measurement usually depends upon what people say about their feelings, beliefs and/or behaviour towards the particular object in question. Attitude questionnaires are not just thrown together haphazardly. There are several fairly sophisticated techniques for ensuring that they measure the attitude in question properly. Two of these are Thurstone scaling and Likert scaling.

In the *Thurstone approach*, or the equal interval scale, the psychologist generates a number of potential questionnaire items, ranging from highly favourable about the topic in question to highly unfavourable – for example, in terms of one's attitude towards working overtime, from 'working overtime is the highlight of my week' to 'there is no conceivable justification for working overtime'. After collecting, say, about a hundred such statements, the psychologist asks a sample group of those ultimately to be assessed to rate each statement on a scale from (for example) 1 to 11 on the degree of favourableness of the attitude statement. The psychologist then includes in the final attitude questionnaire only those statements where (i) there is a high degree of agreement between evaluators on its degree of favourableness, and (ii) the average scale value of the item ranges up the 11-point scale at equal intervals from 1 to 11. Perhaps 20–22 statements are included in the final questionnaire, each of which is separated from the previous one by a scale value of, say, roughly half a point. A person's attitude score is the mean or median scale value of all the statements with which they express agreement.

The second approach is the *Likert technique*, which is sometimes known as the summated scale. This is generally much easier and quicker than Thurstone scaling. In this approach, the psychologist selects a large number of statements that relate to the attitude object concerned. They should either be clearly in favour of the object, or clearly against it. Unlike Thurstone scaling, there is no requirement to establish all points between the extremes. Respondents indicate their agreement or disagreement with each statement. Statements are included in the final scale only if they: (i) tend to be responded to in the same way as others covering apparently similar ground, and (ii) elicit the same responses on two occasions. Whereas in the Thurstone method the respondents might reply with 'yes', 'no' or 'not applicable', in the Likert method a five-, seven- or ten-point response scale is utilised for each statement, usually in terms of strongly agree to strongly disagree. For example, with a five-point response scale, respondents might have the options 'strongly agree' (score 4), 'agree' (score 3), 'neither agree nor disagree' (score 2), 'disagree' (score 1) and 'strongly disagree' (score 0). Scores are reversed (i.e. 4 changes to 0, 3 to 1, etc.) for statements worded negatively (e.g. 'overtime is a real nuisance'), and the person's overall attitude score is the sum or mean of their responses to the statements. Because the scores for negative statements have been reversed, a high score indicates a favourable attitude.

One difficulty with both of these techniques is that they are subject to the *social desirability effect* – that is, to respondents giving the socially desirable answer, as, for instance, 'Of course I don't think war is glorious' when, in fact, they think just the opposite. There are techniques available to minimise this effect. For example, in

Key Learning Point

Attitude measurement is systematic and quantitative. In line with the positivist research philosophy (see Chapter 2), it is usually assumed that attitudes exist independently of attempts to articulate or measure them.

the questionnaire in Table 7.2, one of the authors wanted to find out what people thought about male and female managers. Instead of asking them directly, he devised two questionnaires that were exactly alike, except that in each version a single line was different – 'male' and 'female'. The two versions of the questionnaire were distributed among a random sample of the general public and the differences between the two forms were assessed, without the issue of male versus female stereotypes ever being raised on the questionnaire.

Table 7.2   Stereotyped attitudes towards male versus female managers

Description of a character you may know

Is 20 years old
Graduate
Trainee manager
Woman/man*
Unmarried
Enjoys films

Whereabouts on these scales would you place this character? Please put a tick in the appropriate box according to where you think she/he* would most probably be best described on the scale.

Will be a 'high flyer'					Will not necessarily be a 'high flyer'
Is inclined to be 'bossy'					Is inclined to be meek
Is a good mixer socially					Is rather shy socially
Is very studious					Is not very studious
Would assume leadership in groups					Would not assume leadership in groups
Contains emotions					Expresses emotions freely
Is self-confident					Is not self-confident
Is ambitious					Is not particularly ambitious
Is assertive					Is not particularly assertive

How much do you think he/she* will be earning   (a) when he/she* is 30? £ ...../p.a.
                                                  (b) when he/she* is 60? £ ...../p.a.

* One or the other given on each form

Whatever the technique of attitude measurement, the result is normally a measure of how *extreme* a person's attitude is: for example, whether he or she strongly likes, mildly likes, is indifferent towards, mildly dislikes or strongly dislikes studying work psychology. Petty and Krosnick (1992) have argued for the more general concept of attitude *strength*. As well as extremity, this includes the amount of certainty people feel about their attitude, its importance to them, how intensely they hold the attitude and how knowledgeable they are about it. Petty and Krosnick suggested that consideration of these factors will improve the predictability of behaviour from attitudes. Along the same lines, Pratkanis and Turner (1994) have referred to attitude *salience*, which concerns the extent to which an attitude is clearly relevant to the situation at hand. Their definition of a strong attitude is one that comes easily to mind. This definition seems quite appropriate because research suggests that beliefs that are important to a person are remembered more completely and more quickly than those that are not (van Harreveld *et al.*, 2000). In fact, some psychologists believe that the speed with which a person reacts to a stimulus could be the most valid indicator of his or her attitude (Greenwald *et al.*, 1998).

It is perhaps too readily assumed that measuring attitudes is necessarily a useful thing to do. Schneider *et al.* (1996) have pointed out that senior managers are often more interested in finding out whether company policies and new initiatives are being implemented successfully than in whether employees have positive attitudes toward those polices and initiatives. So Schneider and colleagues devised a questionnaire that asked employees of a very large service company about whether new policies to promote customer focus were being carried out (for example by their bosses). They asked very specific questions about events and behaviours, not attitudes, and discovered that the extent to which policies were being implemented predicted customer satisfaction several months later.

A more fundamental challenge to the way that most psychologists think of attitudes has been provided by Verkuyten (1998) among others. Verkuyten argues that it is a mistake to see attitudes as quantitatively measurable phenomena that in some sense exist inside a person's head. Like other discursive social psychologists, Verkuyten argues that attitudes are expressed in conversation as part of an attempt to achieve the personal goals of the speaker. These might be to convince others of one's correctness, morality, acceptability, rationality and so on. They might be very transient, and they might depend very much on how the object of the attitude is defined. Verkuyten analysed a transcript from a Dutch television programme in which the organisers of an 'erotic fair' in Utrecht debated with a group called 'Christians for Truth' which objected to the fair. Verkuyten (p. 314) commented:

> The fact that the nature of the attitude object was subject to debate also implies that it would be difficult to compare the attitudes of the participants using traditional measures. For some participants the fair was about pornography, whereas for others it represented eroticism and lifestyle. Their views about eroticism [good] and pornography [bad] did not seem to differ, but their attitudes toward the fair were difficult to compare because of the different ways that the fair was defined.

Attitude change through persuasion

Changing attitudes is an important part of many people's work. Sales staff try to persuade potential customers to hold a positive attitude to whatever they are selling. Politicians and others interested in social or economic change try to influence public attitudes concerning those issues (*see*, for example, Eiser and van der Pligt, 1988, Chapter 7). Managers may seek to change the attitudes of colleagues and subordinates on issues such as marketing strategy or work practices. It should be noted that such attempts are ultimately aimed at changing behaviour, and/or the behavioural component of attitudes. The connection between attitudes and behaviour is examined further in the section on 'Attitudes and behaviour'. Now, however, let us examine some of the factors that determine the success or otherwise of attempts by one person to change the attitudes of another. Most of this material is drawn from social psychology. It is important to remember that attempts to change people's attitudes to something they experience personally and often (such as work) solely through verbal persuasion are unlikely to be successful.

Communicator credibility

The credibility of a communicator rests partly on his or her expertness and trustworthiness as perceived by the person on the receiving end of the communication (Hovland and Weiss, 1951). Expertness concerns how much the communicator knows about the subject of the communication. Trustworthiness usually depends mainly on whether the communicator has a record of honesty, and on whether he or she appears to be arguing against his or her own interests (Eagly *et al.*, 1978). For example, although BAT (the British American Tobacco Company) would be low in credibility if it argued that there was no relationship between smoking and lung cancer, it would have great credibility if it argued that smoking definitely leads to lung cancer. This highlights the fact that credibility depends not only on the communication source, but also on the particular issue and arguments presented.

However, the picture is not quite so simple. Sometimes a low-credibility communicator has as much persuasive effect as a high-credibility one – but not immediately; not until a few weeks later. This has been termed the *sleeper effect*, and is thought to be due to the person remembering the message but forgetting the source (Cook *et al.*, 1979). So there is hope even for unpopular politicians and propagandists!

Communicator attractiveness

Tannenbaum (1956) and others since have found that the amount of attitude change is directly related to the degree of attractiveness of the change agent. In Tannenbaum's work, the attractiveness of the communicator was measured through the use of the semantic-differential technique. The ratings of the subjects on the following six evaluation scales were obtained: fair–unfair, dirty–clean, tasty–distasteful, good–bad, pleasant–unpleasant, worthless–valuable. The power of attractiveness may well rest on the desire of the message receiver to be like the communicator. There is also some evidence that attractiveness is especially useful when the message is likely to be unpopular (Eagly and Chaiken, 1975), though its power can be undone if the communicator is perceived to be deliberately exploiting his or her attractiveness.

Key Learning Point

The perceived integrity, expertise and attractiveness of the communicator of a persuasive message partly determine whether the recipients of the message are persuaded by it.

One-sided versus two-sided arguments

Is it better to give both sides of an argument (though portraying the favoured one more convincingly), or is a one-sided message more persuasive? This issue was first examined by Yale University researchers many years ago (Hovland *et al.*, 1949) in their studies of training and indoctrination films used by the American armed forces during the Second World War. One-sided and two-sided communications were used to evaluate the effectiveness of messages in convincing the soldiers that a long, hard war was likely with Japan. They found:

■ That the two-sided presentation was more effective for men who initially held the opposite opinion that the war with Japan would be a short one (less than two years). For men who initially favoured the position of the communication (that war would last longer than two years) the one-sided presentation was more effective. This finding was subsequently replicated in a study by McGinnies (1966).

■ That better educated men were influenced less by the one-sided than by the two-sided presentation. Thus, persons who value their own independence of judgement and their own intellectual competence may view the acceptance of a one-sided communication as incompatible with maintaining self-esteem.

More recent research has suggested some reasons why one-sided or two-sided arguments might be more effective in different situations. For example, a number of studies have indicated that one-sided arguments may allow the individual more time to contemplate the arguments they receive (Chattopadhyay and Alba, 1988).

This may be necessary to persuade people with limited cognitive ability and/or low familiarity with the issues. Also, as Tesser and Shaffer (1990) have contended, 'perhaps the need to decide the relative merits of two sides of an unfamiliar issue leads people to concentrate on receiving the message at the expense of thinking about its implications in detail'.

Use of fear

Is the use of threat effective in changing attitudes? Janis and Feshbach (1953) studied the effects of different intensities of fear-arousing messages in an illustrated lecture on dental hygiene. They found that change in attitude and behaviour tended to be greater when intensity of fear arousal was fairly low. Of subjects exposed to the mild fear appeal, 36 per cent followed the recommendations (e.g. tooth-brushing) of the lecture, but only 8 per cent of those who heard the high-fear lecture did so.

Subsequent research has shown that moderate amounts of fear increase the effectiveness with which people process information, but high amounts of fear tend to immobilise them (Jepson and Chaiken, 1990). The amount of fear depends not only on how scary the message is, but also on how optimistic a person is about his or her ability to deal with the threat described in it. This is in line with Rogers and Prentice-Dunn's (1997) *protection motivation theory*, which proposes that attempts to induce fear will be successful in changing behaviour when they convince a person that:

■ the problem is serious;

■ the problem may affect the person;

■ he or she can avoid the problem by taking certain specific action;

■ he or she is capable of performing the behaviour required to avoid the problem.

This bears some resemblance to expectancy theory of motivation (*see* Chapter 9). Protection motivation theory has received considerable support in research (e.g. Mulilis and Lippa, 1990). But offering reliable strategies to avoid the feared fate is often difficult. Many insurance companies present fear-arousing messages (e.g. about having a disabling accident), and then suggest that buying one of their insurance policies is an effective strategy. They forget that, for most people, monetary reward neither avoids such an occurrence nor fully compensates for it.

Social pressures in persuasion

Requiring people to commit themselves publicly to a change in attitude has long been used by change agents (Kiesler, 1971). One might term this requirement the 'Billy Graham effect'. If people make their stand public, they will be less likely to change their position as a result of persuasion in the opposite direction. This is demonstrated by various religious groups that encourage public commitments in the hope of preventing public reconversion or a lapse in faith. As Krech *et al.* (1962) noted, 'Public commitment has been found to be an effective procedure; private commitment has been found to be ineffective'.

Research on group decision-making (*see* Chapter 12) has sought to explain why groups tend to arrive at more extreme positions than those initially held by the individual members of the group, an effect that has been labelled *group polarisation*. It seems that people are persuaded to adopt more extreme positions by hearing arguments that they regard as both valid and novel (Isenberg, 1986). As Turner (1991, pp. 67–72) pointed out, though, it is likely that attitudes are also changed by repeated exposure to arguments that people have heard before and that are therefore not novel to them. For example, Arkes *et al.* (1991) showed that simply repeating a statement causes it to be judged more true by those who hear it. It is also possible that *social comparison processes* play a part. If a member of a group hears other group members advocating a certain position, he or she may draw two conclusions: first, that this position is socially acceptable, and second, that 'anything (s)he can do, I can do better', leading the person to adopt a position more extreme than the one he or she has just heard.

Wood (2000) has emphasised that attitude change that occurs as a result of social pressures is not necessarily superficial and temporary. One might expect that it would be, because a person might appear to conform for the sake of good relations with other people. On the other hand, we are often required to justify ourselves in public, and this tends to make us think carefully about our attitudes, and thus become more certain about what they are (Cowan and Hodge, 1996). This is one of many lines of argument which suggest that a person's attitudes at work are likely to be influenced by those of people around them. Attitudes and attitude change are truly social phenomena.

Key Learning Point

The social context in which the persuasive message is received can affect the extent to which it is successful.

Events before the persuasive message

If the recipients of a persuasive message have been forewarned about that message, they are more likely to resist it if they feel threatened or demeaned by that attempt. Generally, people tense up (both physically and psychologically) if they are led to expect a challenge (Cacioppo and Petty, 1979). But if the recipients are already amenable to being persuaded, forewarning can soften them up, and perhaps produce some attitude change even before they have heard the arguments (Hass, 1975).

Another relevant factor concerns what has sometimes been called inoculation. Some attitudes are widely held in our society. For example, it is commonly believed that fresh fruit is good for you. Such beliefs are never challenged or questioned, or only very rarely. In some classic research, McGuire and Papageorgis (1961) found that it was easier to change attitudes that had not earlier been challenged than those that had. Challenge leads the recipient to think of reasons why he or she was correct all along (Pfau, 1997). These reasons act as 'antibodies' against subsequent attempts at persuasion.

Overview of attitude change: central versus peripheral routes to persuasion

Petty and Cacioppo (1985) made a distinction between the central route to persuasion (which involves careful thought and weighing up of arguments) and the peripheral route, which relies more on emotional responses but relatively little thought. They argued that attitude change through the central route is longer lasting and more closely associated with behaviour than that through the peripheral route. Chaiken (1987) came up with a similar distinction between systematic and heuristic processing of information.

Persuasive messages processed through the central route need to contain strong arguments that stand up to scrutiny. People who enjoy thinking, are able to concentrate, feel involvement in the issues in question and feel personally responsible for evaluating the message are most likely to process persuasive messages by the central route. For them, the fate of the persuasive message depends more on their weighing up of the arguments than simply remembering those arguments (Cacioppo and Petty, 1989), though the latter is also important when evaluating two-sided messages (Chattopadhyay and Alba, 1988; *see also* the section on 'One-sided versus two-sided arguments', above). A persuasive message that accurately targets the *function* served by the relevant attitude for the recipient of the message is likely to succeed. For example, someone who cares about the social consequences of his or her actions is more likely to respond to a persuasive message emphasising the social acceptability of the new point of view than to one which stresses how it will help make them wealthy (Lavine and Snyder, 1996).

Peripheral processing of information occurs when the recipient of the persuasive message is unwilling or unable to pay it very much attention. When this is the case, the strength of the arguments matters less, and peripheral cues matter more, in determining the success or otherwise of the attempt at attitude change. These peripheral cues include communicator attractiveness and expertise, sheer length of the message (irrespective of the quality of its content), and reactions of other recipients of the message (*see*, for example, Wood and Kallgren, 1988). It seems that peripheral processing is likely when the recipient of the message is in a good mood. Good moods seem to reduce the extent to which messages are critically examined, and weak arguments are sometimes as convincing as strong ones (Eagly and Chaiken, 1992).

Key Learning Point

How persuasive a message is depends partly on which cognitive processes are used by the recipient when thinking about it.

Clearly the distinction between central and peripheral processing is important for those who wish to change the attitudes of others. It gives some guidance about which aspects of the message, its contents and its context are important to different audiences in different situations. Whatever the route, though, it is worth remembering that persuasive messages can focus either on changing the attitude or on changing the definition and meaning of the attitude object (Wood, 2000). Changing the meaning will often automatically change the evaluation. For example, Bosveld *et al.*, (1997) found that people adopted a more favourable attitude to 'affirmative action' in the workplace when it was presented in terms of equal opportunity rather than actively favouring minorities.

Exercise 7.2	Were you persuaded?

Try to think of a recent occasion when someone tried to persuade you to change your attitude to something or someone. It might have been a friend attempting to change your attitude to someone you both know, or a place such as a nightclub or bar. It might have been a politician making a speech. It could even have been an advertiser.

To what extent were the following statements true for this persuasion attempt? (Refer to the text if you are not sure what some of them mean.)

- The persuader had credibility.
- The persuader was attractive to me.
- The persuader used two-sided arguments.
- The persuader tried to frighten me.
- There was pressure from others to change my mind.

How successful was the attempt to persuade you, and why? If you think it was successful, how is your *behaviour* different now?

Attitudes and behaviour

It could be argued that attitudes only matter if they influence actual behaviour. For example, racial prejudice in the workplace is damaging to the extent that it finds expression in discrimination or other negative behaviour towards minority groups. To what extent do attitudes predict behaviour? The answer based on an early review of the research evidence seemed to be 'not very much' (Wicker, 1969). People's avowed feelings and beliefs about someone or something seemed only very loosely related to how they behaved towards that person or object. If true, this would mean that people who say they like their job do not necessarily work harder or better, work longer hours, or relate better to customers than people who say they do not like their job. It would also mean that all the many attitude surveys conducted in workplaces were a waste of time.

A number of possible reasons were suggested for this lack of correspondence. One was social pressures of various kinds: laws, societal norms and the views of specific people can all prevent a person behaving consistently with his or her attitudes. So can other attitudes, limitations on a person's abilities, and, indeed, a person's general activity levels. There was also some suggestion that the research on this issue was badly designed, and therefore failed to find correspondence that did in fact exist between attitudes and behaviour. In particular, it was argued that measures of attitude were often general (e.g. attitudes about law-breaking) whereas measures of behaviour were specific, reflecting only one of many elements of the attitude (e.g. committing motoring offences). Also, behaviour was assessed on only one occasion or over a short time period. Longer-term assessments of multiple instances of the behaviour would be a fairer test of whether attitudes predict behaviour.

In the article referred to earlier, Pratkanis and Turner (1994) summarised observations from earlier research and added some of their own in discussing when the link between attitudes and behaviour is likely to be strong. Here are four of the factors they suggest will increase the correspondence between attitudes and behaviour:

1   When the object of the attitude is both well-defined and salient. An example of a poorly defined object would be where a person was not sure whether his or her immediate supervisor should be classed as a member of management. This would make it uncertain whether that person's attitudes to management would affect his or her behaviour towards the supervisor. Salience concerns the extent to which the object of the attitude is perceived as relevant to the situation at hand.

2   When attitude strength is high – that is, when the attitude comes easily to mind.

3   When knowledge supporting the attitude is plentiful and complex. This increases a person's certainty about what he or she thinks, as well as his or her ability to act effectively towards the object of the attitude.

4   When the attitude supports important aspects of the self. For example, an accountant may have positive attitudes towards other accountants because he or she believes that accountants (and therefore by extension himself or herself) perform an important role in the national economy.

Key Learning Point

The lack of correspondence between attitudes and behaviour found in much research is partly due to poor research design, and partly to a neglect of cognitive processes concerning attitudes.

Ajzen and Fishbein (1980) developed a model of the relationship between attitudes and behaviour designed to overcome these difficulties. This model was called the *theory of reasoned action*. It assumed that actions are best predicted by intentions, and that intentions are in turn determined by a person's attitude and his or her perception of social pressure. The theory of reasoned action was then adapted by Ajzen and Madden (1986), and its name was changed to the *theory of planned behaviour* (Fig. 7.1). It now includes the concept of perceived behavioural control. This reflects the extent to which the person believes that he or she can perform the necessary behaviours in any given situation. It can affect both intention and the extent to which intention translates into actual behaviour.

Note that in the theory of planned behaviour, 'attitude' is defined in precise and rather unusual terms – it concerns beliefs and personal values about the consequences of a specific behaviour, and not general beliefs or feelings about an object or person. This is similar to expectancy theories of motivation (*see* Chapter 9). Note also that 'subjective norm' takes into account both the opinions of other people and the person's wish (or lack of it) to comply with those opinions. The theory of planned behaviour also acknowledges that people vary in the relative importance of attitude and subjective norm in determining their intentions. The theory has proved quite successful in predicting behaviour in a wide range of settings. However, relatively few of these directly concern work behaviour (though many concern consumer behaviour). This is perhaps an example of how work psychology sometimes neglects theoretical advances in social psychology.

Key Learning Point

The theory of planned behaviour takes ideas from cognitive theories of motivation in proposing that actions are the product of attitudes, social pressures and intentions. It is effective in explaining both intentions and actual behaviour.

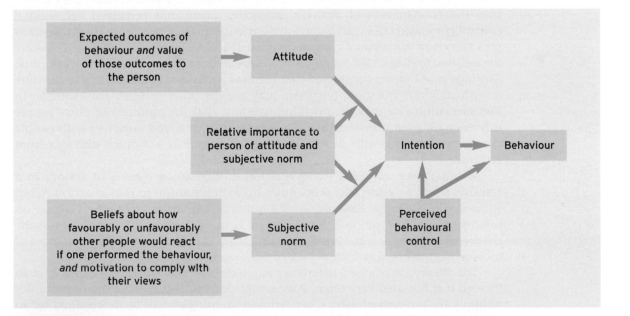

Figure 7.1	Theory of planned behaviour

Source: Reprinted from *Journal of Experimental Social Psychology*, 22, Ajzen, I. and Madden, J. T., 'Prediction of goal-directed behavior: attitudes, intentions, and perceived behavioral control', pp. 453-74, Copyright (1986), with permission from Elsevier

Ajzen (1991) has provided a thorough account of the theory of planned behaviour and research on it. He pointed out that, as the theory suggests, intentions to perform particular behaviours are often accurately predicted by attitudes towards the behaviour, subjective norms and perceived behavioural control. Also, intentions, together with perceived behavioural control, are quite good at predicting a person's actual behaviour. Ajzen also draws attention to some additional points. First, the relative importance of the various factors in predicting intention might be expected to vary with different behaviours and different situations, but little is known beyond this very general proposition about how particular situations/behaviours might exert such an influence. Second, perceived behavioural control really does matter – so the theory of planned behaviour is an improvement on the theory of reasoned action. But the usefulness of perceived behavioural control will be limited if the perception is wildly inaccurate. If a person believes that he or she is in control of a situation, but is mistaken, then no amount of belief will translate an intention into behaviour. Third, the influence of subjective norms on intentions and behaviour is often quite weak. Ajzen suggests that some people may be more responsive to their own perceptions of moral obligations than to the opinions of other people, at least in individualistic Western cultures. These observations suggest areas in which the theory of planned behaviour may be improved in future. Also, comparison of the theory of planned behaviour with material presented earlier in this chapter shows that it ignores factors such as the salience of the attitude and the extent to which it is supported by knowledge.

Recent reviews of the theory of planned behaviour by Ajzen (2001) and Armitage and Conner (2001) have reinforced many of the points already made. Armitage and Conner conducted a meta-analysis of tests of the theory. Based on a total sample of nearly a million people across many research studies, they found that the combination of attitude, subjective norm and perceived behavioural control correlated 0.63 with behavioural intention. They also found that intention plus perceived behavioural control correlated 0.52 with actual behaviour. These are impressive findings. Subjective norm appeared to be a relatively weak link. Armitage and Conner considered that this was partly due to a tendency to measure it with only one question, but there may also be other reasons. For example, in Western culture we may be unwilling to admit that the opinions of other people influence us, even if they really do. Also, we may surround ourselves with people who generally agree with us, so that subjective norm is not much different from attitude.

Another issue concerns the evaluation of alternative courses of action. In a research study, a person may score quire high on intention to pursue action A, but what we do not know (because we did not ask) is that they score even higher on intention to pursue action B. Finally, there is some considerable debate about the nature of perceived behavioural control. Is it, in effect, self-efficacy, or does it include external factors such as lack of opportunity?

The theory of planned behaviour can easily be used in the workplace, even though it is not used very often. For example, a person may have the opportunity to apply for promotion. His or her attitude to doing so will be determined by an assessment of the potential consequences of doing so (both good and bad), the probability that those consequences might include increased pay, a better car, a more interesting job, a requirement to work longer hours, and the risk of being turned down. For a person with fragile self-esteem and/or a concern about personal image, this last possibility might be extremely important. Subjective norm would reflect whether other people (for example partner and colleagues) thought it was a good idea to apply for promotion, and how much the person cared about their opinions. Perceived behavioural control should not be a problem, since it refers simply to the person's ability to apply for the promotion, not to do so effectively. And intention should lead fairly reliably to behaviour in this instance, unless for example the promotion opportunity is unexpectedly withdrawn.

Exercise 7.3   A lunchtime drink

Jerry Lander felt that there was nothing wrong with drinking a glass or two of beer during his lunchbreak. He could afford it easily enough. He claimed that he had never seen any evidence that a lunchtime drink harmed his work performance during the afternoon. He found that it helped him feel more relaxed and happy at work. Nevertheless, he could do without a drink without much difficulty if he had to. Jerry liked the friendship and approval of other people, and at lunchtime the nearby bar was full of acquaintances he could chat to. Work was an important part of Jerry's life and he was keen to gain promotion. Unfortunately his boss did not approve of alcoholic drink at lunchtime – or indeed at any other time. Nor did most of his colleagues, with whom he had to work closely. They seemed to view it as a sign of personal inadequacy.

Use the theory of planned behaviour to decide whether Jerry Lander is likely to drink a glass of beer during his lunchbreak on most working days.

So far in this chapter we have deliberately avoided discussing specific attitudes, in order to ensure that we cover the important general points. Now it is time to be more specific. We therefore conclude this chapter by looking at two concepts central to work psychology: job satisfaction and organisational commitment. The first concerns a person's evaluation and feelings about his or her job, while the second reflects how attached he or she is to the employing organisation. Both have been the subject of much research and practical interest over many years.

Job satisfaction

Job satisfaction has been seen as important for two main reasons. First, it is one indicator of a person's psychological well-being, or mental health. It is unlikely (though not impossible) that a person who is unhappy at work will be happy in general. So psychologists and others who are concerned with individuals' welfare are keen to ensure that high job satisfaction is experienced. Second, it is often assumed that job satisfaction will lead to motivation and good work performance. We have already noted that such connections between attitudes and behaviour do not necessarily occur. The link between job satisfaction and work performance is a good example of how it is often assumed that attitudes affect behaviour, but it is not easy to demonstrate that this is indeed the case.

What is job satisfaction?

Locke (1976) defined job satisfaction as a 'pleasurable or positive emotional state resulting from the appraisal of one's job or job experiences'. The concept generally refers to a variety of aspects of the job that influence a person's levels of satisfaction with it. These usually include attitudes toward pay, working conditions, colleagues and boss, career prospects and the intrinsic aspects of the job itself. Even as long ago as 1976, job satisfaction had been the topic of huge amounts of research. Locke found well over 3000 published studies.

Judge and Hulin (1993), among others, have suggested that in the field of job satisfaction there are three different approaches. The first is that work attitudes such as job satisfaction are dispositional in nature; that is, they are 'stable positive or negative dispositions learned through experience' (Griffin and Bateman, 1986; Staw *et al.*, 1986), or based on a person's genetic inheritance. If this was the case, job satisfaction might be considered more a personality characteristic than an attitude, and attempts to improve satisfaction by changing jobs would be doomed to failure. The second approach is the 'social information processing' model, which suggests that job satisfaction and other workplace attitudes are developed or constructed out of experiences and information provided by others at work (Salancik and Pfeffer, 1978; O'Reilly and Caldwell, 1985). In other words, at least in part, job satisfaction is a function of how other people in the workplace interpret and evaluate what goes on. The third approach is the information processing model, which is based on the accumulation of cognitive information about the workplace and one's job. In a sense, this is the most obvious approach – it argues that a person's job satisfaction is influenced directly by the characteristics of his or her job (Hackman and Oldham, 1976; *see also* Chapter 9), and the extent to which those characteristics match what that person wants in a job.

Key Learning Point

Job satisfaction can be seen in three ways – as a function of (i) a person's general personality or disposition; (ii) the opinions of other people in the person's workplace; or (iii) the features of a person's job.

Measuring job satisfaction

There have been many measures of job satisfaction in the workplace. Examples include the very widely used Job Description Index (JDI; Smith *et al.*, 1969), the Job Satisfaction Scales of Warr *et al.* (1979) and the job satisfaction scale of the Occupational Stress Indicator (OSI; Cooper *et al.*, 1987). They all involve questions or statements asking respondents to indicate what they think and/or feel about their job as a whole (so-called global satisfaction) and/or specific aspects of it, such as pay, work activities, working conditions, career prospects, relationship with superiors and relationships with colleagues (so-called facet satisfaction). Likert scaling (see earlier in this chapter) is usually employed. In Table 7.3 we provide an example of a measure of job satisfaction from the OSI, which contains all of the elements that usually make up a job satisfaction measure.

It is generally assumed in attitude measurement that it is better to ask lots of questions than only one. The argument is that this increases accuracy, for example by including many different facets of the attitude concerned and by avoiding the possibility that a careless response to a single question will mess everything up. However, Nagy (2002) has shown that having just one question to measure global

Table 7.3	A job satisfaction measure

How you feel about your job

Very much satisfaction	6	Much satisfaction	5
Some satisfaction	4	Some dissatisfaction	3
Much dissatisfaction	2	Very much dissatisfaction	1

1	Communication and the way information flows around your organisation	6 5 4 3 2 1
2	The relationships you have with other people at work	6 5 4 3 2 1
3	The feeling you have about the way you and your efforts are valued	6 5 4 3 2 1
4	The actual job itself	6 5 4 3 2 1
5	The degree to which you feel 'motivated' by your job	6 5 4 3 2 1
6	Current career opportunities	6 5 4 3 2 1
7	The level of job security in your present job	6 5 4 3 2 1
8	The extent to which you may identify with the public image or goals of your organisation	6 5 4 3 2 1
9	The style of supervision that your superiors use	6 5 4 3 2 1
10	The way changes and innovations are implemented	6 5 4 3 2 1
11	The kind of work or tasks that you are required to perform	6 5 4 3 2 1
12	The degree to which you feel that you can personally develop or grow in your job	6 5 4 3 2 1
13	The way in which conflicts are resolved in your company	6 5 4 3 2 1
14	The scope your job provides to help you achieve your aspirations and ambitions	6 5 4 3 2 1
15	The amount of participation which you are given in important decision-making	6 5 4 3 2 1
16	The degree to which your job taps the range of skills which you feel you possess	6 5 4 3 2 1
17	The amount of flexibility and freedom you feel you have in your job	6 5 4 3 2 1
18	The psychological 'feel' or climate that dominates your organisation	6 5 4 3 2 1
19	Your level of salary relative to your experience	6 5 4 3 2 1
20	The design or shape of your organisation's structure	6 5 4 3 2 1
21	The amount of work you are given to do, whether too much or too little	6 5 4 3 2 1
22	The degree to which you feel extended in your job	6 5 4 3 2 1

job satisfaction, and/or one question to measure each facet of job satisfaction, can be just as good. Nagy's point is that people generally know how satisfied they are, and do not need a whole set of questions to express this.

Taber and Alliger (1995) have investigated the extent to which overall job satisfaction can be thought of as the total or average of people's opinions about each task in their job. They asked over 500 employees of a US medical college to describe the tasks of their job, and to rate each task according to its importance, complexity, level of supervision, level of concentration required, how much they enjoyed it, and the amount of time spent on it each week. Taber and Alliger found that the percentage of time spent in enjoyable tasks correlated 0.40 with satisfaction with the work itself, and 0.28 with global job satisfaction. The importance of the task, closeness of supervision and concentration required did not have much impact on job satisfaction. The correlations show that the accumulation of enjoyment across the various tasks involved in the job did, not surprisingly, say something about overall job satisfaction. But the correlations were also low enough to indicate that other factors also matter. As the authors noted (p. 118):

> Perhaps workers form a gestalt – a perception of pattern – about their jobs that is not a simple linear function of task enjoyment ... a worker might perform 15 different enjoyable tasks; nevertheless, the worker's global job satisfaction still could be low if the 15 tasks were so unrelated to one another that the total job was not meaningful, or did not relate clearly to the mission of the organization.

The coverage of attitudes earlier in this chapter suggests that job satisfaction is likely to be used by people to help make sense of their work, and to define who they are, or are not. So in a brief reply to Taber and Alliger, Locke (1995) pointed out that job satisfaction will depend partly on how well people's tasks fit their long-term purposes, how much their self-esteem depends on their job and which job experiences are processed most thoroughly in their memory. One could add that the opinions of others, as discussed by O'Reilly and Caldwell (1985), will also influence a person's overall feelings about his or her job.

Key Learning Point

Job satisfaction is more than how much the person enjoys the job tasks. It also depends on how important the job is to the person, and how well it fits in with his or her long-term aims.

Another issue, particularly for global organisations, is whether questionnaire measures of job satisfaction (or indeed anything else) travel well across cultures. Possible problems are that translations between languages are imperfect, that people in different countries understand the same words in the questions (e.g. 'stress') in different ways, and that they interpret response scale options such as 'quite' or 'often' in different ways. These problems are difficult to identify, let alone solve, but they might matter to managers who want to know, for example, whether employees working in a factory in one country are more satisfied than those in a factory in another country. Ryan *et al.* (1999) give an example, using complex statistics, of how some of the problems of comparing across cultures can be investigated. They found only relatively minor differences between data obtained from employees of one large company in the United States, Spain, Mexico and Australia.

Causes and consequences of job satisfaction

The major determinants of job satisfaction seem to derive from all three of the theoretical approaches identified earlier. Thus, regarding the job itself, for most people the major determinants of global job satisfaction derive from the intrinsic features of the work itself. These are most commonly based on the Hackman and Oldham (1976) core constructs of skill variety, task identity, task significance, autonomy and feedback (*see also* Chapter 9). Hackman and Oldham (1976) defined their constructs as:

- *skill variety*: the extent to which the tasks require different skills;

- *task identity*: the extent to which the worker can complete a 'whole' piece of work, as opposed to a small part of it;

- *task significance*: the extent to which the work is perceived as influencing the lives of others;

- *autonomy*: the extent to which the worker has freedom within the job to decide how it should be done;

- *feedback*: the extent to which there is correct and precise information about how effectively the worker is performing.

In addition, as Griffin and Bateman (1986) observed, 'in general, most studies find significant and positive correlations between leader behaviours such as initiating structure and consideration, and satisfaction'. So leader behaviour is also important in satisfaction at work. Of course, it is also possible that job satisfaction causes job perceptions. People who are satisfied may be given the more interesting tasks to do by their bosses, and/or they may optimistically rate their job more favourably than those who are dissatisfied. Wong *et al.* (1998) collected data over a two-year period and found both that perceived job characteristics lead to job satisfaction and vice versa.

Other social factors have more subtle influences on job satisfaction, as predicted by the social information processing approach. For example, Agho *et al.* (1993) found that perceptions of distributive justice (the fairness with which rewards were distributed in the organisation) predicted job satisfaction. O'Reilly and Caldwell (1985) demonstrated that both task perceptions and job satisfaction of workers were influenced by the opinions of others in their workgroups.

Of particular interest to researchers has been whether the saying 'A happy worker is a productive worker' is true. Work and organisational psychologists have usually examined this in the form of whether job satisfaction (happiness) correlates with work performance (productivity). For some years the general consensus was that there was little connection. Iaffaldano and Muchinsky (1985) conducted a meta-analysis and found a mean correlation of 0.17, which is pretty low. But Judge *et al.* (2001) have pointed out several things that were wrong with Iaffaldano and Muchinsky's analysis. They conducted an up-to-date reanalysis and discovered that the mean correlation corrected for measurement unreliability between job satisfaction and job performance was 0.30. As they point out, this still is not huge but is comparable to correlations between some of the more valid employment selection techniques and job performance. Correlations tended to be highest for complex jobs, i.e. those requiring a range of skills.

Of course, demonstrating that two variables are correlated is not the same as demonstrating that one *causes* the other. Judge *et al.* (2001) identify six possible reasons why job satisfaction and job performance might be related. These are shown and briefly explained in Fig. 7.2. The last of the six abandons the usual pattern of treating job satisfaction as the measure of happiness and reflects the idea we have already explored that job satisfaction may partly reflect a person's disposition. This has both an advantage and a disadvantage. The advantage is that it recognises that job satisfaction is only one aspect of happiness. The disadvantage is that it risks repeating the old problem in attitude–behaviour research of having one measure (happiness) that is more general than the other (job performance). Wright and Staw (1999) reported two studies in social services settings that strongly suggest that people's characteristic tendency to experience positive emotion (i.e. happiness) does predict their subsequent work performance as assessed by supervisory ratings. What is more, the characteristic tendency is a better predictor of performance than mood. So all in all it is beginning to look as if happy workers do tend to be productive workers after all, and it may be that they are productive *because* they are happy.

Key Learning Point

Happiness and productivity have often been investigated using measures of job satisfaction and work performance. Contrary to earlier evidence, there does seem to be a tendency for happy/satisfied people to have higher work performance/productivity than unhappy/dissatisfied people.

The dispositional approach to job satisfaction has also received some support. That is, there is some evidence that some people are simply more satisfied than others by their nature. In a review of research, Arvey *et al.* (1991) suggested that somewhere between 10 per cent and 30 per cent of the variation in job satisfaction depends on genetic factors. They argued that 'there is less variability in job satisfaction between genetically identical people [i.e. identical twins] who hold different jobs than there is among genetically unrelated people who hold the same job' (p. 374). However, it is difficult to be sure about what proportion of job satisfaction is a function of a person's disposition. Most research has construed it as what is left over when situational factors have been considered. But this assumes that all of the important situational factors have been taken into account – surely an optimistic assumption. According to Judge and Hulin (1993), research has also tended to use small samples and/or data originally collected for other purposes,

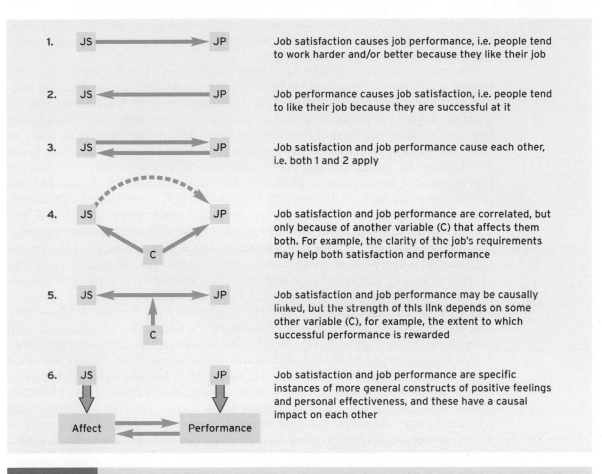

| Figure 7.2 | **Some possible relationships between job satisfaction (JS) and job performance (JP)** *Source:* **Adapted from Judge *et al.* Copyright © 2001 by the American Psychological Association. Adapted with permission** |

and has been unclear about what aspects of a person's disposition might be expected to affect his or her job satisfaction.

Judge and Hulin (1993) obtained data from 255 people working in medical clinics, and for 160 of them they also got the opinions of other individuals who knew them well. The researchers wanted to examine the linkages between affective disposition (that is, a person's tendency to feel positive or negative about life), subjective well-being (how they feel about life right now), job satisfaction and job characteristics. Their data were most consistent with the causal model shown in Fig. 7.3. Affective disposition not surprisingly had a substantial effect upon subjective well-being. That is, a person's tendency to take an optimistic and happy approach to life influenced how optimistic and happy he or she felt day to day. Subjective well-being (and therefore, indirectly, affective disposition) had a substantial impact on job satisfaction, and job satisfaction had almost as much effect upon subjective well-being. Intrinsic job characteristics affected job satisfaction, as one would expect, but scarcely more strongly than subjective well-being. The research of Judge and Hulin suggests: (i) the nature of the job really does matter for job satisfaction; (ii) so, indirectly, does a person's disposition; and (iii) job satisfaction has an impact on more general well-being – work does spill over, psychologically, into other areas of life.

Dormann and Zapf (2001) have reported findings that emphasise that the impact of a person's disposition on his or her job satisfaction is indeed largely indirect. They reviewed studies reported up to September 1997 and found that, on average, people's job satisfaction on one occasion was quite highly correlated (about 0.5) with their job satisfaction on a later occasion (on average, three years later). In their own study of people in the Dresden area of Germany, Dormann and Zapf found a correlation for job satisfaction over 5 years of 0.26 among people who changed jobs during that time. However, when they statistically adjusted for changes in those people's job characteristics, the stability of job satisfaction scores fell virtually to zero. They interpreted this as meaning that people's disposition leads them to seek and find jobs of certain kinds, and that the nature of these jobs affects job satisfaction.

Another angle on the idea that job satisfaction is more a feature of the person than the job is expressed in research on sex differences in job satisfaction. A number of studies have, for example, found that on average women's job satisfaction is lower than men's. This has fuelled stereotypical views of women as being less interested and involved in work than men. Often this is assumed to be because women's earnings are, or have been, the subsidiary income of the household, whereas men tend to be the main breadwinners. On the other hand, a less often considered possibility is that women might be less satisfied simply because they tend to have less good jobs than men. Indeed, this was what Lefkowitz (1994) found. Lefkowitz obtained a diverse sample of 371 men and 361 women from nine organisations. As predicted, men scored significantly higher on average than women on work satisfaction and pay satisfaction. However, these differences disappeared when variables such as actual income, occupational status, level of education and age were held constant.

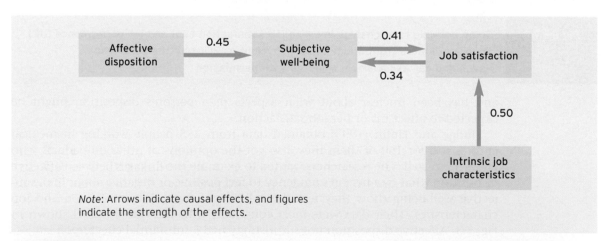

Note: Arrows indicate causal effects, and figures indicate the strength of the effects.

Figure 7.3　**A causal model of job satisfaction**
Source: Reprinted from *Organizational Behavior and Human Decision Processes*, 56, Judge, T. A. and Hulin, C. L., 'Job satisfaction as a reflection of disposition: a multiple source causal analysis', pp. 388-421, Copyright (1993), with permission from Elsevier

Does job satisfaction change over the lifespan?

Some research has suggested that job satisfaction tends to increase fairly steadily through working life. If accurate, this could be for a variety of reasons. First, older people may be in objectively better jobs than younger ones, since they have had longer to find a job that suits them. Second, older people may have lowered their expectations over the years, so that they are more easily satisfied. Third, older people might always have been more satisfied than younger ones – a so-called *cohort effect*. Fourth, dissatisfied older people may be more likely than younger ones to opt for early retirement or voluntary redundancy, so that those remaining in employment represent a biased sample of older people. In the most thorough recent study of the relationship between job satisfaction and age, Clarke *et al.* (1996) found in a sample of over 5000 UK employees that job satisfaction started fairly high in a person's teens, then dipped in the 20s and 30s, then rose through the 40s (back to teenage levels) and further in the 50s and 60s. After controlling for various factors, Clarke *et al.* reckoned that, on average, job satisfaction bottomed-out at age 36. The dip and subsequent rise were more marked for men than for women. Because the study was cross-sectional, the researchers were, however, unable to rule out any of the first three possible explanations described above.

Key Learning Point

Job satisfaction is partly determined by a person's general disposition, but not so much so that it is constant over a person's working life.

Organisational commitment

What is organisational commitment?

The concept of organisational commitment has generated huge amounts of research from the 1980s onwards. This is no doubt partly because it is what some employers say they want from employees – organisational commitment is a managerial agenda to a greater extent than job satisfaction. In recent years particularly, this can be seen as exceptionally one-sided: as Hirsh *et al.* (1995) have pointed out, what some employers now appear to want is totally committed but totally expendable staff. Exactly *why* employers should want committed staff is less obvious, partly because, as we shall see below, commitment does not guarantee high work performance.

Organisational commitment has been defined by Mowday *et al.* (1979) as 'the relative strength of an individual's identification with and involvement in an organisation'. This concept is often thought to have three components (Griffin and Bateman, 1986): (i) a desire to maintain membership in the organisation, (ii) belief in and acceptance of the values and goals of the organisation, and (iii) a willingness to exert effort on behalf of the organisation. If a person is committed to an organisation, therefore, he or she has a strong identification with it, values membership, agrees with its objectives and value systems, is likely to remain in it, and, finally, is prepared to work hard on its behalf. More recently, it has also been suggested that commitment will lead to so-called organisational citizenship behaviours, such as helping out others and being particularly conscientious.

Some work psychologists have divided organisational commitment slightly differently from the way described above. For example, Allen and Meyer (1990a) have distinguished between the following:

- *Affective commitment*: essentially concerns the person's emotional attachment to his or her organisation.

- *Continuance commitment*: a person's perception of the costs and risks associated with leaving his or her current organisation. There is considerable evidence that there are two aspects of continuance commitment: the personal sacrifice that leaving would involve, and a lack of alternatives available to the person.

- *Normative commitment*: a moral dimension, based on a person's felt obligation and responsibility to his or her employing organisation.

There is good evidence for the distinctions between these forms of commitment (Dunham *et al.*, 1994). Interestingly, they approximate respectively to the affective, behavioural and cognitive components of attitudes identified at the start of this chapter.

Other observers have pointed out that people feel multiple commitments at work – not only to their organisation, but also perhaps to their location, department, work group or trade union (Reichers, 1985; Barling *et al.*, 1990). There is also a wider issue here: what exactly *is* the organisation? Complexities such as parent companies and franchises can make it difficult to identify exactly which organisation one belongs to. But more than that, some psychologists (e.g. Coopey and Hartley, 1991) have been critical of the whole notion of organisational commitment because it implies that the organisation is unitarist – that is, it is one single entity with a united goal. A moment's thought reveals that most organisations consist of various factions with somewhat different and possibly even contradictory goals. Faced with these ambiguities, it seems that most people think of the term organisation as meaning top management. This is clearly different from commitment to (for example) one's supervisor or work group, which employees may also feel (Becker and Billings, 1993). Further, it is possible to distinguish between (yet more!) different bases of commitment to the various constituencies in an organisation. Two such bases are identification and internalisation. As Becker *et al.* (1996, p. 465) have put it:

> Identification occurs when people adopt attitudes and behaviours in order to be associated with a satisfying, self-defining relationship with another person or group ... Internalization occurs when people adopt attitudes and behaviours because their content is congruent with their value systems.

Key Learning Point

Organisational commitment concerns a person's sense of attachment to his or her organisation. It has several components, and is only one of a number of commitments a person may feel.

Measuring organisational commitment

A number of questionnaires have been developed to measure the various aspects or theories of commitment discussed above. For example, a widely used scale is the Organisational Commitment Questionnaire (OCQ), which was developed by Mowday *et al.* (1979). It is a 15-item questionnaire which has been used as a total commitment scale, but has also been broken down into subscales by various researchers (Bateman and Strasser, 1984). The OCQ comprises items such as 'I feel very little loyalty to this organisation', 'I am willing to put in a great deal of effort beyond that normally expected in order to help this organisation be successful' and 'I really care about the fate of this organisation'. The OCQ was designed before the distinctions between affective, normative and continuance commitment were articulated in the literature. Subsequent research has clearly shown that the OCQ chiefly reflects affective commitment. There are other scales in use as well. For example, Warr *et al.* (1979) developed a nine-item scale. An example item is 'I feel myself to be part of the organisation'. This measure also tends to concentrate on affective commitment. Allen and Meyer (1990a) have developed their own questionnaire measure of affective, normative and continuance commitment, with each of the three components assessed by eight items. Although not perfect, this measure has stood up well to psychometric scrutiny, and is now commonly used. There are also plenty of other questionnaire measures designed to measure other components and concepts of commitment.

All the commonly used measures of commitment are self-report: that is, a person indicates how committed he or she is. In many ways this makes good sense. After all, the person is in the best position to comment on his or her own commitment. Yet perhaps we are biased. Perhaps other people could provide a more dispassionate view of how committed we are. Goffin and Gellatly (2001) found that self-ratings of commitment were only moderately correlated with ratings given by supervisors and work colleagues. In line with much other research on self *vs* other ratings, ratings of people's commitment made by their supervisors and colleagues were more similar to each other than either was to self-ratings. This suggests that an external perspective is providing something over and above self-perceptions. It is also likely that the word commitment means different things to different people. Singh and Vinnicombe (2000) have shown that, for many people, it has more to do with taking a creative and assertive approach to one's work than with involvement in and loyalty to one's employing organisation.

Key Learning Point

Like job satisfaction, organisational commitment is usually measured with questionnaires using Likert scaling.

Causes and consequences of organisational commitment

Much research has investigated how organisational commitment relates to other experiences, attitudes and behaviour at work. This is discussed below. Some of this has presented quite complex models indicating causal connections between commitment, satisfaction, motivation, job characteristics and other variables (see, for example, Eby *et al.*,1999). Figure 7.4 represents our attempt to summarise what is known, and what seems likely.

As with job satisfaction, there are several distinct theoretical approaches to organisational commitment. One of these, the behavioural approach, sees commitment as being created when a person does things publicly, of his or her own free will, and that would be difficult to undo (Kiesler, 1971). Rather like Bem's (1972) self-perception approach, it is suggested that people examine their own behaviour and conclude that since they did something with significant consequences in full view of others, when they could have chosen not to do so, they really must be committed to it. So if a person freely chooses to join an organisation, and subsequently performs other committing behaviours (e.g. voluntarily working long hours), he or she will feel more committed to it. This is a neat theory and there is a certain amount of evidence in favour of it (Mabey, 1986).

More commonly, however, it has been suggested that people's commitment can be fostered by giving them positive experiences. This reflects a kind of social exchange approach. The person is essentially saying 'if this work organisation is nice to me, I will be loyal and hardworking'. Many researchers have tried to identify exactly which pleasant experiences matter most for organisational commitment. On the whole, it seems that factors intrinsic to the job (e.g. challenge, autonomy) are more important in fostering commitment than extrinsic factors such as pay and working conditions (Mathieu and Zajac, 1990; Arnold and Mackenzie Davey, 1999). This seems especially true for the affective component of commitment (i.e. commitment based on emotional attachment). On the other hand, continuance commitment (that is, the extent to which leaving would be costly for the person) is more influenced by the person's perception of his or her past contributions to the organisation and present likely attractiveness (or lack of it) to other employers (Meyer *et al.*, 1989). Finegan (2000) reported an interesting study of how organisational values might affect commitment. The extent to which the organisation was perceived to value 'humanity' (e.g courtesy, fairness) and 'vision' (e.g initiative, openness) was correlated with affective commitment, while the value of 'convention' (e.g cautiousness) was correlated with continuance commitment.

But there is also some suggestion that commitment is partly a function of the person rather than what happens to him or her at work (Bateman and Strasser,

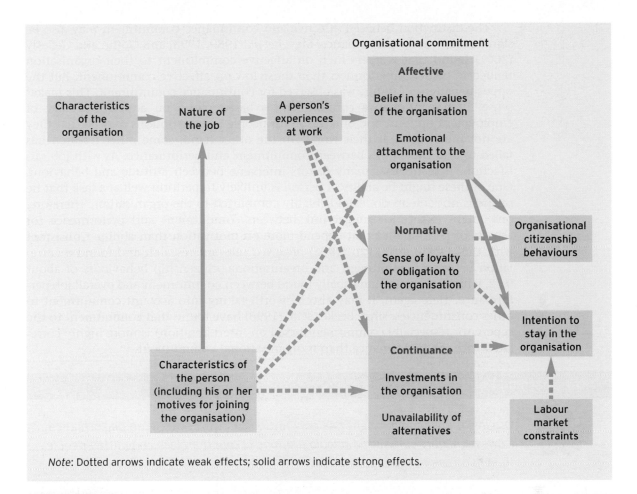

Organisational commitment

Figure 7.4   A model of organisational commitment

1984). That is, perhaps some people are, through their personality or disposition, more prone to feel committed than others, just as some seem more likely than others to feel satisfied with their job. Given the research on job satisfaction, that looks like a reasonable proposition. However, research on organisational commitment has not yet gone down that route.

Key Learning Point

It is usually assumed that organisational commitment is fostered by positive experiences at work, and to a lesser extent by the circumstances in which the person joined the organisation. The possibility that some people may be more predisposed to be committed than others is less often investigated.

The distinction between affective and continuance commitment may also be significant for work performance. Meyer *et al.* (1989, 1993) and Goffin and Gellatly (2001) found that workers high on affective commitment to their organisation tended to be better performers than those low on affective commitment. But the opposite pattern of results was observed for continuance commitment. This makes sense: high continuance commitment is based partly on a perceived lack of employment options, and one reason for people lacking options may be that they are not much good at their work! On the other hand, some other research has failed to find these links between commitment and performance. As with job satisfaction, it seems that many factors intervene between attitude and behaviour. One of these might be ability. A person is unlikely to perform well at a task that he or she is not able to do, even if highly committed to the organisation. Therefore, one might expect a stronger link between commitment and performance for aspects of performance that depend more on motivation than ability. Consistent with this, Organ and Ryan (1995) reviewed relevant research and found a correlation between commitment and organisational citizenship behaviours of about 0.32, which is higher than usually found between commitment and overall job performance. Here again, it may also be worth taking into account commitment to other constituencies, since Becker *et al.* (1996) have found that commitment to the supervisor (especially commitment based on internalisation) is more highly correlated with job performance than is organisational commitment.

Key Learning Point

Organisational commitment has only loose links with overall job performance. However, highly committed people are more likely than less committed people to help others in the organisation.

As one would expect, a person who does not feel committed to his or her employing organisation is more likely to want to leave it, and actually to do so, than a person who feels more committed (Mathieu and Zajac, 1990). In fact, intention to leave the organisation is the strongest and most often reported correlate of low organisational commitment. This appears especially the case for affective commitment (Meyer, 1997). However, intention to leave does not necessarily translate into actual leaving. For example, if a person believes that it would be difficult to obtain another job (low perceived behavioural control in terms of the theory of planned behaviour), then low commitment is unlikely to lead him or her to leave the employing organisation. This once again illustrates how attitudes do not necessarily find expression in behaviour.

| Exercise 7.4 | Satisfaction and commitment |

Using your own experience of work, what factors most affect your job satisfaction? And what factors affect how committed you feel towards an employer? Are they the same things?

Consider the extent to which you think people can be 'made' more satisfied and/or committed by changing things in their work environment. In your experience, are some people just contented (or not) by nature, almost no matter what happens to them?

Summary

In this chapter we have taken a close look at attitudes. In particular, we have focused on what they are, how they can be measured, how they can be changed, and their links with behaviour. Like most social psychological phenomena, attitudes are more complicated than they seem at first sight. They have several different components which may or may not fit together nicely. Changing attitudes is difficult, but it is not impossible – and easier if the persuader is aware of research findings on attitude change. A person's attitudes may predict his or her behaviour quite well in some circumstances, if the right attitude is assessed, and if the person's perceptions of social pressures and his or her own capabilities are also taken into account. Two key work attitudes are job satisfaction and organisational commitment. Job satisfaction concerns a person's evaluation of his or her job, while organisational commitment refers to the extent to which a person feels attached to his or her employing organisation. They can both be measured satisfactorily, both are influenced by the nature of the person's job, and both appear to have quite complex connections with a range of behaviours and attitudes at work. However, they may both say more about whether a person stays in their employing organisation than about his or her job performance.

| Closing Case Study | Attitudes to Job Search |

Imagine that you are a careers adviser at a university or college. You have become concerned at the number of students who do not seem to start thinking about what they will do after graduation until well into their final year of study. You know that it usually takes at least six months to obtain a job, and sometimes a lot longer. You also know that while some graduates seem happy enough to be unemployed or doing casual work for some months after graduation, many others are not. They regret not having begun to plan for their future early enough.   ▶

You decide that you should try to change students' approach to planning for their future career. You decide to compose a handout of not more than 200 words which will be distributed to students during their penultimate year of study.

Suggested exercise

Using the information in this chapter, compose a handout of not more than 200 words designed to persuade students to start their career planning earlier. Let someone else read your handout. Ask them to tell you whether or not they find it persuasive, and why. Justify your wording of the handout to that person.

Test your learning

Short-answer questions

1 Define three aspects of an attitude.

2 Why are attitudes useful for a person?

3 Compare and contrast Likert and Thurstone attitude scaling.

4 List the features of the communicator of a persuasive message which affect the success of that message.

5 List the features of a persuasive message which affect the success of that message.

6 Draw a diagram to show the theory of planned behaviour, and define its key concepts.

7 Briefly describe three general phenomena that can influence job satisfaction.

8 Define organisational commitment and its component parts.

Suggested assignments

1 In what circumstances do attitudes determine behaviours at work?

2 Examine how much is known about what factors determine *either* job satisfaction *or* organisational commitment.

3 To what extent does the research evidence about organisational commitment suggest that managers in organisations should care about how committed their staff are?

Relevant websites

The Social Science Information Gateway (SOSIG) provides links to many sites about attitudes, and indeed to most other topics covered in this book. Go to http://www.sosig.ac.uk/ and try typing attitudes into the search box on that page. You will get brief descriptions of many sites concerned with attitudes in and out of the workplace. Many of these offer useful summaries or applications of attitude theory. For more specific items, try searching on work attitudes.

A good example of how public opinion survey companies work and present their findings can be found at http://www.mori.com/europe/index.shtml. This is MORI's summary of opinion surveys carried out recently about attitudes to Europe, mainly but not only about the UK population's attitudes toward aspects of the European Union.

Another example of commercial work on attitudes, this time regarding how office workers view the city they live in is available at http://www.cushmanwakefield. de/german/publikationen/marktberichte/de/working_in_europe_today.pdf.
Comparisons are made between eight different European cities. Notice the contrast between the straightforward descriptive data presented here and the analyses of data reported in psychological research articles. Notice also how the table showing how the eight cities compare can be interpreted in more than one way, according to whether you pay most attention to the proportion who strongly like their city, or to the proportion who either strongly or mildly like their city. You might wonder whether there are cultural differences in the way people respond to attitude surveys, as well as perhaps real differences between the cities.

For further self-test material and relevant, annotated weblinks please visit the website at http://www.booksites.net/arnold_workpsych.

Suggested further reading

Details of all the references are given in the list at the end of this book.

1   John Meyer's chapter in the 1997 *International Review of Industrial and Organizational Psychology* provides a very thorough analysis of the literature on organisational commitment.

2   Ajzen's 2001 article in the *Annual Review of Psychology* describes the influential theory of planned behaviour, as well as other research on how attitudes work. Not an especially easy read, but very informative about attitude theory.

3   The paper by Pratkanis and Turner in the journal *Human Relations* is an excellent example of how the study of attitudes has profited from the social cognitive tradition in psychology. Elements of the paper have been briefly summarised in this chapter.

4   Timothy Judge and colleagues have produced a very thorough examination of
     the nature of the relationship between job satisfaction and job performance
     in the journal *Psychological Bulletin*.

CHAPTER 8

The analysis and modification of work behaviour

LEARNING OUTCOMES

After studying this chapter, you should be able to:

1 describe the behaviourist view of psychology;

2 briefly summarise the two main types of conditioning in the behaviourist approach;

3 explain what is meant by reinforcement schedules and the reinforcement hierarchy;

4 explain what contiguity and contingency mean;

5 describe Luthans and Kreitner's five-step procedure for using OB Mod techniques;

6 state some of the rewards that might be used for reinforcement;

7 describe the effect on preceding behaviour of five different consequences;

8 state and define the main concepts involved in social cognitive theory.

Opening Case Study   Compensation Systems

There are four main types of reward programmes. First, salaries or wages are the regular payments people receive for their services while employed by a company. Second is bonus or incentive pay, based on the performance of the individual, business unit or company – commonly known as variable compensation. The amount depends on results and is not guaranteed. The difference between a stable salary and variable compensation varies widely.

Third, most organisations provide financial security or services for which people would normally have to pay themselves – known as benefits. Such services include health insurance, pensions and retirement benefits, and transport. They are not considered tools needed to do the job. Finally, companies are increasingly using formal recognition programmes to award individuals for achievements and special contributions. These awards usually take the form of certificates, public recognition, commendation letters or promotions. The value of these awards is largely symbolic, though this is not to minimise their importance.

Consider this example:

Two medium-sized service companies each had an annual goal-sharing programme for managers and employees. Payouts were based on the annual results of the entire organisation. Both achieved about the same results for the initial year of the programme.

In the first company, senior managers conducted a series of employee meetings. They discussed the company's annual results and the impact of these results on their customers and market position. They held open discussions of the challenges faced and what people did to overcome them. When it came time to make the awards, executives randomly passed out the envelopes containing each individual's cheque. They asked them to find the person who was named on the envelope and, as they handed over the envelope, tell them something they appreciated about what they had done during the year. For without the combined efforts of all individuals, managers said, there would be no cheques to distribute.

In the other company, better managers sent e-mails or held brief discussions with the employees about their bonus payments; most did nothing. Otherwise, bonuses were deposited directly into the individual's bank account. Little else was said.

What is the difference in the impact of these two approaches? What do you believe would be the value given to the bonus cheques in each case? Which approach provided the highest return on investment?

Source: 'Rewards that Work', by Tom Wilson, Financial Times, 5 November 2001

Introduction

This opening case study provides a clear illustration of the following three points. First, rewards are intended to be linked with past behaviour. Second, they are intended to influence future behaviour. Third, part of their impact may depend on social processes associated with their distribution. Behaviourist psychology has much to say about the first two of these points, whilst social learning theory helps us understand the last point (*see* Chapter 1 for more on behaviourist and social learning theory).

The scientific study of human *behaviour* has a central role in the development of psychological knowledge. The italics in the previous sentence stress the point that many believe the focus of attention in psychology should be on what people actually do, rather than what they may be thinking or feeling. Indeed, it is obviously extremely difficult to form an impression of what anyone thinks or feels without attending to their behaviour, whether the behaviour involved is their speech, speed of movement, facial expression or whatever. This focus on behaviour as the crucial unit of analysis is particularly important in work psychology. What people actually do at work is critical to organisational success, and it is no accident that the field of organisational *behaviour* has become an important area of research and study within business and management schools.

In the early 1980s Davis and Luthans (1980, p. 281) made the following comment:

> There is today a jungle of theories that attempt to explain human behaviour in organizations. Unfortunately, many of the theoretical explanations have seemed to stray from behaviour as the unit of analysis in organizational behaviour. There is a widespread tendency for both scholars and practitioners to treat such hypothetical constructs as motivation, satisfaction and leadership as ends in themselves. We think it is time to re-emphasize the point that behaviours are the empirical reality, not the labels attached to the attempted explanation of the behaviours.

The viewpoint that Davis and Luthans proposed is derived from the ideas of behaviourist psychology (e.g. Skinner, 1974). Behaviourist ideas have a long and influential history within psychology (*see* Chapter 1) and in many areas of applied psychological research and practice. In rudimentary terms, the behaviourist view argues that a satisfactory and useful science of psychology must be based on the observation and analysis of external, observable behaviour. Behaviourists argue that to focus attention on internal psychological processes that cannot be directly observed is both unscientific and unlikely to provide a coherent or systematic understanding of human behaviour. Thus, internal psychological states, processes, emotions, feelings and many other aspects of human subjective experience are rejected as topics for study. Instead, priority is given to an examination of behaviour, the external conditions in which the behaviour is exhibited and the observable consequences of behaviour. For some this represents a limited and restricting view of human psychology, but for behaviourists it represents a philosophically clear and practical view from which to develop an understanding of behaviour. As this chapter demonstrates, the research of the behaviourists has produced a variety of interesting ideas, many of which have been applied with enthusiasm and some success in organisational settings. In some areas of applied research, the pure form of behaviourism (which rejects any form of internal mental process as unscientific) has been diluted with the acceptance of ideas and techniques from other theoretical perspectives.

This chapter provides several examples of the use of behaviourist ideas in practice and also shows how behaviourist concepts may be incorporated into more general theories such as social cognitive theory (Bandura, 1977b, 1986) to produce useful organisational applications.

Key Learning Point

The behaviourist approach focuses on observable behaviour, not thoughts or feelings.

Conditioning and behaviour

The application of behaviourist ideas within organisations is explored later in this chapter, but first an outline of the major research findings and key concepts of behaviourism is provided (*see* Chapter 1 for a brief introduction to some of these). Two main types of conditioning provide the basis of the behaviourist approach: classical (respondent) conditioning and instrumental (operant) conditioning.

Classical conditioning

Classical conditioning is a simple but important form of learning first identified by the Russian physiologist Pavlov, who was studying the digestive and nervous system of dogs. He did in fact win a Nobel Prize in 1904 for this work, but it was a chance discovery resulting from this original research that earned him lasting fame. Like all dogs, the ones in Pavlov's laboratory would salivate when food was placed in their mouths. Pavlov noticed, however, that once the dogs had been in the laboratory for some time, the sight of their food dish arriving, or even the approaching footsteps of the attendant who fed them, would be enough to cause salivation. Pavlov recognised that the salivation that occurred in response to the dish or the attendant's footsteps involved some form of very basic learning on the part of the animals. After his initial observations, Pavlov went on to investigate the phenomenon in a controlled, experimental setting. He arranged for the amount of saliva produced by the dogs to be measured. Then he sounded a tone slightly before food was placed in the animals' mouths. After several trials it was found that the tone by itself would produce salivation; therefore the dogs had been conditioned to respond to the tone.

The general form of classical conditioning involves an unconditioned stimulus (UCS), such as food, which produces an automatic unconditioned response (UCR), such as salivation. Conditioning occurs when the unconditioned stimulus becomes associated with a conditioned stimulus (CS), such as a bell. In fact, classical conditioning is an extremely widespread phenomenon and it is clear that Pavlov had discovered something of considerable importance and generality. Although we can only guess at the scope and variety of phenomena that can be explained in terms of classical conditioning, such conditioning is often closely involved in our emotional or 'gut reaction' to various experiences. Many people experience strong emotional reactions to certain situations, often because in the past these have been paired with particularly vivid, painful or pleasant experiences. For example, some years ago one of the authors moved house and the deal almost fell through at the last minute. If it had done so, the author would have lost a lot of money. There was much consultation required with lawyers. Ever since then (but not before) the author feels a twinge of anxiety at the thought of meeting a lawyer, even if the meeting concerns a routine matter such as drawing up a will.

Exercise 8.1 — Classical conditioning of emotional responses

Review some of your own typical strong emotional reactions. For example, what makes you behave in an anxious or fearful way? Try to imagine how these reactions could have been established through classical conditioning.

In his original work Pavlov went on to pair other conditioned stimuli (e.g. a shape) with the tone. After several trials the dogs salivated to the shape alone. This procedure of introducing a second stimulus to which the organism can be conditioned to respond is known generally as higher-order conditioning. The specific example above would be referred to as second-order conditioning. Although Pavlov was only ever able to achieve third-order conditioning with his dogs, modern scientists accept that humans may be conditioned to higher orders. Such higher-order conditioning may play an important part in many of our emotional reactions.

Key Learning Point

Classical conditioning may help to explain some strong emotional reactions.

Operant conditioning

The idea that certain basic phenomena such as classical conditioning may be used to explain the behaviour of a range of organisms, from laboratory rats, pigeons or dogs to humans, is one of the mainstays of the behaviourist tradition. The behaviourists began their work in the hope that by studying simple forms of learning in simple animals, it would be possible to uncover the basic laws and principles of learning. These could then be generalised and used to explain human learning and behaviour.

The most famous contemporary behaviourist, B. F. Skinner, is often described as the most influential psychologist of the twentieth century. Skinner distinguished between two types of behaviour: respondent and operant. Respondent behaviour refers to the kind of behaviour shown during classical conditioning when a stimulus triggers a more or less natural reaction such as the salivation produced by Pavlov's dogs or other automatic responses such as excitement, fear and sexual arousal. Operant behaviour (behaviour that operates on the environment) deals with the forms of behaviour that are not the result of simple, automatic responses. Most human behaviour, in fact, is operant behaviour – going to work, driving a car, solving a mathematical problem and playing tennis are all examples of operant behaviour. According to Skinner, such behaviour is learned and strengthened by a process of operant conditioning.

The key elements involved in operant conditioning are the stimulus, the response, and reinforcement or reward. As an example of the operant conditioning process at work, consider an executive who is asked to speak at a management meeting. The stimulus is the request for the executive to speak. The executive responds by giving certain views, and this response may be reinforced (rewarded) by nods and smiles from a senior manager. The effect of this reinforcement is to increase the likelihood that the executive will respond with the same or similar views at future meetings. The learning involved is sometimes described as instrumental conditioning because the response of the person or other organism involved is instrumental in obtaining the reinforcement.

Although the example given above involves human behaviour, much of the work on operant conditioning has been carried out with laboratory animals. In some classic experiments, mostly with rats and pigeons, Skinner was able to show that by providing them with reinforcement (usually food) at appropriate times, animals could be taught to exhibit a wide range of behaviour. Many of the experiments were conducted with the aid of an operant chamber often called a 'skinner box'. Reinforcement is provided when the animal in the box exhibits certain operant behaviour (e.g. pressing the lever or pecking a certain region of the box).

Operant techniques, unlike classical conditioning, can be used to produce behaviour that is not normally part of the organism's repertoire. For example, pigeons have been taught to play ping-pong and 'Priscilla the Fastidious Pig' was taught to turn on the radio, eat breakfast at table, drop dirty clothes in a washing hamper, vacuum the floor and select her sponsoring company's food in preference to brand X (Breland and Breland, 1951). According to Skinner, the same fundamental processes of operant conditioning are involved regardless of whether we are concerned with a pigeon learning how to obtain food in an operant chamber, a child learning to talk and write, or a subordinate learning how to deal with a difficult manager. Operant behaviours (pecking in the right spot, pronouncing a difficult word correctly or saying the appropriate thing at a committee meeting) produce reinforcement (food, the praise of parents or the manager), and as a consequence the behaviour that produced the reinforcement is learned and strengthened. The process of operant conditioning is often described with the aid of a three-term framework: *antecedents* (A), *behaviour* (B) and *consequences* (C). Antecedents refer to the conditions or stimuli that precede the behaviour, and consequences refer to the reinforcing or punishing outcomes that the behaviour produces.

With animals, reinforcement often takes the form of food, but for humans, reinforcement may take a wide variety of forms – smiles, gifts, money, complimentary words – and a wide range of other things may provide reinforcement for behaviour. Broadly, reinforcement is anything which follows operant behaviour and increases the probability that the behaviour will recur. In many circumstances, of course, during our daily lives we administer reinforcement to others in a fairly unsystematic and uncontrolled fashion. Smiles, nods, praise and so on are all given with little thought for the consequences on the operant behaviour of others, or the learning that we are unwittingly encouraging. A common example occurs when parents say 'no' to a child's request for something and at first resist even when the child cries and makes them feel mean and unfair. Eventually, when they can stand it no longer, they give in and comply with the child's request, thus unintentionally reinforcing the child's persistent crying.

Key Learning Point

Operant conditioning can be used to shape behaviour and to produce behaviour that will not appear spontaneously.

The behaviourist research into operant learning has proved to be a rich source of information about certain types of learning experience; many of the basic principles have been applied in a wide range of organisational and other contexts. Over the next few pages some of the more important principles derived from behaviourist research are discussed.

Extinction

So far we have looked at the effect that reinforcement has on strengthening behaviour. What happens when reinforcement is not produced as a result of behaviour? When reinforcement is withdrawn or perhaps never given at all, the operant behaviour associated with it will gradually cease to occur. In technical terms, it is extinguished. Learned behaviour will continue only if the person is being reinforced. For many things we learn during formal education, at work and in everyday life, reinforcement is so frequent and common that we do not notice it. Nevertheless, as Zohar and Fussfeld (1981) pointed out, when operant techniques are used to change employees' behaviour in organisations, the new behaviour will sometimes extinguish quite rapidly if reinforcement is removed.

Schedules of reinforcement

Sometimes reinforcement takes place on a continuous basis. An employee who is rewarded every time a satisfactory piece of work is produced is being reinforced on a continuous basis. Most reinforcement at work and in everyday life, however, occurs on a partial basis: few parents praise their children every time they exhibit good manners; good work often goes unnoticed by superiors; people do not always laugh uproariously at our jokes (well, not mine anyway!). In general, behaviour that is based on a partial reinforcement schedule is much more persistent and likely to continue even when reinforcement is removed. This is true despite the fact that on partial reinforcement schedules less reinforcement is provided. In fact, the general rule is that the lower the percentage of correct responses that are rewarded, the more persistent the behaviour will be. An experiment reported long ago by Lewis and Duncan (1956) helps to explain this apparent paradox. In the experiment people were allowed to gamble, using slot machines. The machines were 'rigged' so that some paid out on every trial (i.e. continous reinforcement). Other machines paid out on a partial bias (as real slot machines do). In the second part of the experiment everyone played on a second machine – rigged so that it would never pay out. People who had been trained on the partial schedules were much more resistant to extinction and they continued to play long after people on a continuous schedule had stopped. In fact, the overall results conformed well with the idea mentioned above, that the lower the percentage of responses rewarded, the more resistant to extinction is the behaviour concerned, demonstrating the powerful effect of partial reinforcement schedules compared with continuous reinforcement.

Partial reinforcement may be given on either an interval or ratio schedule. *Interval reinforcement* occurs when a specified amount of time has passed. The next response that occurs will then produce reinforcement. For example, a telephone salesperson might be told to take a break by the supervisor as soon as the last call in any 45-minute period is completed. *Ratio reinforcement* is based not on the passage of time, but on the number of responses that has occurred (e.g. a worker is given a break after every 50 components produced). Schedules of reinforcement can also be either *fixed* (that is, occur regularly every so many minutes or responses), or they may be *variable* and occur, on average, every *x* minutes or responses, but the actual gap between each reinforcement is varied (*see* Fig. 8.1).

Figure 8.1a shows a fixed-interval (FI) schedule. Reinforcement occurs on a regular, timed basis. Typically, responding slows down immediately after reinforcement and begins to increase as the time for the next reinforcement approaches. Figure 8.2b shows a variable ratio (VR) schedule. Reinforcement occurs 'on average' every so many responses (e.g. VR10 = every 10 responses on average), but the occurrence of each specific reinforcement is irregular and unpredictable. Responding is frequent and regular.

Key Learning Point

Partial reinforcement produces more effective changes in behaviour than continuous reinforcement.

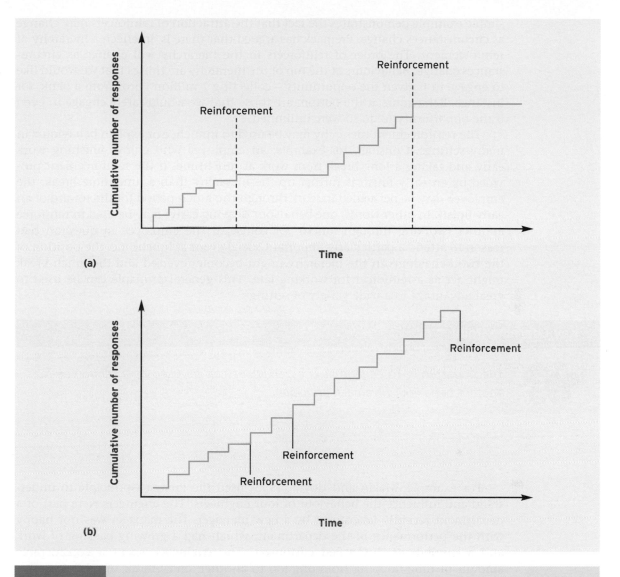

Figure 8.1   **Different schedules of reinforcement**

The reinforcement hierarchy

Some ideas concerning reinforcement, which seem particularly valuable within the context of organisational behaviour, were proposed and developed by Premack (1965), who demonstrated by experiment that an event that serves as a reinforcer for some behaviour may not have a reinforcing effect on other, different behaviour. In addition, he demonstrated that reinforcers may sometimes change places with the behaviour that produces them. For example, a thirsty laboratory animal will run to obtain water; equally, an animal subjected to a long period of inactivity will drink in order to take an opportunity to run. In other words, drinking may reinforce running, but in some circumstances running may reinforce drinking. This simple example demonstrates the fact that the attraction of reinforcers may change as circumstances change. Premack has argued that there is, in effect, a hierarchy of reinforcement. The order of reinforcers in the hierarchy will change as circumstances change. Behaviours at the top of the hierarchy are things that we would like to engage in if given the opportunity – collecting 1 million Euros from a bank, for instance. Behaviours at the bottom are those that we would rarely engage in even if the opportunity to do so were unlimited.

The reinforcement hierarchy may be used to influence or explain behaviours in many settings. Consider, for example, an employee who enjoys finishing work early and taking a long break from work at lunchtime. If the reinforcement provided by an early finish is further up the hierarchy than a lunchtime break, the employee may be persuaded to work through the lunch period for the reward of an early finish. In other words, one behaviour (leaving early) may be used to reinforce another (working through lunch). Of course, if the employee in question had reason to attend a particularly important social event at lunchtime, the position of the two behaviours in the hierarchy might become reversed and the lunch-break might act as a reinforcer for working late. This general principle can be used to great advantage in a wide variety of settings.

Key Learning Point

The opportunity to engage in one behaviour can be used as a reinforcer for another behaviour (Premack principle).

For example, Makin and Hoyle (1993) used the Premack principle to understand and influence the behaviour of four engineers. The engineers were part of a department recently taken over by a new manager. The manager was not happy with the performance of the department, which had a growing backlog of work and a number of dissatisfied customers. The engineers 'spent a considerable amount of time hopping from one job to another' and 'An air of crisis management pervaded' (Makin and Hoyle, 1993, p. 16). Makin and Hoyle found that all of the engineers were putting considerable effort into their work and overall motivation appeared to be high. The problem was that the engineers were directing their attention to tasks that they found reinforcing, rather than those necessary for production. The use of a combination of feedback, praise and recognition was linked to an increase in performance for the section of 73 per cent. The output of the individual engineers improved by between 31 per cent and 270 per cent!

Punishment

Just as reinforcement will increase the likelihood of a response, punishment (the use of aversive or unpleasant stimuli) will decrease the likelihood of the behaviour that immediately precedes it. At first sight, punishment may seem to be a useful means for suppressing or eliminating certain behaviours. It is – but only when used correctly.

Consider the case of a supervisor who always raises disciplinary problems at the company's weekly progress meetings and, in so doing, reveals that he has consistently made bad decisions and errors of judgement when supervising his staff. At first, at the meetings, his manager responds with tactful and diplomatic assistance and tries to point out the errors to the supervisor, suggesting how they might be avoided in future. Eventually, however, the manager becomes exasperated, loses her temper and punishes the supervisor with strong words and a public dressing-down. For the next few months there are no more reports of discipline problems and the manager begins to feel that the 'short, sharp shock' has worked. Suddenly, however, the manager is confronted with a deputation of employees from the supervisor's department who claim that discipline has grown progressively worse and that their working conditions are now intolerable. What went wrong? Had the punishment not worked? The punishment had worked, but inevitably – as anticipated above – it had decreased the likelihood of the behaviour immediately preceding it, which in this case was the *reporting* of problems by the supervisor at the weekly meetings. The supervisor had learned that this was not a successful thing to do. Consequently, he deliberately neglected raising the issue at meetings and thus avoided the possibility of punishment occurring, which was not the outcome the manager had intended. On the contrary, the behaviour the manager had tried to punish had continued unchecked and the supervisor continued making errors of judgement.

In many cases it is not possible to give punishment at the appropriate time. In most countries employment law and/or agreements between management and unions limit the type and amount of punishment that can be meted out. For this and many other reasons (e.g. a classically conditioned aversion to the punisher, and the fact that avoiding punishment may provide a form of reinforcement and therefore encourage avoidance behaviour), most people feel that punishment is not a very effective means of controlling behaviour.

Punishment – the presentation of an aversive stimulus – should not be confused with negative reinforcement. Negative reinforcers are stimuli that have the effect of increasing the probability of occurrence of the response that precedes them when they are *removed* from the situation. For example, a lecturer may mark students' work more quickly if doing so stops unwelcome interruptions from students visiting the lecturer's office to ask when their work will be returned.

Key Learning Point

Punishment is not a very effective way of changing behaviour.

Fundamentals of conditioning: contiguity and contingency

The general overview of the work of the behaviourists given above has illustrated their use of certain key concepts such as response, stimulus, reinforcement and extinction. The research on punishment mentioned immediately above illustrates two important concepts, one of which is contiguity – that is, for conditioning to occur there should be only a small delay between behaviour and reinforcement (or punishment). In broad terms, the longer the gap between these two events, the less likely it is that the target behaviour will be strengthened or diminished. The other fundamental concept, not mentioned explicitly so far, is the idea of contingency. This emphasises that reinforcement is contingent on the response; in other words, for conditioning to occur, reinforcement should be provided only when the desired behaviour occurs. This is – loosely – what the pay-for-performance methods described in the opening case study are designed to ensure. Strictly speaking, though, they tend to be based on *outcomes* of behaviour, not the behaviour itself.

Reinforcing other behaviour makes it likely that this will be influenced and that the intended behaviour will not be affected. Contiguity and contingency are seen as fundamental elements involved in understanding how conditioning takes place and, taken together with concepts of stimulus, response, reinforcement and extinction, represent the core of the behaviourist position. One consistent champion of the operant approach in organisational settings is Komaki who, in her work, has extended the operant approach well beyond the straightforward attempts to manipulate behaviour into a variety of interesting and important areas, such as leader behaviour and supervision (e.g. Komaki *et al.*, 1989); and performance measurement (Komaki *et al.*, 1987).

Organisational behaviour modification

The principles of operant conditioning and systematic procedures of behaviour analysis have been applied in educational and clinical settings for many years (Ulrich *et al.*, 1974; Rimm and Masters, 1979). More recently, they have also been used within organisational settings to modify behaviour. Comprehensive coverage of the application of operant techniques to *organisational behaviour modification* (OB Mod) has been presented by Luthans and Kreitner (1975) and Hellervik *et al.* (1992). The essence of the OB Mod approach involves focusing on critical behaviours that are important for satisfactory work performance and the application of reinforcement principles attempting to strengthen appropriate behaviour patterns. Luthans and Kreitner described a five-step procedure for using OB Mod techniques:

1   identify the critical behaviours;

2   measure the critical behaviours;

3   carry out a functional analysis of the behaviours;

4   develop an intervention strategy;

5   evaluate whether the intervention strategy has led to behaviour change.

Critical behaviours represent the activities of the personnel within the organisation that are influencing organisational performance and are to be strengthened, weakened or modified in some way. Such behaviour might be identified in a variety of ways, including discussion with relevant personnel, systematic observation or tracing the cause of performance or production deficiencies. An important point, however, is that only specific, observable behaviour is used. To say that it is critical to have a 'positive attitude' would not be acceptable and the behaviour that demonstrated such qualities (low absenteeism, prompt responses to requests, instructions etc.) would need to be identified. Wilson (2000) discusses OB Mod interventions in health and safety at work. He suggests that in most organisations there are between 10 and 20 critical behaviours which lead to accidents. So the task of identifying them is considerable but not insurmountable.

Once the critical behaviours are identified, a baseline measure of their frequency of occurrence is obtained, either by direct observation or recording, or perhaps from existing company records. This baseline measure is important in two main ways. It provides an objective view of the current situation, indicating, for example, that the scale of a problem is much bigger or smaller than it was at first thought to be, and it provides a basis for examining any change that might eventually take place as a result of intervention.

Functional analysis involves identifying:

- the cues or stimuli in the work situation (antecedent conditions) that trigger the behaviour;

- the contingent consequences (i.e. the consequences in terms of reward, punishment, etc.) that are maintaining the behaviour.

This stage is critical for the success of any programme of OB Mod, since it is essential to have an accurate picture of the antecedents and consequences that may be maintaining the behaviour in question. For example, an OB Mod programme may be considered by a sales manager as a means of encouraging sales personnel to make fewer visits to base – visits that are spent in unproductive chats with colleagues. The sales manager may be concerned about the behaviour because of the time-wasting involved and because the sales director keeps making comments about large numbers of the salesforce 'sitting at base together doing nothing'. The apparently rewarding consequences of returning to base may be the opportunity to relax and avoid the pressures of being on the road. It could be, however, that the important consequence for the sales staff is the opportunity for social interaction with colleagues and that it is the reinforcing effect of this social interaction that is maintaining their behaviour. Any attempt to modify their behaviour by providing opportunities for relaxation away from base, or by staggering their visits to base so that only small numbers are there at any time, would be founded on an inaccurate view of the behaviour–consequence contingencies. Of course, the problem may be of a different kind altogether. Perhaps the products the sales team are trying to sell are poor and they have little success in finding customers. Their returning to base may be a consequence of a dispiriting lack of reinforcement derived from sales visits. Probably the only remedy here is to improve the product.

Once the functional analysis has been conducted an intervention strategy designed to modify the behaviour concerned must be developed. The purpose of the intervention strategy is to strengthen desirable behaviour and weaken undesirable behaviour. A central feature of human behaviour is the range and variety of rewards that might be used to provide reinforcement. Money provides an obvious example, but many other potential rewards can be identified. Table 8.1 provides some examples. It is worth noting that some rewards, such as friendly greetings and compliments, do not incur direct costs for the organisation. Various intervention strategies may be used, but most involve the use of positive reinforcement in some way. Punishment appears to have had a lesser role in most studies, although it has received some attention (*see* Arvey and Ivancevich, 1980). It is also possible to make use of Premack's reinforcement hierarchy principle mentioned earlier, whereby employees are rewarded for engaging in behaviour low down in the hierarchy (e.g. working at a job until it is finished, even if it means staying late) by being allowed to engage in behaviours higher up it (e.g. being given more challenging and responsible work). The choice of appropriate reinforcers is crucial for successful interventions, since the effects of specific potential rewards vary according to the people involved. To some people, for instance, the allocation of more challenging and responsible work would not be as rewarding as the opportunity to leave work on time every evening; some people would find money more attactive than time off, and so on (*see also* Chapter 9 on motivation).

Key Learning Point

OB Mod is based on the systematic analysis of the antecedent conditions and the consequences of behaviour at work.

OB Mod in practice

Table 8.2 illustrates the primary consequences that can follow behaviour and gives references to some illustrative OB Mod studies. Although it is not an exclusively behaviourist concept, feedback is included in Table 8.2 because of its widespread usage in OB Mod studies, often in conjunction with reinforcers such as praise (Alavosius and Sulzer-Azaroff, 1986) or money and free gifts (Haynes *et al.*, 1982). Feedback is an important aspect of many other theoretical positions and behaviour change strategies, such as goal setting (Locke and Latham, 1990). Within the behaviourist framework, feedback is construed as a consequence of behaviour, and since behaviour may be influenced by adjusting consequences, feedback may be used to help to shape behaviour. Despite this, feedback and its role in helping to shape behaviour is a troublesome concept for pure behaviourism since it is difficult to see how it can have any influence on subsequent behaviour without the informational (i.e. cognitive) component of feedback being important (*see* Bandura 1986; Locke and Henne, 1986).

Table 8.1	Possible rewards for use in organisational behaviour modification				
Contrived on-the-job-rewards				Natural rewards	
Consumables	Manipulatables	Visual and auditory	Tokens	Social	Premack
Coffee-break Treats Free lunches Food baskets Easter hams Christmas turkeys Dinners for the family on the company Company picnics After-work wine and cheese parties Beer parties	Desk accessories Wall plaques Company car Watches Trophies Commendations Rings/tie-pins Appliances and furniture for the home Home shop tools Garden tools Clothing Club privileges Special assignments	Office with a window Piped-in music Redecoration of work environment Company literature Private office Popular speakers or lecturers Book club discussions Feedback about performance	Money Stocks Stock options Passes for films Trading stamps Paid-up insurance policies Dinner and theatre tickets Holiday trips Coupons redeemable at local stores Profit-sharing	Friendly greetings Informal recognition Formal acknowledgement of achievement Invitations to coffee/lunch Solicitations of suggestions Solicitations of advice Compliments on work progress Recognition in house journal Pat on the back Smile Verbal or non-verbal recognition or praise	Job with more responsibility Job rotation Early time off with pay Extended breaks Extended lunch period Personal time off with pay Work on personal project on company time Use of company machinery or facilities for personal projects Use of company recreation facilities

Key Learning Point

A wide variety of reinforcers are used in attempts to change behaviour. These include financial reward, praise and the use of secondary reinforcers, such as tokens.

Table 8.2	Consequences of behaviour and organisational behaviour modification	
Consequence	**Effect on preceding behaviour**	**Usage in OB Mod**
Positive reinforcement	A consequence which, when introduced, increases the frequency of Immediately preceding behaviour recurring	Widely used, although praise and social reinforcers are more common than monetary reinforcers
Negative reinforcement	A consequence which, when removed, increases the frequency of the immediately preceding behaviour recurring	Not used explicitly very often, but may be a side effect of intervention in some studies
Extinction	The absence of any rewarding or punishing consequence. Causes the subsequent frequency of the preceding behaviour to decrease. Often difficult to differentiate from punishment (e.g. if a reinforcer is deliberately withdrawn in order to extinguish some specific behaviour)	Often explicitly or implicitly used in conjunction with positive reinforcement to strengthen desirable behaviour and weaken undesirable behaviour
Feedback	Providing information about the outcomes of behaviour – or actual behaviour (e.g. how close behaviour is to a target behaviour)	One of the most frequently used intervention strategies

Exercise 8.2　　The sad case of Mal

Half way through the first semester of your degree course, you begin to notice that one of your flatmates, Mal Adaptive, seems to be experiencing some problems with his work. Basically, he doesn't do very much, and what he does do seems not very good. He has received low marks in his coursework tests. Although he sometimes expresses concern about this state of affairs, he never seems to do anything to improve it. You obtain the following information. Mal went to school where the teachers set quite a lot of work and regularly checked up on whether pupils were doing it. They were vigorous in ensuring that those who did not complete their work were punished. But apart from making sure that the work had been done, the teachers spent little time marking it or giving feedback to pupils about its quality. They did give a grade, but this did not contribute to pupils' overall marks, and poor grades did not usually lead to punishment. However, grades were an important input to decisions about which pupils should receive school prizes on speech day. Mal found it difficult to understand why he got the grades he did. Sometimes he put a lot of effort in and received a poor mark; other times he scarcely tried at all yet received quite a good mark. He greatly valued the approval of his friends, and most of them seemed to respect others more on the basis of sporting and social skills than school-work accomplishments. In spite of this, Mal had obtained good school grades through intensive last-minute revision. There was no problem with his academic ability.

At university, there seemed to Mal to be much less pressure to produce work immediately. He had missed several coursework deadlines but nothing much seemed to happen to him as a result – unlike at school. He knew that coursework contributed to his end-of-semester grades, but somehow the end of the semester seemed a long time away. It took a long time for the work he did complete to be marked. Mal had joined lots of student societies, especially sporting ones, and had already started to play a leading role in several. He had made two particularly good friends, and together the three of them rarely missed an opportunity to go out in the evening. But unlike Mal, the other two were careful to set time aside for their academic work.

1   Use what you know about behaviour modification to explain why Mal is not doing much work at university.

2   As friends of Mal Adaptive, devise a strategy that uses behaviour modification to change his behaviour. Be as detailed as you can about your strategy. What would you (or others) need to do, and what do you think would be the chances of success?

Several early studies focusing on work quality, absenteeism, supervisory training and other aspects of work behaviour showed that the operant-based systematic application of OB Mod techniques could produce important changes in behaviour (*see* O'Brien *et al.*, 1982; Luthans and Martinko, 1987, for examples). An illustrative study involving the application of behaviourist principles is that of Zohar and Fussfeld (1981). This study was conducted in a textile factory in which noise levels were extremely high (106 dB A). Despite these dangerously high levels of noise, the employees were reluctant to wear ear defenders and only 35 per cent were normally wearing them. Zohar and Fussfeld first made contact with the personnel involved and established some reinforcers that the personnel found attractive (consumer durables, such as radios and televisions). After taking baseline measures of the frequency of ear defender usage, Zohar and Fussfeld then introduced a variable ratio token economy system. Under this scheme, tokens were secondary reinforcers, since they had no direct rewarding value themselves, but they could be exchanged for the consumer durables, when an operative had collected enough tokens. The tokens were given to operatives by supervisors, who distributed them on an irregular basis only to operatives who were wearing ear defenders. The token economy had the almost immediate effect of increasing ear defender usage from 35 to 90 per cent. Furthermore, when the investigators collected follow-up data nine months after the token economy (which ran for only two months) had been discontinued, ear defender usage was still at 90 per cent. This study is a good example of OB Mod at work since it shows how a previously intractable problem – the company had already tried poster campaigns and other means to improve ear defender usage – may be resolved permanently at relatively little cost.

Not all OB Mod interventions are quite so successful though. Beard *et al.* (1998) report in some detail on an intervention at an American manufacturing plant designed to increase employee attendance. Positive reinforcements such as letters of commendation, a carparking space and a 100 dollar gift voucher were used to reward perfect or near-perfect attendance over several months or longer. Slightly less good attenders received counselling and coaching attention from their supervisors, and were required to create action plans to improve their attendance. This was negative reinforcement because these measures were removed if and when the person's attendance improved. Punishment was used with the worst attenders. They were not paid for time absent. Beard and colleagues collected very thorough data about attendance by the 500 or so employees over a 20-month period. They found that even though the management considered the scheme a great success, the improvement in attendance was only about one half of 1 per cent, and furthermore most of this improvement had melted away by the end of the study. Estimated cost savings peaked at about 47 000 dollars a year, and fell back to about 7000. The authors speculate that the rewards were given insufficiently frequently, and one might add that perhaps also the rewards for good attendance were simply too small. They also suggest that the real costs and benefits are hard to quantify. There may well have been hidden benefits in terms of improved team relationships and there were certainly costs (albeit quite small) associated with running the OB Mod scheme and administering rewards.

Stajkovic and Luthans (1997) have reported a meta-analysis of research examining the impact of OB Mod on task performance. Overall they found an average 17 per cent increase in task performance as a result of using OB Mod. The impact tended to be greater in manufacturing than service organisations, possibly because quality of task performance is more objectively observable and measurable. The same authors (Stajkovic and Luthans, 2001) conducted a field experiment using different forms of reinforcement. They found that, despite the use of a wide range of reinforcers in OB Mod research, straightforward monetary reward produced the most positive change in performance (26 per cent) compared with 13 per cent for social recognition and 9 per cent for performance feedback. This may not be a general rule though. For example, Hartshorn (2000, p. 125) argues that praise from others is often enough to enhance safe behaviour:

> The key to effectively reinforcing an unsafe worker is to find those times when he or she happens to be working safely and reinforce that safe behavior. The quickest, easiest, and often the most effective type of reinforcement for behavioral shaping is positive personal feedback.

Saari (1994) has argued that the impact of OB Mod on organisational success is often much greater than might be expected given the amount of change that is observed in the behaviours being modified. She suggests this is for two reasons. First OB Mod may prompt people to start thinking about their behaviour more generally, and possibly change it. Second, people who are not part of the OB Mod may see or hear about the behaviour change and decide they want to change too.

Key Learning Point

OB Mod often but not always produces significant changes in behaviour. Which reinforcers are most effective may vary between individuals and between types of behaviour.

As some of the studies just cited suggest, *evaluation* is an important element in the application of any OB Mod programme. Various designs can be used to conduct the evaluation phase of an OB Mod programme. The primary aim of the evaluation is, of course, to examine if, and to what extent, the intervention has modified the target behaviours. The most widely used designs are the reversal or ABAB design and the multiple baseline design. The reversal (ABAB) design involves alternating use of the OB Mod programme and removal of the programme over a period of time (*see* Fig. 8.2). In such a design the frequency of the target behaviour is assessed before the programme begins. This provides a baseline (the A phase). The next phase involves intervening and using reinforcement, punishment and so forth to modify behaviour (the B phase). After the intervention has produced stable new rates for the behaviour, it is removed (the reversal) and conditions revert to baseline. Usually the behaviour will also revert, or at least show some return towards baseline levels.

Although this design can provide impressive evidence of the effect of the intervention, there are obvious problems. The return to baseline may not always be desirable. Furthermore, the intervention may have been deliberately designed to ensure lasting behaviour change so that even when the specific reinforcers used in the intervention phase are removed, the behaviour should not revert to baseline levels (Zohar and Fussfeld, 1981).

The multiple baseline design can help to deal with these problems. In this design, baseline data are collected across two or more behaviours, then a specific intervention strategy to change each behaviour in turn is introduced (*see* Fig. 8.3). Each behaviour should change only when the relevant intervention strategy is used. If this happens it provides convincing evidence (without the need for reversals) that the intervention is causing the change. Further details on these and other methods may be found in Kazdin (1980), Luthans and Martinko (1987) and Komaki and Jensen (1986). Beard *et al.* (1998) have pointed out that most evaluations of OB Mod are relatively short term, so that the truly long-term impact of interventions is not really known.

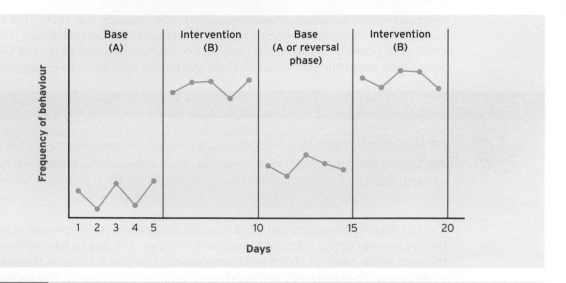

Figure 8.2   **The reversal (ABAB) design for evaluating an OB Mod programme**

Putting more thought into OB Mod

Despite its obvious success in bringing about useful behaviour change, traditional OB Mod has frequently been criticised (e.g. Locke, 1977) and its potential for theoretical growth and conceptual development has been constrained by the rigorous emphasis, in pure behaviourism, on directly observable and measurable phenomena. The difficulties encountered in trying to incorporate such obviously

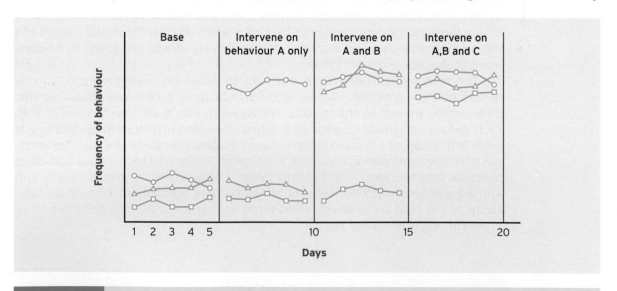

Figure 8.3   **The multiple baseline design for evaluating an OB Mod programme**

cognitive concepts as feedback into such a resolutely anti-mentalistic framework have already been mentioned. Problems such as this, together with the theoretical developments which have extended behaviourist theory into the cognitive domain (Bandura, 1986), have led to an integration of OB Mod with more cognitive approaches.

The cognitive approaches of most relevance to contemporary organisational behaviour and analysis are social cognitive theory (Bandura, 1986) and goal-setting theory (Locke and Latham, 1990). Goal setting is discussed in Chapter 9. Essentially, goal setting is a cognitively based theory which proposes that specific, difficult goals, when they are accepted by the individual, will lead to effective performance. Goals influence cognitions by directing attention. Feedback on goal attainment is necessary for goal setting to be maximally effective. Many behaviour-change studies have made use of both goal setting and feedback, and extremely effective interventions have been produced (e.g. Chokkar and Wallin, 1984). A behaviourist interpretation of goals would see them as antecedent conditions. It has, however, become increasingly accepted by researchers that cognitive states concerning goal commitment, acceptance and attributions are important concepts in understanding how goal setting works.

Social cognitive theory does not reject the operant-based view of behaviour development which is at the heart of behaviourism. This theory does, however, extend the operant view and makes use of important additional cognitive concepts. The essence of social cognitive theory (formerly called social learning theory) is that the role of cognitive processes in determining behaviour is given prominence.

Social cognitive theory accepts the basic tenets of the behavioural approach (i.e. reinforcement, contingency and contiguity and the impact of schedules of reinforcement) but goes on to add further novel concepts. Some of these novel concepts involve significant departures from traditional operant approaches to behaviour. The overall framework within which these concepts are developed involves the concept of 'reciprocal determinism' (see Fig. 8.5).

Social learning theory emphasises that the interaction of situation and person factors may be a better theoretical basis for organisational behaviour than the purely situational view based on operant conditioning only. Social learning theory differs from the traditional operant approach in many ways (see also Chapter 1).

One of the important differences concerns the acceptance that internal cognitive processes are important determinants of behaviour. For example, whereas traditional reinforcement theory argues that behaviour is regulated by its immediate, external consequences only, social learning theory suggests that internal psychological factors such as expectancies about the eventual consequences of behaviour have a role in controlling behaviour. The opening case study in this chapter shows how reward systems at work are based on this assumption. Bandura (1977b, p. 18) expresses it as follows:

> Contrary to the mechanistic view, outcomes change behaviour largely through the intervening influence of thought .... Anticipatory capacities enable humans to be motivated by prospective consequences. Past experiences create expectations that certain actions will bring valued benefits, and that still others will avert future trouble .... Homeowners, for instance, do not wait until they experience the distress of a burning house to purchase fire insurance.

Improving attendance with OB Mod

Absenteeism at SJR Foods' plant had been getting steadily worse for many years. Radha El-Bakry, the production manager, felt that it would be worth investing some money in solving the problem. In consultation with the company unions she developed and installed a lottery scheme which involved the issuing of free tickets to employees who attended work. Each full day's attendance entitled the employee to one free lottery ticket. Full attendance for a week produced a bonus of two extra tickets. The lottery was drawn every Friday evening and prizes were available for collection on the spot. Within two weeks of its introduction the scheme was more than paying for itself in improved attendance (see Fig. 8.4).

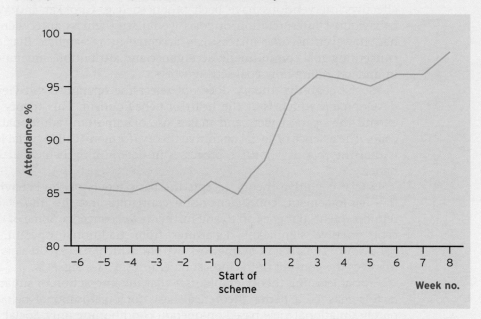

Figure 8.4   **Attendance rates at SJR Foods**

At the same time as she introduced the lottery system, Radha had agreed a goal with the employee representatives of 90 per cent attendance. At the end of each week a chart in the canteen (similar to Fig. 8.4) was completed, which showed the attendance rate for that week.

1   Using the terminology and concepts of OB Mod, explain what had been done at SJR Foods.

2   Discuss the extent to which this intervention adopted a pure behaviourist approach.

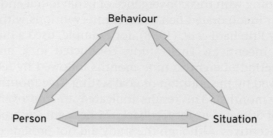

Figure 8.5	Reciprocal determinism

Social learning theorists also argue that, as well as responding to the influence of reinforcement in the environment, people often control and develop behaviour patterns through the use of self-reinforcement: 'self-appraisals of performance set the occasion for self-produced consequences. Favourable judgements give rise to rewarding self-reactions, whereas unfavourable appraisals activate punishing self-responses' (Bandura, 1977b, p. 133). Bandura and other social learning theorists argue that internal psychological events and processes such as self-reinforcement and expectancies help to determine behaviour. This behaviour will, to some extent, influence the situation surrounding the person, and in turn external situational factors, such as the behaviour of others, and help to determine expectancies and the other internal cognitive factors. In other words, there is a constant cycle of interaction between person and situation factors, a process described by Bandura as reciprocal determinism. This view is quite different from the traditional operant view that: 'A person does not act upon the world, the world acts upon him' (Skinner, 1971, p. 211).

Another important aspect of social learning theory is the proposal that people often develop their own patterns of behaviour by observing and then copying or modelling the behaviour of others. The concept of observational learning or modelling is difficult for those holding the traditional, operant behavioural view to explain. For example, the act of copying a model provides no direct reinforcement in itself. Social learning theorists argue that this sort of action can, however, be explained if we accept that the modelling occurred because the learner had expectancies about what might eventually occur as a consequence of modelling. Thus, junior members of an organisation model their dress, attitudes and behaviours on those of successful senior personnel, based on expectancies, goals and plans that they have about the eventual consequences of their behaviours. Luthans and Kreitner (1975) have provided a framework for OB Mod which is rooted firmly in the concepts of social cognitive theory.

Key Learning Point

OB Mod changes behaviour through influencing thought processes and social norms, as well as through behavioural reinforcement.

In keeping with this convergence of behavioural and cognitive theories, studies have often incorporated behavioural interventions within a cognitive framework. A study by Pritchard *et al.* (1988), for example, used a mixture of goal setting, feedback and incentives. Their study, conducted in a military setting, involved a baseline period of eight to nine months followed by feedback (five months); this was followed by the addition of goal setting (five months); finally, incentives were used (five months). The results indicated an improvement in productivity over baseline of 50 per cent for feedback, 75 per cent for group goal setting and 76 per cent for incentives. Although the study did not provide conclusive proof of the different effects of the various interventions, the authors felt that incentives added little to the improvements brought about by feedback and goal setting. This finding from one study must, however, be set against the results obtained by Guzzo *et al.* (1985) in their meta-analytic investigation of many studies, which showed that incentives do generally improve performance, although the effect depends on the method of application and circumstances.

It is clear from other work (e.g. Duff *et al.*, 1994) that behaviour change may be brought about very effectively without the use of incentives. In their study Duff *et al.* (1994) focused on the safety behaviour of operatives on construction sites in the north of England. The design for the study used many of the features mentioned earlier in this chapter, including a multiple baseline, with reversal. As an integral part of the study the investigators developed a comprehensive measure of safety on construction sites. This measure was then used by trained observers to record safety levels on the specific sites involved in the study. Feedback and goal-setting procedures were then introduced and safety levels were monitored regularly (three times per week). Two features of this study illustrate important points. The first is that, as already noted, no incentives were offered nor were any rewards given. Some would argue that rewards are implicit in the feedback, which, when positive, could impact on factors such as self-esteem and feelings of greater security or job satisfaction. Saari (1994, p. 12), also referring to safety behaviour, has put it like this:

> Many studies have shown that plain feedback i.e. information about the prevalence of the correct behaviour, is enough to modify behaviour. Social praise or economic consequences ... have been used by some researchers. However, these do not really seem to be necessary.

Whatever mechanism is involved, feedback (*see* Algera, 1990) and goals (*see* Locke and Latham, 1990), even without reward, can provide a base for behaviour change.

The second point to note is that in the Duff *et al.* (1994) study, the measures and feedback information did not focus on behaviour only. Some of the items in the safety measure did indeed focus on behaviour (e.g. wearing and use of safety equipment); but others focused on the *consequences* of behaviour (e.g. evidence of objects thrown down from height, ladders not tied off properly). In behaviour-change studies it is often impossible to observe behaviour as it happens but this does not preclude the use of the methods described in this chapter.

Saari and Nasanen (1989) used feedback to reduce accidents in a shipyard, achieving a reduction of 70–90 per cent in accidents, persisting to a three-year follow-up. This study is interesting in another sense since, like that of Duff *et al.*

(1994), it was conducted outside the United States, in this case in Finland. Most of the research on behaviour change cited in this chapter has been conducted in the United States, and some authors (e.g. Hale and Glendon, 1987) have expressed the view that feedback techniques may not work as effectively in European cultures as they have done in the United States.

Another illustration of the importance of social cognition is provided by Geller (2001). His analysis of the role of OB Mod in safety includes some important insights derived from very old and well-known social psychological studies, as well as not so old social cognition. The most fundamental point is that lasting behaviour change most often occurs when a person believes that they really *want* to change for their own reasons rather than because they are being rewarded for doing so. As Geller (2001, p. 26) puts it: 'When the only justification people give for their behavior is external consequences, they will not likely develop an internal rationale for their actions.'

Thus it is important to use small rather than large rewards and punishments, and to avoid direct attempts to persuade or give positive feedback because these are all too obvious and allow a people to believe they are changing their behaviour because in a sense they are being bribed. But on the other hand, if a person believes they have changed their behaviour because they wanted to, then this feeds on itself. The person observes him- or herself behaving in (for example) a safe way at work, and concludes 'I must be the kind of person who takes proper care at work'. This self-perception then influences subsequent behaviour.

A final point about OB Mod is that it can seem rather naive. Recommendations about reinforcing behaviour with occasional small rewards are all very well, but what will those on the receiving end think of it, and will it even be legal? As Sturmcy (1998, p. 27) says: 'Explicit disagreement on issues such as staff performance targets and staff reinforcement may be hard to avoid'. This is indeed the case, and is perhaps the most telling illustration of how behavioural techniques are insufficient on their own.

Summary

In many ways what people do (i.e. their behaviour) at work is the most important aspect of work psychology. Behaviourally orientated psychologists have developed concise and powerful frameworks which have been shown to be effective in changing behaviour in organisational settings. These frameworks are rooted in behaviourist psychology and use ideas about how the nature, timing and contingency of rewards can shape behaviour. The work of Luthans and Kreitner (1975) and others has provided a range of examples of the use of behavioural techniques in what has become known as organisational behaviour modification, or OB Mod for short. Even the major exponents of behaviour modification (based on purely behavioural frameworks) recognise that there are also theoretical and practical shortcomings. Nevertheless, OB Mod techniques often have major impacts on behaviour such as work performance, observance of health and safety rules and attendance at work. More recent research has shown that the inclusion of ideas from social cognitive theory provides a theoretically more advanced, yet still practical, basis for bringing about behavioural change. This is because they allow the recognition that people do not necessarily respond to rewards in a knee-jerk way. Instead, they think about their behaviour and rewards in the light of such things as their own personal goals, self-perceptions, the opinions of other people, and even fairness and morality.

Closing Case Study   The Effects of Punishment on Behaviour

Barry Cavanagh's new job as safety manager with Castell Construction was extremely challenging. The construction industry in general had one of the worst accident records of all industries in the country and although Castell's safety record was better than some companies, it was still a source of great concern. Barry felt that he understood the general causes of accidents very well: it was easier and quicker to take short cuts when it came to safety. For example, when a small number of breeze blocks needed cutting down to a smaller size with a power cutter, it was inconvenient and time consuming to get protective goggles, gloves and face mask from the stores. So the job would be done without protection. To make matters worse, because they were often under intense pressure from senior managers to work to agreed production targets, site managers and supervisors were often prepared to turn a blind eye to unsafe practices, if it meant that the job would get done on time.

Barry was a direct, no-nonsense kind of person and felt sure that it was a waste of time to try to educate the construction workers and to change their underlying attitudes to safety. He knew that to have any impact their behaviour needed to change. He also knew that various previous attempts to improve safety, initiated by his predecessor, had failed. These had included poster campaigns and talks from medical staff.

Barry decided that the best approach was to come down very heavily and severely on any examples of unsafe behaviour. Barry and his site managers began a campaign in which unsafe acts were punished severely with reprimands and other more severe forms of punishment such as loss of earnings. Most of their reprimands were given to accident victims or (when it was not the victim's fault) others involved in causing the accident.

At first Barry's policy seemed to be working. He maintained a close watch on accident reports and even within the first weeks of the campaign there was a clear decrease, particularly in minor accidents. After a routine meeting with site managers Barry had been a little disappointed that they did not share his pleasure at the decrease in accident rates. After the meeting one of the site managers took Barry to one side and explained why this was so, and, furthermore, that the scheme was doing more harm than good. There had actually been no change in accident rates – but to avoid punishment operatives were covering up and not reporting all but the most serious and noticeable incidents! Not only was there no improvement in accidents but the relationships between site managers and operatives had deteriorated. Site personnel were angered by the behaviour of managers, who were reprimanding operatives who were often still shaken and in pain after an accident.

Suggested exercises

1   Using the concepts and terminology of behaviour modification, explain what went wrong and why.

2   Make suggestions about how Barry might have gone about achieving his goal by a more successful route, using OB Mod techniques.

Test your learning

Short-answer questions

1   Give an example of classical conditioning.

2   Give an example of operant conditioning.

3   Why is behaviour based on partial reinforcement more persistent than behaviour based on continuous reinforcement?

4   Explain why punishment does not work under most circumstances.

5   What are the two items that need to be identified when functional analysis of behaviour is carried out?

6   Give details of the study carried out by Zohar and Fussfeld (1981), involving the application of behaviourist principles.

7   What is the reversal or ABAB design?

8   Outline the concept of 'reciprocal determinism'.

9   What is modelling behaviour?

Suggested assignments

1   Critically evaluate the OB Mod approach to work performance and discuss its ethical basis.

2   Show how behaviourist concepts may be incorporated into more general theories such as social cognitive theory.

Relevant websites

http://www.gabbai.com/Management/Psychology/Psychology_OBMod.html provides a brief overview of some of the principles of OB Mod and related concepts, and also some examples including one from the catering industry.

http://www.keilcentre.co.uk/downloads/case_study_report.pdf consists of a report prepared by consulting psychologists at the Keil Centre, Edinburgh, Scotland, on four attempts to use OB Mod on offshore oilrigs. It provides some interesting observations about the circumstances in which OB Mod does or does not work.

http://www.whsc.on.ca/Publications/hazardbulletins/spring2003/BBS_pdf.pdf provides a Canadian perspective on how to (and how not to) use behaviour modification principles to improve safety at work. This is part of the website of the Workers Health and Safety Centre, Ontario, Canada.

For further self-test material and relevant, annotated weblinks please visit the website at http://www.booksites.net/arnold_workpsych.

Suggested further reading

Note: full references for all three pieces of suggested further reading are given in the reference list at the end of this book.

1   The review of behavioural approaches in organisations by Luthans and Martinko (1987) covers the background to OB Mod and gives a scholarly account of its use and development.

2   A good example of a thorough and carefully reported attempt at OB Mod is provided by Beard *et al*. (1998). It illustrates many of the principles and dilemmas of OB Mod.

3   An easy to read analysis of how behaviour change is not adequately accounted for by behaviourist principles can be found in Scott Geller's (2001) article.

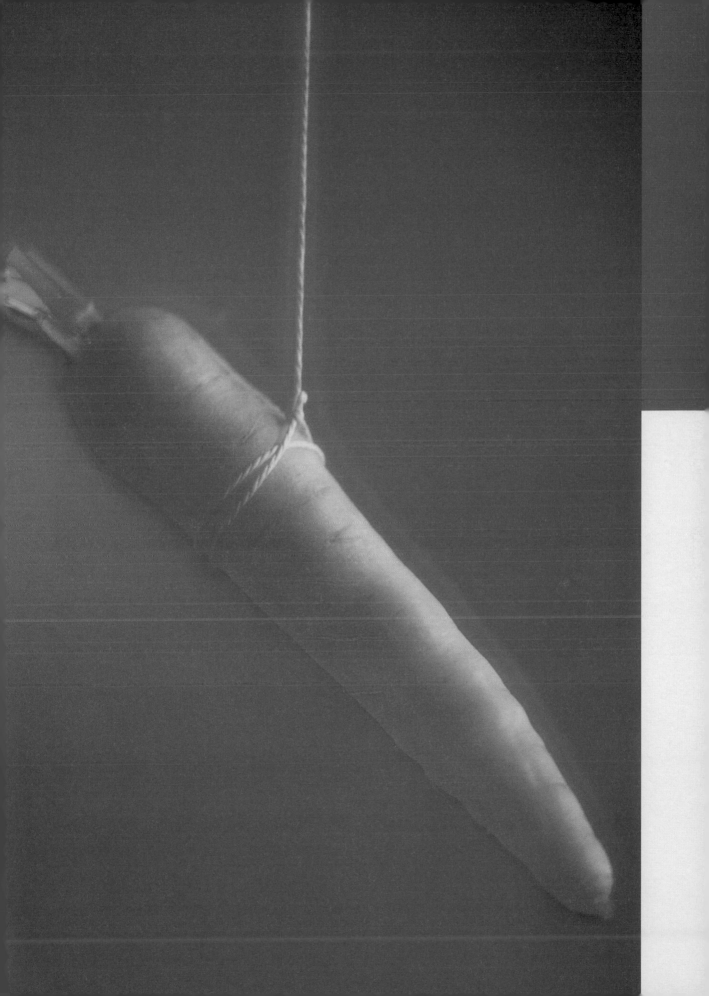

CHAPTER 9

Approaches to work motivation and job design

After studying this chapter, you should be able to:

1 describe three 'common-sense' approaches to motivation;

2 describe Maslow's hierarchy of needs;

3 specify the characteristics of a 'self-actualising' person;

4 specify the strengths and weaknesses of need theories;

5 define valence, instrumentality and expectancy;

6 explain the key features of motivation theories based on justice and equity;

7 describe four types of organisational citizenship behaviour;

8 outline the features of goals that enhance motivation;

9 suggest how material rewards can affect motivation;

10 describe how the following play a part in goal-setting theory: (i) self-reactions; (ii) performance and learning orientations; (iii) action and state orientations;

11 describe the typologies of individual differences in motivation proposed by Leonard *et al.* and Kanfer and Ackerman;

12 describe the key features of scientific management (Taylorism);

13 list four techniques of job redesign;

14 define the five core job characteristics identified by Hackman and Oldham;

15 suggest four ways in which the job characteristics model could be improved.

Opening Case Study **Shop-floor Reorganisation at Land Rover**

Marin Burela, the new head of manufacturing at Land Rover, bounces gently up and down beside the refurbished assembly line at the carmaker's plant in Solihull, England. Looking at the floor, Mr Burela points out the springy 'anti-fatigue matting' as one sign of the transformation of once dingy and cramped working conditions. 'We have made a hell of a difference here. They don't call this the Bat Cave any more,' he says.

Mr Burela is one of a corps of Ford executives dispatched to Land Rover following its Euros 2.9bn (Pounds 1.7bn) takeover this year. He is charged with turning round the loss-making brand, abandoned by Germany's BMW after the break-up of Rover Group. 'We have got to unlock the value in our assets and get the creative juices flowing,' he says. 'It's about instilling a sense of passion in Land Rover people.'

Ford executives privately admit they were shocked by some of what they found at Solihull. The production methods on the Defender line were antiquated. Other areas were poorly lit and untidy. Given the employees' dismay after BMW's sudden withdrawal this year, part of the task before Ford has been to hide its concerns and persuade the employees that they can make better cars. The trick for Land Rover's owners has been to win employees' backing for a restructuring that begins and ends with them. Ford is trying to persuade the workforce that it believes they are a top-quality asset that was either under-used or neglected by the former owner.

To preach its message, senior managers have held a series of US-style 'town hall meetings' with 200–500 workers at a time. Workers have been urged to match the best standards of Ford's premier automotive group, which includes Jaguar, Volvo, Lincoln and Aston Martin. Executives, rarely seen on the shop floor in the past, have been instructed to walk the line. They take cars at random from the assembly line for testing; they hold impromptu meetings with groups of workers. Everyone is encouraged to be on first-name terms. 'We're looking for visual management,' says Bob Dover, the new chief executive installed at Land Rover by Ford. 'You cannot expect high standards and a sense of passion if the management is invisible or if the roof leaks and the place is a mess.'

Mr Dover, formerly chief executive of Aston Martin, wants to start by removing unused temporary buildings: 'We probably have the biggest collection of Portakabins in the Midlands,' he says. 'We could start a Portakabin museum'. That effort and the investment in facilities will be coupled to what Mr Dover calls a 'culture of openness'. 'It sounds soft and stupid but we have to start by concentrating on people.' That means changing the outlook and profile of Land Rover's staff. Mr Dover points out that Land Rover sells cars to 140 countries. 'We have to include people from different backgrounds and more women.' Part of that overhaul mirrors the transformation of Jaguar, another neglected British brand acquired by Ford.

As Jaguar, Land Rover's people are invited to sign up to a system whereby they can suggest changes in production. If a junior employee feels quality is suffering, he or she can stop the entire line. In future, such employees are likely to have spent time on Volvo assembly lines in Gothenburg or Jaguar factories near Coventry. 'Nothing like this has happened in Land Rover's history,' says Mr Burela. 'There is tremendous enthusiasm . . . It's changing the way we do business.'

Source: Financial Times, *27 October 2000*

Introduction

The Ford executives in charge of the Solihull Land Rover plant clearly have some ideas about what will motivate employees there. We suggest you take a few minutes now to identify what they are. The senior managers are looking for 'passion' from the staff, and think they know how to get it. But perhaps they are less clear about what behaviour would signify passion. Also it might be asked whether a person has to exhibit passion in order to be motivated at work.

In this chapter we therefore examine the concept of motivation and explore some of its implications. We look at some conflicting so-called 'common-sense' ideas about motivation. The chapter then turns to a description and evaluation of some of the old but enduring approaches to motivation, including need theories, the motivation to manage, expectancy theory, justice theories and goal-setting. The roles of the self and personality are also considered. Both theoretical and practical issues are covered. The idea that jobs can be designed to be motivating is also examined: this suggests that motivation is as much a feature of the job as of the person. Behaviourist theories are also relevant to motivation, and are described in Chapter 8. The topic of motivation has received huge attention from work psychologists over very many years, so it is not possible to cover every relevant theory. The earlier ones were often designed to be big theories of human nature, whereas later ones have tended to confine themselves to specific aspects of motivated behaviour. In fact, some recent approaches scarcely have the label 'motivation' at all. So although motivation continues to be a very significant concept in work psychology, its boundaries are not easy to define.

Overview of motivation

As with many important concepts in psychology, there is no single universally accepted definition of motivation. Nevertheless, the word itself gives us some clues. To use a mechanical analogy, the motive force gets a machine started and keeps it going. In legal terms, a motive is a person's reason for doing something. Clearly, then, motivation concerns the factors that push us or pull us to behave in certain ways. Specifically, it is made up of three components:

1   *Direction*: what a person is trying to do.

2   *Effort*: how hard a person is trying.

3   *Persistence*: how long a person continues trying.

In a study of bank tellers (cashiers) Gary Blau (1993) assessed *effort* by filming each teller for a day and calculating the proportion of the time he or she was engaged in work behaviours. He assessed *direction* using a questionnaire that asked tellers to indicate how often they engaged in each of 20 different behaviours. Blau found that both the overall effort and the type of behaviours tellers engaged in (i.e. direction) predicted the quality of their work performance. This suggests that effort and direction are indeed separable, and that both are important.

Some key points should be remembered:

- People are usually motivated to do *something*. A person may try hard and long to avoid work – that is motivated behaviour! Hence we should always remember the 'direction' component.

- It is easy to make the mistake of thinking that motivation is the only important determinant of work performance. Other factors, such as ability, quality of equipment and co-ordination of team members' efforts also affect performance.

- Like most concepts in work psychology, motivation is abstract. It cannot be observed directly. Quite often a person's work performance is used as a measure of his or her motivation. But as we have just seen, many factors other than motivation influence performance. Individuals' reports of how hard they are trying (i.e. effort) are sometimes used as an indicator of motivation, but direction and persistence rarely feature (Ambrose and Kulik, 1999). This needs to change. Many people have jobs that offer choices in what to do and pay attention to (i.e. direction), and in many jobs it is necessary to keep trying over a long period in order to succeed.

One often-made distinction is between *content* theories and *process* theories of motivation. The former focus on *what* motivates human behaviour at work. The latter concentrate on *how* the content of motivation influences behaviour. In fact, most theories have something to say about both content and process, but they do vary considerably in their relative emphasis.

Key Learning Point

Motivation concerns what drives a person's choice of what to do, how hard they try, and how long they keep trying. It is not the only factor that influences work performance.

'Common-sense' approaches to motivation

McGregor (1960), Argyris (1964), Schein (1988) and others have collectively identified three broad 'common-sense' approaches to motivation which are endorsed by different individuals or even by the same individual at different times. McGregor (1960) termed two of the three *theory X* and *theory Y*, though the reader should be clear that in neither case is the word 'theory' used in its formal academic sense. Schein (1988) added what can be called the *social* approach. In all three cases, we are essentially uncovering a general perspective on human nature. Briefly, they are as follows:

■ *Theory X*: people cannot be trusted. They are irrational, unreliable and inherently lazy. They therefore need to be controlled and motivated using financial incentives and threats of punishment. In the absence of such controls, people will pursue their own goals, which are invariably in conflict with those of their work organisation.

■ *Theory Y*: people seek independence, self-development and creativity in their work. They can see further than immediate circumstances and are able to adapt to new ones. They are fundamentally moral and responsible beings who, if treated as such, will strive for the good of their work organisation.

■ *Social*: a person's behaviour is influenced most fundamentally by social interactions, which can determine his or her sense of identity and belonging at work. People seek meaningful social relationships at work. They are responsive to the expectations of people around them, often more so than to financial incentives.

As you can probably see, theory X and theory Y are in most respects opposites, with the social approach different from both. Which of these 'common-sense' approaches do you find most convincing? The authors' experience with business/management undergraduates is that, if forced to choose one, about half go for the social approach, about 40 per cent for theory Y and about 10 per cent for theory X. Interestingly, most of that 10 per cent can usually be found right at the back of the lecture theatre! Which of the three approaches do you think is most evident in the opening case study of this chapter?

Key Learning Point

Common-sense views of motivation contradict each other but all have some truth.

None of these three 'common-sense' accounts is universally correct. But, as Schein (1988) pointed out, over time people may be socialised into their organisation's way of thinking about motivation. Ultimately, managers can influence their staff to see motivation their way. Of course they may also attract and select staff who are already inclined to see things their way. Nevertheless, none of the approaches can be forced on all of the people all of the time. Indiscriminate use of any could have disastrous results. Hence, although each of these approaches finds some expression in theories of motivation, the match between theory and common sense is not particularly close.

So what are the theories? Let us now examine some of the most widely known and extensively researched. Bear in mind that several of the theories are old, and nowadays rarely feature in research regarded as leading edge. That does *not* mean they are useless. They contain ideas that have found expression in subsequent work, and some practising managers say they are still useful in managing their staff.

Need theories

What are they?

Need theories are based on the idea that there are psychological needs, probably of biological origin, that lie behind human behaviour. When our needs are unmet, we experience tension or disequilibrium which we try to put right. In other words, we behave in ways that satisfy our needs. Clearly the notion of need reflects the *content* of motivation as opposed to process. But most need theories also make some propositions about how and when particular needs become salient – i.e. process. The notion of need has a long history in general psychology. It has, for example, formed the basis of at least one major analysis of personality (Murray, 1938). Two major traditions have been evident in the work setting. First, there are models based on the notion of psychological growth. Second, there are various approaches which focus on certain quite specific needs.

Need theories based on psychological growth

Easily the best known of these theories is that of Abraham Maslow (1943, 1954). Maslow was a humanistically orientated psychologist (*see* Chapter 1) who offered a general theory of human functioning. His ideas were applied by others to the work setting.

Maslow proposed five classes of human need. Briefly, these are:

1 *Physiological*: need for food, drink, sex, etc., i.e. the most primitive and fundamental biological needs.

2 *Safety*: need for physical and psychological safety, i.e. a predictable and non-threatening environment.

3 *Belongingness*: need to feel a sense of attachment to another person or group of persons.

4   *Esteem*: need to feel valued and respected, by self and significant other people.

5   *Self-actualisation*: need to fulfil one's potential – to develop one's capacities and express them.

Maslow proposed that we strive to progress up the hierarchy shown in Fig. 9.1. When one need is satisfied to some (unspecified) adequate extent, the next one up the hierarchy becomes the most important in driving our behaviour.

Other psychologists produced rather similar analyses. For example, Alderfer (1972) proposed three classes of need: existence, relatedness and growth. Existence equated to Maslow's physiological and safety needs. Relatedness can be matched to belongingness and the esteem of others. Growth is equivalent to self-esteem and self-actualisation. Both Maslow and Alderfer made propositions about how particular needs become more or less important to the person (i.e. process), but need theories are often thought of as examples of content theories because of their emphasis on describing needs.

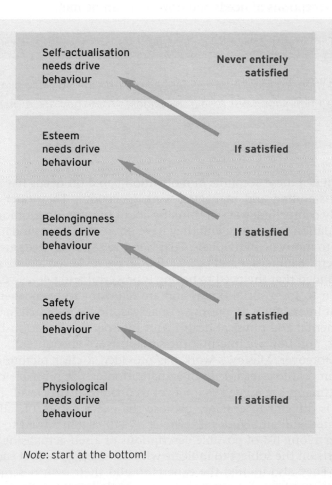

Self-actualisation
needs drive
behaviour   Never entirely
                                    satisfied

Esteem
needs drive
behaviour   If satisfied

Belongingness
needs drive
behaviour   If satisfied

Safety
needs drive
behaviour   If satisfied

Physiological
needs drive
behaviour   If satisfied

Note: start at the bottom!

Figure 9.1   Maslow's hierarchy of needs

For some years, need theories (especially Maslow's) dominated work motivation. Unfortunately, evaluations of them (e.g. Wahba and Bridwell, 1976; Salancik and Pfeffer, 1977; Rauschenberger *et al.*, 1980) revealed a number of significant flaws, such as:

- needs did not group together in the ways predicted;

- the theories were unable to predict when particular needs would become important;

- there was no clear relationship between needs and behaviour, so that (for example) the same behaviour could reflect different needs, and different behaviours the same need;

- needs were generally described with insufficient precision;

- the whole notion of need as a biological phenomenon is problematic. It ignores the capacity of people and those around them to construct their own perceptions of needs and how they can be met.

Key Learning Point

Need theories have intuitive appeal and provide possible explanations for some human behaviour, but research suggests that they are difficult to use at work.

Hence these accounts of motivation based on needs have only limited value in understanding and managing work behaviour. They offer interesting and intuitively compelling ways of thinking about human functioning, but their theoretical foundation is doubtful and they have offered no clear guidance to managers about how to motivate individuals. That is not to say that needs are unimportant or non-existent. Baumeister and Leary (1995) have reviewed a wide range of literature and concluded that the need to belong is powerful and pervasive. People seem strongly driven to form social bonds and are reluctant to break them. Deprivation of frequent interactions of a positive or at least non-conflictual nature has consequences for mental and physical health. Our interpersonal relationships affect the way we think, and how we interpret the situations we encounter.

Moreover, Maslow's work has provided a clear picture of the self-actualising person. Maslow regarded self-actualisation as the pinnacle of human growth and adjustment, but argued that few of us operate at that level. The truth of this assertion is difficult to evaluate because the exact nature of self-actualisation is both disputed and ambiguous. Leclerc *et al.* (1998) have tried to resolve this by developing a long list of possible descriptions of a self-actualising person and asking 30 experts on the subject to indicate whether they agree that each description is accurate. They also invited the experts to add their own descriptions if they wished. Eventually there was consensus about 36 descriptions. Some of them are shown in Table 9.1. Leclerc *et al.* emphasised that this view of self-actualisation suggests that it is not some kind of special state of being, nor is it necessarily the highest stage of being. Instead, it portrays the characteristics of people who function well in the sense that they are open to all aspects of reality, are able to understand and communicate with others, and act accordingly. These observations led Leclerc and colleagues to suggest that self-actualisation can be defined as 'a process through which one's potential is developed in congruence with one's self-perception and one's experience' (pp 78–9).

Examine Table 9.1 to see whether you think you could be described as a self-actualising person. In the opening case study to this chapter, what evidence (if any) is there that Land Rover senior managers wanted a self-actualising workforce?

Maslow's ideas still enjoy some support. In our experience students can often relate to his theory. Even some of those who want to amend his theory believe that it says something profound about human nature. For example, Rowan (1998, p. 81) says 'I am merely trying to tidy up the Maslow theory, which seems to me extraordinarily useful in general.' He proposes three amendments to the need hierarchy theory:

1   There are two types of esteem needs, and they need to be separated. One is the need for the esteem and respect of other people. This is really about self-image rather than the true self, and in some ways reflects needs for relatedness. The other type of esteem is that which we give ourselves. It comes from inside the self, not from other people.

Table 9.1	Fifteen characteristics of self-actualisating people (based on Leclerc et al., 1998)

1   Have a positive self-esteem

2   Consider themselves responsible for their own life

3   Give a meaning to life

4   Are capable of establishing meaningful relationships

5   Take responsibility for their actions

6   Are aware of their feelings

7   Are capable of intimate contact

8   Have a realistic perception of themselves

9   Are capable of commitment

10   Act according to their own convictions and values

11   Are able to resist undue social pressure

12   Are capable of insight

13   Feel free to express their emotions

14   Are able to accept contradictory feelings

15   Are aware of their strengths and weaknesses

2   The need for competence should be added to the hierarchy, probably between safety and belongingness. This need reflects our desire to master certain skills and do something well for the pleasure in being able to do it. It is evident from very early in life.

3   There may be two kinds of self-actualisation. The first is where a person is able to express his or her real self. The second is something more mystical – a sense of closeness with God or humanity as a whole which goes beyond (transcends) the self. This distinction was evident in some of Maslow's later work, which drew open ideas from Asian psychology and religion including Taoism and Zen Buddhism (Cleary and Shapiro, 1996).

Key Learning Point

There are at least two types of esteem, and also of self-actualisation. The need for competence is an important omission from some need theories.

Achievement, power and motivation to manage

Considerable success has been enjoyed by need-based approaches to motivation which concentrate on a small number of more specific needs. Need for achievement was one of the 20 needs underlying behaviour proposed by Murray (1938). It concerns the desire 'to overcome obstacles, to exercise power, to strive to do something difficult as well and as quickly as possible' (Murray, 1938, pp. 80–81, quoted by Landy, 1989, p. 73). Typically, people with high need for achievement seek tasks that are fairly difficult, but not impossible. They like to take sole responsibility for them, and want frequent feedback on how well they are doing. Need for achievement formed the basis of McClelland's (1961) theory of work motivation. McClelland argued that a nation's economic prosperity depends partly on the level of need for achievement in its population. He also believed that people could be trained to have high need for achievement. As for personal success, Parker and Chusmir (1991) found that people with high need for achievement tend to feel more successful regarding status/wealth, professional fulfilment and contribution to society than those with lower need for achievement.

Need for achievement has attracted considerable attention in both theoretical and applied contexts (e.g. *see* Beck, 1983). It is not a simple construct, however, and several attempts have been made to identify its components (e.g. Cassidy and Lynn, 1989). Sagie *et al.* (1996) argue that it is important to restrict analysis to the level of tasks, as opposed to wider considerations of status and power. They propose six task preferences that signal high need for achievement:

1   Tasks involving uncertainty rather than sure outcomes.

2   Difficult tasks rather than easy ones.

3   Tasks involving personal responsibility, not shared responsibility.

4   Tasks involving a calculated risk, rather than no risk or excessive risk.

5   Tasks requiring problem-solving or inventiveness, rather than following instructions.

6   Tasks that gratify the need to succeed, rather than ensuring the avoidance of failure.

Sagie *et al.* report a five-country study of levels of achievement motivation. People from the United States generally scored highest on most components, followed by people from the Netherlands and Israel, with those from Hungary lower and those from Japan lower again, except on the first component, where Japanese people scored close to Americans. However, it is important to remember that need for achievement is not the only route to successful work performance. Also, need for achievement may be a very Western and individualistic concept, of little relevance to some other cultures.

A person's need for achievement is often assessed using *projective* tests, which involve the person interpreting ambiguous stimuli. For example, a person may be asked to make up a story about what is happening in a short series of pictures. It is assumed that people *project* their personality onto the stimuli through their interpretations. This general technique is derived from psychoanalytic theory (*see* Chapter 1). Need for achievement can also be assessed in a more straightforward manner using questions about the person's behaviour, thoughts and feelings as in a personality questionnaire. Spangler (1992) reviewed the relevant literature and found that scores on most assessments of need for achievement are indeed correlated with outcomes such as career success. Also, despite the generally poor record of projective tests in psychology, projective measures of need for achievement correlated more highly with outcomes than did questionnaire measures.

Key Learning Point

Need for achievement is a sufficiently specific and valid construct to explain some aspects of work behaviour, including managerial behaviour, at least in Western contexts.

John Miner (1964) developed the concept of *motivation to manage*. He also devised a measure of it, called the Miner Sentence Completion Scale (MSCS), which requires people to complete 35 half-finished sentences. Their responses are then scored by a carefully trained expert on the various components of motivation to manage. These are shown in Table 9.2. The need for power and self-control, and low need for affiliation probably underlie motivation to manage. So do some of the components of need for achievement.

Miner believes that levels of managerial motivation have a substantial effect on a nation's economic performance, and few have disagreed with that. Carson and Gilliard (1993) reported that over a number of research studies, the higher a manager's motivation to manage as assessed by the MSCS, the higher his or her work performance, status and salary, other things being equal. So motivation to

Table 9.2	Components of the motivation to manage

Component	Meaning
Authority figures	A desire to meet managerial role requirements in terms of positive relationships with superiors
Competitive games	A desire to engage in competition with peers involving games or sports
Competitive situations	A desire to engage in competition with peers involving occupational or work-related activities
Assertive role	A desire to behave in an active and assertive manner involving activities that are often viewed as predominantly masculine
Imposing wishes	A desire to tell others what to do and to utilise sanctions in influencing others
Standing out from the group	A desire to assume a distinctive position of a unique and highly visible nature
Routine administrative functions	A desire to meet managerial role requirements of a day-to-day administrative nature

Source: Miner and Smith (1982, p. 298). Copyright © 1982 by the American Psychological Association. Adapted with permission.

manage is associated with personal success in managerial occupations. We cannot, however, be certain that motivation to manage necessarily leads to success. It is possible that the requirements of higher level jobs lead to people feeling more motivated to conform to traditional expectations of how managers should behave.

Some psychologists have investigated the applicability of the concept of motivation to manage across cultures, countries and genders. Thornton *et al.* (1997) have found that, among a sample of students in United States, whites scored higher on average than blacks on the MSCS, but not on a practical test of management potential. This practical test was a so-called in-basket test, where the test-taker is presented with a pile of letters and other documents from a simulated workplace and is required to indicate what actions they would take and in what priority order if they were a manager in that workplace. Similarly, men scored higher than women on average on the MSCS but not on the in-basket test. Hence although motivation to manage scores may predict job success, it is not necessarily fair to use them to compare people of different genders and ethnicities.

Interesting studies by Miner *et al.* (1991) and Chen *et al.* (1997) investigated motivation to manage in China. They suggested that although China is a more collectivist society than Western ones, it is nevertheless sympathetic to competition and hierarchy, and that this would be one reason why the motivation to manage would be applicable there. Consistent with their arguments, they found that people in higher-level jobs scored higher on the MSCS than people in lower-level jobs. They also found that women scored no lower than men, and suggested that this might be a consequence of the assertive roles women were encouraged to take in China's cultural revolution of the late 1960s and 1970s, together with the Chinese government policy of no more than one child per family.

Exercise 9.1   The motivation to manage

Marie Herzog is an administrative assistant at a large packaging factory in Lyons. She had previously been promoted from the factory floor and is keen to go higher. Her boss, Simone Trouchot, is not so sure – how keen is Marie? Simone made the following observations. Marie seemed rarely to impose her will on her clerical subordinates, even when they were obviously in the wrong. She got on well with the higher managers at the factory, and seemed willing to work closely to the remit they gave her. On the other hand, Marie rarely volunteered her department for trying out experimental new ideas. She seemed uncomfortable when the spotlight was turned on her and her department, even if the attention was congratulatory. Marie seemed happiest dealing with the routine administrative tasks she knew well. She was an accomplished athlete, and had recently been Lyons 400 metres champion two years in succession. Marie was extremely keen to get her department working better than other similar ones, and to ensure that she dealt with problems faster and better than others in similar jobs at the factory.

Consult Table 9.2 to judge the extent and nature of Marie Herzog's motivation to manage. Are there particular kinds of managerial roles in which she would feel particularly motivated?

Exercise 9.2   Need theory in the car factory

Look back at the opening case study of this chapter. Which of the needs described in this section do you think the Ford managers believe govern the motivation of the shop-floor workers? If possible, compare your answers with somebody else's, and discuss whether needs offer a useful guide to managers in improving motivation.

Expectancy theory: what's in it for me?

Whereas need theories place heavy emphasis on the content of motivation, expectancy theory concentrates on the process. Originally proposed by Vroom (1964), expectancy theory (also sometimes called VIE (valence, instrumentality, expectancy) theory or instrumentality theory) aimed to explain how people choose which of several possible courses of action they will pursue. This choice process was seen as a cognitive, calculating appraisal of the following three factors for each of the actions being considered:

1 *Expectancy*: if I tried, would I be able to perform the action I am considering?

2 *Instrumentality*: would performing the action lead to identifiable outcomes?

3 *Valence*: how much do I value those outcomes?

Vroom (1964) proposed that expectancy and instrumentality can be expressed as probabilities, and valence as a subjective value. He also suggested that force to act is a function of the product of expectancy, instrumentality and valence: in other words, V, I and E are multiplied together to determine motivation. This would mean that if any one of the components was zero, overall motivation to pursue that course of action would also be zero. This can be seen in Fig. 9.2, where, for example, the instrumentality question is not even worth asking if a person believes he or she is incapable of writing a good essay on motivation.

If correct, VIE theory would have important implications for managers wishing to ensure that employees were motivated to perform their work duties. They would need to ensure that all three of the following conditions were satisfied:

1 Employees perceived that they possessed the necessary skills to do their jobs at least adequately (expectancy).

Motivation to write an essay on motivation

Expectancy	X	Instrumentality	X	Valence
Question: How likely is it that I am capable of writing a good essay on motivation?		*Question:* How likely is it that I will receive rewards for writing a good essay on motivation?		*Question:* How much do I value those rewards?
Considerations: General self-efficacy		*Considerations:* The weight attached to the mark in the assessment system		*Considerations:* Importance of passing the course
Specific self-rated abilities		The accuracy of the marking		Interest in the subject
Past experience of essay writing		Likelihood of intrinsic rewards such as learning or satisfaction		Extent of commitment to self-development

Figure 9.2   **Example of VIE theory in action**

2 Employees perceived that if they performed their jobs well, or at least adequately, they would be rewarded (instrumentality).

3 Employees perceived the rewards offered for successful job performance to be attractive (valence).

Referring again to the Land Rover case study at the start of this chapter, to what extent do you think each of these three components of motivation was likely to have been a problem?

Key Learning Point

Expectancy theory proposes that people's choice of course of action depends upon their beliefs of (i) their own capabilities; (ii) whether the course of action will lead to rewards; (iii) how valuable the rewards are.

Although it looks attractive, VIE theory has not done especially well when evaluated in research. Like need theories, it has rather gone out of fashion. Van Eerde and Thierry (1996) found 74 published research studies on VIE theory prior to 1990 but only ten subsequently. Van Eerde and Thierry (1996), and also Schwab *et al.* (1979), have summarised the available research and drawn the following conclusions:

■ Research studies that have not measured expectancy, or have combined it with instrumentality, have accounted for effort and/or performance better than studies that assessed expectancy and instrumentality separately.

■ Behaviour is at least as well predicted by adding the three components V, I and E as it is by multiplying them.

■ The theory does not work where any of the outcomes have negative valence (i.e. are viewed as undesirable) (Leon, 1981).

■ The theory works better when the outcome measure is an attitude (for example intention or preference) than when it is a behaviour (performance, effort or choice).

■ Self-report measures of V, I and E have often been poorly constructed.

■ Most research has compared different people with each other (i.e. between-participants research design), rather than comparing different outcomes for the same person (i.e. within-participants design). The latter enables a better test of VIE theory because the theory was designed to predict whether an individual will prefer one course of action over another, rather than whether one person will favour a course of action more than another person does. Where within-participant designs are used, results tend to be more supportive of the theory.

The first four of these points reflect badly on VIE theory as a whole. The other two are more to do with limitations of research design rather than the theory itself. But even if the theory is less than perfect, it is still useful to identify the potential determinants of the motivation process, even if they do not combine as predicted by VIE theory. As Landy (1985, pp. 336–7) put it:

> The cognitive nature of the approach does a good job of capturing the essence of energy expenditure .... A manager can understand and apply the principles embodied in each of the components of the model. Instrumentalities make sense. The manager can use this principle to lay out clearly for subordinates the relationships among outcomes (e.g. promotions yield salary increases, four unexcused absences yield a suspension of one day). Similarly, the manager can affect effort-reward probabilities by systematically rewarding good performance.

Key Learning Point

Instrumentality theory may over-complicate the cognitive processes involved in motivation, but is a helpful logical analysis of key factors in the choices made by individuals.

Finally, notice how little attention VIE theory pays to explaining *why* an individual values or does not value particular outcomes. No concepts of need are invoked to address this question. VIE theory proposes that we should ask someone how much they value something, but not bother about *why* they value it. This is another illustration of VIE theory's concentration on process, not content.

Justice and citizenship theories: am I being fairly treated?

Justice theories are like expectancy theory in that they focus on the cognitive processes that govern a person's decision whether or not to expend effort. But unlike expectancy theory they suggest that people are motivated to obtain what they consider fair return for their efforts rather than to get as much as they can. Some students and managers find it hard to believe that people might not always seek to maximise their gains, but let us suspend disbelief for the moment and consider the propositions of the original justice theory: equity theory.

Equity theory was derived from work by Adams (1965), originally in the context of interpersonal relationships. Huseman *et al.* (1987, p. 222) have described the propositions of equity theory like this:

1   Individuals evaluate their relationships with others by assessing the ratio of their outcomes from and inputs to the relationship against the outcome/input ratio of a comparison other.

2   If the outcome/input ratios of the individual and comparison other are perceived to be unequal, then inequity exists.

3   The greater the inequity the individual perceives (in the form of either over-reward or under-reward), the more distress the individual feels.

4   The greater the distress an individual feels, the harder he or she will work to restore equity. Equity restoration techniques include altering or cognitively distorting inputs or outcomes, increasing or decreasing the amount of effort devoted to the task, acting on or changing the comparison other, or terminating the relationship.

In other words, a person is motivated to maintain the same balance between his or her contributions and rewards as that experienced by salient comparison person or persons.

Laboratory experiments have generally provided reasonable support for equity theory. Because rewards and availability of comparison others are closely controlled by the experimenter, the only way that people participating in the experiment could establish equity was to increase or decrease the quantity or quality of their work. And this they did, on the whole (Pritchard, 1969). But in the 'real world' things are of course more complicated. People have much more choice of strategy to establish equity and choice of comparison other. They often, but not always, choose similar workers in other organisations (Dornstein, 1988).

Perhaps it is not surprising that the predictions of equity theory are less often supported by research when people receive more than their share as opposed to when they receive less (Mowday, 1991). In other words, we are more likely to do something in response to feeling under-rewarded than over-rewarded. Furthermore, rather like need theories, equity theory is vague about exactly what people will do when they are dissatisfied. They might adopt any or all of the equity restoration devices listed above, and equity theory is not good at specifying which (Greenberg, 2001).

Equity theory has been broadened into theories of organisational justice from the late 1980s onwards (*see*, for example, Cropanzano *et al.*, 2001). A distinction is made between *distributive justice* and *procedural justice*. The former concerns whether people believe they have received (or will receive) fair rewards. The latter reflects whether people believe that the procedures used in an organisation to allocate rewards are fair (Folger and Konovsky, 1989). For example, is the reward system impartial, not favouring one group above another? Does it take into account all of the appropriate information? Is there a way of noticing and correcting errors? So if people believe that they are poorly paid relative to people doing similar jobs in other organisations, they may perceive distributive injustice. But if at the same time they think their employing organisation is making available as much reward as possible, and operating fair systems to distribute them, then they may perceive procedural justice. Their satisfaction with pay would probably be low, but their commitment to their employer (*see* Chapter 7) might well be high (McFarlin and Sweeney, 1992).

Ideas about justice have now been prominent long enough to attract some close scrutiny. Many potential limitations of justice concepts mirror those of equity theory. In addition, Greenberg (2001) among others has questioned what are the true motives underlying justice. It could simply be that when people feel a sense of injustice, they are saying that they are getting less than they hoped, rather than less than they deserved. In other words, (in)justice could be a smokescreen for self-interest. Also, a sense of injustice can arise in a number of ways, described by Folger and Cropanzano (2001) as Would, Could and Should. These respectively refer to comparisons with what *would* have happened if events had turned out differently; what *could* have happened if another person had behaved differently; and what *should* have happened if principles of morality had been followed. These three are likely to elicit different responses, and indeed different individuals may interpret the same situation in different ways. From the information given in the opening case study, how much and what kind of injustice do you think members of the Land Rover workforce might have been experiencing?

One likely consequence when people in an organisation feel they have been treated unjustly is that they will be less willing to be 'good citizens' at work. Since the early 1990s psychologists have shown a lot of interest in what have become known as organisational citizenship behaviours (OCBs) (see, for example, Moorman, 1991). This partly reflects a realisation that successful work organisations need people who help each other out in addition to doing the core tasks of their jobs well. OCBs are an interesting area for scholars of motivation, because OCBs are usually thought to be discretionary – that is, a person has choice over whether they perform them. OCBs include the following:

- Altruism: helping another person with a work task or problem.

- Conscientiousness: going well beyond minimum role requirements.

- Civic virtue: participation and involvement in the life of the organisation.

- Courtesy: preventing inter-personal problems through polite and considerate behaviour.

- Sportsmanship: willingness to tolerate less than ideal circumstances without complaining.

There is some reason to question whether it is appropriate to consider OCBs 'extras' , over and above the job. Research by Kam *et al.* (1999) suggested that to a considerable extent bank employees across four countries felt that the five OCBs listed above were indeed part of their job. Their supervisors thought so even more! There were some differences between countries, though. Courtesy and sportsmanship were expected to a greater extent in Japan and Hong Kong than in the United States and Australia. Another common assumption about OCBs is that they enhance organisational performance. This can be questioned. Perhaps OCBs simply distract people from doing their own jobs properly. However, Podsakoff *et al.* (1997) found that OCBs had a small beneficial effect on the performance of a paper mill, so perhaps the fear is unjustified.

Key Learning Point

The role of fairness and justice in motivation is becoming more prominent, and increasingly concerns a person's perceptions of the fairness of organisational systems.

The possible role of justice in motivation has become more apparent in recent years. The downsizing, delayering and other changes that have occurred in many work organisations have meant that the deal, or psychological contract, that many employees felt they had with their organisation has been broken (*see also* Chapter 14). Some people feel a strong sense of injustice about this. To the extent that they can, they are likely to reduce their contribution to their organisation both in terms of their own work performance and other 'good citizen' behaviours such as helping others and attending functions on behalf of their employer (Parks and Kidder, 1994). Figure 9.3 shows how this process might work. It suggests that justice, especially procedural justice, plays a large part in determining reactions to a broken psychological contract, and so does a person's perception of the reasons why the organisation fell short of his or her expectations. There is some evidence for elements of this process (Daly and Geyer, 1994). But it is still likely that people's perceptions of what is fair are heavily influenced by self-interest, so that, for example, you or I tend to believe that we are less fairly treated than other people think we are.

Key Learning Point

The motivation to perform 'good citizen' behaviours is currently a topic of considerable interest to psychologists. This motivation is undermined by a sense of injustice.

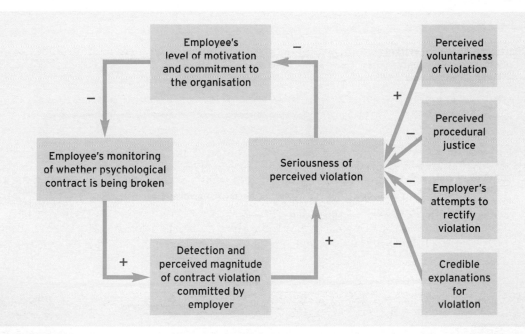

Figure 9.3	**Justice and motivation**
	Source: **Based on Rousseau (1995, p. 118), reprinted with permission. Note that this same process is depicted to illustrate features of the psychological contract in Fig. 14.2**

Goal-setting theory: how can I achieve my aims?

The theory

This approach to motivation was pioneered in the United States by Ed Locke and his associates, starting in the 1960s and continuing with increasing strength and sophistication ever since – so much so, that by the 1990s, well over half the research on motivation published in leading academic journals reported tests, extensions or refinements of goal-setting theory.

As Locke *et al.* (1981, p. 126) put it, 'A goal is what an individual is trying to accomplish; it is the object or aim of an action. The concept is similar in meaning to the concepts of purpose and intent'. Locke drew on both academic writing on intention (Ryan, 1970) and the much more practical 'management by objectives' literature in formulating his ideas. Figure 9.4 represents goal-setting theory, and shows that the characteristics of a goal and attitudes towards it are thought to be influenced by incentives, self-perceptions and the manner in which goals are set. In turn, those goal characteristics and attitudes are thought to determine behavioural strategies, which lead to performance within the constraints of ability. Knowledge of results (also called feedback) is thought to be essential to the further refinement of behavioural strategies.

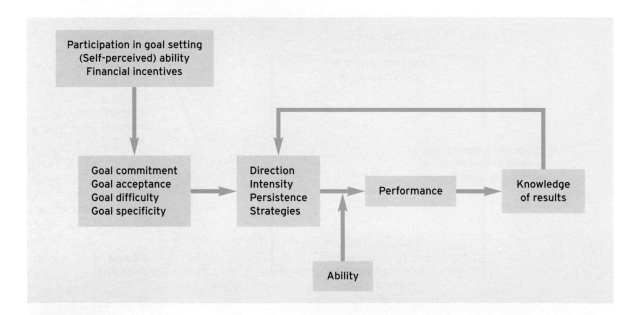

Figure 9.4 **Goal-setting theory**
Source: **Adapted from *Psychology of Work Behavior* by F. Landy. Copyright ©**
1989, 1985, 1980, 1976 Brooks/Cole Publishing Company, a division of
International Thomson Publishing Inc. By permission of the publisher

What does research say about goal-setting? Many of the main features of the theory are now well-established having been researched thoroughly (some would say exhaustively) in the 1970s and 1980s. Reviews by Locke and Latham (1990) and Mento *et al.* (1987) arrived at a number of conclusions, most of which fully or substantially support goal-setting theory. Most fundamental was overwhelming confirmation of the following phenomena:

■ Difficult goals lead to higher performance than easy goals, so long as they have been accepted by the person trying to achieve them. This follows from the fact that people direct their behaviour towards goal achievement, so that difficult goals produce more effective behaviour than easy ones.

■ Specific goals lead to higher performance than general 'do your best' goals. Specific goals seem to create a precise intention, which in turn helps people to shape their behaviour with precision.

■ Knowledge of results (feedback) is essential if the full performance benefits of setting difficult and specific goals are to be achieved. Locke *et al.* (1981) have pointed out that although feedback may exert its main effect through providing a person with information, it may also itself have motivating properties. The optimal timing, frequency and amount of feedback are at present somewhat uncertain,

■ The beneficial effects of goal-setting depend partly on a person's goal commitment: that is, his or her determination to try to achieve the goal, and unwillingness to abandon or reduce it (Hollenbeck *et al.*, 1989).

These findings establish the core of goal-setting and make it probably the most consistently supported theory in work and organisational psychology. Locke *et al.* (1981) observed that 90 per cent of laboratory and field research studies produced results supporting the fundamental elements of goal-setting theory. Mento *et al.* (1987) reinforced that conclusion, and further commented (pp. 74–5) that:

> If there is ever to be a viable candidate from the organizational sciences for elevation to the lofty status of a scientific law of nature, then the relationships between goal specificity/difficulty and task performance are most worthy of serious consideration. [There is also] clear support of the efficacy of coupling feedback with hard specific goals. Both knowledge and motivation, it would seem, are necessary for enhanced performance.

Key Learning Point

The setting of performance goals that are specific and difficult (but not impossible), and to which the person feels committed, is likely to improve his or her work performance as long as he or she receives feedback on progress.

Locke (2000) has elaborated on this last point by proposing that one way in which goals work is to unlock or mobilise existing knowledge and skills that are relevant to the task in hand. Some further comments can be made on the basis of research evidence. First, financial incentives can indeed enhance performance. Locke and Latham (1990) report that this occurs either through raising goal level, or through increasing commitment to a goal – so long as the amount of money on offer is considered significant, and not tied to goals perceived as impossible. Second, and unsurprisingly, knowledge and ability also affect performance. As Locke (2000, p. 409) has pointed out 'It is a virtual axiom that human action is a consequence of . . . knowledge (including skill and ability) and desire'. Third, research on goal-setting has been carried out in a range of contexts. Much work has been in laboratories using students who tackle tasks such as solving anagrams or brainstorming, but some has been conducted with groups such as truck drivers and lumberjacks in their work settings. Fourth, goal-setting is magnificently clear about how managers can enhance the performance of their employees. Research results also show that goal setting is worth doing – Locke *et al.* (1981) reported that in goal-setting field experiments, the median improvement in work performance produced by goal setting was 16 per cent.

Key Learning Point

The impact of difficult and specific goals on a person's work performance occurs through the focusing of his or her strategies and intentions.

The notion of goal commitment has become very important in goal-setting theory. It can be defined as an unwillingness to abandon or lower the goal (Wright *et al.*, 1994). It is routinely argued that if individuals do not feel commitment to the goal, then they will not exert effort in pursuit of goals – even difficult and specific ones. Commitment is construed as more than simple acceptence of a goal, and it has been argued that one way of ensuring goal commitment is to allow people to participate in discussions about what goals to set (Latham *et al.*, 1988). It is usually treated as a moderator variable – that is, one that affects how much impact goals have on performance. The more committed a person is to the goal, the better he or she will do, other things being equal (*see also* Chapter 7 for more on commitment). But it could be argued that the notion of commitment is just another word for motivation – if I am committed to a goal, then that could be another way of saying I am motivated to achieve it. Tubbs (1994) suggests that one way of looking at it is to say that goal commitment is a function of (i) the closeness of one's personal goals to the goal that has been assigned, and (ii) the importance of that personal goal.

Goal commitment influences a person's persistence in pursuing his or her goal and the formation of strategies to achieve it. At least, that's the usual argument. However, Donovan and Radosevich (1998) conducted a meta-analysis of research on goal commitment and found that it had surprisingly little impact on performance. On the other hand, Klein *et al.* (1999) criticised the way Donovan and Radosevich conducted their work. Klein *et al.*'s analysis of existing research showed that commitment to goal achievement is essential for goals to affect performance.

Other work has shown, perhaps not surprisingly, that people's sense of self-efficacy influences the difficulty level of the goals they set themselves and their commitment to those goals as well as their performance (Wooford *et al.*, 1992). We will return shortly to the role of the self in motivation.

Key Learning Point

The impact of a goal on work performance is small or non-existent if the person does not feel committed to it.

Possible limits to the effectiveness of goal-setting

Austin and Bobko (1985) identified four respects in which goal-setting theory had not, at that time, been properly tested. Their work reflected the concerns of many researchers in goal-setting, and subsequently a significant amount of research has been carried out on each of the four issues. First, goals that reflect quality of work (as opposed to quantity) were rarely set in goal-setting research. Yet in many people's work, quality is more important than quantity. But quantity is usually more readily measurable and immediately apparent than quality, so the temptation to produce a lot rather than produce well may be hard to resist (Gilliland and Landis, 1992). Second, real jobs often have conflicting goals: achieving one may mean neglecting another. This could complicate or even undermine the application of goal-setting. For example, Ycarta *et al.* (1995) found some evidence that setting difficult goals may have actually impaired the work performance of the research scientists they studied. They suggest that goal-setting distorted the scientists' choices of work activities, so that they paid too much attention to short-term tasks on which they could obtain clear feedback.

Austin and Bobko's third point was that goal-setting research has used goals for individual people and assessed performance of individuals. In the world of work, however, group goals and group performance often matter more. Fourth, Austin and Bobko argued that goal-setting had not adequately demonstrated its effectiveness outside laboratory settings. Since Austin and Bobko published their work, evidence suggests that the latter two of their concerns are in fact dealt with by goal-setting theory (*see*, for example, Pritchard *et al.*, 1988; de Haas *et al.*, 2000). Goal setting can work for groups and it can work outside the laboratory. Crown and Rose (1995) found that the setting of a group goal can improve group performance as long as the group goal is consistent with individuals' goals. This consistency is probably measured by the individual's commitment to group goals. Durham *et al.* (1997) reported that the overall self-efficacy of a group of people affects the goals group members set for themselves and also the group's performance. So overall it seems that goal-setting for groups works in a similar way to goal-setting for individuals.

Some other research has investigated other potential limitations of goal-setting. Meyer and Gellatly (1988) argued that one function normally served by an assigned goal is to signal what constitutes an appropriate level of performance, or *performance norm*. They manipulated subjects' beliefs about performance norms on a brainstorming (i.e. creative idea generation) task so that they were sometimes different from the goal set. They found that this affected performance and reduced the impact of goal-setting. The practical implication is that goal-setting may be undermined in the workplace where people already have clear ideas (perhaps widely held within a workgroup) about what constitutes acceptable performance. This is consistent with the findings of the Hawthorne studies 60 years earlier (*see* Chapter 1).

| Exercise 9.3 | Goal-setting in a car repair shop |

Giovanni Ronto was dissatisfied with the performance of the mechanics at his car repair workshop. He did not keep detailed records, but in his opinion too many customers brought their cars back after repair or servicing, complaining they were still not right. Others found that their cars were not ready by the agreed time. The garage had recently become the local dealer for one of the smaller car manufacturers. The mechanics had been relatively unfamiliar with cars of that make, and were still often unsure how to carry out certain repairs without frequently checking the workshop manual. Giovanni had decided to introduce performance targets for the mechanics as a group. He told them that complaints and delays must be 'substantially reduced', and to sweeten the pill he immediately increased the group's pay by 8 per cent. The increase would continue as long as performance improved to what he regarded as a satisfactory extent. He promised to let the mechanics know each month whether he regarded their collective performance as satisfactory.

Use goal-setting theory and research to decide whether Giovanni Ronto's attempt at goal-setting is likely to succeed.

Earley *et al.* (1989) suggested that goal-setting may be harmful where a task is novel and where a considerable number of possible strategies are available to tackle it. They asked students to undertake a stock market prediction task, and, sure enough, they found that people who were assigned specific, difficult goals performed *worse* than those assigned a 'do your best' goal. They also changed their strategy more. It seems, then, that when people are tackling unfamiliar and complex tasks, goal-setting can induce them to pay too much attention to task strategy and not enough to task performance itself. A major innovative piece of work by Kanfer and Ackerman (1989), which combined motivation theories with cognitive ability theories, produced a similar conclusion. Kanfer and Ackerman focused on skill acquisition as opposed to performance of established skills, and concluded (p. 687):

Our findings indicate that interventions designed to engage motivational processes may impede task learning when presented prior to an understanding of what the task is about. In these instances, cognitive resources necessary for task understanding are diverted towards self-regulatory activities (e.g. self evaluation). Because persons have few spare resources at this phase of skill acquisition, these self-regulatory activities can provide little benefit for learning.

Kanfer *et al.* (1994) asked students to attempt a simulated air traffic control task and repeated the findings that goal-setting can harm performance of unfamiliar complex tasks. But they also found that giving people time to reflect on their performance between attempts eliminated that effect. The breaks enabled them to devote attentional resources to their strategies without having simultaneously to tackle the task itself.

Key Learning Point

Goal-setting can harm work performance when it takes attention away from learning a complex and novel task.

Goals and self-regulation

Goal-setting could be criticised in its early days for being a technology rather than a theory. It successfully described how goals focus behaviour, without really addressing why or through what processes goals influenced behaviour. During the 1980s and 1990s, developments within the goal-setting tradition (e.g. Latham and Locke, 1991) and outside it have helped progress on these issues. For example, VIE theory predicts that (other things being equal) people will tend to be motivated by tasks where they feel certain they can succeed. Goal-setting, on the other hand, suggests that people are most motivated by difficult tasks where success is (presumably) not certain. In fact Mento *et al.* (1992) showed that most people perceive trying for difficult goals as more likely to bring benefits such as a sense of achievement, skill development and material rewards (instrumentality) than trying for easy goals. This more than offsets the lower expectancy of success associated with difficult as apposed to easy goals.

Other motivation theories can also be integrated with goal-setting in order to explain further how people choose, change and implement strategies for achieving and reviewing goals (Kanfer, 1992). Social learning and social cognitive theories of *self-regulation* (*see* Chapter 1) suggest some processes through which people do these things. Bandura (1986) points out that goals provide a person with a cognitive representation (or 'image') of the outcomes they desire. Depending on the gap between goal and the current position, the person experiences *self-reactions*. These include emotions (e.g. dissatisfaction) and self-efficacy expectations (that is, perceptions of one's ability to achieve the goal). These reactions, together with other factors, affect the level and direction of a person's future effort as well as his or her self-concept. For example, suppose a student is attempting to achieve the difficult task of writing a good essay in one evening's work, but by midnight only half the essay has been written. The student's self-efficacy expectations are likely to be reduced somewhat, especially if high to begin with. But if self-efficacy is still fairly high, and so is dissatisfaction, the student is likely to persist until the essay is finished. If his or her self-efficacy has dropped a lot, or was low to start with, the student may give up even if dissatisfied with the lack of progress.

Other work relevant to the processes involved in goal setting has been reported by Dweck (1986). She developed a theory of motivation and learning which distinguishes between *learning goal orientation* and *performance goal orientation*. Farr *et al.* (1993, p. 195) have described these as follows:

> When approaching a task from a learning goal perspective, the individual's main objective is to increase his or her level of competence on a given task ... Alternatively, when a task is approached from a performance goal orientation, individuals are primarily concerned with demonstrating their competency either to themselves or to others via their present level of task performance.

Farr *et al.* (1993) argue that people who adopt a performance goal orientation will tend to be more fearful of failure, less willing to take on difficult goals, and perhaps less effective in using thought processes to achieve them, than those who adopt a learning goal orientation. They are also less likely to feel they have control over whether they achieve their goals, because by definition the goals of a performance goal orientated person depend partly on what other people are doing. In short, Farr and his colleagues suggest that goal-setting as a theory may be more applicable to, and useful for, learning goal orientated people than performance goal orientated ones. They also believe that in the long run, learning goal orientation is more likely to produce high performance and competence than performance goal orientation. They suggest that there is an increasing and ironic tendency in work organisations for goals to be set which are defined in terms of performance relative to other people, thus encouraging performance goal orientation rather than learning goal orientation.

Key Learning Point

A person's characteristic tendencies to be concerned (or not) with learning, performance and goal achievement influence the extent to which goal setting affects his or her work behaviour.

Another theory concerning self-regulation which is also applicable to goal-setting has been put forward by Kuhl (1992). Kuhl is concerned to explain how we regulate our behaviour in order to achieve goals, and stop ourselves going to do other things before our goals have been achieved. Kuhl distinguishes between *action orientation*, in which people use self-regulatory strategies to achieve desired goals, and *state orientation*, where they do not. He argues that (i) clear intentions, and (ii) moderate discrepancies between current and desired situation both encourage an action orientation. In other words, we 'swing into action' when we think there is a significant but not hopelessly large gap between where we are and where we want to be, and where we can establish a clear picture of what we are trying to do. The similarity with difficult, specific goals should be obvious!

Kuhl has argued that various self-regulatory strategies are part of action orientation. These include *selective attention* to information relevant to current intention, and *emotion control*, which prevents feelings blocking the implementation of intentions. In contrast, state orientation is characterised by *preoccupation* (with past experiences), *hesitation* (in initiating new behaviour) and *volatility* – frequent impulsive switching between different activities. Diefendorff *et al.* (2000) conducted a number of studies to develop self-report questionnaire measures of action and state orientation, and to see whether individuals' scores on these questionnaires correlate with work performance. They found that state-orientated people tended to receive lower performance ratings from their supervisors, and to report fewer organisational citizenship behaviours than their action-orientated counterparts. The hesitation aspect of state orientation seemed particularly important.

Action versus state orientation is probably partly a characteristic of individuals. Consistent with that, Diefendorff and colleagues found that scores on their questionnaire correlated moderately highly with personality test measures. For example, people who scored high on preoccupation tended to be emotionally unstable. However, action and state orientations are probably also partly induced by the situation. If so, there are two ways in which Kuhl's ideas contribute to goal setting. First, goal-setting is likely to encourage action orientation. Second, goal-setting motivational techniques are more likely to work for people who characteristically have an action orientation than for those with a state orientation.

Self-concept and individual differences in motivation

Many of the most recent approaches to motivation have focused on how our sense of who we are, i.e. our self-concepts, personalities and values influence the direction, effort and persistence of our behaviour (Leonard *et al.*, 1999). To some extent this is reflected in research on the role of self-efficacy in goal-setting and on action and state orientations described ealier in this chapter.

However, some work in this area draws on other areas of social psychology, particularly self-categorisation and social identity (Turner and Onorato, 1999). For example, it is proposed that a person does not have just one self-concept (i.e. set of perceptions about his or her own nature), but many. One distinction is between *personal identity*, which represents how we see ourselves relative to others in the same social groups, and *social identity*, which is those aspects of self-concept we think we have in common with others in the same group, and which differentiate us from members of other groups (*see also* Chapter 12). We have many different personal and social identities, depending on which social group is most salient to us at any given time. Furthermore, we are motivated to behave in ways that are consistent with our identity, or perhaps in some cases our ideal self – i.e. how we would *like* to be. In a work context this might mean that if our social identity as (for example) a member of the marketing department is most salient, then we will be motivated to perform behaviours that support the value of marketing and perhaps our marketing colleagues. On the other hand, if our personal identity as an ambitious young manager is most salient, we are more likely to pursue behaviours that we see as being in our own interest, such as concentrating on our own work or making ourselves look good in front of the boss in case there is a promotion opportunity on the horizon (Haslam *et al.*, 2000; Van Knippenberg, 2000).

Leonard *et al.* (1999) suggest that our identities are composed of three elements. Traits are broad tendencies to react in certain ways. Competencies are perceptions of one's skills, abilities, talents and knowledge. Values are beliefs about desirable ways of being and/or patterns of behaviour that transcend specific situations. It is difficult to predict which of these three aspects of self will motivate behaviour at any given time. Leonard *et al.* suggest that various psychological processes involving the processing of information and integrating it with our sense of self lead to the following types of motivation:

- **Intrinsic process motivation:** the pursuit of activities because they are fun, whether or not they help in goal attainment.

- **Extrinsic/instrumental motivation:** the pursuit of individual or group goals because they lead to rewards other than satisfaction, especially material ones.

- **External self-concept:** the pursuit of success in order to gain affirmation from others for a social identity as a member of a successful group, or a personal identity as a competent person.

- **Internal self-concept**: the pursuit of success in order that the individual is able to feel competent, irrespective of what others might think of him or her.

- **Goal internalisation:** the pursuit of goal-achievement for its own sake, because it is valued by the individual.

Key Learning Point

People are motivated to act in accordance with their self-concepts and identities. Different aspects of these are salient (and therefore influence their behaviour) in different situations.

Kanfer and Heggestad (1997) and Kanfer and Ackerman (2000) have proposed another way of looking at individual traits in motivation. They argue that standard personality measures do not adequately reflect motivational traits, and that over the last 30 years of the twentieth century there was a narrowing focus on certain motivational traits. This meant that there was room for self-report measure of motivation, and good guidance available about what traits it should measure. Their Motivational Trait Questionnaire (MTQ) assesses the following:

1   Personal mastery.

1a Desire to learn new skills and knowledge.

1b Mastery of tasks in order to achieve goals.

2   Competitive excellence.

2a Other – referenced goals i.e. comparing one's performance with that of other people.

2b Competitiveness, i.e. a determination to do better than other people.

3   Motivation related to anxiety.

3a Worry – about being evaluated and/or failing.

3b Emotionality – the extent to which the person feels emotion concerning his or her performance.

Kanfer and Ackerman (2000) report that women tend to score higher than men on both Mastery and Emotionality. However, as yet there is little evidence available concerning how scores on the MTQ link with behaviour at work. The value of this approach will depend greatly on whether such links can be demonstrated.

Exercise 9.4   **Self and identity in motivation**

Magnus Johannson was the captain of what he considered to be the best fishing crew in the Baltic Sea. Again and again his boat, *The Seagull*, brought back the highest quantity and quality catch of all the trawlers he knew about – and all the catches conformed perfectly to European Union regulations. In a very difficult era for all fishing fleets, he considered this to be a major achievement. And he valued the fact that his crew and other crews recognised it. He felt his particular talent was sensing where the best shoals of fish were likely to be, given currents and weather conditions. This was rarely the same place two days running, and sometimes Magnus's hunches proved more reliable than the ship's technical gadgets. Often his intuition about it differed from some members of his crew, but they had learned that Magnus was usually right. Indeed, it had become a standing joke on *The Seagull* that there was no point arguing with him. That was one of the things he liked best about his crew. They could laugh and joke but they still respected their captain and worked hard partly out of loyalty to him. Other crews did not seem to have that same mix of lightheartedness and purpose, as far as he could see. But Magnus sometimes felt concerned that many people with great reputations eventually fail, and he feared that a day might come when he was no longer able to find the fish or command the respect of his crew.

Which elements of the motivation themes described in the section 'self-concept and individual differences in motivation' do you think help us understand Magnus Johannson's work motivation?

Pay and motivation

Do pay increases affect motivation? Pay is certainly used in many attempts to increase motivation. Performance-related pay (PRP) has been tried in many organisations. PRP involves attempts to link pay directly to work performance of individuals or (occasionally) groups. Often there is only a certain amount of pay available in total, so individuals compete to win greater increases (or smaller decreases) than their colleagues (Torrington and Hall, 1991, Chapter 35).

What do the theories presented in this chapter say about pay and motivation? For Maslow, pay would be a motivator only for people functioning at the lower

This of course bears a strong resemblance to the 'theory X' view of human nature (described earlier in this chapter). Observers agree that jobs in many, perhaps most, organisations are implicitly or explicitly based on Taylorism.

Key Learning Point

Scientific management, also known as Taylorism, emphasises standardised methods and minimisation of costs in the design of work.

Taylorism might make for a well-ordered world, but is it a happy and productive one? During the 1960s, a number of studies seemed to show that work organised along scientific management principles was associated with negative attitudes towards the job, as well as poor mental and/or physical health (e.g. Kornhauser, 1965; Turner and Lawrence, 1965). It was also often assumed that poor productivity would accompany such outcomes, and that simplified work actually *caused* poor mental health, motivation and satisfaction, rather than the reverse causal direction.

These studies of simplified work led to considerable concern about what came to be called *quality of working life* (QWL). Several theoretical perspectives were brought to bear on QWL. One was *job enrichment* – a concept developed through the work of Herzberg (1966). Herzberg proposed a basic distinction between *hygiene factors* and *motivators*. Hygiene factors included pay, conditions of employment, the work environment and other features extrinsic to the work activities themselves. Motivators included job challenge, recognition and skill use – that is, features appealing to growth needs. On the basis of his data, Herzberg proposed that hygiene factors could not cause satisfaction, but that dissatisfaction could result if they were not present. On the other hand, motivators led to satisfaction: their absence produced not dissatisfaction, but a lack of satisfaction. Although Herzberg's data and conclusions can be criticised on several grounds, his recommendation that motivation and/or satisfaction can be enhanced by increasing skill use, job challenge, etc. is consistent with much subsequent work.

Another relevant theoretical tradition is *socio-technical systems* (Cherns, 1976, 1987; Davis, 1982; Heller, 1989). Arising from studies in the immediate post-1945 years, socio-technical theory emphasises the need to integrate technology and social structures in the workplace. Too often, technology is introduced with scant regard for existing friendship patterns, work groups and status differentials. Socio-technical theory attempts to rectify this, but it also makes wider propositions. For example, it states that job activities should be specified only in so far as necessary to establish the boundaries of that job. It also emphasises that boundaries should be drawn so that they do not impede transmission of information and learning, and that disruptions to work processes should be dealt with at source wherever possible, rather than by managers further removed from the situation. Such principles may seem self-evident, but close examination of many organisations will demonstrate that they are not adhered to. Socio-technical job design therefore emphasises autonomy, decision-making and the avoidance of subordinating people to machines.

Interest in job redesign has been stimulated in more recent years by concerns about the quality of products and services, the need for customer responsiveness, and the increasing use of teams. Another factor is the need for staff who can fulfil more than one function in the organisation – so-called functional flexibility (Cordery *et al.*, 1993). In other words, job redesign is part of hard-headed business strategy rather than (or as well as) a philanthropic concern with the quality of working life. This is well illustrated by a survey of 181 human resource managers in the United States reported by McCann and Buckner (1994). From a list of 12 statements about work redesign, the one most often agreed with (by 69 per cent of the managers) was 'Work redesign is part of an overall quality/productivity improvement effort – all parts of our organization are being examined and changed'.

Whatever their exact theoretical origin, most attempts to redesign jobs centre on increasing one or more of the following (Wall, 1982):

- *variety* (of tasks or skills);

- *autonomy* (freedom to choose work methods, scheduling and occasionally goals);

- *completeness* (extent to which the job produces an identifiable end result which the person can point to).

This may be attempted in one or more of the following ways:

- *Job rotation*: people rotate through a small set of different (but usually similar) jobs. Rotation is frequent (e.g. each week). It can increase variety.

- *Horizontal job enlargement*: additional tasks are included in a person's job. They are usually similar to tasks already carried out. This too can increase variety.

- *Vertical job enlargement*: additional decision-making responsibilities and/or higher-level challenging tasks are included in the job. This increases autonomy, variety and possibly completeness. An increasingly commonly used term for this is *empowerment*: a person does not necessarily achieve an increase in formal status, but he or she is given more freedom to take decisions and implement them according to the needs of the situation at the time (Conger and Kanungo, 1988).

- *Semi-autonomous work groups*: similar to vertical job enlargement, but at the level of the group rather than the individual. In other words, a group of people is assigned a task and allowed to organise itself to accomplish it. Semi-autonomous workgroups have been introduced in some car factories.

- *Self-managing teams*: more often composed of managers and professionals than semi-autonomous work groups, these teams are often given considerable freedom to accomplish a group task, and perhaps even to define the task in the first place.

Another aspect of job redesign has been discussed by Campion and McClelland (1993). They distinguish between *knowledge enlargement*, where there is an increase in the amount of understanding required of procedures relating to the different parts of an organisation's operation, and *task enlargement*, where further tasks relating to the same part of an organisation's operation are added to a job. Campion and McClelland found some evidence that knowledge enlargement had a more positive effect than task enlargement on work performance and satisfaction.

Wall (1982) reviewed earlier work on job redesign. He concluded that attempts to redesign jobs usually had some effect as long as they did not confine themselves to increasing variety. Redesign often succeeded in improving job satisfaction,

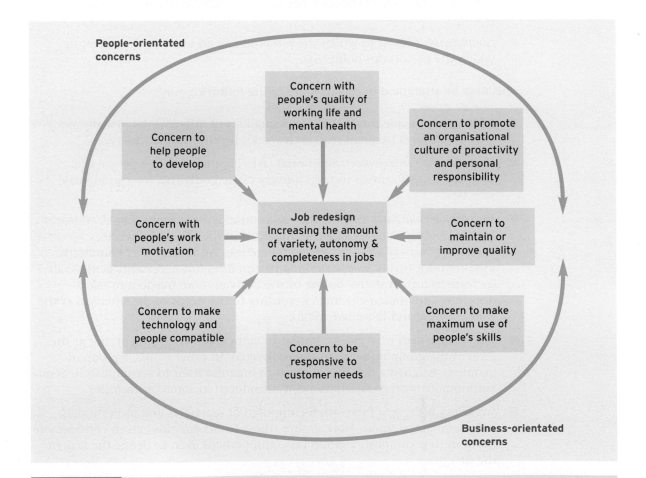

Figure 9.5   Concerns leading to job redesign

motivation, employee mental health and performance. However, Wall also acknowledged that this conclusion was not definitive. Redesign rarely occurred in the absence of other changes, such as pay rates and staffing levels. It was therefore impossible to be sure what caused any change in employee attitudes and behaviour. More recently, there has been some scepticism about the genuineness of attempts to empower employees at lower levels of the organisation. It might be considered exploitation, in so far as it means that staff take on more responsibility without an increase in pay. There is also some suggestion that managers only really give away control over things they regard as unimportant, thus rendering empowerment something of a sham.

The job characteristics model

The *job characteristics model* (JCM) of Hackman and Oldham (1976, 1980) has been very influential. It is depicted in Fig. 9.6, which shows that Hackman and Oldham identified five 'core job characteristics':

1   *Skill variety* (SV): the extent to which the job requires a range of skills.

2   *Task identity* (TI): the extent to which the job produces a whole, identifiable outcome.

3   *Task significance* (TS): the extent to which the job has an impact on other people, either inside or outside the organisation.

4   *Autonomy* (Au): the extent to which the job allows the job holder to exercise choice and discretion in his or her work.

5   *Feedback from job* (Fb): the extent to which the job itself (as opposed to other people) provides information on how well the job holder is performing.

The core job characteristics are said to produce 'critical psychological states'. The first three core job characteristics are believed to influence *experienced meaningfulness of the work*. Autonomy affects *experienced responsibility for outcomes of the work*, and feedback from the job impacts on *knowledge of the actual results of the work activities*. Collectively, the critical psychological states are believed to influence three outcomes: motivation, satisfaction and work performance. But this whole process is said to be moderated by several factors (*see* Fig. 9.6). The most often investigated of these is growth-need strength. This refers to the importance to the individual of Maslow's growth needs (*see* earlier in this chapter). The model is said to apply more strongly to people with high growth needs than to those with low ones.

Key Learning Point

The job characteristics model specifies five features of jobs that tend to make them intrinsically motivating and satisfying.

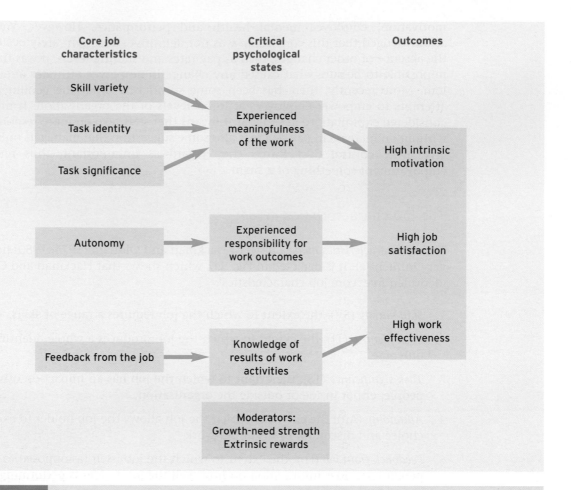

The job characteristics model provoked a huge amount of research, especially in the United States. This is not surprising, since it provides specific hypotheses about exactly which job characteristics matter, how they affect people's psychological states, what outcomes they produce, and which individual differences affect the whole process. Also, Hackman and Oldham produced a questionnaire called the Job Diagnostic Survey (JDS) which assesses the constructs shown in Fig. 9.6. The JDS is completed by job holders.

Several helpful reviews of research on the JCM were published (see, for examples, Roberts and Glick, 1981; Fried and Ferris, 1987). They made a lot of well-observed points about it. In summary, it seems that the job characteristics identified by Hackman and Oldham do indeed seem to correlate with motivation and satisfaction. However, there were few studies in which attempts were actually made to *change* jobs so that they had more of the core job characteristics (which is, after all, the whole point of job redesign). There was also quite a lot of doubt about whether the effects on attitudes and behaviour of each core job characteristic were mediated by the critical psychological states specified by Hackman and Oldham. Indeed, in general the core job characteristics seemed to have more effect on people's attitudes to their work than on their work performance. It was also recognised that there may be additional job characteristics that matter. Warr (1987) suggested availability of money, physical security, interpersonal contact and valued social position as likely contenders.

The JCM is a very tightly defined theory which focuses on a limited range of variables. Kelly (1993) argued that research had failed to establish that changes in job characteristics lead to changes in motivation, satisfaction and performance. Part of the reason for this may be poor research design (Kelly, 1993, p. 754):

> Control groups are rare and measurement of post-redesign change has often been carried out within a relatively short time-span of around 12 months. Longitudinal studies spanning several years are still the exception.

Out of several hundred research reports on job redesign, Kelly found only 31 that were sufficiently rigorous and well designed to warrant his attention. Of these, 17 reported that job redesign led to improved perceptions of job content, but 8 reported no change (the other 6 did not investigate this). Job redesign by no means always led to improvements in satisfaction or motivation; and even when it did, increases in job performance did not necessarily follow. However, improvements in job performance *did* tend to happen when pay rises and/or job losses occurred along with job redesign.

On the basis of his review of research, Kelly (1993) proposed what he called the twin-track model of job redesign (*see* Fig. 9.7). One track concerns satisfaction/motivation and the other job performance. He argued that changes in work methods, pay rates, job security, goals and individual rewards can occur as a result of job redesign, as well as (or instead of) changes in job characteristics. Changes in job characteristics affect satisfaction and motivation, but the other changes have a more direct impact on job performance, Kelly argued.

Key Learning Point

Improvements in job performance do not usually occur as a direct consequence of changes in job characteristics, even if motivation and/or satisfaction do improve.

Key Learning Point

Research suggests considerable support for the job characteristics model, but also that it needs some refinement.

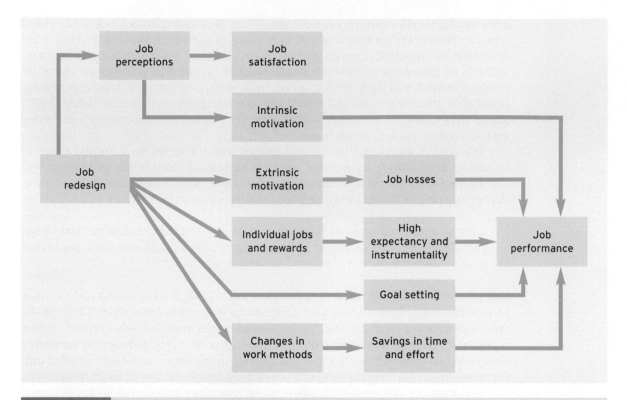

Figure 9.7   **Kelly's twin-track model of job redesign**
Source: Kelly, J. E. (1993) 'Does job redesign theory explain job re-design outcomes?' *Human Relations*, vol. 45, pp. 753-74. Reprinted with permission.

Exercise 9.5   Bicycle assembly at Wheelspin

The Wheelspin bicycle company produces a range of bicycles for adults and children. At their factory, already-manufactured components are painted and assembled. Assembly is carried out on assembly lines which move at constant speeds. The factory manager decides which line will assemble which bicycle. Each member of staff has a specific part or parts which they screw, weld or otherwise fix onto the basic frame at a specified point on the assembly line. They carry out the same tasks about 80 times a day. Staff are recruited to a specific job: they generally remain on the same assembly line and deal with the same parts. Once every two or three months, the model being assembled changes, but generally the assembly tasks required are more or less constant. Noise levels are low enough to allow staff to chat to immediate neighbours as they work. Work quality is assessed at the end of the production line, where performance of the assembled bicycle is examined by quality control staff.

Examine the characteristics of the assembly jobs at Wheelspin. How might those characteristics be changed?

Nevertheless, the JCM has stood empirical test reasonably well, especially considering the relatively large number of connections between specific variables it proposes. Even the more recent reviews acknowledge that the JCM specifies much that is important about jobs and job redesign (Parker and Wall, 1998). However, it is not the whole story, and paradoxically it still has not been tested much in the context of job redesign. There have been even fewer long-term investigations to see whether any effects of job redesign are maintained over a long period. The few studies that have appeared (e.g. Griffin, 1991; Campion and McClelland, 1993) suggest that the impact of job redesign on attitudes and behaviour may wane over time. Also, jobs that become too complex may not be motivating because employees perceive a low probability of achieving satisfactory performance.

Ambrose and Kulik (1999) have pointed out that research interest in the JCM decreased very markedly in the latter half of the 1990s. They argue that this may be appropriate, since it is now quite well understood. More attention now needs to be devoted to the roles of technology and the work context (such as the physical environment and salary structures) and requirements for efficient production while also offering stimulating work. The question of whether it is possible to design jobs that are both efficient and motivating has been investigated by Morgeson and Campion (2002). They conducted a detailed analysis of a set of jobs in one part of a pharmaceutical company and then redesigned some of them to include more 'scientific management' efficiency-based elements, some to include more variety and autonomy, and some to include more of both. They found that it was possible to increase both elements at the same time, and that this produced some small benefits for efficiency and satisfaction.

Twenty-first century work design

It is often pointed out that jobs, and the nature of work, are changing greatly (*see also* Chapters 1 and 14). The older job redesign theories were largely based on male shop-floor workers in large-scale manufacturing industry during what might be described as the late-middle part of the twentieth century. Since then, of course, the proportion of women in the workforce of most countries has increased. In many countries, jobs are now much more in the service sector than in manufacturing, and the technology involved in jobs in all sectors has become more sophisticated. The need for employees to be responsive to customers and willing to change and learn is said to be much greater. So is the need to acquire new information rapidly and share it with others who need it. Some argue that it is better to use the term 'work', because the word 'job' implies a fixed set of duties – a situation that is now relatively rare.

These changes and others have meant that a much wider range of factors needs to be considered in job redesign than those appearing in, for example, the job characteristics model. The following observations seem particularly important (Parker *et al.*, 2001):

■ In an era when many jobs are less clearly defined and less closely supervised than they were, it is inappropriate to assume that jobs have characteristics that remain fixed until someone tries to redesign them.

- There are more features of jobs that affect attitudinal and behavioural outcomes. In fact, those features probably always did matter; it is just that they are more obvious now. These include the extent to which the job is compatible with home commitments, and the various cognitive demands it makes (for example, problem-solving, vigilance). Another is whether the job requires so-called emotional labour – that is, the display of positive or negative emotion in order to (for example) empathise with customers.

- The processes by which jobs affect people may well not be confined to motivational ones, as assumed by traditional job redesign theories. Other processes may include the extent to which a speedy response to events is possible, and also whether employees are able to use their local knowledge to solve problems as and when they arise.

- The outcomes of job redesign should be evaluated at individual, group and organisational levels. As well as motivation, satisfaction and profitability, relevant outcomes might include creativity, innovation, customer satisfaction, accident rates, absence and turnover.

- A much greater range of factors than those suggested in the JCM may affect the impact of job characteristics (and changes in them) on outcomes. These include the extent to which tasks within an organisation are interdependent, and the extent to which the organisation is operating in an ambiguous and/or rapidly changing environment.

- Clearer thinking is needed about when it is best to redesign jobs at the individual level, and when at the group level. Factors such as task interdependence (see above) will probably be important here.

These points are encapsulated in Fig. 9.8, which is adapted from Parker *et al.* (2001). It demonstrates how much expansion on the older models of job redesign might be required. It also suggests how difficult it might be to conduct research that includes all the relevant factors, and to provide managers with straightforward, easy-to-understand advice about what jobs in their organisations should look like.

Although the words used are not always the same, the model shown in Fig. 9.8 encompasses many of the management techniques that have been used to try to improve individual and organisational outcomes. A good example is empower-ment (Wilkinson, 1998), which refers to attempts to transfer more responsibility and scope for decision-making to people at low levels in an organisation. As Wall *et al.* (2002) have pointed out, empowerment often means increases in job control, performance monitoring, cognitive demands, and possibly role conflict and social contact. It is likely to be embraced most wholeheartedly by people with a proactive personality, and perhaps have most impact in conditions of environmental uncer-tainty, where it is more likely that local quick decisions will be needed.

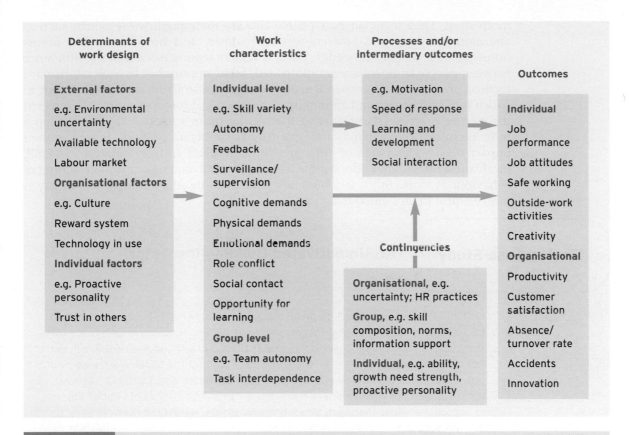

Determinants of work design	Work characteristics	Processes and/or intermediary outcomes	Outcomes

External factors

e.g. Environmental uncertainty

Available technology

Labour market

Organisational factors

e.g. Culture

Reward system

Technology in use

Individual factors

e.g. Proactive personality

Trust in others

Individual level

e.g. Skill variety

Autonomy

Feedback

Surveillance/ supervision

Cognitive demands

Physical demands

Emotional demands

Role conflict

Social contact

Opportunity for learning

Group level

e.g. Team autonomy

Task interdependence

e.g. Motivation

Speed of response

Learning and development

Social interaction

Contingencies

Organisational, e.g. uncertainty; HR practices

Group, e.g. skill composition, norms, information support

Individual, e.g. ability, growth need strength, proactive personality

Individual

Job performance

Job attitudes

Safe working

Outside-work activities

Creativity

Organisational

Productivity

Customer satisfaction

Absence/ turnover rate

Accidents

Innovation

Figure 9.8	**An elaborated model of work design** *Source:* Adapted from Parker *et al.* (2001), adapted with permission

Summary

Work motivation is a wide-ranging topic of considerable practical and theoretical importance. It concerns the direction, intensity and persistence of work behaviour. Some psychologists view motivation as a product of innate human needs. Others see it as a calculation based on the question 'how can I maximise my gains?' Still others take the view that we are motivated to achieve what we perceive as a fair situation relative to that experienced by other people. But perhaps the most effective approach to motivation is goal-setting. It is based on the premise that intentions shape actions. If work goals (e.g. target levels of performance) are specific and difficult, and if they are accompanied by feedback on how well one is doing, work performance is usually enhanced. There are some circumstances, however, in which goal-setting is less effective. Another approach that has enjoyed some success is viewing motivation as something that is elicited by the right kinds of task. Here motivation is viewed as a property of the job, not the person. So the task for managers is to make jobs more motivating, not people more motivated. The most recent analyses of motivation use ideas from other theories to account for limitations in earlier theorising and thus further develop our understanding of motivation. They focus on how people allocate their cognitive resources such as attention, thinking and problem-solving to tasks, and how their self-concepts influence their thought processes. There is also increasing interest in the difference between people in how they are motivated. Some approaches to motivation have focused on the job rather than the person. Early versions identified the extent to which jobs had variety and autonomy as being crucial for motivation. More recent theory and practice has broadened the picture quite a lot in order to develop a fuller picture of the demands and opportunities inherent in work, as well as their impact on a wider range of outcomes for individual and organisation. Overall, motivation theories have done quite a good job of advancing our understanding of behaviour at work. But it is sometimes difficult to be sure about which theory is most helpful in any individual case.

Closing Case Study

An Unmotivated Building Inspector

Nobody at Kirraton Council planning department knew what to do about Simon Lucas. Simon was a building inspector. It was his job to approve proposals for small alterations to buildings (such as extensions and loft conversions) which did not need formal planning permission, and to check that the building work carried out was consistent with the approved plans. The trouble was, he didn't - at least, not often and not quickly. There had been a number of complaints about delays in approval of plans that were Simon's responsibility. He did not seem to keep up to date with the frequent changes in building regulations, which meant that he sometimes made decisions that contradicted them. This had led to some appeals by builders and homeowners, and on three occasions the Council had been forced to change its decision.

This was embarrassing and costly, and it was Simon Lucas's fault. He only rarely carried out site inspections. This meant that some of the less scrupulous builders got away with unauthorised changes to plans, and others who genuinely wanted his advice did not get it. This damaged the Council's reputation and also increased the changes of a structurally unsound building being constructed.

However, it was difficult to point to specific rules that Simon Lucas was breaking. Council guidance was vague: plans should be dealt with 'within a few weeks'; site inspections conducted 'as and when necessary', and decisions made 'within the spirit', not the letter, of some of the less vital regulations. In any case, it wasn't always clear which of the regulations, if any, could be treated as less vital.

Simon's boss, Katherine Walker, decided that she would check his records and unobtrusively observe him at work - it was an open-plan office, so this was feasible. She discovered that Simon was 26-years-old, and had qualified as a building inspector two years earlier. Simon had been recruited by Katherine's predecessor, apparently partly because Simon had 'come up the hard way'. Rather than attending college full time to obtain the necessary qualifications, he had worked for several years as an architect's draughtsman and attended college night classes. In fact, he had been almost the last person to qualify in that way. The building inspectors' professional institute had subsequently decided that part-time study could not develop the necessary skills and knowledge for work as a qualified building inspector. Katherine knew it was true that the part-time route was often seen as 'second class'. She heard it said that this had prevented Simon from getting a job in another area of the country where he very much wanted to live. Few senior building inspectors held the view of Katherine's predecessor that Simon's route into the profession was superior to full-time study. Simon was certainly sensitive about it himself. He frequently mentioned how difficult it had been to combine study with work, but at the same time also remarked that he did not know enough about some things because his training had been 'too basic'.

Katherine observed that Simon often seemed not to be doing very much. He sat at his desk doodling quite a lot. He sometimes had to phone people more than once because he had forgotten to check something the first time. He seemed to have difficulty finding things on his shelves and desk. Sometimes he would give up after only a short and not very systematic search. He also sometimes jumped from one task to another without finishing any of them. As far as she could tell, his home life was not a particular problem. Simon was married, apparently happily, and seemed to participate in many social and leisure activities judging from his lunchtime conversations, not to mention his phone calls to squash clubs, campsites, etc. during work time! He was especially keen on long-distance walking, and could often be seen at lunchtime reading outdoor magazines and carefully planning his walking club's next expedition. He joked to Katherine that he should have her surname because it described what he liked most.

Simon's job was relatively secure. Ultimately he could be dismissed if he demonstrated continuing incompetence, but he had successfully completed his probationary period (Katherine wasn't sure how). Because Kirraton Council covered only a small area, and because Simon's job was a specialist one, he could not be moved to another town or department. Building inspectors' pay depended on age and length of service, with slightly higher rates for those with a relevant college degree. Outstanding performance could only be rewarded with promotion, and this was extremely unlikely for anyone with less than ten years' service. Katherine established that Simon would like promotion because of the extra money it would bring rather than the status. But he correctly perceived that he had virtually no chance of achieving it. Apart from the fact he had been at Kirraton for a relatively short time, he thought he was not scoring very well on Katherine's recently implemented building inspector performance criteria of no lost appeals, high client satisfaction, at least 15 complete projects per month, and acknowledgement of receipt of plans within four working days.

The other four building inspectors were quite a close-knit group of building sciences graduates who had worked together for several years before Simon's arrival. Simon didn't really see himself as a member of the group, preferring instead to emphasise how he, unlike them, was 'on the same wavelength' as local people. He had found it hard to establish a relationship with them, and now it was even harder because they felt his apparently poor performance reflected badly ▶

on them all. They did not involve him much in their activities, nor did they appear to respect him. Simon was afraid that the others thought he wasn't doing his job properly and Katherine suspected that secretly he agreed with them. Katherine knew something had to be done, but what, and how?

Suggested exercises

1   Review the motivation theories discussed in this chapter. How would each one describe and explain the problems with Simon Lucas's motivation?

2   To what extent does each theory provide guidance to Katherine Walker about what she should do? What actions would they recommend?

3   Apply concepts from the job redesign literature to Simon's job. Do they explain why he is not motivated?

Test your learning

Short-answer questions

1 Describe the key features of the theory X and theory Y 'common-sense' views of motivation.

2 Suggest three ways in which Maslow's hierarchy of needs theory might helpfully be amended.

3 List five features of the 'self-actualising' person.

4 What are the components of the motivation to manage?

5 Define valence, instrumentality and expectancy. According to Vroom, how do they combine to determine motivation?

6 Name and define three kinds of organisational citizenship behaviour *and* two kinds of perceived injustice at work.

7 Draw a simple diagram that shows the key elements of goal-setting.

8 What are the key differences between performance goal orientation and learning goal orientation?

9 Name and define the five types of motivation suggested by Leonard *et al.* (1999).

10 What self-regulatory strategies are features of an action orientation?

11 Draw a diagram which represents the main features of the job characteristics model (JCM).

12 Suggest three limitations of the JCM as a framework for job redesign.

13 Describe three characteristics of jobs that have recently been identified as being important in job redesign.

Suggested assignments

1   Examine the usefulness of need theories in understanding and predicting behaviour at work.

2   In what ways, if any, do academic theories of motivation improve upon so-called 'common sense'?

3   It is often claimed that goal-setting is a theory of motivation which works. Examine whether it works better in some situations than others.

4   In what ways have motivation theories based on individual differences in personality and self-identity advanced our understanding of work behaviour?

5   When and how is pay a motivator?

6   To what extent do we know how to design work so that everyone benefits?

Relevant websites

There are very many sites which describe training courses in motivational techniques (for managing self or others) and provide very brief accounts of some well-known motivation theories, usually the oldest and most straightforward ones. Here are a few examples:

http://www.bizhelp24.com/personal_development/motivation_theory_importance. shtml is part of a managers' self-help site. This particular item gives prominence to Herzberg's theory. It also encourages managers to take on responsibility for the motivation of the people who work for them.

A site with a lot of interesting material, including an original article by Maslow, is http://www.themanager.org/Knowledgebase/HR/Motivation.htm. This is another managers' self-help resource site.

A good example of one of the many conferences where consultants and others gather to consider how to motivate workforces can be found at http://www. motivationatwork.nl/. You will need to be familiar with Dutch to understand most of it.

An example of how Singapore is approaching work redesign (and other aspects of work psychology and HRM) can be seen on the website of the Singapore Productivity and Standards Board at http://www.spring.gov.sg/portal/newsroom/epublications/pd/2001_01/mwmc_index.html

For further self-test material and relevant, annotated weblinks please visit the website at http://www.booksites.net/arnold_workpsych.

Suggested further reading

1   Maureen Ambrose and Carol Kulik (1999; full reference in the list at the end of the book) provide a good account of how various motivation theories have developed (and in some cases emerged) in recent years. It is quite a technical article, but worth the effort of reading carefully, because it presents both the fundamentals of theories and the details of how they are being extended and tested.

2   Sharon Parker and Toby Wall's 1998 book called *Job and Work Design* (published by Sage) provides a good analysis of the nature of early twenty-first century jobs, and their impact on individuals and organisations (full reference in the list at the end of this book).

3   Craig Pinder's book *Work Motivation in Organisational Behaviour* published in 1998 by Prentice Hall presents a detailed and scholarly analysis of many of the theories covered in this chapter. Some other approaches are also covered, for example the role of emotion in motivation.

CHAPTER 10

Training

After studying this chapter, you should be able to:

1 identify and explain the three components of the learning cycle;

2 describe how training and development activities in organisations have changed over the past 30 years;

3 describe and explain the purpose of three different levels of training needs analysis;

4 explain how learning theories can inform training design;

5 identify potential barriers to the successful transfer of learning to the workplace and how these might be addressed;

6 understand the importance of training evaluation in determining the cost-effectiveness and utility of training interventions;

7 describe two different models of evaluating training;

8 discuss the overlap between training and other organisational systems aimed at enhancing performance such as performance appraisal;

9 identify how individual differences can impact upon trainee learning;

10 understand how training activities can contribute to the development of a learning organisation.

Opening Case Study

Training for Excellence

Fastcar is a global car manufacturer with major production facilities around the world. The company headquarters are in Orlando (US), and European operations are managed out of Bristol (UK) and Munich (Germany). Recent developments in the global market for car manufacturers have meant that, in order to survive, the company has recognised that it must become increasingly innovative and competitive. It must, for example, significantly reduce the time traditionally taken to develop and introduce new models. Fastcar must also ensure that customers are no longer merely satisfied with their new cars, but surprised and delighted by the inclusion of new 'extras'.

Senior managers in the United Kingdom and Germany have worked closely together to identify ways in which they can facilitate these changes and improvements. They have recognised that, although their engineers are among the most highly skilled in the world, their traditional training has not always focused on the skills needed for team-based working, often involving team members from several different countries. Typically these engineers prefer to work on technical problems by themselves, and can forget that people may be working on similar problems in other parts of the company. They are also poor at communicating new ideas or asking for help. In addition, while the engineers complain that they are under increasing pressure to reduce the development time for new products, the managers feel that they do not recognise wider economic pressures faced by the organisation.

Although Fastcar has an active and respected training unit, the majority of training provided relates to specific technical skills. The training unit does occasionally outsource more specialist training, such as interviewer or assessor training for the HR function, but as a rule does not get involved in what it considers to be 'soft-skills'. The senior management strategy group invites the training managers to a briefing where they describe their plans to implement a training programme aimed at developing engineers' skills in a radical approach to challenge the way in which the engineers typically work. It has been decided that, unlike previous training (which has focused on the development of knowledge of a technical skill such as the use of a new engineering tool), this training will combine technical and social skills training. The ultimate objective will be to change the organisation's culture such that the engineers interact with one another in a different, more proactive and innovative way. The new training programme, delivered in-house by the current training unit, will involve 10 two-day modules over a two-year period for 10 000 engineers in Germany and the United Kingdom. The senior managers have committed significant funds to this new training intervention, but would now like to hear the views of the training managers themselves.

Try to imagine yourself as a manager in Fastcar, and then as one of the engineers who is expected to take part in this training. What might your

initial reactions be? What factors might make you feel enthusiastic about the training, and are there any reasons why you might feel hesitant or even resistant to this training? Think about the questions that you would have as a manager responsible for sending employees on the training, and as a prospective trainee yourself. In the next sections you will learn about how and why training takes place in organisations. As you read through, try to relate this material to the Fastcar example.

Introduction

Training and development activities have the potential to benefit individuals, organisations and society as a whole. As a consequence of training, employees can develop portfolios of skills, enhance their promotion opportunities, take part in more interesting work, and move more easily between jobs and organisations. Skilled individuals perform their jobs faster and more safely. They make fewer mistakes and produce higher-quality work. Therefore training can benefit organisations in terms of increased productivity, safer work environments, improved employee well-being, and lower levels of absenteeism and employee turnover. Investment in training and development is important for society as a whole, because the economic competitiveness of a nation is related to its skill-base. Not only is it important that organisations are able to attract and recruit skilled workers, inward investment from overseas companies can also depend upon the existence of a pool of skilled workers. A good example of this is the Japanese investment in the UK car industry that took place during the 1990s. Furthermore, today's global economy has meant that there is an increasing demand for people with high-level skills and the ability to adapt quickly to changing requirements (DTI, 2001). For this reason governments often direct considerable efforts towards encouraging organisations to invest in the training and development of their staff. Efforts are also directed towards educational institutions in an attempt to ensure that students develop the skills needed for national and international economic prosperity.

While the training and development of employees is clearly important, other recent trends have meant that these activities are taking an increasingly prominent role within organisations. Historically within Europe, training has had a strong association with craft apprenticeship. Indeed training was traditionally viewed as a means of equipping individuals with a set of skills at the beginning of their career that were unlikely to change over the course of their working life. Organisations could afford to provide apprentices with five years of training in a specific area, such as machine tooling, carpentry and precision engineering, because people stayed with the company for their working lives. However, much has changed and apprenticeships are now hard to find. The speed with which technological developments now occur means that jobs are constantly changing and individuals must therefore continually learn new techniques, and how to use new tools and systems. The evolution of new flatter organisational structures has also meant that in order to progress, employees are expected to move sideways into new roles in order to develop a diverse portfolio of skills. This provides a flexibility that enables organis-ations to move people to new positions when required and therefore adapt more quickly and effectively to changing environments.

Given these widespread changes it is not surprising that the activities of trainers and training departments have become more complex. Rather than pro-viding discrete individual training courses that focus on specific needs, training departments are increasingly viewed as central organisational functions. Their primary responsibility is now seen as one of helping to develop learning organis-ations, where employees and managers engage in continual learning as part of their roles. There has also been a growing overlap between training and perform-ance management activities such as appraisal. There is a useful distinction between: 'competence-based training' that involves training staff to achieve the required performance standards in their current job; 'personal development' that involves broadening and growing staff to achieve potential within their current job level (i.e. promotional seniority); and 'career development' that involves challenging motivated and high-performing staff to prepare for progression. All of these overlap with training and development activities, but for the purposes of this chapter, we focus on the first of these. We define 'training' in terms of the organised efforts by organisations to provide employees with structured opportunities to learn and develop within their work-roles. These may include 'one-off' courses devoted to customer service skills, induction training for new employees and more compre-hensive training plans for employees that tie in with organisational change objectives. Another important factor to note at this point, however, is that although learning in organisations can occur at any point – and generally does (a new member of a team may learn how he or she is expected to behave simply by observing other members of the team interacting) – in this chapter we focus on development and change that takes place in a more controlled and planned fashion.

Key Learning Point

Training activities are now a continual feature of organisational life.

The training cycle

Although we have suggested that training and development activities can benefit individuals, organisations and society as a whole, we need to include a very important caveat at this point. Training *per se* is not necessarily beneficial – too little, or too much, training can be problematic (Davies, 1972). More specifically, training that is misdirected, or inappropriate for the specific needs of the individual or the organisation can be worse than no training at all. In short, training is only beneficial if it is based upon a needs analysis and is designed in a way that ensures that this need is met. Moreover, we can only know if training is beneficial if we evaluate its success. Training needs analysis (TNA), training design (TD) and training evaluation (TE) are the three components that constitute the Training Cycle (see Fig. 10.1).

As Fig. 10.1 shows, the training and development process moves from an assessment of need, through the development of programmes, to evaluation of what has taken place. This is described as a cycle, because the information gained through TE should be used to improve future training activities as part of a continuous feedback system. Each of these three elements is considered in more detail over the next sections.

Key Learning Point

Training needs analysis (TNA), training design (TD) and training evaluation (TE) constitute the three stages of the training cycle.

Training needs analysis

Before setting in motion any systematic training or development activity, those responsible should satisfy themselves that it will produce worthwhile results and is therefore necessary. Unfortunately, while this might seem rather obvious, a detailed analysis of training needs does not always happen. On occasions, training programmes can take on a more or less independent 'life of their own' and can occur regardless of any clear and established need for them. It may be, for example, that managers believe that training (any training) is simply a 'good thing'. Consequently, an employee may find him- or herself attending a training course because a manager is fulfilling a performance objective of their own stating that he or she should ensure that all employees attend a minimum of five days of training per year. However, if no assessment of employees' specific needs has been undertaken, how do we to know that the time spent away from their work attending this training will be worthwhile?

In broad terms, poorly conceived training programmes are extremely costly for organisations. Consider the financial investment required to develop, implement

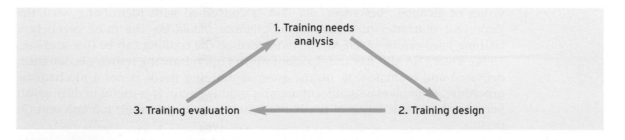

| Figure 10.1 | The training cycle |

and manage the training. On top of that comes the potential impact upon productivity from having employees away from their work. Senior managers at Fastcar intend that 10 000 engineers will each receive ten days of training. The financial implications of 100 000 missed days for the organisation are immense. Can Fastcar justify this expense in terms of likely levels of improved productivity?

Exercise 10.1   Training customer skills

Mercom, a company providing telephone support for organisational clients, has received a growing number of complaints about its customer service department. The senior managers conclude that their staff lack skills, and invite an external training agency in to run a mandatory two-day training course in customer service skills. Had they undertaken a training needs analysis, however, they would have discovered that the problem was not one of poor skills, but low morale caused by an autocratic section leader.

1   What might be the consequences of sending staff on this customer service training?

2   What could the senior managers have done to establish the reasons behind the high number of customer complaints?

3   How might you assess this section leader's training needs?

A TNA is the important first step in developing a training programme. Its primary aim is to identify the training objectives (TOs) or, put simply, 'what the training needs to achieve'. Training objectives can be diverse and as part of the training needs analysis they will include objectives beyond behavioural changes associated with trainees. They might, for example, include an objective that: all members of the marketing department will be fully trained in the new client database system within three months. At an individual level, a training course designed to equip staff with skills necessary to work in a nightclub bar might include several objectives such as: (1) 'trainees should develop knowledge of different spirits and wines and use the appropriate measures and glasses when serving customers'; (2) 'trainees should be able to demonstrate high levels of customer service by responding to customers in a friendly and courteous manner'; and (3) 'trainees should demonstrate knowledge of health and safety legislation governing the provision of alcoholic beverages'. As TNA is concerned with identifying what the important outcomes of a training programme *should* be, the more precisely a training need can be specified, the more focused the training can be (Bee and Bee, 1994). Thus TNA also has an important impact upon how the training is designed, delivered and evaluated. In reality, assessing training needs is not a mechanistic procedure. It involves a significant amount of judgement. It is useful to distinguish between three basic levels of needs analysis: (1) organisation, (2) job/task and (3) person.

Organisational analysis

The purpose of undertaking a TNA at the organisational level is to understand where training activities fit into the wider organisational systems and how they relate to organisational strategy. In simple terms organisational analysis asks 'what are the training needs of the whole organisation?' A first step might therefore be to examine aims and objectives of the organisation. These can often be identified in general terms by examining plans and statements of policy and by discussion with senior personnel in the organisation. Very broadly, organisational training needs exist when there is some sort of barrier hindering the achievement of organisational aims and objectives. This could be either in the present or the future. For example, an insurance company setting up a new call centre on a greenfield site may need to recruit 100 new employees, all of whom will require training. Alternatively, the senior strategy team at Fastcar have identified a need for employees to become more innovative and skilled in team-working. In this instance the company has recognised that it needs to change its culture in order to better meet the challenge from competitors, and that it will achieve this through a large-scale training programme. However, it is important to stress that such problems represent training needs *only* if the barrier to the achievement of aims and objectives might be best removed by training rather than by some other activity. For example, in the case of Mercom mentioned above, training staff rather than dealing with an ineffective manager may make it seem like the senior managers are colluding with the section leader and cause further demotivation among staff. Similarly, in certain instances production problems could be solved more effectively by redesigning the job or equipment, improving recruitment and selection procedures, or by providing job aids.

Another reason for undertaking an organisational TNA might be to determine whether the organisation's investment in training provision for different areas is appropriate. As senior managers play a key role in determining the level of resources devoted to training within an organisation, they need information regarding the specific needs, costs and effectiveness of training interventions. Linking training interventions with strategic plans is an important means of ensuring that funds invested in training are used most effectively.

Task analysis

Task analysis involves determining what important tasks need to be performed and the KSAs (knowledge, skills and attitudes) that an individual requires in order to be able to perform them. In short, the second level of TNA asks: 'what skills and abilities are required to perform this task?' In many ways task analysis is similar to job analysis (*see* Chapter 4), but for training purposes, task analysis focuses more specifically on the objectives or outcomes of the tasks that people perform. It provides an extremely flexible and useful method of analysis, the main unit of analysis of which is the operation. An operation is defined by Annett *et al.* (1971) as 'any unit of behaviour, no matter how long or short its duration and no matter how simple or complex its structure, which can be defined in terms of its objective'. One of the important features of the procedures developed by Annett *et al.* (1971) is that tasks are analysed and broken down into increasingly specific operations in a hierarchical fashion. Because of this approach to analysis the technique is known as *hierarchical task analysis* (HTA). The starting point for HTA involves a general description of the main operation(s) involved in the job or job components being analysed. These operations are then divided into sub-operations and, in turn, the sub-operations themselves may be subdivided. For example, this approach has been used to break down the components of the job of a person working in a call centre service department. As a demonstration, try requesting information by ringing the help-desk for a mobile phone. At each level there are a number of options that the customer can choose from. This represents a hierarchical decision tree structure, but the questions also represent the different questions that a receptionist might ask a customer phoning for assistance. They can therefore be seen as sub-operations.

Several other analytical procedures can be useful in the training needs assessment phase. It is often helpful to employ questionnaires to collect relevant information. Such questionnaires may be targeted at any level of analysis and derive information from various people, or groups of people. Interviews or discussion-based data collection procedures also come in useful, and in many settings, some detailed observation of relevant jobs and job holders is essential. Probed-protocol analysis (see Kraiger *et al.*, 1993) is a technique developed from interviews that is particularly useful in the case of roles where knowledge and cognitive skills form the basis for task performance. For example, computer programmers undertake much of their work in their heads. In such roles, observation of behaviour would not be particularly useful. Useful additional references include Goldstein (1993) who lists and evaluates nine basic needs assessment techniques. Patrick (1992) also gives a review of the various techniques that are of use for training analysis and provides a consideration of general methodological issues relevant to the use of these techniques.

Person analysis

While task analysis determines the skills that are needed to be able to perform for a task or job, person analysis essentially involves identifying who needs training and what kind of training they need. Person analysis may take place in response to a specific organisational need to determine whether a group of individuals possess specific skill levels. This can happen during selection procedures when an applicant's performance at an assessment centre leads to specific training recommendations. However, person analysis is also an on-going part of many performance management schemes. In an appraisal interview, managers and employees may be expected to discuss training needs with respect to the current role, as well as any requirements that may result from future development and role changes. In this instance the manager and employee are working together to conduct a person-level analysis of training needs. Devolving responsibility for training needs analysis appears to be an on-going trend and it fits with the notion that, in a learning organisation, employees and managers should take responsibility for their own learning. However, problems can occur when there are discrepancies between what individuals identify as being their needs and those identified by their managers. Similarly, identification of training needs can be effective only if the appropriate training is available to meet those needs.

In practical terms it is traditional to make distinctions between the development of KSA. Rather confusingly, contemporary American industrial/organisational psychologists use the term KSAs to refer to knowledge, skills and *abilities*, rather than attitudes. According to this distinction, knowledge is concerned with the recall and understanding of facts and other items of information. Skills may be used with reference to the psychomotor movements involved in practical activities such as operating equipment or machinery, but may also incorporate higher-order cognitive or interpersonal processes. Attitudes refer primarily to the emotional or affective feelings and views that a person has, although attitudes also have other components (*see* Chapter 7). For example, a person might be able to operate a drilling machine (skill) and might also be aware that certain safety procedures should be observed (knowledge) but feel that observing such procedures is time wasting and unnecessary (attitude). The six types of learning developed by Gagné (1977) provide a much more comprehensive description than the knowledge/skills/attitudes distinction. These are shown in Table 10.1.

In summary, a training needs analysis identifies the objectives of the training in terms of required outcomes, and can occur at one of three levels. Organisational needs analyses assess whether training fits with the overall strategy and needs of the organisation. The second level is concerned with determining the training needs associated with a particular job or task, and the third level, with the training needs of the individual. Training can be thought of as part of a wider system. Organisations change, as do jobs and people; therefore, ideally, training needs analysis should be a continuous process feeding into the development of training programmes and ensuring that they adapt to the changing needs of individuals and companies.

Training design

Training design (TD), the second component of the training cycle, relates to the content of the training programme. This includes the information presented to

Table 10.1	Gagné's six types of learning:

1 **Basic learning:** stimulus–response associations and chains. This represents the formation of simple associations between stimuli and responses such as those that occur during classical conditioning.

2 **Intellectual skills** (divided into the following hierarchy):
   (a) Discriminations, being able to make distinctions between stimulus objects or events.
   (b) Concrete concepts, classification of members of a class by observation (e.g. red, circular).
   (c) Defined concepts, classification by definition (e.g. mass, personality).
   (d) Rules, use of a relation or association to govern action.
   (e) Higher order rules, generation of new rules (e.g. by combining existing rules).

3 **Cognitive strategy:** skills by which internal cognitive processes such as attention and learning are regulated (e.g. learning how to learn or learning general strategies for solving problems).

4 **Verbal information:** ability to state specific information.

5 **Motor skills:** organised and purposeful physical movements.

6 **Attitude:** evaluations of elements of a person's perceptual world (see Chapter 7).

trainees and methods of how that information is conveyed. Essentially, training needs analysis tells us what needs to be learnt and training design is concerned with how that learning occurs. Training methods concern the ways in which the material to be learned is presented to learners and can include training media (is the material presented in a lecture, on a video or via a computer?), instructional settings (where does the learning take place – in a lecture theatre, a multimedia learning environment, or the learner's own home?), and the sequencing of material (can the learner control the pace at which the material is presented?). Training activities are designed to bring about changes in people's behaviour through the acquisition of knowledge and skills, therefore the way in which the training is delivered has an important impact upon the extent to which the knowledge and skills are acquired.

The first step in training design builds upon a training needs analysis by specifying the aims and objectives of training. Aims involve general statements of intent: examples might be that a programme sets out to provide participants with 'a grasp of the basic principles of management accountancy' or 'an awareness of the relevance of industrial psychology to the management process'. By contrast, objectives are much more specific and precise and can be thought of as a sub-set of the training objectives identified as part of the TNA. These training objectives focus specifically on what trainees should be able to do as a consequence of the training. Objectives can be expressed in the following, three-component form:

1 *The criterion behaviour*: a statement of what the trainee should be able to do at the end of training. Because of this emphasis on criterion behaviour, objectives expressed in this way are often referred to as behavioural objectives.

2   *The conditions* under which the behaviour is to be exhibited.

3   *The standard of performance* of the behaviour.

It is important to recognise that objectives specify what the person should be able to do at the end of training – they do not describe what will happen during training. For example, the statement 'participants will gain experience of various personnel selection interviewing techniques' would not be acceptable as an objective. It says what will happen on the course but not what the outcomes will be. These behavioural objectives are therefore crucial for determining at a later point whether or not the training has been effective – an issue that we will return to later.

In many training situations a full description of the expected outcomes of training is not provided in the form described above. Sometimes competence at the end of training is assessed by the use of various tests, or job simulation exercises. The behaviours that produce satisfactory performance on these exercises represent the targets for the programme of training. Regardless of whether behavioural objectives or other methods are used to define these targets, it is important that the desired outcomes of training are clear at an early stage so that programmes can be designed to enable trainees to reach the targets.

Key Learning Point

Training objectives give a clear description of what the trainee should be capable of doing at the end of training.

Exercise 10.2   Your course

What are the aims and objectives for the course that you are studying? Are these in the course literature? Do they state what you should be able to know *and* do at the end of your course?

Theories of learning

In order to design a training programme, it is important to first understand how people learn. Theories of learning represent ideas about how learning occurs. They are important because they feed into training practice by identifying the most appropriate methods of instruction. Although there is no single, universally accepted theory for the learning process there are several widely accepted underlying principles and points of agreement among psychologists. Within the history of psychology the most prominent approach to learning originates in the work of the behaviourist school. According to this school, learning is seen to result from strengthening stimulus (S)–response (R) links through reinforcing appropriate behaviour (reward) and, in some cases, punishing inappropriate behaviour (*see* Chapter 8). Behaviour modification is a procedure that has been used to help people learn new behaviour. It involves a sequencing of small steps towards behavioural objectives. In fact, many parents use behaviour modification strategies to teach young children appropriate behaviour such as learning to feed themselves. By sequencing small steps such as baby holding the spoon, baby dunking spoon into custard, baby moving spoon in the direction of their mouth, and rewarding these behaviours with smiles and praise, the baby will finally learn how to get most of the custard into his or her mouth as opposed to on the floor.

Behaviour modification has also played an important role in training contexts where the reward of appropriate behaviour still plays a central role in helping trainees to achieve certain skill levels. However, as a technique it has important limitations. According to behaviourists, learning largely occurs through trial and error; but clearly not all learning takes place through the reinforcement of S–R links as this would take too long. More importantly, it ignores the cognitive components underlying the learning of new concepts. The development of social learning theory (SLT) provided a considerable improvement to our understanding of learning by allowing a bigger role for internal, mental processes (Bandura, 1986). Here key cognitive processes, such as expectancies about what might happen and the capacity of individuals to learn without direct experience, are seen as having a crucial role to play in learning (*see also* Chapters 1 and 8).

SLT involves three stages. First, trainees' attention is focused by using a model to perform the target behaviour (e.g. customer service skills). Second, learning takes place by observing the model and the reward or punishment that he or she receives following their performance. Third, trainees' learning is strengthened through rehearsal and practice. A typical training intervention concerning teamwork, based upon SLT principles, might include the following:

1   The trainer emphasises the importance of communication skills for team-working success.

2   The trainees watch a video of a model effectively handling a situation involving communication of information between members of a team.

3   Key points are drawn from the modelling by the trainer, and group discussion takes place.

4   Trainees take part in a role-play with feedback from the trainer and other group members.

5   Trainees return to work to practise new behaviour with members of their own teams.

6   The trainer and trainees meet two weeks later to discuss their experiences and how they dealt with them.

Thus trainees are told why effective communication is important, they observe the skills required, they practise these skills and receive feedback, and finally, they attempt to generalise this learning to other situations when they return to work. Research has shown that simple ways to improve learning include using models who are high status and the same race or sex as the trainees, as well as models who are friendly and helpful, and who are seen by the trainees to receive rewards for their behaviour (Bandura, 1977b). Finally, models who control resources desired by the trainee are also more effective. This may simply be perceived popularity. Indeed, a good example of how SLT has been used in training design has been in the production of videos involving well-known actors using humour to illustrate how, and how not, to perform work-related tasks such as interviewing, negotiating and customer service.

More recently research has begun to explore the effectiveness of different forms of role-play. Baldwin (1992) makes an interesting and important point. He states that simply providing trainees with examples of how they should perform tasks ignores the fact that they may already have become quite skilled at performing a particular behaviour in a way that is not desired by the organisation. For example, in an effort to promote effective communication in a team environment, Fastcar has decided to provide trainees with an opportunity to learn listening skills. However, it may be that Fastcar's 'old' culture encouraged autocratic behaviour. Consequently, trainees may arrive at the training having learned as a consequence of years in this work environment that the most effective communication strategy is to be authoritative and challenging. One individual may have become very skilled at intimidating colleagues into accepting his or her ideas. As a consequence, not only does this individual need to learn the new skills, he or she also needs to 'unlearn' or 'unfreeze' old skills before doing so. Unfortunately many training programmes fail to address the fact that many trainees will arrive at training programmes 'pre-programmed'. This has potentially important consequences for evaluating training, as we will see later.

An important limitation of SLT becomes clear when we consider that many work tasks are not suitable for behavioural modelling (Gist, 1989). Take the example of creativity and innovation. Fastcar managers would like their engineers to be more innovative, it would like them to design more features for new cars that will surprise and delight their customers. Yet it is difficult to see how observing a person 'being creative' would help, because most of this activity may be cognitive rather than behavioural. Similarly, it is difficult to see how modelling could help when learning strategic thinking or how to develop a computer system. Certainly, the theories of cognitive psychologists have become increasingly relevant and influential in training design. One of their central concerns has been to explain the development that takes place as a person moves from being an unskilled novice to becoming an expert. This is a significant question because it holds the key to understanding how skilled performance develops.

Fitts (1962) proposed a theory that has been well regarded by psychologists with an interest in training. In essence, he suggested that skill development progressed through three distinct phases: (a) cognitive, (b) associative and (c) autonomous. These are summarised in Table 10.2. Although the phases can be separated conceptually, Fitts recognised that there might well be some practical overlap between them. In the cognitive phase the learner is attempting to get some intellectual understanding of the tasks involved. During the cognitive phase, actions are deliberate and in the forefront of consciousness as the learner concentrates on the key features of skilled performance. At this stage a novice golfer will, for example, concentrate on which club to select, how to stand, how to hold the club, and so on. For skills that are not trivially easy to learn, practice is the key feature of the next (associative) phase as the learner attempts to reproduce skillful performance. During this phase there is less and less ponderous concentration on the steps involved and, usually through practice and feedback, a gradual improvement in the smoothness and accuracy of performance. The autonomous phase is reached as the skill becomes more and more automatic. In this phase performance of the skill requires less in the way of psychological resources, such as memory or attention, and is increasingly resistant to interference from distractions or competing activities. The skilled driver can drive a car and talk. The novice is safer not to attempt this!

Key Learning Point

In developing a skill the learner passes through a series of stages, with each one producing performance that is more and more automatic.

Anderson (1983, 1987) also proposed a very influential theory that, in some ways, reflects the ideas put forward by Fitts (1962) within the context of contemporary cognitive psychology, (see Table 10.2). Anderson's theory also has three stages, but a central feature of this approach is the distinction between *declarative* and *procedural* knowledge. Declarative knowledge is essentially factual knowledge that may be stated (declared) and made explicit. An example of this would be a skilled counsellor who is able to provide a definition of clinical depression and list the chief symptoms. By contrast, procedural knowledge may be involved when the counsellor deals with a client who is threatening self-harm. Procedural knowledge is the basis for knowing how to do something, whereas declarative knowledge is knowing that something is or is not the case. For example many people know *that* to ride, and stay on, a horse involves gripping with the knees, sitting upright, holding the reins in a particular way and maintaining balance as the horse moves. Not all of the people who know this have the procedural knowledge to know *how* to stay on a difficult horse for any length of time. Anderson proposes that, as the development of a new skill begins, people move into the declarative stage. Here important facts are learnt and the learner attempts to use them in working out how to conduct the tasks involved. In this stage demands on attention and memory are considerable. During the knowledge compilation stage the trainee develops better and better specific procedures for conducting the tasks. By the end of this stage the procedural knowledge, usually incorporating the application of guiding rules, is in place. As the tuning stage is reached, the underlying rules are refined and streamlined so that performance is increasingly efficient and automatic. The interested reader should also consult a text that deals with the psychology of training and skill acquisition in some detail (e.g. Patrick, 1992).

Individual differences and training design

As we have seen, the theoretical ideas about skill development are extremely useful when it comes to the selection or development of training methods. The training

Table 10.2	Phases of skill development	
Fitts		**Anderson**
Cognitive phase: learning the basic ingredients that make up skilled performance. Performance is prone to error and some lack of understanding of how to conduct task(s) may be apparent		*Declarative stage*: establishing the basic 'facts' about the tasks. The trainee is beginning to grasp what is involved in the task(s) (i.e. declarative knowledge)
Associative phase: establishment of the appropriate patterns of behaviour, underpinned by the knowledge acquired in the first phase. Initially rather a lot of errors but improvement with repeated practice		*Knowledge compilation stage*: physical mechanisms are developed for transforming the declarative knowledge into procedural knowledge (i.e. knowing how to accomplish the task(s))
Autonomous phase: the task(s) are performed increasingly smoothly with relatively low demands on memory or attention. Performance is very resistant to interference or stress		*Tuning stage*: performance strengthens and generalises across tasks within the relevant skill domain

Source: Fitts (1962), Anderson (1983, 1987)

method may be selected on the basis of the kind of learning outcome that is intended: motor skills, for example, require repeated practice to develop adequately. The training needed will also depend on the stage of skill development that the trainees are likely to have reached. It would be pointless to design a series of high-speed practice exercises for trainees who were still at the first (declarative knowledge) stage of skill development. The benefit to be gained from identifying learning capabilities involved in a training programme is that they can often provide guidance on the methods or sequences of training that might be most useful. Guidance about training methods and sequence can thus be arrived at by moving from task analysis, to learning capabilities, to sequence and method of instruction.

However, the learning process and the development of skill and knowledge are complex and depend on a variety of related aspects of an individual's psychological functioning. Perception, memory, motivation, cognitive ability and personality are all of some importance in understanding how and what any individual might learn (Warr and Bunce, 1995). One consequence of this is the possibility that individuals may benefit most from different methods of learning such as lecture-based learning or self-paced learning using computer-based training materials. Evidence that individuals benefit most from different types of training methodology is known as 'aptitude–treatment interaction' (Cronbach, 1967). There are clearly important practical issues that need to be considered by organisations when it comes to tailoring training provision for individual needs. In some instances, it may simply not be financially viable. However, it is clearly important to understand how broad individual differences impact upon the effectiveness of training interventions. Similarly, there have been many advances in the technology available to support training interventions. We now have, among others, web-based learning, e-learning and multimedia learning environments. Such advances in training methodology have meant that groups of individuals who have historically missed out on training opportunities (for example, homeworkers, women workers with family responsibilities and individuals working in far-flung geographical locations) are able to participate more easily in training activities. However, we have relatively little research to support or refute the utility of such methods and there is clearly a need for more studies in this area. We will consider the importance of individual differences and training methods in more detail in the section concerned with the transfer of learning.

Key Learning Point

Individual differences can mean that different trainees may be better suited to different training methods.

Training evaluation

Training evaluation (TE), the third component of the training cycle, is concerned with establishing whether or not the training has worked. Techniques for evaluating training provide a way of examining the success of training programmes and identifying areas where change is needed. Akin to examining the validity of a selection process (*see* Chapter 5), training evaluation considers the validity of the training programme by assessing the extent to which trainees have reached the training objectives. However, the evaluation of training is usually taken to be a much broader concept than validation, as it also deals with the overall benefits of a training programme for an organisation. These might include financial benefits such as increased sales, as well as reduced absenteeism and increased organisational commitment.

Probably the most popular framework for training evaluation is that developed by Kirkpatrick (1967), involving four levels of data collection: (1) reaction, (2) learning, (3) behaviour, and (4) results. This is shown in Fig. 10.2.

Collecting reaction data represents the first and minimal level of evaluation for a training programme. In Kirkpatrick's model, this type of information relates to trainees' views of the training. Obviously trainees' views are valuable, but they can easily give a misleading impression of the value of a training programme and an incomplete view of training effectiveness. For example, trainees may be enthusiastic about a training programme simply because it was an enjoyable break from routine. They may also provide poor reports for a training programme that required them to work extremely hard, or one that involved an unpopular instructor. None of this feedback tells us whether the training was actually effective in terms of promoting new learning. For this reason, while most training designers

REACTION

This involves collecting data directly from trainees about their *reactions* to the training. It might focus on issues such as the length of training (did trainees feel it was too long?), the depth, pace, difficulty level, etc.

LEARNING

Data at this level are concerned with new knowledge acquired by trainees. Information is often collected with the aid of some test or assessment process. An actual assessment is needed – merely asking trainees if they feel more knowledgeable or skilful is not sufficient.

BEHAVIOUR

A direct test of new skills is usually what is involved here – can the trainee perform to the appropriate standard?

RESULTS

This level of evaluation focuses on the extent to which the training produces results in the workplace.

Figure 10.2   Levels of training evaluation

ask trainees for their comments about the training (in many cases this is the only information collected) such feedback has often been dismissed as 'happy sheets'. However, recent studies have identified simple ways in which reaction level information can be improved. For example, in addition to questions relating to enjoyment of the course, questions about how difficult and how useful trainees found the course have been shown to be more effective at predicting later learning and the application of skills (e.g. Warr *et al.*, 1999).

Key Learning Point

Reaction level evaluation data can be improved by asking trainees how difficult and useful they found the training.

Level two of Kirkpatrick's framework involves collecting learning data and represents a considerable improvement over the use of reaction data only. Learning criteria are concerned with whether or not the trainees show evidence that they have attained the immediate learning outcomes of the programme. This may involve administering pre- and post-programme written tests to check participants' understanding of the material covered during training. Although learning results are typically collected immediately after training is over, recent studies have suggested that the extent to which trainees retain material in the period following the training programme should also be considered an important indicator of the success of the training programme. Consequently, the assessment of learning might also take place six months post-training. However, like reaction data, learning data are useful but incomplete – trainees may have learned the relevant knowledge, but do they apply it?

Kirkpatrick's third level of evaluation relates to behaviour change – the extent to which trainees demonstrate the skills they have learned on the training programme once they return to work. We know that various factors can influence the transfer of learning (and we will discuss these in more detail in the next section), but in terms of collecting data at this level the criteria and methods used are similar to those used in assessing many aspects of job performance (*see* Chapter 6). They might include managers' assessments of whether or not the employee's performance on the job, or a specific part of it, has improved. However, this information should be treated with caution. Managers' ratings may well be influenced by an expectation that training will be effective – particularly if it was the manager's idea that the employee should attend the training! In addition to managers' ratings, level three data might include more objective assessments of changes in the number of mistakes an employee makes, or the number of customer complaints received. But, as learning a new skill can often involve unlearning a previously automatic way of behaving, it can take time for an individual to generalise the new skill to their workplace. Similarly, it will take time to move from novice to expert status. Therefore, it is just as important to decide *when* to collect data, as it is to decide *what* type of data to collect when conducting a training evaluation.

The fourth and final level of evaluation proposed by Kirkpatrick is described as 'results'. This involves assessing the extent to which the training has had an impact on organisational effectiveness. Results criteria, although conceptually clear, are extremely difficult to assess in a controlled fashion and it is often more or less impossible to be certain whether or not changes in organisational effectiveness have been brought about by the effect of training, or whether some other factors may also be partly or entirely responsible. In the case of Fastcar, the senior managers obviously intend that, ultimately, their investment in this training programme for engineers will mean creating more attractive new cars, more cars sold and improved organisational profitability. However, there are many other factors that can influence the number of cars sold: examples include the state of the economy, the effectiveness of the salesforce, and the organisation's investment in manufacturing technology. So while the engineers may have successfully become more innovative and effective team-players, the number of cars sold is not a good criterion of success. Moreover, improvement in engineers' performance might also occur because they have been given more sophisticated design equipment. Consequently, although data at this level might be highly desirable in terms of determining the ultimate effectiveness of a training programme, they are also the most difficult to collect and interpret. Perhaps it is not so surprising, therefore, that in their meta-analysis of training studies, Alliger and Janak (1997) identified only two investigations that had attempted to collect such data and relate them to training effectiveness.

Key Learning Point

Although important, results level evaluation data are often difficult to collect and interpret.

Exercise 10.3   Course feedback evaluations

Universities often ask students to complete feedback sheets for the courses they have studied and the lecturers who have taught them. How might you change these feedback sheets to improve the quality and utility of the evaluation information collected?

Criticisms of Kirkpatrick

Although Kirkpatrick's model has provided a popular and clear framework for evaluating training, it has not been without criticism. Perhaps the strongest criticism has centred on the argument that the four levels are hierarchical. For example, successful learning of the training material is viewed as being dependent upon an individual's level of enjoyment of the course. Similarly, the model assumes that behaviour change in the workplace is determined largely by the trainee's successful acquisition of knowledge. In their meta-analysis of the results of training evaluation studies based upon Kirkpatrick's model, however, Alliger *et al.* (1997) found that the associations between the four levels were consistently low. Clearly it is possible to dislike a particular course, yet learn some of the material. It is also possible to learn the material, yet not apply it in the workplace. For example, trainees may like material and understand it perfectly well, yet they may still not demonstrate their learning by changing their behaviour when they return to work if they receive no encouragement from managers or colleagues.

Kraiger *et al.* (1993) argue that because Kirkpatrick's model lacks specificity, it is not easy to identify those methods that are best suited to assessing different stages of learning. Focusing at this second level of 'learning', they proposed a more detailed framework for evaluation based upon three broad, conceptually different categories of learning outcomes: (a) cognitive, (b) skill-based, and (c) affective (*see* Figure 10.3). Kraiger *et al.* suggest that by identifying the specific changes that result from these categories of learning, it is possible to identify the most appropriate assessment techniques. For example, in the category of skill-based outcomes it is possible to differentiate between a trainee's learning in the compilation stage and their learning in the automaticity stage. In the compilation stage learning can be assessed using methods such as targeted behavioural observation, hands-on testing and structured situational interviews. In comparison, learning at the automaticity stage can be assessed by looking at how trainees respond to interference problems such as requesting them to perform secondary tasks simultaneously.

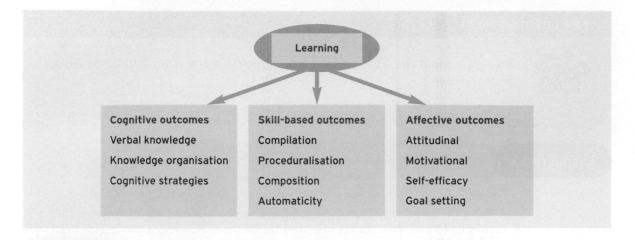

Finally, affective learning outcomes can be assessed using self-report questionnaires that can, for example, assess a trainee's confidence in their ability to demonstrate a particular skill before and after training. This type of model allows us to investigate the causes and processes of learning in much greater detail than we might gain from Kirkpatrick's model.

Threats to accurate evaluation

A simple learning point with respect to training evaluation is that in most instances no single method is capable of providing sufficient information regarding the effectiveness of a training programme. In most cases, evaluation will involve a multi-method approach, focusing on different types of data, in order to build up a picture of the effectiveness of the training process. If the training objectives have not been achieved, it is important to determine why this is the case and how the training might be amended. Yet Patrick (1992) points out that only about 10 per cent of companies evaluate on-the-job behaviour change and even fewer companies conduct longitudinal analyses of training effectiveness. There are important practical reasons for this. Individuals within the organisation may simply lack the skills necessary for conducting this type of analysis. There may also be political reasons – no one who has been responsible for committing large amounts of money to a training intervention likes to see it fail, or indeed, be associated with its failure. Yet, only by evaluating training can we determine whether it is necessary to change or adapt the training, and how this is best achieved. In the case of successful training interventions, it is also important to be able to provide evidence of this success to reinforce the likelihood that organisational resources for training and development continue.

Transfer of learning

In the last section we suggested that although trainees may acquire new knowledge and learn new skills, they might still not apply this learning or use these skills when they return to their place of work. Identifying the factors that contribute to successful transfer of learning to the workplace has been an important focus for research. Those identified include: trainee characteristics (ability, personality and motivation); training design (use of sound principles of learning, appropriate sequencing and content); and work environment (support and opportunities to use) (Baldwin and Ford, 1988).

A number of trainee characteristics, including personality variables, self-efficacy, cognitive ability, and demographics such as age, have all been associated with failure to transfer learning (Colquitt *et al.*, 2000). For example, we know that there is a positive relationship between cognitive ability and learning. We also know that an increased level of anxiety is negatively related to learning, as are low levels of achievement motivation and training motivation. Individual differences that have received most attention from researchers include age and personality. In the case of age, there have been suggestions that older workers learn more slowly than younger workers (a cognitive speed of processing argument) or that older workers are more resistant to learning new methods (competing schema argument). Demographic changes and an ageing work population have led to increasing concern about the importance of training for older workers. Efforts to determine what training methods might be more effective with an older population have led researchers such as Warr and Bunce (1995) to evaluate the use of self-paced learning programmes.

A personality construct that has received widespread attention from training researchers is self-efficacy (*see also* Chapters 1 and 8) . This refers to an individual's belief in his or her ability to perform specific tasks. It is therefore seen as being integral to individuals' ability to master a particular skill and then to perform this skill once they return to their place of work. It has been suggested that individuals who possess high levels of self-efficacy are more likely to learn material and new skills more quickly. They are also more likely to use these skills in the workplace (Stevens and Gist, 1997). Self-efficacy regulates behaviour by determining task choices, effort and persistence. It is not concerned with the skills that individuals have, but with their judgements of what they can do with whatever skills they possess.

However, organisational factors also play an important role in determining whether learning is transferred to the workplace (Baldwin and Ford, 1988). For example, it is quite possible that trainees may not transfer their learning once they return to the workplace simply because they have a fear of looking foolish in the eyes of their established work colleagues, who may not have been exposed to the training. In fact, the most important organisational factors that influence how effectively an individual employee transfers what they have learnt on a training course to their place of work include organisational climate and support. Organisational barriers to successful transfer include inertia, bureaucratic procedures, work overload, and fear of change. Tracey *et al.* (1995) found that both organisational climate and culture were directly related to post-training behaviours. In particular, the social support system played a central role in the transfer of learning. Tannenbaum and Yukl (1992) found that elements of the post-training environment can encourage (e.g. rewards, job aids, recognition), discourage (e.g. ridicule from peers) or actually prohibit the application of new skills and knowledge (e.g. lack of the necessary equipment). Employees need encouragement from their managers and peers. For example, Birdi *et al.* (1997) found that managers' support for trainees returning to the workplace was positively related to the extent to which learning was transferred. However, in an investigation of a training programme designed to change the culture of an organisation, Silvester *et al.* (1999) found that senior managers and the trainers were less optimistic about the likely success of the change programme than the trainees themselves.

Managers of trainees returning to the workplace therefore have a key responsibility in the development of a positive climate for transfer of learning. To take Fastcar as an example, this will mean that the managers of engineers participating in the training need to ensure that there are adequate resources for the trainees when they return from attending a training programme. They should provide cues that serve to remind trainees what they have learned (possibly from their own behaviour), as well as opportunities for trainees to use the skills they have learned. Managers need to provide frequent feedback and reward trainees for using the skills they have learnt. From this it is clear that managers themselves may need to be trained in specific skills in order to understand their importance and facilitate their development among employees. For this reason, many training programmes are cascaded down within organisations, beginning with managers and then training the people they manage. However, managers and other senior staff within organisations also have wider responsibilities. First they are responsible for facilitating the development of a learning culture by actively promoting the benefits of training for the individual and the organisation. Second, they determine relevant organisational policies regarding training and allocate resources to ensure that training provision is adequately integrated and supported within the organisation. Third, they need to offer an example to others in the organisation through their own actions and involvement in training.

Key Learning Point

Individual and organisational factors can serve to determine whether learning is transferred to the workplace.

Threats to accurate evaluation

The problem of establishing whether training, rather than some other factor, is responsible for causing observed changes is one that makes the effective evaluation of training a technically complex and extremely time-consuming endeavour. The most thorough consideration of experimental designs that can be used by evaluators to examine the effectiveness of training programmes is presented by Cook *et al.* (1990). Fundamentally, the goal of training evaluation is to provide the training designer with information about effectiveness that can be *unambiguously* interpreted and is *relevant* to the question of training effectiveness. To illustrate the problems involved in conducting good evaluation work we will consider some of the common difficulties that may arise. These difficulties are usually referred to as internal or external threats to *validity*, since they affect (or threaten to affect) the validity of conclusions that can be drawn from the evaluation. The validity of training may be divided into two broad types: internal validity is concerned with the extent to which the training has brought about new learning; questions of external validity are to do with the extent to which the training will generalise to subsequent groups of trainees and settings.

Threats to internal validity are concerned with the factors or problems that can make it appear that a training programme has been responsible for changes in learning, behaviour or results, when in fact the changes were caused by some other factors. For example, a group of new entrants to an organisation may be given a pre-training test of knowledge of the organisation's rules and procedures. After a period of induction training (one hour per day for their first week) they may be tested again. If their test scores have improved, does this mean that the induction training was responsible? Of course not – the improved knowledge could have been gained in the six or seven hours per day spent in the organisation outside the induction course. An obvious solution to this problem is to administer the tests immediately before and after training. Would any differences now be attributable to the training? It seems more likely now, but, for example, there is the possibility that trainees might benefit from the formal training only when they have spent some of the previous day doing their normal duties in the organisation. This could be important, for instance, if, for any reason, the organisation wanted to run the induction training in one block all at once, instead of spreading it over the first week. The question here is partly one of internal validity: did the training bring about the change? It is also partly a question of external validity: will the programme be effective for different trainees in different circumstances?

Evaluation designs

In an attempt to control various threats to the validity of training, evaluation investigators will often make use of experimental designs. Most training evaluation has to be conducted within real organisational settings, and under these circumstances it is often not possible to obtain the conditions necessary for perfect experimental designs (*see* Chapter 2). In such circumstances it is common for what Campbell and Stanley (1963; *see also* Cook *et al.*, 1990) have called quasi-experimental designs to be utilised. Campbell and Stanley (1963) also described what they term pre-experimental designs. Such designs are unfortunately commonplace in the training world, although they produce results with so many threats to validity that they are uninterpretable and not capable of providing clear findings about training effectiveness (*see* Wexley, 1984, pp. 538–9). Two of the best-known pre-experimental designs are shown in Fig. 10.4, together with more complex designs which overcome some of the problems inherent in the pre-experimental designs.

Key Learning Point

Pre-experimental designs, such as the one-group post-measure-only design, are common in the training world but they are not capable of providing clear results.

One group, post-measure only

X ⟶ M_2

One group, pre-measure/post-measure

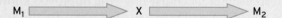

M_1 ⟶ X ⟶ M_2

Pre-measure/post-measure control group

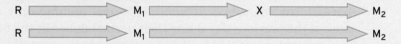

R ⟶ M_1 ⟶ X ⟶ M_2
R ⟶ M_1 ⟶ M_2

Non-equivalent control group

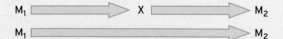

M_1 ⟶ X ⟶ M_2
M_1 ⟶ M_2

Key:
M_1 = pre-measure (administered prior to training)
M_2 = post-measure (administered after training)
X   = training programme
R   = random assignment of people to groups

Figure 10.4   Pre-experimental, experimental and quasi-experimental designs for training evaluation studies

Exercise 10.4   Assessing the effectiveness of training

The Midland Provincial Bank was going through a difficult period. Changes in the status and aims of many financial services organisations meant that competition for business was getting tougher and tougher. Like many banks, Midland Provincial was a fairly traditional organisation and most of its longer-serving employees had spent their careers in an industry where competition was restrained and relationships with customers were of less significance than financial acumen. In recent years this had all changed, and attracting and holding customers was of increasing importance. Interpersonal skills, customer care programmes and sales and marketing know-how were crucial qualities for the bank's employees to develop.

The bank's senior management team decided that the only way forward was to invest heavily in training in order to develop the required characteristics in their staff. Several commercial training consultancies were invited to discuss the situation with the board, and three were invited to tender for the job of retraining the bank's personnel. The board of the bank were impressed with all of the proposals and found it very difficult to choose between the two consultants who submitted the best tenders.

Eventually the decision was delegated to a small working group involving the personnel director, the controller of training and the head of human resources. The working group invited each consultant to prepare and run one pilot training course for branch managers in two different regions of the country. The personnel director visited both courses and at the end of the course conducted private (i.e. without the consultants) interviews with the course participants. He felt that the branch managers trained by one of the consultants had gained much more from the course and eventually the steering group awarded the contract to this consultancy.

Decide whether or not you feel that the steering group adopted a suitable procedure for choosing between the consultants. Explain why. Suggest ways in which the choice could have been made more effectively.

Clearly, the single-group, post-test-only design controls for none of the possible threats to internal or external validity and it is quite impossible to interpret the data. It is impossible to tell whether scores are better after training than before – let alone whether training or some other factor is responsible for any changes. The one-group, pre–post measure design goes some way towards resolving the problems by making it possible to measure change. Nevertheless, it is not possible with this design to assess whether training may have caused any difference. This may be done only if there is also an untrained control group, who are similar to the trained group and whose performance has also been measured at the appropriate times. To conduct a true experiment, trainees should be assigned to the experimental and control groups on a random basis since systematic differences between groups before the experiment could bias the results. Often this degree of control is impossible in field research and the kind of quasi-experimental design shown in the non-equivalent control group example of Fig. 10.4 is the best that can be done. Typically pre-existing groups in the organisation, such as all of the members of a particular job group, region or unit, form the groups. This is obviously administratively much more convenient than random assignment and does control for some of the main threats to validity. Even the pre–post measure control group design is subject to some threats to validity, and for totally unambiguous results more complex designs are needed (*see* Campbell and Stanley, 1963).

Key Learning Point

In general research offers support for the effectiveness of training.

Training and the learning organisation

In recent years there has been a growing recognition that training can play an important role in organisational change. More specifically, it has been suggested that, in order to survive in today's changing environments, unstable economies and global markets, organisations must learn to thrive on change. However, central to this is the willingness of employees to engage in learning as an ongoing feature of their jobs – essentially to create 'learning organisations' (Easterby-Smith *et al.*, 1999). Only through individual learning, supported by organisational development and performance management systems that identify needs and provide structured learning opportunities, can learning organisations exist. To this end, training and development activities are slowly being incorporated as part of the essential infrastructure of most large organisations. Indeed, many employees are attracted into companies that offer systematic and structured training opportunities that allow them to build marketable portfolios of skills. Arguably a company's provision of training opportunities is now seen as being a more important determinant of an applicant's choice of company than more traditional long-term benefits such as pensions and career structure.

In terms of the activities of work psychologists, the creation of learning organisations presents new and exciting challenges. For example, we need to know more about how to effectively integrate organisational training programmes with individual development programmes. How can we design training in a way that is sufficiently flexible to accommodate organisational and individual needs? How should we evaluate training in an environment where roles are in a state of flux and where individuals are expected to learn continuously? How does individual learning contribute to organisational learning – indeed, can organisations (rather than individuals) actually learn? These and many other questions are in need of exploration. However, for work psychologists, the really interesting questions relate to the interface between individual and organisational change. Too often 'training' is viewed as a 'one off' intervention to skill an individual to use a particular piece of machinery. Yet this betrays the historical view of training discussed at the beginning of this chapter. Organisations have changed dramatically over the past 20 years and training is beginning, once again, to take centre stage because of its focus on how people change. It is quite possible that work psychology will see a resurgence of interest in this area as focus shifts away from static traits as predictors of performance, to the ability of individuals to adapt, learn and change to fit their environments, or indeed to change the environment to fit them.

Summary

Constant social and technological change provides the context for organisational life. This coupled with individual growth and career development means that training has a key role in many organisations. The adequate analysis of training needs (at organisation, task and personal levels) provides the basis for training activities. Although the analysis of needs, together with a clear statement of training aims and objectives, is important, there is still a certain degree of judgement involved in choosing appropriate training methods. This essential subjectivity can be checked and assessed by the application of systematic procedures for evaluating the effectiveness of training. Evaluation at reaction, learning, behaviour and results levels provides a way of determining the overall value of training and assessing necessary improvements. In general, research has shown that training is an effective way of bringing about behaviour change, although there are often problems in ensuring that the potential for change provided by training activities actually transfers to the work setting.

Closing Case Study   Training and Organisational Change

Premier TV had undergone enormous changes in the last few years. The most important of these concerned the new agreement that had been reached between management and unions. This provided a much more flexible rostering system so that unit managers could use people's time more effectively. The previous system had involved fixed rosters and set numbers of personnel for specific tasks. All this was now history and managers (in consultation with programme makers) could decide who should work on which job and how many people were needed. However, the new agreement had been achieved at a cost and it was only after severe management pressure, including threats of compulsory redundancy, that the unions finally accepted the new agreement. This had left smouldering bad feeling between many employees and the company's senior managers.

Other changes in the organisational structure of the company had also taken place. Financial controls on what was spent to make programmes were now much tighter and each department or unit was accounted for as a separate cost centre and was expected to operate at a profit by selling its services to other units within Premier TV or to outside companies. ▶

During the period of change the human resources staff at Premier had had little opportunity to assess training needs or to organise training events – so, apart from induction training and some specialist technical training nothing had taken place for the last five years. Kathy Lamb, the human resources manager, was well aware that this could not continue and resolved to take some positive action.

Suggested exercise

Decide what Kathy Lamb should do. Explain why.

Test your learning

Short-answer questions

1   What are the three key phases in the training system?

2   Why is training needs analysis important and what are the levels at which this can occur?

3   Explain the function of learning outcomes in the design of training.

4   Describe Anderson's three stages of skill development.

5   Explain how a consideration of individual differences in learning capabilities can help in training design.

6   Name and explain (briefly) Kirkpatrick's four levels of evaluation data.

7   How can we improve reaction level data?

8   Give a brief critical explanation of two designs that might be used for an evaluation study.

Suggested assignments

1   Why is it important to position training as a central HR function linking with other selection and performance management systems?

2   Explain how you would review the training needs of an organisation and design relevant training programmes.

3   Consider what value and understanding the psychology of learning offers for a training manager.

Relevant websites

The Academy of Human Resource Development (AHRD), based in Oklahoma USA, provides via its website some useful resources about the ethical and effective use of training and development practices. http://faculty.okstate.edu/ahrd/.

An example of how training can be important in basic skills as well as high level professional and management ones can be seen at http://www.literacytrust.org. uk/socialinclusion/adults/benefits.html. This site also shows how, at national level, economic and social policy have implications for training provided by the state and employers.

For further self-test material and relevant, annotated weblinks please visit the website at http://www.booksites.net/arnold_workpsych.

Suggested further reading

Full details are given in the reference list at the end of the book.

1   John Patrick's (1992) book *Training: Research and practice* provides thorough coverage of the psychology of learning and the whole area of training. He covers operative training particularly well.

2   A useful human resources perspective on training is provided by Rosemary Harrison in her book *Employee Development*.

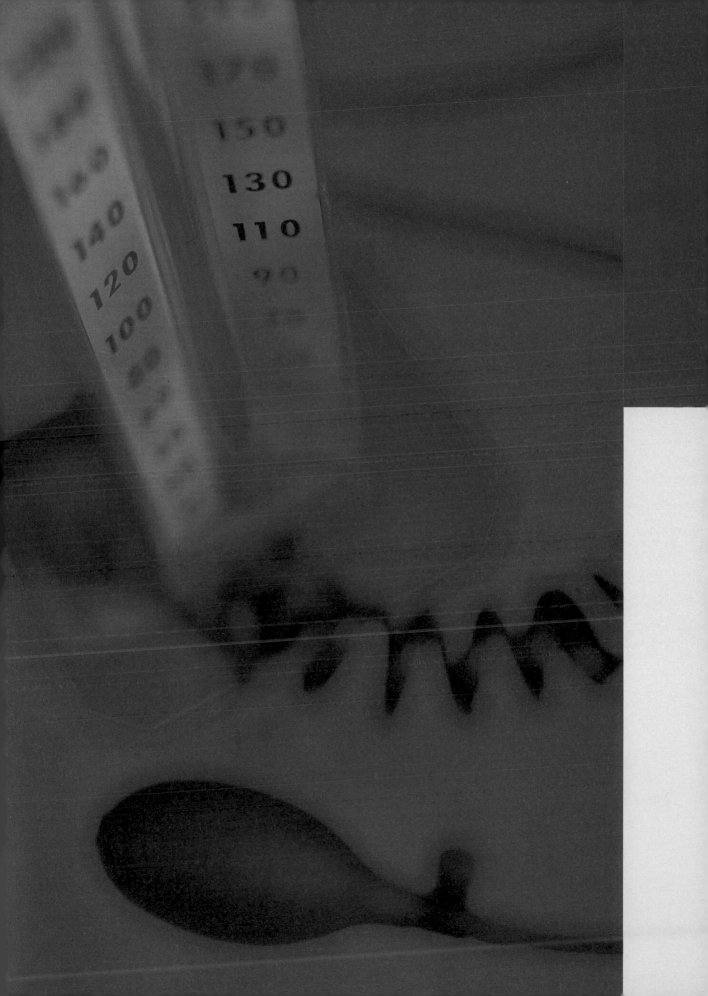

CHAPTER 11

Stress in the workplace

LEARNING OUTCOMES

After studying this chapter, you should be able to:

1 define what stress is and highlight its costs;

2 identify the sources of workplace stress;

3 explain the stress of being unemployed;

4 identify your own Type A stress-prone behaviour;

5 list three criticisms of the concept of stress;

6 distinguish between primary, secondary and tertiary stress interventions;

7 understand the role of the employee assistance programme (EAP);

8 use a problem-solving framework for dealing with occupational or organisational stress.

Opening Case Study

Stress Among the Paper Clips

The unkind stereotype harboured by many UK private sector workers about their public sector colleagues is that they are a lazy bunch. The vision is of a working day spent unbending paper clips, until the office clock hits ten to five and it is time to go home.

That is not an environment where stress should be a problem. The private sector likes to believe it has something of a monopoly here, thanks to volatile stock markets, unpredictable sales patterns and big redundancy programmes triggered by restructurings.

A survey published late last year by the Chartered Institute of Personnel and Development, a body representing personnel managers, therefore made surprising reading. This showed that public sector employees felt significantly more stressed and undervalued than people who work for companies.

Researchers who polled 1000 workers for the CIPD found only 21 per cent of those employed in the private sector reported being 'very or extremely stressed'. In contrast, the figure was 28 per cent for central government employees, a category ranging from civil service chiefs working in Whitehall (central London) to staff at employment advice centres in towns and cities throughout the United Kingdom. It rose to 30 per cent for local government, a category that included teachers, taking another step up to 38 per cent for the National Health Service (NHS).

In the hard-bitten world of commerce, with its dictatorial bosses and boardroom coups, just 21 per cent of staff thought their organisations cared about their opinions. But the total fell to 16 per cent for the NHS and local government and slumped to 7 per cent for central government.

Similarly, only 12 per cent of central government respondents 'strongly agreed' that their organisation cared about their well-being. This rose to 18 per cent for the NHS and 20 per cent for local government, with the private sector just a whisker ahead, again with 21 per cent.

'The message for central government, which trails in every category, is stark,' says Mike Emmott, employment relations adviser at the CIPD. 'It is worse managed than every other sector and has a massive amount of work to do to catch up.' By now, you should not be surprised to learn that central government workers came bottom for job satisfaction too, with an average of 6.1 out of 10. Mr Emmott says this reflects 'ambiguity about what the job is because of the political element'.

Owen Tudor, a health and safety expert at the Trades Union Congress, believes stress has risen sharply in the public sector as a result of Labour's triumphant return to government in 1997. He says: 'It has become a much tougher place to work, because the current government wants to do so much more but until recently has not provided the extra resources needed.'

NHS staff meanwhile, who cope with heavy pressures and terrifying responsibilities, averaged 6.9 out of 10 for job satisfaction, the same as for company employees. Helping people get well – however indirectly – means many staff have formidable motivation. 'The psychological contract is very healthy,' says Mr Emmott. 'People feel they have a mission, that they are not just pen-pushers.'

The apparent purpose of a role, particularly in Whitehall, may shift constantly, he says, depending on political imperatives. 'Messages are always geared to the electorate and to ministers - members of staff are only a tertiary audience,' he says. At the same time, there is little invigorating contact with 'real end users', such as homeowners, pupils, patients or customers.

Ministerial reshuffles mean central government departments, despite the continuity provided by civil service working practices, can be surprisingly insecure places to work. 'Senior managers find it harder to create a space where their employees can feel protected,' Mr Emmott says.

Source: Adapted from a report in the Financial Times, *6 March 2003.*

Introduction

Stress at work is costing a great deal of money. It has been estimated that nearly 10 per cent of the United Kingdom's GNP is lost each year due to job-generated stress in the form of sickness absence, high labour turnover, lost productive value, increased recruitment and selection costs and medical expenses. This chapter looks at what stress is, how you can identify it, what it costs, what its sources in the workplace are and what can be done about it. We also acknowledge the other side of the coin, and discuss the nature of well-being, health and positive emotion at work. In identifying organisational sources of stress we will focus on factors intrinsic to a job, role problems, relationships at work, career development, organisational climate and structure, and the work–home interface (*see* Cooper *et al.*, 2001, for a more detailed account). As the opening case study shows, the causes of stress are not necessarily obvious, and can be very specific to certain kinds of work. We also provide a brief examination of the stressful effects of being without work, i.e. unemployed. The chapter concludes with a description and analysis of different forms of intervention for reducing stress in the workplace.

What is stress?

Stress is a word derived from the Latin word *stringere*, meaning to draw tight. Early definitions of strain and load used in physics and engineering eventually came to influence one concept of how stress affects individuals. Under this concept, external forces (load) are seen as exerting pressure upon an individual, producing strain. Proponents of this view argue that we can measure the stress to which an individual is subjected in the same way that we can measure physical strain upon a machine (Hinkle, 1973).

While this first concept looked at stress as an outside stimulus, a second concept defines stress as a person's response to a disturbance. The idea that environmental forces could actually cause disease rather than just short-term effects, and that people have a natural tendency to resist such forces, was seen long ago in the work of Walter B. Cannon (1929). Cannon studied the effects of stress upon animals and people, and in particular the 'fight or flight' reaction. Through this reaction, people, as well as animals, will choose whether to stay and fight or try to escape when confronting extreme danger. Cannon observed that when his subjects experienced situations of cold, lack of oxygen, and excitement, he could detect physiological changes such as emergency adrenalin secretions. Cannon described these individuals as being 'under stress'.

One of the first scientific attempts to explain the process of stress-related illness was made by physician and scholar Hans Selye (1946), who described three stages an individual encounters in stressful situations:

1   Alarm reaction, in which an initial phase of lowered resistance is followed by countershock, during which the individual's defence mechanisms become active.

2   Resistance, the stage of maximum adaptation and, hopefully, successful return to equilibrium for the individual. If, however, the stress agent continues or the defence mechanism does not work, the individual will move on to a third stage.

3   Exhaustion, when adaptive mechanisms collapse.

Newer and more complete theories of stress emphasise the interaction between a person and his or her environment. By looking at stress as resulting from a misfit between an individual and his or her particular environment, we can begin to understand why one person seems to flourish in a certain setting, while another suffers. Cummings and Cooper (1979) have designed a way of understanding the stress process:

■   Individuals, for the most part, try to keep their thoughts, emotions and relationships with the world in a 'steady state'.

■   Each element of a person's emotional and physical state has a 'range of stability', in which that person feels comfortable. On the other hand, when forces disrupt one of these elements beyond the range of stability, the individual must act or cope to restore a feeling of comfort.

■   An individual's behaviour aimed at maintaining a steady state makes up his or her 'adjustment process', or coping strategies.

A stress is any force that pushes a psychological or physical factor beyond its range of stability, producing a strain within the individual (Cooper, 1996). Knowledge that a stress is likely to occur constitutes a threat to the individual. A threat can cause a strain because of what it signifies to the person. This description is summarised in Fig. 11.1.

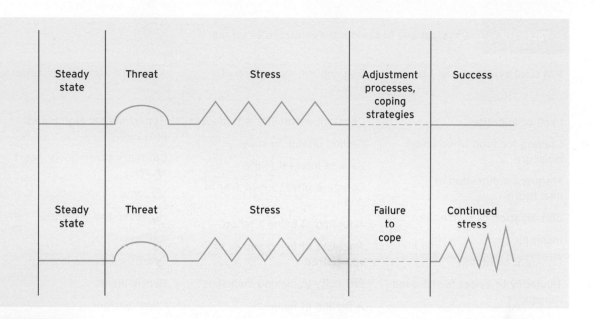

Steady state	Threat	Stress	Adjustment processes, coping strategies	Success
Steady state	Threat	Stress	Failure to cope	Continued stress

Figure 11.1   The Cooper-Cummings framework
Source: Cummings, T., and Cooper C. L. (1979) 'A cybernetic framework for the study of occupational stress', *Human Relations*, vol. 32, pp. 395-419. Reprinted with permission

As stress begins to take its toll on the body and mind, a variety of symptoms can result. Doctors have identified the physical and behavioural symptoms of stress listed in Table 11.1 as commonly occurring before the onset of serious stress-related illness. They have also identified those ailments having a stress background, meaning that they may be brought on or aggravated by stress.

Key Learning Point

When pressure exceeds the individual's ability to cope, he or she enters the stress arena.

The costs of stress

To the individual whose health or happiness has been ravaged by the effects of stress, the costs involved are only too clear. Whether manifested as minor complaints of illness, serious ailments such as heart disease, or social problems such as alcoholism and drug abuse, stress-related symptoms exact a heavy payment. It has also long been recognised that a family suffers indirectly from the stress problems of one of its members – suffering that takes the form of unhappy marriages, divorces, and spouse and child abuse. But what price do organisations and nations

Table 11.1	Physical and behavioural symptoms of stress

Physical symptoms of stress	Behavioural symptoms of stress	Ailments with stress aetiology
Lack of appetite	Constant irritability with people	Hypertension: high blood pressure
Craving for food when under pressure	Feeling unable to cope	Coronary thrombosis: heart attack
Frequent indigestion or heartburn	Lack of interest in life	Migraine
Constipation or diarrhoea	Constant or recurrent fear of disease	Hayfever and allergies
Insomnia	A feeling of being a failure	Asthma
Constant tiredness	A feeling of being bad or of self-hatred	Pruritus: intense itching
Tendency to sweat for no good reason	Difficulty in making decisions	Peptic ulcers
Nervous twitches	A feeling of ugliness	Constipation
Nail-biting	Loss of interest in other people	Colitis
Headaches	Awareness of suppressed anger	Rheumatoid arthritis
Cramps and muscle spasms	Inability to show true feelings	Menstrual difficulties
Nausea	A feeling of being the target of other people's animosity	Nervous dyspepsia: flatulence and indigestion
Breathlessness without exertion	Loss of sense of humour	Hyperthyroidism: overactive thyroid gland
Fainting spells	Feeling of neglect	Diabetes melitus
Frequent crying or desire to cry	Dread of the future	Skin disorders
Impotency or frigidity	A feeling of having failed as a person or parent	Tuberculosis
Inability to sit still without fidgeting	A feeling of having no one to confide in	Depression
High blood pressure	Difficulty in concentrating	
	The inability to finish one task before rushing on to the next	
	An intense fear of open or enclosed spaces, or of being alone	

pay for a poor fit between people and their environments? As studies of stress-related illnesses and deaths show, stress is taking a devastatingly high toll on our combined productivity and health (Cooper, 1996; Sutherland and Cooper, 2000).

With the increasing pace of life, the changing nature of the family and of work, stress is increasingly implicated in a range of illnesses. Cooper and Quick (1999) contend that in the developed world, stress is directly implicated in four causes (heart disease, strokes, injuries and suicide and homicide) and indirectly involved in a further three (cancer, chronic liver disease and bronchial complaints such as emphysema).

Costs in the workplace

All of the potential stress costs outlined so far combine both to lessen the satisfaction obtained from work and to reduce on-the-job performance. Later in this chapter, we look more closely at how work influences stress levels, but it is relevant here to mention the ways in which stress is reflected in the workplace.

Work has dramatically changed since the early 1990s, with more and more workplaces downsizing, merging and restructuring (*see also* Chapters 1 and 14). The impact is reflected in the job satisfaction figures in many countries, particularly the United Kingdom. The International Survey Research 5-yearly report on European employee satisfaction showed that between 1985 and 1995 Britain saw a marked decline in job satisfaction among employees from 64 per cent to 53 per cent. Many other countries in Europe were reporting declines as well, as the European workforce became more Americanised in terms of intrinsic job insecurity, long hours and constant restructuring.

Certain occupations, such as mining, piloting, police work, advertising and acting, are believed to provide the highest stress levels (Cooper, 1997). Stress on the job becomes an occupational hazard for certain 'helping' professionals, such as physicians, dentists, nurses and health technologists, who have higher than expected rates of suicide and alcohol/drug abuse. 'Burnout', or the premature withdrawal from one's career due to stress, appears particularly common among nurses. Nurses and others in the health field suffer from mental ill health to the extent that more of them are being admitted to hospitals and clinics for the treatment of mental disorders than in previous years. Yet at least health workers have a clear mission and are in personal contact with the people for whom they work. As noted in the opening case study, central government workers might appear to have an easy time, but rapidly shifting government policies and remoteness from the people served can lead to a sense of rolelessness.

Experiments and studies have shown that, within certain limits, an individual's performance actually improves with increased levels of stress. After a point, however, stress clearly results in reduced performance. The Yerkes–Dodson law, as shown in Fig. 11.2, reflects this phenomenon in medical terms. As Melhuish (1978) suggested:

> the portion of the graph between B and C represents pressures which the individual can tolerate: within these limits his health and quality of life improve with increased pressure (challenge). At C, however, increased pressure loses its beneficial effect and becomes harmful. Pressure becomes stress and in the portion C–D, health and quality of life decrease. C is the threshold (as is B, for boredom is also a potent stress and the portion B–A also represents increasing risk of stress illness).

Absenteeism is one of the obvious costs of stress to employers. The UK Confederation of Business and Industry (CBI) found that 'workplace stress' was the second biggest cause of absence in the UK workforce (CBI, 2001). However, if you also add up home–family responsibilities, personal problems, poor workplace

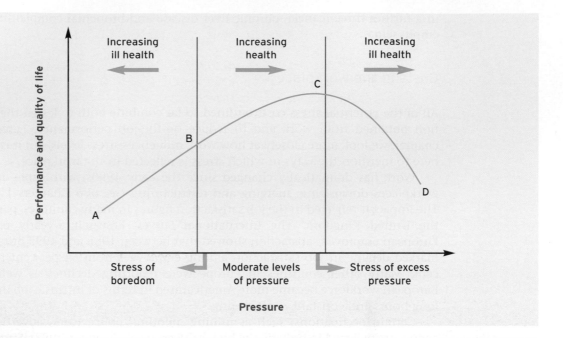

Figure 11.2   Medical extension of Yerkes-Dodson law
Source: **Extract from EXECUTIVE HEALTH by Dr Andrew Melhuish published by Random House Business Books. Used by permission of The Random House Group Limited**

morale, impact of long hours, lack of commitment and drink and drug problems (some of the other categories in addition to workplace stress – all of which are sources or outcomes of stress), then stress at work generally is the single biggest cause of absence. This is one conclusion drawn by the CBI (2001), which reported that in 2000 absence averaged 7.8 days per employee, at a probable cost to British business of about £11 billion (approx €16 billion). On the bright side however, the absence rates were lower than they had been a decade earlier.

High rates of employee turnover can become quite expensive to a company – they raise training costs, reduce overall efficiency and disrupt other workers. Although it is hard to estimate the actual costs of labour turnover, it is thought that they often equal about five times an employee's monthly salary (Quick and Quick, 1984).

Employers are paying directly for stress-related illnesses through workers' compensation claims (Earnshaw and Cooper, 2001). Ivancevich *et al.* (1985) reviewed landmark court cases which resulted in American corporations increasingly being held responsible for workplace stress. For example, in 1955, an iron worker named Bailey saw a fellow scaffolding worker fall to his death. Bailey returned to work, but gradually he began to have frequent blackouts and became paralysed. He also suffered from sleeping difficulties and extreme sensitivity to pain. In the resulting court case, Bailey *vs* American General, a Texas court ruled in Bailey's favour. The physical accident and psychological trauma were held responsible for the onset of the subsequent paralysis and other problems. Although not a radical decision, it paved the way for compensation cases under existing laws. Many employers are being held responsible for employee stress due to the belief that they are doing little to cut down the stressful aspects of many jobs. This may help to explain the growth in corporate health and stress management programmes in America and elsewhere. Those employers who are at least seen to be doing something about workplace stress may be able to put forward a better defence in the courts.

According to a US government report (NIOSH, 1993), one specific type of compensation claim, 'gradual mental stress', has shown significant growth in recent years. As the report explained, this type of claim refers to 'cumulative emotional problems stemming mainly from exposure to adverse psychosocial conditions at work ... Emotional problems related to a specific traumatic event at work, or to work-related physical disease or injury, such as witnessing a severe accident, are not included'. According to the report, about 11 per cent of all occupational disease claims involve gradual mental stress. Over the last decade in the United Kingdom, from the High Court judgment in the John Walker *vs* Northumberland County Council case in 1994, employee stress claims have been rising. There are literally hundreds of cases in the UK courts and the ones that were settled around the turn of the century averaged over £250 000 (€365 000) each (for details of all of these see Earnshaw and Cooper, 2001).

Key Learning Point

Stress costs industrialised economies around 10 per cent of GNP, through sickness absence, ill health and labour turnover.

What are the most common sources of stress at work?

Stress-related illness is not confined to either high- or low-status workers (Cooper *et al.*, 2001). Regardless of how one job may compare to another in terms of stress, it is helpful to recognise that every job has potential stress agents. Researchers have identified seven major sources of work stress (Cooper *et al.*, 1988a; Sutherland and Cooper, 2000). Common to all jobs, these factors vary in the degree to which they are found to be causally linked to stress in each job. The seven categories (Fig. 11.3) are:

1   factors intrinsic to the job;
2   role in the organisation;
3   personality and coping strategy;
4   relationships at work;
5   career development;
6   organisational culture and climate;
7   home–work interface.

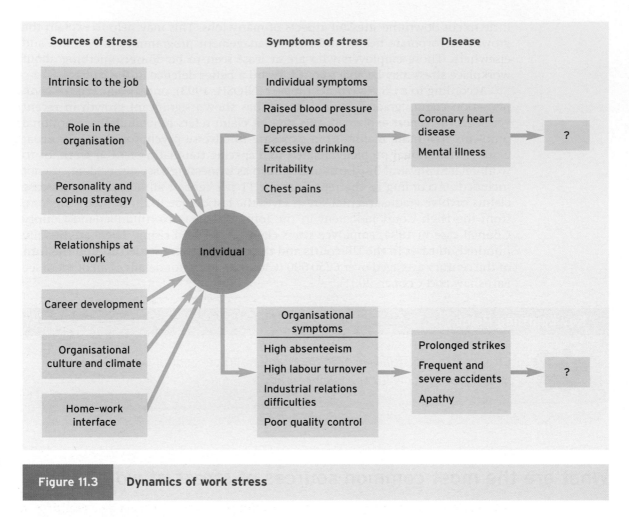

Sources of stress	Symptoms of stress	Disease

Sources of stress
- Intrinsic to the job
- Role in the organisation
- Personality and coping strategy
- Relationships at work
- Career development
- Organisational culture and climate
- Home-work interface

→ Indvidual

Symptoms of stress

Individual symptoms
- Raised blood pressure
- Depressed mood
- Excessive drinking
- Irritability
- Chest pains

Organisational symptoms
- High absenteeism
- High labour turnover
- Industrial relations difficulties
- Poor quality control

Disease

- Coronary heart disease
- Mental illness
→ ?

- Prolonged strikes
- Frequent and severe accidents
- Apathy
→ ?

Figure 11.3   Dynamics of work stress

Factors intrinsic to the job

As a starting point to understanding work stress, researchers have studied those factors that may be intrinsic to the job itself such as: poor working conditions, shift work, long hours, travel, risk and danger, new technology, work overload and work underload.

Working conditions

Our physical surroundings – noise, lighting, smells and all the stimuli that bombard our senses – can affect our moods and overall mental state, whether or not we find them consciously objectionable. Considerable research has linked working conditions to mental health. Kornhauser (1965) long ago suggested that poor mental health was directly related to unpleasant working conditions, the necessity to work fast and to expend a lot of physical effort, and to excessive and inconvenient hours. Others have found that physical health is also adversely affected by repetitive and dehumanising work settings, such as fast-paced assembly lines (Cooper *et al.*, 2001). In one study of stress factors associated with casting work in a steel manufacturing plant, poor working conditions such as noise, fumes and to a lesser extent heat, together with the social and psychological consequences, including isolation and tension among workers, had significant impact (Kelly and Cooper, 1981).

Health workers, too, often face a variety of noxious stimuli. Hospital lighting, for example, is usually artificial, monotonous, and too bright or garish. One study of the problems experienced by nurses working in intensive care units in the United States found that an oppressive visual environment became particularly stressful to nurses over a period of time (Hay and Oken, 1972). This factor, combined with the incessant routine nature of many of the activities, led to feelings of being trapped, claustrophobia and dehumanisation. In addition, the high noise level of a busy ward adds to the stress factors faced by health professionals. All of this, of course, is in addition to the stress encountered in dealing daily with death and pain (Cooper and Quick, 1999).

Each occupation has its own potential environmental sources of stress. For example, in jobs where individuals are dealing with close detail work, poor lighting can create eye strain. On the other hand, extremely bright lighting or glare presents problems for air traffic controllers. Similarly, as Ivancevich and Matteson (1980) stated,

> noise, in fact, seems to operate less as a stressor in situations where it is excessive but expected, than in those where it is unexpected, or at least unpredictable. The change in noise levels more than absolute levels themselves, seems to be the irritant. This, of course, is simply another way of saying that noise, like any stressor, causes stress when it forces us to change.

The physical design of the workplace can be another potential source of stress. If an office is poorly designed, with personnel who require frequent contact spread throughout a building, poor communication networks can develop, resulting in role ambiguity and poor relationships.

Shift work

Many workers today have jobs requiring them to work in shifts, some of which involve working staggered hours. Studies have found that shift work is a common occupational stress factor. It has been demonstrated that shift work affects blood temperature, metabolic rate, blood sugar levels, mental efficiency and work motivation, not to mention sleep patterns and family and social life. In one study of nurses, for example, Demir *et al.* (2003) found that working night shifts might lead to greater exhaustion, sense of depersonalisation and loss of energy than working day shifts.

In a study of offshore oil rig workers, the third most important source of stress found was a general category labelled 'work patterns', such as shift work, physical conditions and travel (Sutherland and Cooper, 1987). The longer the work shift – for example '28 days on, 28 days off' versus '14 days on, 14 days off' – the greater the stress. The shift work patterns were a predictor of mental and physical ill health, particularly when the oil rig workers were married and had children.

As the last comment indicates, shift work comes in a variety of forms. In particular, shifts can be at somewhat different times, they can be different lengths, and there are variations in the extent and frequency with which staff are required to change shifts. On this last point, a study (again with nurses) by Tasto *et al.* (1978) compared nurses working fixed shifts with those working rotating shifts. They found that the rotating nurses fared the worst, followed closely by night-shift workers. Shift rotators reported a greater use of alcohol, a higher frequency of problems with their health and their sex lives, and less satisfaction in their personal lives than other shift workers. Rotating shift nurses were significantly more confused, depressed and anxious than nurses on non-rotating shifts.

Regarding shift length, Hoffman and Scott (2003) found that nurses working 12-hour shifts experienced no more stress than those working 8-hour shifts. Mitchell and Williamson (2000) reported that power station workers on 12-hour shifts experienced fewer problems in domestic life, and better sleep and mood, than those on 8-hour shifts. However, and rather ominously, some aspects of work performance showed an increase in error rates towards the end of a 12-hour shift (somehow this brings up images of Homer Simpson!). The possible performance losses brought about by extended shifts are also discussed by Sparks *et al.* (2001).

Work hours and load

The long working hours required by many jobs appear to take a toll on employee health. One early research study has made a link between long working hours and deaths due to coronary heart disease (Breslow and Buell, 1960). This investigation of light industrial workers in the United States found that individuals under 45 years of age who worked more than 48 hours a week had twice the risk of death from coronary heart disease than did similar individuals working a maximum of 40 hours a week. Another early study of 100 young coronary patients revealed that 25 per cent of them had been working at two jobs, and an additional 40 per cent worked for more than 60 hours a week (Russek and Zohman, 1958). Many individuals, such as executives working long hours and some medics who might have no sleep for 36 hours or more, may find that both they and the quality of their work suffer.

It seems that in many Western countries the average number of hours worked per week is slowly reducing. However, this is not the case in some countries, particularly those with relatively deregulated economies such as the United Kingdom, the United States and New Zealand (OECD, 1999). Typical working hours in some developing countries can be twice those in some of the industrialised developed countries.

It is now commonly recognised that beyond 40 hours a week, time spent working is increasingly unproductive and can create ill health. In fact, in a meta-analytic investigation of a large number of international studies linking hours of health, it was found that consistently working long hours damaged individuals' physical and/or psychological health – and 'long' was considered any hours over 40 (Sparks *et al.*, 1997). Of course, it may not only be the long hours that create this effect. People who choose to work long hours may be especially driven individuals who are prone to health problems. Their jobs may be demanding in many different ways (for example overload, responsibility), which may lead the person to work long hours in order to complete their tasks.

Key Learning Point

Long and/or unsociable work hours have clear negative psychological and behavioural effects on people who experience them.

Two different types of work overload have been described by researchers. *Quantitative overload* refers simply to having too much work to do. *Qualitative overload* refers to work that is too difficult for an individual (French and Caplan, 1972). In the first case, too much work often leads to working long hours with the attendant problems described above. Too heavy a work burden has also been connected with increased cigarette smoking and other ill health behaviours.

Cox (1980) and Sutherland and Cooper (2000) have described the problem of not being sufficiently challenged by work. Job underload associated with repetitive routine, boring and understimulating work is associated with ill health. Certain workers, such as pilots, air traffic controllers and nuclear power workers, face a special aspect of work underload. They must deal with long periods of time in which they have little to do, while facing the possibility that they may suddenly be required to spring into action in a crisis. On a smaller scale, this is also the fate of some workers with advanced manufacturing technology who (depending on how jobs are configured) may become relatively unskilled machine-minders but who nevertheless have to respond quickly if the machine malfunctions (Chase and Karwowski, 2003).

Risk and danger

A job that involves risk or danger can result in higher stress levels. When someone is constantly aware of potential danger, he or she is prepared to react immediately. The individual is in a constant state of arousal, as described in the 'fight or flight' syndrome. The resulting adrenalin rush, respiration changes and muscle tension are all seen as potentially threatening to long-term health. On the other hand, individuals who face physical danger – such as police, mine workers, firefighters and soldiers – often appear to have reduced stress levels, particularly those who are adequately trained and equipped to deal with emergency situations. Young and Cooper (1995) found that high-risk public sector workers such as firefighters, ambulance workers, etc., also suffered from lack of control at work, unable to influence the change process and managing work–life balance.

New technology

The introduction of new technology into the work environment has required all workers, blue-collar workers and management, to adapt continually to new equipment, systems and ways of working. Having a boss trained in the 'old ways' may be an extra burden for the new employee trained in the latest methods, and raises questions about the adequacy of supervision and about those in senior positions (*see also* Chapter 1). As well as the sheer amount of change, the introduction of new technology can also mean that jobs become less fulfilling yet in some ways more demanding, thus increasing stress, though these patterns are not inevitable (Chase and Karwowski, 2003).

The use of IT has also increased the pressure, particularly the introduction of e-mail. More and more communication within and between workplaces is done by e-mail, but the prioritising and management of this vast amount of communication and information is under-developed, with little emphasis in organisations on information management (Lantz, 1998). Other technologies have also radically changed the work environment, such as mobile phones, lap-top computers and others that now increasingly encourage people to work 24-7, while travelling, in hotels, on holidays – with less and less personal disposable time for ourselves.

Role in the organisation

When a person's role in an organisation is clearly defined and understood, and when expectations placed upon the individual are also clear and non-conflicting, stress can be kept to a minimum. But as researchers have clearly seen, this is not the case in many workplaces. Three critical factors – role ambiguity, role conflict and the degree of responsibility for others – are seen to be major sources of stress.

Role ambiguity and role conflict

These are two concepts with very long histories in stress research. Their impact is summarised in Fig. 11.4. Role ambiguity arises when individuals do not have a clear picture about their work objectives, their co-workers' expectations of them, and the scope and responsibilities of their job. Often this ambiguity results simply because a supervisor does not lay out to the employee exactly what his or her role is. As Warshaw (1979) stated, 'The individual just doesn't know how he or she fits into the organization and is unsure of any rewards no matter how well he or she may perform'.

A wide range of events can create role ambiguity (Beehr, 1995). These include starting a new job (*see* Chapter 14), getting a new boss, the first supervisory responsibility, a poorly defined or unrealistic job description, or a change in the structure of the existing organisation – all of these events, and others, may serve to create a temporary state of role ambiguity. The stress indicators found to relate to role ambiguity are depressed mood, lowered self-esteem, life dissatisfaction, low motivation to work and high intention to leave a job.

Role conflict exists when an individual is torn by conflicting job demands or by doing things that he or she does not really want to do, or things which the individual does not believe are part of the job. Workers may often feel themselves torn between two groups of people who demand different types of behaviour or who believe the job entails different functions. Conflict situations can clearly act as stress factors upon the individuals involved. Research has indicated that role conflict leads to reduced job satisfaction and higher anxiety levels (e.g. Nystedt *et al.*,

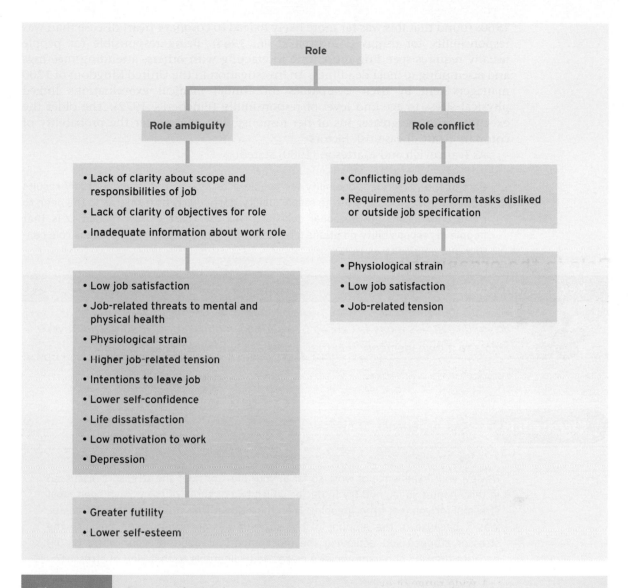

| Figure 11.4 | **Sources of role stress at work** |

1999). Other research has shown that role conflict can lead to cardiovascular ill health risks, such as elevated blood pressure and abnormal blood chemistry (Ivancevich and Matteson, 1980).

Responsibility

Responsibility has been found to be another organisational role stress agent. In an organisation, there are basically two types of responsibility: responsibility for people, and responsibility for things, such as budgets, equipment and buildings. Responsibility for people has been found to be particularly stressful. Studies in the

1960s found that this was far more likely to lead to coronary heart disease than was responsibility for things (Wardwell *et al.*, 1964). Being responsible for people usually requires spending more time interacting with others, attending meetings and attempting to meet deadlines. An investigation in the United Kingdom of 1200 managers sent by their companies for annual medical examinations linked physical stress to age and level of responsibility (Pincherle, 1972). The older the executive and the greater his or her responsibility, the greater the probability of coronary heart disease risk factors.

As Ivancevich and Matteson (1980) stated:

> Part of the reason responsibility for people acts as a stressor undoubtedly results from the specific nature of the responsibility, particularly as it relates to the need to make unpleasant interpersonal decisions. Another part of the reason ... is that people in responsibility positions lend themselves to overload, and perhaps role conflict and ambiguity as well.

Key Learning Point

Workplace stress today is caused by overload, job insecurity, information overload and a management style that punishes rather than praises.

Exercise 11.1   Your experience of stress

Review your experience of work so far in your life. Consider the stressors discussed in this chapter so far, and try to decide which two or three of them have been most stressful for *you* (not other people). Then think about *why* you found them stressful. Was it because (i) the amount of the stressor was so great, or (ii) because the stressor stopped you achieving the most important goals of your work, or (iii) because the kind of person you are makes you vulnerable to that kind of stressor?

Personality and coping

Most models of stress construe personality as having one or more of the following roles in the stress process:

■ A direct effect on stress outcomes – for example, anxious people may be more tense across all kinds of situations, which can lead to psychological and/or physical health problems.

■ A moderating effect in the stress or strain relationship. In other words, certain personality characteristics may mean that some people are more affected than others by an aspect of their work situation. So, for example, extrovert people may find a socially isolated job more stressful than introverts.

■ A direct perceptual effect. Personality may have some impact on a person's perceptions of what his or her job is like. For example, people with a high need for control may be very aware of limitations on their autonomy, and rate their work autonomy as lower than it really is.

As might be expected, studies have shown that people with high anxiety levels suffer more from role conflicts than do people who are more flexible in their approach to life. Anxiety-prone individuals experience role conflict more acutely and react to it with greater tension than people who were less anxiety prone; and more flexible individuals respond to high role conflict with lesser feelings of tension than their more rigid counterparts (Warr and Wall, 1975). In other studies, when the individual has had stronger needs for cognitive clarity or lower levels of tolerance for ambiguity, job-related stress has been found to be higher and more prolonged. More recent studies (Sparks and Cooper, 1999; Cooper *et al.*, 2001) have shown that locus of control, the hardy personality and type A behaviour are moderators between the stressors and strains in the stress process. That is, personality, or lifestyle factors can mitigate the *effects* of a stressor, as well as by eliminating or minimising the stressor itself. Locus of control refers to the extent to which a person believes he or she has control over his or her life. In many circumstances having an internal locus of control (i.e. believing one is in control) is helpful because it encourages a person to do something about their stressful situation. This is fine unless there really is not anything a person can do, in which case an internal locus of control will simply increase his or her frustration. The so-called hardy personality refers to a combination of internal locus of control, self-confidence and motivation (especially to recover from disappointments).

The Type A behavioural pattern is another concept that has a long history in stress research (Lee *et al.*, 1993). Many managers and other white collar and professional people who may be vulnerable to stress at work seem to display a pattern of behaviour termed Type A stress-prone behaviour (Rosenman *et al.*, 1964). The questionnaire shown in Exercise 11.2 was developed by Bortner (1969) to assess an individual's Type A behaviour. People who exhibit the Type A personality are more prone than others to the effects of stress.

Exercise 11.2   Type A behavioural pattern

Fill in the following questionnaire and then score it as suggested. If you are a high Type A it means that you are very competitive, high achieving, aggressive, hasty, impatient, time conscious and hard driving. Type B, which is the other end of the continuum, is the opposite of this characterisation.

Type A behaviour

Circle one number for each of the statements below which best reflects the way you behave in your everyday life. For example, if you are generally on time for appoint- ▶

ments, for the first point you would circle a number between 7 and 11. If you are usually casual about appointments you would circle one of the lower numbers between 1 and 5.

Casual about appointments	1 2 3 4 5 6 7 8 9 10 11	Never late
Not competitive	1 2 3 4 5 6 7 8 9 10 11	Very competitive
Good listener	1 2 3 4 5 6 7 8 9 10 11	Anticipates what others are going to say (nod, attempts to finish for them)
Never feels rushed (even under pressure)	1 2 3 4 5 6 7 8 9 10 11	Always rushed
Can wait patiently	1 2 3 4 5 6 7 8 9 10 11	Impatient while waiting
Takes things one at a time	1 2 3 4 5 6 7 8 9 10 11	Tries to do many things at once, thinks about what will do next
Slow deliberate talker	1 2 3 4 5 6 7 8 9 10 11	Emphatic in speech, fast and forceful
Cares about satisfying him/herself no matter what others may think	1 2 3 4 5 6 7 8 9 10 11	Wants good job recognised by others
Slow doing things	1 2 3 4 5 6 7 8 9 10 11	Fast (eating, walking)
Easy-going	1 2 3 4 5 6 7 8 9 10 11	Hard-driving (pushing yourself and others)
Expresses feelings	1 2 3 4 5 6 7 8 9 10 11	Hides feelings
Many outside interests	1 2 3 4 5 6 7 8 9 10 11	Few interests outside work/home
Unambitious	1 2 3 4 5 6 7 8 9 10 11	Ambitious
Casual	1 2 3 4 5 6 7 8 9 10 11	Eager to get things done

Plot total score below:

Type B		Type A
14	84	154

The higher the score on this questionnaire, the more firmly an individual can be classified as Type A. For example, 154 points is the highest possible score and indicates the maximum Type A stress-prone personality. It is important to understand that there are no distinct divisions between Type A and Type B. Rather, people fall somewhere on a continuum leaning more towards one type than the other. An average score is 84. Anyone with a score above that is inclined towards Type A behaviour, and below that towards Type B behaviour. What does your score say about your likely vulnerability to stress?

Source: Cooper's adaptation of the Bortner Type A scale scoring

With the emergence of the so-called 'Big Five' personality characteristics (*see* Chapter 3) there will no doubt be more research on their role in the stress process. Hart and Cooper (2001) make some suggestions about this. For example, the personality characteristic of conscientiousness may be helpful in situations where sticking at the task is a good coping strategy.

Key Learning Point

Personality has a major role in influencing both how people perceive stressors and how they respond to them.

On the subject of coping, how individuals cope with stress has been the focus of quite a lot of research and practice (see for example Zeidner and Endler, 1996). Coping is usually defined as the efforts people make, through their behaviour and thoughts, to alter their environment and/or manage their emotions. Coping strategies include analysing the situation, planning a course of action, seeking information from others, seeking support and comfort from others, relaxation techniques, counselling, and using alcohol, tobacco or other drugs.

One general distinction is between problem-focused strategies (dealing with the original cause of stress) and emotion-focused strategies (dealing with how one feels about the stressful situation). Logically, when it is possible to change the situation, problem-focused strategies would seem to be the better option. But research suggests that the results of coping are hard to predict, perhaps not only because of the coping strategy a person uses, but also because how effectively he or she uses it, matters a lot.

Another distinction is between a person's coping *resources* and the coping *strategies* he or she actually uses. Some people may have certain resources, such as sympathetic close friends, but not use them. Underlying this is a debate about whether people choose coping strategies on the basis of the current situation, or of their personality and prior learning.

Relationships at work

Other people – and our varied encounters with them – can be major sources of both stress and support (Makin *et al.*, 1996). At work, especially, dealings with bosses, peers and subordinates can dramatically affect the way we feel at the end of the day. Selye (1974) suggested that learning to live with other people is one of the most stressful aspects of life. This is in spite of the fact that most people, given the opportunity, seek out social contact and relationships at least some of the time.

It is an interesting fact, however, that little research has been done in this area. Lazarus (1966) suggested that supportive social relationships with peers, supervisors and subordinates at work are less likely to create interpersonal pressures, and will directly reduce levels of perceived job stress. Poor relationships were defined by researchers at the University of Michigan as those which include low trust, low supportiveness and low interest in listening or trying to deal with problems that confront the organisational member.

Most studies (e.g. Cartwright and Cooper, 1997; Sparks and Cooper, 1999) have concluded that mistrust of fellow workers is connected with high role ambiguity, poor communications and psychological strain in the form of low job satisfaction, and feelings of job-related threat to one's well-being. There are three critical relationships at work: relationships with superiors, relationships with subordinates and relationships with colleagues or co-workers.

Relationships with superiors

Physicians and clinical psychologists support the idea that problems of emotional disability often result when the relationship between a subordinate and a boss is psychologically unhealthy for one reason or another. More optimistically, Sosik and Godshalk (2000) among others have shown that an inspiring leadership style (*see also* Chapter 13) can significantly reduce the amount of stress experienced by subordinates. This style of leadership includes giving priority to the development needs of specific individuals, setting a personal example, and establishing clear mission for the workgroup or organisation. Note how, in the opening case study, several of these features appeared to be absent in the opinion of UK central government employees.

As Sparks *et al.* (2001) have pointed out, competitive pressures on organisations in turn usually mean pressure on individual managers. Some managers find this hard to cope with, and many respond by behaving in unpleasant ways towards their subordinates. For example, some reports suggest that bullying is disturbingly common (Hoel *et al.*, 1999). More subtly, a boss under stress many change the nature of a subordinate's job so that it becomes more stressful – for example by supervising the subordinate much more closely (Lobban *et al.*, 1998).

To understand how to *manage* the boss, it is important to be able to identify different species of boss. Cooper *et al.* (1993) found that there were various boss prototypes: the bureaucrat, the autocrat, the wheeler-dealer, the reluctant manager and the open manager. Each has to be dealt with differently if the stress is to be minimised. For example, the bureaucrat is likely to respond most positively to structured and relatively formal communication which respects established procedures.

Relationships with subordinates and colleagues

The way in which a manager supervises the work of others has always been considered a critical aspect of his or her work. For instance, the inability to delegate has been a common criticism levelled against some managers. It now appears that managers face a new challenge: learning to manage by participation. Today's emphasis on participation can be a cause of resentment, anxiety and stress for the managers involved.

Stress among co-workers can arise from the competition and personality conflicts usually described as 'office politics'. Adequate social support can be critical to the health and well-being of an individual and to the atmosphere and success of an organisation (Bernin and Theorell, 2001). Because most people spend so much time at work, the relationships among co-workers can provide valuable support or, conversely, can be a huge source of stress. French and Caplan (1972) found that strong social support from co-workers eased job strain. This support also reduced the effects of job strain on cortisone levels, blood pressure, glucose levels and the number of cigarettes smoked.

Key Learning Point

Relationships with others at work have much potential to create stress or to reduce it.

Career development

A host of issues can act as potential stress factors throughout one's working life. Lack of job security, fear of redundancy, obsolescence or retirement, and numerous performance appraisals can cause pressure and strain. In addition, the frustration of having reached one's career ceiling or having been over-promoted can result in extreme stress. Ivancevich and Matteson (1980) suggested that individuals suffering from 'career stress' often show high job dissatisfaction, job mobility, burnout, poor work performance, less effective interpersonal relationships at work and so on. Career-related issues are considered more fully in Chapter 14.

For many workers, career progression is of overriding importance. Through promotion, people not only earn more money, but enjoy increased status and new challenges. In the early years in a job, the striving and ability required to deal with a rapidly changing environment is usually rewarded by a company through monetary and promotional rewards. At middle age, however, many people find their career progress has slowed or stopped. Job opportunities may become fewer, available jobs can require longer to master, old knowledge may become obsolete, and energy levels can flag. At the same time, younger competition threatens (*see also* Chapter 14).

The transition to retirement can in itself be a stressful event. While a job is a socially defined role, retirement has been described as the 'roleless role'. The potential vagueness and lack of structure of retirement can bring problems for the ill prepared. For some individuals, becoming 'pensioners' or 'senior citizens' presents a situation in which they are uncertain about how to obtain the social rewards they value. In contrast, those individuals who have maintained balance in their lives by developing interests and friends outside their work can find retirement a liberating period in their lives. Hanisch (1994) found that people who have positive reasons for retiring (such as travel) rather than negative ones such as poor health or job dissatisfaction were more likely to plan ahead for retirement and enjoy it.

The process of being evaluated and appraised can be a stressful experience for all of us (Fletcher, 2001; *see also* Chapter 6). It must be recognised that performance appraisals can be anxiety provoking, for both the individual being examined and the person doing the judging and appraising. The supervisor making performance judgements faces the threat of union grievance procedures in some cases, as well as interpersonal strains and the responsibility of making decisions affecting another person's livelihood.

The way in which an evaluation is carried out can affect the degree of anxiety experienced. For example, taking a written examination can be a short-term stress factor, while continuous and confidential appraisals by supervisors can have a more long-term effect, depending on the structure and climate of the organisation.

Key Learning Point

The concept of career is changing, with more and more people pursuing short-term contracts and freelance careers as organisations outsource more and more, leading to insecurity and ill-health for some people.

Organisational culture and climate

Much has been written about organisational climate and culture (e.g. Schein, 1992; Ashkanasy and Jackson, 2001). There has also been quite a lot of argument concerning what is the most appropriate definition of each concept. Broadly speaking, organisational climate is about employees' perceptions of how their organisation functions, while organisational culture refers to the values, assumptions and norms that are shared by organisational members, and which influence individual and collective behaviour.

An individual is likely to experience stress if he or she does not share the values etc. inherent in the employing organisation. Several factors could cause this. For example, the mismatch between individual and culture may lead the person to feel isolated and unable to communicate effectively with colleagues. It may mean that the person's role includes activities that he or she finds distasteful, and that conflict with personal preferences (a form of role conflict – see above).

Organisational climate can be a source of stress if a person believes that the way the organisation functions is unfair, or perhaps unclear and unpredictable (which could lead to role ambiguity). As early as the 1940s, researchers began reporting that workers who were allowed more participation in decision-making processes produced more and had higher job satisfaction (Coch and French, 1948). They also found that non-participation at work was a significant predictor of strain and job-related stress, relating to general poor health, escapist drinking, depression, low self-esteem, absenteeism and plans to leave work. Participation in the decision-making process on the part of the individual may help increase his or her feeling of investment in the organisation's success, create a sense of belonging and improve communication channels within the organisation. The resulting sense of being in control seems vital for the well-being of the workforce (Sauter *et al.*, 1989; Spector, 2000).

Exercise 11.3	Sources of stress on male managers at work and home

See if you can see yourself in Herbert Greenberg's (1980) description of a stressed manager: George's week hadn't been going too well. Last night he'd been up late. He and his wife had had another talk about their fifteen-year old son, a talk that had degenerated into a blaming argument. When he awoke, he was weary and unrested. He felt restless, and during breakfast he was clearly irritable and not very pleasant to be around. When he finally got off to work, the traffic was heavy. He impatiently changed lanes a lot and honked his horn several times. Later, when he arrived at work, his desk seemed overflowing with unfinished business. Today was no exception – problems and headaches. Several people, too, were waiting with dissatisfactions and complaints. He wasn't able to listen to them very patiently – he certainly wasn't particularly tolerant of their points of view. Throughout the morning, he found his mind wandering as other people talked to him. He just couldn't focus on several big projects he had planned to tackle.

He drank five or six cups of coffee during the morning and stuffed in a doughnut or two with each cup. When lunch time arrived, he felt a need for a drink and wanted nothing more than to escape – get away from it all. But he had an early afternoon meeting, so he gulped a quick lunch and went back to his office to get ready for it. All he remembered of the meeting was his indigestion. The rest of the afternoon was quieter but not much better. He snapped at his secretary once or twice and was curt with colleagues. He felt weary, tense and tight. He again postponed several decisions. He finished one report but wasn't pleased with it.

When he arrived at home he wanted nothing more than a drink and a chance to complain about how hard he worked and how lousy his job was.

What causes and symptoms of stress are evident here? If you were in George's position, how well do you think you would cope?

Home-work interface

People (most of us anyway!) have lives outside work. There are many reasons why the interface between home and work lives has become increasingly prominent in stress research and practice (Frone, 2002). These include the following:

- The increasing proportion of women in the workforce – traditionally women have tended to shoulder most of the responsibility for managing the home and caring for children, so fitting home and work lives together is seen as an important issue (Greenhaus and Parasuraman, 1999).

- The rise of the so-called 'boundaryless career' (*see* Chapter 14), where work and home lives are thought of as intertwined and (ideally) existing in harmony with each other.

- The increasing pressure that some people feel to work harder and/or for longer hours than was formerly the case.

- The increasing number of dual-career households, where the total burden of employment and domestic responsibilities tends to be high, and personal resources stretched.

Home–work interface issues are usually given the label 'conflict' in the stress literature. This conflict can be in either or both of two directions: work interference with family (where the demands of work create difficulties for home life) and family interference with work (where the demands of home life create difficulties for work).

This interference or conflict can be manifested in a variety of ways. Most obviously, the sheer amount of time required by roles in one domain (home or work) may make it difficult to give enough time to roles in the other domain. Slightly more subtly, the amount of cognitive, emotional or physical energy required to fulfil roles in one domain may mean that insufficient energy remains for roles (including tasks and relationships) in the other. Less obviously again, the kinds of values, attitudes and behaviours required in one domain may be different from (or clash with) those required in the other. For example, a salesperson may be expected to be aggressive and dominant at work, but gentle and co-operative at home. The many human resource management practices designed to reduce home–work interface stress (e.g. workplace crèches, family leave) can help with some forms of conflict, but probably not all (Cooper and Lewis, 1993).

Conflict between work and home can produce a variety of symptoms of stress (Kossek and Ozeki, 1998). Time-based conflict might lead to guilt or anxiety that one is not fulfilling one's roles properly, and perhaps low satisfaction. Energy-based conflict can produce exhaustion and irritability, while value-based conflict can lead to a sense of alienation and/or loss of self-identity.

Of course, the picture is more complicated than this. One issue is what 'home' means. Does it mean anything that is not work? If so, perhaps the term is too broad, and if not, maybe it would be more helpful to distinguish between various domestic and leisure commitments a person may have (e.g. parent, spouse, fitness fanatic, amateur photographer, etc.). Also, to some extent there are differences between cultures/countries in the importance typically assigned to work *vs* home roles, and in the extent to which work and home roles are typically seen as necessarily separate or compatible (Trompenaars and Hampden Turner, 1998). So although the interface between work and other aspects of life can produce stress, there is much still to be understood about which interfaces, and why and how stress is produced.

Key Learning Point

Stress at work can (i) be caused by factors outside the workplace and (ii) have an impact on a person's non-work roles.

The stress of being unemployed

Ever since the high levels of unemployment in the United Kingdom and many other countries throughout the 1980s, into the early 1990s, the stress of being unemployed has been a major topic of concern. It is a problem faced by many, from the unskilled to the professional worker. Reviews of the research on the psychological experience of being unemployed (e.g. Winefield, 1995; Fryer, 1998; Wanberg *et al.*, 2001) conclude that people who experience unemployment tend to suffer from lower levels of personal happiness, life satisfaction, self-esteem and psychological well-being than (i) people who are employed and (ii) when they themselves were in employment. They also tend to report increased depression, difficulty in concentrating and other minor to severe behavioural and physical problems. Although there are differences of opinion about the relationship between unemployment and mortality, evidence is emerging of a positive association, with studies indicating that long-term unemployment may adversely affect the longevity of the unemployed by as much as two to three years, depending on when the person had been made redundant.

Murphy and Athanasou (1999) conducted a meta-analysis of 16 longitudinal studies of unemployment published between 1986 and 1996. They found that moving involuntarily from employment to unemployment was associated with a fall, on average, of 0.36 standard deviations (*see* Chapter 2) on measures of well-being. This is a substantial though not huge effect. Regaining employment brought, on average, an improvement in well-being of 0.54 standard deviations. This suggests that, at least for a time, regaining employment may lead to better well-being than the person had experienced in his or her pre-unemployment job. However, much depends on the coping strategies of the individual (Kinicki *et al.*, 1999). It seems that problem-based coping (e.g. trying to find a job) rather than emotion-focused coping (e.g. telling oneself that employment is not very important) does not necessarily help people feel better at the time, but it does help them find a new job. This, as we have already noted, leads to a recovery of mental and physical health.

Of course, some people experience more than average falls and rises in well being while others experience less. What determines this? Researchers have investigated a number of factors (Wanberg *et al.*, 2001) and have mostly reported unsurprising findings. Greater financial hardship is associated with lower well-being, and so is the extent to which a person feels committed to the idea of being employed. High levels of social support and a high ability to structure time tend to reduce the impact of unemployment on well-being. Finally, it is important to remember that not all jobs are psychologically enriching (*see* Chapter 9), so it is possible that unemployment is a less bad experience than some of the least pleasant jobs.

Key Learning Point

It is clear that, for most people, unemployment leads to a significant deterioration in psychological and physical health.

Some psychologists have tried to identify exactly what it is about unemployment that leads people to feel psychologically bad. Jahoda (1979) wrote of the manifest function of employment (income), but also its latent functions – structuring of time, social contact outside the family, linkage to wider goals/purposes, personal status/identity and enforced activity. A person who becomes unemployed is deprived of both the manifest and the latent functions of employment, and it is this, Jahoda argued, that leads to negative psychological states. Others have seen Jahoda's approach as too limited. Warr (1987) pointed out that not all employment fosters mental health, and identified features of 'psychologically good' employment. These included money, variety, goals, opportunity for decision-making, skill use/development, security, interpersonal contact and valued social position. This pays more attention than Jahoda to characteristics of the job itself. Warr argued that becoming unemployed would have negative psychological effects to the extent that it led to loss of these features in day-to-day life. Fryer (1998) has taken a rather different approach. He has criticised conventional treatments of unemployment for taking an overly passive view of the person. The psychological effects of unemployment are, he argues, the result of frustrated attempts to create a better future rather than memories and regrets about loss of a more satisfying past.

Critiques of stress

Stress is a topic (or perhaps more accurately a word) that has generated huge amounts of research and media interest over many years. Yet not everyone agrees that the term is entirely helpful. This is for various conceptual and practical reasons. First, in spite of many writers offering definitions of stress, these are not all the same. It is therefore difficult to know exactly what is being referred to.

Second, following on from the first point, the word stress tends to refer to almost anything unpleasant that happens, and/or as anything that leads a person to feel negative emotion. Many would argue this is far too broad a domain for just one word, and risks hiding important differences between different kinds of negative events and emotions. In turn, this increases the difficulty of devising research and management practices that effectively address key issues.

Third, much of the literature seems to construe stress as entirely negative. Yet in some circumstances it is possible for both stress and positive emotions to arise from the same experience – for example in the opening case study of this chapter, NHS workers were seen as coping with heavy pressure but also experiencing quite high job satisfaction. Indeed, sometimes it seems that some stress may even be necessary in order for other more positive things to happen, such as personal development (see, for example, Nicholson and West's 1988 analysis of how people react to new jobs). So as Hart and Cooper (2001) argue, it is possible to experience what we might call satisfaction and stress at the same time. This means that looking at stress would get only half the picture of a person's current experience of work.

Fourth, and developing the third point, it is tempting to see stress as the negative end of the single dimension of well-being and/or emotion. But many psychologists argue that this is too simplistic. It seems that the extent to which a person is experiencing pleasant emotion (positive affect) is more or less independent of the extent to which he or she is experiencing unpleasant emotion (negative affect). So any individual at any given moment could be high on one and low on the other, or high on both, or low on both (Agho *et al.*, 1992). It is also possible to distinguish between high arousal and low arousal. This creates four quadrants of emotion that can be experienced (see Fig. 11.5). Again, this helps us gain a more complete picture of a person's work experience than simply examining 'stress'.

Fifth, as we shall see in a moment, many attempts to manage stress focus on what the individual who is experiencing it can do to help him or herself. This conveniently sidesteps the question of whether employing organisations are doing all they should to prevent stress-inducing conditions arising in the first place (see, however, the closing case study of this chapter for an employer-focused approach). Also, of course, psychologists and others who make a living helping people and/or organisations deal with stress have a vested interest in not only promoting the concept of stress, but also ensuring that it continues to be seen as prevalent. They also need to be able to argue that stress has serious negative consequences, and that attempts to manage it remove or at least reduce these. Some (e.g. Briner and Reynolds, 1999) are very sceptical about that.

Key Learning Point

Some people believe that stress is an over-used word and a poorly defined concept that obscures important subtleties of human experience at work and encourages a range of poorly focused interventions.

Stress management

As we have already seen in this chapter, stress at work is costly to the individual and the organisation. We therefore will now examine the role of stress management training and stress counselling in the workplace and their likely effects. In

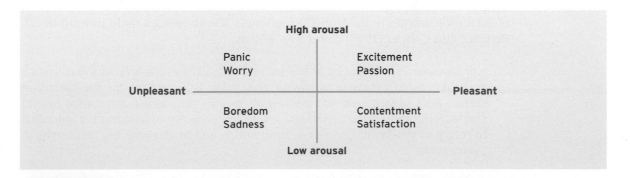

| Figure 11.5 | **Four types of emotion** |

addition, we will highlight organisation-directed strategies to reduce stress, interventions that get at the root of the job or organisational problem or stressor (e.g. changing an autocratic management style, redesigning a job, introducing more flexible working arrangements, etc.).

DeFrank and Cooper (1987) suggest that stress interventions can focus on the individual, the organisation or the individual–organisational interface. Murphy (1988) emphasised three levels of intervention: (i) primary, or reducing the *sources* of organisational stress, (ii) secondary, or stress management training, and (iii) tertiary, or health promotion and workplace counselling.

As Cartwright and Cooper (1997) highlight, most workplace initiatives operate at the secondary or tertiary levels, which focus on stress management training or counselling and health promotion. Health promotion/education programmes aim to modify behavioiurial risk factors that lead to disease and poor health, whereas health screening is concerned with the diagnosis and detection of existing conditions. The form these activities take varies widely. They may involve the provision of keep-fit facilities on site, dietary control, cardiovascular fitness programmes, relaxation and exercise classes, stress management training or psychological counselling, or some combination of these.

Employee assistance programmes and stress management training

While organisation-directed interventions are attempting to eliminate the source of job or organisational stress, most workplace stress initiatives have been directed at helping employees as individuals learn to cope with any stressors, be they job or organisational, that occur at work. This is achieved by improving the adaptability of individuals to their environment by changing their behaviour and improving their lifestyle or stress management skills. Such an approach is commonly described as the 'Band-Aid' or 'inoculation' treatment. Inherent in this approach is the notion that the organisation and its working environment will not change, therefore the individual has to learn ways of coping that help him or her to 'fit in' better (Cartwright and Cooper, 1997).

Increasingly, these initiatives have been in the form of employee assistance programmes (EAPs) (Berridge *et al.*, 1997). In the United States, it has been estimated that over 75 per cent of all Fortune 500 companies, together with about 12 000 smaller companies, now have such programmes (Feldman, 1991). The introduction of such programmes in the United Kingdom is also showing a rapid upward trend. Berridge and Cooper (1993) defined an EAP as:

> a programmatic intervention at the workplace, usually at the level of the individual employee, using behavioiurial science knowledge and methods for the control of certain work related problems (notably alcoholism, drug abuse and mental health) that adversely affect job performance, with the objective of enabling the individual to return to making her or his full contribution and to attaining full functioning in personal life.

An EAP can take various forms. It may involve the provision of on-site fitness facilities, dietary control, cardiovascular fitness programmes, relaxation classes, or stress and health education, but most often psychological counselling. EAPs have proved more popular with organisations than primary-level interventions or dealing with the sources of the job/organisational stress, for several reasons:

- Cost–benefit analysis of such programmes has produced some impressive results. For example, the New York Telephone Company's 'wellness' programme designed to improve cardiovascular fitness saved the organisation $2.7 million in absence and treatment costs in one year alone (Cartwright and Cooper, 1997).

- The professional 'interventionists' – the counsellors, physicians and clinicians responsible for health care – feel more comfortable with changing individuals than changing organisations (Ivancevich *et al.*, 1990).

- It is considered easier and less disruptive to business to change the individual than to embark on an extensive and potentially expensive organisational development programme, the outcome of which may be uncertain (Cooper and Cartwright, 1994).

- They present a high-profile means by which organisations can 'be seen to be doing something about stress' and taking reasonable precautions to safeguard employee health. This is likely to be important, not only in terms of the message it communicates to employees, but also to the external environment. This latter point is particularly important, given the increasing litigation fears that now exist among employers throughout the United States and Europe. It is not difficult to envisage that the existence of an EAP, regardless of whether or not an individual chooses to use it, may become an effective defence against possible legal action.

Evidence as to the success of stress management training, frequently a component of EAPs, is generally confusing and imprecise (Elkin and Rosch, 1990), which possibly reflects the idiosyncratic nature of the form and content of this kind of training. Studies that have evaluated the outcomes of stress management training, have found a modest improvement in self-reported symptoms and psychophysiological indices of strain (Reynolds *et al.*, 1993; Cooper, 1996; Cooper and Quick, 1999), but little or no change in job satisfaction, work stress or blood pressure. Similarly, studies that have assessed the impact of psychological counselling (Allison *et al.*, 1989; Cooper and Sadri, 1991) have shown significant improvements in the mental health and absenteeism of counselled employees, but little change in levels of organisational commitment and job satisfaction. Counselling and stress management training may have short-term effects, particularly if employees return to an unchanged work environment and its indigenous stressors. If, as has been discussed, such initiatives have little impact on improving job satisfaction, then it is more likely that the individual will adopt a way of coping that may have positive individual outcomes, but possibly negative implications for the organisation.

Health promotion activities are another key feature of most stress management and EAP initiatives. Research findings that have examined the impact of lifestyle and health habits provide further support that any benefits may not necessarily be sustained. Lifestyle and health habits appear to have a strong direct effect on strain outcomes, in reducing anxiety, depression and psychosomatic distress, but do not necessarily moderate the stressor–strain linkage (Baglioni and Cooper, 1988).

Cardiovascular fitness programmes, such as the New York Telephone Company's 'wellness' programmes, have been shown to dramatically improve employee health, but, again, any benefit may be relatively short term, particularly if, as suggested (Ivancevich and Matteson, 1988), after a few years, 70 per cent of individuals fail to maintain a long-term commitment to exercise habits and are likely to revert to their previous lifestyle.

Key Learning Point

A useful way to view stress management is to think of primary *(e.g. dealing with the source of the stress),* secondary *(e.g. training) and* tertiary *(e.g. EAPs) prevention.*

Changing the *sources* of workplace stress

Although there is considerable activity at the stress management, counselling and health promotion level, the organisational-level strategies are comparatively rare. It has been argued that the simplistic philosophy of 'one size fits all' (Elkin and Rosch, 1990), implicit in the current stress management interventions, may be appropriate for smoking cessation programmes, but is less appropriate for workplace stressor reduction. Cardiovascular fitness programmes may be successful in reducing the harmful effects of stress on the high-pressured executive, but such programmes will not eliminate the job stressor itself, which may be 'overpromotion' or a poor relationship with a boss. Identifying and recognising the source itself, and taking steps to tackle it, might arguably arrest the whole 'stress process' (Cartwright and Cooper, 1997).

Elkin and Rosch (1990) summarised a useful range of possible organisation-directed strategies to reduce stress:

- ■ redesign the task;
- ■ redesign the work environment;
- ■ establish flexible work schedules;
- ■ encourage participative management;
- ■ include the employee in career development;
- ■ analyse work roles and establish goals;
- ■ provide social support and feedback;
- ■ build cohesive teams;
- ■ establish fair employment policies;
- ■ share the rewards.

Many of these strategies are directed at increasing employee participation and autonomy. It is recognised that social support, control/job discretion or autonomy

(Karasek, 1989) and coping behaviour play an important role in moderating the stress response. Tertiary- and secondary-level interventions may be useful in improving and extending an individual's coping strategies and social support, but they do not directly address the important issue of control in the workplace.

Indirectly, many strategies that focus on changing the style of work organisation are a vehicle for culture change, moving the organisation towards a more open and 'employee empowered' culture. Previous reviews of the organisation behaviour literature have demonstrated that employee participation has a positive impact upon productivity and quality control (Guzzo *et al.*, 1985). Quality circle programmes, which it has been suggested represent the ultimate form of employee involvement, have been shown to impact favourably upon productivity and employee attitudes (Dale *et al.*, 1998).

The healthy organisation

A healthy organisation, therefore, can be defined as an organisation characterised by both financial success (e.g. profitability) and a physically and psychologically healthy workforce, which is able to maintain over time a healthy and satisfying work environment and organisational culture, particularly through periods of market turbulence and change (Cartwright and Cooper, 1997; Hart and Cooper, 2001). Healthy work organisations are those in which:

- levels of stress are low;
- employee organisational commitment and job satisfaction are high;
- sickness, absenteeism and labour turnover rates are below the national average;
- industrial relations are good and strikes/disputes are infrequent;
- safety and accident records are good;
- fear of litigation is absent (i.e. professional negligence, worker compensation, product liability claims etc. are rare and insurance premiums generally are below the sector average);

and

- Profitability and/or efficiency of resource-use are good;
- Impact on the physical environment is positive or neutral.

Therefore, it could be argued that the truly 'healthy' organisation, which has been successful in creating and maintaining a healthy and relatively stress-free environment, will be an organisation in which stress management and counselling interventions are unnecessary. Such an organisation will have effectively targeted its interventions at reducing or eliminating job and organisational stressors before their longer-term consequences on employee and organisational health (in all its aspects) adversely affect the bottom line. Indeed, although organisations have recognised the benefits of providing regular health screening for employees, they have been less concerned or slower to recognise the potential diagnostic benefits of conducting regular 'stress audits' to ascertain the current state of health of their organisation as a whole (and its constituent parts), through occupational/organisational stress screening.

Key Learning Point

Dealing with the job and organisational sources of stress requires job redesign, flexible working arrangements, a supportive corporate culture and better organisational communications.

Dealing with workplace stress: a problem-solving framework

If the constructs and framework of problem solving are applied to the problem of workplace stress, then both the individual and the organisation need to:

- be aware and accept that a problem exists;

- be able to identify and isolate the problem/stressor;

- attempt to change the problem/stressor in a way that provides a solution which is mutually beneficial;

- if the problem/stressor cannot be changed, then find a way of coping with the problem;

- monitor and review the outcome.

Cartwright and Cooper (1997) suggest the following steps.

Step 1: Being aware and accepting that a problem exists

It is widely accepted that recognising that one has a problem is the crucial first step towards solving it. Ownership of the problem is considered to be the most significant factor in the clinical treatment of problems such as alcoholism, drug abuse or a damaging relationship. The first step in dealing with stress, therefore, requires an awareness by the individual and the organisation that stress is a feature of modern working life, which at some time or other everybody is likely to experience, irrespective of their position in the organisation and, furthermore, that *it is not necessarily a reflection of their incompetence*. It is important that the individual is able to 'tune in' to the problem and recognise his or her own stress symptomatology early in the stress process, and that the organisation seeks to create a climate which is perceived to be openly supportive rather than punitive.

Organisations can tune into the problem of stress by monitoring a variety of behavioural indices. Aside from the more obvious ones such as rate of labour turnover, sickness and absence data, other more subtle indices might include error

and accident rates, insurance claims, tardiness, levels of job satisfaction and industrial relations generally. Organisations can also provide training in symptom
recognition and basic counselling skills for their supervisors and managers to help
them to be more responsive to employee stress. It would seem desirable, if not
essential, that this first step in the coping process requires an organisational
initiative in demonstrably acknowledging and communicating to employees that
stress has a legitimate place on the organisation's agenda alongside other more traditional issues that fall into the category of health and safety at work.

Steps 2 and 3: Identifying the problem/stressor and attempting to eliminate it or change it

At the individual level, stressor identification can be achieved by the maintenance
of a stress diary. By recording on a daily basis the incidents, types of situation and
person(s) involved that cause distress, over a period of time (e.g. four weeks), this
information will reveal any significant themes or common stressor patterns and
help the individual to identify specific problems or problem areas. It is also useful
if the individual records show how he or she responded to the situation at the time,
whether the strategy was successful in both the short and longer term, and how,
on reflection, they might have handled it better.

On the basis of this information, the individual can then move towards developing an action plan as to how they could either eliminate the source of stress or
change or modify it. For example, if a boss consistently undermines you at work,
you can either confront or avoid him or her, or consider the options for employment elsewhere. If the stressor cannot be changed, however, then the individual
has to accept the situation and explore ways of coping with the situation as it is.
By cataloguing current responses and ways of coping and reviewing these with the
benefit of retrospection, the individual can (i) identify areas where his or her
coping skills could be improved and (ii) develop a repertoire of successful contin-
gency-based coping methods which can be applied to similar situations in the
future. The review process is particularly important, as has been suggested, when
cognitive processes are frequently impaired under stress to the extent that the
range of possible alternative strategies for coping is unlikely to be fully considered
or evaluated. An awareness of potential stressors can also help the individual to
develop anticipatory coping strategies (i.e. pre-stressor).

At the organisational level, an employee survey or organisational stress audit
can be used to assess and monitor employee health and well-being, and identify
the source of stress which may be operating at an organisation-wide, departmental
or work group level. Instruments such as the Occupational Stress Indicator (Cooper
et al., 1988b) or ASSET (Cartwright and Cooper, 2001) can be used, which also
incorporate personality measures of Type A behaviour, locus of control and
employee coping strategies. Different stressors are likely to suggest different organisational solutions. For example, eliminating or reducing stressors relating to
factors intrinsic to the job may involve ergonomic solutions to the problem of
poorly designed equipment, whereas if a significant source of stress among
employees relates to career issues, then this may possibly be addressed by the introduction of regular appraisals, career counselling or retraining opportunities.
Diagnostic stress audits can be advantageous in terms of directing organisations to

areas when they can engage in anticipatory coping strategies and so arrest the stress process before its negative impact on employee health manifests itself, for example, in circumstances where the currently reported stress levels among employees are high, but the previous baseline outcome measures of physical and mental health and job satisfaction are comparable with normative data. At the more local work-group level, there are less formal means by which potential stress-related problems can be identified through the introduction of regular workgroup review meetings or quality circle type initiatives.

Step 4: If the problem/stressor cannot be changed, then find ways of coping with it

There are likely to be certain stressors which neither the individual nor the organisation is able to change, but which have to be 'coped with' in the conventional sense of the word. It is in relation to stressors of this nature that secondary and tertiary levels of intervention have a definite role to play. It is also important to recognise that not all of the stress that impacts on the workplace is necessarily or exclusively caused by the work environment. Financial crisis, bereavement, marital difficulties and other personal life events create stress, the effects of which often spill over into the workplace. Tertiary-level interventions, such as the provision of counselling services, can be extremely effective in dealing with non-work-related stress, as evidenced by the experiences of the UK Post Office (Cooper and Sadri, 1991).

Step 5: Monitoring and reviewing the outcome

The final stage in any problem-solving process involves the evaluation of the implemented solution. As already discussed, the discipline of maintaining a stress diary can help the individual to review the efficacy of his or her own coping strategies. Similarly, stress audits can provide a baseline measure whereby the introduction of any subsequent stressor reduction technique implemented by an organisation can be evaluated. If, as has been argued, stressor reduction provides the most effective means of tackling the problem of occupational stress, the criteria by which an organisation may also assess its effectiveness would be in terms of the extensiveness of its secondary- and tertiary-level programmes, for one would expect that the more successful the organisation is in eliminating or modifying environmental stressors, the less demand there would be for stress management training and employee assistance programmes.

Key Learning Point

Managing stress at work requires a stage-by-stage approach: identifying a problem, intervening to change it or find ways of coping with it, and monitoring and reviewing progress.

Exercise 11.4   Managing your stress

7.30 a.m. The day starts badly. You forgot to set the alarm and you're running late. You have an important client meeting at 9.30 a.m. and you intended to get into the office early to reread the papers in preparation for the meeting. You have to stop for fuel on the way in, which further delays you. Traffic is heavy and there are roadworks on the motorway. You find yourself in a tailback of slow-moving traffic and it's at least seven kilometres until the next exit. As you're crawling along, you suddenly become aware that you have developed a flat tyre. You limp on to the hard shoulder and look at your watch. It's 8.50 a.m. and you're still some fifteen kilometres from your office. You're not going to make that meeting!

Assuming a typical response to the previous scenario, the day might continue as follows:

9.45 a.m. You eventually arrive at your office. You go to collect the file for the client meeting and the phone rings. A subordinate is having some problems accessing information on the computer; brusquely, you give hasty instructions. You then spend a further ten minutes wading through the huge piles of paper stacked on your desk, searching for the right file. You notice a new pile of correspondence and phone messages on the desk, some marked 'urgent'. You contemplate dealing with these but you're now already 30 minutes late for this meeting. Suddenly, you realise that before you left last night your boss popped in and suggested a meeting at 10.30 a.m. You're going to be late for that one too.

What is the most effective way of handling the various problems in the above scenario? Discuss how you would have coped with each of the problems as they occurred.

Summary

Stress in the workplace has become the black plague of the late twentieth and twenty-first centuries. This is likely to get worse as international competition increases with the development of the European Union, the Pacific Basin and the economic and political liberation of Eastern Europe. These pressures at work are also likely to lead to less rather than more concern for the 'people management' aspects of the workplace. Much of the stress at work is caused not only by work overload and time pressures, but also by a lack of rewards and praise, and, more importantly, by not providing individuals with the autonomy to do their jobs as they would like (Makin *et al.*, 1996). We are seeing an increasing army of human resource professionals, such as stress counsellors, entering the arena of work (Berridge *et al.*, 1997). We need them, but they are only part of the answer. Organisations must begin to manage people at work differently, treating them with respect and valuing their contribution, if we are to enhance the psychological well-being and health of workers in the future.

Closing Case Study | Setting Standards for Stress at Work

Adapted from a Press Release from the UK Government's Health and Safety Executive (HSE), 30 October 2003

A new practical guidance pack to enable employers and employees to develop solutions to workplace stress problems is being launched today in London. The guidance, called 'Real solutions, real people – A manager's guide to tackling work-related stress', contains examples of clear, practical measures which provide a starting point for the workforce to agree how to tackle the findings of a stress risk assessment.

The guidance pack includes an introduction on how to use it, learning points, prompt cards, and an action plan to record and monitor what needs to be done.

The new guidance will cover each of the following stressor areas. These are:

- Demands

- Control

- Support

- Role

- Relationships

- Change

Launching the guidance, Bill Callaghan, Chair of the Health and Safety Commission (HSC) which oversees the work of the HSE said, 'The Health and Safety Commission wants workplace health and safety to be a cornerstone of a civilised society and is committed to ensuring that HSE's work remains relevant to the changing world and changing economy.'

' "Real solutions, real people" provides a tool to help managers and staff develop solutions to tackle work-related stress that are specifically relevant to their organisation. It then encourages them to tailor their energy to the particular needs identified by risk assessment. The launch of this guidance today, and the innovative stress management standards pilot, already well under way, are fine examples of how the HSE is seeking to help organisations reduce the incidence of occupational ill health.'

The 'Real solutions, real people' conference forms part of the HSC's Priority Programme on Stress. A key element of that programme is the development of clear, agreed standards of good management practice to prevent work-related stress. These standards are currently being piloted by 25 organisations, most of which were at the conference. The pilot process is now being evaluated, and the management standards will be revised and developed for further public consultation by HSE in Spring 2004. Six of the case studies from Real solutions, real people (one for each of the six stressor areas) is available on HSE's website at http://www.hse.gov.uk/stress.

Suggested exercise

Using the material in this case study (and perhaps the HSE website) consider whether you think it is appropriate to specify acceptable standards for stress levels in an organisation, and whether the HSE is going about it in the right way. For example, is it taking all major sources of stress into consideration and is it seeking to assess them in the right way, do you think?

Test your learning

Short-answer questions

1 What are Hans Selye's three stages of stress?

2 How does the Yerkes–Dodson law apply to workplace stress?

3 Which workplace stressor, in your view, is the most damaging to the individual employee? Why?

4 Define the following: role ambiguity, role conflict and Type A behaviour.

5 How can bosses be managed?

6 What is an EAP?

7 What are the range of organisation-directed strategies to reduce stress?

8 What is a stress audit?

9 Define the main features of a 'healthy organisation'.

Suggested assignments

1 What are the major sources of stress at work? Why are they stressful?

2 Is the concept of stress a useful one?

3 What is the impact of job loss on the individual, and why?

4 Why might stress management programmes be less effective than organisation-orientated interventions?

Relevant websites

Many websites with material on stress are also concerned with health and safety at work more generally. For example, Croner's Health And Safety Centre, which can be found at http://www.healthandsafety-centre.net/cgi-bin/croner/jsp/Croner HomeHealthAndSafety.do, covers a range of issues. However, if you type 'stress' into the site search facility, you will be directed to material that relates closely to the content of this chapter, especially recent news items.

Practical concern with how to manage (and/or reduce) stress at work is always high, and seems to be growing. One manifestation of that is the International Association for Stress Management, which can be found at http://www.1do3.com/uk/page.php?x=19,935,4606. This site offers links to ideas and resources for managing stress, and although it is UK-based, there are also links to equivalent sites in some other countries.

A concise account from a manager's perspective of how stress is construed and what might be its causes and consequences can be found at http://www.businesshr.net/docs/guides/stress.html. You might like to compare the content of that analysis with the contents of this chapter.

For further self-test material and relevant, annotated weblinks please visit the website at http://www.booksites.net/arnold_workpsych.

Suggested further reading

Full details of these books are given in the reference list at the end of the book.

1   *Organizational Stress: A review and critique of theory, research and application* by Cary Cooper, Phil Dewe and Mike O'Driscoll, published by Sage Publications in 2001, is a comprehensive review of theory and research in the field of organisational and occupational stress.

2   *Strategic Stress Management* by Val Sutherland and Cary Cooper, published by Macmillan Books in 2000, highlights what *organisations* should do to manage the structural aspects of workplace stress.

3   *Conquer Your Stress* by Cary Cooper and Stephen Palmer, published by CIPD Press in 2000, explores how *individuals* can and should cope with stress.

4   *Employee Assistance Programmes and Workplace Counselling* by John Berridge, Cary Cooper and Carolyn Highley-Marchington, published by John Wiley in 1997, is a comprehensive review of all research on EAPs, as well as a guide for human resource professionals about how to choose one, how to evaluate them and the costs/benefits of EAPs for organisations.

CHAPTER 12

Decisions, groups and teams at work

LEARNING OUTCOMES

After studying this chapter, you should be able to:

1 describe information-processing biases that can occur when a person is making a decision involving risk or uncertainty;

2 specify how the ways in which information is presented may exacerbate those biases;

3 explain how individuals or groups can become over-committed to a poor decision, and suggest how this can be prevented;

4 explain how and when 'brainstorming' can succeed in producing many new ideas;

5 outline the main features of the 'groupthink' model of group decision-making, and suggest two ways in which it may not be entirely accurate;

6 define group polarisation and explain why it occurs;

7 explain why relations between groups at work depend partly on individuals' sense of personal identity;

8 define stereotypes and specify two reasons why they can affect relations between groups at work;

9 describe some evidence suggesting the incidence of teamwork in Europe is lower than some people assume;

10 explain the stages of development some teams go through;

11 describe Belbin's nine team roles;

12 explain the ways in which the diversity of team members can affect team functioning;

13 define negotiation and distinguish between different types of negotiator behaviour;

14 define the main features of 'interest-based negotiation'.

Opening Case Study | Playing the Game

Team-building used to be about going to the pub on a Friday evening and helping your colleagues into a taxi when they'd had one drink too many. Gone are those days. Even team-building through paintballing is old news. These days nothing less than an African safari, hot air ballooning or sailing on the high seas will do, it seems.

The team is now the norm at work. Office life is no longer the atomised existence it once was. 'Teams have become a way of organising work,' says Rob Briner, organisational psychologist at Birkbeck College, London.

'The problem is that these teams are normally very artificial,' Briner says. 'One of the defining characteristics of a team is that you have to be interdependent, but that's rarely true of workplace teams. Part of the reason for recent interest in team-building is that these teams often aren't actually working properly.'

As team-building has become the buzz word of HR departments, training providers have proliferated and their offerings diversified. Prices vary from £50 per person for a half-day activity up to several thousand pounds for week-long team-building activities overseas.

Team activities centre on forcing people into new situations. 'Getting people out of the mould and out of the existing hierarchy that they're used to is crucial,' says Alan Kiff, managing director of Campfire Adventures, which runs safaris in South Africa and dog-sledding in Finland. During week-long trips, activities include guiding a blindfold driver through an obstacle course using whistles, and doing a treasure hunt around a safari park.

Get to know your fellow workers in challenging and unfamiliar situations. Then you'll all work together better – that's the theory. But experts dispute this assumption. 'There is no strong evidence that team cohesion aids team effective-ness,' says Michael West, professor of organisational psychology and director of research at Aston University. 'People assume they work more effectively if they like the people they're with, but may simply conspire to do less work, spend longer ensuring they don't fall out, or even decide they don't like each other.'

But the blame may lie with client companies and not the training providers, says Neil Russell, managing director of Eos Yacht Charters. 'Some companies really want to build a team in a genuine sense, but these are few and far between.' Many man-agers remain cynical about skills training and development, he says. 'People are much more into developing technical knowledge rather than teamworking skills.'

Team-building events are big business these days. And while doubts remain about the exact nature of their benefits, training providers and clients insist that they bond staff, build company loyalty and help break down barriers.

Source: Adapted from an article in People Management, *30 May 2002*

Introduction

The opening case study shows that teams and groups are a fashionable topic in the workplace, and allegedly a fashionable way of organising workers. However, the case study also shows that there is some scepticaism about whether teams are necessarily a good way of organising work, and about whether teambuilding in exotic ways succeeds in enhancing team effectiveness.

Some teams are primarily concerned with making decisions. Decisions concern choices between more than one possible course of action. For many people, work involves frequent decisions. Some are perhaps made almost automatically – so much so, that some writers (e.g. Hunt, 1989) have argued that the whole notion of deliberate, conscious choice has been taken too seriously by work psychologists. Others disagree, contending that understanding how decisions (conscious or otherwise) are made in the workplace, and how they might be improved, is crucial to enhancing the performance of organisations and even national economies. This chapter therefore examines decision-making by individuals and groups in the workplace from a psychological perspective. The strengths, weaknesses and biases of decision-making processes are discussed, and their implications in the workplace identified.

The prevalence and impact of teamworking is examined, and some of the important psychological processes that occur in teams are identified. These include creativity and innovation, and the role of diversity in team membership. The functioning of teams of top managers in strategic decision-making in organisations has attracted a lot of attention from researchers, and that is reflected in this chapter. Teams can be argued to be a special case of groups. How we perceive and behave towards members of our own group and members of other groups has been of great interest to social psychologists, and some of the key themes of that work are included in this chapter. We also discuss decisions made in conditions of potential conflict: that is, negotiations. What happens in negotiations, and can the outcomes of a negotiation be predicted? Negotiations in the workplace often involve trade union representatives, and this chapter ends with a brief consideration of some issues at the interface of work psychology and employee relations.

Decision-making by individuals

Information processing in decision making

Much of psychologists' work on individual decision-making has focused on how we deviate from strictly 'rational' processes. 'Rationality' is often defined as choosing the option that has the *highest expected value* among those potentially open to us. For example, suppose you can choose between a 40 per cent chance of winning €2000 (with a 60 per cent chance of winning nothing) and the certainty of winning €600. The expected value of the first option is €800 (40 per cent ×

€2000), and that of the second is €600 (100 per cent × €600). The 'rational' decision would therefore be the 40 per cent chance of winning €2000. Much research on decision-making has used problems of this general kind.

It is true, of course, that the first option is preferable, *other things being equal*. But suppose you had no money at all, and your bank manager had written telling you that your debts would be called in, thus causing your business to fail, unless you paid at least €500 into your account immediately. In such circumstances, the 'rational' decision could be argued to be the less attractive. This illustrates the general point that it can make more sense to consider total assets than gains or losses. It also brings to mind the adage 'don't bet if you can't afford to lose'. More broadly, in different circumstances people may have different motives and goals for a decision (Tetlock, 1992). Hence a manager may make an investment decision that conforms to the above definition of 'rational', but the next day decide not to make some staff redundant because of the organisation's avowed policy of caring for its people. Thus, it is important to recognise that the attractiveness, or expected utility, of various possible outcomes of decisions varies between people and between situations: that is, it is *subjective*. Furthermore, the true probabilities of different decision outcomes are often unknown, and therefore subject to individual perception. Using the notion of subjective expected utility (SEU), psychological research has uncovered some interesting phenomena, some of which will be described shortly. Much of this research was conducted (often with students in laboratories) by Kahneman, Tversky and colleagues (Kahneman and Tversky, 1979, 1981, 1984; Tversky and Kahneman, 1981, 1986).

Key Learning Point

What is a rational decision from a strictly logical viewpoint may not be the most appropriate one for a particular person given his or her values and/or circumstances.

There are many systematic strategies for decision-making apart from a thorough search for the maximum gain. For example, one can evaluate options on a very limited range of important criteria. Ignoring less crucial criteria may not have important costs, but it is of course possible that the cumulative effect of those criteria would be significant. Another possible strategy is to search for an option that one considers good enough, and stop the search as soon as one is found. This approach has been termed *satisficing* and can be contrasted with *maximising*, where a thorough search is conducted for the best possible solution. Clearly, strategies such as satisficing cut corners. But they may be justified if a person does not have the time and/or ability to use more thorough ones, or if the decision is not particularly important.

Frisch and Clemen (1994) have argued that SEU is not an entirely redundant concept. Once people know what the decision is that they are trying to make, it is logical to try to maximise SEU. But they also argue that the earlier stages of decision-making are of great importance. These include generating options, deciding which consequences to consider and identifying the relevant risks. So, in line with many other writers, they argue that more attention must be paid to the *process* of decision-making. In order to understand decision-making well, and to make better decisions, we need to take account of the following:

- *Consequentialism*: making decisions on the basis of expected personal consequences rather than habit or tradition.

- *Thorough structuring*: more than one option must be considered, and the likely consequences thought through carefully.

- *Compensation*: most decisions involve trade-offs of one benefit against another, and this should be recognised.

Despite the limitations of the notion of expected utility (subjective or otherwise), some interesting phenomena in decision-making have been uncovered by research on it.

Information processing in decision-making

Certainty, uncertainty and risk

We seem to give huge weight in our decisions to the difference between, for example, a 95 per cent chance of a particular outcome, and a 100 per cent chance of it, or that between a 5 per cent chance and 0 per cent. In other words, when something is 95 per cent certain, we are very aware of the 5 per cent chance that it will not happen. And when there is only a 5 per cent chance of something happening, we are very conscious that 'there's a chance'. In both examples, this reflects the difference between absolute certainty and near certainty. We give less weight to a difference of similar magnitude between intermediate probabilities (e.g. 60 per cent versus 55 per cent). As Kahneman and Tversky (1984) pointed out, this means that we tend to be less attracted than we should be to a highly likely (but not certain) pleasant outcome. Similarly, we are likely to be more attracted than we should be to a highly unlikely but pleasant outcome. Hence we tend to be less inclined to take a small risk for a gain, and more inclined to bet on a long shot, than is indicated by objective probability. The popularity of lotteries in many countries is a good example of this.

Monetary gambles are relatively simple contexts for the study of risk. Many other contexts are less simple, and then the meaning of risk is ambiguous. Mellers *et al.* (1998, pp. 451–2) cite the example of coal mines, where during one 20-year period, fatal accidents per ton of coal mined decreased, while accidents per employee increased. So did coal mines become more or less risky places to work?

Gains versus losses

As Kahneman and Tversky put it, the attractiveness of a possible gain is less than the aversiveness of a loss of the same amount. This leads to risk-averse decisions concerning gains and risk-seeking decisions concerning losses. Thus, Kahneman and Tversky have pointed out that while most people prefer the certainty of winning €800 over an 85 per cent chance of winning €1000, a large majority of people prefer an 85 per cent chance of *losing* €1000 (with a 15 per cent chance of losing nothing) over a certain loss of €800. Such risk-seeking over losses has also been found in (laboratory) studies where non-monetary outcomes such as hours of pain or loss of human lives are at stake. This has some interesting implications. For example, an unpopular government facing an election may be more inclined to risk a new policy initiative that could lose votes than a popular government in the same position. Firms in financial difficulties may take more risks (because they are trying to eliminate losses) than firms doing well (which are dealing with gains) (Fiegenbaum and Thomas, 1988).

As one might expect, there appear to be some cultural differences in how gains and losses are evaluated. Bontempo *et al.* (1997) asked students in four countries to rate the riskiness of monetary gambles. Students in the United States and Netherlands were inclined to place emphasis on the *probability* of incurring a loss, while students in Hong Kong and Taiwan were more concerned about the *magnitude* of a potential loss.

Framing

The same information can be presented in different ways. This can affect decisions made on the basis of that information. Thus, for example, organisers of conferences often advertise a special low fee for people who register early rather than expressing it as a surcharge for people who register late. The organisers may privately think in terms of the latter, but use the label 'discount' rather than 'surcharge' in order to keep customer goodwill, and hopefully increase the number of attenders. There are also links here with the previous subsection, because some choices can be framed in terms of either gains or losses. An often-used scenario in laboratory experiments concerns the choice of medical programmes to combat a killer disease. The potential benefits of these programmes are presented either in terms of the number of people who will be saved (equivalent to gains), or the number who will die (equivalent to losses). According to Kahneman and Tversky (1981) when the options are presented in terms of number of deaths, people tend to prefer a programme that might succeed completely or fail completely (i.e. a risk) over one with a guaranteed moderate success level. The reverse is true when the same figures are presented in terms of number of lives saved. However, Fagley and Miller (1987) found no such effect, and questioned its generality. Although their hypothetical scenario was not exactly like that of Kahneman and Tversky, the results of Fagley and Miller do indeed cast doubt on this particular aspect of framing.

Key Learning Point

The way situations requiring decisions are described, and whether they involve gains or losses, can significantly influence the decision that is made.

Emotion, action and inaction

The role of emotion in decision-making has recently received increasing research attention. This reflects the move away from instrumental rationality we noted earlier. There is some evidence that people who are experiencing positive emotion are able to be more creative than those who are not, and more able to process information (Isen, 1993). On the other hand, it also seems that positive emotions can lead people to be unrealistically optimistic about future events and outcomes (Nygren *et al.*, 1996). However, as Mellers *et al.* (1998, p. 454) point out, the well-known dimensions for distinguishing between emotions (pleasant–unpleasant and high arousal–low arousal) are probably too broad to capture the impact of different emotions on decision-making processes.

People also seem to consider their likely future emotions when making decisions. One emotion that has been studied a lot is regret. Kahnenan (1995) argues that people regret actions (what they have done) more than inactions (what they failed to do, or decided not to do), probably because actions are more salient in our memory and their consequences are more tangible. Consistent with this, Baron (1994) found that worries about future regrets tended to make people prefer inaction to action. This might suggest that, for example, people may tend to stay in jobs or occupations they do not like very much if the alternative is a step into the unknown.

Escalation of commitment

Some approaches to commitment (*see* Kiesler, 1971; *see also* Chapter 7) emphasise that if a decision is made freely and explicitly, the person making it feels a need to justify it to self and others. The person is *committed* to it, and seeks retrospectively to find reasons why he or she 'did the right thing'. There is some evidence for this concerning choice of organisation to work in (e.g. Mabey, 1986). It also seems to happen in some managerial decisions (Staw, 1981; McCarthy *et al.*, 1993) and other related areas such as wastefulness (Arkes, 1996). In laboratory simulations, people who are told that their own earlier financial investment decisions have so far been unsuccessful tend to allocate more additional funds to that investment than if the earlier decisions were made by another member of their (imaginary) organisation. They feel compelled to prove that ultimately their own wisdom will be demonstrated, but observers are more likely to think they are 'pouring good money after bad'. This 'escalation of commitment' phenomenon is now well established. The next question is therefore how it can be reduced or eliminated. In a laboratory study of a simulated marketing decision, Simonson and Staw (1992) asked decision-makers to specify in advance minimum outcome levels that would have to be achieved for the decision to be considered successful. If their decisions did not achieve that level, they were less likely to invest further in it than decision-makers who did not specify a minimum outcome level. Simonson and Staw also found that further investment in a losing course of action was less likely if decision-makers were told that, owing to the artificiality of the task, their performance on this task did not reflect their managerial abilities – in other words, some of the threat to decision-makers' dignity was removed. Finally, escalation of commitment was also reduced if decision-makers were told that their performance would be evaluated on the quality of decision-making processes, not the outcomes (which in the real world depend partly on factors outside the decision-maker's control). While the second strategy is rather laboratory-specific, the first and last strategies can and should be used by decision-makers and those who appraise their performance at work.

Heuristics

Heuristics are 'rules of thumb' that people use to simplify information processing and decision making (Eiser, 1986, p. 220). These can be social – for example, 'I will ignore everything person X tells me' – or abstract – such as, 'Never do anything without checking the production figures first'. In their early work, Tversky and Kahneman (1974) identified three particularly common heuristics. The *representativeness* heuristic is analogous to the finding in person perception that we do not use base-rate information. We judge someone or something purely according to how representative it appears of a particular category, and we ignore the naturally occurring probability of belonging to that category in the first place. So if we meet a young person wearing a tracksuit and looking fit, we might be inclined to believe he or she is a professional athlete, even though statistically the probability of any individual (even a young, fit one) being a professional is low. We are swayed by the person's appearance. The *anchoring* bias refers to our failure to change our views as much as we should in the light of new information. We seem 'anchored' by our starting point. This too finds expression in person perception, in the same sense that first impressions can be hard to dislodge. Finally, the *availability* heuristic concerns our tendency to consider an event more probable if it can easily be imagined than if it cannot. Hence an employee relations manager contemplating policy changes might overestimate the risk of a strike (vivid event), and underestimate the risk of a persistently resentful and not particularly co-operative workforce (less vivid).

Heuristics, or rules, can be especially useful when the impact of a course of action being considered only becomes clear in the long term and/or with repetition – for example, being slightly abrupt with a work colleague. In such situations, evaluating the expected costs and benefits of a course of action is time-consuming and in any case ignores the long-term impact of repeating it. It might be better to follow a rule something like 'I will only be abrupt if I am angry with my colleague and am willing to tell him/her about my anger and the reason for it'. Rules like this tend to take us beyond calculations of gain and loss to a broader consideration of what kind of person we are and what behaviours and decisions are moral (Fiske and Tetlock, 1997).

Key Learning Point

Some of the ways in which we habitually think about decisions are bad in the sense that they distort the real situation.

Exercise 12.1	An upmarket move?

Three years ago, Harry Milento gave up a highly-paid job in insurance in order to opt for a 'quieter life' running his own guest house in a scenic coastal location. Redecoration and improvements to the large old house he purchased proved more expensive and time consuming than he had expected. Business was not good: a difficult economic climate had adversely affected the holiday trade, and a new guest house such as Harry's inevitably had trouble getting established. The result was that he was certain to make a loss for the third successive year, albeit one which would not exhaust his financial reserves. In spite of the difficulties, Harry felt fairly happy with his life and past decisions, and in some ways enjoyed the unexpectedly challenging nature of his new lifestyle. An established traditional hotel nearby had recently gone upmarket with some success, and Harry was considering the same strategy. After all, he could relate well to successful and wealthy people, having once been one himself. The area had historically offered middle-to-low budget family holidays rather than more luxurious ones, but maybe things were changing, Harry thought. But, for him, a move upmarket would need extensive further alterations to his premises, and these would swallow up his remaining reserves.

Use psychological findings about decision-making to suggest what Harry Milento is likely to do. Is this what he should do?

Group decision-making

Groups versus individuals

Although many people are very cynical about the value of meetings and committees, the fact is that their work tends to involve a lot of them. In work organisations most major decisions and many lesser ones are made by groups of people, not individuals. Hence groups have attracted a lot of interest, an increasing proportion of which is from organisational psychologists (Guzzo and Dickson, 1996). If handled in the right way, a decision made by a group can evoke greater commitment than one made by an individual because more people feel a sense of involvement in it. On the other hand, group decisions usually consume more time (and more money) than individual ones, so they need to justify the extra costs. One often-asked question over many years is whether individual or group decisions are superior (Davis, 1992). At one extreme is the 'many heads are better than one' school of thought, which holds that, in groups, people can correct each other's mistakes and build on each other's ideas. On the other hand there is the 'too many cooks spoil the broth' brigade, which contends that problems of communication, rivalry and so on between group members more than cancel out any potential advantage of increased total available brain power. In fact it is not possible to generalise about whether individuals or groups are universally better. It depends on the abilities and training of the individuals and groups, and also on the kind of task being tackled (Hill, 1982).

McGrath (1984) identified eight different types of task that groups can face: four of these directly concern decision-making. These are:

- generating plans;

- generating ideas;

- solving problems with correct answers;

- deciding issues with no identifiably correct answer at the time the decision is made.

The second and third of these provide the best opportunities for comparing group and individual performance. *Brainstorming*, for example, is a technique for generating ideas with which many readers will already be familiar. It was originally advocated by Osborn (1957), who argued that if a group of people agree that (i) the more ideas they think of the better, and (ii) members will be encouraged to produce even bizarre ideas, and not be ridiculed for them, then individuals can think up twice as many ideas in a group as they could on their own. In fact, some research has indicated that lone individuals who are encouraged to think of as many ideas as possible generate more ideas per individual than groups do (e.g. Lamm and Trommsdorf, 1973). A number of possible explanations have been suggested for this phenomenon. These include *evaluation apprehension*, where a person feels afraid of what others will think, despite the brainstorming instructions, and *free-riding*, where group members feel that other group members will do the work for them. Diehl and Stroebe (1987) devised experiments to test different explanations, and came out in favour of a third explanation: *production blocking*. Simply, only one person at a time in a group can talk about their ideas, and in the meantime other members may forget or suppress theirs. Nevertheless, there is also clear evidence that exposure to the ideas of other people enhances creativity, especially if those people are diverse (Paulus, 2000), so the key seems to be to achieve that exposure without incurring production blocking or other negative group effects. Advances in information and communication technology can help here, by transmitting information between group members in a clear and impersonal way (e.g. Valacich *et al.*, 1994). It seems that groups linked by computer produce more ideas than those meeting face to face, and also have greater equality of participation (Hollingshead and McGrath, 1995), although they also tend to make more extreme decisions and have some hostile communications. There is more about virtual teams in Chapter 1.

Key Learning Point

The production of new ideas tends to be greater when individuals brainstorm alone with information about other people's ideas, rather than in the physical presence of others.

Psychologists have conducted a number of experiments comparing individual and group performance on problems with correct answers. For example Vollrath *et al.* (1989) found that groups recognised and recalled information better than individuals. However, McGrath (1984) pointed out that the extent to which the correct answer can be shown to be correct varies. On one hand there are 'Eureka' tasks – when the correct answer is mentioned, everyone suddenly sees that it must be right. There are also problems where the answer can be proved correct with logic, even though its correctness is not necessarily obvious at first sight. Then there are problems where the correct (or best) answer can only be defined by experts, whose wisdom may be challenged by a layperson.

An example of the second kind of problem, often used in research, is the so-called 'horse-trading task'. A person buys a horse for €60 and sells it for €70. Then he or she buys it back for €80 and again sells it for €90. How much money does the person make in the horse-trading business? Many people say €10, but the answer is €20 – though strictly this assumes that the person does not have to borrow the extra €10 to buy back the horse, and it ignores the opportunity cost of using the €10 in that way rather than another.

Some early research with problems of this kind (e.g. Maier and Solem, 1952) produced several important findings. First, lower-status group members had less influence on the group decision than higher-status ones, even when they (the lower-status people) were correct. Second, even where at least one person in the group knew the correct answer, the group decision was by no means always correct. Third, group discussion made people more confident that their consensus decision was correct, but unfortunately the discussion did not in fact make a correct decision more likely! For problems like the horse-trading one, it typically needs two correct people, not one, to convince the rest of the group. Put another way, on average *the group is as good as its second-best member*. This could be taken to mean that, for solving problems with correct answers, groups are on average better than individuals, but inferior to the best individuals.

Key Learning Point

For problems with demonstrably correct answers, groups are on average as good as their second-best member. However, groups can do better or worse than this average depending on their membership and process.

However, conclusions of this kind cannot easily be generalised. Many decisions in organisations do not have a provable correct answer, or even an answer that experts can agree on. Also, even if groups typically do badly, perhaps they can be improved. This latter issue has been the subject of much popular and academic debate, and we now turn to it.

Group deficiencies and overcoming them

Some social scientists have concentrated on identifying the context within which groups can perform well (e.g. Larson and LaFasto, 1989). They point out necessities such as having group members who are knowledgeable about the problem faced, having a clearly defined and inspiring goal (*see* Locke's goal-setting theory in Chapter 9), having group members who are committed to solving the problem optimally, and support and recognition from important people outside the group. Other work has attempted to identify the roles that group members should adopt in order to function effectively together. Perhaps the most influential has been Belbin (1981, 1993), who identified the roles required in a team. We return to his work later in this chapter. Other observers of groups have concentrated more on procedural factors (e.g. Rees and Porter, 2001, Chapter 16). Prominent here are the practices of the chairperson in facilitating discussion and summing it up, ensuring that everyone has their say and that only one person speaks at a time, and making sure that votes (if taken) are conducted only when all points of view have been aired, and with clearly defined options, so that group members know what they are voting for and against.

Social psychologists have noted many features of the group decision-making process that can impair decision quality. Many of these underlie the practical suggestions noted in the previous paragraph. Hoffman and Maier (1961) noted a tendency to adopt 'minimally acceptable solutions', especially where the decision task is complex. Instead of seeking the best possible solution, group members often settle on the first suggested solution that everyone considers 'good enough'. In certain circumstances this might be an advantage, but on most occasions it is probably not a good idea. Hackman (1990) pointed out that groups rarely discuss what strategy they should adopt in tackling a decision-making task (i.e. how they should go about it), but that when they do, they tend to perform better. In our experience, simply telling groups to discuss their strategy before they tackle the problem itself is usually not enough – strategy discussion has to be treated as a separate task if it is to be taken seriously.

Motivational losses in groups can also be a problem. Experimental research has repeatedly shown that as the number of people increases, the effort and/or performance of each one often decreases – the so-called *social loafing* effect (e.g. Latane *et al.*, 1979). On the other hand, this motivational loss can be avoided if individuals in the group feel that their contribution can be identified, *and* that their contribution makes a significant difference to the group's performance (Williams *et al.*, 1981; Kerr and Bruun, 1983). Hence a group leader would be well advised to ensure that each group member can see the connection between individual efforts and group performance both for themselves and other group members.

Interestingly, there is some evidence that social loafing does not occur in collectivist societies. Earley (1989) found that while American management trainees exhibited this effect in a laboratory-based management task, trainees from the People's Republic of China did not. In collective societies, one's sense of shared responsibility with others (in contrast with individualistic Western cultures) is perhaps the source of this difference. Once again, this is a reminder of the culture-specific nature of some phenomena in applied psychology. More than that, Erez and Somech (1996) found that subcultural differences in individualism–collectivism even within one country (Israel) made a difference to the social loafing effect. But even then, groups in an individualistic subculture showed social loafing only when they lacked specific goals. As Erez and Somech pointed out, most groups in the workplace have members who know each other, who communicate, have team goals that matter to them, and whose individual performance can be identified. So social loafing may be the exception, not the rule, in the real world, even in individualistic cultures.

Key Learning Point

Group members tend to reduce their efforts as group size increases, at least in individualistic cultures. This problem can, however, be overcome.

It seems that groups may be even more likely than individuals to escalate their commitment to a decision even if it does not seem to be working out well (Whyte, 1993). This can occur even if the majority of group members start off with the opinion that they will not invest any further resources in the decision. The essentially risky decision of the group may be even more marked if it is framed in terms of avoiding losses rather than achieving gains. As noted earlier in this chapter, most people are more inclined to accept the risk of a big loss in the hope of avoiding a moderate loss than they are to risk losing a moderate profit in pursuit of a big profit.

Groupthink

Janis (1972, 1982a,b) arrived at some disturbing conclusions about how some real life policy-making groups can make extremely poor decisions that have serious repercussions around the world. He analysed major foreign policy errors of various governments at various times in history. One of these was the Bay of Pigs fiasco in the early 1960s. Fidel Castro had recently taken power in Cuba, and the new US administration under President John F. Kennedy launched an 'invasion' of Cuba by 1400 Cuban exiles, who landed at the Bay of Pigs. Within two days they were surrounded by 20 000 Cuban troops, and those not killed were ransomed back to the United States at a cost of $53 million in aid. Janis argued that this outcome was not just bad luck for the United States. It could and should have been anticipated. He suggested that in this and other fiascos, various group processes could be seen, which collectively he called *groupthink*.

According to Janis, groupthink occurs when group members' motivation for unanimity and agreement over-rides their motivation to evaluate carefully the risks and benefits of alternative decisions. This usually occurs in 'cohesive' groups – i.e. those where group members are friendly with each other, and respect each other's opinions. In some such groups disagreement is construed (usually unconsciously) as a withdrawal of friendship and respect. When this is combined with a group leader known (or believed) to have a position on the issues under discussion, an absence of clear group procedures, a difficult set of circumstances, and certain other factors, the group members tend to seek agreement. This leads to the symptoms of groupthink shown in Fig. 12.1. The symptoms can be summarised as follows:

■ *Overestimation of the group's power and morality*: after all, group members have positive opinions of each other.

■ *Closed-mindedness*: including efforts to downplay warnings and stereotype other groups as inferior.

■ *Pressures towards uniformity*: including suppression of private doubts, leading to the illusion of unanimity and 'mindguards' to shield group members (especially the leader) from uncomfortable information.

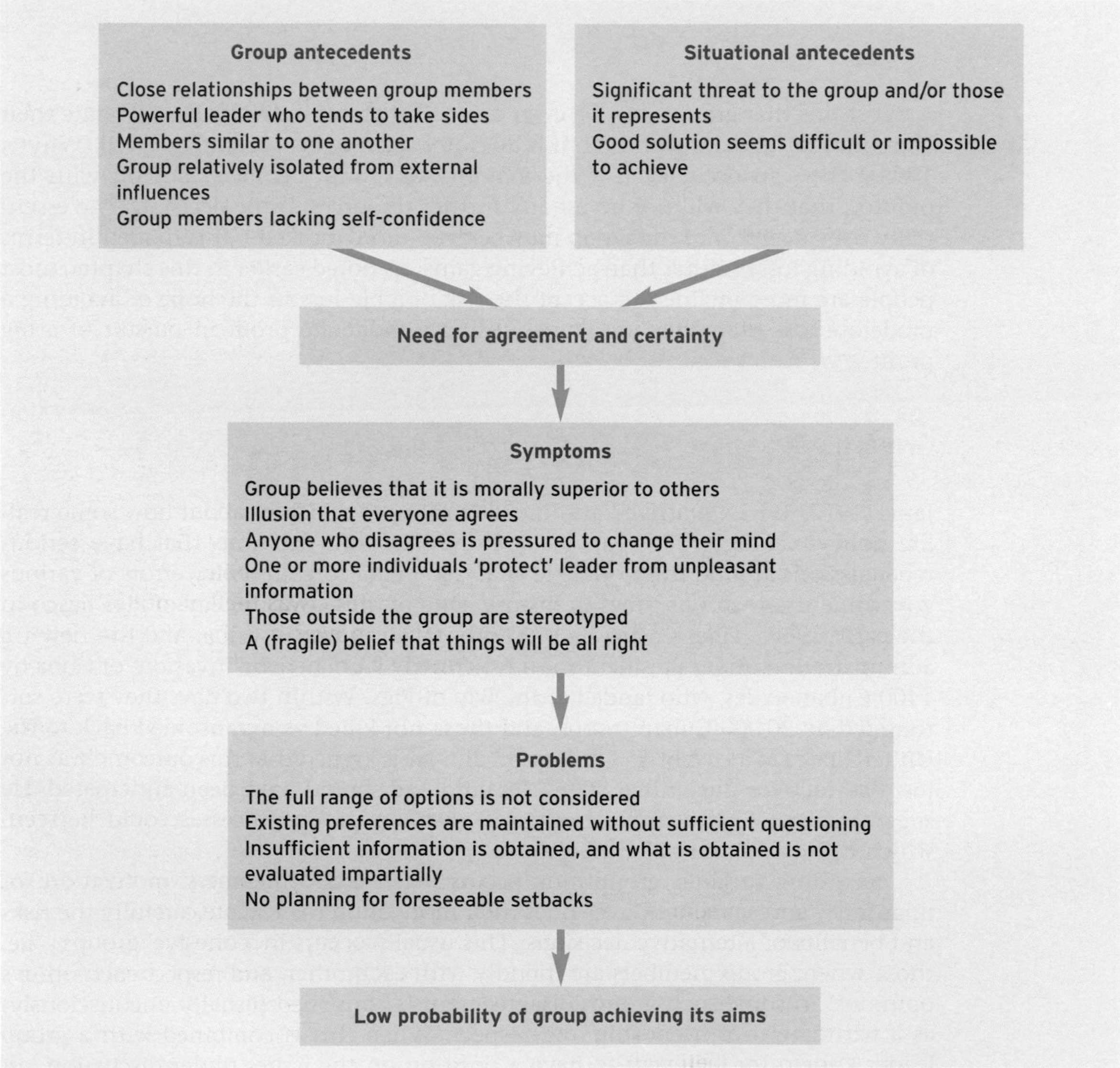

Group antecedents

Close relationships between group members
Powerful leader who tends to take sides
Members similar to one another
Group relatively isolated from external influences
Group members lacking self-confidence

Situational antecedents

Significant threat to the group and/or those it represents
Good solution seems difficult or impossible to achieve

Need for agreement and certainty

Symptoms

Group believes that it is morally superior to others
Illusion that everyone agrees
Anyone who disagrees is pressured to change their mind
One or more individuals 'protect' leader from unpleasant information
Those outside the group are stereotyped
A (fragile) belief that things will be all right

Problems

The full range of options is not considered
Existing preferences are maintained without sufficient questioning
Insufficient information is obtained, and what is obtained is not evaluated impartially
No planning for foreseeable setbacks

Low probability of group achieving its aims

Figure 12.1   The Janis groupthink model

Key Learning Point

Groupthink is a set of group malfunctions that occurs when group members are more concerned (although they may not realise it) to achieve unanimity and agreement than to find the best available solution to a problem or situation.

Janis (1982b) has argued that certain measures can be taken to avoid groupthink. These include:

- impartial leadership (so that group members are not tempted simply to 'follow the leader');

- each person in the group should be told to give high priority to airing doubts and objections;

- experts should be in attendance to raise doubts;

- 'second chance' meetings should be held where members express their doubts about a previously made but not yet implemented decision.

One might add the necessity of fostering a group norm that disagreeing with another group member does *not* signal disrespect or unfriendliness towards him or her.

Key Learning Point

It is possible for groups to use formal procedures to combat groupthink, even though these may be tiresome and time consuming.

Janis's work has not gone unchallenged (e.g. Aldag and Fuller, 1993). It has been argued that the groupthink syndrome is really simply a collection of phenomena that do not occur together as neatly as Janis claims, and that anyway have already been investigated by other social scientists. Also, Janis obtained much of his information from published retrospective accounts, which (some argue) may be much too inaccurate and/or incomplete. On the other hand, most research investigating groupthink has been carried out in laboratories, where groups do not have the history implied by some of the antecedents listed in Fig. 12.1. Whyte (1989) argued that so-called groupthink is not itself a unitary phenomenon. Instead, it is a product of groups seeking risks when they perceive that losses are at stake (*see* 'Information processing in decision-making', above), and of group polarisation (*see below*).

Aldag and Fuller (1993) have pointed out that some research has found that group cohesiveness actually helps open discussion of ideas, rather than inhibiting it as Janis has argued. In fact, Mullen and Copper (1994), in a review of 66 tests of the relationship between group cohesiveness and group performance, found that cohesiveness was on average a significant (though not large) aid to performance, especially when groups were small. They also found that successful group performance tended to foster cohesiveness more than cohesiveness fostered performance. This is not surprising. If we think of cohesiveness as a combination of interpersonal attraction, commitment to the task and group pride, we would expect all of these to increase when the group succeeds in its tasks.

Park (2000) presents a review of 28 tests of the groupthink model that was reported between 1974 and 1998. Eleven of these tests were experiments using students, while most of the others were case studies of real-life events. Nine of the experiments produced partial support for the groupthink model, two produced no support and none was fully or almost fully supportive. The case studies did better: seven supported all or nearly all of the model, three offered partial support and three offered little or no support. The greater support from case studies might be because the experiments were artificial situations or alternatively because case studies are inherently more ambiguous and open to interpretation in line with the groupthink theory. Park (2000) conducted another experiment, testing all the relationships between variables proposed by the groupthink model with 64 groups of four students. Park found partial support for the groupthink model. Some of Park's findings were:

- high group cohesiveness was associated with more symptoms of groupthink than low group cohesiveness;

- groups with members who had high self-esteem showed more symptoms of groupthink than where members had low self-esteem;

- group members' feelings of invulnerability and morality were associated with fewer symptoms of defective decision-making;

- incomplete survey of alternative solutions was associated with poor decision quality.

You might find it helpful to refer back to Fig. 12.1 and think about which of these findings are as Janis predicted, and which are not.

Some other research not in the groupthink tradition has investigated some phenomena similar to those identified by Janis. For example, Schulz-Hardt *et al.* (2002) found that groups of managers who had similar points of view even before they met tended to seek yet more information that supported their existing view. Genuine disagreement in initial points of view led to a much more balanced information search. The presence of people instructed to be a 'devil's advocate' (i.e. to argue the opposite view of the group's preference whatever their own private opinion) also had some limited effect in reducing a group preference for information agreeing with their initial opinions. Taken as a whole, these findings support Janis's ideas that groups where the members agree are prone to restricting their information search and that appointing a devil's advocate may go some way towards correcting that.

All of the criticisms of groupthink have some force. Nevertheless, Janis has provided rich case studies that graphically illustrate many potential problems in group decision-making, and that should dispel any comforting belief we might cling to that really important decisions are always made rationally.

Exercise 12.2   Your experiences of group decision-making

Try to recall a time when you participated in a group that had to make a decision (for example, choose between alternative courses of action). Bring to mind as much as you can about what happened, then consider the following questions. If you can do so with someone else who was there, so much the better.

1   How cohesive was the group, and what consequences do you think that had for (i) the way the group went about its task and (ii) how you felt about participating?

2   Do you think the group members were (i) excited about the possibility of accomplishing something really worthwhile or (ii) fearful about making a mistake? Either way, how did that affect the discussion and the decision?

3   If there was a leader of the group, to what extent was he or she admired and trusted by the other members? What was the impact of this on how the group conducted itself?

4   To what extent were alternative options carefully considered? Think about why.

5   Finally, was the eventual decision actually implemented? Why (or why not)? Did the decision work out well, and if not, could that have been foreseen?

6   Consider how well (or not) your observations match the theory and research discussed in this chapter so far.

Key Learning Point

The groupthink model appears not to be entirely accurate, but it includes many ideas that have had a big impact on research on groups and teams.

Group polarisation

One often-voiced criticism of groups is that they arrive at compromise decisions. But in fact this is often not so. Instead, it seems that groups tend to make more extreme decisions than the initial preferences of group members (Bettenhausen, 1991). This has most often been demonstrated with respect to risk. If the initial tendency of the majority of group members is to adopt a moderately risky decision, the eventual group decision is usually more risky than that. Conversely, somewhat cautious initial preferences of group members translate to even more cautious eventual group decisions.

Psychologists have reduced no fewer than 11 possible explanations of group polarisation down to just 2, using systematic research (Isenberg, 1986). The *social comparison* explanation is that we like to present ourselves in a socially desirable way, so we try to be like other group members, only more so. The *persuasive argumentation* explanation is that information consistent with the views held by the majority will dominate discussion, and (so long as that information is correct and novel) have persuasive effects. Both explanations are valid, though the latter seems to be stronger. While polarisation is not in itself inherently good or bad, clearly group members need to ensure that they air all relevant information and ideas so that arguments rejecting the initially favoured point of view are heard. They also need to avoid social conformity, which reflects one of Janis's arguments. Chen *et al.* (2002) have shown that using a quantitative decision aid can reduce the impact of overly biased persuasive arguments on group members, albeit only slightly.

Key Learning Point

Contrary to popular opinion, groups often produce more extreme decisions, and fewer compromises, than individuals.

Minority influence

Minorities within groups only rarely convert the majority to their point of view. But how can they maximise their chances? Many people say that they should gain the acceptance of the majority by conforming wherever possible, and then stick out for their own point of view on a carefully chosen crucial issue. Moscovici and colleagues argued otherwise (Moscovici and Mugny, 1983; Moscovici, 1985). They found that, if it is to exert influence, a minority needs to disagree consistently with the majority, including on issues other than the one at stake. Minorities do not exert influence by being liked or being seen as reasonable, but by being perceived as consistent, independent and confident. Consistent with this, Van Hiel and Mervielde (2001) have found that group members believe that being assertive and consistent is an effective strategy for minorities, while being agreeable is better for majorities than for minorities. This has connections with the previous section concerning group polarisation. A minority that demonstrates these characteristics will tend to express many arguments that oppose the majority point of view, thereby limiting the extent of group polarisation.

Much debate has centred on why and how minorities in groups exert influence (e.g. Nemeth, 1986; Smith *et al.*, 1996; McLeod *et al.* 1997). The predominant view is that minorities and majorities exert influence in different ways. Nemeth (1986) suggested that majorities encourage convergent, shallow and narrow thinking, while consistent exposure to minority viewpoints stimulates deeper and wider consideration of alternative perspectives. Nemeth (1986, p. 28) concluded from experimental data that:

> Those exposed to minority viewpoints ... are more original, they use a greater variety of strategies, they detect novel solutions, and importantly, they detect correct solutions. Furthermore, this beneficial effect occurs even when the minority viewpoints are wrong.

This emphasises again that groups need to encourage different points of view, not suppress them.

Key Learning Point

Minority views may be tiresome, but their expression typically leads to better group functioning, even if they are incorrect.

Wood *et al.* (1994) reviewed 143 studies of minority influence, and found that minorities do indeed have some capacity to change the opinions of people who hear their message. This effect is stronger if recipients of the message are not required to publicly acknowledge their change of opinion to the minority. Opinion change is also much greater on issues indirectly related to the message than on those directly related to it. Indeed, although the opinion of the majority usually has more effect than that of the minority, this seems not to be the case on issues only indirectly related to the message. Ng and Van Dyne (2001) have found in an experimental study with students, that group members who (i) value collectivist beliefs (i.e. act according to social norms and stressing interpersonal harmony) and (ii) do *not* value individualist beliefs (i.e. focus on personal goals and perspectives) are less influenced than others by minority views. This tends to impair their decision-making. Ng and Van Dyne also found that when a one-person minority happens to be the leader of the group, he or she has more influence than when the one-person minority is not the leader.

Exercise 12.3   A soft drink product decision

Rudi Lerner was managing director of a medium-size soft drinks company. His father had founded and then managed the business for nearly 30 years before handing over to his son four years ago. Rudi felt he knew much more about the business than his colleagues on the top management team. They agreed about that, and they liked and respected their boss as well as each other. They usually went out of their way to avoid contradicting him. On the rare occasions they did so, they received a friendly but firm reminder from the chairman that he had been in the business much longer than they had. That was true, but the team membership had not changed for five years now, so nobody was exactly ignorant. However, it was hard to argue – after all, the company had been successful relative to its competitors over the years. Rudi attributed this to frequent takeovers of competitors by people from outside the business. He rarely commissioned market research, relying instead on his 'gut feeling' and extensive prior experience. Now a new challenge faced the company: should it go into the low-calorie 'diet' drinks market, and if so, with what products? The demand for diet drinks was recent but might be here to stay.

How likely is it that Rudi and the rest of the management team will make a good decision about entering the 'diet' market? Explain your answer.

Relations between groups at work

So far we have examined what goes on within groups that are attempting to generate ideas and/or solve problems. Another important perspective is what happens *between* groups at work. Most workplaces are composed of a large number of overlapping groups – for example different departments, committees, occupations, locations, project teams or hierarchical levels. Some of these groups have responsibilities for making and/or implementing decisions, while others are defined simply in terms of members having something in common. Work organisations need groups to co-operate and relate well to each other, both for organisational effectiveness and for the well-being of people within them.

It is widely thought that our need for a clear and positive personal identity leads us, on occasions, to define ourselves in terms of our group membership(s), and to evaluate those groups positively (and in particular more positively than other groups). So in effect we use groups we belong to, to give ourselves a positive sense of who we are. These are the fundamental ideas behind social identity theory (Tajfel and Turner, 1979) and self-categorisation theory (Turner, 1999).

A review of the inter-group literature by Hewstone *et al.* (2002) makes the following points:

■ Usually we tend to favour the group(s) we belong to (termed the 'in-group') more than we derogate out-groups, and this often happens without us even realising it.

■ Successful inter-group bias enhances self-esteem, as predicted by social identity theory. Some have also predicted that when people's self-esteem is low or threatened, they will be even keener to evaluate their in-group positively. However, there is much less evidence for this.

■ Groups of high status and numerical superiority tend to show more in-group bias than those of low status and low membership numbers. However, dominant groups may show generosity when the status gap is very wide, and low-status groups show high in-group bias when they have a chance of closing the gap and/or see their low status as unfair.

■ Various methods have been tried to reduce in-group bias, on the assumption that this will improve relations between groups. The methods include teaching people to suppress their biases; inducing them to behave positively towards out-groups so that they infer from their own behaviour that they must have a positive attitude; increasing people's knowledge about out-group members, so that they are seen as individuals more than group members; finding superordinate groups (for example, everyone in the company) which allow people to re-categorise out-group members as in-group members.

■ In some situations, and some cultures, people tend to define themselves in terms of their group memberships, but in others they do so more in terms of their characteristics as an individual (Ellemers *et al.*, 2002). So the nature and extent of in-group bias may change almost minute by minute.

Key Learning Point

Relations between groups at work are affected, often negatively, by group members' wishes to see themselves in a more positive light than members of other groups.

A closely related issue concerns stereotypes. Stereotypes are generalised beliefs about the characteristics, attributes and behaviours of members of certain groups (Hilton and Von Hippel, 1996, p. 240). Groups can be defined on any number of criteria. Obvious possibilities are race, sex, occupation and age, but research suggests that most people do not have a stereotype of all women or all men or all old people. Stereotypes tend to be based on rather more specific groups, such as old men or old white women (Stangor *et al.*, 1992). Some stereotypes held by a person refer to quite specific groups, as in the following examples:

- Trade union officials are mostly militant ideologues.

- Most police are violent authoritarians.

- Managers in this company are honest.

- Accountants are more stimulating than anybody else.

- Production managers usually speak their mind.

Clearly, then, stereotypes vary in their favourability. They also differ in their extremity. The third and fourth above do not allow for any exceptions, but the others do because they refer to 'most' rather than 'all'. Often stereotypes have some validity, in the sense that *on average* members of one group differ from members of another. On average, middle managers are doubtless more intelligent in some respects than building site labourers. But there is equally certainly a large overlap – some building site labourers are more intelligent than some middle managers. In fact, formation of stereotypes may lead to overestimation of the differences between groups (Krueger, 1991).

We may develop stereotypes of groups based on very limited information about them – perhaps confined to what we see on television. Other stereotypes can arise when a generalisation is true of a very few people in one group and practically none in another group. Suppose for a moment that 1 in 500 shop stewards are members of revolutionary left-wing political groups, compared with 1 in 3000 of the general population. Would it be a good idea to expect that a shop steward you were about to meet for the first time would be a revolutionary left-winger? Clearly not. It is more probable that he or she holds such views than someone who is not a shop steward, but is still not very likely.

Perhaps most of us like to think that we are free of stereotypes. If so, we are probably fooling ourselves. At a university where two of the authors were employed, a small number of students came each year from Norway. One of us (who shall remain nameless!) caught himself feeling slightly surprised that many of these students were *not* blond and tall – his stereotype of Scandinavians.

Some of the causes and consequences of stereotypes are shown in Fig. 12.2, and discussion of the role of stereotypes in assessing people at work appears in Chapter 6. Devine (1989) argues that we cannot avoid starting out with stereotypes. The difference between prejudiced and non-prejudiced individuals is that the latter deliberately inhibit the automatically activated stereotype and replace it with more open-minded thoughts (Devine, 1989, p. 15):

> [This] can be likened to the breaking of a bad habit . . . The individual must (a) initially decide to stop the old behavior; (b) remember the resolution, and (c) try repeatedly and decide repeatedly to eliminate the habit before the habit can be eliminated.

Other work has shown that simply instructing people to try to suppress stereotypic thoughts can actually be counterproductive. Ironically, the instruction itself leads people to be more conscious of the stereotype they are trying to suppress (Bodenhausen and Macrae, 1996). As Devine implied, what matters seems to be a personal commitment to changing one's perception or behaviour. Often this will involve changing one's assumptions about why a particular person is the kind of person he or she is – for example, poor because of lack of opportunity, not laziness.

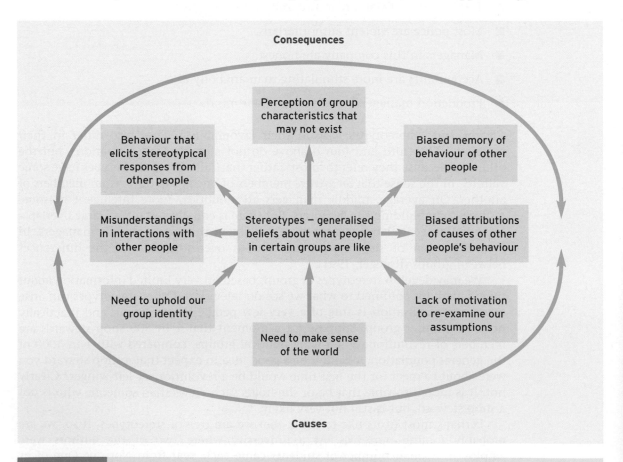

Figure 12.2   Some causes and consequences of stereotypes

Finally, Hewstone *et al.* (2002, p. 594) acknowledge that social psychology does not have all the answers to problems of inter-group bias:

> It would be a mistake, however, to consider ethnic and religious mass murder as a simple extension of intergroup bias. . . . Real-world intergroup relations owe at least as much of their character to intragroup variables such as self-esteem, in-group identification . . . and group threat.

Teams in the twenty-first century workplace

How prevalent is teamwork?

Much of the previous section focused on the effectiveness of teams, mainly in so far as they make decisions. Chapter 13, on leadership, has a lot to say about how to manage teams. In this section we look at team functioning from a broader perspective. Teams are increasingly common in organisations as functional boundaries break down and work is increasingly based on projects requiring input from people with different expertise and experience.

It is quite difficult to distinguish between groups and teams at work. Indeed, Guzzo and Dickson (1996) think it is more or less impossible, and probably pointless. They argue that a work group is made up of individuals who:

- see themselves and are seen by others as a social entity;
- are interdependent because of the tasks they perform;
- are embedded in one or more larger social systems;
- perform tasks that affect others such as co-workers or customers.

Perhaps teams differ from groups in the extent to which (i) members are interdependent (more so in teams) and (ii) the team as a whole (rather than the individuals in it) has performance goals. As Mohrman *et al.* (1995, p. 39) have put it, a team is 'a group of individuals who work together to produce products or deliver services for which they are mutually accountable'.

Many observers think that more and more people are working in teams rather than as individuals. Sometimes it is not clear exactly what is meant by the words 'team' and 'teamwork', but it is clear that they refer to work that involves a group of colleagues who co-operate quite closely and are interdependent in achieving collective work goals. This is in contrast to individual work, where individuals rather than teams have work goals and there is less close co-operation and interdependence. It is argued by some (e.g. Morita, 2001) that teamworking has two distinct origins. The first is the concern in Europe, especially during the 1960s and 1970s, for the quality of working life. Teamworking was thought to provide people with more satisfying work than individual working. The second origin was Japanese management, with its emphasis on multifunctional employees, loyalty to the collective, and collective responsibility for the quality and quantity of work.

So how much teamworking is really happening? Predictably, it depends on how teamworking is defined, who is asked about it, and exactly how the question is asked. Perhaps the most informative analysis has been provided by Benders *et al.* (2001). They obtained data from nearly 6000 workplaces across ten European countries. They asked a senior manager in each workplace to describe the extent to which people in the largest occupational group in that workplace worked in teams which had the authority to make their own decisions in each of the following eight areas:

- allocation of work;

- scheduling of work;

- quality of work;

- timekeeping;

- attendance and absence control;

- job rotation;

- co-ordination of work with other internal groups;

- improving work processes.

Benders *et al.* decided that, in order to qualify as a 'group-based workplace', at least four of the eight decision areas should be assigned to teams, *and* at least 70 per cent of core employees should work in such groups. Only 217 workplaces (about 4 per cent of the total) met both criteria. In fact, only 1404 (24 per cent) of the workplaces assigned *any* of the eight decision areas to teams. Country-by-country, the 24 per cent were distributed as shown in Table 12.1 – apologies if the list rather resembles scoring in the Eurovision Song Contest!

It is perhaps to be expected that Sweden would be top of this league, with its tradition of participative democracy, socio-technical work design, and high-profile

Key Learning Point

Most European workplaces appear not to be predominantly organised in teams, but there is wide variation in this respect between European countries.

Table 12.1	The incidence of teamworking in ten European countries	
	Percentage with at least one decision area assigned to teams	**Percentage of workplaces 'team-based'**
Sweden	44	11
Netherlands	38	5
France	27	5
UK	27	5
Germany	26	4
Denmark	24	3
Ireland	22	3
Italy	22	1
Portugal	6	0
Spain	4	0

Source: Adapted from Benders *et al.* (2001)

examples of teamworking – for example Volvo. More surprising is that this did not spill over the border to Denmark. The low incidence of teamwork in the southern European countries is consistent with evidence that their cultures tend to emphasise status and hierarchy quite highly. Regarding which decisions teams made for themselves, improving work processes and scheduling were the most common, and job rotation and attendance and absence control the least common. Benders *et al.* note that 'headline' figures from studies of teamwork in the United States are higher than theirs (e.g. Gittleman *et al.*, 1998, 32 per cent of workplaces using teamwork). However, on closer inspection it appears that because of differences in sampling methods and the way that questions were asked, if anything teamwork is more prevalent in Europe than in the United States.

In spite of a lot of enthusiasm for teamwork, it still seems to be more the exception than the rule.

Attitudes to teamwork

What does teamworking do for members' work attitudes and performance? Harley (2001) points out that on the one hand are job redesign enthusiasts who argue that teamwork increases the amount of control people have over their work, while on the other hand theorists from the 'critical management' school maintain that teamworking leads to more work and less discretion for individuals, with senior managers effectively allowing pressure and scrutiny from other team members to substitute for formal supervisory control. Harley analysed data from the 1998 British Workplace Employee Relations Survey, and found that people who were described as working as part of a team were on the whole no more and no less happy in their work, and committed to their employer, than people who were not so described. Harley (2001, p. 737) concludes:

> The results leave [both] positive and critical accounts of teamwork looking rather forlorn. While teamwork does not, according to this analysis, herald a transformation of work in which employees regain the discretion denied to them by Taylorist work organisation, nor does it appear to involve reductions in discretion and hence increased work intensification.

Some case-study based work also suggests that teamwork may have multiple and complex meanings, the overall impact of which is difficult to discern. For example, Procter and Currie (2002) studied a local branch of the United Kingdom's tax collection system, the Inland Revenue. It had reduced its layers of management during the 1990s and reorganised work so that tasks were allocated to teams rather than individuals. There was a general belief that teamwork was partly intended by management to elicit more workless resources. Procter and Currie note (2002, p. 304) that in some ways teamworking had meant little substantive change in jobs, yet in other ways it had had an impact:

> The range of work is little changed; employees exercise little in the way of new skills; they appear reluctant to adopt responsibility for the work of others; and the performance management system operates on the basis of individual performance. Nonetheless, teamworking appears to work in the Inland Revenue. It does so by having a team rather than an individual allocation of work, and by encouraging individual identity with the team target.

Steijn (2001) points out that one reason why some studies find little or no impact of teamworking may be that non-teamworkers in fact comprise two very different groups. One is people who work in mundane jobs with low skill requirements and little discretion. The other is professional or craft workers who exercise both skill and discretion in pursuing their individualised un-teamlike work. In a survey of 800 Dutch workers, Steijn found that the mundane jobs are less pleasant for the people who do them than either professional/craft work or teamwork, but that those two types of work differed little from each other.

A sophisticated analysis of some aspects of teamwork has been offered by Griffin *et al.* (2001). Like many others, they suggested that the introduction of teamwork reduces the role of supervisors and that this can be a difficult transition for those involved. Griffin and colleagues obtained data from nearly 5000 employees in 48 manufacturing companies in the United Kingdom, and also made their own assessments of the extent to which each company had introduced team-working. As they hypothesised, employees' job satisfaction was influenced by the extent to which they felt their supervisors supported them, but (again as hypothe-sised), this effect was smaller in companies which used teamwork a lot than in those which made little use of it. In other words, teamworking does indeed reduce (but not eliminate) the impact of employees' supervisors on their job attitudes. On the whole, the use of teamworking seemed to lead to a small reduction in job sat-isfaction. This was an outcome of two conflicting forces: on the one hand teamwork reduced the amount of supervisor support employees experienced, and this in turn eroded job satisfaction quite a lot. On the other hand, teamwork also led to more enriched jobs (e.g. multiskilling, responsibility) which tended to increase job satisfaction. These two opposite effects cancelling each other out may be another reason why Harley (2001) among others found little or no overall impact of teamwork on people's job attitudes.

Key Learning Point

Teamworking appears to have little association with work attitudes. This is partly because the introduction of teamworking may leave some work practices unchanged, and partly because people who do not work in teams have many different kinds of job.

Another important issue concerns the images and concepts people use to describe a team. This is likely to indicate quite a lot about, for example, what they expect from a team leader (*see also* Chapter 13). Such images are also likely to vary somewhat between cultures. Gibson and Zellmer-Bruhn (2002) present an analysis of how employees in pharmaceutical firms in Europe, Southeast Asia, Latin America and the United States talk about teams. They invoke the concept of metaphor, which they define (p. 102) as 'mechanisms by which we understand our experiences. We use metaphors whenever we think of one experience in terms of another. They help us to comprehend abstract concepts and perform abstract rea-soning.'

From a careful analysis of how people talked about teams, Gibson and Zellmer-Bruhn identified five types of teamwork metaphor:

1   Sports: engage in specific tasks with clear objectives and performance measurement; members have clear roles; interaction between team members

is largely confined to task-related matters; relatively little hierarchy; focus on winning and losing.

2   Military: also engage in tasks with limited scope and clear objectives, but have a clear and indisputable hierarchy; focus on life, death, survival and battle.

3   Family: engage in broad-ranging tasks and interact across most domains of life; relatively low emphasis on goals; clear roles (e.g. 'brothers' and 'sisters') and hierarchy ('father', 'mother').

4   Community: like families, communities are broad in the scope of interactions between members. However, roles are quite informal and ambiguous; goals sometimes quite ambiguous and the team quite amorphous.

5   Associates: limited activity, with interactions only in the professional domain; little hierarchy; roles may be clear but can change; ties between group members quite loose.

Where a team leader holds a teamwork metaphor that differs from those held by other team members, problems are likely to arise. For example, if the leader tends to construe a team as a sports team but the others see it more like a community, the members may feel confused or alienated by their leader's concern with meeting targets and restricting interaction to the task.

Different countries tend to exhibit somewhat different cultures (*see also* Chapter 1). This has implications for multinational companies where managers are assigned to countries other than their own, and where teams are often made up of people of various nationalities. For example, as Gibson and Zellmer-Bruhn (2002) point out, Latin American countries tend to emphasise both collectivism and status differentials, which would tend to imply a family team metaphor. If a leader is from a highly individualist and low power distance culture such as the United States, he or she may find it easier to think in terms of sports teams or associates.

Team development, roles and diversity

Teams are not constant. As well as changes in personnel, they change over time in terms of how they approach their tasks and how team members relate to each other. One early analysis (Tuckman, 1965) suggested that teams tend to go through a series of stages in their development:

1   *Forming*: there is typically ambiguity and confusion when a team first forms. The members may not have chosen to work with each other. They may be guarded, superficial and impersonal in communication, and unclear about the task.

2   *Storming*: this can be a difficult stage when there is conflict between team members and some rebellion against the task as assigned. There may be jockeying for positions of power and frustration at a lack of progress in the task.

3   *Norming*: it is important that open communication between team members is established. A start is made on confronting the task in hand, and generally accepted procedures and patterns of communication are established.

4   *Performing*: having established how it is going to function, the group is now free to devote its full attention to achieving its goals. If the earlier stages have been tackled satisfactorily, the group should now be close and supportive, open and trusting, resourceful and effective.

Most teams have a limited life, so it is probably appropriate to add another stage called something like *disbanding*. It would be important for team members to analyse their own performance and that of the group, to learn from the experience, and agree whether to stay in touch, and if so what that might achieve.

Not everyone agrees that these stages are either an accurate description or a desirable sequence. Teams composed of people who are accustomed to working that way may jump straight to the norming stage. The members may already know each other. Even if they do not, they may be able quickly to establish satisfactory ways of interacting without conflict. In any case, many teams are required to perform right from the start, so they need to bypass the earlier stages, at least partially. West (1994, p. 98) has argued that key tasks in team start-up concern the establishment of team goals and individual tasks that are meaningful and challenging, and of procedures for performance monitoring and review.

Key Learning Point

Some teams go through stages in their development, but many need to achieve high performance straight away.

West (2002) has argued that teams at work are often required both to think of new ideas and to implement them. He refers to the former as creativity and the latter as innovation. Creativity is encouraged by diversity of perspectives in the group, coupled with participation of all members, feelings of respect for each other, and expectations that it is acceptable to argue constructively with each other. These factors also help innovation. However, pressures from the environment have opposite effects on creativity *vs* innovation. These pressures include uncertainty (e.g. about market conditions), probably by increasing team members' anxiety and consuming their cognitive resources. On the other hand, they encourage innovation because innovation involves action and active problem-solving to improve a possibly difficult situation.

Teams at work sometimes use people from outside the team to help them improve their effectiveness. This is usually called team-building, and it can focus on some or all of the following:

- the team's goals or priorities;
- the work required and its distribution between team members;
- the team's deliberate and accidental procedures, processes and norms;
- relationships with other groups and teams.

in the employing organisation. They suggest that functional diversity tends to lead to task-related conflict (that is, disagreement between group members about preferred solutions and methods) and that this (as long as it is handled well) helps group performance. On the other hand, diversity in race and tenure leads to emotional conflict between group members, and this can undermine group performance. Jehn *et al.* (1999, p. 742) point out that 'No theory suggests that a workgroup's diversity on outward personal characteristics such as race and gender should have benefits except to the extent that diversity creates other diversity in the workgroup, such as diversity of information or perspective'.

Consistent with this assertion, Jehn *et al.* found that, among a sample of 545 employees, informational diversity in teams was associated with good group performance. Social category diversity (in the form of age and gender) made people more satisfied with their team, while value diversity (defined as disagreement about what the teams goals should be) tended to produce more relationship conflict within the team, and to undermine slightly the performance of the team.

Key Learning Point

Research on diversity in teams has shown the value for team performance of task-related disagreement and differences in knowledge and skill amongst team members.

Exercise 12.4   Roles and diversity in a team

Recall your experience of working in a group or team that you used for Exercise 12.2. This time, consider the following questions:

1   How diverse were the group members in terms of (for example) age, sex, ethnic or religious affiliation, outlook, personality, past experience, social class? What consequences did the diversity (or lack of it) have for how the group went about its task, and for the final decision?

2   Which of Belbin's nine team roles were most often adopted by members of the group? Consider whether this was helpful or not, and whether more (or less) of certain roles would have been helpful.

The wider organisational context

Guzzo and Dickson (1996) have pointed out that improved group performance does not guarantee improved organisational performance. It depends on the appropriateness of what the group is being asked to do, and how well the efforts of different groups are co-ordinated. Macy and Izumi (1993) found that organisational financial performance improves most when a range of change initiatives (*see* Chapter 15) are used, such as organisational structure, technology and human resource management techniques. But team development interventions were among the more effective of those initiatives. So group interventions do appear to be useful in the wider organisational context.

Decisions in organisations can be divided into various types, and each decision has various phases (Mintzberg *et al.*, 1976; Heller and Misumi, 1987). As regards types, there are (i) operational decisions (usually with short-term effects and of a routine nature); (ii) tactical decisions (usually with medium-term effects and of non-routine nature but not going so far as reviewing the organisation's goals); and (iii) strategic decisions (usually with long-term effects and concerning the organisation's goals). In line with leadership research (*see* Chapter 13), it is also possible to distinguish between people-orientated and task-orientated decisions within each type. Phases of decision-making include (i) start-up, when it is realised that a decision is required; (ii) development, when options are searched for and considered; (iii) finalisation, when a decision is confirmed; and (iv) implementation, when the finalised decision is put into operation or fails (Heller *et al.*, 1988).

Much attention has been focused on who in organisations really makes decisions, and how their influence is distributed across the decision types and phases described above (e.g. Mintzberg, 1983; Heller *et al.*, 1988; Vandenberg *et al.* 1999). The concept of *power* is frequently invoked. Power concerns the ability of an individual or group to ensure that another individual or group complies with its wishes. Power can be derived from a number of sources, including the ability to reward and/or punish; the extent to which a person or group is seen as expert; and the amount of prestige or good reputation that is enjoyed by a person or group. These sources of power are distinct, though they tend to go together (Finkelstein, 1992). Especially if they are in short supply, individuals and groups often use *organisational politics* to maximise their chances of getting their way. Politics consists of tactics such as enlisting the support of others, controlling access to information, and creating indebtedness by doing people favours for which reciprocation is expected. In extreme forms politics can also involve more deceitful activities such as spreading rumours. In general, however, the effectiveness and morality of power and politics depend on their intended goals. The distinction between the two goals of self-aggrandisement and organisational effectiveness is often blurred. After all, most of us probably construe ourselves as playing important and legitimate roles in our work organisations, and it is easy to jump from there to a belief that what is good for us must therefore also be good for the organisation.

Several large studies over the years have explored the question of who participates in organisational decisions. Heller *et al.* (1988), for example, conducted a detailed longitudinal study of seven organisations in three countries (the Netherlands, the United Kingdom and the former Yugoslavia). Not surprisingly, they found that most decision-making power was generally exercised by top management. The lower levels and works councils typically were merely informed or at best consulted. The distribution of power did, however, vary considerably between organisations and also somewhat between countries, with Yugoslavia (as it then was) generally having the most of participation by people at low organisational levels, and the United Kingdom least. There was also some variation between types and phases of decision-making. Top management was most influential in strategic decisions. Within tactical decisions, workers had quite high influence at the start-up phase of people-orientated decisions but little thereafter. This led to frustration. But for tactical task-orientated decisions, they had much influence in the finalisation phase. This was often less frustrating, since the right of management to initiate decisions of this kind was rarely challenged (i.e. high legitimate power).

Senior managers are often tempted to make decisions in quite an autocratic way, involving only a few senior colleagues with little or no consultation. This is not necessarily because those managers have autocratic personalities. In fast-moving environments it may be necessary to make decisions quickly, and the participation of a large number of people slows things down. However, Ashmos *et al.* (2002) have argued for a simple management rule: use participative styles of decision-making. Although this can be time-consuming and confusing, it has a number of benefits, including:

- using the skills and knowledge available in the organisation;

- developing people's sense of involvement in the organisation;

- increasing information flow and contacts among members of the organisation;

- making decisions that reflect the real (and changing) nature of the organisation's environment.

Ashmos *et al.* argue that most organisations tend to have complex systems of rules and procedures that ensure that organisational decisions are predictable and standardised. The use of established procedures tends to eliminate real participation by organisational members. If the simple rule 'use participation' is followed, decisions are made and actions taken in less predictable and comfortable ways, but they are better suited to the specific situation. Ashmos *et al.'s* ideas are summarised in Fig. 12.4. They are consistent with the proposition in the Vroom–Yetton theory of leadership (*see* Chapter 13) that participative methods are appropriate in most situations.

Key Learning Point

The amount and type of workforce participation in organisational decision-making varies between countries, between types of decision, and between phases of the decision-making processs.

Finally, examinations of strategic decision-making by senior management have been undertaken (e.g. Forbes and Milliken, 1999). Some interesting findings have emerged. For example, Papadakis and Barwise (2002) have examined strategic decisions in medium and large Greek companies. They were interested in how comprehensive and rational the decision-making process was, how hierarchically decentralised it was, how much lateral communication occurred, and how political it was. They found that the personalities and other characteristics of the Chief Executive Officer and top management team had relatively limited impact on how decisions were made. Instead, the extent to which the decision would have an impact on the firm seemed to matter. Encouragingly perhaps, higher impact was associated with a more comprehensive process with more decentralisation and communication.

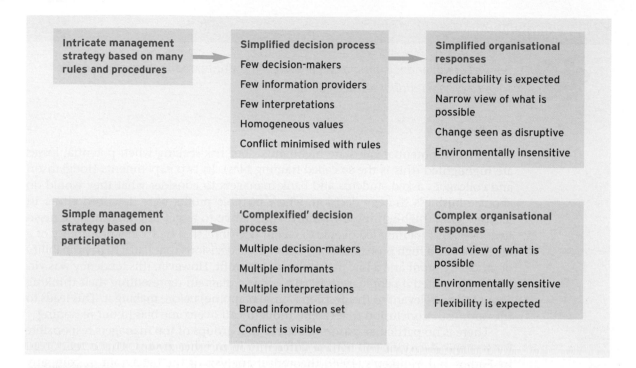

Figure 12.4　**Participation in organisational decision-making**
Source: Adapted from Ashmos *et al.*, 'What a mess! Participation as a simple managerial rule to "complexify" organizations', *Journal of Management Studies*, 39 (2), pp. 189–206, Blackwell Publishing Ltd

Dean and Sharfman (1996) investigated the process and outcomes of 52 strategic decisions in 24 companies. The most common types of strategic decision concerned organisational restructuring, the launch of a new product, and organisational change. Dean and Sharfman used multiple in-depth interviews with senior managers involved in the decisions. Their findings are summarised in Fig. 12.5. The procedural rationality of the decision-making process (that is, the extent to which relevant information was sought, obtained and evaluated) had a significant impact on decision effectiveness, particularly when the business environment was changeable, requiring careful monitoring of trends. But even more important was the thoroughness and care with which the decision was implemented. This is an important reminder that managers cannot afford simply to make decisions – the decisions must be followed through. However, not everything is under decision-makers' control. Dean and Sharfman found that the favourability of the business and industrial environment also had an impact on decision effectiveness. Political behaviour by those involved was bad for decision effectiveness. So, behaviour such as disguising one's own opinions, and negotiations between factions of the decision-making group, should not be accepted as an inevitable part of organisational life. They impair organisational performance, though of course they may serve the interests of individuals or subgroups.

There are also plenty of demonstrations that the biases in individual decision-making described early in this chapter occur in strategic decision-making. For example, Hodgkinson *et al.* (1999) demonstrated the tendency for people to be risk

Key Learning Point

Taking care over decision-making and implementation really does make a difference to organisational effectiveness.

averse when potential gains are highlighted, but risk-seeking when potential losses are highlighted (this is the so-called framing bias). In two experiments Hodgkinson and colleagues asked students and bank managers to consider what they would do about a business strategy decision, where possible profits were described either in terms of cash (highlighting the positive) or relative to target (highlighting the negative). Negative framing led people to favour decisions that had a low probability of a big profit and a high probability of no profit over decisions that had a high probability of moderate profit and a low probability of no profit. However, this tendency was virtually eliminated if people were asked to draw a diagram representing their thinking about factors relevant to the decision (causal mapping) before making it. This leads to the optimistic conclusion that careful thought can overcome bias in our reasoning.

There is no particular reason to believe that groups of top managers responsible for strategic decisions will behave differently from other groups. This is reinforced by Forbes and Milliken's (1999) theoretical analysis of the behaviour of company Boards of Directors. They make a number of propositions that are very consistent with more general theorising about groups and teams, particularly concerning the impacts of cohesiveness and diversity. For example, they suggest that Board members feeling a sense of cohesiveness is good up to a point, but too much cohesiveness impairs decision-making. This is a similar prediction to that made by Janis in his groupthink model discussed earlier in this chapter. Also, Forbes and Milliken predict that cognitive conflict (i.e. disagreements about the best solutions to prob-

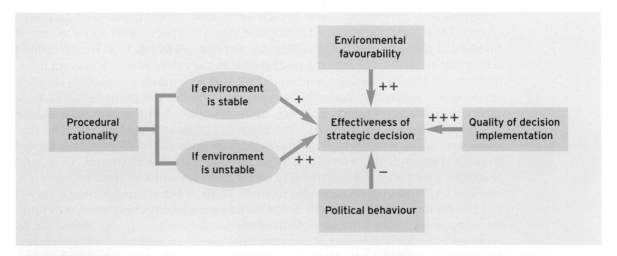

Figure 12.5	**Influences on the effectiveness of strategic decisions**
	Source: **Adapted from Dean and Sharfman (1996), adapted with permission**

lems) will increase the Board's effectiveness, but reduce its cohesiveness. This is closely in line with the findings of Jehn *et al.* (1999) also noted earlier in this chapter.

Key Learning Point

Analyses of strategic decisions in organisations support the findings and perspectives of much other research on groups and teams.

Negotiation and conflict at work

Some decisions involve discussion between two or more individuals or groups who have different opinions about what the decision should be, at least at the outset. The process of attempting to resolve these differences through discussion is called *negotiation*. The most obvious form of negotiation in the workplace is that between management and employees in organisations, the latter often represented by a trade union. Rather like group decision-making, psychologists have tried to describe what happens in negotiations and also in some cases to recommend strategies for success as a negotiator. They have tended to concentrate on what happens in the negotiation itself, and placed less emphasis on the economic and political context in which a negotiation takes place (Lewicki *et al.*, 1992). Although some research has involved real negotiations, much has been conducted in laboratories with students tackling standard tasks under varying conditions.

The negotiation process

As Pruitt (1981) pointed out, at certain key decision points during a negotiation, a negotiator can choose between three types of behaviour:

1   *Unilateral concession*: the negotiator lowers his or her demands, or agrees to something desired by an opposing negotiator.

2   *Standing firm, or contention*: the negotiator restates his or her demands, or refuses to give something desired by an opposing negotiator. This can involve strong uncompromising arguments in support of one's own position, and even threats.

3   *Collaboration*: the negotiator tries to work with, rather than against, opposing negotiators to find a mutually acceptable solution.

In an early and influential piece of work, Walton and McKersie (1965) distinguished between *distributive bargaining* and *integrative bargaining*, which are similar to Pruitt's competition and collaboration, respectively. In distributive bargaining the negotiators assume that there is a fixed amount of reward available, so that one negotiator's gain is another's loss. But integrative bargaining involves an attempt to increase the size of the overall reward available to both sides. One phenomenon often observed in research is that negotiators tend to treat the task as distributive even though they could gain more by taking an integrative approach. For example, suppose that negotiators A and B are trying to reach an agreement over the sale of A's house, which B wishes to buy. A wants €200 000, and B begins by offering €180 000. After some discussion, A agrees to accept €195 000 and B increases the offer to €190 000. Neither side is prepared to shift further on the price so it looks like a deal will not be struck. However, if A and B then search together for other ways of viewing the problem, they may reach an agreement. Perhaps A has little use for the carpets and curtains in the house because the one she is moving to has them fitted already. In fact, she would prefer to avoid the hassle of removing them. B on the other hand very much wants A to leave the carpets and curtains because he likes them and is too busy to arrange new ones. So A and B may agree a price of €195 000 including carpets and curtains. B considers the extra €5000 a fair price for the carpets and curtains, and A is also happy because the carpets and curtains are of no value to her, and she has got the price she wanted.

This kind of outcome, sometimes referred to as 'win–win' (Pruitt and Rubin, 1986), often depends on the negotiators having complementary priorities so that each can make concessions over issues where their subjective loss is smaller than the corresponding gain experienced by another negotiator. To engage in problem-solving implies that a negotiator has some concern for the other party's outcomes as well as his or her own, and can tolerate the possiblity that the other party will be seen to have got at least some of what they wanted. Indeed, a negotiator's predominant negotiating style can be predicted on the basis of the extent of his or her concern about outcomes of the participating parties. This is shown in Fig. 12.6.

Although quite simple, Fig. 12.6 has three important lessons. First, a negotiator has more options than those of conceding or not conceding. Second, a negotiator may not be concerned only with his or her own outcomes. Especially if one negotiator anticipates having to work with another in the future, he or she would be wise to pay attention to the other's wishes because this helps to maintain their relationship. Third, compromise is not in the middle of Fig. 12.6 as one might expect. Instead it is near the top. This indicates that compromise requires a strong concern about the other party's outcomes. A contentious negotiator is almost as unlikely to compromise as to make a concession (Van de Vliert and Prein, 1989).

Key Learning Point

Effective negotiators pay attention to the interests of the other side as well as their own.

As Carnevale and Pruitt (1992) have pointed out, whatever a negotiator's preferred or typical style, the state of the negotiation may dictate his or her behaviour. This is another illustration of the fact that situation sometimes overrides personality (*see* Chapter 1). Indeed, some research has suggested that negotiators typically

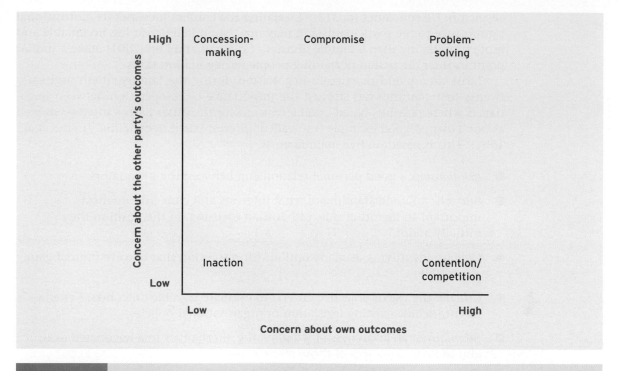

Figure 12.6 **Negotiator concerns and characteristic strategies**
Source: Adapted from Carnevale and Pruitt (1992), with permission from the
Annual Review of Psychology, vol. 43. © 1992 by Annual Reviews Inc.

behave in a contentious fashion early in a negotiation, adopting a problem-solving approach only when their position has been stated clearly and repeatedly. Up to a point this seems to be a sensible strategy. Research suggests that early in negotiation, uncompromising statements by one negotiator may produce concessions, or at least a rather lower opening bid, from the other than would otherwise have been the case (Pruitt and Syna, 1985). However, making high initial demands *and* sticking to most of them is a high-risk strategy because it is likely that no agreement at all will occur. In most work settings, failing to reach agreement is unsatisfactory for both or all parties – a so-called 'lose–lose' outcome. On the other hand, making low initial demands and many concessions produces a quick agreement but a rather one-sided one! It may also be a mistake to start with moderate demands and then refuse to move – the moderation raises the expectations of the other negotiator(s) but then the inflexibility frustrates them and leaves them unable to point to concessions they have won for their supporters (Hamner, 1974). The best approach may often be to start with high demands and make frequent concessions. Making meaningful concessions is easier if the negotiator has some awareness of, and empathy with, the concerns of the other party. It implies a willingness to be co-operative as opposed to (or as well as) competitive. Deutsch (2002), in a summary of research on the social psychology of conflict, argues that a wholly competitive approach has many negative effects, including impairment of communication, reduced self-confidence in both self and other party, and mutual suspicion. He concludes (p. 312): 'Escalating the conflict increases its motivational significance to the participants and may make a limited defeat less acceptable and more humiliating than a mutual disaster'. Coleman and Lim (2001) make a similar point in their discussion of training people in negotiation skills.

Most theory and practice in negotiation during the late twentieth and early twenty-first centuries has stressed the importance of co-operation between negotiators where possible, based upon a concern for the other party's interests as well as one's own. A good example is so-called 'interest-based negotiation' (Fisher *et al.*, 1991). This is based on five main factors:

- *Relationship:* a good personal relationship between the negotiators.

- *Interests:* an understanding of what interests and concerns are most important to the other side, rather than focusing on the position they initially adopt.

- *Options:* identifying as many options for resolution that involve mutual gain as possible.

- *Criteria:* the use of objective criteria to evaluate possible outcomes. Criteria might include existing legislation or organisational policies.

- *Alternatives:* an awareness of what are the alternatives to a negotiated deal, and the consequences of those alternatives.

Senger (2002) offers an interesting account from an American perspective of how interest-based negotiation operates (or does not) in various cultures. He takes most of his examples from the customer–shopkeeper negotiation, and discusses the many ways in which sellers use the five factors described above. For example, a *relationship* might be established by offering the customer a cup of tea, or free use of the shop's telephone to make a call. This can in turn create an *interest* on the part of the customer – for example an interest in repaying a favour. An illustration of *options* has been given earlier in the example of negotiation over a house sale. *Criteria* can be seen operating in the charging of higher taxi fares to tourists staying in five-star hotels than others: the criterion is the place in which they are staying, which signals their wealth. Often in buyer–seller transactions, one party will have better knowledge of *alternatives* than the other, for example, a market trader may have a pretty good idea of how much money he or she can typically get for a particular item, which helps the decision about whether to accept a potential customer's offer.

Senger (2002) also shows how interest-based negotiation can be manipulated. For example, one party may pretend they feel more warmly towards the other than they really do; or lie about what other customers have offered in an attempt to manipulate a potential customer's wish to appear a reasonable person. There is also the possibility that interest-based negotiation may break down if one party decides to be the ultimate hard bargainer.

As Lewicki *et al.* (1992) have pointed out, much research on negotiation seems to rest on the assumption that the only negotiation worth considering occurs at the negotiating table. Yet Walton and McKersie (1965) argued that much significant negotiation occurs when negotiators try to persuade their constituents to accept a deal as the best that can be achieved, and when negotiators on the same side discuss with each other how they should respond to a certain situation. Negotiators tend to believe (sometimes correctly) that their constituents are more anxious to win than they are themselves. This makes them more inclined to engage in contentious negotiation tactics, perhaps in the real hope of getting a good deal, or perhaps just to impress their constituents even if there is no hope of further progress. On the other hand, when negotiators have to justify their behaviour to their constituents *and* when they want a continuing relationship with the other side, they are quite likely to engage in problem-solving tactics. This is presumably because problem-solving is the strategy most likely to maintain their credibility with both their constituents and the opposing negotiators.

Ideas from cognitive and social psychology have also contributed to our understanding of negotiator behaviour. For example, we have already seen in this chapter how people are more inclined to take a risk in the hope of avoiding a loss than in the hope of making a gain. When applied to negotiation, this means that a negotiator who perceives that he or she is trying to avoid a loss will be more inclined to resist concessions (thus risking failure to reach agreement) than a negotiator who construes the position as trying to make a gain (Bazerman *et al.*, 1985). Negotiators also run the risk of escalating commitment to their initial position, especially if they are inexperienced.

Negotiators also have expectations or scripts concerning how negotiations will unfold. One common element of such a script is that a concession, once made, is not withdrawn. This expectation means that such a withdrawal is less likely to happen, and that if it does happen it will be viewed with outrage.

Employee relations

Negotiation is often conducted by representatives of owners and/or managers on one side and representatives of employees on the other. But negotiation is only one aspect of *employee relations*, which have been defined by Walker (1979, p. 11) as

Exercise 12.5   A negotiation at Micro

Employee relations at the Micro electronics company had reached a critical point. The company was performing well in its markets and making a good profit. In order to maintain this, managers wanted to abandon one of the company's products, for which demand was declining. This might mean some redundancies. When rumours broke out that voluntary redundancy might be available there was interest from a few people, but not enough to avoid some compulsory redundancies. At the same time, the employees who remained would undertake more varied and sometimes more skilled work. Employee attitude surveys had consistently indicated that this was what many of them wanted, and many of them claimed to want it more than an above-inflation pay rise. Perhaps swayed by this information, managers at Micro had underestimated the strength of opposition to their plans for implementing the changes they desired. Although there had not yet been industrial action, it was a clear possibility in the near future. New pay discussions were also due. Recent pay deals in similar companies to Micro had been slightly above inflation, even though all those companies faced similar dilemmas to Micro about which products to discontinue and how to manufacture the rest at the lowest possible cost. The details of those recent pay deals were described in the current issue of an industry magazine. The union negotiator, Nils Gunderson, was generally felt by union members to have achieved a poor deal in the last pay discussions two years ago. He was keen to move out of his job at Micro into a full-time union post. He had had a cordial relationship with the previous managing director, but his few encounters with the new one, Stephanie Viken, had not been so pleasant during the six months she had been in the post. Nils and Stephanie had had several arguments about relatively unimportant matters and knew little about each other as people. For her part, Stephanie was anxious to secure active union co-operation (as opposed to passive compliance) with company plans. She knew that she would need the employees on her side if the company was to remain competitive. She was also worried by the possibility that many might change to another, more militant, union.

What insights do the five factors of interest-based negotiation offer concerning (i) how Nils and Stephanie are likely to approach this negotiation, and (ii) the scope for a mutually satisfactory outcome?

being to do with 'the accommodation between the various interests that are involved in the process of getting work done'. This definition does not assume that the parties involved are necessarily management and other employees, nor that the latter are represented by trade unions, nor that there is necessarily conflict between the parties. However as Brotherton (2003) has pointed out, employee relations (and its earlier label industrial relations, IR) have been dominated by research on institutions (such as government, trade unions and employers) rather than individuals. This plus the perceived tendency of psychologists to adopt a managerialist perspective has meant that psychology has been rather marginalised in the field of employee relations (see also Kelly, 1998).

Hartley (1992) has provided a helpful account of many aspects of employee relations. Figure 12.7 is an adaptation of her picture of the field.

Figure 12.7 reflects trends in many Western countries during the late twentieth and early twenty-first centuries. The references to human resource management (HRM) and employee participation and involvement reflect a decreasing emphasis on collective, formal employment relationships. Instead, there is an increasing tendency for workplace-specific employment agreements; more emphasis on management for quality; training and flexibility of employees; and a greater concern with the commitment of individuals to their employing organisation (Guest and Hoque, 1996). Attempts to increase employee commitment and performance include share ownership, quality circles (where groups of employees jointly review the quality of output), and empowerment. The last of these involves trusting people to recognise and solve problems themselves rather than referring them to someone 'higher up', or not noticing them at all. Kelly and Kelly (1991) conclude that while many employees react positively to such interventions, they do not change their fundamental attitudes to managers. This is because employees often

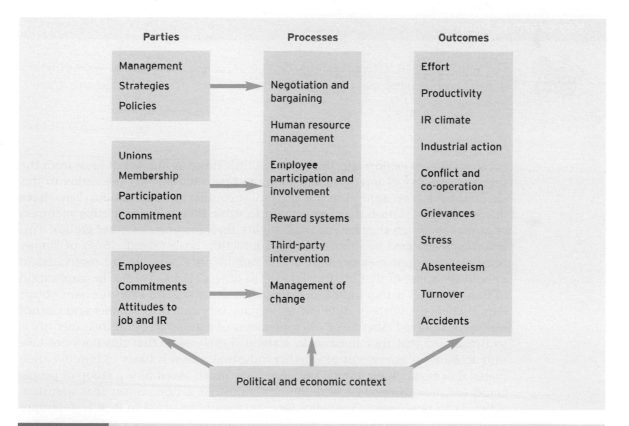

Figure 12.7   **Psychology in employee relations**
Source: **Adapted from J. Hartley (1992), 'The psychology of employee relations' in C.L. Cooper and I.T. Robertson (eds) *International Review of Industrial and Organizational Psychology*, vol. 7. Copyright John Wiley and Sons Ltd. Reproduced with permission**

believe, rightly or wrongly, that powerful groups in the organisation are still in control and might at any time choose to exert their control in a more draconian manner.

This trend towards the individualising of employee relations (at the expense of institutional perspectives) should mean that psychology's relevance is increasing, Brotherton (2003) identifies three aspects of psychology for which this is particularly true:

■ Commitment (*see* Chapter 7), and in particular the circumstances in which people feel committed to both their employer and their trade union.

■ The psychological contract (*see* Chapter 14). This refers to individuals' perceptions of their rights and obligations in the employment relationship.

■ Social identity and social categorisation theories, which seek to explain how and when people incorporate group memberships into their personal identities.

Key Learning Point

The ways in which different power blocs in organisations relate to each other depend partly on the wider legal and cultural contexts in which the organisation operates.

We will now explore this third aspect a little more. A number of ideas from the social psychology of inter-group relations and personal identity (*see* earlier in this chapter) have been applied to the analysis of conflict in organisations. They have in common the notion that people tend to value themselves and other members of groups to which they belong more highly than members of other groups. This may be engendered by groups having conflicting goals (Sherif, 1966) or simply because our group memberships define our identity, and we are motivated to uphold the value of that identity relative to others (Tajfel, 1972). The implication of these theories is that industrial action such as strikes and overtime bans occurs either when the goals of different groups are very much in conflict and cannot readily be resolved (Sherif), or when members of a group feel that their identity is so threatened that they must make a stand (Tajfel). Note that this does not take into account an assessment of whether industrial action is likely to improve their material or psychological state, nor does it say much about how a group of people could (or should) organise and conduct industrial action. Given that industrial action is an unpleasant experience for most people involved in it, it is important for a group taking industrial action to maintain cohesion and a sense of purpose without undue escalation of commitment to an unwinnable battle.

Aspects of social identity have been used more in understanding who participates in union activities. Kelly and Kelly (1994) studied 350 union members in a UK local government organisation. They divided participation into 'easy' (e.g. reading union journals, attending union meetings) and 'difficult' (e.g. being a union delegate, speaking at branch meetings). Perhaps not surprisingly, the extent to which people engaged in either form of participation was predicted by the extent to which they identified with the union. In addition, 'easy' participation was affected by the extent to which union members had stereotypical 'us and them' perceptions of management – the more stereotypical the perceptions, the more the 'easy' participation. Interestingly, these aspects of social identity were better predictors of participation than the extent to which members felt they were badly off relative to comparison groups.

The quality of inter-group relations in the workplace, and whether poor relations lead to industrial action, depends partly on the extent to which members of the different groups have accurate perceptions of each other. Allen and Stephenson (1984) have found that when members of groups overestimate differences in attitudes and beliefs between their own group and other groups, industrial action is more likely than when the differences are underestimated. This is another illustration of the importance of social factors: not only the real difference in views, but also the perceived difference, can influence whether industrial action occurs.

Involvement in industrial action is stressful (Barling and Milligan, 1987). But stress is not confined to times of industrial action. It is easy to see how people with trade union or other representative duties might experience stress from role conflict, role ambiguity, interpersonal conflict, split loyalties and work overload (*see* Chapter 11), especially perhaps if they are working in an 'ordinary' job and not as a full-time union official. Nandram and Klandermans (1993) found that much of union officials' stress was induced by role ambiguity *within* the union role rather than ambiguity about whether they should be acting as an employee or a union representative at any given time. That is, they were not clear what they, or their union, were trying to achieve. More optimistically, Shirom and Mayer (1993) reported that although trade union officials among teachers experienced high role overload and conflict, they did not experience more stress. This suggests that union activities have some compensatory advantages which might cancel out some of the unpleasant features. These advantages may include greater job challenge, a sense of being useful to one's colleagues, and perhaps also the esteem and gratitude of those colleagues.

Key Learning Point

For individuals, union participation can depend on their social identity, and can lead to significant stress related to conflicts between union and employee roles.

Summary

Decisions by individuals and groups are influenced by many psychological phenomena. For individuals, the subjective evaluation of risk and rewards is rarely the same as an objective mathematical calculation. This does not necessarily imply that people are typically irrational, although some features of decision-making can be construed as biased or ineffective in certain circumstances. Groups are usually more effective than the average individual but less so than the best individual in decision-making tasks. Groups can make terrible decisions, especially if characterised by the 'groupthink' syndrome. However, the typical effectiveness of groups should not be viewed as the best they can do. Possible ways in which groups and teams can improve include more consideration in advance of the problem-solving strategy they wish to adopt, a clear expectation that members should challenge each other, and an understanding that such challenges do not signal hostility or disrespect. Members of groups and teams need to fulfil a wide range of roles and to respect diversity. The nature of decision-making tasks, their importance and their subject matter all have implications for the way they are handled. Some decisions require negotiation with other parties. Negotiations are often perceived as 'fixed-pie' or 'zero sum' scenarios where one party's gain is equal to another's loss. However, this is not necessarily the case, and negotiations that produce an agreement satisfactory to both (or all) parties usually involve some collaborative problem-solving, which may uncover a solution that gives all involved the rewards that they value. Negotiations are just one part of employee relations, which concern the adjustments groups make to each other in the workplace. Theories from social psychology help to explain how industrial action arises as well as why people do or do not participate in trade union activities.

Closing Case Study

To Expand or not to Expand?

The management team of the Fastsave retail chain store company had a decision to make. Should they build a new store in Danesville, a medium-size town in which the company owned a suitable patch of land? Fastsave was doing quite well, and had more than enough financial resources to make the necessary investment in a town that did not currently have a major supermarket. On the other hand, there were two existing large superstores within 25 kilometres. It was agreed that there was no significant danger of substantial losses: the question was more whether the time and effort involved in expansion would be worth the return.

The management team consisted of the general manager (GM), finance manager (FM), marketing manager (MM), operations manager (OM), personnel manager (PM) and company secretary (CS). Each member of the team had been supplied with reports on the demographic make-up of the town, a market research survey, detailed costings of building the store, and the likely attitude of the local council planning authority.

Group members were accustomed to working together and there was rivalry (at present friendly) among them about which of them if any would succeed GM when she retired in about three years. At the outset of the meeting, GM made it clear that she would act as an impartial chairperson, and not reveal her own opinions until the end. In the past, however, she had usually been cautious about business expansions. The following extract is representative of the group's deliberations:

FM: I suspect the time is not right. We are currently upgrading six other stores, and to start a completely new one would run the risk of spreading our resources too thin. In purely financial terms we can do it, but would we do a good job?

OM: Yes, we've certainly got our hands full at present. In fact, I would be in favour of reviewing two of our already-planned store upgradings because I'm not sure they are really worth it either. Generally we're doing all right as we are – let's consolidate our position.

MM: I can't believe I'm hearing this! According to our market research report, the population of Danesville wants its own big supermarket, and what's more the 45+ age group particularly likes our emphasis on low price rather than super de luxe quality.

CS: Come on, as usual you're taking an approach which could possibly pay off but could land us in trouble . . .

MM: Like what?

CS: Well, there has been a lot of housing development in Danesville, and the local council is under pressure to preserve what it sees as the charm of the town. It would be very bad public relations to be perceived as undermining that. And having a planning application refused wouldn't be much better.

FM: That's right, and being seen as an intruder would probably reduce sales too.

PM: I can't comment on that last point, but as a general principle we should not stand still. Our competitors might overtake us. If resources are spread too thin, we can recruit more staff: we have the money, and experience suggests that the labour force in the region has the necessary skills.

FM: You've had a rush of blood to the head, haven't you? You're normally telling us how difficult it is to manage expansion of staff numbers. I must say I share the concern about a couple of our existing upgrading plans, let alone building an entirely new store. Do those stores really need refitting yet? They are doing all right.

CS: I notice that Danesville has an increasingly young, mobile population these days. In spite of the market research report, will they really be interested in a local store, especially with our position in the market?

MM: They can be made to be. Anyway, who says that a Danesville store should not go slightly more upmarket? Tesco seem to manage to have both upmarket and downmarket stores.

OM: Well yes, but I don't think we are big enough to be that versatile . . .   ▶

Suggested exercises

1   Examine this case study from the following perspectives:

(a)   the likely attitude to risk

(b)   group polarisation

(c)   minority influence.

2   Given this examination, what do you think the group is likely to decide? What is your evaluation of that decision?

Test your learning

Short-answer questions

1   Explain the distinction between satisficing and maximising in decision-making.

2   Define escalation of commitment to a decision and briefly describe the circumstances in which it is likely to occur.

3   Describe the main features of social categorisation theory.

4   Suggest three possible negative consequences of stereotypes in the workplace.

5   What strategies should minorities in groups use in order to maximise their chances of influencing a group decision?

6   What is group polarisation and why does it happen?

7   List the team roles identified by Belbin and explain why they are needed for team effectiveness.

8   Briefly outline three reasons why groups sometimes make poor decisions.

9   Define power and politics in organisations.

10   Describe the main principles of interest-based negotiation.

11   Briefly describe the topics within employee relations studied by psychologists.

Suggested assignments

1   Examine the importance of the work of Tversky and Kahneman for understanding decision-making by individuals.

2   Discuss the proposition that Janis's groupthink model adequately accounts for failures in group decision-making.

3   Examine the potential benefits and problems of diversity in teams.

4   To what extent has teamwork become a normal feature of working life?

5   What factors affect the occurrence of industrial action and how it is resolved?

6   Critically assess the proposition that compromise in negotiation is not the same as weakness.

Relevant websites

The International Society for Performance Improvement, as its name suggests, is concerned with promoting techniques which will raise performance levels of individuals and organisations at work. It carries some articles which relate to specific topics. One on virtual teams can be found at http://www.pignc-ispi.com/articles/cbt-epss/virtualteam.htm. Its home page http://www.pignc-ispi.com/ shows the full range of material there on various topics, including some covered in other chapters of this book. Some of the material is in Spanish.

An Australian site which offers a lot on teams can be found at http://www.productivesolutions.com.au/workteams.htm. This site contains a brief diagnosis of what constitutes a self-managing team, and also links to many other relevant pages.

Reviews of books and other resources on teamwork for managers and trainers can be found at http://reviewing.co.uk/reviews/teambuilding.htm. This shows the range of material available, including some pretty scary outdoor exercises.

The negotiation Academy Europe's home page at http://www.negotiationeurope.com/ provides many resources which show how ideas from negotiation research are used in management development.

For further self-test material and relevant, annotated weblinks please visit the website at http://www.booksites.net/arnold_workpsych.

Suggested further reading

All four suggested readings are listed in detail in the reference list at the end of the book.

1   Michael West's chapter entitled 'The human team: Basic motivations and innovations' in volume 2 of the 2001 *Handbook of Industrial Work and Organizational Psychology* gives an up-to-date and scholarly but accessible review of many team processes and outcomes.

2   R. Meredith Belbin's book *Beyond the Team* (published in 2000) is a good example of a genre that attempts to use everyday language to help people understand how to make teams work.

3   Chris Brotherton's 2003 chapter on the psychology and industrial relations in the book *Understanding Work and Employment* provides a personal and wide-ranging analysis of the field.

4   Although now quite old, the 1984 article in *American Psychologist* by Daniel Kahneman and Amos Tversky provides a good summary of research on the psychological processes involved in decision-making by individuals.

CHAPTER 13

Leadership

LEARNING OUTCOMES

After studying this chapter, you should be able to:

1 suggest reasons why leadership at work in the twenty-first century might be more challenging than ever before;

2 identify various criteria of leader effectiveness;

3 specify some common personality characteristics of leaders;

4 define consideration and structure;

5 name and define four aspects of transformational leadership and two aspects of transactional leadership;

6 examine the nature of charismatic leadership, and discuss the extent to which transformational and charismatic leadership influence performance at work;

7 define the key concepts and propositions of Fiedler's contingency and cognitive resource theories of leadership;

8 name and define five leader styles varying in participativeness, and at least five features of the problem situation, identified by Vroom and Jago in their theory of leadership;

9 describe how concepts of leadership held by subordinates and in society generally give an alternative perspective on leadership;

10 examine the circumstances in which leadership might be seen as relatively unimportant;

11 explain why and in what ways effective leader behaviour may differ between countries and cultures;

12 list the cultural groupings within Europe, and their distinctive views of leadership.

Opening Case Study   Corporate Leaders on a Quest for Meaning

Chief executives are reluctant to talk publicly about the difficulties of the job. In private, however, they admit to a fear of failure, qualms about their leadership style and worries about winning employees' commitment. Anonymous interviews with 30 European chief executives over the past three months reveal consistent concerns despite wide variations in culture and management style.

'The things keeping them awake at night would be to do with their own personal performance as a leader, not their business performance,' says Mike Walsh, chairman of Ogilvy Europe, Africa and Middle East, part of Ogilvy & Mather, the advertising company, which carried out the research. Strikingly, only two of the 30 had been groomed for the job, highlighting the rapid rate of CEO turnover and the difficulties, or even absence, of succession planning. While they were worried about handling external economic pressure, they felt the absence of 'textbook' solutions most acutely in relation to their personal style and effectiveness.

'Coming fresh to this role, many were tempted or persuaded to do things in which they did not believe,' says the report, *Today's CEO*. 'They learned that this did not work, primarily because the people who were expected to follow and implement such decisions could detect their lack of sincerity. The greatest mistake was to try to be something one was not: to claim to know more, do more, be more than one actually was.'

The interviewees said they wanted to build relaxed, non-hierarchical working cultures. But in many cases they were part of a much larger organisation for which that was too big a step. Many needed to understand better how their employees think and feel, especially as they tried to squeeze more productivity out of them. Increasingly, they realised this need. 'There is a degree of introspection today that wasn't there three years ago, inspired by a fear of failure and loss of office' the report says.

Senior executives are increasingly searching for meaning in their lives, says Mark Watson, a coach, and director or Purple Works, a UK learning and communications group. Top jobs confer less influence and power than most people think but entail huge responsibility, and life can be a grind. 'In big organisations you're hemmed in by board committees, corporate governance protocol and expectations to perform. Many of these people also find themselves detached from the real operations.'

Source: Financial Times, *21 September 2001.*

Introduction

If the article above is to be believed, corporate leaders are not happy people. They think a lot about how they should go about being a leader. The styles they adopt are influenced by their own past experience and by the opportunities and constraints of their current situation. In many cases they feel they are expected to pay attention to the needs of others while their own needs are overlooked. They want to (or feel they must) increase the productivity of their workgroups and organisations and they wonder how to achieve that without inducing burnout and alienation.

Many observers argue that demands on leaders are changing in their nature and also increasing (Dess and Picken, 2000). Work organisations are increasingly reliant upon rapid and skilful innovation and use of information at all levels. Leadership based upon monitoring and control of subordinates is no longer appropriate. Subordinates and leaders sometimes work in different locations, which makes close supervision very difficult. The task of leaders, even at quite low levels in an organisation, is said to be managing continuous change and delegating responsibility while maintaining an overall sense of direction. Yet this may not come naturally to either leaders or followers. To quote an analysis of leadership from South African and American perspectives:

> What is killing us is the illusion of control: that things can be predictable, consistent and forever under control. What is also killing us is that followers require their leaders to be in control, on top of things, and to take the blame when things go wrong. Nearly all the new management programmes on TQM, re-engineering, right-sizing, just-in-time, this or that, are really old wine in new bottles – more efforts to design control systems that ask the workers to try harder; do better and be even more productive. (April *et al.*, 2000, p. 1)

Key Learning Point

Leadership is especially challenging nowadays because of the pace of change, the illusion of control and the high expectations of followers.

In this chapter we examine some of the many approaches to leadership. There is quite a long history of psychological theory and research in this area, and it would be impossible to cover all of it. So work that has been particularly influential will receive most of the attention, along with some discussion of whether it is applicable in twenty-first century workplaces. We will also examine the extent to which national cultures affect perceptions and impact of leaders.

Some important questions about leadership

A leader can be defined as the 'person who is appointed, elected, or informally chosen to direct and co-ordinate the work of others in a group' (Fiedler, 1995, p. 7). This definition acknowledges the important truth that the formally appointed leader is not always the real leader. But it also confines the notion of leader to a group context. If we take the word 'group' literally, this definition excludes leaders of nations, large corporations and so on, except in so far as they lead a small group of senior colleagues.

So much for the leader. Leader*ship* can be considered to be the personal qualities, behaviours, styles and decisions adopted by the leader. In other words, it concerns how the leader carries out his or her role. Hence while the role of leader can be described in a job description, leadership is not so easily pinned down. The point is frequently overlooked that the dynamics of leadership when most followers do not have direct contact with the leader may differ from those when they do. Waldman and Yammarino (1999) have argued that similar concepts can be used to describe leadership styles in these two situations, but the ways in which followers form impressions of the leader differ. For those close to him or her, impressions are derived from day-to-day interaction, whereas for others, impressions depend more on the leader's stories, vision and symbolic behaviours and also on how well his or her organisation performs.

Key Learning Point

The real leader of a group may not be the person who was formally appointed to the role.

Over the years several distinct but related questions have been asked about leaders and leadership. These include the following:

- Who becomes a leader?

- How do leaders differ from other people?

- How can we describe their leadership?

It is in fact difficult to consider these questions without bringing in the notion of effectiveness. So we can also ask:

- What are effective leaders like?

- How do effective leaders differ from ineffective ones?

- What characteristics of situations help or hinder a leader's effectiveness?

At this point it is worth pausing to consider how we can tell whether or not a leader is effective. The most obvious method is to assess the performance of his or her group relative to other similar groups with different leaders. Quite apart from the assumption that such comparison groups will be available, there is also the problem that performance is often determined by many things other than leadership. The reader can probably think of several straight away. Performance is itself often difficult to define and measure, especially in the long term. Sometimes grievance rates against the leader, and/or group members' satisfaction with the leader, have been used as a measure of leader effectiveness. But who is to say that, for example, low grievance rates are a good thing? Perhaps a group needs 'shaking up', and it could be argued that a good leader should ruffle a few feathers. Similar considerations apply to voluntary turnover among group members as a measure of leader effectiveness. In short, there is no perfect measure of leader effectiveness. Group performance is used most often, probably correctly. But we must remember not to expect an especially strong association with leadership: too many other factors come into play.

Key Learning Point

There is no one perfect indicator of leadership effectiveness, but the work performance of his or her workgroup or organisation is probably the best.

In recent years further questions about leadership have been raised. When and why is leadership seen as being important? How do leaders come to be perceived as such? Are these perceptions the same across cultures? These three questions emphasise that leadership is an interpersonal issue as well as a personal one. The social psychology of relationships between pairs of people, and within groups, is seen as crucial. There is also a perception that theories that concentrate on leader effectiveness have tended to neglect adequate description of interactions between leader and subordinates. Hence this more recent approach is to some extent returning to a descriptive rather than an evaluative orientation. However, its sophistication ensures that it does not simply cover old ground.

The early leader-focused approaches to leadership

It seems reasonable to look for the simple before resorting to the complex. This has indeed been the case in leadership research. Most theory and practice up to the 1960s, and plenty since then, has had two key features:

1 Description of the leader rather than the dynamics of the leader's relationship with subordinates.

2 Attempts to identify the characteristics/behaviour of a 'good leader' regardless of the situation.

Leader characteristics

Some early work (reviewed by Stogdill, 1974; House and Baetz, 1979) found that leaders tended to be higher than non-leaders on:

- intelligence;
- dominance/need for power;
- self-confidence;
- energy/persistence;
- knowledge of the task.

Many other personality characteristics (for example adjustment, extroversion) have also been found in some studies to be more characteristic of leaders than non-leaders. In addition, intelligence and sociability seem characteristic of emergent (as opposed to appointed) leaders. But characteristics that help leaders to reach the top may subsequently prove their undoing. For example, a high level of dominance and need for personal power may prevent a leader maintaining good relationships with his or her team or superiors, and this may precipitate his or her removal (Conger, 1990). Further, the characteristics of people who attain leadership positions depend partly on their motives for being leaders, and the acceptability of those motives to those who appoint them. So if a leader subscribes to Robert Greenleaf's (1983) concept of the servant leader, then his or her primary aim will be to help others, through an attitude of humility and concern for people as individuals. Servant leadership means a move away from controlling towards encouraging and listening (Spears, 1995). This is a far cry from dominance and personal power.

House and Baetz (1979) argued that the very nature of the leadership role must mean that sociability, need for power and need for achievement are relevant. However, they also acknowledged two insights, which are nowadays accepted by many people involved in leadership:

1 A leader's personal characteristics must be expressed in his or her behaviour if those characteristics are to have an impact on performance.

2 Different types of tasks may require somewhat different leader characteristics and behaviours.

Of course, one of the most evident and difficult-to-change personal characteristics is one's gender. It can be argued that most leadership roles are typically described in stereotypically masculine terms, which might mean that women have more difficulty in being selected for them, and being seen as good leaders even when they are selected. On the other hand, one might expect women to do better precisely because only the most able ones make it to leadership roles. In a meta-analysis of 96 studies, Eagly *et al.* (1995) found no overall difference in leadership performance between men and women. However, men had an advantage in military and outdoor pursuits (i.e. stereotypically masculine settings), while there was no difference or a slight advantage for women in business, education and government settings. Research by Lewis (2000) suggested a rather subtle disadvantage for women leaders relative to men. Lewis asked undergraduate students to view videotapes showing a male or female company chief executive displaying either anger or sadness or emotional neutrality about the company's poor performance. The student's ratings of leader effectiveness tended to be lower if the leader expressed emotion than if he or she was neutral. However, displays of anger damaged the ratings of women leaders much more than those of men leaders. Lewis suggested that whereas a man's anger might be taken to signal assertiveness, a woman's might be perceived as aggression or instability.

Key Learning Point

Personality characteristics in themselves do not make leaders effective. What matters is how those characteristics are expressed in their behaviour, and how that behaviour is understood by others.

Task orientation and person orientation

Way back in the 1950s, one research team at Ohio State University and another at Michigan University launched major projects on leader behaviour. They worked more or less independently of each other, and approached the task from opposite directions. The Ohio group sought to uncover the central features of leader behaviour by asking subordinates, and to a lesser extent leaders themselves, to describe the leader's behaviour. From an initial list of almost 2000 questions, ten dimensions of leader behaviour were identified. It was then discovered that two more general dimensions underlay the ten. These two have consistently emerged in subsequent work, and have been described as follows (Fleishman, 1969):

1   *Consideration*: the extent to which a leader demonstrates trust of subordinates, respect for their ideas, and consideration of their feelings.

2   *Structure*: the extent to which a leader defines and structures his or her own role and the roles of subordinates toward goal attainment. The leader actively directs group activities through planning, communicating information, scheduling, criticising and trying out new ideas.

The Michigan team started by classifying leaders as effective or ineffective. They then looked for behaviours that distinguished between the two groups. One distinction was that effective managers seemed concerned about their subordinates whereas ineffective ones were concerned only with the task. Clearly this bears considerable resemblance to the distinction between consideration and structure described above. It seemed that consideration was a good thing, and structure a bad one if it was not accompanied by consideration. Blake and Mouton's (1964) Managerial Grid (which is much used in management training, even today) encourages leaders to examine their own style on these two dimensions. It assumes that leaders can be high on both, low on both or high on one and low on the other. Blake and Mouton proposed that it is usually best to be high on both.

Research suggests that in many situations a certain level of consideration is essential for maintenance of satisfactory relations between leader and group. However, where group performance is the outcome measure, it is far from clear whether consideration and structure are always good, bad or indifferent.

In any case, structure and consideration refer to quite specific styles of day-to-day behaving. They give little indication of how *well* the leader structures tasks or expresses consideration, and no indication of how well (if at all) the leader is thinking strategically about what the workgroup is trying to achieve, and by what routes. The extent to which leaders of large organisations show structure and consideration to their immediate subordinates may in any case have little or no impact on the attitudes and behaviour of other organisational members.

Key Learning Point

Consideration and structure are useful concepts that have stood the test of time in analysing leadership. However, they focus on the leader's day-to-day behaviour rather than his or her overall strategy.

Participation and democracy

Another dimension of behavioural style that has received much attention is participativeness. This concerns the extent to which the leader is democratic or autocratic. It is clearly related to the dimensions already discussed, but arguably not identical. For example, the definition of structure given earlier does not necessarily exclude subordinates from influencing the direction given by the leader. Gastil (1994) has discussed the nature of the democratic leadership, and made the general point that it is certainly not just a case of letting the subordinates get on with their work. According to Gastil, the three key elements of democratic leadership are as follows:

1 *Distributing responsibility*: ensuring maximum involvement and participation of every group member in group activities and setting of objectives.

2 *Empowerment*: giving responsibility to group members, setting high but realistic goals, offering instruction but avoiding playing the role of the 'great man'. Keller and Dansereau (1995) have found that use of empowerment by leaders can both help them get the performance they want from subordinates and increase subordinates' satisfaction with their leadership.

3 *Aiding deliberation*: by playing an active part in the definition and solution of group problems, without dictating solutions.

In the aftermath of the Second World War it was hoped and believed that democratic or participative leadership was superior to autocratic. In fact, the evidence is that on the whole participation has only a small positive effect on performance and satisfaction of group members (Wagner, 1994). As Filley *et al.* (1976) observed, where the job to be done is clearly understood by subordinates, and within their competence, participation is not going to make much difference because there is little need for it. On the other hand, in many less straightforward situations, participation does aid group performance. We will return to that theme later in this chapter.

Key Learning Point

A democratic leader is active in group affairs: he or she does not just sit back and let the rest of the group sort everything out.

Transformational leadership and charisma

Much of the early research on leadership viewed the leader as a tactician, not as an inspirational figure. Yet successful real leaders in business and politics (not to mention fictional leaders in films and literature) are frequently portrayed as heroes and heroines. They unite and motivate their followers by offering shared visions and goals usually based on a better tomorrow. Leaders deemed to be non-charismatic (for example, former American president George Bush senior and former British prime minister John Major) are often seen as lacking what it takes, even though of course that did not prevent their rise to the top. Psychologists have therefore turned their attention to charisma and related concepts.

A currently influential approach to leadership makes a distinction between so called transactional and transformational leadership (Burns, 1978). Transactional leaders try to motivate subordinates by observing their performance, identifying the rewards they desire and distributing rewards for appropriate behaviour. They also play the leading role in defining work goals and the behaviour deemed appropriate for reaching them. The underlying idea is that transactional leadership is based on exchanges, or transactions, with subordinates. The leaders offer clarity and rewards, and in return subordinates contribute effort and skill.

Transformational leaders, on the other hand, go beyond the skilled use of inducements by developing, inspiring and challenging the intellects of followers in order to go beyond their self-interest in the service of a higher collective purpose, mission or vision. This is ambitious but realistic, and articulated clearly and in inspirational ways. Leaders encourage followers by setting a personal example (Bass, 1990, 1998). Followers feel motivated and emotionally attached to the leader. They are aware of the leader's vision and goals, and accept them. All this means that a leader can transform an organisation – hence the term 'transformational'. This notion of transformational leadership has captured the imagination of psychologists: according to Judge and Bono (2000), over half of the research papers on leadership published in psychological journals in the 1990s focused on transformational leadership.

Bass (1985) has developed a questionnaire called the Multifactor Leadership Questionnaire (MLQ) to assess the extent to which subordinates feel that their leader exhibits transformational and transactional leadership. Questions in the

MLQ assess four components of transformational leadership, two of transactional leadership and also a 'laissez-faire' (i.e. do nothing) approach to leadership. These are described in Table 13.1.

Key Learning Point

Transformational leadership is about inspiring and challenging subordinates and setting a personal example.

For the sake of conceptual clarity, it is helpful to distinguish between the components of transformational and transactional leadership described in Table 13.1. However, psychologists have investigated whether, in practice, the components are separable. It does seem as if leaders' MLQ scores on the four components of transformational leadership often go together very closely. For example, Den Hartog *et al.* (1997) found correlations of 0.61 to 0.75 between components of transformational leadership in ratings of their leaders made by a sample of about 700 people in eight Dutch organisations. Geyer and Steyrer (1998) also report very high corre-

Table 13.1   Components of transformational, transactional and laissez-faire leadership

The four components of transformational leadership

1 *Individualised consideration*: the leader treats each follower on his or her own merits, and seeks to develop followers through delegation of projects and coaching/mentoring

2 *Intellectual stimulation*: the leader encourages free thinking, and emphasises reasoning before any action is taken

3 *Inspirational motivation*: the leader creates an optimistic, clear and attainable vision of the future, thus encouraging others to raise their expectations

4 *Idealised influence,* or *charisma*: the leader makes personal sacrifices, takes responsibility for his or her actions, shares any glory and shows great determination

The two components of transactional leadership

1 *Contingent reward*: the leader provides rewards if, and only if, subordinates perform adequately and/or try hard enough

2 *Management by exception*: the leader does not seek to change the existing working methods of subordinates so long as performance goals are met. He or she intervenes only if something is wrong. This can be *active* where the leader monitors the situation to anticipate problems, or *passive* where the leader does nothing until a problem or mistake has actually occurred

Laissez-faire leadership
The leader avoids decision-making and supervisory responsibility, and is inactive. This may reflect a lack of skills and/or motivation, or a deliberate choice by the leader.

lations (0.69 to 0.75) in their sample of over 1400 employees in 20 Austrian banks who rated their supervisors (over 200 of them in total) on a German version of the MLQ. Higher again were the correlations recorded by Tracey and Hinkin (1998) – between 0.81 and 0.91 in their sample of about 300 hotel employees in the United States. What does this array of statistics mean? Simply that the components of transformational leadership tend to 'hang together' in perceptions of leader behaviour. It would be unusual for a leader to be (for example) high on two components and low on the other two.

Furthermore, one of the components of transactional leadership, contingent reward, also tends to go hand in hand with transformational leadership. In other words, transformational leaders also administer contingent rewards. In some studies it seems that they also tend to engage in active management by exception.

It has often been argued over the years that transactional and transformational leadership are not mutually exclusive (e.g. Bryman, 1992), and that leaders can demonstrate one or the other, both or neither. That is true, but more recent research studies suggest that both and neither are more common than one or the other. It is almost as if leaders vary simply in how active they are. The active ones engage (or are perceived by their followers to engage) in both transformational and some aspects of transactional behaviour, and the passive ones engage in neither. This conclusion is further supported by a tendency for passive management by exception (see Table 13.1) to be an aspect of a laissez-faire leadership style rather than of transactional leadership (Den Hartog *et al.*, 1997). Not surprisingly, the extent to which a leader is transformational seems to depend partly on his or her personality. For example, Judge and Bono (2000) found that transformational leaders tended to score higher than others on the personality traits extraversion, agreeableness and openness to experience. However, they concluded that the connections between personality and leadership style were not strong enough to consider transformational leadership a personality-based theory. It also concerns learned behaviour.

Key Learning Point

The four components of transformational leadership tend to go together in the behaviour of real leaders.

Other work has taken a closer look specifically at charismatic leadership (Conger and Kanungo, 1998). Charisma tends to be viewed by researchers as a perception of a leader held by followers as well as a characteristic of the leader him- or herself.

As Gardner and Avolio (1998) put it, perceptions of charisma do not always stem directly from the leader's behaviour. A leader is not charismatic unless described as such by his or her followers. Conger *et al.* (2000) collected data from about 250 managers which suggested five aspects of charismatic leadership:

1 The leader formulates a strategic vision, and articulates that vision.

2 The leader takes personal risks in pursuit of the vision.

3   The leader is sensitive to the opportunities and limitations provided by the environment (e.g. in terms of technology, money, people).

4   The leader is sensitive to others' needs.

5   The leader sometimes does unusual or unexpected things.

Although this is labelled charisma, it clearly has a wider meaning than the charisma component of transformational leadership (see Table 13.1). Sensitivity to others' needs looks similar to individualised consideration, and strategic vision resembles inspirational motivation. So Conger and Kanungo's model of charismatic leadership is really an alternative way of viewing transformational leadership, and it may be superior to Bass's in some ways. For example, the five components described above are much more distinguishable from each other than the four components of transformational leadership (Conger *et al.*, 2000). In other words, it seems to be quite possible for leaders to be perceived as exhibiting some aspects of charismatic leadership but not others. Although one might think that charisma is something a leader is (or is not) born with, Frese and Beimel (2003) report an interesting study which suggests that leaders can be trained to perform some of the behaviours associated with charisma.

Key Learning Point

The components of charisma as defined by Conger and Kanungo go beyond transformational leadership as defined by Bass.

Of course, there is great interest in whether transformational and/or charismatic leadership helps improve the work performance of individuals, groups and organisations, and if so how. Many people also want to know whether transformational leadership has a measurable impact on the satisfaction and other attitudes of followers. In other words, does transformational leadership 'work'? The simple answer seems to be yes. The extent to which leaders are perceived (by themselves, their subordinates or their supervisors) to use elements of transformational leadership is consistently positively correlated with perceptions of their effectiveness, satisfaction with their leadership, and effort exerted by their subordinates. It is also associated with performance measures such as percentage of group targets reached, and supervisory evaluations of workgroup performance (e.g. Hater and Bass, 1988; Bass and Avolio, 1994). There is also consistent evidence that the active management by exception element of transactional leadership is associated with positive workgroup performance and attitudes, albeit to a lesser extent than transformational leadership (Lowe *et al.*, 1996). Research by Conger *et al.* (2000) found that when followers perceive their leader as charismatic, they form more of a sense of group identity, empowerment and reverence (i.e. awe or extreme admiration) for the leader. House *et al.* (1991) even found that the perceived success of US presidents was associated with how charismatic they were thought to be.

The work by Geyer and Steyrer (1998) already mentioned is a particularly good piece of research on transformational leadership. As well as taking a careful look at the nature and measurement of transformational leadership, Geyer and Steyrer obtained objective measures of the performance of bank branches in Austria such as volumes of savings, loans and insurance products. They took into account the local market conditions for each branch – for example, the average income in the area. Staff in branches rated their branch manager on a German translation of the MLQ. What the researchers called Core Transformational Leadership (which mainly concerned intellectual stimulation, inspirational motivation and charisma) was a significant predictor of branch performance. So was contingent reward, though to a slightly lesser extent. Both core transformational leadership and contingent reward were strongly associated with the effort branch staff said they exerted. So was individualised consideration. Passive management by exception was associated with less effort and lower branch performance. In statistical terms the correlations between ratings of branch manager leadership styles and branch performance were not especially high (around 0.25) but with a large number of branches and high volume of business, a small effect of transformational leadership could mean a big impact on profitability.

Key Learning Point

Transformational and charismatic leadership are associated with good performance of workgroups and organisations.

The concepts of transformational and charismatic leadership clearly represent an important advance in our understanding of how leadership can be described and of how to be an effective leader. Even in the complex twenty-first century world (perhaps especially in the complex twenty-first century world) we need a leader we can believe in. However, the evangelical zeal of some leadership researchers, and their use of quasi-religious terms such as charismatic, inspirational and reverence, cannot disguise some limitations. Four seem particularly apparent.

First, writers such as Tourish and Pinnington (2002) argue that the notion of transformational leadership is moving too close to resembling cult leaders who are revered by their followers as people who can do no wrong, almost God-like. It also encourages authoritarianism. This is not helpful for democracy, nor for the development of mature and responsible adults. As we will see later in this chapter, Gemmill and Oakley (1992) had similar concerns. Second, transformational leadership glosses over the issue of whether the leader is forming and articulating an *appropriate* vision of the future. History tells us that some transformational leaders fail, or even cause terrible harm. In any case, followers may reject the leader's vision as being inappropriate. Third, until the very late 1990s there seems to have been an implicit assumption that the leader is the source of most of what happens. The reality may be that followers have as much impact on the leader as vice versa. Barker (1997) has complained that too much leadership research – especially on transformational leadership – ignores the fact that any workplace has conflict and competition. Leaders and followers do not necessarily have the same goals. Barker argues that the 'ship' in leadership has too often led to leadership being seen as a set of skills (as in craftsman*ship*) rather than a political phenomenon (as in relation*ship*). Fourth, researchers have speculated but so far scarcely investigated whether the type of situation in which leaders and followers find themselves affects the suitability of transformational leadership. This last observation leads nicely to our next section.

Key Learning Point

Transformational leadership construes the leader as a 'great person', and pays little attention to followers or the situation.

Exercise 13.1   Transactional and transformational leadership

Marc LeBlanc is manager of the claims department of a medical insurance company. He is rather unlike many of his colleagues, in that he dresses unconventionally and has long hair, which he ties into a pony tail. The department's job is to process claims by clients who have spent time in hospital. Marc considers himself scrupulously fair with his staff of 17 administrators and clerks. He thinks that if something (such as a training course) is good for one of them, then it is good for all. He has successfully resisted senior management's wish for performance-related pay, arguing that group solidarity will ensure that everyone pulls their weight. Marc thinks of his job as making sure that the members of the department know where it is going and why. In contrast to his predecessor, he never tires of telling his staff that their job is to 'play a proper part in the client's return to good health' rather than to contest every doubt, however tiny, about a client's claim. He has been known to invite claimants to the office when he thinks they are being treated badly by the company, and to force his bosses to see them. Marc has a noticeboard for displaying complimentary letters from clients grateful for prompt and trouble-free processing of their claims. He frequently emphasises the need to look at things from the client's point of view. He tells his staff to focus on certain key aspects of the long and complicated claim form, and only briefly inspect most of the rest of it. Marc checks whether they are doing this, but only when a complaint is received from a client or the company's own internal claims auditors. In such cases he defends his staff, provided they have conformed to the department's way of doing things. He is less sympathetic if they have taken decisions about claims on other criteria, even if those claims have some unusual features.

1   Marc LeBlanc scores high on just one aspect of transformational leadership. Which one?

2   He scores high on one aspect of transactional leadership. Which one?

3   In what respects, if any, might Marc's leadership be described as charismatic?

4   The performance of the claims department could be measured with more than one criterion. Think of one respect in which Marc's style enhances the department's performance, and one respect in which his style hinders performance.

Contingency theories of leadership

The above approaches to leader behaviour vary in their sophistication. They have all left their mark, and each contributes something to our understanding of what leaders actually do and what it is best for them to do. In their original forms they have an important feature in common. They all seek to describe leader behaviour without paying much attention to the situation. In essence, they are stating that in order to be effective, leaders need to perform certain behaviours and do so whatever the situation.

In fact, concepts such as consideration, structure, participation, and transactional and transformational leadership can all be used more flexibly. Indeed, some of them have been. The key idea is that some situations demand one kind of behaviour from leaders, while other situations require other behaviours. Do we really need a leader high on consideration and low on structure in an emergency such as a bomb scare? Probably not – we need someone who will quickly tell us where to go, and what to do. We can do without a leader who asks us, at that moment, how we feel about the bomb scare. On the other hand, if a leader is responsible for allocating already well-defined tasks to a group of junior managers, we might hope for some sensitive consideration of the managers' preferences, career development plans, etc.

This brings us to contingency theories; so called because they assume that optimal leader behaviour is contingent upon (i.e. depends upon) the situation. Contingency theories are necessarily fairly complex and they reflect very clearly the different elements of psychological theory described in Chapter 1. Their task is not easy. They have to specify not only which leader behaviours are crucial, but also which aspects of the situation matter most, and how leader and situation interact. Needless to say, there is plenty of room for disagreement about this. We will now take a look at the most influential and controversial contingency theories.

Key Learning Point

Contingency theories of leadership propose that different situations demand different leader behaviours.

Fiedler's contingency theory of leadership

Fred Fiedler put forward his contingency theory of leadership way back in the 1960s (Fiedler, 1967). He built his theory from data collected over the previous decade. Fiedler argued that leaders have fairly stable personal characteristics, which in turn lead to a characteristic style that they (and their subordinates) are stuck with. For Fiedler, the key personal characteristic concerns how positively the leader views his or her least preferred co-worker. He developed a questionnaire measure of this concept called LPC (which stands for least preferred co-worker). The measure consists of 16 dimensions, such as pleasant–unpleasant, boring–interesting and insincere–sincere. The leader describes his or her least preferred co-worker on these dimensions. A high LPC score signifies a positive view of the least preferred co-worker. A low LPC score indicates a negative opinion.

There is some dispute about exactly what a leader's LPC score means. It could be quite similar to consideration (high LPC) and structure (low LPC), though this assumes that consideration and structure are opposite ends of the same continuum rather than independent constructs. Indeed, high LPC leaders are often referred to as person-orientated – after all, they must be if they can be positive even about people they do not like! Low LPC leaders are often thought of as task-orientated. There is no doubt considerable overlap between LPC on the one hand and consideration and structure on the other. But Fiedler and others have argued that LPC also reflects the leader's deeper pattern of motivation. Some have suggested that LPC involves cognitive complexity. High LPC leaders are sometimes said to be more cognitively complex than low LPC leaders because they can differentiate between a person's inherent worth and his or her work performance.

Key Learning Point

In his original contingency theory Fiedler assumed that a leader's perception of his or her least preferred co-worker indicates how person-orientated the leader is.

Whatever LPC is, Fiedler argued that in some situations it is best to have a high LPC leader at the helm, while in others a low LPC leader is preferable. Specifically, Fiedler proposed three key aspects of the situation which together define its favourableness to the leader. In descending order of importance, these are:

■ leader–member relations: whether or not the subordinates trust and like their leader;

■ task structure: the extent to which the group's tasks, goals and performance are clearly defined;

■ position power: the extent to which the leader controls rewards and punishments for subordinates.

Fiedler concluded from his data that in highly and fairly favourable situations, and in very unfavourable ones, group performance was better if the leader had a low LPC score (i.e. was task-orientated). In situations of moderate to quite low favourability, high LPC scores were best (i.e. person-orientated). These predictions are summarised in Table 13.2. It is not altogether clear why this should be. One common-sense explanation is, however, plausible. Where the situation is good, the leader does not need to spend time on interpersonal relationships. Where the situation is bad, things are so difficult that it is not worth spending time on interpersonal relationships. In both cases, forging ahead with the task is best. But where the situation falls between the two extremes, keeping group members happy becomes more important. A leader needs high LPC to hold the group together so that its tasks can be tackled.

Fiedler's theory asserts that because leaders have a fairly stable LPC score, there is little point trying to train them to cope with different situations. They cannot change their style. Instead, he has argued (Fiedler and Chemers, 1984) that it is important to match leader to situation. Placement is more useful than training. So if you are a high LPC leader, you cannot expect to be placed in the most favourable leadership situations!

Key Learning Point

Fiedler proposed in this original contingency theory that task-orientated leaders are best in very favourable and unfavourable situations, and that people-orientated leaders are best in moderately favourable or moderately unfavourable situations.

Many problems with Fiedler's theory have been pointed out. Apart from the unclear nature of LPC, there is doubt about whether the LPC score is as stable as Fiedler assumes. Perhaps it depends too much on just how undesirable the leader's least preferred co-worker really is – that is, the LPC score may say more about the co-worker than the leader. Another issue concerns Fiedler's concept of the situation. For example, in the medium and long term, leader–member relations are perhaps a function of the leader and subordinates themselves. Is it therefore valid to treat leader–member relations as part of the situation?

Despite these doubts, it is clear that Fiedler was on to something. Peters *et al.* (1985) reported a thorough meta-analysis of tests of Fiedler's theory. They observed that the data on which the theory was originally based supported it very well. Hence the theory was appropriately constructed given the data then available. Subsequent research testing the theory gave it partial support. Laboratory-based studies produced results more consistent with the theory than field studies. Schriesheim *et al.* (1994) reviewed only the research studies which compared leader performance in different situations. They too found general support for Fiedler. Low LPC leaders did better in the two most favourable situations and the one least favourable one. High and low LPC leaders were about equal in the third most favourable situation. High LPC leaders did somewhat better in moderately favourable situations and much better in moderately unfavourable situations. The authors point out that if we assume that most leadership situations are moderately favourable, we can simply say that high LPC leaders are better, rather than going to the trouble of engineering situations to fit different leader styles.

Table 13.2	Predictions of Fiedler's contingency theory of leadership						

	Situation highly favourable I	II	III	IV	V	VI	VII	Situation highly unfavourable VIII
Leader–member relations	Good	Good	Good	Good	Poor	Poor	Poor	Poor
Task structure	Structured	Structured	Un-structured	Un-structured	Structured	Structured	Un-structured	Un-structured
Leader position power	Strong	Weak	Strong	Weak	Strong	Weak	Strong	Weak
Desirable leader LPC score	Low	Low	Low	High	High	High	High	Low

Cognitive resource theory

Fiedler himself has built on his earlier work (e.g. Fiedler and Garcia, 1987). His more recent cognitive resource theory (CRT) examines how the cognitive resources of leaders and subordinates affect group performance. As Fiedler (1995, p. 7) has put it: 'the relationship between cognitive resources and leadership performance is strongly dependent on such factors as the leader's situational control over the group's processes and outcomes, and the stressfulness of the leadership situation.' The reference to situational control demonstrates the links between CRT and Fiedler's earlier contingency theory, since situational control is presumably determined by leader–member relations, position power and task structure. The stressfulness of the situation is also partly tied up with this: less favourable situations are presumably more stressful. But Fiedler (1995) also sees stress as coming from the leader's own boss, if he or she is unsupportive, hostile or over-demanding.

Some of the key predictions of CRT are shown in Fig. 13.1. Fiedler argues that cognitive performance is inhibited in high-stress situations. That is, when leaders feel anxious or overloaded, they are unable to think clearly. In difficult situations they are likely to fall back on well-learned patterns of behaviour that result from their experience (Fiedler, 1996). Hence, in high-stress situations experience is a more important attribute of leaders than intelligence – indeed, high intelligence seems actually to be a small disadvantage.

Sternberg (1995) makes the point that experience is in fact a disguised measure of so-called crystallised intelligence; that is, our store of know-how and knowledge about the world. This contrasts with fluid intelligence, which is relatively context-free logic and problem-solving, and which is essentially what Fiedler is referring to when he uses the word intelligence. When a lot of our cognitive resources are being used in coping with a difficult situation, we use 'automatic' behaviour, which we can do without having to think. That behaviour is more likely to be appropriate if it is based on long experience.

Key Learning Point

Fiedler's cognitive resource theory introduces new factors about the leader and the situation. It proposes that, in difficult situations, leaders need to use their experience rather than their intelligence.

Not all psychologists are very convinced by CRT. Vecchio (1990, 1992) has argued that there is not much support for it, but Fiedler *et al.* (1992) claim that this is because it has not been tested properly. Fiedler (1995) reports a number of studies consistent with his predictions, and most of the commentators on his article (in the same issue of the journal *Applied Psychology: An International Review*) do not challenge them fundamentally.

Thus, Fiedler is now introducing more characteristics of the leader over and above LPC. As he points out, experience and intelligence are often key criteria in selecting leaders. His recent work suggests that the concept of matching leader to situation must be based on the leader's intelligence and experience as well as LPC and situational characteristics. Stress-reduction programmes are now thought to have a role in helping leaders to utilise their cognitive resources. But one important practical implication of Fiedler's work remains the same: try to determine the characteristics of the situation you are selecting a leader for, and thereby specify the characteristics you most desire in the leader.

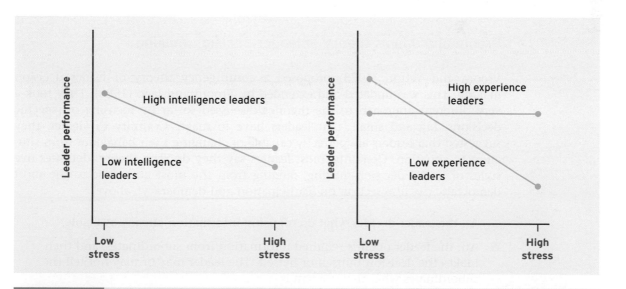

Figure 13.1   **Predictions of leader performance in Fiedler's cognitive resource theory**

Exercise 13.2   **Using Fiedler's theories of leadership**

For the last year, Debbie Walsh has been head of the ten staff of the market analysis department of a garden furniture company. The company sells its products through selected garden centres and do-it-yourself shops. The department's tasks are well established. For example, it monitors sales of each product at each outlet. It evaluates the viability of potential alternative outlets. It checks the products and prices of competitors. Debbie is a 'high-flyer' academically, having obtained a first-class honours degree and an MBA with Distinction. The managing director has great faith in her, and has given her complete discretion over awarding salary increases to her staff and most other aspects of people management in the marketing department. This is Debbie's first marketing job: most of her previous four years' work experience were spent in general management at a knitwear company. Other staff do not resent Debbie. They feel her appointment demonstrates the truth of the company's pledge to put ability ahead of experience in promotion decisions. They may in future benefit from that policy themselves, since most of them are young and well qualified.

Debbie takes a 'no-nonsense' approach to her work and colleagues. She responds well to businesslike people who come straight to the point. She has little patience with those who are slower to get to the heart of a problem, or who do not share her objectives. Most of her present staff have a similar approach to hers. But in one of Debbie's previous jobs her hostility toward several slow and awkward colleagues was a major factor in her decision to leave.

1   In Fiedler's terms, how favourable is Debbie Walsh's leadership situation?

2   Using Fiedler's contingency and cognitive resources theories, decide whether Debbie is well suited to her situation.

Vroom and Jago's theory of leader decision-making

Vroom and Yetton (1973) proposed a contingency theory of leader decision making. This was updated and extended by Vroom and Jago (1988). They took a very different approach to the theories discussed so far by focusing on specific decisions, big and small, that leaders have to make. Contrary to Fiedler, they suggested that leaders are perfectly capable of changing their behaviour from situation to situation. Certainly, most leaders say they do. The theory identifies five styles of leader decision-making, ranging from the most autocratic to the most democratic (*see also* section on 'Participation and democracy', above):

■   AI: the leader decides what do to, using information already available.

■   AII: the leader obtains required information from subordinates, and then makes the decision himself or herself. The leader may or may not tell the subordinates what the problem is.

■   CI: the leader shares the problem with each subordinate individually, and obtains their ideas. The leader then makes the decision.

- CII: the leader shares the problem with subordinates as a group, and obtains their ideas. The leader then makes the decision.

- GII: the leader shares the problem with subordinates as a group. They discuss options together and try to reach collective agreement. The leader accepts the decision most supported by the group as a whole.

Vroom and Jago (1988) also identified some key features of problem situations that leaders should consider. Taken together, these features indicate the style a leader should adopt in that particular situation. The situational features are shown in Fig. 13.2.

Also, Vroom and Jago (1988) argued that two further factors are relevant if the situational factors shown in Fig. 13.2 allow more than one recommended style. These are the importance to the leader of (i) minimising decision time and (ii) maximising opportunities for subordinate development. Computer software has been developed that allows a leader to input his or her answers to the questions listed above. It then calculates an overall 'suitability score' for each possible style. The formulae used are too complex to examine here, but some general rules of thumb governing use of the leader styles in the Vroom and Jago model include the following:

- where subordinates' commitment is important, more participative styles are better;

- where the leader needs more information, AI should be avoided;

- where subordinates do not share organisational goals, GII should be avoided;

- where both problem structure and leader information are low, CII and GII tend to be best.

Key Learning Point

Vroom and Jago assume that leaders are able to alter their style to fit the decision-making situation they are in. The nature of the situation is determined by many factors, including time pressure, clarity of the decision parameters, and attitudes of subordinates.

There is some evidence that the skill with which the leader puts his or her style into action is at least as important as choosing a style deemed appropriate in the first place (Tjosvold *et al.*, 1986). The Vroom and Jago model has still not been examined much in published literature, and does not figure very prominently in most reviews of leadership. Nevertheless it was based on 15 years of research and development by its originator and on an earlier version of the model, so it should have considerable value. On the other hand, its complexity makes it difficult for leaders to use quickly and easily, even with computer support. It is also possible that a leader's answers to the questions posed by the Vroom and Jago model (e.g. whether subordinates share organisational values) say as much about the leader's personality and ways of viewing the world as about the true situation. Vroom and

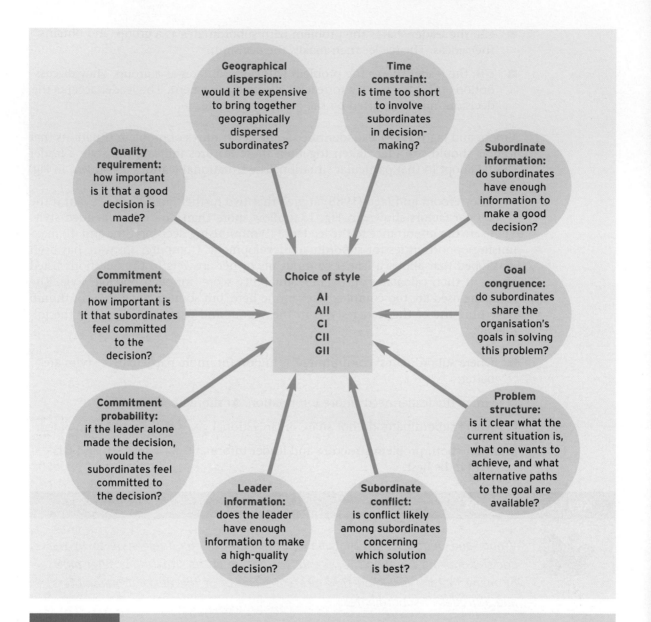

| Figure 13.2 | Vroom and Jago's features of leadership situations |

Jago (1988) nevertheless expressed the hope that knowledge of general principles, including those presented here, will often be sufficient.

Other contingency approaches: is a leader really necessary?

In their situational leadership theory (SLT), Hersey and Blanchard (1982) proposed that leader effectiveness depends on the interplay between leader style and follower maturity. They considered two leader styles: relationship orientation and task orientation. These are more or less equivalent to consideration and structure, respectively. Follower maturity refers to the subordinates' understanding of the job and their commitment to it, but length of time in the job is often used to measure it in research.

Vecchio explained the theory as follows (1987, p. 444):

> During the early stages of an employee's tenure, a low level of relationship orientation coupled with high task orientation is considered to be ideal. As an employee (or group of employees) gains in maturity, the need for supervisory social-emotional support increases, while the need for structuring declines. At the highest levels of employee maturity, supervisory task and social behaviours become superfluous to effective employee performance.

In other words, employees first need to be introduced to their tasks. Then as they are coping with tasks they need sympathetic help and advice. After that they should have come to grips with both task and social relationships, and are best left to get on with it. If we consider follower maturity as part of the situation, we can see that SLT is very similar to Fiedler's contingency theory.

Vecchio (1987) declared that SLT is much used by managers but rarely tested. He found that among 303 teachers in America, the theory's predictions were fairly accurate for subordinates with low maturity, reasonably accurate for those with moderate maturity, and not at all accurate for those with high maturity. His measure of maturity was school principals' ratings of teachers' task-relevant and psychological maturity.

Perhaps the crucial message of Vecchio's results is that even when subordinates are mature, it is not a good idea for their leader to neglect both task and relationships. This echoes the finding from research on transformational leadership described earlier that laissez-faire leader style is unlikely to be effective. This rather argues against an extension of SLT principles proposed by Kerr and Jermier (1978). They developed the idea that in some circumstances leaders are unnecessary. Their approach has been termed substitutes for leadership, though it also includes the notion that some factors can neutralise the impact of leadership (as opposed to substitutes, which do the leadership job for the leader). Examples of proposed substitutes for leadership are: intrinsically interesting tasks; ability, experience, training and knowledge of subordinates; and availability of senior staff other than subordinates' own leader.

Consistent with Vecchio (1987), research has tended to find that the presence of substitutes for leadership does not eliminate effects of leadership style on subordinate satisfaction and performance. This may be partly because measures of substitutes for leadership are not very good (Williams *et al.*, 1988). However, it is hard to escape the conclusion that leadership does matter. The apparent lack of efficacy of substitutes for leadership suggests either that leadership tasks cannot easily be distributed around a group, or that we have an in-built psychological need for a leader. We now turn to further consideration of that latter possibility.

Perceiving leadership

In recent years, increasing attention has been paid to how and when we perceive leadership to be important. A related issue is how we identify someone as leader. As we will see in a moment, some authors have explicitly tackled these questions, using ideas from the social psychology of person perception (Meindl, 1992). More subtly, other analyses of leadership, including some covered in this chapter, also recognise that leadership is at least partly in the eye of the beholders – for example, see the earlier coverage of charismatic leadership.

However, Meindl and colleagues (e.g. Meindl, 1995) are inclined to go further. They argue that perceptions of leadership are entirely constructed by followers and observers – and these have little to do with the specific behaviour of their leader. In an article appropriately entitled 'The romance of leadership', Meindl *et al.* (1985, p. 79) argued that:

> we may have developed highly romanticised, heroic views of leadership – what leaders do, what they are able to accomplish, and the general effects they have on our lives. One of the principal elements in this romanticised conception is the view that leadership is ... the premier force in the scheme of organisational processes and activities.

Meindl *et al.* (1985) further argued that our conception of leadership as important and influential should lead us to consider leadership a key factor where performance is either very good or very bad. When things go really well, we attribute it to the leader's skill. When things go really badly, we blame the leader's ineptitude. But when things go averagely well, we are unlikely to say it was primarily due to average leadership. This is because we see leadership as a big concept which has big effects, not moderate ones.

Meindl *et al.* (1985) produced support for their point of view in a number of interesting ways. First, they searched the *Wall Street Journal* (WSJ) between 1972 and 1982 for articles about 34 firms representing a range of American industries. They then related the proportion of WSJ articles about each company which mentioned the leadership of top management to the company's performance. Sure enough, they found that a higher proportion of 'leadership' articles appeared when firms were doing especially well or especially badly – particularly the former. Second, they surveyed dissertations by postgraduate students and related that to overall American economic performance. Increasing numbers of dissertations about leadership were associated with downturns in the US economy two to four years earlier (it usually takes two to four years to produce a dissertation). Third, they conducted a similar analysis with business journals, where the articles generally take less time to produce than dissertations. In this case upturns in the US economy were associated with increasing numbers of articles about leadership. Perhaps academics want to understand what goes wrong whereas business people want to understand (and presumably copy) what goes right.

Finally, Meindl *et al.* (1985) conducted a series of laboratory experiments where case studies of corporate success and failure were presented, and students were asked to rate the importance of various possible causes, including leadership. Again, leadership was seen as a more important cause of extreme (especially good) performance than of medium performance. Alternative causes were generally seen as less important than leadership, and at a fairly constant level of importance across the range of performance outcomes. Pillai and Meindl (1991) expanded on this by finding that the charisma of the Chief Executive Officer in a hypothetical case study of a fast food company was indeed rated very high if the case described a crisis followed by success for the company, and very low if the crisis was followed by decline.

Gemmill and Oakley (1992) have argued that leadership is indeed a culturally defined concept, which has no objective existence. We use it to protect ourselves from anxiety brought about by uncertainty concerning what we should do ('no need to worry, the leader will decide'), and from various uncomfortable emotions and wishes that arise when people try to work together. One cost of using the concept of leadership to organise our social world is *alienation* – that is, feeling distant from our true self and devoid of authentic relationships with others. Because we give too much responsibility to people we label leaders, we find it difficult to lead purposeful lives, or to view ourselves as purposeful, self-managing individuals. This radical view of leadership draws partly on psychoanalytic theory (*see* Chapter 1). It challenges both 'common-sense' and academic theories of leadership. Most people working in organisations would probably find it difficult to agree that leadership is illusory, or that it is a harmful concept. Yet Gemmill and Oakley do convincingly make the point that as individuals we may try to transfer tasks to leaders that it would be better to do ourselves. This brings us back to a point made by Gastil (1994): democratic leaders may have to insist that their subordinates take a share of the responsibility.

All of this seems like very good evidence for a 'romanticised' view of leadership, where we grossly overestimate its importance. Meindl has argued that current interest in charisma and transformational leadership shows even more clearly just how romanticised it is. But this is not necessarily true. Meindl *et al.* (1985) did not demonstrate that we are wrong to make these attributions about leadership, only that we do make them. Others, such as Yukl (1998), argue forcefully that the quality of leadership really does make a difference to outcomes that matter in the real world.

Key Learning Point

Leadership is partly in the eye of the beholder. We may be inclined to overestimate the impact of leaders, particularly when performance is very good or very bad.

Global leadership

The globalisation of markets brought about by communications technology and the mobility of production resources mean that more and more people work in countries and cultures that are novel to them. For many managers, this means leading people of different backgrounds and outlooks to their own. There has been much recent interest in identifying the cultural dimensions along which countries can differ. The work which started it all was carried out by Hofstede (1980, 2001), who collected data from employees of IBM across many countries. He identified four cultural dimensions:

- *Power distance:* the extent to which members of a society accept that there should be an unequal distribution of power between its members.

- *Uncertainty avoidance:* the extent to which members of a society wish to have a predictable environment, and have set up institutions and systems designed to achieve this.

- *Masculinity* vs *femininity:* a masculine society values assertion, success and achievement, while a feminine one is orientated more towards nurturing and caring.

- *Individualism* vs *collectivism:* the former reflects a belief that individuals should be self-sufficient while the latter emphasises people's belongingness to groups in which there is mutual support.

It would be strange if there were not differences between countries with respect to the most used and most effective leadership styles. Using Hofstede's cultural dimensions we might expect autocratic styles to be more effective in high power distance cultures than in low ones. Leaders whose style is high on structure will probably be more appreciated in high uncertainty-avoidance cultures than others. Dickson *et al.* (2003) provide a very informative review of research on cross-cultural leadership. They discuss in detail some of the reasons why the dimensions of culture identified by Hofstede and others might affect which styles of leadership are expected and effective. They also argue that the search for leadership styles that work across the whole world is (or should be) over, and instead more attention is being paid to exactly how culture and leadership affect each other.

There is also the general issue of whether leader behaviour is interpreted differently in different cultures and countries. Some research (Smith *et al.*, 1989; Peterson *et al.*, 1993) sought to discover whether leader styles are described using the same dimensions across different cultures. Using data from electronics firms in the United Kingdom, the United States, Japan and Hong Kong, Smith *et al.* (1989) concluded that what they call maintenance and performance leadership styles (approximately equivalent to the consideration and structure dimensions described earlier in this chapter) do indeed exist in different cultures. However, they also stated that 'the specific behaviours associated with those styles differ markedly, in ways which are comprehensible within the cultural norms of each setting' (p. 97). For example, one of the questions asked by Smith *et al.* was: 'When your superior learns that a member is experiencing personal difficulties, does your superior discuss the matter in the person's absence with other members?' In Hong Kong and Japan, this behaviour is seen as highly characteristic of maintenance (consideration). In the United Kingdom and the United States it is not – probably most Western subordinates would regard this as 'talking about me behind my back'. Not that all other British and American perceptions were identical: as Smith *et al.* (1989) noted, in the United Kingdom, consideration can be expressed by talking about the task, but this is not so in the United States.

Political changes in some countries, for example in Eastern Europe, also have implications for the way managers are expected to lead. Maczynski (1997) has shown that Polish leaders' preferred problem-solving styles shifted towards more participation between 1988 and 1994, during which time communism was toppled. Smith *et al.* (1997) found some differences even between neighbouring Eastern European countries. Managers in the Czech Republic and Hungary tended to report that they made great use of their own experiences and those of others around them. This is an individualistic style consistent with those countries' long-standing links with Western Europe, and contrasted with Romanian and Bulgarian managers' self-reported reliance on widespread beliefs held in their country to guide their behaviour.

Some more recent work offers further insights into leadership across Europe. Brodbeck *et al.* (2000) have reported a very large study of perceptions of what makes a good leader at work amongst managers in the food, finance and telecommunication industries in 22 European and ex-Soviet countries. This is part of a worldwide research effort called the GLOBE project. Brodbeck and colleagues asked managers to indicate the extent to which 112 words (such as foresight, honest, logical, dynamic, bossy) were characteristic of outstanding leaders. The 112 words were grouped into 21 scales, which were given names such as Visionary, Diplomatic, Administrative and Conflict inducer. The researchers then searched their data for consistent patterns both within and between countries. There were some substantial similarities across all countries regarding perceptions of good leadership. For example, Integrity and Inspirational were almost universally seen as highly desirable leader characteristics, and Face-saver and Self-centred as highly undesirable. But there were also some differences. To a large extent these replicated other work (Ronen and Shenkar, 1985) suggesting the European cultural groupings and characteristics shown in Table 13.3. France did not clearly fit into any of the groupings.

It is clear that some of the differences between clusters are quite small. Nevertheless, it is notable that, for example, the Anglo cluster is the only one to have Performance at the top of the list, whereas Performance is not even in the top 5 for the Central and Near East clusters. Integrator is more important in South and East Europe (i.e. clusters 4, 5 and 6) than in North and West Europe. Although not shown in Table 13.3, it is also the case that Status consciousness was seen as slightly unhelpful to good leadership in North and West Europe but slightly helpful in the south and east.

Further data from the GLOBE project have been reported by Abdalla and Al-Homoud (2001). The five most highly valued leadership characteristics in both Qatar and Kuwait were Integrity, Administratively competent, Diplomatic, Visionary and Inspirational (however, the ordering of these five differed somewhat between the two countries). The second and third of these also appeared in the top five for the Central Europe cluster but none of the other European clusters.

Table 13.3	Cultural groupings in Europe	
Grouping	**Countries**	**Five most valued leadership attributes (most important first)**
1. Anglo	UK, Ireland	Performance, Inspirational, Visionary, Team Integrator, Integrity
2. Nordic	Sweden, Netherlands, Finland, Denmark	Integrity, Inspirational, Visionary, Team Integrator, Performance
3. Germanic	Switzerland, Germany, Austria	Integrity, Inspirational, Performance, Non-Autocratic, Visionary
4. Latin	Italy, Spain, Portugal, Hungary	Team Integrator, Performance, Inspirational, Integrity, Visonary
5. Central	Poland, Slovenia	Team Integrator, Visionary, Administratively competent, Diplomatic, Decisive
6. Near East	Turkey, Greece	Team Integrator, Decisive, Visionary, Integrity, Inspirational

Source: Adapted from Brodbeck *et al.* (2000)

Although not in the top five, Status consciousness was seen as positive in Qatar and Kuwait, to a greater extent than in Europe.

These insights are very important as work organisations become increasingly international. Assuming that leaders can identify which style they wish to adopt, they need to make sure they behave in ways which are interpreted as consistent with that style. Those behaviours differ somewhat between countries and cultures. The very fact that people are willing to try to describe leaders in terms of personal characteristics supports the attributional view that we carry around in our heads conceptions of what leaders are like. It also suggests that we believe we know what a good leader is like, regardless of the situation. Nevertheless, historically the situations faced by countries may well have influenced cultural norms about what constitutes good leadership.

Key Learning Point

Both long-standing cultural differences and major social and political change can influence actual leader behaviour and the behaviour desired by subordinates.

Summary

This chapter has explored many approaches to leadership. Consideration, structure, charisma, cognitive complexity/intelligence, and participativeness have been identified as some key leader characteristics and behaviours. Other less complex notions such as the extent of the leader's knowledge of the industry and organisation must not be overlooked. There is considerable overlap between the various leadership concepts, and some tidying up and increased precision is needed. The same is true of the various situational variables proposed by contingency theorists. For example, take another look at the Vroom and Jago decision questions (Fig. 13.2). At least two relate closely to Fiedler's notions of leader–member relations and task structure. The theories are in some respects more similar than they might seem. It is therefore not surprising that several of them are equally (and moderately) good at explaining leadership phenomena. Several approaches, especially that of Vroom and Jago, and transformational leadership, contain useful practical guidance about how to go about being a leader. Future theory and practice in leadership need to combine concepts from the better theories in a systematic way. There is also increasing recognition that leadership is not only about leaders. It also concerns followers, relationships between leaders and followers, and cultural and individual perceptions of what leaders should be. Greater attention must also be paid to whether and how leaders can be trained or selected not only to do the desirable things, but to do them well.

Exercise 13.3   Leadership and policy implementation

It was a turbulent time in the health and safety department of Super Chem's Hamburg plant. The multinational chemical company had recently adopted a policy of developing managers by giving them international experience. A consequence of this policy had been that a 32-year-old Spaniard, José Alonso, had been put in charge of the department. José's German was more than adequate for the task, but this was his first assignment outside Spain, a country seen by many in the company as ▶

peripheral to its operations. He had much to learn when he first arrived, especially about German health and safety legislation. He was, however, an experienced health and safety manager, having been head of health and safety at two plants in Spain for two years each.

Almost as soon as he arrived, José was pitched into an interesting situation. Two major accidents at other plants had caused a high-level health and safety policy review. The resulting report had come out in favour of more stringent inspection and a tougher approach from company health and safety departments. The recommendations were clear and specific, and had quickly become company policy.

José knew that his presence was resented by his six staff, who had worked together for some time and tended to think alike. They felt they had more specialist knowledge than he did. Most were older than him, and they could not understand why the deputy head, Gunter Koenig, had not been promoted. Koenig himself was understandably especially bitter. José felt that he could not follow his staff around as they inspected the plant: it would look too much like snooping. On the other hand, he needed to tap into his staff's knowledge of the plant and of how things had always been done there. Existing documents were too incomplete or too out of date to be of much help.

José had reason to believe that his staff typically adopted a collaborative approach with the plant managers whose areas they inspected. They preferred to use friendly persuasion and gentle hints rather than the precise written reports and threats for non-compliance required by the new policy. It had always worked at that plant, they said, and it would continue to do so. Yet José knew that exactly the same had been said at the plants where major accidents occurred. What was worse for José, it was fairly clear that the plant manager privately agreed with José's staff. José's position was all the more difficult because he was known to be on a two-year secondment, after which the previous head (who had herself been seconded elsewhere) was expected to return in his place. Therefore he was not in a position to exert a long-term influence on the careers of his staff. His inclination would have been to intervene in his subordinates' work only when something was clearly wrong, but the new policy did not permit that approach. José himself was answerable not only to the plant manager but also to the company health and safety chief, who was the chief proponent of the new policy.

José knew that he was not a particularly creative or imaginative individual. He enjoyed the precision and rules and regulations of health and safety work. He preferred to focus on implementing the detail of policies rather than the big picture. He was usually inclined to draw up detailed plans of work for himself and others, and to keep a careful check on implementation of those plans. He liked to formulate work plans in a collaborative manner, encouraging his subordinates to think for themselves about what was required and how best to go about it. He felt he could understand how his staff felt about his appointment as their head without their consent: he had been landed with an unwelcome boss himself a few years earlier. He did not blame them for their attitude, and, characteristically, he was always keen to emphasise what he genuinely saw as the many strengths of his subordinates. He took time to discuss their work with each of them individually and tried to assign them work that would broaden their skills.

Despite the complicated situation, José felt that his task was clear enough. A decision had to be made concerning exactly how the department's practices would need to change in order to implement the new health and safety policy. Also, it had to be made in time for a visit by the health and safety chief six weeks later.

1   Analyse this case study using Fiedler's theories. What kind of situation is it? How well suited to it is José Alonso? What should he do next? What important features of this case study, if any, are neglected by Fiedler's ideas?

2   Analyse this case study using the Vroom and Jago theory. What kind of situation is it? What should José Alonso do next? What important features of this case study, if any, are neglected by Vroom and Jago?

3   In what respects, if any, can Jose's leadership style be described as (i) transformational and (ii) transactional? What scope is there for him to change, and would it make any difference if he did?

4   In what respects are national and cultural differences in perceptions of leadership relevant to this case study?

Closing Case Study   Lion King and the Politics of Pain

Junichiro Koizumi is the most popular prime minister in Japan's history and he is turning on its head the country's staid political world. For most of the past half-century, the country's politics have been predictable and dull, with barely a change of government, let alone the earth-shaking of the past few months. Until Koizumi took power in April 2001, the possibility of the country producing an iconic statesman capable of inspiring both hope and fear was unimaginable.

When Koizumi appears in parliamentary debates, millions tune in to watch live broadcasts. When he handed out a trophy at a recent sumo tournament, he stole the show, and the following day's headlines, from the sumo champion. The prime minister is a fashion leader, too. His Armani suits and permed 'Lion King' hairstyle are the talk of afternoon TV gossip shows. Fans are so desperate for a piece of 'Jun'chan', as he is nicknamed, that schoolgirls are queuing up at his party head-quarters to buy mobile phone straps decorated with little Koizumi dolls. Off-duty salarymen wear T-shirts printed with their hero's chiselled profile drawn in the style of the famous Che Guevara poster, with the message: 'It's not just my challenge, it's our challenge.' Housewives subscribe to his personal webzine, Lionheart, where he shares insights into his family life. Depicted as a cartoon cuddly, big-hearted lion, Koizumi confides that high office feels 'like being trapped in a cage'. Among Tokyo's Asian neighbours, however, his unapologetic nationalism and mass appeal ignite fears that he may become a Japanese Hitler, a dictator who will lead the country back down the path of militarism.   ▶

Last month, Koizumi's approval ratings hit a staggering 90%. Almost entirely as a result of his personal popularity, the ruling Liberal Democratic Party, which looked dead and buried at the start of the year, won a convincing victory in the upper house election. And his means of achieving such pre-eminence defy conventional political logic: Koizumi has wooed his party and the public with the bleakest of messages. Ask any Japanese citizen what words they most associate with the prime minister, and the answer will almost certainly be 'pain, pain and more pain'. Koizumi says he is willing to accept two years of recession, unemployment and bankruptcy as the price for restructuring an economy that has been described by former prime minister Yasuhiro Nakasone as 'the sick man of Asia'.

It all looked very different in 1989, when Tokyo was the envy of the world. From the ruins of the second world war, the 'Japanese miracle' had transformed this nation of 126 million, small geographically, into the richest country on the planet. People worked hard, but in return they had the smallest gap between rich and poor in the world, the safest streets and the longest average lifespan.

Since 1989, shares on the Tokyo stock exchange have lost three-quarters of their value and land prices have more than halved. Economic growth – the *raison d'être* of postwar Japan – has virtually ground to a halt. Two years of falling prices have left the country on the edge of a deflationary spiral not seen in an industrialised nation since the great depression of the 1930s. The government has already pushed most of the emergency levers, to little effect. Even a 'money-for-nothing' policy of zero interest rates put in place by the Bank of Japan has failed to find takers.

All this would be a nightmare in any country, but it hurts more in Japan because the entire social system is built on the assumption of growth and the principle of deferred reward: men put up with low pay, long hours and short holidays; in return, they are guaranteed a job for life, steady promotion and a generous allowance when they retire. Women carry the burden in the home in return for a share of the security provided for their husbands. But with a prolonged economic contraction, this unwritten contract has been broken. Faced by the trauma of restructuring, so many middle-aged salarymen are committing suicide that the average male lifespan has actually gone down.

The prime minister's family background and political record raise many questions about his claim to be a daring reformer who will shake up the country's semi-feudal political system. Like almost a third of Japanese MPs, Koizumi is a political aristocrat who inherited his father's constituency, support group and factional allegiances. He won the family seat in 1972 and has been re-elected 10 times, pushing him higher and higher up the LDP hierarchy. He has been consistently ambitious – running twice for the party leadership before this year's victory.

'He is a very unusual Japanese leader because he has a broad vision of society and culture, rather than a deep understanding of particular issues of industries', observed the governor of Okinawa, Kenichi Inamine. 'He's a weirdo', said LDP lawmaker Tanaka, before she became foreign minister and declared herself

Koizumi's 'political wife'. In office, Koizumi has already shaken the old hierarchy with the formation of a cabinet that, for once, does not merely reflect the old Confucian bias towards geriatric male timeservers. In terms of sex, age and background, Koizumi has picked the most diverse administration in the country's history. Many in the cabinet stress their loyalty to the premier ahead of the party. 'I'm not doing this for LDP, I'm doing it for Koizumi', says Tanaka. For the public, this is thrilling stuff. For the first time, politics is being played out in the open rather than in smoke-filled rooms. There is a clear diversity of opinion in the cabinet and public debate about key issues. It is chaotic, exciting and not a little frightening.

It is more for his promise of economic reform than for his nationalism that the public love Koizumi. But, at times, they are disturbingly protective of their would-be saviour. Opposition politicians who dare criticise the prime minister are bombarded with hate mail. The two parties that launched the most vociferous opposition to the government's policies were almost wiped out in the last election. 'It frightens me that parties who criticise Koizumi or Tanaka during parliamentary debates receive death threats', says Kyosen Ohashi, an opposition lawmaker. 'LDP candidates think they can get elected just by posing for a campaign poster with Mr Koizumi. It is so far away from democracy that it worries me.'

Source: The Guardian, *August 2001.*

Suggested questions

1   To what extent and in what ways can Koizumi be considered a successful leader?

2   Which leadership characteristics are most evident in this article?

3   What aspects of the situation and the followers (i.e. the Japanese population) might have contributed to perceptions of Koizumi's leadership?

Test your learning

Short-answer questions

1 Describe the strengths and weaknesses of alternative measures of leader effectiveness.

2 What are the major pressures facing corporate leaders in the early twenty-first century?

3 Briefly, what factors other than the leader's personality traits influence his or her effectiveness?

4 Define consideration and structure.

5 Describe the key features of democratic leadership.

6 Name and define four aspects of transformational leadership and two aspects of transactional leadership.

7 Briefly describe three possible weaknesses or limitations of the notion of transformational leadership.

8 Outline the main features of Fiedler's contingency theory. Suggest two strengths and two weaknesses of the theory.

9 Outline the main features of Fiedler's cognitive resource theory.

10 List the leadership styles and problem-situation features identified in Vroom and Jago's theory of leadership.

11 List the main cultural groupings of European countries in terms of perceptions of leadership.

Suggested assignments

1 Discuss the proposition that all of the aspects of leadership style identified in research essentially amount to person-orientation and task-orientation.

2 Examine the extent to which different contingency theories of leadership share the same key ideas.

3 Examine the implications for leadership of research which views leadership as a socially constructed phenomenon.

4 Discuss how and why leaders need to adjust their behaviour to different cultures.

5 Do theories of leadership concentrate too much on the leader as an individual?

6 Discuss the proposition that theories of leadership pay too much attention to specific aspects of the leader's behaviour, and not enough to his or her overall strategy.

Relevant websites

In the UK, the Council for Excellence in Management and Leadership has been working since 2000 to promote good practice – as indicated by its strap-line of 'Managers and Leaders: Raising our Game'. Its web address is http://www.managementandleadershipcouncil.org/. You can find quite a lot of useful information there, including reports prepared for the Council.

The Executive Speaker Internet Library contains several thousand speeches by leading executives over many years. Not surprisingly, leadership is a favourite topic. Most speeches are available by subscription only, but an exception can be found at http://www.executive-speaker.com/spch0024.html. This gives some good insights into how people at the 'sharp end' might see the task of leadership.

A good example of how some consultancy companies promote leadership training can be found at http://www.ldl.co.uk/inspirational-leadership-management-training-course.htm. This shows the close connections between leadership and motivation, as well as the current concern with leaders who are inspirational.

One of the most influential and long-standing organisations promoting leadership research and practice is the Center for Creative Leadership, which is based in the USA but also has substantial operations in Europe (Brussels) and Asia (Singapore). Its home page is http://www.ccl.org/CCLCommerce/index.aspx?CatalogID=Home. There is a lot there to illustrate how ideas from theory and research are applied in management development.

For further self-test material and relevant, annotated weblinks please visit the website at http://www.booksites.net/arnold_workpsych.

Suggested further reading

1   *Business Leadership* by Viv Shackleton, published by Routledge in 1995, is a readable overview of leadership theory and practices which expands on many of the themes of this chapter.

2   Keith Grint's edited book published in 1997 entitled *Leadership: Classical, contemporary and critical approaches* provides a scholarly and quite detailed analysis of a variety of leadership theories (full details are in the reference list at the end of the book).

3   Gary Yukl has produced a thorough text called *Leadership in Organizations*. The fifth edition was published in 2001 by Prentice Hall.

CHAPTER 14

Careers and career management

After studying this chapter, you should be able to:

1 define career and list three significant features of that definition;

2 list six ways in which careers are changing;

3 name and describe the career anchors identified by Ed Schein;

4 define the psychological contract and briefly explain its significance;

5 name and define Holland's six vocational personality types, and draw a diagram to show their relationship to each other;

6 identify the conclusions that can be drawn from research on Holland's theory;

7 describe three styles of career decision-making;

8 name, describe and compare the stages in two developmental theories;

9 name and describe the stages of the transition cycle;

10 describe the psychological processes associated with each stage of the transition cycle;

11 name and briefly describe at least ten career management interventions that can be used in organisations;

12 explain the circumstances in which career management interventions are most likely to be successful.

Careers in Changing Times

Phil Schneidermeyer is a 'chief talent scout' but his clients are not footballers or Hollywood hopefuls. He is one of a small but growing number of agents who manage the careers of high-flyers in the corporate world.

The uncertain economic climate, with waves of job cuts being announced each week, may seem the obvious time for employees to make contingency plans. But career management has been growing during economic boom as well. The ill-fated leaps that many made to new jobs during the dotcom frenzy highlight the need for careful planning at all times.

'Executives are being a lot more proactive about their careers,' says Shannon Kelley, marketing director of the Association of Executive Search Consultants in New York. 'I think it's a mindset that's developing, independent of the economic cycle. People know companies won't necessarily be loyal and they also want a varied career, not necessarily within the same company.'

Personal career agents target an exclusive clientele. The website of STI, a Californian executive management firm, boasts that it will 'define your personal brand vision' using consultants such as Richard Greene, presentation coach to the late Diana, Princess of Wales. But the emergence of such agents reflects a wider trend for professionals and managers to take control of their careers.

What has caused this shift? The cuts that signalled the end of 'jobs for life' were not forgotten as the last recession gave way to economic growth. Nor did they end there. Redundancies continued throughout the upswing as companies merged, restructured and shed staff to meet changing needs. Not surprisingly, it became more acceptable for employees to move to a rival company or to start their own business.

The corporate response to these changes has been to sponsor career development and coaching for employees, particularly the most prized. In-house programmes have been the fastest-growing form of executive education in the past decade. But in-house career development programmes are limited in that they tend to assume employees will stay put. Who helps those who want to move on? In the past few years, most of the big executive search firms have launched online career management services aimed at individual candidates.

People who have been wedded to a single career might find the idea of breaking out on their own a little daunting. A new type of counselling agency, focusing on individual potential rather than labour market need, is emerging in response. One example is New Directions, a Boston-based outplacement company which has set up a 'portfolio programme' for senior people who want a change from a traditional career. The mix of options on offer ranges from business and entrepreneurship to education, charitable work, 'spiritual' work, and leisure time, says Bill Reading, vice-president of marketing and sales. 'We find out what their personal interests are. We don't have an endgame when we start.' This is a service for older, well-heeled clients or for people whose companies are paying because they are being made redundant or taking early retirement: fees range from 8,000 to 35,000 dollars.

The fees charged by Careers by Design, a London-based agency, are more modest at 650 to 1,500 pounds sterling, and clients vary widely in age and background. Many are highly successful but feel something is missing in their lives, says Elizabeth Klyne, who founded the agency three-and-a-half years ago. 'There's an increasing unwillingness for people to sacrifice their whole life for the sake of their careers,' she says. Her programmes aim to discover what each person has to offer – their 'unique contribution' – and what changes are needed to make this contribution a central part of their working lives.

One former client is Phyllis Santa Maria, a 57 year old consultant in electronic learning, who explains what this new approach to career development means to her. 'So often we live our lives in a big rush and just don't stop and listen,' she says. 'The question is not what am I doing in my career, but what am I doing in my life?'

Source: Financial Times, *30 April 2001*

Introduction

This case study nicely illustrates a number of important themes in careers. Increasingly volatile labour markets mean that people are more inclined than they once were to take control of their own careers, to seek advice and support throughout their working life (not just at the start), and to view a career as part of life as a whole rather than as a separate compartment. The case study also shows that some employing organisations make attempts to manage the careers of some of their employees.

A distinction is often made between people who have careers and people who have jobs. Those with careers tend to be better educated, more highly paid, and with better promotion prospects than those with jobs. However, this distinction between so-called careers and so-called jobs was never very helpful, and has become even less so. It can be argued that everyone has a career, but that those careers differ a great deal from each other.

In this chapter we examine alternative definitions of career, and also some of the contextual factors that affect the careers experienced by individual people. One common definition of career is as an occupation or line of work. Most young people, and nowadays some older people too, are faced with decisions about what line of work to enter. Psychologists have been very interested in that, so in this chapter we also examine alternative approaches to career choice, and some of the practical applications arising from them. But careers are not just about choosing a type of work. They also concern what happens after that – particularly changes as a person moves between jobs and grows in experience and age. We will therefore also examine starting work and subsequent work-role transitions; as well as some theories of human development over the lifespan.

Individuals and organisations are paying increasing attention to planning and managing careers. This is partly because the fast pace of economic change makes careers much less clearly defined and predictable than they once were. Ideas and perspectives from psychology play a central part in understanding and managing careers. The techniques that are available to help manage careers in organisations are described and analysed. Overall the chapter aims to help readers to understand career theory and practice, and to apply key concepts to their own careers and also the careers of other people.

The context of careers

Definitions

Many definitions of career have been proposed. Cohen (2001) and Arnold (2001) briefly discuss some of them. Like many concepts in applied psychology, there is not complete agreement about what a career is. For our purposes, we can consider a career as: *the sequence of employment-related positions, roles, activities and experiences encountered by a person.* This definition reflects ideas from several sources (e.g. Greenhaus *et al.*, 2000). Several points can be made about it:

■ The notion of *sequence* means 'more than one'. Instead of looking at a person's present job in isolation, we are interested in how it relates to his or her past and future.

■ The inclusion of *experiences* emphasises that careers are subjective as well as objective. Hence, for example, a person's feeling of having been successful in his or her own career may differ from an 'objective' assessment of success such as status or salary. One person may regard reaching deputy managing director as a great success, another as a disappointment. Some people may be more concerned about how effectively they integrate work and home life than about promotion (Peluchette, 1993).

■ Careers are *not* confined to professional and managerial occupations, nor to 'conventional' career paths involving increasing seniority within a single occupation and/or organisation.

■ The term *employment-related* means that activities such as training, education and voluntary work, as well as *un*employment (*see* Chapter 11), can be considered elements of a person's career. Employment includes self-employment and short-term contracts.

Key Learning Point

Careers include any sequence of work-related experiences, not just conventional or orderly ones.

Current trends in careers

The changing employment scene has major implications for careers (*see also* Arnold, 1997, Chapter 2). Some of the changes and their implications for work psychology are reviewed in Chapter 1 of this book. Briefly, features of the changing labour market in the United Kingdom and most other Western countries include the following:

- *Increasing workload for individuals*, both in terms of hours worked per week, and the intensity of effort required during each working hour.

- *Organisational changes*, particularly the elimination of layers of management (delayering) and reductions in the number of people employed (downsizing).

- *More global competition*, which means that organisations in Western countries need to control costs and also make maximum use of employees' skills and ideas.

- *More team-based work*, where individuals with different types of expertise are brought together for a limited period to work on a specific project with clear goals, such as the development of a new product.

- *More short-term contracts*, where the length of a person's employment is specified at the outset. Renewal of the contract when that time has expired may be the exception, not the norm.

- *Increasingly frequent changes in the skills required in the workforce*, because of the changing requirements of work partly brought about by new technology (*see* Chapter 1).

- *More part-time jobs*. Most part-time jobs are occupied by women, and many part-time workers have two or more part-time jobs.

- *Changing workforces*. Relatively low birth rates and increasing longevity mean that the average age of people in work or available for it is increasing quite rapidly in most Western countries. Historic patterns of immigration and other factors mean that the workforce is more diverse in terms of ethnicity, values and gender.

- *More self-employment and employment in small organisations*. One might cynically say that a small organisation is a big one after downsizing, but in reality most small organisations have never been big. Nearly half of the people in work in the United Kingdom are either self-employed or work in organisations with fewer than 20 employees.

■ *Working at or from home*. Advances in communications technology and cost-cutting by employers mean that more people, currently around 3–5 per cent of those in employment, either work at home or are permanently based there.

■ *Increasing pressure on occupational and employer-based pension schemes*, owing to the ageing population and more mobility between occupations and organisations.

It is pretty clear that these labour market changes mean significant changes in the nature of jobs and careers. Careers are different from what they were, and also on the whole more difficult to manage. Figure 14.1 illustrates this. The differences include the following:

■ A greater need for individuals to look ahead and ensure that they update their skills and knowledge in order to remain employable. One consequence is the necessity of viewing learning as lifelong, not confined to childhood and early adulthood.

■ Organisations, too, need to look ahead in order to develop the skills and knowledge required for future survival.

■ Less frequent promotions within organisations, and (because of delayering) bigger increases in status and responsibility when promotions do happen. This means that it is very important to make good decisions about who to promote, and that a promoted person's new job is likely to be very challenging.

■ Less time (and often less energy) is left over for a person to consider his or her future. This is ironic because, as already noted, the need to do so is increasing.

■ A greater need for individuals to make an effort to build up and maintain their networks of contacts. Also these networks need to consist of people who can collectively offer a wide range of new perspectives, information and introductions to valuable people (Seibert *et al.*, 2001a, b).

■ A greater need for older people, as well as younger ones, to initiate and cope with change.

■ A greater need for skills of entrepreneurship, self-management and small business management.

■ A greater need for individuals to be able to handle uncertainty;

■ A greater need for individuals to be flexible in terms of the work they are prepared to do, and the people with whom they are able to work constructively.

■ An increasing need for effective management of one's personal finances.

There is wide agreement that there have been some important changes in the context of careers since the 1980s – hence the discussion in this chapter so far. But there is also some vigorous debate over just how fundamental and lasting those

Changes in:	Lead to:	Changes in careers and their management

Organisations

Greater competitive pressures
Fewer levels
Fewer employees
Smaller size
More dispersed (e.g. working at home)

Jobs

More teamworking
More short-term
More part-time
Changing skill requirements
Harder work

People

Older on average
More women
More diverse
More mobile

More need to look ahead and develop staff, but less time or resources to do it

Less frequent promotion

More need for networking by individuals

More need for individuals to tolerate ambiguity

Greater need for lifelong learning by individuals

More need for individuals to look ahead

Less time/energy for individuals to look ahead

More skills of entrepreneurship required

Everyone must be able to cope with change

More personal financial management skills required

Greater need to understand others' values and cultures

Greater need to understand one's own values, skills, interests

Figure 14.1   The changing context of careers

Key Learning Point

Careers are becoming more varied and more difficult to manage for both individuals and organisations.

changes are. For example, Doogan (2001) found that, in the United Kingdom, 42 per cent of employed managers and 38 per cent of professionals had been with their current employer for more than 10 years. This seems quite a high proportion if times are truly changing quickly. Nevertheless, these people could be the ones who dig in as a strategy to deal with insecurity, while many others not included in Doogan's survey become freelancers.

A good example of controversy is the exchange between Jacoby and Cappelli in the journal *California Management Review* in 1999. Jacoby argues that, at least in the Western world, the welfare capitalist approach remains in place. There has been a 'transfer of risk' from organisations to individual employees in the sense that organisations are less likely to shield employees from economic trends, but this trend has probably already gone about as far as it can. Jacoby also asserts that we tend to mistake cyclical change for permanent change, and to be misled by the fact that job losses in the 1990s affected the middle classes much more than those in earlier decades. Jacoby thinks that, in reality, change is happening within a largely stable broader scenario:

> For women and for those in service ocupations and industries, long-term employment has become *more* prevalent over the last twenty years. Also, the [United States] economy is creating new jobs that are predominantly neither low-wage nor part-time. Hence the majority of displaced workers are finding re-employment in career type positions (Jacoby, 1999, pp. 133–4).

As an aside, notice how in this quote 'career' is taken to mean a steady job with promotion prospects – a definition that many feel is too old-fashioned.

Cappelli (1999) disagrees with Jacoby. He believes that although career-type jobs do still exist, there is clear evidence that jobs are becoming less secure and less stable, especially white collar and managerial ones. This means that prospects of long-term advancement within the same organisation are becoming ever slimmer. And although broad labour force statistics may suggest that change is incremental rather than fundamental, the experience of individual workers is that old assumptions can no longer be taken for granted. For example, by the 1990s it was common for organisations to be downsizing while the economy was expanding. This is a contrast that was largely unknown in earlier years.

Key Learning Point

There is disagreement about whether or not recent trends in the labour market reflect a big and lasting change.

Career forms

It is still tempting to view careers in the narrow sense of predictable moves to jobs of increasing status, usually within a single occupation or organisation. This is what Kanter (1989) has called the *bureaucratic career*, and indeed many people do still see career in that narrow way. For example Jacoby and Cappelli (see above) both did so. But Kanter (1989) also identified two other career forms. The first is *professional*, where growth occurs through development of competence to take on complex tasks rather than through promotion to another job. A person's status depends more on his or her reputation with other professionals or clients than on level in an organisation hierarchy. Kanter's other career form is *entrepreneurial*, which rests on the capacity to spot opportunities to create valued outputs and build up one's own organisation or operation. The experience of many people is that careers are becoming more like the professional and/or entrepreneurial form, and less like the bureaucratic form, because of the changing context noted earlier.

The boundaryless career

In recognition of this changing nature of careers, Michael Arthur and colleagues (1999) refer to the *boundaryless career*. They define the boundaryless career in rather general fashion as 'A range of career forms that defy traditional employment assumptions' (Arthur and Rousseau, 1996, p. 3). Careers are boundaryless in the sense that, either by choice or necessity, people move across boundaries between organisations, departments, hierarchical levels, functions and sets of skills. Movement across these boundaries is made easier by the fact that they are tending to dissolve anyway. Such movement is necessary for individuals to maintain their employability and for organisations to maintain their effectiveness. In some ways the boundaryless career is very similar to Kanter's notion of the professional career because a person's marketability and affirmation are derived from outside their present employer and sustained through outside networks. Another boundary that is being broken down (in Arthur's opinion) is that between work and non-work. This is because people are increasingly likely to consider the impact of a job on their home life before taking it, and because more and more work is done at (or from) home. Arthur *et al.* (1999) have found some evidence of boundaryless careers in action among a varied sample of people in New Zealand. They argue that career is a verb, not a noun. Individuals are careering.

All this might sound very individualistic, and certainly the concept of the boundaryless career is a product of individualistic western culture, where many situations are what Weick (1996) among others calls 'weak' – that is, they have relatively few constraints and allow individuals to express themselves. Nevertheless, Arthur *et al.* (1999) point out that successful boundaryless careering does require communion (relating closely to others, recognising interdependence) as well as agency (individual action on the environment). More critically, Hirsch and Shanley (1996) among others argue that although the boundaryless career might look liberating, for many people it is deeply threatening and confusing. They believe it is a recipe for the strong to prosper even more and the weak to be further disadvantaged. Also, as noted earlier, some observers doubt whether things are really changing so much that boundaryless careers are the norm. An example is Gunz *et al.* (2000) who found plenty of evidence that bounded careers were still being pursued in the Canadian biotechnology industry.

The concept of the boundaryless career is a popular one, but it might overestimate the power individuals have over their own careers as well as the extent to which career forms are changing.

Career anchors

Another way to examine types of career is to concentrate on the subjective experience. Edgar Schein (1993) has used some research he carried out many years ago to develop the concept of *career anchors*. This has become very popular in recent years. Schein defined a person's career anchor as an area of the self-concept that is so central that he or she would not give it up even if forced to make a difficult choice. He felt that people's anchors develop and become clear during their early career, as a result of experience and learning from it. Schein's list of alternative anchors people hold is shown in Table 14.1. We might look at the list of anchors and feel that several or even all of them are important to us, but which would win if we had to choose? That is our real anchor. Career anchors consist of a mixture of abilities, motives, needs and values. They therefore reflect quite deep and far-reaching aspects of the person. It is perhaps the career anchor that a person questions when he or she is in the transitional periods identified by Levinson (*see* later in this chapter).

Key Learning Point

Career anchors are areas of the self-concept that a person would not give up, even if faced with a difficult choice.

Being able to identify one's career anchor is clearly important for the effective management of one's own career. It is also important that people in organisations responsible for managing careers are aware of the prevalence of the various anchors in their organisation. This might inform human resource policies such as job placement and transfer, promotion hierarchies and control systems. For example, problems are likely if there is an attempt to impose standard working hours and methods on people who most value the autonomy/independence anchor. Also, a common issue in organisations is how far up the hierarchy specialists such as scientists and engineers can rise without becoming general managers. Often the answer is not very far, which may create a problem for some talented staff who subscribe to the technical/functional competence career anchor. People with a security anchor are likely to have quite a difficult time because security is now harder to attain than it was. The technical/functional competence anchor could be a problem in organisations with project-based multidisciplinary teams, while the lifestyle integration anchor is increasingly difficult to honour when workloads are increasing (Schien, 1996).

Table 14.1	Career anchors

1 *Managerial competence.* People with this anchor are chiefly concerned with managing others. They wish to be generalists, and they regard specialist posts purely as a short-term means of gaining some relevant experience. Advancement, responsibility, leadership and income are all important.

2 *Technical/functional competence.* These people are keen to develop and maintain specialist skills and knowledge in their area of expertise. They build their identity around the content of their work.

3 *Security.* People with a security anchor are chiefly concerned with a reliable, predictable work environment. This may be reflected in security of tenure - i.e. having a job - or in security of location - wanting to stay in a particular town, for example.

4 *Autonomy and independence.* These people wish most of all to be free of restrictions on their work activities. They refuse to be bound by rules, set hours, dress codes and so on.

5 *Entrepreneurial creativity.* Here people are most concerned to create products, services and/or organisations of their own.

6 *Pure challenge.* This anchor emphasises winning against strong competition or apparently insurmountable obstacles.

7 *Service/dedication.* This anchor reflects the wish to have work that expresses social, political, religious or other values that are important to the individual concerned, preferably in organisations that also reflect those values.

8 *Lifestyle integration.* People who hold this anchor wish most of all to keep a balance between work, family, leisure and other activities, so that none is sacrificed for the sake of another.

Exercise 14.1	A medical career

Rashid Kassim has been appointed a consultant doctor at a general hospital. This is the fourth hospital he has worked in since qualifying as a doctor at the age of 25. The consultant grade is the most senior type of post available for doctors who continue to specialise in clinical work as opposed to taking on major managerial responsibilities. Rashid is delighted to have achieved this promotion because he believes that the status of consultant will allow him more freedom to shape his medical work in the ways he thinks most appropriate. Also, he is very active in his professional association and believes that having the status of consultant will help him make changes that he sees as necessary, as well as making him more visible to other senior doctors, with whom it might be possible to share ideas, experiences and knowledge. And who knows, perhaps one day one of them might offer him a job!

Even now, Rashid is thinking ahead a few years, and wondering how long it will be before he gets bored. He suspects that one day he will want to move to a higher-paid consultant post in a bigger hospital attached to a university medical school. This is ▶

mainly because he would be likely to see a wider range of medical conditions, to have better equipment available, and be more closely in touch with the latest developments in medical research.

On the basis of the information given here, try to specify the career type(s) and anchor(s) that fit Rashid Kassim's career so far. How easy is this to do? Do your conclusions depend on whether you focus mainly on the observable moves he has made and hopes to make, or on his motives?

Career success

How can we measure the success of a career? Perhaps the most obvious way is to see how high in a status hierarchy a person has risen, and/or how much his or her earnings have grown. These objectively verifiable indicators are indeed used in the majority of research on career success. Yet although status and earnings are important to many people, other indicators of success may be more significant to some. Earnings and promotions are well geared to the traditional or bureaucratic concept of career, but probably much less so to other career forms. They are often referred to as objective career success, in contrast to attitudes and feelings (see below), which are subjective career success.

Some psychologists have therefore used other criteria for assessing career success. For example, there are measures available of people's feelings of career satisfaction. However, some of these measures are rather unimaginative because they tend to ask people how satisfied they are with their advancement and/or earnings, rather than tapping altogether different concepts. Other psychologists have used measures of *job* satisfaction, but this is not particularly helpful because they refer solely to the present job, not the career as a whole.

Research by Sturges (1999) has provided a more sophisticated analysis of the ways in which people might experience career success. She interviewed employees of a large company and obtained quantitative data about how they viewed career success. Sturges discovered that factors such as personal influence, being recognised for one's achievements, a sense of accomplishment or achievement, enjoyment, working with integrity and achieving a balance between work and non-work were frequently mentioned as criteria of career success.

Of course, there is great interest in identifying what factors help a person achieve career success. If we know what those factors are, we may be able to do something about some of them. A model of career success is shown in Fig. 14.2. It shows the range of factors that might influence the objective and subjective career success a person experiences. These factors can be divided into three types. First are structural/social in which a person's career takes place. This includes quite impersonal factors such as the nature of the labour market, as well as more personal ones such as the biases and prejudices held by people who select others for jobs. Second are features of the individual, often termed human capital because they partly reflect what the person brings to his or her work through inherited and acquired characteristics. Of course, the significance and meaning of these characteristics depend on how they are interpreted by others, and on how they influence the individual's behaviour. So the third set of factors concerns the person's behaviour, such as how much they network with other people and how much effort they exert in their work.

Key Learning Point

Career success can be based on observable things such as status and salary, or on more subjective things such as a sense of accomplishment and having a balanced life.

Mirvis and Hall (1994, p. 367) have pointed out that success in a boundaryless career is likely to be both difficult to define and difficult to achieve:

it seems likely, too, that many of the factors that have supported and reinforced feelings of psychological success including job security, increasing levels of income, and

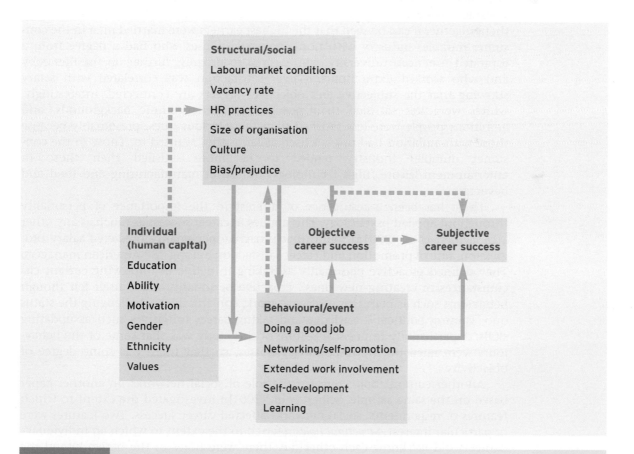

Structural/social
Labour market conditions
Vacancy rate
HR practices
Size of organisation
Culture
Bias/prejudice

Individual (human capital)
Education
Ability
Motivation
Gender
Ethnicity
Values

Objective career success

Subjective career success

Behavioural/event
Doing a good job
Networking/self-promotion
Extended work involvement
Self-development
Learning

Figure 14.2   A possible model of career success

the status that derives from one's position and employer, will be less accessible and more chancy ... since this career will provide so few external guideposts and guarantees of success, there will be little choice but to look inside and probe personal values.

This may be one reason why most research investigates objective rather than subjective career success – it is easier to understand and measure, and in truth is still of key importance to many people. It is likely that there are still some large organisations that operate what Rosenbaum (1989) among others has referred to as career tournaments. This is where progress up the status hierarchy is determined by a series of competitions. People who, for whatever reason, fail in an early round of the tournament find it very difficult to catch up later, even if they have high ability. In this respect the tournament is a knock-out one, used by those at the top of the organisation to filter the flow of people. This is of course a very bureaucratic view of career, and it illustrates how structural/social factors (*see* Fig. 14.2) can in some settings override human capital ones.

However, other research has confirmed that a wide range of factors influences success. For example a study of nearly 1400 US executives by Judge *et al.* (1995) evaluated the impact on salary, status and career satisfaction of a large range of variables. Table 14.2 shows how some of those variables affected salary. Taking them together it can be seen that the highest earners were married men in the consumer durables industry with non-employed spouses who had a degree from a top-rated American university, who desired to progress further up the hierarchy and who worked extra hours. Career satisfaction was correlated with salary showing that the subjective and objective careeers are connected. Interestingly, whites were less satisfied than people from other ethnic backgrounds, and ambitious people were less satisfied than unambitious ones, presumably because those with ambition had not yet risen as far as they wanted to. Those in the consumer durables industry tended to be more satisfied than those in entertainment/leisure, high technology, industrial manufacturing and food and beverages.

There has been a resurgence of interest in the importance of personality throughout applied psychology. This applies to career success as much as any other area. Seibert *et al.* (2001a) found that proactive personality predicted salary progression, rate of promotion and career satisfaction among 180 American managers. They defined proactive personality as 'taking initiative in improving current circumstances or creating new ones'. Proactive personality made itself felt though behaviours such as being innovative at work, constructively challenging the status quo, gaining political knowledge and taking career initiatives such as updating skills. A particularly impressive feature of this study was that some of the behaviours were rated by the respondents' bosses, so that there was some degree of objectivity.

Another current topic concerns the role of social networks. In another paper based on the same sample, Seibert *et al.* (2001b) investigated the extent to which features of respondents' social networks affected career success. Two features were of particular interest. *Structural holes* referred to the extent to which an individual's contacts did *not* know each other (i.e. there were holes in the network) and the number of *weak ties* reflected the extent to which the person had many contacts they knew slightly, rather than a few they knew well. Social network theory suggests

Table 14.2	Which American executives are the best paid?	
Predictor	**Salary value in US dollars (in mid-1990s)**	
Working in consumer durables industry	54 195	
Being a graduate of a top university	30 929	
Being a law graduate	30 328	
Being married	27 845	
Having a non-working spouse	22 011	
Having a high performance rating	11 816	
Each 7 years of age	10 262	
Ambition (per level up the hierarchy aspired to)	9 238	
Being male	6 575	
Working extra (per evening per week)	3 855	

Source: Based on T. Judge *et al.* (1995), reprinted with permission
Note: the predictors' effects are *not* cumulative – for example, being a law graduate from a top university does not mean a salary advantage of over $60 000.

that the most effective networks have both of these properties because they allow the person to access many different perspectives without getting too attached to any of them. Seibert and colleagues found that the number of weak ties and structural holes both predicted the number of contacts at higher levels a person had, which in turn influenced their career satisfaction (but interestingly not so much their salary and promotions).

Much of the research on career success focuses on how women fare versus men. Some of this is discussed in a later section of this chapter.

Exercise 14.2   Meanings of career success

Imagine your career unfolds in ways which please you. Now try to write your 'Career Epitaph' - that is, a statement about you and your career rather like the statements that sometimes appear on the headstones of graves.

Now examine your epitaph carefully. Which career forms and which notions of career success are embedded in it?

The psychological contract

The *psychological contract* is a concept that is proving very useful in explaining people's responses to the changing context of careers. A quite large research literature on the psychological contract has been produced in only a short time, with the key players being, in the United States, Denise Rousseau (e.g. Rousseau, 1995, 2001) and in the United Kingdom, Peter Herriot and Carole Pemberton (Herriot and Pemberton, 1995) and David Guest (Guest, 1998). Although much of the interest in the psychological contract is recent, its roots go back a long time, it having originally been discussed by Argyris (1960).

The psychological contract has been defined in several slightly different ways. We will use the following definition (Robinson and Rousseau, 1994, p. 246):

> An individual's belief regarding the terms and conditions of a reciprocal exchange agreement between that focal person and another party ... a belief that some form of a promise has been made and that the terms and conditions of the contract have been accepted by both parties.

So, in the context of careers, the psychological contract represents informal, unwritten understandings between employer and employee(s). From the employees' point of view, the psychological contract is the agreement that they think they have with their employer about what they will contribute to the employer via their work, and what they can expect in return. The trends described earlier in this chapter have changed the careers landscape, and for the worse in many people's opinions. The deal many employees thought they had with their employer has turned out to be worth less than the paper it wasn't written on. As Herriot and Pemberton (1995, p. 58) put it in their book entitled *New Deals*, captains of industry 'have set in motion a revolution in the nature of the employment relationship the like of which they never imagined. For they have shattered the old psychological contract and failed to negotiate a new one'.

So what was the old psychological contract that has been broken? Herriot and Pemberton draw on a well-established distinction between a relational and a transactional contract. The former refers to a long-term relationship based on trust and mutual respect. The employees offered loyalty, conformity to requirements, commitment to their employer's goals, and trust in their employer not to abuse their goodwill. In return, the organisation supposedly offered security of employment, promotion prospects, training and development, and some flexibility about the demands made on employees if they were in difficulty. But global competition, new technology, downsizing, delayering and the rest of it have put an end to all that. Many employers no longer keep their side of the bargain. The new deal is imposed rather than agreed; it is transactional rather than relational. Instead of being based on a long-term relationship, it is much more like a short-term economic exchange. The employee offers longer hours, broader skills, tolerance of change and ambiguity, and willingness to take more responsibility. In return the employer offers (to some) high pay, rewards for high performance and, simply, a job.

According to Herriot and Pemberton (1995), many people have understandably responded very negatively to these changes. This might be particularly the case for managers, many of whom identify with the organisation rather than a profession. Their sense of identity and self-worth is therefore particularly threatened when their organisation 'rats' on the deal. Reactions vary, but include outrage, disappointment, anger, sullen conformity, fear, anxiety and probably lots of other negative things besides. Herriot and Pemberton describe typical reactions to violation of the psychological contract as get out, get safe or get even – or, to put it another way: to leave, to stay and keep your head below the parapet, or to stay and take your revenge. It is clear that many employees feel that their psychological contract has been violated by their employer. For example, Robinson and Rousseau (1994) found that 70 of their sample of 128 managers thought that their employer had violated their psychological contract (i.e. what they thought they had been promised) in the first two years of employment. Violations most commonly concerned training and development, pay and benefits, and promotion opportunities. When employees felt that their employer had violated the psychological contract, they were not surprisingly inclined to feel less sense of obligation and less commitment (see Chapter 7) to their employing organisation.

The apparent frequency with which psychological contracts are violated has led psychologists to try to clarify what is coming to be called the 'violation process' (e.g. Robinson and Morrison, 2000). Figure 14.3 illustrates this. One important but rather confused debate here concerns the distinction between contract breach and contract violation. The former is often thought of as the realisation that what has been promised has not materialised. Sometimes violation is also defined in that way. But violation is also on occasions defined either as the belief that a breach was deliberate, or as negative emotional reaction to a breach – usually because it is perceived to have been deliberate. The main point underlying all this is that contract breach does not necessarily lead to reduced employee loyalty and commitment. If it is felt that the breach was neither the employer's fault, nor intended, then the impact on the employee's loyalty is likely to be small, particularly if it is put right quickly. Further, there is of course a lot of scope for individual interpretation in this process. For example, a person who starts out favourably disposed towards his or her employer might be less likely to notice breaches than somebody who already mistrusts the employer. They might also be less likely to construe breaches as violations. Some psychologists have tried to be specific about when breaches and violations will be perceived, how they will be interpreted, and what will be the consequences for employee behaviour and attitudes (Turnley and Feldman, 1999; Robinson and Morrison, 2000).

Key Learning Point

The psychological contract concerns an individual employee's perceptions of his or her rights and obligations with respect to the employing organisation. In the eyes of individuals, employers frequently break their side of the contract.

The psychological contract is perhaps in danger of overuse, and it does have some limitations (Arnold, 1996). These limitations were the subject of a vigorous debate between David Guest (1998) and Denise Rousseau (1998). It revolved around the following issues:

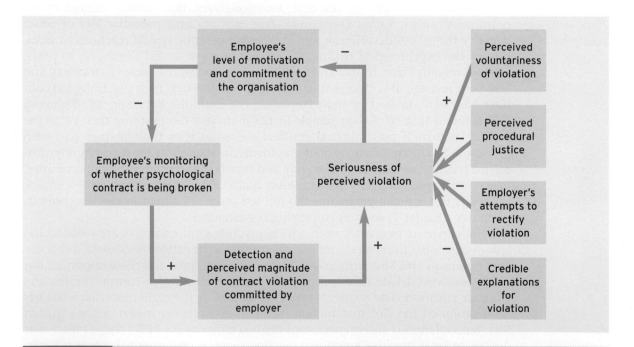

Figure 14.3   The process of psychological contract violation
Source: Adapted from Rousseau (1995, p. 118), reprinted with permission. Note that this same process is depicted to illustrate features of motivation in Chapter 9.

■ If the psychological contract exists purely in the mind of an employee, it is doubtful whether it can be considered a contract at all. There is no agreement, written or unwritten, with any other party. On the other hand, if it is explicit and agreed between parties along the lines advocated by Herriot and Pemberton, it is more legal than psychological.

■ An organisation is not a person, and therefore cannot be a party to a psychological contract. Organisations consist of many different individuals and groups, and each employee may have quite specific expectations about his or her rights and obligations vis-à-vis those individuals (e.g. supervisor) and groups (e.g. departments).

■ Violation of the psychological contract carries a clear implication of a broken promise. This is more emotionally charged than the more neutral notion of unmet expectations, and more complicated than simply asking how pleasant a person's experiences have been within a work organisation. In spite of Rousseau's (1998) assertions to the contrary, it is not yet clear whether the psychological contract explains people's work behaviour any better than more neutral and simpler concepts (*see also* Schurer Lambert *et al.*, 2003).

■ The psychological contract may be a somewhat redundant and/or over-complicated concept. It is possible that its overlap with other psychological constructs such as job satisfaction and organisational commitment (*see* Chapter 7) is too great.

Guest (1998) tentatively concludes that the psychological contract *is* a useful concept in spite of its limitations. This is because it is consistent with the spirit of the times, helps to make sense of current employment relationships, and helps to highlight who has power. Rousseau (1998) is much more enthusiastic than Guest. She argues that all agreements are open to interpretation and therefore psychological. She thinks that the limitations identified by Guest are based on his misunderstandings of what the psychological contract is, and believes that it is worthy of study *not* simply because changes in the labour market make it appear relevant.

It seems likely that attention to the psychological contract will continue to increase in the psychological literature. By capturing important aspects of people's experience of work, it offers considerable possibilities for understanding work attitudes and behaviour.

Career choice

Psychologists have long been interested in how people choose an occupation, and how they can be helped to do so effectively. Here the term career is usually taken to mean occupation or line of work. Three basic requirements of effective career choice were proposed long ago by Frank Parsons (1909, p. 5, described in Sharf, 1992, Chapter 2):

1   A clear understanding of ourselves, our attitudes, abilities, interests, ambitions, resource limitations and their causes.

2   A knowledge of the requirements and conditions of success, advantages and disadvantages, compensation, opportunities and prospects in different lines of work.

3   True reasoning on the relations of these two groups of facts.

This nicely describes the nature of the task, but does not in itself help people to do it well. We now examine psychologists' attempts to take things further.

Holland's theory

John Holland has developed over many years an influential theory of career choice. The most recent version can be found in Holland (1997). He summarises his approach in the preface of that book. In some ways it is a much more narrowly focused, personal and pragmatic approach than what has appeared in this chapter so far:

> I have become addicted to seeing careers from an individual's perspective – how can a person's difficulties be resolved within the present personal and environmental resources? I have neglected the restructuring of educational institutions, businesses, and public policy, although I have indicated some of the implications of the theory for these institutions. My concern for individuals has led to a related goal – to construct a formulation that can be understood and used by practitioners. Consequently, I have stuck to simple measures of all theoretical constructs. Fortunately, these simple measures usually work as well as more complex ones. (p. vi)

In the course of his earlier work as a careers counsellor in the United States, Holland thought he could discern six pure types of vocational personality. He also felt that he could see the roots of these types in traditional personality theory. He developed his concepts and measures of them. Subsequent work has sought to validate these, and to test Holland's hypotheses about career choice (*see below*). Very briefly, Holland's six personality types are as follows:

1   *Realistic*: outdoor-type. Tends to like, and be good at, activities requiring physical strength and/or co-ordination. Not keen on socialising.

2   *Investigative*: interested in concepts and logic. Tends to enjoy, and be good at, abstract thought. Often interested in the physical sciences.

3   *Artistic*: tends to use imagination a lot. Likes to express feelings and ideas. Dislikes rules and regulations; enjoys music, drama, art.

4   *Social*: enjoys the company of other people, especially in affiliative (i.e. helping, friendly) relationships. Tends to be warm and caring.

5   *Enterprising*: also enjoys the company of other people, but mainly to dominate or persuade rather than help them. Enjoys action rather than thought.

6   *Conventional*: likes rules and regulations, structure and order. Usually well organised, not very imaginative.

Holland proposed that the types can be arranged in a hexagon in the order described above to express their similarity to each other (*see* Fig. 14.4). This ordering is usually referred to as RIASEC. Each type is placed at a corner of the hexagon. Types on opposite corners of the hexagon (i.e. three corners apart) are in many senses opposites. Types on adjacent corners (e.g. *Realistic* and *Conventional*) are quite similar to each other. Nobody exactly matches any single type, but nevertheless each of us resembles some types more than others. In fact, Holland suggests that people are most usefully described in terms of the three types they resemble most, in descending order of similarity. Hence, for example, for an ISE person, the *investigative* type comes closest to describing him or her, the *social* type comes next and *enterprising* third. Holland proposed that occupations can also be described in terms of the six types. He has argued that any environment exerts its influence through the people in it. Hence occupations are described in terms of the people in them, again using the three most prevalent types in descending order. In the United States, Holland's classification of occupations has been widely applied in, for example, the *Dictionary of Holland Occupational Codes* (Gottfredson and Holland, 1996).

Key Learning Point

John Holland has identified six vocational personality types. These types map on to different occupations.

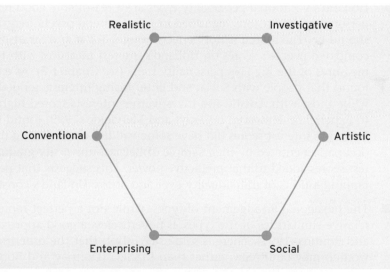

Figure 14.4	**Holland's six types of vocational personality**

Source: Holland (1997, p. 6). Reproduced by special permission of the Publisher, Psychological Assessment Resources, Inc., from *Making Vocational Choices*, Third Edition, copyright 1973, 1985, 1992, 1997 by Psychological Assessment Resources, Inc. All rights reserved

Some of Holland's main theoretical propositions (*see* Holland, 1997, pp. 67–8) are as follows:

■ People find environments satisfying when environmental patterns resemble their own personality patterns. This situation (often referred to as *congruence*) encourages stability of behaviour because people receive a lot of reinforcement of their already-preferred styles. Congruence also tends to enable a person to perform well in his or her work.

■ Incongruent interactions stimulate change in behaviour. A person may seek a more congruent environment, remake the present one, or change to become more congruent in behaviour and/or perceptions.

■ An environment expels incongruent people, seeks new congruent ones, or changes its demands on inhabitants.

Holland has said he is irritated by what he sees as a lack of attention to the more dynamic social-psychological elements of his theory. However, his fundamental hypothesis is relatively straightforward and states: people will be most satisfied, and most successful, in occupations that are congruent with (i.e. match) their personality. Thus Holland's theory reflects a well-established tradition in work psychology: the matching of person and work, with the assumption that both are fairly stable over time. The large volume of research on this and other aspects of Holland's theory has been reviewed by Spokane *et al.* (2000) and Tranberg *et al.* (1993), among others. Several conclusions can be drawn:

■ Holland's vocational personality types are a reasonably good reflection of basic personality dimensions identified in more general psychology, as indeed they should be. The match is not perfect though. Tokar and Swanson (1995) compared people's scores on Holland's interest measures with their scores on measures of the Big Five personality traits (*see* Chapter 3). As expected, they found that people with Social and Enterprising interests tended to be extroverts while those with Artistic and Investigative interests scored high on Openness to Experience. However, De Fruyt and Mervielde (1999) found that although Holland's interest scores did have some validity in predicting the type of occupation entered by their sample of Belgian university graduates, personality test scores added to that predictive power. This suggests that personality is tapping aspects of individuality over and above Holland's constructs.

■ The hexagonal arrangement of types, while not a perfect representation of the relative similarities of the types, is nevertheless a good approximation (Tracey and Rounds, 1993). There is some suggestion that the ordering of types for women may be IRASEC rather than RIASEC (Donnay and Borgen, 1999).

■ There is some evidence that congruence is correlated with satisfaction and success, but it is surprisingly weak. Even when the correlation is observed we cannot be sure that congruence *leads* to satisfaction and success. Spokane *et al.* (2000) have conducted a detailed analysis of the congruence issue. They estimate that the correlation between congruence and job satisfaction in most studies is about 0.25. They argue, correctly, that this is a strong enough relationship to take seriously. They also point out a huge range of problems with most research on congruence. For example, some research has examined the congruence between a person and his or her career *choice*, rather than the person and his or her actual career or educational environment. A choice is not an environment, and is therefore an inappropriate basis for assessing congruence. Also, there are very many different statistical formulae measuring congruence, some of which may be overly simple or unnecessarily complicated. Defining the occupation as a person's environment may not adequately reflect his or her day-to-day work situation. The environment might also be defined partly by the organisation, workgroup, etc. A further limitation is that job satisfaction is nearly always the dependent variable. Alternatives might be job performance ratings, occupational commitment, frequency of absence from work, or intention to stay in the occupation.

Key Learning Point

Congruence between person and environment, as defined in Holland's theory, is less good at predicting a person's satisfaction in an occupation than might be expected.

Holland's approach to personality assessment is a little unusual. He has developed the *Self-Directed Search* (SDS) (see Holland, 1998, for a recent edition), which asks the respondent about his or her preferred activities, reactions to occupational titles, abilities, competencies and even daydreams. People can score their own SDS, establish their three-letter code, and then examine an 'occupation finder' to check which occupations might be appropriate for them. There is also a 'leisure activities finder' for people who are seeking congenial spare-time pursuits. They are encouraged to try various permutations of their three-letter code, especially if their three highest scores are of similar magnitude. All of this is unusual in a number of respects. First, it is rare for questions about both abilities and interests to be included in a vocational guidance instrument. Second, the SDS is deliberately transparent – people can see what it is getting at (Reardon and Lenz, 1998). Third, it is rare for psychologists to allow the people they assess to score and interpret their own data. Holland feels that most people simply need reassurance that their career ideas are appropriate, and that the SDS generally provides this much more quickly and cheaply than careers counselling.

More generally, there are many tests of occupational interests on the market – some paper-and-pencil, others computerised. Few have such a strong theoretical and empirical basis as Holland's. One that does is the *Strong Interest Inventory* (Harmon *et al.*, 1994), which has been revised to reflect the Holland types. Data from it have contributed to the classification of occupations in Holland's terms.

Key Learning Point

Holland's self-directed search makes it easy for a person to see for him- or herself what occupations seem to be most suitable.

Even if research on congruence has not always supported Holland's hypotheses, his approach is very valuable because it provides a structure for understanding and assessing individuals and occupations. Even so, some have suggested that alternative structures are even better. Prediger and Vansickle (1992) complained that Holland's hexagon does not allow placement of a person or occupation in two- or three-dimensional space. They proposed instead two dimensions, *data–ideas* and *things–people*. So any person could be described by his or her position on each of these dimensions, the relationships of which with Holland's hexagon are shown in Fig. 14.5. Hogan (1983) has suggested that the two personality dimensions of sociability and confirmity underlie the Holland types. This is also shown in Fig. 14.5. Both of these alternatives to Holland have some validity (see Tokar and Fischer, 1998). However, they lack the vividness and ease of understanding offered by Holland's six types.

Making career decisions

Theories such as Holland's describe the *content* of actual and ideal decisions, but not the *process*. How can a person make an effective career decision? Several factors are relevant.

Self-awareness

First, a person needs to have an accurate appraisal of his or her own strengths and weaknesses, values, likes and dislikes. Numerous exercises and techniques are available for this, some in published books (e.g. Bolles, 2001; Hirsh and Jackson, 1998) and others homegrown in (for example) college careers advisory services. Most are designed to help people to examine systematically their experiences in the work

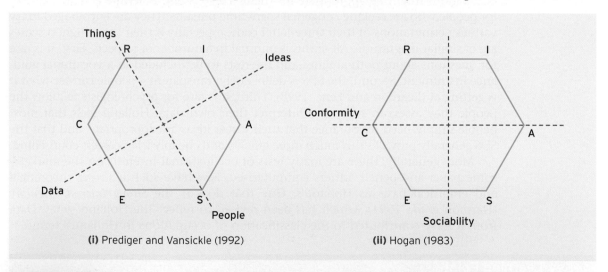

(i) Prediger and Vansickle (1992)   **(ii)** Hogan (1983)

Figure 14.5   **Alternative configurations of Holland's hexagon**
Source: Reprinted from *Journal of Vocational Behavior*, 52, D. M. Tokar and A. R. Fischer, 'More on RIASEC and the five-factor model of personality: direct assessment of Prediger's (1982) and Hogan's 1983 dimensions', pp. 246-59, Copyright (1998) with permission from Elsevier

setting and outside it, in order to arrive at the most accurate and complete self-assessment that their past experience allows. The importance of examining emotions as well as thoughts, and negative experiences as well as positive ones, is usually stressed. Careful self-assessment is important because research (e.g. Church, 1997) has shown that self-assessments often fail to agree with assessments by objective tests or by other people. Most correlations are around 0.25. Mabe and West (1982) did, however, find that if people have previous experience of self-assessment and if they think carefully about how they compare with other people, their self-assessments are more likely to be accurate or at least plausible. Schrader and Steiner (1996) found that any comparison point for self-ratings (e.g with other people, or with minimum standards required to get by in the current environment) was much better than none.

Knowledge of occupations

Again, there are many workbooks that give guidance on how to find out about occupations (e.g. Hopson and Scally, 2000; Bolles, 2001). Apart from reading published information, methods include talking to a person in that occupation, and 'shadowing' such a person for a period of time in order to see what he or she actually does. Emphasis is placed on avoiding stereotypes of occupations, and ensuring that one pays attention not only to positions one might ultimately occupy in an occupation, but also to those one will have to fill on the way.

Putting self-knowledge and occupational knowledge together

Often it is surprisingly difficult for people to relate what they know about occupations to what they know about self (Yost and Corbishley, 1987, Chapter 5). This is especially the case when a person is trying to choose between fairly similar occupations. One advantage of the better-developed vocational measures is that they do describe people and occupations in the same language, but even then there are usually several occupations to which the person seems well suited. It is the choice between these which is often difficult.

Career exploration and job search

Becoming aware of self and of the world of work requries exploration. Stumpf *et al.* (1983) produced a questionnaire measure of the extent to which a person has engaged in career exploration, intends to do so and is satisfied with how he or she is going about it. This career exploration survey (CES) has been used in a lot of subsequent research. Blustein *et al.* (1994) showed that engaging in career exploration does aid progress in career decision-making. On the other hand it is difficult to identify what characteristics of a person determine the extent to which he or she will explore (Bartley and Robitschek, 2000). It seems that exploration of the environment helps successful job search more than exploration of self does (Werbel, 2000). This is perhaps because engaging in self-exploration signals that a person does not yet feel ready to engage in the process of making a career decision. It may also be because exploring the environment also involves some self-exploration when the person asks 'would I like it?'

Computers and career decision-making

Computer-assisted career exploration and decision-making have been available in various forms for many years, and have developed hugely (Harris-Bowlsbey and Sampson, 2001). Examples of packages available are DISCOVER in the United States and CAREERBUILDER and ADULT DIRECTIONS in the United Kingdom. The most common pattern is still for users to be invited to input information about themselves, which is then matched against information about occupations held in the package's database. Some packages – for example Adult Directions – are supported by enormous amounts of regularly updated occupational information. Others are less thorough. The value of these packages depends partly on the validity and reliability of the information held and of the questions they put to users. Nevertheless, there is some evidence that people find computer-assisted careers guidance useful in many (though possibly not all) circumstances, and that it helps move them towards decision-making (Mau, 1999; Gati *et al.*, 2001).

The rapid expansion of sources of career information on the Internet makes issues of quality control even more critical. It also adds new issues such as the confidentiality of the information provided by users, and the availability of support for people who might be confused or upset by what a website 'tells' them (Sampson and Lumsden 2000). That said, there are many interesting sites available that attempt to help people with their careers. Examples are Monster.com, Proteus-net.co.uk, and Self-directed-search.com. As one might expect from its name the last of these specialises in Holland's theory. Another site is www.jobhuntersbible.com, which is a supplement to Richard Bolles' best-selling book *What Color is Your Parachute?* (2001).

Decision-making styles and self-efficacy

Phillips *et al.* (1985) identified three styles of career decision-making: *rational*, where advantages and disadvantages of various options are considered logically and systematically, *intuitive*, where various options are considered and the decision is made on 'gut feeling', and *dependent*, where the person essentially denies responsibility for decision-making and waits for other people or circumstances to dictate what he or she should do. Not surprisingly, it seems that the dependent style is the least successful. The other two are about equally successful when aggregated across large numbers of individuals, though one or the other may suit any particular person best.

However, some of the findings in this area may be somewhat culture-specific. Mau (2000) compared the decision-making styles of a large sample of American and Taiwanese students. Some 32 per cent of the Taiwanese students reported a predominantly dependent style, compared with 11 per cent of the Americans. But in Taiwan, activities such as consulting parents and friends (which might be considered rather weak in the West) are normal and indeed expected activities. It may be misleading to call them dependent.

It is becoming increasingly clear that self-efficacy is also important in effective career decision-making. Self-efficacy had been defined as the extent to which a person believes he or she is capable of performing the behaviour required in any given situation (Bandura, 1977a) – in this case making an appropriate career decision. The concept is prominent and explicit in the attempt by Lent *et al.* (1994)

to combine various traditions in vocational psychology in their social cognitive theory of career interests, choice and performance. The key idea is that self-efficacy influences task performance over and above measured ability. In other words, it dictates whether people will perform as well as they are capable. There is some evidence that career decision-making self-efficacy does affect progress through career decision-making among college students (Taylor and Betz, 1983) and among older people too (Gianakos, 1999). Saks and Ashforth (1999) found that students' sense of self-efficacy about searching for a job predicted the vigour with which they actually did so, and in turn that vigour predicted their success in getting a well-paid job. Furthermore, Donnay and Borgen (1999) found that self-efficacy in each of Holland's six areas helped to predict the occupations chosen by a large sample of American people. This was even after their Holland occupational interest scores had been accounted for. In other words, like personality, self-efficacy appears to be useful over and above John Holland's typology.

Key Learning Point

The quality of a person's career exploration, his or her style of decision-making, and belief in his or her own abilities, all affect how successful his or her career decision-making is.

Exercise 14.3   Your own career decision-making

1   How clear are you about your abilities and interests? How specific can you be about this? For example, it is not much good simply saying you like being with people. In what situations, and for what purposes do you like being with people? If you are not clear, you might like to reflect further on your past experiences, or seek new ones to find out more about yourself.

2   How much do you know about different occupations? How clear are you about what people in particular occupations actually do, and the conditions (hours, pay, environment) in which they work? If you are not clear, you might like to read more about certain occupations, and/or ask people working in them to tell you what they know.

3   What is your typical decision-making style – rational, intuitive or dependent? How successful have your decisions been in the past? If you tend to make decisions in a dependent manner, you might try to develop one of the other styles, perhaps by practising with small decisions.

4   How much have you engaged in career exploration, and how confident are you about your ability to do so? On the basis of your answers to the previous three questions you may want to consider what aspects of exploration should be your priority.

All change: approaches to lifelong career development

Development through the lifespan

Many social scientists have sought to map out human development in adulthood (*see*, for example, Perlmutter and Hall, 1992). They have often identified age-linked stages of development, each with its own specific concerns and tasks for the person. The aim is ambitious: to map out motivation and development across the whole course of life. Other psychologists have taken a quite different approach. They have focused on specific changes experienced by the person such as starting work, relocation, unemployment and retirement.

Let's take the lifespan approach first. Within the context of careers, the work of Donald Super (e.g. 1957, 1990) was influential over a long period of time. Super identified four career stages in his early work:

1   *Exploration* of both self and world of work in order to clarify the self-concept and identify occupations which fit it. Typical ages: 15–24.

2   *Establishment*: perhaps after one or two false starts, the person finds a career field, and makes efforts to prove his or her worth in it. Typical ages: 25–44.

3   *Maintenance*: the concern now is to hold onto the niche one has carved for oneself. This can be a considerable task, especially in the face of technological changes and vigorous competition from younger workers. Typical ages: 45–64.

4   *Disengagement*: characterised by decreasing involvement in work and a tendency to become an observer rather than a participant. Typical ages: 65+.

Super's theory reflected some others at the time, in that he saw the late teens and twenties as a time of exploration and self-concept clarification. He viewed the following years as a time when people 'get stuck in' and make themselves indispensable. Super saw this 'getting stuck in' as achievement-orientated, though some others thought more in terms of developing a sense of involvement and belonging. Super's view of middle-age essentially concerns hanging on, while some others have placed more emphasis on creative striving.

Some older research examined whether people's career concerns do indeed match Super's stages (e.g. Veiga, 1983; Isabella, 1988). The results suggest some distinctions between stages, but they are not very clear cut. As Hall (1986, Chapter 4) pointed out, it is difficult to identify what career stage a person is in, especially if, for example, he or she enters a career relatively late in life. Also, of course, the changing nature of careers makes it much more difficult to link stages with ages. In fact, Super (1980, 1990) acknowledged this, and developed a much more flexible framework for mapping a person's life and career. He identified six roles people typically perform in Western societies: homemaker, worker, citizen, leisurite, student and child. The importance of each of these roles in a person's life can rise and fall over time. Also, at any given time, a person can be at different stages (exploration, establishment, etc.) in different roles. In other words, the original notion of career stages has now become priorities, or concerns, that an individual may have at any point in his or her adult life. These insights do not in themselves create a theory, but they do help people to consider their lives in a systematic way (Super, 1990). Some self-assessment devices such as the *Adult Career Concerns Inventory* (Super *et al.*, 1985) and the *Salience Inventory* (Super and Nevill, 1985) have been developed to assist in this process.

Key Learning Point

Donald Super proposed stage theories of career development. He later loosened the connection between ages and stages, and broadened the focus from career to other domains of life.

Of the many other attempts to map out adult life, that of Levinson and colleagues (1978) has been the most influential. This influence is perhaps surprising, given that Levinson and his colleagues conducted interviews (albeit in-depth ones) with only 40 American-born men between the ages of 35 and 45. Nevertheless, Levinson came up with some interesting conclusions. He proposed that in each of three eras of adulthood (early, middle and late) there are alternating stable and transitional periods (Fig. 14.6). For example, early adulthood (ages 17–40) begins with the *early adult transition* (ages 17–22), where the person seeks a niche in the adult world. Then comes a stable phase *entering the adult world* (ages 22–28), where the task is to explore various roles while keeping one's options open. Next, between 28 and 33, comes the *age 30 transition*, where the person appraises his or her experiences and searches for a satisfactory lifestyle. This is followed by a stable settling down phase, when that lifestyle is implemented. This was called Boom (Becoming One's Own Man) by Levinson, who felt that it was a key time for men to achieve in their occupational lives.

The *midlife transition* (ages 40–45) identified by Levinson has often been considered the most significant aspect of his work. He argued that the lifestyle is reappraised at this age, often with considerable urgency and emotion – so much so, that it is sometimes referred to as the 'midlife crisis'. People realise that their life is probably at least half over and this concentrates their minds on what they should be doing with the rest of it. In the eyes of their children they are now symbols of authority, old-timers. Physical signs of ageing become unmistakable. There are by now clear indications of whether or not earlier career ambitions will be achieved. These factors can lead to substantial life changes: for example, a change of career or a change of spouse. Alternatively, a commitment to the current lifestyle may be reaffirmed, and increased effort put into it.

After the midlife transition comes *entering middle adulthood* (45–50), then the *age 50* transition (50–55), then the *culmination of middle adulthood* (55–60). These all concern implementing and living with midlife decisions. The *late adult transition* and *late adulthood* follow. Levinson was very clear that his stages were closely linked with age. He argued that the lives of particular individuals may look very different on the surface, but underlying them are similar personal issues (Levinson, 1986).

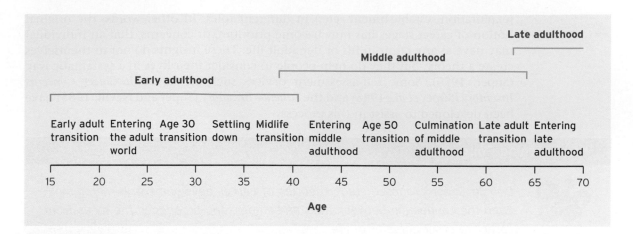

Figure 14.6	**Phases of development in adulthood** *Source:* **Adapted from Levinson and colleagues (1978)**

Key Learning Point

Levinson proposed a closely age-linked series of phases in adult life. The phases were alternately transitional and stable in terms of tasks facing the person.

These approaches to adult development have implications for career management in organisations. If people are going to work effectively, the needs and concerns of their life stage should be taken into account. Therefore, in early adulthood, people must be given the opportunity to integrate themselves into an organisation and/or career, and demonstrate their worth to themselves and others. This may involve special efforts to give the newcomer significant work assignments and social support. In mid-career, it may be necessary to provide opportunities for some people to retrain, perhaps in the light of a midlife reappraisal. They could also be given opportunities to allow them to keep up to date in their chosen field. It may also be helpful to give people in their mid to late career a chance to act as mentor or guide to younger employees (*see* 'Mentoring', below) – this is, after all, a way of handing on one's accumulated wisdom and thereby making a lasting impression. But these developmental theories are all vulnerable to the accusation that they really only reflect the lives of middle-class males in Western countries in the mid- to late-twentieth century.

Transitions between jobs

Now we turn to psychologists' insights concerning specific transitions people may experience during their working lives. Since the start of the 1980s, increasing attention has been paid to the processes involved in changing jobs (e.g. Sokol and Louis,

Exercise 14.4   Career stages

Jenny Peterson was 36 years old and had been working in the sales function of a large retailer since she was 18. She had found her early years quite difficult, and for a time wondered how she had ended up in the job. During those years, however, she gradually found that she could handle the tasks, and that some of them were quite enjoyable. By the time she was 23, she felt confident that she could cope with anything that came her way, but wondered whether she really wanted to work for the company. She thought a great deal about whether or not she liked its people and philosophy. Over the next decade, she slowly but surely found herself feeling more attached to both. Now a different matter was bothering her. Some of the younger staff seemed to know more than she did about sales techniques and marketing strategies. Was she already obsolete at age 36, she wondered?

Consider the extent to which Jenny Peterson's career so far is consistent with Super's and Leivinson's stages.

1984). This has included international job moves, which can make particularly severe demands on the person (Black *et al.*, 1991). Such attention is appropriate because it appears that people change jobs with increasing frequency and often involving change of organisation, status and type of work (Inkson, 1995; Arthur *et al.*, 1999).

Key Learning Point

Moves between jobs are happening with increasing frequency.

Nicholson (1990) proposed a *transition cycle* model of job change. The cycle consists of four stages undergone by a person making a job change: *preparation*, *encounter*, *adjustment* and *stabilisation*. These are described in Fig. 14.7, along with some of the problems often encountered at each stage, and strategies for dealing with them. Nicholson (1990) pointed out that there is *disjunction* between stages – or put another way, each stage has its own characteristics that differentiate it from the others. At the same time, the stages are *interdependent*: that is, what happens in one stage has implications for the next. Successfully managing one stage makes it easier to manage the next successfully, and vice versa. Wider aspects of the context in which a transition occurs can also be important – see Exercise 14.5.

Preparation

The preparation stage concerns what both individual and future employer can do before the individual starts the job. From the individual's perspective some of this

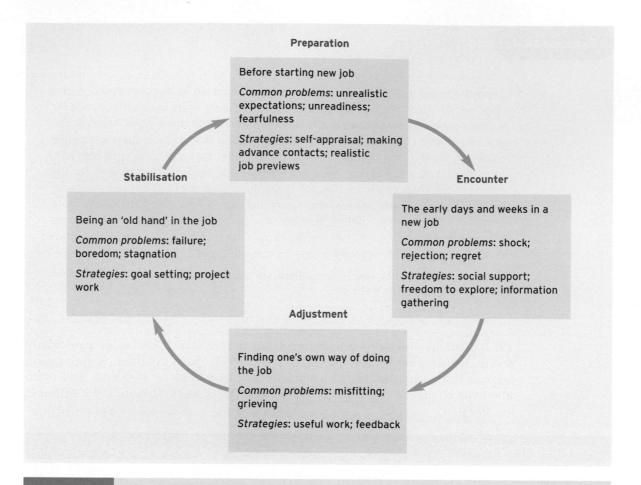

Preparation

Before starting new job

Common problems: unrealistic expectations; unreadiness; fearfulness

Strategies: self-appraisal; making advance contacts; realistic job previews

Encounter

The early days and weeks in a new job

Common problems: shock; rejection; regret

Strategies: social support; freedom to explore; information gathering

Stabilisation

Being an 'old hand' in the job

Common problems: failure; boredom; stagnation

Strategies: goal setting; project work

Adjustment

Finding one's own way of doing the job

Common problems: misfitting; grieving

Strategies: useful work; feedback

Figure 14.7	The transition cycle
	Source: Adapted from Nicholson (1990)

involves making an effective career or job choice. It is likely that both sides will try to make themselves seem as attractive as possible: the individual, so that he or she will be offered the job, and the organisation, so that the person to whom they offer the job is likely to accept it. This creates the likelihood that each side will have unrealistically high expectations about how wonderful the other is.

One technique for helping an applicant have accurate expectations of the job and organisation is to use a *realistic job preview* (RJP) during the selection process. An RJP can be a written booklet, a videotape, or a chance to do the job for a day or two. It represents an attempt to describe the job and organisation as seen by those in it. Crucially, it includes bad points as well as good ones. Although managers often fear that good applicants will be deterred by hearing about the disadvantages as well as the advantages, research suggests that RJPs have modest but significant success in reducing the number of people who leave their jobs quickly, in increasing positive work attitudes among those who experience an RJP, and in increasing the number of people who voluntarily drop out of the selection process, presumably because they realise the job is not suitable for them (Wanous *et al.*,

1992). Implementing an RJP well is not straightforward. It is possible to formulate it badly (for example *too* negatively) or deliver it at the wrong time in the wrong way. Wanous (1989) has offered some advice for avoiding these pitfalls.

How RJPs work has been a matter of some debate. Hom *et al.* (1999), with help from some other psychologists who critiqued their work, suggest that:

■ RJPs increase the newcomer's perception of the employer's concern and honesty, which in turn helps the newcomer feel more committed.

■ RJPs reduce the newcomer's initial expectations, which encourages him or her to focus on how to cope with the new job, and this improves job satisfaction.

Encounter

RJPs are a good example of how what happens at one stage of the transition cycle can affect subsequent ones. RJPs occur at the preparation stage, but their benefits are seen at the encounter and adjustment stages. The task at the encounter stage is for the newcomer to establish a 'mental map' of his or her new environment: to understand who's who, what 'social rules' operate, what is expected of him or her, and so on. If any of this is not what the newcomer was led to expect, or if the newcomer feels it is in some sense wrong, then he or she may regret taking the job (and those who employed him or her may regret it too).

Chao *et al.* (1994) pointed out six types of information a newcomer needs to obtain:

1 *Performance proficiency*: learning and performance of the tasks required in the job.

2 *People*: establishment of successful and satisfying work relationships with organisational members.

3 *Politics*: understanding of formal and informal work relationships and power structures within the organisation.

4 *Language*: understanding of the necessary technical language and organisation-specific acronyms, slang and jargon.

5 *Organisational goals and values*: learning what the organisation is trying to achieve and what its members value.

6 *History*: knowledge of the past of the organisation and of particular organisation members.

Research by Morrison (1993), among others, has shown that active attempts by newcomers to find this information tend to be successful, and that this leads to better satisfaction, performance and commitment. A particularly useful strategy seems to be *monitoring* – that is, observing and listening to what goes on. It tends to work better than asking direct questions or consulting written documents.

Adjustment

Adjustment is the stage when the person has already developed an understanding of the work environment and now seeks to use it to establish how to go about doing the job in the long term. Clearly, how individual and organisation have dealt with each other up to this point will influence the mode of adjustment adopted by the individual. Of importance here is research on *innovation*. For example, Schein (1971) long ago identified three orientations a person may adopt in a job:

1   *Custodianship*: where the person accepts the role requirements as given.

2   *Content innovation*: where the person accepts the goals of the role but adopts his or her own ways of achieving them.

3   *Role innovation*: where the person redefines the goals of the job and probably the methods too.

In the long run, role innovators are probably vital for societal advance. In the short term, many work organisations claim to value content innovators (though they would not use that term) but probably in truth they reward custodians more highly because they conform to the existing organisational culture.

Van Maanen and Schein (1979) specified some key aspects of organisational 'people-processing' strategies that would, they proposed, influence whether a person became a custodian or an innovator. These dimensions all concerned the extent to which the newcomer's socialisation was *institutionalised* or *individualised*. Institutionalised socialisation involves sending newcomers on structured training courses together as a group, and separate from other members of the organisation, with a clearly defined timetable and career plan. Individualised socialisation involves ambiguous timings of assignments, on-the-job learning with established members of the organisation, and relative isolation from other newcomers (perhaps because there aren't any). The institutionalised approach tends to lead to a custodial orientation (Ashforth and Saks, 1996). This is because institutionalised socialisation exposes all newcomers to similar and quite narrow experiences. On the other hand, it gives newcomers a comforting feeling of predictability and being 'looked after' by the organisation, which leads them to feel committed to it (Allen and Meyer, 1990b). The challenge is now to find ways of socialising newcomers that foster *both* innovation and commitment.

Stabilisation

Nicholson (1990) has commented that much of work psychology seems to be built on the assumption that people are in the stabilisation stage. Yet the pace of change in the early twenty-first century is such that many people spend little or no time in this stage before moving on. Those who do reach it and experience it for any length of time are presumably both sufficiently satisfied with their job and satisfactory to the organisation in terms of their performance in it. This is a key proposition of the theory of work adjustment (Dawis and Lofquist, 1984). Satisfaction is not necessarily static though – there may be frequent minor but significant changes in work duties, colleagues, etc., which are too small to count as transitions but which nevertheless require adjustment.

For some people, the effect of organisations reducing the number of levels in their management hierarchy and disbanding well-established career routes is to keep them in a job for much longer than they had anticipated. This is sometimes termed a *career plateau*, which Feldman and Weitz (1988) defined as the point in a person's career where the likelihood of additional increases in responsibility is very low.

It is often assumed that the plateaued person is unhappy about this situation and that this unhappiness is likely to produce negative work attitudes and poor performance. This pattern does indeed sometimes happen (Goffee and Scase, 1992). But plateauing can occur for many reasons, and produce many reactions, not all negative (Ettington, 1998). A person may have all the responsibility he or she wants already. Howard and Bray's (1988) longitudinal research over 20 years showed that people are often able to reduce their ambitions quite painlessly. Plateauing may therefore be something that some people are reconciled to by the time it happens. And given the decline of the bureaucratic career noted earlier, plateauing may in any case be a less relevant concept than it was. Indeed, people may *choose* not to take on additional responsibility even though they are seen as capable of handling it. Even if this is not the case, it is important to consider exactly why an individual is plateaued in order to determine what should be done about it (Tan and Salomone, 1994). A lack of ability may be rectifiable by retraining. A lack of experience can be made good by a sideways move to another job which will provide the required experience, or by project work within the existing job. In some cases of possible discrimination on the basis of (for example) ethnicity or gender, senior members of the organisation may need urgently to review organisational career management practices.

Transitions into and out of the employment market

Aside from the transition cycle, there are certain transitions and aspects of transitions that have received some special attention. The first is the transition into work from education. For some years there has been a tendency to assume that this

Exercise 14.5   Comparing two work-role transitions

Jo Smith

Last month Jo Smith (a UK national) started her new job as the Human Resource Director (Eastern Asia) of Stockitt & Sellitt department stores, having previously been training manager for the company in the United Kingdom. Jo is thrilled to have got the job. She is 48-years-old, whereas most HR Directors are more like 38 or 40 when first appointed. Certainly she had anticipated making the grade (if at all) some years earlier. Still, she thought, at least it's a case of better late than never. A number of people in the company were delighted about her appointment, both because they felt she deserved it and because it seemed to show that the company wasn't only for young people. Jo would have a lot more freedom in her new job to do things the way she wanted, and she felt confident about handling this. Although the Eastern Asia HR Director job had many different duties from her training manager job, earlier in her career she had built up wide-ranging experience across all aspects of HR, albeit in the United Kingdom, and she was looking forward to using that. Jo had talked to a number of HR Directors both in Stockitt & Sellitt and outside, and discovered that most of them had had her sort of background, including a lack of overseas experience, when first appointed. They had given her a lot of information about what their jobs involved. Nevertheless, it had been a surprise when this job came Jo's way. The previous Director of HR (Eastern Asia) had left suddenly. Even though Jo had more or less given up hope of reaching HR Director level, within days she had been earmarked for the job and then quickly appointed without any other candidates being interviewed. Jo enjoyed greatly her training manager job, and it was clear that she would have continued to have the company's support if she had chosen to stay in that role. However, she wanted the Director's job, not least because it meant a significantly higher salary.

Harry Brown

Last month Harry Brown (a UK national) started his new job as Quality Manager in the UK data processing centre of Round the World Bank. Harry had previously been long-serving manager of a branch of the bank in Singapore, where he had lived for many years. Harry is very pleased and relieved to have got the Quality Manager's job. He is 48-years-old, and for several years has been acutely aware of his insecure position, what with reductions in the bank's headcount and the virtual disappearance of staff over 50 years of age. He is even keeping the same salary, status and employment conditions, although he will have to move to the United Kingdom largely at his own expense. The bank gave him fully a year's notice of his redeployment to the data-processing centre but it is only very recently that Harry found out what his new job would involve. It is the only one of its kind within Round the World Bank. Although he has been involved in quality issues in the bank's Singapore operation, Harry is fairly inexperienced in the quality area, and not clear about the duties his new job will involve. In general terms he has always expected a move in this late 40s – in the past it has been the bank's policy to move employees on at around that age to keep them flexible and interested. But he would have expected a move to a job and a culture a little more familiar than this. He had not lived in the United Kingdom for over 20 years and nowadays felt much more at home in Asia. But Harry felt he must accept the offer because the likely alternative was redundancy. People have proved rather reluctant to talk to him about his move, being unsure whether to congratulate him about keeping a good job or commiserate with him for being shunted to one side.

1   What are the similarities and differences between the transitions experienced by Jo and Harry?

2   What are the likely consequences of these for their performance and adjustment in their new jobs?

transition is likely to be difficult for young people because they are entering an unfamiliar world, making important decisions about their future, and simultaneously making the transition from childhood to adulthood. But in fact most young people who enter employment do so without undue stress (Arnold, 1990). They are often pleasantly surprised by the friendliness and informality of their workplace, and sometimes their work is actually better than they expected (Arnold, 1990). Unpleasant surprises include the political and apparently irrational ways in which decisions are made in work organisations. Perhaps less obvious, at least to many psychologists, is the role of wider factors that can influence the way a young person has been brought up, and the opportunities available to him or her (Mortimer, 2003). These factors include social class, education systems and changes at national and international levels – for example the reunification of Germany during the 1990s.

As Schein (1978) observed, a key task for young people entering the world of work is to accept that this is the way things are, and to decide how to handle it rather than merely complaining about it. The task facing young people is *not* to find an occupation that they can pursue for the rest of their working lives. Rather, it is to find work which suits them for the present and to continue their learning and expand their interests and abilities for the sake of their futures (Krumboltz and Worthington, 1999).

At the other end of the career, the transition out of work – *retirement* – has also received some attention. Just as the transition into work is becoming less clearcut than it was due to the increasing number of part-time jobs, work experience schemes in schools etc., so the same is happening to the transition out of it. Retirement is often a gradual *disengagement* (to use Super's term) from the labour force rather than a sudden change in status (Reday-Mulvey and Taylor, 1996). Also, there is sometimes a gap between subjective and objective retirement. A person may not consider himself or herself retired even if classified as retired on the basis of the (small) number of hours worked and being in receipt of a pension (Feldman, 1994). As is the case for the transition into work, retirement is often experienced quite positively, though not always. Good health, retiring voluntarily as opposed to compulsorily, adequate income and personal preparation for retirement all help a person adjust well to being retired (Bosse *et al.*, 1991).

Key Learning Point

Transitions at the start and end of working life are, for most people, less diffi-cult than is often assumed.

Relocation

The management by organisations of people transferring from one job to another within that organisation is often covered under the label *relocation*. Brett *et al.* (1992) have identified three main forms of relocation:

1 *Job transfer*: a within-country move between jobs in the same organisation.

2 *International transfer*: an international move between jobs in the same organisation.

3 *Group moves*: a relocation of a relatively large group of employees who normally work together.

Employees have become more reluctant to relocate in recent years. This is partly because relocation affects the whole family. Lawson and Angle (1994), among others, have found that disruption to children's education and friendships, and dif-ficulties of house buying and selling were more important than work concerns to relocating employees and their partners. Eby and Russell (2000) studied a sample of 872 pairs of employees and spouses from 74 organisations in America. They found that easily the best predictor of employee willingness to relocate for the firm was the spouse's attitude to moving. Less important, but still somewhat influential, were employee age (younger people were more willing), employee commitment to the organisation and desire for career progression.

Increasing numbers of relocations involve movement between countries. These international relocations can of course present greater difficulties of adjustment than domestic ones. Black *et al.* (1991) presented a thorough analysis of many of the key issues. Along with a number of other authors, they estimated the failure rate of international assignments (failure was defined as returning early) as between 16 and 40 per cent. However, Forster (1997) showed that this figure was based on speculation rather than data. In his study the failure rate appeared to be between 8 and 28 per cent. Then again, some would argue that a person who stays in their assignment for the planned period of time but is ineffective represents a greater failure than someone who returns home early.

Family issues appear to be even more important in international relocations than in domestic ones (Harvey, 1998). Some employing organisations are responding to this by offering cross-cultural training before departure not only to the employee but also to his/her family. Even so, it seems that additional training in understanding the new culture after arrival is also often useful (Mendenhall and Stahl, 2000). How well the family adusts to the new environment has a substantial impact on how well the employee is able to perform at work. Family factors seem to be more of a barrier for women than men on international relocation (Linehan and Walsh 2001).

Selection of staff to undertake international relocation is often based on specific job-related skills rather than on interpersonal skills or openness to other cultures. This is probably a significant cause of problems, though as Selmer (2001) has pointed out, often the problem is to find *anyone* willing to go rather than to select between enthusiastic candidates. It is also important not to assume that pre-departure issues of selection and training are all that matters.

Support from the home office during the assignment helps to prevent early returns (Garonzik *et al.*, 2000), and a carefully thought-out policy for how to reintegrate returning assignees helps to avoid subsequent disillusion. This is because it is easy for people based overseas to believe that they have been forgotten and will not be considered for good opportunities when they return. Also, other staff who have never been overseas can benefit a lot from what the returned international assignee has learned, especially if some thought is given to how that learning opportunity is best organised (Mendenhall and Stahl, 2000).

Key Learning Point

The management of relocation requires great attention to family-related concerns.

Gender and careers

Much research on careers has focused on males, and often white, middle-class ones at that. This is not a satisfactory state of affairs. Since the 1980s there have been some attempts to rectify the imbalance (*see*, for example, Larwood and Gutek, 1987; Davidson and Burke, 2000). There is no doubt that women are at a disadvantage relative to men in the labour market (Davidson and Cooper, 1992) so to what extent do existing theory and practice reflect women's needs and career problems? Not very much, many would answer.

The lifespan theories of Levinson and Super described earlier in this chapter have been particularly heavily criticised for focusing on the experiences and personal concerns of men to the exclusion of those of women. For example, Bardwick (1980) and Gallos (1989), among others, argued that women focus more on attachment and affiliation in their development, in contrast to men, who emphasise separateness and achievement. Nevertheless, although some developmental issues are more problematic for women than for men, Levinson would argue that the same underlying concerns arise at the same ages for both sexes. So whereas for a man the age 30 transition might focus mainly on occupational concerns, for a woman it might concern whether and when to have children. The issues are different but the theme of fine-tuning the direction of one's life is the same (Roberts and Newton, 1987).

A number of psychologists have developed theories concerning aspects of women's career development. For example, White *et al.* (1992) developed a model of the careers of successful women managers. Betz and Hackett (1981) examined how self-efficacy influences women's career choices and aspirations. Gattiker and Larwood (1988) have discussed what career success means for women. These and other analyses have in common a recognition that the socialisation of girls and societal expectations of women's and men's roles are likely to have profound effects on the way women think about their careers. The same is true for men, but this is less often recognised because of the temptation to take male socialisation and values as an unquestioned norm. There is some suggestion, however, that the new so-called boundaryless career is favouring women bacause they are more accustomed to having to change their work and balance multiple priorities. Their orientation towards relationships, often termed 'communion' is said to be well-suited to an era of networking and teamworking. Men's orientation is more towards problem-solving and acting upon the world (often called agency), which may still be useful but not sufficient in a complex world.

When women's career success is assessed on the basis of conventional criteria of salary progression and promotion, there is generally bad news. In a well-designed and influential study, Stroh *et al.* (1992) found that women members of a large sample of American managers, who were comparable to men in education, qualifications, experience, proportion of family income generated and willingness to relocate, still suffered from slightly less good salary progression than the men. Furthermore, Brett and Stroh (1997) found that the men gained more in salary by moving between employing organisations, but the women did not. Schneer and Reitman (1995) found that women MBA graduates, up to 18 years after obtaining their degree, earned on average 19 per cent less than men, and that only a small part of this could be explained by possibly legitimate factors such as years of work experience. Tharenou *et al.* (1994) found that training helped men's advancement in terms of status and salary more than women's, and that women's success depended on receiving encouragement from other people more than men's success did. Lyness and Thompson (2000) found relatively few differences between high-flying men and women, but even among this highly successful group there were some small differences. For example, women reported more difficulty getting geographical mobility opportunities, and more concern that they did not fit the dominant culture.

Key Learning Point

Women and men tend to have different developmental paths. Career theory and practice still reflect men's perspectives better than women's.

One way in which women's careers have traditionally differed from men's is, of course, their likelihood of being interrupted by child-bearing and child-rearing, and by the fact that in most households a woman does more of the childcare and housework than a man, no matter what her employment situation. The presence of two people in a household pursuing careers (usually called dual-career couples) adds extra stresses for both partners (*see* Chapter 11), but again these seem to fall more on the woman than on the man (Cooper and Lewis, 1993). A variety of measures designed to help people with family responsibilities are used by some employers. One of these is the use of flexible working patterns, such as total annual working hours, which people can distribute through the year as they wish (within certain fairly broad limits). Career breaks have been used relatively extensively, most notably by financial services organisations. People can suspend their career with the organisation for several years, normally in order to make a start on raising a family. During that time they must report for refresher training for a small number of weeks per year. These may look like expensive schemes, but what evaluation evidence there is suggests that they are cost-effective for organisations because they help to retain skilled labour. On the other hand, there is some feeling that people who make use of them may find that their subsequent progress is handicapped by others perceiving that they are not really serious about their career. Judiesch and Lyness (1999) report that leaves of absence for family responsibilities are almost always taken by women not men, and that leaves result in fewer subsequent promotions and smaller salary increases.

Career management in organisations

Some organisations have responded to the trends described earlier in this chapter by giving up any attempt to manage the careers of employees. Because traditional career paths have disappeared and organisational structures are continually changing, some believe that there does not seem much point in attempting corporate management of careers. The term 'self-development' is now frequently used. As the words suggest, it means that individual employees are responsible for identifying their own development needs, and for doing something about them. Refer back to the opening case study of this chapter for good illustrations of how some people approach this. But self-development seems to mean slightly different things in different places. On the one hand, it can be quite an aggressive message: 'You're on your own; look after yourself'. Alternatively, it can be more supportive: 'Don't expect the organisation to tell you how you need to develop, but we can play a part in helping you to make and implement your own decisions'.

Table 14.3 describes some of the interventions that can be used in organisations to manage careers. It is difficult to obtain accurate figures on which interventions are used most, though evidence from Iles and Mabey (1993) and Baruch and Peiperl (2000) is helpful. It looks as if internal vacancy advertising is nearly universal. Lateral moves and succession planning seem to be used by more than half of the organisations questioned. Perhaps surprisingly, so is counselling either by the line manager or human resources staff – though this may be slightly wishful thinking by those reporting on behalf of their organisation. Mentoring seems to be becoming increasingly common, with perhaps 50 per cent of medium to large-size organisations either running organised schemes or actively encouraging the formation of informal mentor–protégé pairings. Formal career path information is (or is said to be) provided in about one-third of organisations, which is perhaps surprising given frequent and major structural changes and the disappearance of career paths in many organisations. Self-assessment materials, development centres, career planning workshops and career counselling probably feature in one quarter-or one-sixth of organisations. Baruch (2003) provides a useful discussion of these and other techniques available for managing careers in organisations.

Key Learning Point

There are many different career management interventions available to organisations, and some organisations use several of them.

Several of the career management interventions shown in Table 14.3 (for example, mentoring, coaching and career action centres) can be used to support self-development rather than organisational control of careers. But on the whole, the interventions are used to pursue organisational goals, and in some organisations the notion of managing careers has rather come back into fashion. This is a reaction to the fact that the choices people make about their self-development do not necessarily serve the needs of the organisation. For example, a company's IT specialists may tend to seek training on a popular software package which helps them to maintain their employability, but which happens to be of little use to that company.

It is neither possible nor desirable to use all of the interventions in the same organisation at the same time. Hirsh *et al.* (1995) point out that it is much better to do a few things well than a lot badly. It is also necessary to be clear about what an intervention is designed to achieve, and on whose behalf. Possible purposes are:

- filling vacancies – that is, selecting one or more people for specific posts;

- assessment of potential, competencies, skills or interests – this might help an organisation to assess its human resources, or individuals to know how well placed they are to obtain specific jobs inside or outside the organisation;

- development of skills and competencies – in order to help an organisation to function effectively in its markets, or individuals to be more effective in future jobs;

- identification of career options – that is, what types of work or specific posts might be obtainable for one or more individuals;

- action to implement career plans.

Key Learning Point

It is important that the purpose(s) of career management interventions are clearly defined and stated.

Table 14.3	Career management interventions in organisations

1 *Internal vacancy notification.* Information about jobs available in the organisation, normally in advance of any external advertising, with a job description and some details of preferred experience, qualifications.

2 *Career paths.* Information about the sequences of jobs that people can do, or competencies they can acquire, in the organisation. This should include details of how high in the organisation any path goes, the kinds of interdepartmental transfers that are possible, and perhaps the skills/experience required to follow various paths.

3 *Career workbooks.* These consist of questions and exercises designed to guide individuals in determining their strengths and weaknesses, identifying job and career opportunities, and determining necessary steps for reaching their goals.

4 *Career planning workshops.* These cover some of the same ground as workbooks, but offer more chance for discussion, feedback from others, information about organisation-specific opportunities and policies. They may include psychometric testing.

5 *Computer-assisted career management.* Various packages exist for helping employees to assess their skills, interests and values, and translate these into job options. Sometimes those options are customised to a particular organisation. A few packages designed for personnel or manpower planning also include some career-relevant facilities.

6 *Individual counselling.* Can be done by specialists from inside or outside the organisation, or by line managers who have received training. May include psychometric testing.

7 *Training and educational opportunities.* Information and financial support about, and possibly delivery of, courses in the organisation or outside it. These can enable employees to update, retrain or deepen their knowledge in particular fields. In keeping with the notion of careers involving sequences, training in this context is not solely to improve performance in a person's present job.

8 *Personal development plans (PDPs).* These often arise from the appraisal process and other sources such as development centres. PDPs are statements of how a person's skills and knowledge might appropriately develop, and how this development could occur in a given timescale.

9 *Career action centres.* Resources such as literature, videos and CD-ROMs and perhaps more personal inputs such as counselling available to employees on a drop-in basis.

10 *Development centres.* Like assessment centres in that participants are assessed on the basis of their performance in a number of exercises and tests. However, development centres focus on identifying a person's strengths, weaknesses and styles for the purpose of development, instead of (or as well as) selection.

11 *Mentoring programmes.* Attaching employees to more senior ones who act as advisers, and perhaps also as advocates, protectors and counsellors.

12 *Coaching.* This is defined in various ways, and can be similar to mentoring. It usually involves one-to-one sessions between coach and 'coachee', where the former helps the latter address issues regarding adjustment and performance at work (and possibly outside it).

13 *Succession planning.* The identification of individuals who are expected to occupy key posts in the future, and who are exposed to experiences which prepare them appropriately.

14 *Job assignments/rotation.* Careful use of work tasks can help a person to stay employable for the future, and an organisation to benefit from the adaptability of staff.

15 *Outplacement.* This may involve several interventions listed above. Its purpose is to support people who are leaving the organisation to clarify and implement plans for their future.

16 *Secondment.* Individuals work temporarily in another organisation, or in another part of the same one.

Any intervention might achieve more than one purpose, but it is important to be clear about what purpose(s) it is designed for. It is also necessary, according to Hirsh *et al.* (1995), to be clear about who in the organisation is eligible to participate in interventions – preferably everyone. The operation of a career management intervention must be consistent with its goals. So, for example, it would be inappropriate for detailed feedback about performance in a development centre to be withheld from participants if an aim of the development centre was to help people identify their career options.

We will now briefly describe three career management interventions that are of particular interest to work psychologists. Notice how two of them feature in the opening case study of this chapter.

Career counselling

This has been defined by Nathan and Hill (1992) as 'a process which enables people to recognise and utilise their resources to make career-related decisions and manage career-related problems'. One might add that this process is an interpersonal one, in order to distinguish counselling from (for example) computer-aided guidance.

There are several different approaches to career counselling, some of which draw very directly on specific traditions in psychology (*see* Chapter 1; *see also* Walsh and Osipow, 1990). One approach relies heavily on the use of psychometric tests and here the counsellor tends to give advice on the basis of the test results. However, the most common approach to counselling can be described as person-centred, based loosely on Carl Rogers' humanist ideas (*see* Chapter 1). The counsellor does not generally give advice, but helps the client clarify his or her ideas about self and world of work by offering unconditional positive regard and asking open-ended questions. Many writers identify different phases of a counselling interaction (e.g. Egan, 1998; Nelson-Jones, 2000). The phases they identify tend to be fairly similar though not identical. Reddy (1987) described them as follows:

1 *Understanding*: the counselling focuses on listening to what the client is saying, and observing the associated non-verbal behaviour. The counsellor seeks to show no more than understanding. Listening requires concentration. Normal everyday conversation often involves surprisingly little listening, so a person who is being a counsellor needs to work on it.

2 *Challenging*: as Reddy (1987) points out, listening helps for a lot longer than one might think, but not for ever. The aim of this second phase is to help a client shift his or her thinking by probing for further information, challenging apparent inconsistency, summarising what the counsellor thinks the client has said, and perhaps by giving information. Suggesting interpretations and picking out themes are other possible counsellor techniques of this stage, *but not before*.

3 *Resourcing*: having clarified the feeling (phase 1) and thinking (phase 2), possible decisions and plans of action often emerge. Here the counsellor's role is often to help the client to fine-tune plans, perhaps by giving coaching in job-seeking techniques, and suggesting sources of further information.

Career counselling is more about listening than giving advice. Also, it concerns any career-related issue, not just choosing an occupation.

Career counselling is offered by a number of individuals and agencies in education and private practice. It can also occur much more informally through work colleagues, friends or relatives. Some organisations offer (and pay for) career counselling for staff, normally delivered by an independent consultant who has no stake in the organisation and who can therefore work purely in the client's interest. Perhaps understandably, it is common for organisations to offer career counselling only when there is an immediate and obvious need, such as when people are being made redundant. Whatever the situation in which counselling occurs, it is important that the counsellor maintains confidentiality. Nothing that is said or done in the counselling sessions can normally be revealed to anyone else, except with the client's permission.

Development centres

Development centres are attractive to work psychologists because of their similarity to assessment centres which are commonly used in selection. Psychologists have over many years studied the effectiveness of assessment centres and also their psychometric properties (see for examples Gaugler *et al.*, 1987). Consequently, development centres tend to be soundly designed with exercises carefully devised to allow assessment of candidates' competencies, and well-trained assessors observing the candidates. The trickier issues concern how the development centre is used in career development. It is often said that development centres are intended to identify people's development needs rather than select them, but in reality development centres are often partly about selection. For example, they may be used to decide who gets on to a fast-track promotion scheme. This can mean that candidates try to hide their weaknesses, thus making it more difficult for assessors to identify their development needs (Woodruffe, 1993).

Studies of development centres in real organisations show that it really is difficult for assessment and development to mix if the assessment process is used to give people an overall grading, and especially if that grading affects their future prospects (Arnold, 2002). Another major issue is whether plans for personal development are drawn up after the centre, and if so whether they are implemented. Carrick and Williams's (1999) review of the field suggests that this is a continuing problem because hard-pressed line managers may be unwilling to devote time and energy to developing others, and in any case may lack the skills for doing so. There may also be ambiguity concerning whose responsibility it is to implement a development plan.

Mentoring

Mentoring has been defined in a number of ways, but perhaps the most widely accepted definition is that of Kram (1985): 'a relationship between a young adult and an older, more experienced adult that helps the younger individual learn to navigate in the adult world and the world of work. A mentor supports, guides and counsels the young adult as he or she accomplishes this important task'.

Mentoring can fulfil a number of specific functions for the person being mentored (who is normally called the protégé). Kram (1985) divided these into *career functions* and *psychosocial functions*. The *career functions* include sponsorship, where the mentor promotes the interests of the protégé by putting him or her forward for desirable projects or job moves; exposure and visibility to high-ranking people; coaching the protégé by sharing ideas and suggesting strategies; protecting the protégé from risks to his or her reputation; and (if the mentor is in a position to do so) providing challenging work assignments for the protégé. The *psychosocial functions* include acting as a role model for the protégé; providing acceptance and confirmation; frank discussion of the protégé's anxieties and fears; and friendship. Mentoring has become a popular technique for developing younger employees; so much so that claims like 'everyone needs a mentor' (Clutterbuck, 2001) are taken seriously.

Psychologists have been very keen to research mentoring, especially its impact on those who receive it. It is potentially an effective way of socialising new employees and passing on accumulated wisdom. It also offers some people in mid or late career the chance to be a mentor, which may appeal to their career and life concerns, and can introduce a motivating new element to their job. On the other hand, there is not yet very much research demonstrating that people who participate in organised mentoring schemes receive benefits that other people do not. What evidence there is suggests that they enjoy better salaries and promotion rates, at least under some circumstances (Whitely *et al.*, 1991; Aryee and Chay, 1994). This seems particularly the case when the mentoring is informal (i.e. it happens spontaneously) rather than formal, where it happens because there is a mentoring scheme that people have to participate in (Chao *et al.*, 1992). But it is less clear whether receiving mentoring is actually what produces the benefits. Perhaps the people who experience mentoring tend to have certain characteristics (for example, an ability to get themselves noticed by effective mentors, or to be selected by organisations offering mentoring) which would have brought them success even without mentoring.

There are certainly examples of mentoring failing to provide significant benefits to any of the parties involved (e.g. Arnold and Johnson, 1997). There has also been some concern that mentoring can actually cause harm – for example a mentor may stifle the protégé or have unrealistic expectations of him/her (Scandura, 1998). This 'dark side' of mentoring seems to be relatively rarely experienced, but it does happen (Eby *et al.*, 2000). There has also been some attention to the mentor's perspective, particularly concerning what makes potential mentors more or less inclined to fulfil the role (Allen *et al.*, 1997).

It is likely that some mentoring schemes work better than others. It is probably important that mentors and protégés want the relationship, and they may well need training and orientation in order to make the most of it. The goals of the mentoring scheme should be clear and specific. The mentor's work performance should be assessed and rewarded partly on the basis of how effectively he or she is carrying out the mentoring role. The culture of the organisation should be one that values personal and professional development. Even then there is a danger that mentors will hand on outdated knowledge and skills to protégés, especially in times of rapid change.

There are some signs that mentoring is being superseded by coaching as a preferred way of developing people. This may simply be a new word for the same activities, but it may also signal a shift to more performance-focused approach where the emphasis is more on improving quality of work now than on long-term career or general psychological well-being.

Key Learning Point

Mentoring has potential benefits for all parties involved, but it is not easy to achieve those benefits with an organised mentoring scheme.

Exercise 14.6   A successful laboratory technician

Pauline Ware was deputy chief laboratory technician at the main factory of a medium-size agrochemicals company. She had been there 11 years, ever since joining from school. This is her story:

'When I left school I didn't really know exactly what I wanted to do. I took my exams, mainly in sciences. I passed but did less well than I had hoped. I had really wanted to be a science teacher, but I wasn't sure whether my grades were good enough to get into a teacher training course, and somehow I never got round to finding out. Also, I wasn't very confident about my abilities at that time, and wondered whether I could really handle lots of youngsters. Mind you, I had helped one of my teachers with one of his classes of younger children a few times, and that seemed to go quite well.

'Anyway, I saw an advert in the local paper for a trainee lab technician job here. It sounded good. They said the person selected would be able to choose which project they wanted to work on, and that in the long term there would be chances to take extra courses and get promotion to a job as development scientist. I was also told ▶

that most of my work would be quite skilled, and that other people were employed to do the most boring bits. Well, they offered me the job and I took it. I soon found out that things weren't quite as I'd imagined. There was no choice of project at that time, the budget for technician education was small, nobody could remember anyone being promoted from technician to scientist, though it was possible in theory, and I found I *was* expected to do many unskilled tasks like sweeping the floor. I complained to Personnel or Human Resources as they are called these days. They were quite surprised, and said that the laboratory must have failed to implement the changes in technician's job descriptions agreed several months earlier.

'So I was quite fed up, but I didn't leave. That was partly because I couldn't think of anything better, and partly because I was planning to get married, and somehow work didn't seem very important. And I did learn quite a lot in that first job. I got little training, and there were no other new technicians joining at the same time as me, so it was a bit scary at first, but I learned my own way of doing things. That stood me in good stead four years later when I was moved to another lab. I soon found out that my predecessor there had not been very effective. Although it was a different lab, I knew more or less what to do. I changed a lot of things for the better, and that got me noticed. In the next six years I was promoted three times. So now here I am as deputy chief technician.

'You'd think that was fine, but actually I'm not so sure. I don't really know where to go next. I wouldn't want the chief's job. She has to go to lots of meetings, argue over financial allocations, draw up five-year plans and all that. Myself, I have to make sure we are getting the right equipment at the right time, and I look after the training of the technicians – so in a way I'm a teacher after all! The point is that I'm still using my scientific know-how.

'In the last five years three chiefs have left because the chief's job does not involve technical work. So have two deputies who can't see any future for them in the chief's work. I have the same problem: I like my work, but I think in a couple of years I will have done all I can in this role. Then what? Nobody knows, least of all me. I want to prove I can handle a higher job because nowadays I feel confident about my abilities. Yet this company has never said anything about where you can go from here. In fact, I'm seeing Human Resources about it next week. Mind you, I still haven't forgotten how out of touch they were when they advertised my job.'

1   Examine the role in this case study of (i) Pauline's self-concept, (ii) realistic job previews, (iii) socialisation and innovation, and (iv) career anchors.

2   If you were the human resources manager, what provision, if any, would you be making to support the career development of laboratory technicians in the company?

Summary

Careers concern the sequence of jobs people hold, and the attitudes and behaviours associated with them. Labour market and organisational changes have made the careers experienced by many people less predictable than they once were, and a sense of injustice and broken promises is quite common among employees in work organisations. It is increasingly recognised that choices frequently have to be re-made later in careers, and that between choices many significant developments can occur. Much career development theory and practice therefore attempts to identify people's concerns at different stages of their lives, though research on career choice still tends to treat it as choice of a type of work made by young people on the basis of their relatively static personal characteristics. Psychologists have produced helpful theories for understanding different types of people and different types of job. They have also produced some practical ways in which individuals can improve their own choice of occupation. There is also some useful guidance concerning what helps people be successful in their careers, but there is a need for more flexible thinking about what career success might mean apart from promotion and pay increases. In general, career theory tends to reflect men's perspectives better than women's. It is based on men's lives and men's values. Given the increasing frequency of job changes, there is also a lot of attention paid to how individuals and organisations can manage transitions from one job to another. Some organisations attempt to manage the career development of their employees. A number of techniques can be used to achieve this, including mentoring, careers counselling and development centres. Current trends are towards increasing flexibility of career structures, and towards identifying how career development systems can be implemented and maintained successfully within organisations.

Closing Case Study   Cleaning Up Careers

Bruno Lundby has had some of the toughest, dirtiest jobs around. He has dug sludge from the bottom of empty crude oil tanks, cleaned up offices and homes after fires and floods and cleared roads for UN troops in the former Yugoslavia. Mr Lundby, 30, was one of the ranks of typically low-paid, low-status workers who fill supermarket shelves, serve fast food, change hotel beds or empty office waste bins, often at unsocial hours and with little expectation of anything better.

Lacking formal qualifications, he drifted from the army into odd cleaning jobs. Then, unexpectedly, he found the opportunity for advancement in a management training programme offered by ISS, the Danish support services group. Today he sits in a spotless, air-conditioned office directing all ISS damage control operations in the greater Copenhagen area.

'I couldn't have imagined getting to where I am today when I started,' he says. 'I was surprised to be offered a future at ISS in 1993 when I became a supervisor.' In the past three years, he has been promoted three times.

ISS, which employs 272,000 people in 36 countries in Europe, Asia and Latin America in cleaning and other contract work, still appears to be an exception in ▶

the services sector in offering career progression to workers. Noel Howell of Uni, the Geneva-based global trade union for skills and services, says that employment conditions and prospects vary from sector to sector within the service industry and some employers are 'diabolical'.

But there are also signs of change: the concentration of ownership in some industries means quality is replacing price as the basis of competition. 'Value added is becoming more important and that often means better qualified staff,' he says. 'We're seeing more resources devoted to training.'

ISS acknowledges that by offering career progression it has changed the nature of its contract with blue-collar employees, raising expectations on both sides that may not always be met. Its 'five-star' management training programme had been in place for more than 10 years, training about 800 people a year. There is also a corporate university in Copenhagen, operating in partnership with IMD, the Swiss business school, to train senior managers.

But some employees' hopes for a management role may be disappointed. So the next step is to devolve power down the ranks, says Martin Christensen, human resources director. Cleaning team leaders will be responsible for profit and loss on their contracts and for the quality of customer care, in addition to training and organising shifts.

Last November, the company launched an intranet job site in Norway to increase cross-border mobility for staff who want it. The aim is to make the portal available in all its locations. Staff with no internet access will receive print-outs of job vacancies.

How effective has ISS been so far in improving the quality of blue-collar jobs? 'We're in an industry where most people are not very well educated and there is high staff turnover, of 80–90 per cent a year,' says Martin Christensen. Within ISS, turnover ranges from just 20 per cent in Denmark, where the company culture is embedded, to more than 80 per cent in Austria, where newly acquired businesses are being integrated.

Another indicator of quality is the proportion of full-time to part-time jobs. Mr Christensen says most cleaning companies hire people part-time or on temporary contracts to keep staff costs low and avoid high social payments. ISS had intended that 80 per cent of its workforce should be employed full-time by 2000. So far, the figure has reached 52 per cent. Mr Christensen says this should be seen in the light of a doubling in staff numbers through acquisitions in the past three to four years. 'I'd be satisfied if we reached that goal (of 80 per cent) by 2005.'

He says not every cleaner will want to work full-time, or to progress and have extra responsibilities. 'But I think there are many people who haven't been given the opportunity, so it's never been in their mind that they have this possibility.'

For Mr Lundby, career progress has induced loyalty to his employer and greater self-esteem. 'Personal skills are often more important than high educational qualifications if you have to deal with people every day,' he says. 'I'm a practical, not an academic, person. I know the business from the bottom. I know the loop-holes and the hardships.'

Source: Financial Times, *3 September 2001*

Suggested exercises

1 In what ways does ISS reflect recent changes in labour markets, and in what ways does it contradict them?

2 What ideas from the literature on psychological contracts can be applied to this case study?

3 In what ways do careers in ISS reflect the bureaucratic form, and in what ways do they reflect other forms?

4 To what extent do you think ISS is achieving competitive advantage through its career management? What other career management techniques, if any, might it use to its advantage?

Test your learning

Short-answer questions

1 Describe the reasons why careers are more difficult to manage than they used to be.

2 List some of the available criteria for assessing objective and subjective career success.

3 What vocational personality types have been identified by John Holland, and how are they related to each other?

4 List three limitations of Holland's theory.

5 In what ways is self-efficacy significant in career decision-making?

6 What phases of adult life were identified by Daniel Levinson, and what are the main characteristics of each stage?

7 Describe the transition cycle and for each stage suggest one problem that might arise for a person experiencing a work-role transition.

8 What is a 'realistic job preview'?

9 According to Schein, what is a career anchor? List at least six of the anchors Schein proposed.

10 Define eight techniques that can be used in organisations to manage careers.

11 Define mentoring and outline its potential benefits.

12 What three stages can be identified in a counselling relationship?

13 Describe two key research findings that show how women are at a disadvantage relative to men in their careers.

Suggested assignments

1 Critically examine the extent to which labour market changes are affecting the careers that people experience.

2 Discuss how the various definitions of career can influence how career success is construed.

3 Examine the extent to which John Holland's theory has improved our understanding of careers.

4 In what ways, if any, does the transition cycle help us to understand and manage job change?

5 What, if anything, can career/life stage theories contribute to effective career management?

6 Using examples, examine the likely impact of career management interventions in organisations.

Relevant websites

A good example of a site geared to helping people manage their own careers (especially in the professions and/or management) is http://www.expatica.com/jobs/careerzone.asp. It gives information about the current job market in several European countries, and also advice about how to present oneself effectively across cultures, and survive and prosper when starting a new job in an unfamiliar culture.

John Holland's Self-Directed Search career choice questionnaire has its own website at http://www.self-directed-search.com/browser.html. You can take a version of the SDS and see what your scores suggest about appropriate occupations for you. Beware: it does cost, though not very much. You get an on-screen report which will probably suggest more possible occupations than you expected.

Another good example of a self-help all-purpose careers site is http://content.monster.com/. You can find advice about many aspects of managing your career, as well as information about various occupations. It's primarily geared to the USA, but travels relatively well.

For further self-test material and relevant, annotated websites please visit the website at http://www.booksites.net/arnold_workpsych.

Suggested further Reading

Full details are given in the reference list at the end of the book.

1 John Arnold's (1997) book *Managing Careers into the 21st Century*, published by Sage, provides a more detailed analysis of all of the topics covered in this chapter.

2 Somewhat similar to Arnold's book but from an American perspective, Jeffrey Greenhaus, Gerard Callanan and Veronica Godshalk's book *Career Management*, 3rd Edition, was published by Dryden Press in 2000. There is quite a strong focus on the individual as opposed to the organisation.

3 *The New Careers* by Michael Arthur, Kerr Inkson and Judith Pringle (1999) published by Sage is a scholarly but readable account of how people live out their careers in new and changing circumstances.

4 *Managing Careers* by Yehuda Baruch, published by Pearson Education in 2003, provides up to date coverage of many of the issues mentioned in this chapter, especially managing careers in global organisations.

CHAPTER 15

Understanding organisational change and culture

LEARNING OUTCOMES

After studying this chapter, you should be able to:

1 identify the two main approaches to organisational change;

2 describe and compare the strengths and weaknesses of the main approaches to change;

3 place these approaches within a wider framework for change;

4 identify the respective roles of managers, employees and change agents;

5 understand the difference between open-ended change and closed change;

6 appreciate how the main approaches view employee involvement and resistance;

7 explain how the different approaches view 'political' behaviour;

8 understand the role of culture both as an objective of, and a constraint on, change programmes;

9 list the main reasons why change projects fail.

Opening Case Study   Shake-up Plan Boosts TPSA Shares

Telekomunikacja Polska's shares jumped 4.5 per cent on Friday on news that the company's new managers were drafting a three-year plan to boost its efficiency. Managers told analysts in a conference call late on Thursday that the plan, to be completed next week, would aim to increase TPSA's revenues, decrease its debt, and reduce capital expenditure. 'I have great optimism that we're looking at a big change in corporate culture,' said George Storozynski, chief financial officer. France Telecom, which has displaced the Polish state as TPSA's dominant share-holder, appointed Mr Storozynski and Marek Jozefiak, chairman, last month. The shake-up came after the French company and its Polish partner, Kulczyk Holding, increased their stake in TPSA from 35 to 47.5 per cent, with an option to increase to majority control next year.

TPSA, one of Poland's largest private owners of real estate, will seek to reduce its debt in part by selling or selling and leasing back some of its sites, Mr Storozynski said. Staff cuts at TPSA will also be 'more aggressive than had been expected,' he said, adding that the company was consulting with lawyers about the scope of reductions allowed under France Telecom's 2000 privatisation agreement with Poland's state treasury. TPSA employed more than 71 000 people last year, but its unions are powerful and with Poland's unemployment rate at 16 per cent, radical cutbacks are likely to be politically sensitive. Pending France Telecom's approval, managers will present their new strategic plan to investors in a roadshow in the second or third week of January.

TPSA claims 10 million customers, but growth of its fixed-line business is slowing due to Poland's economic downturn and competition from mobile providers. Last week the company reported a 10 per cent drop in net profit for the first three quarters of the year to 862.8m zlotys ($210m).

Source: Adapted from article in Financial Times, *19 November 2001*

Introduction

The above case study illustrates three key aspects of organisational change in the modern world. Firstly, foreign ownership and control are increasing facts of life for many organisations, even (and perhaps especially) ex-public utilities. Secondly, despite much talk of 'a third way' and caring capitalism, organisations that underperform are likely to face swift and brutal job cuts and restructuring, regardless of previous agreements and assurances. Lastly, the prime aim of many of these restructuring programmes is to create an appropriate corporate culture. Nevertheless, what is an appropriate culture in one European country may not be so appropriate in another; changes driven by France Telecom and designed to reassure financial analysts in France may not seem that appropriate when implemented in an ex-public utility in Poland.

Without doubt, the ability to identify the right changes and implement them successfully is a prime task facing managers today. Despite the high level of interest in cultural change over the past two decades, it is not the only form of change organisations undertake. Whether change is small scale or large scale, strategic or operational, people-centred or technology-focused, it needs to be planned and implemented effectively. This chapter provides a critical review of the main approaches to planning and implementing change that have been developed since the 1950s. It begins by examining the importance and complexity of organisational change and illustrates this with an examination of organisational culture. From this, it is argued that an understanding of the theory and practice of change management is crucial to organisational effectiveness and success. The chapter then goes on to review the two main approaches to organisational change: the Planned Approach, and the Emergent Approach. It is shown that the Planned Approach, which was developed by Kurt Lewin in the 1940s and forms the core of organisation development (OD), views organisational change as essentially a process of moving from one fixed state to another through a series of predictable and pre-planned steps. However, it will be seen that the Emergent Approach, which came to the fore in the 1980s, starts from the alternative assumption that change is a continuous, open-ended and unpredictable process of aligning and realigning an organisation to its changing environment. Advocates of Emergent change argue that it is more suitable to the turbulent environment in which firms now operate because, unlike the Planned Approach, it recognises the need for organisations to align their internal practices and behaviour with changing external conditions. Proponents of Planned change, though, dispute this criticism and argue that as OD has developed it has come to incorporate more organisation-wide and transformational approaches to change.

The review of these two approaches will reveal that, despite the large body of literature devoted to the topic of change management, and the many tools and techniques available to change agents, there is considerable disagreement regarding the most appropriate approach. In an effort to bring clarity to the issue, the chapter concludes by presenting a *framework for change* which shows that neither the Emergent nor Planned Approach is suitable for all situations and circumstances. Instead, it is maintained that approaches to change tend to be situation-specific and that the potential exists for organisations to influence the constraints under which they operate in order to exercise choice over what to change and how to change.

The importance of change management

Change management would not be considered particularly important if products and markets were stable and organisational change was rare: however, that is not the case, nor has it ever been so. Change is an ever-present feature of organisational life, though many leading management thinkers such as Tom Peters (1995), Rosabeth Moss Kanter (1989), John Kotter (1996) and Charles Handy (1994) do argue that the place, magnitude and necessity of change have increased significantly over the past two decades.

Certainly, there is more than just anecdotal evidence to support this view, such as evidence from the UK Institute of Management, which surveyed its members throughout the 1990s. In 1991, the Institute reported that 90 per cent of organisations in its survey were becoming 'slimmer and flatter' (Coulson-Thomas and Coe, 1991, p. 10). In 1992, it reported that 80 per cent of managers responding to its survey had experienced one or more corporate restructurings in their organisations in the previous five years (Wheatley, 1992). In its 1995 survey (Institute of Management, 1995), 70 per cent of respondents reported that their organisations had restructured in the previous two years. A similar picture emerged from a study carried out at the University of Manchester Institute of Science and Technology (UMIST) in the early 1990s. This study found that 51 per cent of respondents' organisations were experiencing major transformations (Ezzamel *et al.*, 1994).

Despite the increasing prevalence of change, the evidence that it is actually bringing benefits to organisations or to those who work in them is debatable. In both the 1995 Institute of Management study and the UMIST study, managers reported considerable levels of dissatisfaction with the outcome of change programmes. The Institute of Management (1995) study found that, as a result of recent organisational changes, managers' workloads had increased greatly and that one in five was working an extra 15 hours per week. Many also reported that increased workloads were preventing them from devoting adequate time to long-term strategic planning or to their own training and development needs. The UMIST study found that while most managers supported the case for change, many were anxious not only about the outcome of change but also about the process of change itself (Ezzamel *et al.*, 1994).

Organisational change comes in many shapes, sizes and forms and, for this reason, it is not easy to establish an accurate picture of the degree of difficulty firms face in managing change successfully. However, there are three types of organisational change which, because of their perceived importance, have received considerable attention: the introduction of new technology in the 1980s; the adoption of total quality management (TQM) over the last 15 years; and, in the last decade, the application of business process re-engineering (BPR). All three, in their time, were hailed as 'revolutionary' approaches to improving performance and competitiveness. Nevertheless, the record of achievement in these areas (or rather the lack of it) indicates why managers are right to be anxious about both the outcome and the process of change.

The impact of the (so-called) microelectronics revolution of the 1980s, which saw the rapid expansion of computers and computer-based processes into most areas of organisational life, was the subject of a great many studies. These found that the failure rate of new technology change projects was anywhere between 40 and 70 per cent (Bessant and Haywood, 1985; Voss, 1985; McKracken, 1986; Smith and Tranfield, 1987; Kearney, 1989; New, 1989).

The move by European organisations to adopt TQM began in the mid-1980s. At its simplest, TQM is an organisation-wide effort to improve quality through changes in structure, practices, systems and, above all, attitudes (Dale and Cooper, 1992). Though seen as pre-eminently a Japanese innovation, the basic TQM techniques were developed in the United States in the 1950s (Crosby, 1979; Deming, 1982; Taguchi, 1986; Juran, 1988). Though TQM appears to be central to the success of Japanese companies, the experience of Western companies has been that it is difficult to introduce and sustain. Indeed, one of the founders of the TQM movement, Philip Crosby (1979), claimed that over 90 per cent of TQM initiatives by American organisations fail. Though a 90 per cent failure rate seems incredibly high, studies of the adoption of TQM by companies in the United Kingdom and other European countries show that they too have experienced a similarly high failure rate – perhaps as much as 80 per cent or more (Kearney, 1992; Cruise O'Brien and Voss, 1992; Economist Intelligence Unit, 1992; Whyte and Witcher, 1992; Witcher, 1993; Zairi *et al.*, 1994).

BPR was hailed as 'the biggest business innovation of the 1990s' (Mill, 1994, p. 26). Wastell *et al.* (1994, p. 23) stated that BPR refers to 'initiatives, large and small, radical and conservative, whose common theme is the achievement of significant improvements in organizational performance by augmenting the efficiency and effectiveness of key business processes.' Though relatively new, and therefore less well documented than either new technology or TQM, Wastell *et al.* (1994, p. 37) concluded from the available evidence that 'BPR initiatives have typically achieved much less than they promised'. Other studies of BPR have come to similar conclusions (Short and Venkatraman, 1992; Coombs and Hull, 1994). Even the founding father of BPR – Michael Hammer – acknowledges that in up to 70 per cent of cases it leaves organisations worse off rather than better off (Hammer and Champy, 1993).

Therefore, even well-established change initiatives, for which a great deal of information, advice and assistance are available, are no guarantee of success. This is perhaps why managers list their ability (or inability) to manage change as the number one obstacle to the increased competitiveness of their organisations (Hanson, 1993).

Key Learning Point

Effective organisational change is crucial to an organisation's competitiveness but, despite the plethora of advice available, the majority of change programmes appear to fail.

There are many reasons why change management programmes fail. Some of these are specific to the particular organisations concerned. However, some relate to the inadequacy or inappropriateness of the various recipes for change that are available to organisations (Burnes, 2000). In addition, it needs to be recognised that change, even in quite small organisations, is a complex process whose consequences can be difficult to predict. Perhaps the prime example of this is culture change. Since the early 1980s the main objective for many organisations has been to change their culture. Indeed, a survey by the Industrial Society (1997) in the United Kingdom found that 94 per cent of its respondents had either recently been involved in or were currently going through a culture change programme. Therefore, to understand and illustrate why change is so complex, the following section will examine organisational culture.

Changing organisational culture

There is widespread agreement that managers and employees do not perform their duties in a value-free vacuum (Brown, 1995). Their work and the way it is done are governed, directed and tempered by an organisation's culture – the particular set of values, beliefs, customs and systems unique to that organisation. Though this view has been around for many years (see Blake and Mouton, 1969; Turner, 1971; Eldridge and Crombie, 1974), it was only in the 1980s, with the work of writers such as Peters and Waterman (1982) and Deal and Kennedy (1982), that culture, rather than factors such as structure, strategy or politics, became seen as central to organisational success. So influential has this view become that, as Wilson (1992) noted, culture has come to be seen as the great 'cure-all' for the majority of organisational ills.

As Allaire and Firsirotu (1984) noted, there are many different definitions of organisational culture. Perhaps the most widely accepted definition is that offered by Eldridge and Crombie (1974, p. 78), who stated that culture refers 'to the unique configuration of norms, values, beliefs, ways of behaving and so on, that characterise the manner in which groups and individuals combine to get things done.' Culture defines how those in the organisation should behave in a given set of circumstances. It affects all, from the most senior manager to the humblest porter. Their actions are judged by themselves and others in relation to expected modes of behaviour. Culture legitimises certain forms of action and proscribes other forms.

There have been a number of attempts to identify and categorise the constituent elements of culture (e.g. Schein, 1985; Hofstede, 1990). Based on an analysis of the different definitions of culture, Cummings and Huse (1989) produced a composite model of culture, comprising four major elements existing at different levels of awareness: basic assumptions; values; norms and artefacts. However, while the various hierarchical models of culture elements are useful, we should always remember that, as Brown (1995, pp. 8–9) notes, '. . . actual organisational cultures are not as neat and tidy as the models seem to imply.'

As well as the numerous attempts to define organisational culture, there have also been a number of attempts to categorise the various types of culture (e.g. Deal and Kennedy, 1982; Quinn and McGrath, 1985). Perhaps the best-known typology of culture, and the one that has been around the longest, is that developed by Handy (1979) from Harrison's (1972) work on 'organisation ideologies'. Handy (1986, p. 188) observed that 'There seem to be four main types of culture . . . *power, role, task* and *person*'. The various attempts to provide a universal categorisation of culture types do have their critics, especially among those who point to the influence of the host society on organisational cultures (Hofstede 1980, 1990).

The debate over culture has significant implications for organisations (Burnes, 2000). Perhaps the most significant of these, as Barratt (1990, p. 23) claims, is that 'values, beliefs and attitudes are learnt, can be managed and changed and are potentially manipulable by management'. O'Reilly (1989) takes a similar view, arguing that it is possible to change or manage a culture by choosing the attitudes and behaviours that are required, identifying the norms or expectations that promote or impede them, and then taking action to create the desired effect.

Therefore, there is a body of opinion that sees culture as something that can be managed and changed. There are also many, many organisations in which, for a variety of reasons, senior managers have decided that their existing culture is inappropriate or even detrimental to their competitive needs and, therefore, must be changed.

Nevertheless, one of the leading writers on culture, Schein (1985), cautions organisations to be wary of rushing into culture change programmes. He believes that before any attempt is made to change an organisation's culture, it is first necessary to understand the nature of its existing culture and how this is sustained. According to Schein, this can be achieved by analysing the values that govern behaviour, and uncovering the underlying and often unconscious assumptions that determine how those in the organisation think, feel and react. His approach, therefore, is to treat the development of culture as an adaptive and tangible learning process. Schein emphasises the way in which an organisation communicates its culture to new recruits. It illustrates how assumptions are translated into values and how values influence behaviour. Schein seeks to understand the mechanisms used to propagate culture, and how new values and behaviours are learned. Once these mechanisms are revealed, he argues, they can then form the basis of a strategy to change the organisation's culture.

In a synthesis of the literature on organisational culture, Hassard and Sharifi (1989, p. 11) proposed a similar approach to Schein's. In particular, they stressed the crucial role of senior managers:

> Before a major [cultural] change campaign is commenced, senior managers must understand the implications of the new system for their own behaviour: and senior management must be involved in all the main stages preceding change.
>
> In change programmes, special attention must be given to the company's 'opinion leaders'.

So most writers consider that organisational culture is very complex. There are a number of influential writers who believe that it can be, and in certain circumstances should be, changed; there are also those who take the contrary view. For example, Meek (1988, pp. 469–70) commented that:

> Culture as a whole cannot be manipulated, turned on or off, although it needs to be recognised that some [organisations] are in a better position than others to intentionally influence aspects of it. ... culture should be regarded as something an organisation 'is', not something it 'has': it is not an independent variable nor can it be created, discovered or destroyed by the whims of management.

In a similar vein, Filby and Willmott (1988) questioned the notion that management has the capacity to control culture. They point out that this ignores the way in which an individual's values and beliefs are conditioned by experience outside the workplace – through exposure to the media, through social activities, as well as through previous occupational activities.

Hatch (1997, p. 235) is also very dubious about attempts to change organisational culture:

> Do not think of trying to manage culture. Other people's meanings and interpretations are highly unmanageable. Think instead of trying to culturally manage your

organization, that is, manage your organization with cultural awareness of the multiplicity of meanings that will be made of you and your efforts.

A further concern expressed by a number of writers relates to the ethical issues raised by attempts to change culture (Van Maanen and Kunda, 1989; Willmott, 1995). This concern is succinctly articulated by Watson (1997, p. 278) who concludes that:

> Employers and managers engaging in these ways with issues of employees' self-identities and the values through which they judge the rights and wrongs of their daily lives must be a matter of serious concern. To attempt to mould cultures – given that culture in its broad sense provides the roots of human morality, social identity and existential security – is indeed to enter 'deep and dangerous waters' . . .

As we can see, most observers see organisational culture as being complex and difficult to understand. However, even among those who believe it can be changed, few appear to believe that such a change is easy or without dangers. This is perhaps why so many organisations have found successful culture change so difficult to achieve (Brown, 1995; Cummings and Worley, 1997; De Witte and van Muijen, 1999). Indeed, it is the fact that organisations are not machines but very complex social systems that makes any form of change potentially hazardous.

Key Learning Point

Organisational culture may be crucial to an organisation's performance but it is also difficult to understand and change.

Exercise 15.1   Take-off delayed by squabbles in the cockpit

The shine is wearing off Europe's most ambitious attempt to restructure and rationalise its defence and aeronautics industry. Deep cracks are appearing in the venture's management and financial prospects. Differences are also surfacing between the industrial partners and their respective political masters. This puts at risk the future of the project, at least in its present form. The European Aeronautic Defence and Space Company [EADS] was born last year . . . with great fanfare, France, Germany and Spain announced the merger of the dominant components of their defence and aerospace industries to make Europe's largest aerospace company and the world's second biggest after Boeing of the US.

'The current crisis has simply amplified the patchwork of incoherence and incompatibilities evident in EADS right from the beginning,' says a veteran of the French aerospace establishment. With its joint Franco-German chairmen and joint chief executives, EADS 'is a double-headed monster' . . . In recent days there have been growing reports that the French and Germans are now looking for a 'third man' to run the company single-handed. But the question of who this would be and – more important – from which country he or she would emerge encapsulates the schism within the company.

EADS has been attempting to break down internal national barriers by setting up a corporate business academy on the model of the US's General Electric. It has been working to make its younger generation of managers feel more integrated into the company, irrespective of their nationalities. Despite these efforts, Franco-German rivalry also occurs lower down the company, where merit was supposed to be the criterion for appointments.

'The Germans must accept European integration. They still have problems accepting this. They are still too nationalistic. And there also important differences between French and German approaches to supporting industry,' explains a French government official, underlining the French government's efforts to promote greater support for the aviation sector. 'The real issue is that both the French and Germans want to run the show,' says a British aerospace official.

Speaking to both sides makes it clear that they already consider the current structure and situation unworkable. National considerations and the very principle of managerial parity are proving severe handicaps. 'We must arrive quickly at a single leadership and a strong independent corporate culture,' stresses one senior insider. 'I don't know exactly when this will happen but current events will accelerate the integration process. It will and must be quick. At present the system does not react swiftly enough. And it must become reactive. If not, the consequences will be dire.'

Source: Financial Times, *16 November 2001*

1   To what extent can the problems of EADS be attributed to an inappropriate organisational culture?

2   To what extent can the problems of EADS be seen as a clash of national cultures or a battle for national interest between the two governments?

3   What are the main barriers to EADS being able to '... arrive quickly at a single leadership and a strong independent corporate culture'?

Despite the adverse experience of many organisations, change, of an increasingly radical form, seems to be the order of the day. Some organisations look to management gurus such as Charles Handy (1994), Rosabeth Moss Kanter (1989), John Kotter (1996) and Tom Peters (1995) for their salvation. Others seek the assistance of management consultants such as McKinsey, PricewaterhouseCoopers and KMPG. However, whether organisations seek outside advice and assistance or whether they rely on their own competence, they cannot expect to achieve successful change unless those responsible for managing it understand the different approaches on offer and can match them to their circumstances and preferences. On this basis, understanding the theory and practice of change management is not an optional extra but an essential prerequisite for survival. However, as the following examination of the two main approaches to change management will show, this is by no means an easy or straightforward exercise.

The Planned Approach to organisational change

Planned change is a term first coined by Kurt Lewin to distinguish change that was consciously embarked upon and planned by an organisation, as opposed to types of change that might come about by accident, by impulse or which might be forced on an organisation (Marrow, 1977). Among those advocating Planned change, a variety of different models of change management have arisen over the years. The Planned Approach to change is most closely associated with the practice of organisation development (OD), and indeed lies at its core. According to French and Bell (1995, pp. 1–2):

> Organization development is a unique organizational improvement strategy that emerged in the late 1950s and early 1960s. ... [It] has evolved into an integrated framework of theories and practices capable of solving or helping to solve most of the important problems confronting the human side of organizations. Organization development is about people and organizations and people in organizations and how they function. OD is also about planned change, that is getting individuals, teams and organizations to function better.

Underpinning OD is a set of values, assumptions and ethics that emphasise its humanistic-democratic orientation and its commitment to organisational effectiveness. These values have been articulated by many writers over the years (Conner, 1977; Warwick and Thompson, 1980; Gellerman et al., 1990). Hurley et al. (1992) found there were five clear values that OD practitioners espoused:

1   Empowering employees to act.

2   Creating openness in communications.

3   Facilitating ownership of the change process and its outcomes.

4   The promotion of a culture of collaboration.

5   The promotion of continuous learning.

Within the OD field, there are a number of major theorists and practitioners who have contributed their own models and techniques to its advancement (eg Argyris, 1962; Beckhard, 1969; French and Bell, 1973; Blake and Mouton, 1976). However, despite this, there is general agreement that OD grew out of, and became the standard bearer for, Kurt Lewin's pioneering work on behavioural science in general, and his development of Planned change in particular (Cummings and Worley, 1997). Lewin was a prolific theorist, researcher and practitioner in interpersonal, group, intergroup and community relationships. The models of the change process that emerged from his work are:

■   the action research model;

■   the three-step model;

■   the phases of Planned Change model.

Action research

This model was designed by Lewin as a collective approach to solving social and organisational problems. Although American in origin, soon after its emergence it was adopted by the Tavistock Institute in Britain, and used to improve managerial competency and efficiency in the coal industry. Since then it has acquired strong adherents on both sides of the Atlantic (French and Bell, 1984). Some comments on action research appear in Chapter 2 of this book.

In an organisation setting, an action research project usually comprises three distinct groups: the organisation (in the form of one or more senior managers), the subject (people from the area where the change is to take place) and the change agent (a consultant who may or may not be a member of the organisation). These three distinct entities form a learning community in and through which the research is carried out, and by which the organisation's problem is solved (Heller, 1970).

Action research is a two-pronged process. Firstly, it emphasises that change requires action, and is directed at achieving this. Secondly, it recognises also that successful action is based on a process of learning that allows those involved to analyse the situation correctly, identify all the possible alternative solutions (hypotheses) and choose the one most appropriate to the situation at hand (Bennett, 1983). The theoretical foundations of this approach lie in gestalt-field theory, which stresses that change can only successfully be achieved by helping individuals to reflect on and gain new insights into their situation (Smith *et al.*, 1982).

Although action research is highly regarded as an approach to managing change (Cummings and Huse, 1989), it is Lewin's three-step model of change that lies at the core of Planned change.

Key Learning Point

Action research is concerned as much with individual and group learning as it is with achieving change.

The three-step model of change

In developing this model, Lewin (1958) noted that a change towards a higher level of group performance is frequently short-lived; after a 'shot in the arm', group behaviour may soon revert to its previous pattern. This indicates that it is not sufficient to define the objective of change solely as the achievement of a higher level of group performance. Permanence of the new level should also be included in the objective. A successful change project, Lewin (1958) argued, should involve three steps:

1 *Unfreezing* the present level.

2 *Moving* to the new level.

3 *Refreezing* the new level.

Step 1 recognises that before new behaviour can be successfully adopted, the old has to be discarded. Only then can the new behaviour become accepted. Central to this approach is the belief that the will of the change adopter (the subject of the change) is important, both in discarding the old, 'unfreezing', and the 'moving' to the new.

Unfreezing usually involves reducing those forces maintaining the organisation's behaviour at its present level. According to Rubin (1967), unfreezing requires some form of confrontation meeting or re-education process for those involved. The essence of these activities is to enable those concerned to become convinced of the need for change. Unfreezing clearly equates with the research element of action research, just as step 2, moving, equates with the action element.

Moving, in practice, involves acting on the results of step 1. That is, having analysed the present situation, identified options and selected the most appropriate, action is then necessary to move to the more desirable state of affairs. This involves developing new behaviours, values and attitudes through changes in organisational structures and processes. The key task is to ensure that this is done in such a way that those involved do not, after a short period, revert to the old ways of doing things.

Refreezing is the final step in the three-step model and represents, depending on the viewpoint, either a break with action research or its logical extension. Refreezing seeks to stabilise the organisation at a new state of equilibrium in order to ensure that the new ways of working are relatively safe from regression. It is frequently achieved through the use of supporting mechanisms that positively reinforce the new ways of working; these include organisational culture, norms, policies and practices (Cummings and Huse, 1989).

The three-step model provides a general framework for understanding the process of organisational change. However, the three steps are relatively broad and, for this reason, have been further developed in an attempt to enhance the practicable value of this approach.

Phases of Planned change

In attempting to elaborate upon Lewin's three-step model, writers have expanded the number of steps or phases. Lippitt *et al.* (1958) developed a seven-phase model of Planned change, while Cummings and Huse (1989), not to be outdone, produced an eight-phase model. However, as Cummings and Huse (1989, p. 51) point out, 'the concept of planned change implies that an organization exists in different states at different times and that planned movement can occur from one state to another.' Therefore, in order to understand Planned change, it is not sufficient merely to understand the processes that bring about change; there must also be an appreciation of the states that an organisation must pass through in order to move from an unsatisfactory present state to a more desired future state.

Bullock and Batten (1985) developed an integrated, four-phase model of Planned change based on a review and synthesis of over 30 models of Planned change. Their model describes Planned change in terms of two major dimensions: change phases, which are distinct states an organisation moves through as it undertakes Planned change; and change processes, which are the methods used to move an organisation from one state to another.

The four change phases, and their attendant change processes, identified by Bullock and Batten are as follows:

1   *Exploration phase*: in this state members of an organisation have to explore and decide whether they want to make specific changes in its operations and, if so, commit resources to planning the changes. The change processes involved in this phase are: becoming aware of the need for change; searching for outside assistance (a consultant/facilitator) to assist with planning and implementing the changes; and establishing a contract with the consultant which defines each party's responsibilities.

2   *Planning phase*: once the consultant and the organisation have established a contract, then the next state, which involves understanding the organisation's problem or concern, begins. The change processes involved in this are: collecting information in order to establish a correct diagnosis of the problem; establishing change goals and designing the appropriate actions to achieve these goals; and getting key decision-makers to approve and support the proposed changes.

3   *Action phase*: in this state, an organisation implements the changes derived from the planning. The change processes involved are designed to move an organisation from its current state to a desired future state, and include: establishing appropriate arrangements to manage the change process and gaining support for the actions to be taken; and evaluating the implementation activities and feeding back the results so that any necessary adjustments or refinements can be made.

4   *Integration phase*: this state commences once the changes have been successfully implemented. It is concerned with consolidating and stabilising the changes so that they become part of an organisation's normal, everyday operation and do not require special arrangements or encouragement to maintain them. The change processes involved are: reinforcing new behaviours through feedback and reward systems and gradually decreasing reliance on the consultant; diffusing the successful aspects of the change process throughout the organisation; and training managers and employees to monitor the changes constantly and seek to improve upon them.

According to Cummings and Huse (1989), this model has broad applicability to most change situations. It clearly incorporates key aspects of many other change models and, especially, it overcomes any confusion between the processes (methods) of change and the phases of change – the sequential states that organisations must go through to achieve successful change.

Key Learning Point

Both the three-step and the phases models view change as a sequential activity involving a beginning, a middle and an end.

The focus of Bullock and Batten's model, just as with Lewin's, is change at individual and group level. However, OD practitioners have recognised, as many others have, that: 'Organizations are being reinvented; work tasks are being reengineered; the rules of the marketplace are being rewritten; the fundamental nature of organizations is changing', and, therefore, OD has to adapt to these new conditions and broaden its focus out beyond individual and group behaviour (French and Bell, 1995, pp. 3–4).

From organisation development to organisation transformation

In the United States at least, OD has become a profession with its own regulatory bodies, to which OD practitioners have to belong, its own recognised qualifications, a host of approved tools and techniques and its own ethical code of practice (Cummings and Worley, 1997). The members of this profession, whether employed in academic institutions, consultancy practices or private and public organisations, exist to provide consultancy services. As with any profession or trade, unless they provide their customers with what they want, they will soon go out of business. Therefore, to appreciate the current role and approach of Planned change, it is necessary to say something of how OD has responded to the changing needs of its customers.

The original focus of OD was on work groups within an organisational setting rather than organisations in their entirety, and it was primarily concerned with the human processes and systems within organisations. However, as French and Bell (1995) and Cummings and Worley (1997) noted, in recent years there has been a major shift of focus within the OD field from improving group effectiveness to transforming organisations. This move to 'transformational' OD stems from three developments in particular:

- Firstly, with the rise of the job design movement in the 1960s, and particularly the advent of socio-technical systems theory, OD practitioners came to recognise that they could not solely concentrate on the work of groups and individuals in organisations but that they needed to look at other and wider systems. Gradually, OD has adopted an open systems perspective that allows it to look at organisations in their totality and within their environments.

- Secondly, OD practitioners have broadened their perspective to include organisational culture. Given that OD had always recognised the importance of group norms and values, it is a natural progression to translate this into an interest in organisational culture in general.

■ Lastly, the increasing use of organisation-wide approaches to change, such as culture change programmes, coupled with increasing turbulence in the environment in which organisations operate, have drawn attention to the need for OD to become involved in transforming organisations in their totality rather than focusing on changes to their constituent parts.

While these major additions to the OD repertoire are understandable, the danger is that they appear to be moving away from the commitment to individual involvement and learning espoused by OD practitioners. This can be seen from the following five-step approach to culture change advocated by Cummings and Huse (1989, pp. 428–30):

1 *A clear strategic vision*: effective cultural change should start from a clear vision of the firm's new strategy and of the shared values and behaviour needed to make it work. This vision provides the purpose and direction for cultural change.

2 *Top management commitment*: cultural change must be managed from the top of the organisation. Senior managers and administrators need to be strongly committed to the new values and the need to create constant pressure for change.

3 *Symbolic leadership*: senior executives must communicate the new culture through their own actions. Their behaviours need to symbolise the kind of values and behaviours being sought.

4 *Supporting organisational changes*: cultural change must be accompanied by supporting modifications in organisational structure, human resource systems, information and control systems, and management style. These organisational features can help to orientate people's behaviours to the new culture.

5 *Organisational membership*: one of the most effective methods for changing culture is to change organisational membership. People can be selected in terms of their fit with the new culture, and provided with an induction clearly indicating desired attitudes and behaviour. Existing staff who cannot adapt to the new ways may have their employment terminated.

Not only does Cummings and Huse's approach exclude all but senior staff from being involved in decisions about what to change and how to implement it, but also those who are deemed not to 'fit' the new culture can have their employment terminated. This all seems to be part of the growing tendency observed by French and Bell (1995, p. 351) for top managers to focus less on people-orientated values and more on 'the bottom line and/or the price of stock. ... [Consequently] some executives have a 'slash and burn' mentality.' Clearly, this tendency is not conducive to the democratic and humanistic values traditionally espoused by OD practitioners. Instead, the emphasis is on the consultant as a provider of expertise that the organisation lacks. The consultant's task is not only to facilitate but also to provide solutions. The danger in this situation is that the learner (the change adopter) becomes a passive recipient of external and, supposedly, objective data: one who has to be directed to the 'correct' solution (Cummings and Worley, 1997).

Therefore, as can be seen, for better or ill, OD has attempted to move considerably away from its roots in Planned change and now takes a far more organisation- and system-wide perspective on change.

Exercise 15.2   Working with suppliers

When Nissan established its British car-assembly operation in the mid-1980s, it recognised that UK component suppliers fell far short of Japanese standards of quality, reliability and cost. As one means of helping suppliers to improve their capability, it established a Supplier Development Team (SDT). The aim of the SDT was to help suppliers to develop their business to the stage where they can meet Nissan's performance requirements.

Though the assistance given by the SDT to suppliers is in effect free consultancy, this is not philanthropy on Nissan's part. Nissan believes that unless its suppliers achieve world-class performance standards, it cannot produce world-beating cars. Therefore, in helping its suppliers, Nissan is helping itself.

The SDT approach is to work co-operatively with suppliers to help them identify areas for improvement, and then to assist them to develop and monitor improvement plans. The basic elements of the SDT's approach are as follows:

- Suppliers are at liberty to choose whether or not to invite the SDT into their plant.

- The SDT begins by explaining to senior managers within suppliers that its objective is to help them to develop a continuous improvement philosophy.

- The SDT seeks to train and guide a supplier's personnel to undertake change projects for themselves, rather than doing the work for them.

- The SDT insists that staff in the area where change is to take place are involved.

- The SDT seeks to promote trust, co-operation and teamworking within suppliers.

- The SDT's own members are extremely well-trained and proficient and, consequently, are able to win the confidence of the people with whom they work.

- The SDT seeks to ensure that those who carry out the improvement get the credit and praise for it, rather than seeking to take the credit itself.

It would be misleading to give the impression that Nissan was in any way 'soft' on suppliers. As Sir Ian Gibson, Nissan's then Managing Director, stated: 'Co-operative supply relationships are not an easy option, as many imagine, but considerably harder to implement than traditional buyer–seller relationships'.

Source: Adapted from Burnes (2000)

1   To what extent does Nissan's approach to supplier development fit in with the planned approach to change?

2   How does the philosophy promoted by Nissan's SDT compare to Lewin's own underlying philosophy of change?

3   Is the SDT approach compatible with 'transformational' OD?

4   What effect might a supplier's culture have on the longer-term success of the SDT approach?

Planned change: summary and criticisms

Planned change is an iterative, cyclical process involving diagnosis, action and evaluation, and further action and evaluation. It is an approach that recognises that once change has taken place, it must be self-sustaining (i.e. safe from regression). The purpose of Planned change is to improve the effectiveness of the human side of the organisation. Central to Planned change is the emphasis placed on the collaborative nature of the change effort: the organisation, both managers and recipients of change, and the consultant jointly diagnose the organisation's problem and jointly plan and design the specific changes. Underpinning Planned change, and indeed the origins of the OD movement as a whole, is a strong humanist and democratic orientation and an emphasis on organisational effectiveness. This fits in well with its gestalt-field orientation, seeing change as a process of learning which allows those involved to gain or change insights, outlooks, expectations and thought patterns. This approach seeks to provide change adopters with an opportunity to 'reason out' their situation and develop their own solutions (Bigge, 1982).

However, the advent of more organisation-wide approaches, which seem to be leading to a move away from OD's original focus and area of expertise (i.e. the human processes involved in the functioning of individuals and groups in organisations), coupled with a more hostile business environment, appear to be eroding the values that Lewin and the early pioneers of OD saw as being central to successful change.

As might be expected, these developments in OD, as well as newer perspectives on organisations, have led many to question not only particular aspects of the Planned Approach to change but also the utility and practicality of the approach as a whole. The main criticisms levelled against the Planned Approach to change are as follows.

Firstly, as Wooten and White (1999, p. 8) observe, 'Much of the existing OD technology was developed specifically for, and in response to, top-down, autocratic, rigid, rule-based organizations operating in a somewhat predictable and controlled environment'. This may account for the assumption by many proponents of OD that, as Cummings and Huse (1989, p. 51) pointed out, 'an organization exists in different states at different times and that planned movement can occur from one state to another'. However, from the 1980s onwards in particular, an increasing number of writers argued that, in the turbulent and chaotic world in which we live, such assumptions are increasingly tenuous and that organisational change is more a continuous and open-ended process than a set of discrete and self-contained events (Nonaka, 1988; Peters, 1989; Garvin, 1993; Stacey, 1993).

Secondly, and on a similar note, a number of writers have criticised the Planned Approach for its emphasis on incremental and isolated change and its inability to incorporate radical, transformational change (Miller and Friesen, 1984; Harris, 1985; Schein, 1985; Dunphy and Stace, 1993).

Thirdly, the Planned Approach is based on the assumption that common agreement can be reached, and that all the parties involved in a particular change project have a willingness and interest in doing so. This assumption appears to ignore organisational conflict and politics, or at least assumes that problem issues can be easily identified and resolved which, as Pfeffer (1992), among many others, has shown, is not always the case.

Fourthly, it assumes that one type of approach to change is suitable for all organisations, all situations and all times. Stace and Dunphy (1993) show that there is a wide spectrum of change situations, ranging from fine-tuning to corporate transformation, and an equally wide range of ways of managing these, ranging from collaborative to coercive. Though Planned change may be suitable to some for these situations, it is clearly much less applicable to situations where more directive approaches may be required, such as when a crisis, requiring rapid and major change, does not allow scope for widespread involvement or consultation. This has led them (Dunphy and Stace, 1993, p. 905) to argue that:

> Turbulent times demand different responses in varied circumstances. So managers and consultants need a model of change that is essentially a 'situational' or 'contingency model', one that indicates how to vary change strategies to achieve 'optimum fit' with the changing environment.

Leading OD advocates, as might be predicted, dispute these criticisms and point to the way that Planned change has tried to incorporate issues such as power and politics and the need for organisational transformation (French and Bell, 1995; Cummings and Worley, 1997). Also, as Burnes (1998) argues, there is a need to draw a distinction between Lewin's original analytical approach to Planned change and the more prescriptive and practitioner-orientated variants that have been developed by the OD profession subsequently. Nevertheless, even taking these points into account, it has to be recognised that Planned change was never intended to be applicable to all change situations and it was certainly never meant to be used in situations where rapid, coercive and/or wholesale change was required.

Key Learning Point

The main criticism of the Planned approach is that it is not suitable for open-ended and unpredictable situations.

The Emergent Approach to organisational change

The Planned Approach to change is relatively well developed and understood, and is supported by a coherent body of literature, methods and techniques. The Emergent Approach, on the other hand, is a relatively new concept that lacks an agreed set of methods and techniques. The proponents of the Emergent Approach to change view it from different perspectives and tend to focus on their own particular concerns. Therefore, they are a much less coherent group than the advocates of Planned change and, rather than being united by a shared belief, they tend to be distinguished by a common disbelief in the efficacy of Planned change.

Dawson (1994) and Wilson (1992) both challenged the appropriateness of Planned change in a business environment that is increasingly dynamic and uncertain. They argue that those who believe that organisational change can successfully be achieved through a pre-planned and centrally directed process of 'unfreezing', 'moving' and 'refreezing' ignore the complex and dynamic nature of environmental and change processes, and do not address crucial issues such as the continuous need for employee flexibility and structural adaptation. Wilson (1992) also believes that the Planned Approach, by attempting to lay down timetables, objectives and methods in advance, is too heavily reliant on the role of managers. It assumes (perhaps rashly) that they can have a full understanding of the consequences of their actions and that their plans will be understood and accepted and can be implemented. Buchanan and Storey (1997, p. 127) maintain that the main criticism of those who advocate Planned change is 'their attempt to impose an order and a linear sequence to processes that are in reality messy and untidy, and which unfold in an iterative fashion with much backtracking and omission.'

Pettigrew (1990a, b) has argued that the Planned Approach, as exemplified by the OD movement, is too prescriptive and does not pay enough attention to the need to analyse and conceptualise organisational change. He maintains that it is essential to understand the context in which change takes place. In particular he emphasises:

■ the interconnectedness of change over time;

■ how the context of change shapes and is shaped by action;

■ the multi-causal and non-linear nature of change.

For Pettigrew (1987), change needs to be studied across different levels of analysis and different time periods. This is because organisational change cuts across functions, spans hierarchical divisions, and has no neat starting or finishing point; instead it is a 'complex analytical, political, and cultural process of challenging and changing the core beliefs, structure and strategy of the firm' (Pettigrew, 1987, p. 650).

Advocates of the Emergent Approach, therefore, stress the developing and unpredictable nature of change. They view change as a process that unfolds through the interplay of multiple variables (context, political processes and consultation) within an organisation. In contrast to the pre-ordained certainty of Planned change, Dawson (1994) in particular adopted a processual approach to change. The processual approach views organisations and their members as shifting coalitions of individuals and groups with different interests, imperfect knowledge and short attention spans. Change, under these conditions, is portrayed as a pragmatic process of trial and error, aimed at achieving a compromise between the competitive needs of the organisation and the objectives of the warring factions within the organisation.

Advocates of Emergent change who adopt the processual approach tend to stress that there can be no simple prescription for managing organisational transitions successfully, owing to temporal and contextual factors. Neither, as Dawson (1994, p. 181) argued, can change be characterised 'as a rational series of decision-making activities and events ... nor as a single reaction to adverse contingent circumstances.' Therefore, successful change is less dependent on detailed plans and projections than on reaching an understanding of the complexity of the issues concerned and identifying the range of available options.

Key Learning Point

The Emergent approach challenges the view that organisations are rational entities and seeks to replace it with a view of organisations as comprising moving coalitions of different interest groups.

The rationale for the Emergent Approach stems from the belief that change should not and cannot be solidified, or seen as a series of linear events within a given period of time; instead, it is viewed as a continuous process. Dawson (1994) sees change as a period of organisational transition characterised by disruption, confusion and unforeseen events that emerge over long timeframes. Even when changes are operational, they will need to be constantly refined and developed in order to maintain their relevance.

From this perspective, Clarke (1994) suggested that mastering the challenge of change is not a specialist activity facilitated or driven by an expert, but an increasingly important part of every manager's role. To be effective in creating sustainable change, according to McCalman and Paton (1992), managers will need an extensive and systemic understanding of their organisation's environment, in order to identify the pressures for change and to ensure that, by mobilising the necessary internal resources, their organisation responds in a timely and appropriate manner. Dawson (1994) claimed that change must be linked with the complexity of changing market realities, the transitional nature of work organisation, systems of management control and redefined organisational boundaries and relationships. He emphasises that, in today's business environment, one-dimensional change interventions are likely to generate only short-term results and heighten instability rather than reduce it.

As can be seen, though they do not openly state it, advocates of Emergent change tend to adopt a contingency perspective. For them, it is the uncertainty of the environment that makes Planned change inappropriate and Emergent change more pertinent. Stickland (1998, p. 76) extends this point by raising a question that many of those studying organisational change appear not to acknowledge: 'To what extent does the environment drive changes within a system [i.e. organisation] and to what extent is the system in control of its own change processes?' Finstad (1998, p. 721) puts this issue in a wider context by arguing that 'the organization is ... the creator of its environment and the environment is the creator of the organization.'

This reciprocal relationship between an organisation and its environment clearly has profound implications for how managers in organisations conceptualise and manage change. It also serves to emphasise that a key competence for organisations is the ability to scan the external environment in order to identify and assess the impact of trends and discontinuities (McCalman and Paton, 1992). This includes exploring the full range of external variables, including markets and customers, shareholders, legal requirements, the economy, suppliers, technology and social trends. This activity is made more difficult by the changing and arbitrary nature of organisation boundaries: customers can also be competitors; suppliers may become partners; and employees can be transformed into customers, suppliers or competitors.

Changes in the external environment require appropriate responses within organisations. Appropriate responses, according to the supporters of the Emergent Approach, should promote extensive and deep understanding of strategy, structure, systems, people, style and culture, and how these can function either as sources of inertia that can block change, or alternatively, as levers to encourage an effective change process (Wilson, 1992; Pettigrew and Whipp, 1993; Dawson, 1994). A major development in this respect is the move to adopt a 'bottom-up' rather than 'top-down' approach to initiating and implementing change. The case in favour of this move is based on the view that the pace of environmental change is so rapid and complex that it is impossible for a small number of senior managers effectively to identify, plan and implement the necessary organisational responses. The responsibility for organisational change is therefore of necessity becoming more devolved.

Key Learning Point

'While the primary stimulus for change remains those forces in the external environment, the primary motivator for how change is accomplished resides with the people within the organization' (Benjamin and Mabey, 1993, p. 181).

Supporters of the Emergent Approach identify five features of organisations that either promote or obstruct success: cultures, structures, organisational learning, managerial behaviour, and power and politics.

Organisational culture

Earlier in this chapter, it was argued that organisational culture is a complex and contentious subject which can be seen both as a constraint on, and an object of, change. In looking at culture from the Emergent perspective, Johnson (1993, p. 64) has taken the view that the strategic management of change is 'essentially a cultural and cognitive phenomenon' rather than an analytical, rational exercise. Clarke (1994) stated that the essence of sustainable change is to understand the culture of the organisation that is to be changed. If proposed changes contradict cultural biases and traditions, it is inevitable that they will be difficult to embed in the organisation.

In a similar vein, Dawson (1994) suggested that attempts to realign internal behaviours with external conditions require change strategies that are culturally sensitive. Organisations, he points out, must be aware that the process is lengthy, potentially dangerous and demands considerable reinforcement if culture change is to be sustained against the inevitable tendency to regress to old behaviours. Clarke (1994) also stressed that change can be slow, especially where mechanisms that reinforce old or inappropriate behaviour, such as reward, recruitment and promotion structures, continue unchallenged. In addition, if these reinforcement mechanisms are complemented by managerial behaviour that promotes risk aversion and fear of failure, a climate where people are willing to propose or undertake change is unlikely. Accordingly, as Clarke (1994, p. 94) suggested, 'Creating a culture for change means that change has to be part of the way we do things around here, it cannot be bolted on as an extra.'

Therefore, for many proponents of the Emergent Approach to change, if an appropriate organisational culture does not exist, it is essential that one is created. However, not all its proponents take this view. Beer *et al.* (1993) suggested that the most effective way to promote change is not by directly attempting to influence organisational behaviour or culture. Instead, they advocate restructuring organisations in order to place people in a new organisational context, which imposes new roles, relationships and responsibilities upon them. This, they believe, forces new attitudes and behaviours upon people. This view is also shared by Tom Peters (1993) who advocates rapid and complete destruction of existing hierarchical organisation structures as a precursor to behavioural and cultural change.

Wilson (1992, p. 91), however, took an even more sceptical approach to culture change, claiming that:

> to effect change in an organization simply by attempting to change its culture assumes an unwarranted linear connection between something called organizational culture and performance. Not only is this concept of organizational culture multi-faceted, it is also not always clear precisely how culture and change are related, if at all, and, if so, in which direction.

It is apparent that, while the Emergent Approach recognises the importance of culture to organisational change, there is a split between those who believe an appropriate culture can be created, where one does not exist, and those who believe that attempting to change culture is something an organisation does at its peril.

Organisational structure

This is seen as playing a crucial role in defining how people relate to each other and in influencing the momentum for change (Clarke, 1994; Dawson, 1994; Kotter, 1996; Hatch, 1997). Therefore, an appropriate organisation structure can be an important lever for achieving change, but its effectiveness is regarded as dependent upon the recognition of its informal as well as its formal aspects.

The case for developing more appropriate organisational structures in order to facilitate change very much follows the arguments of the contingency theorists (Child, 1984). Those favouring an Emergent Approach to change point out that the last 20 years have witnessed a general move to create flatter organisational structures in order to increase responsiveness by devolving authority and responsibility (Senior, 1997). As Kotter (1996, p. 169) remarks, the case for such structural changes is that 'An organization with more delegation, which means a flat hierarchy, is in a far superior position to manoeuvre than one with a big, change-resistant lump in the middle.'

One aspect of this is the move to create customer-centred organisations with structures that reflect, and are responsive to, different markets rather than different functions. Customer responsiveness places greater emphasis on effective horizontal processes and embodies the concept that everyone is someone else's customer.

One result of attempts to respond rapidly to changing conditions by breaking down internal barriers, disseminating knowledge and developing synergy across functions is the creation of network organisations or, to use Handy's (1989) term, 'federal' organisations. Snow *et al.* (1993) suggested that the semi-autonomous nature of each part of a network reduces the need for and erodes the power of centrally managed bureaucracies, which, in turn, leads to change and adaptation being driven from the bottom up rather than from the top down. They further argue that the specialisation and flexibility required to cope with globalisation, intense competition and rapid technological change can only be achieved by loosening the central ties and controls that have characterised organisations in the past.

Key Learning Point

Adopting an Emergent Approach to change may require organisations to move towards radically different structures and cultures.

Organisational learning

In many instances, a willingness to change only stems from the feeling that there is no other option. Therefore, as Wilson (1992) suggests, change can be precipitated by making impending crises real to everyone in the organisation (or perhaps even engineering crises) or encouraging dissatisfaction with current systems and procedures. The latter is probably best achieved through the creation of mechanisms by managers that allow staff to become familiar with the marketplace, customers, competitors, legal requirements, etc., in order to recognise the pressures for change.

Clarke (1994) and Nadler (1993) suggested that individual and organisational learning stems from effective top-down communication and the promotion of self-development and confidence. In turn, this encourages the commitment to, and shared ownership of, the organisation's vision, actions and decisions that are necessary to respond to the external environment and take advantage of the opportunities it offers. Additionally, as Pugh (1993) pointed out, in order to generate the need and climate for change, people within organisations need to be involved in the diagnosis of problems and the development of solutions. Carnall (1990) took this argument further, maintaining that organisational effectiveness can be achieved and sustained only through learning from the experience of change.

Clarke (1994, p. 156) believed that involving staff in change management decisions has the effect of 'stimulating habits of criticism and open debate' which enables them to challenge existing norms and question established practices. This, in turn, creates the opportunity for innovation and radical change. Benjamin and Mabey (1993) argued that such questioning of the status quo is the essence of bottom-up change. They consider that, as employees' learning becomes more valued and visible within a company, then rather than managers putting pressure on staff to change, the reverse occurs. The new openness and knowledge of staff puts pressure on managers to address fundamental questions about the purpose and direction of the organisation which previously they might have avoided.

Managerial behaviour

The traditional view of organisations sees managers as directing and controlling staff, resources and information. However, the Emergent Approach to change requires a radical change in managerial behaviour. Managers are expected to operate as facilitators and coaches who, through their ability to span hierarchical, functional and organisational boundaries, can bring together and motivate teams and groups to identify the need for, and achieve, change (Mabey and Mayon-White, 1993).

To be effective in this new role, Clarke (1994) believed that managers would require knowledge of and expertise in strategy formulation, human resource management, marketing/sales and negotiation/conflict resolution. But the key to success, the decisive factor in creating a focused agenda for organisational change is, according to Clarke (1994), managers' own behaviour. If managers are to gain the commitment of others to change, they must first be prepared to challenge their own assumptions, attitudes and mindsets so that they develop an understanding of the emotional and intellectual processes involved (Buchanan and Boddy, 1992b).

For supporters of the Emergent Approach, the essence of change is the move from the familiar to the unknown. In this situation, it is essential for managers to be able to tolerate risk and cope with ambiguity. Pugh (1993) took the view that, in a dynamic environment, open and active communication with those participating in the change process is the key to coping with risk and ambiguity. This is echoed by Clarke's (1994, p. 172) assertion that because 'top-down, unilaterally imposed change does not work, bottom-up, early involvement and genuine consultation' are essential to achieving successful change. This in turn requires managers to facilitate open, organisation-wide communication via groups, individuals, and formal and informal channels.

An organisation's ability to gather, disseminate, analyse and discuss information is, from the perspective of the Emergent Approach, crucial for successful change. The reason for this, as Wilson (1992) argued, is that to effect change successfully, organisations need consciously and pro-actively to move forward incrementally. Large-scale change and more formal and integrated approaches to change (such as TQM) can quickly lose their sense of purpose and relevance for organisations operating in dynamic and uncertain environments. However, if organisations move towards their strategic vision on the basis of many small-scale, localised incremental changes, managers must ensure that those concerned, which could (potentially) be the entire workforce, have access to and are able to act on all the available information. Also, by encouraging a collective pooling of knowledge and information in this way, a better understanding of the pressures and possibilities for change can be achieved, which should enable managers to improve the quality of strategic decisions (Buchanan and Boddy, 1992a; Quinn, 1993).

As well as ensuring the free flow of information, managers must also recognise and be able to cope with resistance to change, and political intervention in it. They will, especially, need to acquire and develop a range of interpersonal skills that enable them to deal with individuals and groups who seek to block or manipulate change for their own benefit (Buchanan and Boddy, 1992a). In addition, supporting openness, reducing uncertainty and encouraging experimentation can be powerful mechanisms for promoting change (Mabey and Mayon-White, 1993). In this respect, Coghlan (1993) and McCalman and Paton (1992) advocated the use of OD tools and techniques (such as transactional analysis, teamwork, group problem-solving, role-playing, etc.) which have long been used in Planned change programmes. However, there is an enormous and potentially confusing array of these; Mayon-White (1993) and Buchanan and Boddy (1992b) argued that managers have a crucial role to play in terms of identifying and applying the appropriate ones. The main objective in deploying such tools and techniques is to encourage shared learning through teamwork and co-operation. It is this that provides the framework and support for the emergence of creative solutions and encourages a sense of involvement, commitment and ownership of the change process (Carnall, 1990; McCalman and Paton, 1992).

Nevertheless, it would be naive to assume that everyone will want to work, or be able to function effectively, in such situations. The cognitive and behavioural changes necessary for organisational survival may be too large for many people, including and perhaps especially managers. An important managerial task will, therefore, be to identify sources of inertia, assess the skill mix within their organisation and, most of all, consider whether their own managerial attitudes and styles are appropriate.

Key Learning Point

The Emergent Approach requires a major change in the traditional role of managers. In future they will need to be facilitators and coaches rather than initiators and directors.

Power and politics

Although the advocates of Emergent change tend to view power and politics from differing perspectives, they all recognise their importance and that they have to be managed if change is to be effective. Dawson (1994, p. 176), for example, concludes that: 'The central argument is that it is important to try and gain the support of senior management, local management, supervisors, trade unions and workplace employees.' Pettigrew *et al.* (1992, p. 293) state that: 'The significance of political language at the front end of change processes needs emphasizing. Closures can be labelled as redevelopments. Problems can be re-coded into opportunities with ... broad positive visions being articulated to build early coalitions ...'. However, in an era in which political 'spin' is increasingly recognised and questioned, the effectiveness and integrity of such 'political language' is debatable. Kanter *et al.* (1992, p. 508) argue that the first step to implementing change is coalition-building: 'involve those whose involvement really matters. ... Specifically, seek support from two general groups: (1) power sources and (2) stakeholders.' In a similar vein, Nadler (1993) advocates the need to shape the political dynamics of change so that power centres develop that support the change rather than block it. Senior (1997), drawing on the work of Nadler (1988), proposes four steps organisations need to take to manage the political dynamics of change:

■ Step 1: Ensure or develop the support of key power groups.

■ Step 2: Use leader behaviour to generate support for the proposed change.

■ Step 3: Use symbols and language to encourage and show support for the change.

■ Step 4: Build in stability by using power to ensure that some things remain the same.

Important though power and politics are in the change process, as Hendry (1996) and Pugh (1993) argue, they are not the be all and end all of change and it is important not to focus on these to the exclusion of other factors. Nevertheless, the focus placed on the political dynamics of change does serve to highlight the need for those who manage change to be aware of and control this dimension of the change process.

Key Learning Point

Though power and politics can play an influential role in managing change, other factors, such as culture, also play an influential role.

Exercise 15.3   Organisational learning

Oticon, the Danish hearing-aid manufacturer, was founded in 1904. In 1979, it was the number one hearing-aid manufacturer in the world. However, by the early 1990s, it was rapidly losing money and market share. A new Chief Executive was appointed to reverse the decline in the company's fortunes.

The Chief Executive believed that the company could no longer compete merely by supplying good technology. Instead it needed to offer its customers a high standard of service as well. It also had to accept that while it operated in a global marketplace, this was composed of a number of distinct and rapidly changing local markets. Each of these demanded a different service mix and, therefore, a different approach.

In short, if Oticon were to survive, the Chief Executive believed it would have to move from a technological orientation to a knowledge orientation; from a technology-based manufacturing company to a knowledge-based service business. The core of this was to build a learning organisation where experts put aside their expertise and worked as a team to create satisfied customers.

1 How can learning facilitate organisational change?

2 How might becoming a learning organisation help Oticon to deal with rapidly changing and diverse customer needs?

Emergent change: summary and criticisms

The proponents of Emergent change are a somewhat disparate group who tend to be united more by their scepticism regarding Planned change than by a commonly agreed alternative. Nevertheless, there does seem to be some agreement regarding the main tenets of Emergent change, which are as follows:

■ Organisational change is a continuous process of experiment and adaptation aimed at matching an organisation's capabilities to the needs and dictates of a dynamic and uncertain environment.

■ Though this is best achieved through a multitude of (mainly) small-scale incremental changes, over time these can lead to a major re-configuration and transformation of an organisation.

■ The role of managers is not to plan or implement change, but to create or foster an organisational structure and climate that encourages and sustains experimentation and risk-taking, and to develop a workforce that will take responsibility for identifying the need for change and implementing it.

■ Although managers are expected to become facilitators rather than doers, they also have the prime responsibility for developing a collective vision or common purpose which gives direction to their organisation, and within which the appropriateness of any proposed change can be judged.

■ The key organisational activities that allow these elements to operate successfully are: information-gathering – about the external environment and internal objectives and capabilities; communication – the transmission, analysis and discussion of information; and learning – the ability to develop new skills, identify appropriate responses and draw knowledge from their own and others' past and present actions.

Though not always stated openly, the case for an Emergent Approach to change is based on the assumption that all organisations operate in a turbulent, dynamic and unpredictable environment. Therefore, if the external world is changing in a rapid and uncertain fashion, organisations need to be continually scanning their environment in order to adapt and respond to changes. Because this is a continuous and open-ended process, the Planned Approach to change is seen as inappropriate. To be successful, changes need to emerge locally and incrementally in order to respond to and take advantage of environmental threats and opportunities.

Presented in this fashion, there is certainly an apparent coherence and validity to the Emergent Approach. However, it is a fragile coherence and of challengeable validity. As far as coherence is concerned, some proponents of Emergent change, especially Dawson (1994) and Pettigrew and Whipp (1993), clearly approach it from the processual perspective on organisations. However, it is not clear that Wilson (1992) and Buchanan and Boddy (1992a, b) would fully subscribe to this view. In the case of Clarke (1994) and Carnall (1990), it is clear that they do not take a processual perspective. Partly, this is explained by the fact that some of these writers (especially Wilson, 1992; Pettigrew and Whipp, 1993; Dawson, 1994) are attempting to understand and investigate change from a critical perspective, while others (notably Carnall, 1990; Buchanan and Boddy, 1992a, b; Clarke, 1994) are more concerned to provide recipes and checklists for successful change. Nevertheless, these differing objectives and perspectives do put a question mark against the coherence of the Emergent Approach.

The validity or general applicability of the Emergent Approach to change depends to a large extent on whether or not one subscribes to the view that all organisations operate in a dynamic and unpredictable environment to which they continually have to adapt. Burnes (1996, 2000) produced substantial evidence that not all organisations face the same degree of environmental turbulence and that, in any case, it is possible to manipulate or change environmental constraints. This does not necessarily invalidate the Emergent Approach as a whole, but it does indicate that some organisations, by accident or action, may find the Planned Approach to change both appropriate and effective in their particular circumstances.

Obviously, the above issues raise a major question mark regarding the Emergent Approach; however, even without reservations regarding its coherence and validity, there would still be serious criticisms of this approach. For example, a great deal of emphasis is given to creating appropriate organisational cultures; but many writers have questioned whether this is either easy or indeed possible (Filby and Willmott, 1988; Meek, 1988). Indeed, as mentioned earlier, even Wilson (1992) was sceptical about the case for viewing culture as a facilitator of change. Similar points can be made regarding the 'learning organisation' approach. As Whittington (1993, p. 130) commented:

> The danger of the purely 'learning' approach to change, therefore, is that ... managers [and others] may actually recognize the need for change, yet still refuse to 'learn' because they understand perfectly well the implications for their power and status. Resistance to change may not be 'stupid' ... but based on a very shrewd appreciation of the personal consequences.

A variant of this criticism relates to the impact of success on managerial learning. Miller (1993, p. 119) observed that, while managers generally start out by attempting to learn all they can about their organisation's environment, over time, as they gain experience, they 'form quite definite opinions of what works and why' and as a consequence tend to limit their search for information and knowledge. So experience, especially where it is based on success, may actually be a barrier to learning, in that it shapes the cognitive structures by which managers, and everyone else, see and interpret the world. As Nystrom and Starbuck (1984, p. 55) observed:

> What people see, predict, understand, depends on their cognitive structures ... [which] manifest themselves in perceptual frameworks, expectations, world views, plans, goals ... myths, rituals, symbols ... and jargon.

This brings us neatly to the topic of the role of managers. As the above quotations indicate, they may neither welcome nor be able to accept approaches to change that require them to challenge and amend their own beliefs, especially where such approaches run counter to their experience of 'what works and why'. It is in such situations that managers may seek to use their power and political influence in an adverse manner.

Advocates of the Emergent Approach have undoubtedly provided a valuable contribution to our understanding of change by highlighting the neglect of these important issues. However, they have also been criticised for overstating their case. Hendry (1996, p. 621) argues that: 'The management of change has become ... overfocused on the political aspects of change', while Collins (1998, p. 100), voicing concerns of his own and of other researchers, argues that:

> in reacting to the problems and critiques of [the Planned Approach], managers and practitioners have swung from a dependence on under-socialized models and explanations of change and instead have become committed to the arguments of, what might be called, over-socialized models of change.

One final and important point which needs to be considered is that, though the Emergent Approach offers valuable insights and guidance, it does not appear to be as universally applicable as its advocates imply. The focus of Emergent change tends to be the organisation and its major subsystems rather than individuals and groups *per se*. It is also the case that, both implicitly and explicitly, the Emergent Approach advocates co-operative change rather than coercive or confrontational change. Though this is to be applauded, it is also clear that there are many situations where change is pushed through in a rapid and confrontational manner (see Edwardes, 1983; Grinyer *et al.*, 1988; Dunphy and Stace, 1992; Franklin, 1997). It is also the case that the Emergent Approach is specifically founded on the assumption that organisations operate in a dynamic environment that requires continuous, coherent and, over time, large-scale change. It is, then, by its own definition, not applicable to organisations operating in stable environments or to those seeking to achieve a large-scale and rapid transition from one fixed state to another. In addition, as mentioned above, if the possibility exists to manipulate environmental variables and constraints to avoid having to undertake radical change, managers may perceive this as a more attractive or viable option.

Key Learning Point

Though the Emergent Approach to change has apparent advantages over the Planned Approach, an examination of it reveals that there are serious question marks over its coherence, validity and applicability.

Organisational change: approaches and choices

A framework for change

As Stickland (1998, p. 14) remarks: 'the problem with studying change is that it parades across many subject domains under numerous guises, such as transformation, development, metamorphosis, transmutation, evolution, regeneration, innovation, revolution and transition to name but a few.' As this chapter has shown, there are two dominant and, in the main, quite different approaches to managing change – the Planned and the Emergent. However, despite their valuable contributions to assisting organisations to manage change more effectively, as has been indicated, they do not cover the full spectrum of change events organisations encounter. Indeed, given the vast array of types of organisation – operating in different industries and different countries – and the enormous variety of change situations – ranging from small to large, from technical to people – and all stages in between, it would be surprising if one or even two approaches could encompass all these situations. Nevertheless, the important point is not to be able to categorise the variety of change situations *per se*, but to provide a framework that matches types of change situations with the appropriate ways of managing them.

This, of course, is no small task. Dunphy and Stace (1992), for example, identify four approaches to managing change based on the degree to which employees are involved in planning and executing change, as follows: collaborative, consultative, directive and coercive. They also argue that consultative and directive approaches tend to dominate, except where rapid organisational transformations are required, when more coercive approaches come into play. Kotter (1996) takes a different view, seeing the overall direction of change as being decided by senior managers, but its implementation being the responsibility of empowered managers and employees at all levels. Storey (1992) takes a slightly different tack. He identifies two key dimensions. The first concerns the degree of collaboration between the parties concerned: varying from change that is unilaterally constructed by management, to change brought about by some form of joint agreement with those involved. The second dimension concerns the form that change takes: ranging from change that is introduced as a complete package, to change comprising a sequence of individual initiatives.

We could cover many pages in this fashion, listing the various ways of managing change that writers have identified. However, the key issues are: how can these approaches be classified and what determines which approach an organisation should take and in what circumstances? In addressing these questions Burnes (2000) constructed *a framework for change* (*see* Fig. 15.1). The horizontal axis of the framework incorporates both the nature of the environment, running from stable to turbulent, and the pace of change, running from slow change, where the focus is on behavioural and cultural change, to rapid change, where the focus is on major changes in structures and processes. This is based on the work of the culture school, who argue that rapid change tends to be effective in changing structures and processes, but achieving attitudinal and/or cultural change is a much slower process (see, for example, Allaire and Firsirotu, 1984; Kanter *et al.*, 1992). The vertical axis covers the magnitude of change events, running from small scale, incremental to large scale, transformational.

These two axes create four quadrants, each of which has a distinct focus in terms of change. Quadrants 1 and 4, on the left-hand side of the figure, identify situations where the primary focus is on cultural and attitudinal/behavioural change. Burnes argues that these are likely to be best achieved through a slow, participative approach, rather than a rapid and directive or coercive one. For relatively small-scale initiatives whose main objective is performance improvement through attitudinal and behavioural change at the individual and group level, the Planned

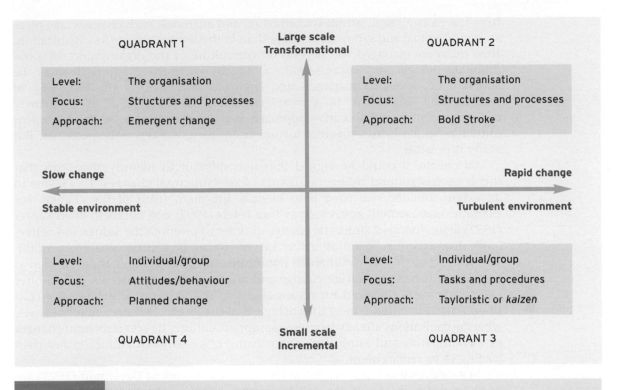

Figure 15.1   A framework for change

Approach, with its emphasis on collaboration and participation, is likely to be most appropriate. For those relatively large-scale initiatives, whose main focus is culture change at the level of the entire organisation or large parts of it, the Emergent Approach, which emphasises both the collaborative and political dimensions of change, is likely to be most appropriate.

Turning to the right-hand side of Fig. 15.1, this identifies situations where the primary focus is on achieving changes in structures, processes, tasks and procedures. Quadrant 2 relates to situations where the focus is on achieving rapid major changes in structures and processes at the level of the entire organisation (i.e. what Kanter *et al.*, 1992, refer to as a 'Bold Stroke' approach). Situations where such changes are required arise for a variety of reasons. It may be that an organisation finds itself in serious trouble and needs to respond quickly to realign itself with its environment. Alternatively, it may be that an organisation is not experiencing a crisis, but that it needs to restructure itself for the future or in response to a merger or acquisition. In such cases, it may not be possible or advisable to change the structure slowly and on a piecemeal basis and, therefore, a major and rapid re-organisation is necessary. Because it involves the entire organisation or major components of it, this is likely to be driven by the centre and to be the focus of a political struggle, given that major structural changes are usually accompanied by major shifts in the distribution of power. Therefore, the new structure will be imposed from the top in a directive or even coercive way, depending on the balance between winners and losers. Quadrant 3 presents a different picture. This is where the changes tend to be small scale and of a relatively technical nature, and have few (if any) implications for behaviour and attitudes. Such changes take place at the individual and group level rather than at the level of the entire organisation. How these are managed will depend on the culture of the organisation. In a traditional, bureaucratic organisation, a directive-Tayloristic approach may be adopted, i.e. specialist managers and engineers will identify the 'best way of working' and impose it. In a more participative culture, such as a Japanese company, a more collaborative approach may be appropriate, such as a *kaizen* initiative, which brings together a team comprising workers and specialists. But either is possible.

Of course, it could be argued that it is difficult to identify situations that involve solely cultural changes or involve solely structural changes. This is true to an extent, but the real issue is to identify the main focus of the change. For example, management gurus such as Tom Peters (1997) and Rosabeth Moss Kanter (1997) argue for rapid structural change in order to promote the values and behaviours necessary for organisations to survive in an increasingly complex world. Therefore, though they recommend significant structural changes, these are seen as part of the process of culture change and not an end in themselves. John Kotter (1996) advocates the need for organisations to restructure themselves on a continuous basis in order to meet the challenges of the future. However, in many cases, where organisations already have an appropriate culture, he sees structural changes as working with and reinforcing the existing organisational culture rather than leading to its replacement.

Where does this leave us? Firstly, drawing on the work of Davenport (1993), we need to distinguish between initiatives that focus on fundamental attitudinal change and those aimed at fundamental structural change. Allaire and Firsirotu (1984) argued that there is a strong relationship between organisational structures and organisational cultures, and so changes in one may require corresponding changes in the other. However, as was also argued earlier, it is much easier and quicker to change structures than to change cultures. Consequently, we need to take into account the timescale for change. Rapid change is likely to be effective or necessary only where the main changes are structural changes, or where the organisation is in such trouble that delay is not an option. In the former case, change may involve some consultation but is likely to have a large element of direction from the centre. In the latter case, because of the speed and nature of the situation, change is likely to be directive and, probably, coercive.

There is one further point that needs to be noted, and that relates to how these various approaches can be used in combination. In a manner reminiscent of Mintzberg's (1994) definition of 'umbrella' strategies, Pettigrew *et al.* (1992, p. 297) write of instances where change is both 'intentional and emergent'. Storey (1992) identifies the need for change projects whose outlines are decided at corporate level with little or no consultation, but whose implementation comprises an interrelated series of change initiatives, some or all of which could be the product of local co-operation and consultation. Kotter (1996) takes a similar perspective. He sees strategic change as comprising a series of large and small projects aimed at achieving the same overall objectives, but that are begun at different times, can be managed differently and vary in nature. Buchanan and Storey (1997) also hint at this when criticising Planned change for attempting to impose order and a linear sequence to processes that are untidy, messy, multi-level and multi-function, and develop in an iterative and back-tracking manner. This is also identified by Kanter *et al.* (1992) when speaking of Long Marches and Bold Strokes. They argue that Bold Strokes often have to be followed by a whole series of smaller-scale changes over a more extended timescale in order to embed the changes brought about by the Bold Stroke. Therefore, when examining the management of major change projects, one should not see them as solely co-operative or solely coercive. They may have elements of both but at different levels, at different times and managed by different people. They may also, indeed probably will, unfold in an unexpected way which will require rethinking and backtracking from time to time.

A framework for choice

As can be seen from Fig. 15.1, what appears to be on offer is a menu approach to change whereby organisations, or more accurately those who manage them, can choose the approach that fits their circumstances. This conception of a multiplicity of approaches is in line with the call by Dunphy and Stace (1993, p. 905) for 'a model of change that is essentially a "situational" or "contingency model", one that indicates how to vary strategies to achieve "optimum fit" with the changing environment'. If we were to stop at this point, it might be considered that we had indeed made significant progress in our understanding of change; yet there would still be one essential question outstanding: what about choice? We have identified situations where these various approaches seem appropriate or not, but does that mean they cannot be used in other situations and does that mean that the context cannot be changed? Supposing organisations, whose management prefer a co-operative approach, find themselves seriously out of alignment with their environment: is their only option rapid and coercive structural change? Or, alternatively, where managers prefer a more directive, less participative style, are they compelled to adopt a more participative style and culture?

These questions revolve around two issues. The first issue concerns the extent to which an organisation can influence the forces driving it to change in one direction or another. If we accept that the speed and nature of the changes that organisations are required to make are dependent upon the nature of the environment in which they are operating, then choice will relate to the extent that organisations can influence, manipulate or recreate their environment to suit their preferred way of working. Over the last decade, there has been a growing tide of support for those who argue that organisations can influence their environment, either to stabilise or to destabilise it (Morgan, 1986; Hatch, 1997; Burnes, 2000). If this is the case, then the important question is not just how organisations can do this, but whether, finding themselves in trouble, they have the time to influence their environment.

This leads on to the second issue – to what extent and for how long can an organisation operate with structures, practices and cultures that are out of line with its environment? The answer to this question revolves around Child's (1972) concept of equifinality. Sorge (1997, p. 13) states that equifinality 'quite simply means that different sorts of internal arrangements are perfectly compatible with identical contextual or environmental states'. Put more simply, there are different ways to achieve the same end result. This does not imply that any structure is suitable for any environment. What it does suggest, though, is that total alignment between structure and environment is not always necessary. The duration for which this non-alignment is sustainable will clearly vary with the degree of non-alignment and the circumstances of the organisation in question; however, at the very least, it does offer organisations the potential to stave off realignment for some time during which they can influence or change their circumstances. It follows that Fig. 15.1 depicts not only a framework for change but also a framework for choice.

Therefore, we can see that the debate between Planned change and Emergent change is too narrow. It is too narrow in the sense that there are other approaches to change that organisations have available to them; especially it tends to ignore the more coercive and directive approaches to change that, in many organisations, may be more prevalent than more co-operative ones. It is also too narrow in the sense that it assumes that change is unidirectional, i.e. is driven by the environment. People in organisations do have the opportunity to make choices about what to change, how to change and when to change. This does not mean that all organisations will exercise such choices or that those that do will be successful. Nor does it mean that choice is not severely constrained. However, it does mean that those who do not recognise that choice exists may be putting themselves in a worse competitive position than those who do.

Summary

This chapter has examined the merits, drawbacks and appropriateness of the Planned and Emergent Approaches to change which have successively dominated the theory and, to a large extent, the practice of organisational change over the past 50 years. It has been argued that just as change comes in all shapes and sizes, so too do models or approaches to change. Therefore, instead of portraying the argument regarding the most appropriate approach to change as a contest between the merits of the Planned and Emergent Approaches, a change framework has been developed (see Fig. 15.1) which provides an overview of the range of change situations and approaches organisations face or are offered and the types of situations in which they can best be applied.

It has also been argued that the environment and other organisational constraints can be manipulated or subject to managerial choice. Consequentially, some organisations will find that the organisational adjustments required to accommodate their position on the environment continuum coincide with the dominant view in the organisation of how it should operate. In that case, whether the approach to change adopted is Planned or Emergent, directive or co-operative, it will fit in with both how the organisation wishes to operate and the needs of the environment. Some organisations will, obviously, find that the dominant view internally of how they should operate is out of step with what is required to align or realign them with their environment. Such organisations face a number of choices ranging from whether to attempt to change their structures, cultures or style of management to accommodate the environment, or whether to attempt to manipulate the environment and other constraints so as to align them more closely with the dominant view within the organisation of how it should operate. Still further, there will be other organisations that face severe problems either because they failed to respond quickly enough or in an appropriate manner to changes in their environment, or because the environment moved too rapidly for an incremental approach to respond adequately. Nevertheless, by showing that a more conducive environment can be brought about, the framework also provides those who wish to promote more co-operative approaches to change with the means to argue their case in situations where previously more directive and coercive measures appeared to be the only option.

The concept of a change framework that allows approaches to change to be matched to environmental conditions and organisational constraints is clearly attractive. The fact that it incorporates the potential for managers, and others, to exercise some choice or influence over their environment and other constraints allows the model to move beyond the limitations of mechanistic and rational perspectives on organisations, and into the heartland of organisational reality.

Key Learning Point

Just as organisations have choice in terms of what to change, they also have choice in what approach they adopt to change.

Closing Case Study   Team-building and Problem-solving

GK Printers Limited is a small, family-run printing business. In the 1980s, in response to increased competition, it upgraded its technology and skills in order to concentrate on providing a full-range design and printing service to its customers. This enabled it to survive and prosper at a time when many companies of its size were going out of business. Nevertheless, by the mid-1990s, GK began to lose significant amounts of business. This was partly due to increased competition, but mainly it was because its customers, in seeking to cut their own costs, were reducing the size and frequency of their orders (though when orders were placed, they were often required far faster than previously). This presented a double threat to GK. Firstly, the fall in overall volumes was having an adverse effect on turnover and profit. Secondly, the reduction in size of individual print runs was having an adverse effect on costs because, though the actual volume was smaller, the design, order processing and set-up costs remained constant.

Therefore, GK appeared to be faced with the dilemma of whether to increase its prices to offset rising costs (and risk more customers going elsewhere) or to maintain or reduce prices and see its profits plunge. The Marketing and Design Manager suggested that GK needed to improve on its already good level of service. In particular, it needed to cut costs in order to cut prices and improve the efficiency of its internal operations to cut delivery times. Other managers ▶

reacted negatively to this suggestion. The Marketing and Design Manager was relatively new to the company, and in some people's eyes, he lacked an in-depth knowledge of the printing industry. In addition, GK had already made significant strides in improving efficiency and cutting costs, and there was doubt as to the scope for any more real improvements in these areas.

Despite this, in the absence of any other credible suggestions, the Managing Director asked the Marketing and Design Manager to put together a plan for reducing costs and set-up times. Within a fortnight he presented his proposals to the Managing Director and other senior staff. He began by identifying what he saw as the main problems the company faced:

■ Though there had been a slight decline in the number of individual orders, the actual reduction in the volume of business was much greater because customers were ordering shorter print runs.

■ The result of this was that, while office staff, marketing, design, administration, etc., were as busy as ever, the print shop was short of work.

■ However, though the printers were underworked, this did not provide much scope for reducing delivery times, because most of GK's lead time was accounted for by non-printing activities – especially design, which could take anything up to two weeks.

His solution was to hire more design staff. The Managing Director and other managers were taken aback by this proposal. They felt it was an outrageous piece of opportunism. The case for more design staff had been raised and rejected in the recent past. The Marketing and Design Manager's colleagues felt that he was using the company's current problems to empire-build. Not surprisingly, the meeting ended acrimoniously and no decision was taken.

The Managing Director was particularly infuriated, as he had genuinely been expecting an acceptable solution to emerge from the meeting. Instead, the friendly working atmosphere he valued had been shattered. After several weeks of indecision, during which tensions within the management team continued to rise, the Managing Director decided to seek outside assistance. He approached a contact at the local university who recommended a colleague with expertise in team-building. Though the Managing Director was sceptical, his contact pointed out that, working together, there was enough experience in GK to solve its current dilemma. Therefore, the issue was how to bring people together, rather than seeking outside solutions.

With some misgivings, the Managing Director met with the team-builder and agreed to his suggested approach. Firstly, all the relevant managers had to be involved. Secondly, the team-builder would meet each of them individually and then, as a group, would take them away from the company for two days to work on the problem. Thirdly, each member of the team would have to agree to operate in an open and constructive fashion during the two days. Lastly, the team would agree to reach a commonly accepted solution by the end of the two days.

Although the GK management later admitted that the first day had been decidedly uncomfortable, they also agreed that the two days had been a success. The proceedings began with the team-builder reporting on his findings from the individual interviews. Though he did not reveal who said what, in a small organisation such as GK, it was relatively easy for managers to make a good guess as to the source of particular comments. This was one of the reasons why they found the first day uncomfortable.

The key issue which emerged from the team-builder's report and the subsequent discussion was the style of the Managing Director. He tended to make decisions either by himself or in consultation with one other manager. This created suspicion among managers excluded from decisions, and led to accusations of favouritism. All the managers, other than the Managing Director, favoured a more open and collective style of management.

The Managing Director was very upset and said so. He wanted, he said, to 'clear the air' there and then. However, the team-builder suggested, and agreement was eventually reached, that they should all reflect on what had been said, and return to the issue at the end of the second day. They then moved on to discuss the immediate problems facing GK: how to reverse the decline in turnover and profitability. With the delicate matter of the Managing Director's approach to decision-making out in the open, they found it much easier to reach an agreement on the way forward which they could all accept. They agreed to:

- Meet with their main customers to identify what their needs were and discuss how these could best be met.

- Review the entire production process, from order intake to dispatch, with the intention of either reducing it for all orders, or possibly shortening it for specific categories of orders.

These actions were to be carried out by two groups comprising managers and employees from the areas involved, who would report directly to the management team.

This then left the thorny issue of the Managing Director's role. Since the issue had been raised on the first day, he had spoken to the team-builder and his colleagues informally, and had come to recognise the strength of feeling on the issue, though he did not fully accept their interpretation of his actions. Nevertheless, he was prepared to try to amend his management style. He agreed that there would be regular management team meetings which would deal with all major decisions. He also agreed that he would not seek to impose a decision on the team unless the managers themselves could not reach agreement.

Six months later

The investigation of customer requirements and the order-to-dispatch process resulted in changes which brought significant improvements in the service GK could offer to its customers, and a reduction in lead times and costs. The ▶

company now offers its customers a choice of lead times and prices: normal – a two-week delivery and a 5 per cent reduction on the standard prices; accelerated – a one-week delivery charged at standard prices; and urgent – a one working day delivery charged at 10 per cent above standard prices.

In addition to these changes, the management team, after some initial difficulties (such as identifying what constituted a major decision), found that working together and having all information out in the open reduced the tension, not only between individual managers but between the individual functions as well.

Suggested exercises

1   Use the Framework for Change shown in Fig. 15.1 to analyse and identify the form of change or changes described in the GK case study.

2   To what extent can the changes in how the management team operates be seen as the beginning of a cultural change or merely an adaptation within an existing culture?

3   Does the GK case study represent an example of Emergent change, or of *ad hoc* and reactive management?

Test your learning

Short-answer questions

1 What was Kurt Lewin's main contribution to the development of organisational change?

2 How does Bullock and Batten's phases of change model differ from Lewin's three-step model?

3 What are the main advantages of the Planned Approach?

4 What are the main disadvantages of the Planned Approach?

5 What are the key components of the Emergent Approach?

6 How does the Emergent Approach view the role of organisational culture?

7 What are the main advantages of the Emergent Approach?

8 What are the main disadvantages of the Emergent Approach?

9 What are the practical benefits of the framework for change shown in Fig. 15.1?

10 In what ways might an organisation influence its environment?

Suggested assignments

1   To what extent can it be said that, in today's rapidly changing world, the Planned Approach to change is no longer relevant?

2   Discuss the proposition that the Emergent Approach is nothing more than an attempt to provide an intellectual justification for allowing managers to adopt an *ad hoc* approach to change.

3   Describe and discuss the Planned and Emergent Approaches' view of the role of managers.

4   What are the main constraints on organisations when deciding on which approach to change to adopt?

5   In what ways can the framework for change, shown in Fig. 15.1, be used to increase managerial choice?

Relevant websites

The Social Science Information Gateway (SOSIG) is a good source of links to the thoughts of well-known writers. In the case of organisational change, this includes the management gurus Peter Drucker and Tom Peters. You can find it at http://www.sosig.ac.uk/roads/subject-listing/World-cat/orgchan.html.

A short account of a practical outlook on organisational change can be found at http://www.galtglobalreview.com/business/what_works.html#focus4. How well do you think what is stated here matches the content of Chapter 15?

A significant proportion of academic work on organisational change is published in the *Journal of Organizational Change Management*. The website for this journal can be found at http://lris.emeraldinsight.com/vl=8297309/cl=80/nw=1/rpsv/jocm.htm. If you are a student at a university, there is a good chance that your university subscribes to this journal, in which case you will probably be able to download articles free of charge.

For further self-test material and relevant, annotated weblinks please visit the website at http://www.booksites.net/arnold_workpsych.

Suggested further reading

1   Bernard Burnes (2004) *Managing Change: A Strategic Approach to Organisational Dynamics (fourth Edition)*, FT/Prentice Hall: Harlow. This book provides a comprehensive review of the development of organisations and organisational change. It expands on this chapter and contains ten detailed case studies of major change projects in European companies.

2   Rosabeth Moss Kanter, Barry A. Stein and Todd D. Jick (1992) *The Challenge of Organizational Change: How companies experience it and leaders guide it*. Free Press: New York. Though research-based, this is less of an academic text and more of a guide book on how to manage change. It contains many examples of change projects in American companies.

3   David Wilson (1992) *A Strategy of Change: Concepts and controversies in the management of change*. Routledge: London. This is a short and readable book that covers some of the key arguments concerning change management.

GLOSSARY OF TERMS

Action orientation A psychological state in which a person uses self-regulatory strategies in order to achieve desired goals. Contrast with **State orientation** (*see below*).

Action research A form of research that concentrates on solving practical problems in collaboration with the people and organisations experiencing them.

Adjustment The extent and ways in which a person is able to function effectively and happily in his or her environment.

Advanced manufacturing technology Computer-controlled machinery that can perform sophisticated production activities once appropriately programmed.

Agreeableness A positive orientation towards others, sympathetic, eager to help – preferring collaboration to conflict.

Alarm reaction When an individual's defence mechanisms become active.

Alienation A state of being where a person does not feel that he or she is in touch with his or her true self, nor does he or she experience fulfilling relationships with others.

Alternative hypothesis (also called the *experimental hypothesis*) The hypothesis that is the alternative to the null hypothesis. The alternative hypothesis essentially proposes that 'something is going on' in the data. That is, that two or more groups of people do differ on a psychological variable, or that two or more variables are correlated with each other.

Analysis of variance A statistical technique used to test whether two or more samples have significantly different mean scores on one or more variables.

Antecedents Events that precede the occurrence of behaviour. In (non-behaviourist) approaches they may be seen to *cause* the behaviour.

Anxiety *See* **Neuroticism**.

Archival data Research information obtained from written, computerised or audiovisual sources that exist independent of the research.

Assessee Person whose behaviour is being assessed by an assessor (either in an interview, performing a work sample task, or on the job).

Assessment centre An assessment process that involves multiple exercises and multiple assessors to rate an assessee's performance on a series of job-related competencies.

Assessor Person who is observing and assessing a target person's behaviour for the purposes of assessing whether they are, or are likely to be able to, perform a role effectively.

Associative phase The second phase of skill acquisition, when the learner begins to combine the actions needed to produce skilled performance.

Attitude A regularity in an individual's feelings, thoughts and predispositions to act towards some aspect of his or her environment.

Attractiveness of communicator The extent to which a person attempting to change the attitude of another is seen as the kind of person that the recipient of the message would like to be.

Attribution The explanation a person constructs for the nature or behaviour of another person.

Autonomous phase The final phase of skill acquisition, when performance becomes increasingly polished. To some degree performance is automatic and control relies less and less on memory or attention.

Autonomy at work When individuals feel that they have some influence and control over their jobs.

Behavioural indicator A description of an observable behaviour related to a specific competency.

Behaviourally anchored rating scales (BARS) Rating scales that use anchors that describe specific behaviour. The behaviours provide anchors for a spread (good–poor) of performance standards and are derived from a systematic development procedure.

Behaviourism An approach to psychology that concentrates on the external (to the person) conditions under which behaviour is exhibited and the observable consequences of behaviour.

Behaviourist tradition The approach that focuses on behaviour, rather than thoughts and emotions.

Behaviour-modelling training An approach to training in which models are reinforced for engaging in the intended behaviour.

Belongingness need The psychological need to feel part of a group, organisation or other collective endeavour.

Bias A psychological assessment procedure is biased if consistent errors of prediction (or classification) are made for members of a particular subgroup.

Biodata Life history information about candidates, usually collected with the aid of a structured questionnaire. Criterion-related validity for biodata is explored by examining statistical links between biodata items and criterion measures.

Bold strokes These are major and rapid change initiatives which are imposed on an organisation from the top in a directive rather than participative manner.

Boundaryless career A term given to careers that cross boundaries for example between employers and job functions.

BPS British Psychological Society – the governing body for psychologists in the United Kingdom.

Brainstorming A technique for generating ideas which involves people thinking of as many things as possible that might be relevant to a given problem, however far-fetched their ideas may seem.

Bureaucratic career The term given by Kanter to a career characterised by predictable upward movement within one organisation and/or occupation.

Career The sequence of employment-related positions, roles, activities and experiences encountered by a person.

Career anchor The set of self-perceived skills, interests, motives and values that form a basis for a person's career preferences, and which he or she would not give up even if required to make a difficult choice.

Career choice The selection made by a person of an area of work or sequence of work roles that they intend to pursue.

Career counselling An interpersonal process that enables people to recognise and utilise their resources to make career-related decisions and manage career-related problems.

Career decision-making The psychological processes involved in making a career choice.

Career development The changes and adjustments experienced by a person as a consequence of a career choice.

Career exploration The process of investigating oneself and the world of work in order to assist in career decision-making and career management.

Career management The techniques and strategies used by individuals and organisations in seeking to optimise careers.

Career plateau The point in a person's career when the likelihood of additional increases in responsibility is very low.

Career stage A period of time in a person's career characterised by a particular set of concerns or motives.

Career success The extent to which a person's career is achieving the goods that matter to the person and/or society as a whole.

Central route to persuasion Attitude change which occurs as a result of a person carefully considering information and arguments relevant to that attitude.

Change agent An internal or external facilitator whose role is to guide an organisation through a process of change.

Charisma A set of attributes of leaders and/or their relationships with subordinates where the leader demonstrates and promotes a sense of pride and mission through personal example.

Chartered psychologist (C. Psychol.) Title conferred by the BPS recognising the qualifications and experience of psychologists in the United Kingdom. Appropriately qualified work psychologists may also use the title Chartered Occupational Psychologist.

Chi-square A statistical technique used to test whether two or more groups of people differ in the frequency with which their members fall into different categories.

Classical conditioning A form of conditioning in which a previously neutral stimulus such as a tone (the conditioned stimulus) is repeatedly linked with the presentation of an unconditioned stimulus (such as food) so that the conditioned stimulus will, after repeated pairings, produce the unconditioned response (e.g. salivation) normally associated with the unconditioned stimulus. In other words (using this example) an animal could be conditioned to salivate at the sound of a tone.

Coaching A form of development where one person advises and demonstrates to another on how to improve their work performance.

Cognitive ability Also referred to as intelligence or general mental ability. Refers to the capacity of individuals to process information and use the information to behave effectively (including the capacity to learn from experience).

Cognitive phase The first phase of skill acquisition, when the learner is developing knowledge about the task but lacks the procedural skill to carry it out.

Cognitive psychology The branch of basic psychology that concerns the study of human perception, memory and information processing.

Cognitive resource theory A theory of leadership proposed by Fred Fiedler which focuses on how the cognitive resources (e.g. intelligence, knowledge) of leaders influence group performance in situations of varying stress and leader control.

Cohort effect Lasting differences in psychological functioning between people born in different eras.

Common method variance The extent to which people's scores on two or more psychological variables are related solely because the variables were assessed using the same research method.

Competency The specific behaviour patterns (including knowledge, skills and abilities) a job holder is required to demonstrate in order to perform the relevant job tasks with competence.

Competency analysis A person or worker-orientated approach to job analysis that focuses on identifying the relevant knowledge skills and abilities relevant to a specific job role.

Concurrent validity A form of criterion-related validity in which data on the predictor and criterion are obtained at the same time.

Conditioned stimulus *See* **Classical conditioning**.

Conditions of worth In phenomenological approaches to personality, conditions of worth are the conditions under which other people are prepared to value us as a person.

Congruence In John Holland's theory, congruence is the extent to which a person's vocational personality matches his or her work environment.

Conscientiousness A predisposition to prefer active control and organisation. A conscientious person will like to be purposeful and well organised and see life in terms of tasks to be accomplished.

Consideration An aspect of leadership style which reflects the extent that the leader demonstrates trust of subordinates, respect for their ideas and consideration of their feelings.

Construct validity An indication of the extent to which the test or procedure measures the psychological construct that it is intended to measure.

Content analysis A technique for analysing qualitative data that sorts the data, or parts of it, into different categories according to its content.

Content theories of motivation Theories which concentrate on *what* motivates people, rather than *how* motivation works. Contrast with **Process theories of motivation** (*see below*).

Content validity A form of validity based on a logical analysis of the extent to which a test or procedure embodies a representative sample of the behaviour from the domain being measured.

Contiguity The existence of only a small delay between behaviour and reinforcement (or punishment).

Contingency This is present if reinforcement (or punishment) is given *only* when specific behaviour precedes it.

Contingency theories of leadership These are theories of leadership that focus on how features of the situation determine what is the most effective leadership style.

Contingency theory An approach to organisation design which rejects any universal best way and instead views organisation structures as being dependent (i.e. contingent) on the particular combination of situational variables each organisation faces. The main situational variables cited in the literature are environment, technology and size.

Control group In an experiment investigating the impact of one or more interventions, the control group of research subjects does *not* experience an intervention. This group provides a comparison with groups which do experience an intervention.

Core job characteristics The five aspects of jobs suggested by Hackman and Oldham as being essential in influencing satisfaction, motivation and job performance. The five are: skill variety, task identity, task significance, autonomy and feedback.

Correlation A statistical technique used to test whether scores obtained from one sample on two variables are associated with each other, such that as scores on one variable increase, scores on the other either increase (positive correlation) or decrease (negative correlation).

Credibility of communicator The extent to which a person attempting to change the attitude of another is seen as expert and trustworthy.

Criterion-related validity The extent to which a predictor (e.g. a selection test score) is related to a criterion (e.g. work performance). In personnel selection, high criterion-related validity indicates that a selection measure gives an accurate indication of candidates' performance on the criterion.

Critical incident technique A technique developed by Flanagan (1954), still widely used, to obtain information about jobs by concentrating on specific examples (incidents) of outstandingly good or poor performance.

Critical psychological states The three immediate psychological effects of the core job characteristics, as proposed by Hackman and Oldham. The three are: experienced meaningfulness of the work, experienced responsibility for outcomes of the work, and knowledge of the actual results of work activities.

Cross-sectional research Research where data are collected at only one point in time.

Cross-validation A research technique where a piece of research is repeated on a second sample to see if the same results as first time are obtained.

Cumulative trauma The gradual build up of stress which leads to some stress-related illness or event; a term also applied to stress litigation cases.

Decision-making style A person's normal or habitual way of going about making decisions.

Declarative knowledge Factual knowledge that may be stated or made explicit.

Defence mechanisms In the psychoanalytic approach to personality, these are the methods we use to deal with intrapsychic conflicts that provoke anxiety.

Demand characteristics Features of experiments that convey clues to subjects about the hypotheses being investigated.

Democratic leadership A leader style that encourages self-determination, equal participation and active deliberation by group members.

Dependent variable The variable on which the impact of one or more independent variables is investigated in an experiment.

Developmental psychology The branch of basic psychology that concerns how people develop and change throughout their life.

Development centre A career management intervention where assessment centre methods are used to identify individual development needs and formulate development plans.

Differential validity This would exist if there was conclusive evidence that a selection procedure had different levels of criterion-related validity for different subgroups of the population.

Discourse analysis A technique for analysing qualitative data where the aim is to interpret what is said or written in the light of how the speaker or writer might be trying to present him- or herself.

Dispositional approach to attitudes An approach which views attitudes as determined by a person's genetic make-up or by other deep-seated stable personality characteristics.

Distributive bargaining A form of negotiation characterised by an assumption by the negotiators that the total rewards available are fixed, so that one negotiator's gain is another's loss.

Diversity A general term given to the ways in which members of a workplace or labour force differ from one another (see also managing diversity).

EAP Employee assistance programme, usually referring to a counselling service provided for employees, most often by outside providers.

e-Business The procurement, production, marketing and selling of goods and services using computer communication, particularly the Internet.

Effect size The magnitude of an association between scores on one or more variables, or of the differences in mean scores between two or more samples.

Ego In the psychoanalytic approach to personality, the ego is the part of the psyche that seeks to channel id impulses in socially acceptable ways.

Emergent change This is a bottom-up and open-ended approach that views organisations as constantly having to adjust to changing environmental circumstances.

Emotional instability *See* **Neuroticism**.

Emotional intelligence A set of characteristics and styles that is thought to enable a person to utilise intellect, emotion and awareness of other people in his or her day-to-day behaviour.

Employee empowerment The degree to which employees have a say in their jobs or the organisation they work for.

Employee relations The accommodations made by the various parties involved in getting work done.

Empowerment A human resource management technique that (i) increases employee involvement in (and responsibility for) decision-making and quality management, and (ii) encourages employees to learn a wide range of skills to ensure their capacity to make an effective contribution to organisational performance.

Entrepreneurial career The term given by Kanter to a career concerned with building one's own business through creating value through new goods or services.

Equal opportunities The attempt to ensure that all people, no matter what their group memberships, are given a fair chance to succeed in the workplace.

Equity theory An approach to motivation which argues that people are motivated to achieve an equitable (fair) return for their efforts in comparison with other people.

Escalation of commitment A process whereby a person makes further investments in a course of action in order to justify to self and others his or her original decision to pursue that action.

Esteem need The psychological need to feel respected by others and also by oneself.

Ethics Rules of conduct that protect the well-being, dignity and other interests of people who participate in the research of work psychologists and/or use their services.

Ethnic identity A person's image of self in terms of cultural, national or racial characteristics (*see also* **Ethnicity**).

Ethnicity A person's cultural, national, or racial group membership (*see also* **Ethnic identity**).

Exhaustion When one's adaptive mechanisms collapse.

Expectancy In expectancy theory, expectancy is the extent to which a person believes that he or she has the ability to perform certain behaviours.

Expectancy theory An approach to motivation that focuses on the rational decision-making processes involved in choosing one course of action from alternatives.

Experiment A research design in which the researcher controls or manipulates one or more independent variables in order to investigate their effect on one or more dependent variables.

Experimental group The group of subjects in an experiment which experiences one or more interventions in an investigation of the impact of those interventions.

Experimental hypothesis *See* **Alternative hypothesis**.

External validity The extent to which one can be sure that some specific training will generalise and bring about results for subsequent groups of trainees or settings.

Extinction This occurs when behaviour is not followed by reinforcement (or punishment). Under these circumstances operant behaviour will cease to occur.

Extrinsic motivation The motivation to perform a task derived from rewards that are not part of the task itself (e.g. money, status). Contrast with **Intrinsic motivation** (*see below*).

Extroversion A personality factor characterised by lively, sociable, excitable and impulsive behaviour.

Face validity A very weak form of validity based on the extent to which a test or procedure appears to measure a particular construct.

Factor analysis A statistical technique used to identify key factors that underlie relationships between variables.

Fairness *See* **Bias**.

Faith validity A blind acceptance by users of the extent to which a selection tool is valid.

Flight-fight reaction Individuals will choose whether to stay and fight or try to escape when confronting extreme danger or stress.

Framing effect The impact on decision making of the way the problem is expressed – for example either in terms of its potential losses or its potential gains.

Freudian slip When a person accidentally says something that reflects his or her unconscious desires.

Functional flexibility The name often given to the second aspect of **empowerment** described above.

Functional job analysis An approach to job analysis that uses a standardised language and concentrates on the tasks (rather than skills) required for the job.

Fundamental attribution error The tendency to attribute our own behaviour to more situational causes (e.g. circumstances, behaviour of others) than internal causes (e.g. personality, intentions), whilst doing the opposite when observing the behaviour of other people.

g *See* **Cognitive ability**.

General mental ability *See* **Cognitive ability**.

Goal commitment In goal-setting theory, goal commitment is the extent to which a person is determined to achieve a goal.

Goal-setting theory This approach to motivation concentrates on how goals (performance targets) can affect a person's work strategies and performance.

Grounded theory Theory that develops during the process of data collection in a research project, and which influences data collection later in the same project.

Group Two or more people who are perceived by themselves and others as a social entity.

Group polarisation A phenomenon where the decision of a group after discussion is more extreme than the original preferences of individual group members.

Groupthink A failure of group decision-making identified by Irving Janis, where the motivation of group members to seek agreement with each other exceeds their motivation to conduct a thorough and open analysis of the situation.

Hawthorne studies A series of investigations of work behaviour conducted at the Hawthorne factory of the Western Electric Company near Chicago, USA in the 1920s.

Heuristic General rules that people use to guide their decision-making about complex problems.

Hierarchical task analysis A procedure for identifying the tasks involved in a job, which proceeds to increasingly detailed task units. Task breakdown ceases when predetermined criteria are satisfied, ensuring that the analysis is sufficiently detailed for the purpose in mind.

Humanism *See* **Phenomenological approach to personality**.

Id In the psychoanalytic approach to personality, the id is the part of the psyche that consists of basic instincts and drives.

Independent variable A variable that is manipulated or controlled in an experiment in order to examine its effects on one or more dependent variables.

Informal assessment On-going observation and assessment of individuals that occurs on a day-to-day basis which is not part of a structured system of assessment and which can be subjective and vulnerable to bias.

Instrumentality In expectancy theory, instrumentality is the extent to which a person believes that performing certain behaviours will lead to a specific reward.

Integrative bargaining A form of negotiation characterised by collaborative problem-solving and attempts by the negotiators to find a mutually beneficial solution.

Intelligence *See* **Cognitive ability**.

Internal validity The extent to which one can be confident that a specific training programme (rather than some other possible cause) has brought about changes in trainees.

Interview method Research method where the researcher asks questions face to face or on the telephone with one or more subjects.

Intra-organisational (or intra-party) bargaining The negotiations that occur between members of the same party.

Intrinsic motivation The motivation to perform a task for rewards that are part of the task itself (e.g. interest, challenge). Contrast with **Extrinsic motivation** (*see above*).

Introversion A personality factor characterised by a lack of enthusiasm for the company of others and a low-key, risk-averse and unexcitable approach to life.

Job analysis Procedures (there is more than one way to do a job analysis) for producing systematic information about jobs, including the nature of the work performed, position in the organisation, relationships of the job holder with other people.

Job characteristics model The name given to Hackman and Oldham's theory (*see also* **Core job characteristics** and **Critical psychological states**).

Job components inventory (JCI) A job analysis technique developed in the United Kingdom (Banks *et al.*, 1983) which can provide profiles of the skills required for the job in question.

Job redesign Collective name given to techniques designed to increase one or more of the variety, autonomy and completeness of a person's work tasks.

Job satisfaction A pleasurable or positive emotional state arising from the appraisal of one's job or job experiences.

Knowledge management A general term given to the attempt by organisations to ensure that the learning, information and experience possessed by individuals or subgroups is made available to all members.

Laissez-faire leadership A leader style in which the leader remains very uninvolved and passive.

Leader The person who is appointed, elected or informally chosen to direct and co-ordinate the work of others in a group.

Leader-member relations Defined as a feature of the situation in Fiedler's contingency theory of leadership, this refers to the extent to which leader and subordinates have relationships characterised by respect and mutual trust.

Learning data Data that are concerned with the extent to which specific skills and knowledge have been attained.

Learning goal orientation An approach people may take to a task where their main concern is to increase their level of competence on the task. Contrast with **Performance goal orientation** (*see below*).

Least preferred co-worker (LPC) In Fiedler's contingency theory, LPC refers to the leader's attitude towards the subordinate he or she likes least. This attitude is assumed to reflect the leader's general orientation towards others at work.

Life stage A period of time in a person's life characterised by a particular set of concerns or motives.

Likert scaling A method of measuring attitudes where people respond by indicating their opinion on a dimension running from (for example) 'strongly agree' at one end to 'strongly disagree' at the other.

Locus of control The degree to which the individual feels that he or she has substantial control over events (internality) or little control over events (externality).

Longitudinal research Research where data are collected at two or more points in time, usually months or years apart.

Long Marches Change initiatives that comprise a series of small-scale, local, incremental changes which have little overall effect in the short term but over the long term can transform an organisation.

Managerial grid Put forward by Blake and Mouton, this is a simple aid to assessing leadership style, based on the leader's person- and task-orientation.

Managing diversity The process of ensuring that all members of a workforce are treated in a way that respects their individuality, group memberships and capacity to make a contribution.

Mentoring An approach to development in which an experienced mentor is paired with a less experienced colleague to offer career advice, support and assistance in the development of new skills.

Meta-analysis A statistical technique for aggregating data from a number of different studies in order to establish overall trends.

Modelling The process by which one person demonstrates certain behaviours which are then learned, and may be performed, by observers.

Motivating potential score Arithmetical combination of Hackman and Oldham's job characteristics designed to summarise the overall quality of a job from a psychological point of view.

Motivation The factors which determine the effort, direction and persistence of a person's behaviour.

Motivation to manage The needs and values which underlie the effort and persistence a person devotes to management tasks.

Multiple regression A statistical technique used to identify which of two or more variables are most strongly correlated with another variable (usually called the criterion variable).

Multi-source feedback (MSF) A system of collecting performance feedback from multiple sources, usually including self, manager, subordinates, colleagues and possibly clients or customers.

National culture The set of values, assumptions and beliefs that are dominant in the population of a particular country.

Need A biologically based desire that is activated by a discrepancy between actual and desired states.

Need for achievement The desire to carry out a task as well and as quickly as possible.

Negative reinforcement This is *not* punishment. Negative reinforcers *increase* the probability of the preceding behaviour when they are *removed* from the situation (for example, putting up an umbrella takes away the rain).

Negotiation The process of attempting to resolve, through discussion, differences of opinion between two or more individuals or groups.

Networking The development and maintenance of social contacts in order to increase one's learning access to information and opportunity, and to help others do the same.

Neuroticism A predisposition to be tense and anxious. Sometimes referred to as emotional instability, or anxiety.

New technology A generic label used to describe any form of computer-based technology.

Normal distribution The term given to a particular distribution of scores on a variable where the distribution curve is symmetrical about the mean, with unit area and unit standard deviation.

Null hypothesis The null hypothesis essentially proposes that 'nothing is happening' in the data. That is, that the variables measured are not correlated, or that there are no differences in mean scores between groups of people.

One-sided argument Attempt at persuasion where all of the points made support the direction of attitude change desired by the communicator. Contrast with two-sided arguments, where points for and against the desired change are presented.

Openness to experience A tendency to be curious about inner (psychological) and outer worlds with a willingness to entertain novel ideas and unconventional values.

Operant conditioning A form of conditioning that shapes (operant) behaviour by the application of reinforcement, punishment or extinction.

Organisational analysis Aims to understand where training activities fit into the wider organisational systems and how they relate to organisational strategy.

Organisational behaviour modification (OB Mod) A systematic approach to influencing the behaviour of people in organisations which is based on the principles of conditioning.

Organisational citizenship behaviours Behaviours that go beyond the requirements of the job description and serve to help an employing organisation and/or individuals within it.

Organisational commitment The relative strength of an individual's identification with and involvement in an organisation.

Organisational culture The distinctive norms, beliefs, principles and ways of behaving that combine to give each organisation its distinctive character.

Organisational development (OD) The application of behavioural science knowledge to the planned creation and reinforcement of organisational strategies, structures and processes.

Organisational justice An approach to motivation that focuses on the extent to which people perceive that rewards are distributed fairly in their organisation, and that the process of deciding reward allocation is fair.

Organisational learning The ability of an organisation to develop and utilise knowledge in order to create and sustain competitive advantage.

Organisational politics Interpersonal processes used by people in an organisation to enhance or maintain their reputation.

Organisational power The capacity of an individual or group within an organisation to make other individuals or groups do what they want them to do.

OSI Occupational Stress Indicator, a measure that assesses an individual's and organisation's stress profile.

Participant observation Research method where the researcher observes events, and perhaps asks the people involved about them, while also participating in the events.

Participants People who contribute data in a research project (they are also sometimes called respondents or subjects, though the latter term is discouraged nowadays as being too impersonal).

Participativeness The extent to which a leader includes his or her subordinates in, and allows them control over, decision-making.

Perceived behavioural control In the theory of planned behaviour, perceived behavioural control concerns the extent to which a person believes that he or she can perform the behaviour required in a given situation.

Performance appraisal A process whereby a manager (usually) observes the performance of an employee, records evidence and feeds back to them about how their performance relates to others in the group and whether it meets expected standards.

Performance goal orientation An approach to a task where people's main concern is to demonstrate their competence to themselves and other people. Contrast with **Learning goal orientation** (*see above*).

Performance-related pay (PRP) Where some or all of a person's pay is based on how successfully they produce results in their work.

Peripheral route to persuasion Attitude change that occurs as a result of 'surface' features of an attempt at persuasion such as communicator attractiveness or an easily recalled slogan.

Personal identity Aspects of our self-concept that reflect us as individuals, differentiated from others, even those in the same social group as we are (contrast with **Social identity** below).

Personality tradition The branch of basic psychology that concerns how and why people differ from each other psychologically.

Person analysis Involves identifying who needs training and what kind of training they need.

Person-job fit The extent to which a person's skills, interests and needs are consistent with the requirements and rewards of their work.

Personnel specification A representation of the demands of a job translated into human terms (i.e. a statement of the attributes needed for successful job performance).

Person-organisation fit A term used to describe the extent to which an individual's values, interests and behaviour fits with the culture of an organisation as a whole rather than a specific role or task.

Phases of change These are distinct states through which an organisation moves as it undertakes planned change.

Phenomenological approach to personality An approach to personality that emphasises how personality is shaped by a person's individual interpretations, experiences and choices.

Phenomenological research See **Social constructionist research**.

Physiological needs The desire to avoid hunger, thirst and other unpleasant bodily states.

Physiological psychology The branch of basic psychology that concerns the relationship between brain and body.

Planned behaviour A theory which attempts to explain how and when attitudes determine intentions and behaviour.

Planned change This is a generic term for approaches to change that have predetermined goals and a distinct starting and finishing point.

Position analysis questionnaire (PAQ) A questionnaire-based procedure for job analysis which produces information about the major job elements involved, broken down into six divisions.

Position power In Fred Fiedler's contingency theory, position power refers to the extent to which a leader is able, by virtue of his or her position in the organisation, to influence the rewards and punishments received by subordinates.

Positivist research In contrast to social constructionist research, positivist research takes the view that human behaviour, thoughts and feelings are substantially influenced by objectively measurable factors which exist independent of the researchers and people being researched.

Practical intelligence A view of intelligent behaviour that focuses on real-world activity, rather than controlled behaviour assessed by conventional intelligence testing.

Predictive validity A form of criterion-related validity in which data on the criterion are obtained after data on the predictor.

Predictor A term sometimes used to refer to a selection procedure, on the grounds that a selection procedure is intended to *predict* candidates' job performance.

Pre-experimental design Study design (e.g. one-shot, post-only data) that does not control for major threats to validity. The results of such designs cannot be interpreted with any certainty since many factors could have been involved in causing the observed outcomes. This design may be useful for case studies.

Premack principle The principle that there is a hierarchy of behaviour in which opportunity to engage in behaviour further up the hierarchy may be used to reinforce behaviour lower down.

Procedural knowledge The kind of knowledge that provides a basis for skilful performance; knowledge of how to do something that may be difficult to articulate.

Process theories of motivation Approaches to motivation that focus on *how* motivation works, rather than *what* motivates behaviour. Contrast with **Content theories of motivation** (*see above*).

Processual approach An approach to change that sees organisations as shifting coalitions of individuals and groups with different interests and aims, imperfect knowledge and short attention spans.

Professional career The term given by Kanter to a career where work is primarily specialised and progress is derived from increasing challenge, competence development and personal reputation rather than promotion up a hierarchy.

Protection motivation theory A theory proposed by Rogers (1983) to explain the effect of fear on attitude change and behaviour.

Psychoanalytic tradition The approach to psychology that focuses on unconscious drives and conflicts as determinants of behaviour.

Psychological contract An individual employee's beliefs about the rights and obligations of both sides in the employment relationship.

Psychology Sometimes defined as the science of mental life, psychology concerns the systematic study of behaviour, thoughts and emotions.

Psychometric tests Standardised procedures (often using pen and paper) embodying a series of questions (items) designed to assess key cognitive or personality dimensions. Must have acceptable levels of validity and reliability to be of value.

Psychophysiological assessment Research method where information is obtained about some aspect of a person's neurological, physiological or medical condition.

Punishment In the behaviourist approach to personality, punishment is the occurrence of an unpleasant stimulus or the removal of a pleasant stimulus following a specific behaviour.

Qualitative data Information expressed in the form of words or images, rather than numbers.

Qualitative overload Work that is too difficult for an individual.

Qualitative research Research design where the researcher aims to obtain a detailed picture of the way in which a limited number of people interpret one or more aspects of their world, normally using words rather than numbers.

Quantitative data Information expressed in the form of numbers.

Quantitative overload Having too much work to do.

Quasi-experimental design Study design that has some, but not all, of the features needed for a perfect experimental design. Such designs are often used in field settings.

Questionnaire A written list of questions designed to obtain information about a person's life history, beliefs, attitudes, interests, values or self-concept.

Random sample A number of people selected from a population in such a way that everyone in that population had an equal chance of being selected.

Range restriction This arises when a limited range of scores (rather than when the full population range) is present in a sample. It can occur when the sample is biased in some way, e.g. selection scores are available *only* for people who were given jobs.

Reaction data Data that are concerned with how trainees react to the training they have been given.

Realistic job preview A technique used in recruitment where an organisation presents a balanced view of a job to applicants rather than only its good points. This can be done using written materials, videos or even a day or two's experience of the job.

Reciprocal determinism The complex interaction between situational, personal and behavioural variables.

Reinforcement In the behaviourist approach to personality, reinforcement is the occurrence of a pleasant stimulus (positive reinforcement) or the removal of an unpleasant stimulus (negative reinforcement) following a specific behaviour.

Reliability An indicator of the consistency which a test or procedure provides. It is possible to quantify reliability to indicate the extent to which a measure is free from error.

Relocation A job move within an organisation to a different location that requires a move of home.

Respondent A term often given to a person who provides data in psychological research, particularly a survey research sample.

Respondent conditioning Another term for classical conditioning.

Retirement There is no single accepted definition of retirement. For most people it is the time when, having experienced a number of years of work, they withdraw from the labour market and do not intend to re-enter it.

Role ambiguity Unclear picture of the nature of the job, its objectives, responsibilities, etc.

Role conflict When an individual is torn by conflicting job demands.

Role innovation The extent to which a person seeks to change the nature of his or her job.

Safety needs The desire to avoid physical or psychological danger.

Sample A number of people drawn from a defined population (e.g. all people; all females; all sales managers).

Sampling error Fluctuations in observed results that arise when small samples are used. Any small sample may contain some unrepresentative cases, but if the sample is small these cases may have an unduly large influence on the results.

Schema In the social cognitive tradition in psychology, a schema is an organised set of beliefs and expectations held by a person.

Science A branch of knowledge based upon systematically collected data under controlled conditions.

Scientific management Also called Taylorism, this is an approach to management that emphasises management control, simplification and standardisation of work activities, and purely financial incentives.

Script In the social cognitive tradition in psychology, a script is an expected sequence of events that a person associates with a particular type of situation.

Selection ratio An indication of the number of positions available compared with the number of candidates. Ten candidates for every post would give a selection ratio of 1:10, i.e. 0.1.

Self-actualisation The need to fulfil one's potential: to develop and express one's capacities.

Self-awareness The capacity to know and understand one's own characteristics, motives and values.

Self-categorisation theory A theory that proposes that we define who we are by placing ourselves into categories, and these categories are often social groups. We seek to defend our identity when threatened. Similar to social identity theory.

Self-concept The total set of beliefs a person holds about himself or herself.

Self-development An approach to staff development which places primary responsibility for identifying development needs and taking action to deal with them on the individual employee.

Self-regulation The strategies a person uses to monitor and direct his or her behaviour in pursuit of a goal.

Servant leadership An approach to leadership that portrays the leader as a helpful facilitator of others' efforts, rather than a dominant agenda-setter.

Situational interviews A form of structured interview in which key work situations (identified through job analysis) are used to provide a basis for questioning and assessing job candidates.

Situational leadership theory A theory of leadership that proposes that the maturity of subordinates dictates the style a leader should adopt.

Sleeper effect Where an attempt at attitude change produces a delayed but not an immediate effect.

Social approach A 'common-sense' approach to motivation that argues that a person is motivated to establish and maintain meaningful social relationships.

Social cognitive theory A theory that developed from behaviourist origins and sees the behaviourist view as incomplete, rather than wrong. In social cognitive theory internal cognitive processes (e.g. expectancies about what might happen) and external (social/situational) factors play a key role in determining behaviour.

Social cognitive tradition The tradition in psychology that emphasises how we process information in a social context.

Social constructionist research Research based on the assumption that there are few objective facts about the social world, and that it is therefore necessary to focus on people's subjective interpretations rather than objectively verifiable causal laws. Sometimes called phenomenological research.

Social identity Aspects of our self-concept that reflect the general characteristics of people in the same social groups as we are, and which differentiate us from members of other group (contrast with **Personal identity** above).

Social identity theory A theory that suggests we define ourselves largely in terms of our membership of social groups, and often tend to value our own group more than others. Similar to self-categorisation theory.

Socialisation The processes by which the person learns and adopts the behaviours, attitudes and values expected in his or her role.

Social loafing The process where some members of a group do not contribute their share of effort, but still obtain the rewards of group membership.

Social psychology The branch of basic psychology that concerns how the social world affects the behaviour, thoughts and emotions of individuals and groups.

Social support networks Refers to informal and formal relationships which can help the individual to explore and deal with stress.

Socio-cognitive An approach to attitudes which stresses how they are encoded in a person's memory and what functions they serve for the person.

Standard deviation A measure of how much variability around the mean there is in a set of numerical data.

State orientation A psychological state in which a person does *not* use self-regulatory strategies to achieve goals. Contrast with **Action orientation** (*see above*).

Statistical power A measure of the probability that a statistically significant effect will be observed in a sample of given size if such an effect does actually exist in the population from which the sample is drawn.

Statistical significance The probability of rejecting the null hypothesis on the basis of data obtained from a sample when it is in fact true for the population from which the sample is drawn. Psychologists are normally only willing to reject the null hypothesis if there is, at most, a 1 in 20 chance of it being true.

Stereotype A generalised belief about what people in a particular group are like.

Strategic decision A decision that affects the overall goals, aims or mission of an organisation.

Stressor Means the source of the stress, the cause or underlying reasons why an employee may show stress symptoms or disease.

Structure Sometimes called initiating structure, this is an aspect of leadership style that reflects the extent to which the leader plans, organises and monitors the work of his or her group.

Structured observation A research method where the researcher remains uninvolved in events, but records what occurs using a predetermined system.

Subjective norm In the theory of planned behaviour, subjective norm is a combination of the (perceived) opinions of other people and the person's motivation to comply with them.

Substitutes for leadership This term, coined by Kerr and Jermier, reflects the idea that in some circumstances the resources of a group are sufficient to make a leader unnecessary.

Superego In the psychoanalytic tradition in psychology, the superego is the part of the psyche that concerns moral values, or conscience.

Survey Research design where a sample of respondents/subjects provides data in a standard form on one or more variables.

Task analysis involves determining what important tasks need to be performed and the KSAs that an individual requires in order to perform them.

Team A group of people who work together towards group objectives.

Team-building Techniques designed to enhance the effectiveness of a new or established team.

Team roles The functions that need to be fulfilled by team members if the team is to be effective.

Teleworking Working from a remote location using information and communication technologies (ICTs).

Terminal behaviour A statement of what the trainee should be able to do at the end of training.

Theories of learning Represent ideas about how learning occurs; they feed into training practice by identifying the most appropriate methods of instruction.

Theory X A 'common-sense' approach to motivation that views people as untrustworthy, to be motivated by financial reward and punishment.

Theory Y A 'common-sense' approach to motivation that views people as inherently trustworthy and responsible, to be motivated by challenge and responsibility.

Three-step model This model views change as a planned and finite process which proceeds through three stages: unfreezing, moving and refreezing.

Thurstone scaling A method of measuring attitudes where statements are graded in terms of their extremity of agreement or disagreement with a particular attitude.

Total quality management A strategic and organisation-wide approach to quality which is associated with Japanese manufacturing organisations.

Trainability tests A form of work-sample test which incorporates a systematic learning period for the candidate, who is then required to attempt the task unaided.

Training Organised efforts to provide employees with structured opportunities to learn and develop within their work role.

Training design Relates to the content of the training programme and includes decisions about what information is presented to trainees and how it is presented.

Training evaluation Considers the validity of training programmes by assessing the extent to which the training objectives have been achieved.

Training objectives These define what the training needs to achieve and can include individual and organisational level objectives.

Training transfer Transfer occurs when new learning is used in new settings (e.g. on-the-job) beyond those employed for training purposes.

Trait A dimension upon which people differ psychologically.

Trait-factor analytic theory An approach to individual differences that uses factor analysis to identify the major structural dimensions (traits) of personality.

Trait tradition The tradition in psychology that emphasises stable differences between people in their position on various personality dimensions.

Transactional leadership A leadership style originally identified by Burns (1978), in which the leader uses rewards for good performance and tends to maintain existing work methods unless performance goals are not being met.

Transformational leadership Another leadership style originally identified by Burns (1978), this refers to the extent to which a leader articulates a clear vision and mission, while treating individuals on their merits and encouraging free thinking.

Transition A relatively permanent move from one environment to another experienced by a person. The sequence of phases a person goes through in adjusting to a new job.

***t*-Test** A statistical technique used to test whether two samples have significantly different mean scores on a variable.

Type A behaviour A hard-driving, time-conscious, aggressive, impatient lifestyle.

Type I error This occurs when the null hypothesis is erroneously rejected on the basis of research data.

Type II error This occurs when the alternative hypothesis is erroneously rejected on the basis of research data.

Unconditional positive regard In the phenomenological tradition in psychology, unconditional positive regard is the acceptance of one person by another, irrespective of his or her behaviour.

Unconditioned response *See* **Classical conditioning**.

Unconditioned stimulus *See* **Classical conditioning**.

Utility (financial) A procedure for estimating the financial gain that may be derived from the improved job performance that is obtained from better personnel selection.

Valence In expectancy theory, valence is the subjective value a person attaches to a particular reward.

Validity A general term indicating the extent to which a test or procedure measures what it is intended to measure.

Vroom-Jago theory of leadership This theory assumes that leaders can vary the participativeness of their decision-making style according to the situation, and identifies key aspects of the situation.

Wash-up session This is a meeting of the assessors at the end of an assessment centre, where the ratings for each assessee are discussed and an overall rating made.

Wellness programme A company-wide programme to promote employee health, both physical and psychological.

Work-role transition Any move between jobs, into a job or out of one, or any substantial change in work duties.

Work-sample tests Personnel assessment procedures that require candidates to conduct tasks that are sampled from the job(s) in question.

z-score An individual's score on a variable expressed as the number of standard deviations above or below the mean.

REFERENCES

Abdalla, I.A. and Al-Homoud, M.A. (2001) 'Implicit leadership theory in the Arabian Gulf States', *Applied Psychology: An International Review*, vol. 50, pp. 506–31.

Abelson, R.P. (1981) 'Psychological status of the script concept', *American Psychologist*, vol. 36, pp. 715–29.

Adair, J.G. (1984) 'The Hawthorne effect: A reconsideration of the methodological artifact', *Journal of Applied Psychology*, vol. 69, pp. 334–45.

Adams, J.S. (1965) 'Inequity in social exchange' in Berkowitz, L. (ed.) *Advances in Experimental Social Psychology*, vol. 2. New York: Academic Press.

Agho, A.O., Price, J.L. and Mueller, C.W. (1992) 'Discriminant validity of measures of job satisfaction, positive affectivity and negative affectivity', *Journal of Occupational and Organizational Psychology*, vol. 65, pp. 185–96.

Agho, A.O., Mueller, C.W. and Price, J.L. (1993) 'Determinants of employee job satisfaction: An empirical test of a causal model', *Human Relations*, vol. 46, pp. 1007–27.

Aiello, J.R. and Kolb, K.J. (1995) 'Electronic performance monitoring and social context: Impact on productivity and stress', *Journal of Applied Psychology*, vol. 80, pp. 339–53.

Ajzen, I. (1991) 'The theory of planned behavior', *Organizational Behavior and Human Decision Processes*, vol. 50, pp. 179–211.

Ajzen, I. (2001) 'Nature and operation of attitudes', *Annual Review of Psychology*, vol. 24, pp. 1251–63.

Ajzen, I. and Fishbein, M. (1980) *Understanding Attitudes and Predicting Social Behavior*. Englewood Cliffs, NJ: Prentice Hall.

Ajzen, I. and Fishbein, M. (2000) 'Attitudes and the attitude–behaviour relation: Reasoned and automatic process' in Stroebe, W. and Hewstone, M. *European Review of Social Psychology*. Chichester: John Wiley.

Ajzen, I. and Madden, J.T. (1986) 'Prediction of goal-directed behavior: Attitudes, intentions, and perceived behavioral control', *Journal of Experimental Social Psychology*, vol. 22, pp. 453–74.

Akgün, A.E., Lynn, G.S. and Byrne, J.C. (2003) 'Organizational learning: A socio-cognitive framework', *Human Relations*, vol. 56, pp. 839–68.

Alavosius, M.P. and Sulzer-Azaroff, B. (1986) 'The effects of performance feedback on the safety of client lifting and transfer', *Journal of Applied Behavior Analysis*, vol. 19, pp. 261–7.

Aldag, R.J. and Fuller, S.R. (1993) 'Beyond fiasco: A reappraisal of the groupthink phenomenon and a new model of group decision processes', *Psychological Bulletin*, vol. 113, pp. 533–52.

Alderfer, C.P. (1972) *Existence, Relatedness and Growth: Human needs in organizational settings*. New York: Free Press.

Algera, J.A. (1990) 'Feedback systems in organisations' in Cooper, C.L. and Robertson, I.T. (eds) *International Review of Industrial and Organizational Psychology*, vol. 5. Chichester: John Wiley.

Algera, J.A. and Greuter, M.A.M. (1998) 'Job analysis' in Drenth, P., Thierry, H. and de Wolf, C.J. (eds) *Handbook of Work and Organizational Psychology*, vol. 3, 2nd edition. Hove: Psychology Press.

Allaire, Y. and Firsirotu, M.E. (1984) 'Theories of organizational culture', *Organization Studies*, vol. 5(3), pp. 193–226.

Allen, N.J. and Meyer, J.P. (1990a) 'The measurement and antecedents of affective, continuance and normative commitment to the organization', *Journal of Occupational Psychology*, vol. 63, pp. 11–18.

Allen, N.J. and Meyer, J.P. (1990b) 'Organizational socialization tactics: A longitudinal analysis of links to newcomers' commitment and role orientation', *Academy of Management Journal*, vol. 33, pp. 847–58.

Allen, P.T. and Stephenson, G.M. (1984) 'The relationship of inter-group understanding and inter-party friction in industry', *British Journal of Employee Relations*, vol. 23, pp. 203–13.

Allen, T.D., Poteet, M.L. and Burroughs, S.M. (1997) 'The mentor's perspective: A qualitative inquiry and future research agenda', *Journal of Vocational Behavior*, vol. 51, pp. 70–89.

Alliger, G.M. and Janak, E.A. (1997) 'Kirkpatrick's levels of training criteria thirty years later', *Personnel Psychology*, vol. 41, pp. 63–105.

Alliger, G.M., Tanenbaum, S.I., Bennett, W. Jr, Traver, H. and Shotland, A. (1997) 'A meta-analysis of the relations among training criteria', *Personnel Psychology*, vol. 50, pp. 341–58.

Allison, T., Cooper, C.L. and Reynolds, P. (1989) 'Stress counselling in the workplace – the Post Office experience', *The Psychologist*, vol. 2, pp. 384–8.

Allport, G.W. (1937) *Personality: A psychological interpretation*. New York: Holt, Rinehart and Winston.

Ambrose, M.L. and Kulik, C.T. (1999) 'Old friends, new faces: Motivation research in the 1990s', *Journal of Management*, vol. 25, pp. 213–92.

Anastasi, A. (1988) *Psychological Testing*. New York: Macmillan.

Anderson, J.R. (1983) *The Architecture of Cognition*. Cambridge, MA: Harvard University Press.

Anderson, J.R. (1987) 'Skill acquisition: Compilation of weak-method problem solutions', *Psychological Review*, vol. 94, pp. 192–210.

Anderson, N. (2003) 'Applicant and recruiter reactions to new technology in selection: A critical review and agenda for future research', *International Journal of Selection and Assessment*, vol. 11(2–3), pp. 121–36.

Anderson, N.R. and Herriot, P. (1997) 'Selecting for change: How will personnel and selection psychology survive?' in Anderson, N.R. and Herriot, P. (eds) *International Handbook of Selection and Assessment*, pp. 1–38. Chichester: John Wiley.

Anderson, N. and Prutton, K. (1993) 'Occupational psychology in business: Strategic resource or purveyor of tests?', *The Occupational Psychologist*, no. 20, pp. 3–10.

Anderson, N., Born, M. and Cunningham-Snell, N. (2001a) 'Recruitment and selection: Applicant perspectives and outcomes' in Anderson, N., Ones, D. S., Sinangil, H.K. and Viswesvaran, C. (eds) *Handbook of Industrial, Work and Organizational Psychology*, pp. 200–18. Thousand Oaks, CA: Sage Publications.

Anderson, N., Herriot, P. and Hodgkinson, G.P. (2001b) 'The practitioner–scientist divide in Industrial, Work and Organizational (IWO) psychology: Where are we now, and where do we go from here?', *Journal of Occupational and Organizational Psychology*, vol. 74, pp. 391–411.

Annett, J., Duncan, K.D., Stammers, R.B. and Gray, M.J. (1971) *Task Analysis*, Training Information Paper No. 6. London: HMSO.

April, K., Macdonald, R. and Vriesendorp, S. (2000) *Rethinking Leadership*. Cape Town: University of Cape Town Press.

Argyris, C.P. (1960) *Understanding Organizational Behavior*. Homewood, IL: Dorsey.

Argyris, C. (1962) *Interpersonal Competence and Organizational Effectiveness*. Homewood, IL: Irwin.

Argyris, C. (1964) *Integrating the Individual and the Organization*. Chichester: John Wiley.

Arkes, H.R. (1996) 'The psychology of waste', *Journal of Behavioral Decision Managing*, vol. 9, pp. 213–24.

Arkes, H.R., Boehm, L.E. and Xu, G. (1991) 'Determinants of judged validity', *Journal of Experimental Social Psychology*, vol. 27, pp. 576–605.

Armitage, C.J. and Conner, M. (2001) 'Efficacy of the Theory of Planned Behaviour: A meta-analytic review', *British Journal of Social Psychology*, 40, pp. 471–99.

Arnold, J. (1990) 'From education to job markets' in Fisher, S. and Cooper, C.L. (eds) *On the Move: The psychological effects of change and transition*. Chichester: John Wiley.

Arnold, J. (1996) 'The psychological contract: A concept in need of closer scrutiny?', *European Journal of Work and Organizational Psychology*, vol. 5, pp. 511–20.

Arnold, J. (1997) *Managing Careers into the 21st Century*. London: Paul Chapman.

Arnold, J. (2001) 'Careers and career management' in Anderson, N., Ones, D., Sinangil, H. and Viswesvaran, C. (eds) *International Handbook of Work and Organizational Psychology*. London: Sage.

Arnold, J. (2002) 'Tensions between assessment, grading and development in development centres: a case study', *International Journal of Human Resource Management*, vol. 13(6), pp. 975–91.

Arnold, J. and Johnson, K. (1997) 'Mentoring in early career', *Human Resource Management Journal*, vol. 7, pp. 61–70.

Arnold, J. and Mackenzie Davey, K. (1999) 'Graduates' work experiences as predictors of organisational commitment, intention to leave, and turnover: Which experiences really matter?', *Applied Psychology: An International Review*, 48(2), pp. 211–38.

Arthur, M.B. and Rousseau, D.M. (1996) 'The boundaryless career as a new employment principle' in Arthur, M.B. and Rousseau, D.M. (eds) *The Boundaryless Career: A New Employment Principle for a New Organizational Era*. Oxford: Oxford University Press.

Arthur, M.B., Inkson, K. and Pringle, J.K. (1999) *The New Careers, Individual Action and Economic Change*. London: Sage.

Arvey, R.D. and Ivancevich, J.M. (1980) 'Punishment in organizations: A review, propositions and research suggestions', *Academy of Management Review*, vol. 5, pp. 123–32.

Arvey, R.D. and Murphy, K.R. (1998) 'Performance evaluation in work settings', *Annual Review of Psychology*, vol. 49, pp. 141–68.

Arvey, R.D., Carter, W.G. and Buerkley, D.K. (1991) 'Job satisfaction: Dispositional and situational influences' in Cooper, C.L. and Robertson, I.T. (eds) *International Review of Industrial and Organizational Psychology*, vol. 6. Chichester: John Wiley.

Aryee, S. and Chay, Y.W. (1994) 'An examination of the impact of career-oriented mentoring on work commitment attitudes and career satisfaction among professional and managerial employees', *British Journal of Management*, vol. 5, pp. 241–49.

ASE (1994) *16PF*, 5th edn. Windsor: ASE.

Ashforth, B.E. and Saks, A.M. (1996) 'Socialization tactics: Longitudinal effects on newcomer adjustment', *Academy of Management Journal*, vol. 39, pp. 149–78.

Ashkanasy, N. and Jackson, C. (2001) 'Organizational culture and climate' in Anderson, N., Ones, D., Sinangil, H.K. and Viswesvaran, C. (eds) *Handbook of Industrial, Work and Organizational Psychology*, vol. 2, pp. 398–415. London: Sage.

Ashmos, D.P., Duchon, D., McDaniel, R.R. Jr and Huonker, J.W. (2002) 'What a mess! Participation as a simple managerial rule to "complexify" organizations', *Journal of Management Studies*, vol. 39(2), pp. 189–206.

Austin, J.T. and Bobko, P. (1985) 'Goal-setting theory: Unexplored areas and future research needs', *Journal of Occupational Psychology*, vol. 58, pp. 289–308.

Bagilhole, B. (2002) 'Challenging equal opportunities; changing and adapting male hegemony in academia', *British Journal of Sociology of Education*, vol. 23, pp. 19–33.

Baglioni, A.J. Jr and Cooper, C.L. (1988) 'A structural model approach toward the development of a theory of the link between stress and mental health', *British Journal of Medical Psychology*, vol. 61, pp. 87–102.

Baldwin, T.T. (1992) 'Effects of alternative modelling strategies on outcomes of interpersonal-skills training', *Journal of Applied Psychology*, vol. 77, pp. 147–54.

Baldwin, T.T. and Ford, J.K. (1988) 'Transfer of training: A review and directions for future research', *Personnel Psychology*, vol. 41, pp. 63–105.

Bandura, A. (1977a) 'Self-efficacy: Toward a unifying theory of behavioral change', *Psychological Review*, vol. 84, pp. 191–215.

Bandura, A. (1977b) *Social Learning Theory*. Englewood Cliffs, NJ: Prentice Hall.

Bandura, A. (1982) 'The self-efficacy mechanism in human agency', *American Psychologist*, vol. 37, pp. 122–47.

Bandura, A. (1986) *Social Foundations of Thought and Action: A social cognitive theory*. Englewood Cliffs, NJ: Prentice Hall.

Bandura, A. (1997) *Self-efficacy: The exercise of control*. New York: Freeman.

Banks, M.H. (1988) 'Job components inventory' in Gael, S. (ed.) *Job Analysis Handbook*. New York: John Wiley.

Banks, M.H., Jackson, P.R., Stafford, E.M. and Warr, P.B. (1983) 'The job components inventory and the analysis of jobs requiring limited skill', *Personnel Psychology*, vol. 36, pp. 57–66.

Bardwick, J. (1980) 'The seasons of a woman's life' in McGuigan, D. (ed.) *Women's Lives: New theory, research and policy*. Ann Arbor, MI: University of Michigan.

Barker, R.A. (1997) 'How can we train leaders if we do not know what leadership is?', *Human Relations*, vol. 50(4), pp. 343–62.

Barling, J. and Milligan, J. (1987) 'Some psychological consequences of striking: A six month longitudinal study', *Journal of Occupational Behaviour*, vol. 8, pp. 127–38.

Barling, J., Wade, B. and Fullagar, C. (1990) 'Predicting employee commitment to company and union: Divergent models', *Journal of Occupational Psychology*, vol. 63, pp. 49–61.

Barnes, C. (1991) *Disabled People in Britain: A case for anti-discrimination legislation*. London: C. Hurst and Co. Ltd.

Barnes-Farrell, J.L. (2001) 'Performance appraisal: Person perception, processes and challenges' in London, M. (ed.) *How People Evaluate Others in Organizations*, pp. 135–50. London: LEA.

Barnett, R.C. and Shen, Y.C. (1997) 'Gender, high and low schedule control housework tasks and psychological distress: A study of dual earner couples', *Journal of Family Issues*, vol. 18 pp. 403–28.

Baron, J. (1994) 'Nonconsequentialist decisions', *Behavioral and Brain Sciences*, vol. 22, pp. 72–88.

Bar-On, R. (1997) *The Emotional Intelligence Inventory (EQ-i): Technical manual*. Toronto: Multi-Health Systems.

Bar-On, R. (2000) 'Emotional and social intelligence: Insights from the Emotional Quotient Inventory' in: Bar-On, R. and Parker, J.D.A. (eds) *The Handbook of Emotional Intelligence*, pp. 363–88. San Francisco, CA: Jossey-Bass.

Barratt, E.S. (1990) 'Human resource management: Organisational culture', *Management Update*, vol. 2(1), pp. 21–32.

Barrett, P. and Sowden, P. (2000) 'Psychophysiological methods' in Breakwell, G., Hammond, S. and Fife-Schaw, C. (eds) *Research Methods in Psychology*. London: Sage.

Bartley, D.F. and Robitschek, C. (2000) 'Career exploration: A multivariate analysis of predictors', *Journal of Vocational Behavior*, vol. 56, pp. 63–81.

Bartram, D. (ed.) (1995) *Review of Personality Assessment Instruments (Level B) for use in Occupational Settings*. Leicester: The British Psychological Society.

Bartram, D. (2000) 'Internet recruitment and selection: Kissing frogs to find princes', *International Journal of Selection & Assessment*, vol. 8, pp. 261–74.

Baruch, Y. (2003) *Managing Careers*. Harlow: Pearson Education.

Baruch, Y. and Peiperl, M.A. (2000) 'Career management practices: An empirical survey and theoretical implications', *Human Resource Management*, vol. 39, pp. 347–66.

Bass, B.M. (1985) *Leadership and Performance: Beyond expectations*. New York: Free Press.

Bass, B.M. (1990) *Bass and Stogdill's Handbook of Leadership: Theory, research and managerial application*, 3rd edition. New York: Free Press.

Bass, B.M. (1998) *Transformational Leadership: Industry, military and educational impact*. Mahwah, NJ: Eplbaum.

Bass, B.M. and Avolio, B.J. (1994) *Improving Organizational Effectiveness Through Transformational Leadership*. Thousand Oaks, CA: Sage.

Bassi, L.J. (1997) 'Harnessing the power of intellectual capital', *Training and Development*, vol. 51, pp. 25–30.

Bateman, T. and Strasser, S. (1984) 'A longitudinal analysis of the antecedents of organizational commitment', *Academy of Management Journal*, vol. 27, pp. 95–112.

Batt, R. (2000) 'Strategic segmentation in front-line services: Matching customers, employees and human "resource systems"', *International Journal of Human Resource Management*, vol. 11, pp. 540–61.

Baumeister, R.F. and Leary, M.R. (1995) 'The need to belong: Desire for interpersonal attachments as a fundamental human motivation', *Psychological Bulletin*, vol. 117, pp. 497–529.

Bazerman, M.H., Magliozzi, T. and Neale, M.A. (1985) 'Integrative bargaining in a competitive market', *Organizational Behavior and Human Decision Processes*, vol. 35, pp. 94–113.

Beard, J.W., Woodman, R.W. and Moesel, D. (1998) 'Using behavioural modification to change attendance patterns in the high-performance, high-commitment environment', *Research in Organizational Change and Development*, vol. 11, pp. 183–224.

Beck, R.C. (1983) *Motivation: Theory and principles*. Englewood Cliffs, NJ: Prentice Hall.

Becker, T.E. and Billings, R.S. (1993) 'Profiles of commitment: an empirical test', *Journal of Organizational Behavior*, vol. 14, pp. 177–90.

Becker, T.E., Billings, R.S., Eveleth, D.M. and Gilbert, N.L. (1996) 'Foci and bases of employee commitment: Implications for job performance', *Academy of Management Journal*, vol. 39, pp. 464–82.

Beckhard, R (1969) *Organization Development: Strategies and models*. Reading, MA: Addison-Wesley.

Bee, F. and Bee, R. (1994) *Training Needs Analysis and Evaluation*. London: Institute of Personnel Management.

Beehr, T.A. (1995) *Psychological Stress in the Workplace*. London: Routledge.

Beer, M, Eisenstat, R.A. and Spector, B. (1993) 'Why change programmes don't produce change' in Mabey, C. and Mayon-White, B. (eds) *Managing Change*, 2nd edition. London: Open University/Paul Chapman Publishing.

Belbin, R.M. (1981) *Management Teams: Why they succeed or fail*. London: Heinemann.

Belbin, R.M. (1993) *Team Roles at Work: A strategy for human resource management*. Oxford: Butterworth-Heinemann.

Belbin, R.M. (2000) *Beyond the Team*. Oxford: Butterworth-Heinemann.

Bell, R.Q. (1979) 'Parent, child and reciprocal influences', *American Psychologist*, vol. 34, pp. 821–6.

Bem, D.J. (1972) 'Self-perception theory', *Advances in Experimental Social Psychology*, vol. 6, pp. 1–62.

Bem, S. (1981) 'Gender schema theory; a cognitive account of sex typing', *Psychological Review*, vol. 88, pp. 354–64.

Benders, J., Huijgen, F. and Ulricj, P. (2001) 'Measuring group work; findings and lessons from a European survey', *New Technology, Work and Employment*, vol. 16(3), pp. 204–17.

Benjamin, G. and Mabey, C. (1993) 'Facilitating radical change' in Mabey, C. and Mayon-White, B. (eds) *Managing Change*, 2nd Edition. London: Open University/Paul Chapman Publishing.

Bennett, R. (1983) *Management Research*, Management Development Series no. 20. Geneva: International Labour Office.

Bernin, P. and Theorell, T. (2001) 'Demand-control-support among female and male managers in eight Swedish companies', *Stress and Health*, vol. 17(4), pp. 231–43.

Berridge, J. and Cooper, C.L. (1993) 'Stress and coping in US organizations: The role of the Employee Assistance Programme', *Work and Stress*, vol. 7, pp. 89–102.

Berridge, J., Cooper, C.L. and Highley-Marchington, C. (1997) *Employee Assistance Programmes and Workplace Counselling*. Chichester: John Wiley.

Bertua, C., Anderson, N. and Salgado, J.F. (in press). The predictive validity of cognitive ability tests: A UK meta-analysis. *Journal of Occupational and Organizational Psychology*.

Bessant, J. and Haywood, B. (1985) *The Introduction of Flexible Manufacturing Systems as an Example of Computer Integrated Manufacture*. Brighton: Brighton Polytechnic.

Bettenhausen, K.L. (1991) 'Five years of group research: What we have learned and what needs to be addressed', *Journal of Management*, vol. 17, pp. 345–81.

Betz, N.E. and Hackett, G. (1981) 'The relationship of career-related self-efficacy expectations to perceived career options in college women and men', *Journal of Counseling Psychology*, vol. 28, pp. 399–410.

Bhavnani, R. and Coyle, A. (2000) 'Black and ethnic minority women managers in the UK – continuity or change?' in Davidson, M.J. and Burke, R.J. (eds) *Women in Management*. London: Sage.

Bigge, L.M. (1982) *Learning Theories for Teachers*. Aldershot: Gower.

Birdi, K., Allan, C. and Warr, P. (1997) 'Correlates and perceived outcomes of four types of employee development activity', *Journal of Applied Psychology*, vol. 82(6), pp. 845–57.

Black, J.S., Mendenhall, M. and Oddou, G. (1991) 'Toward a comprehensive model of international adjustment: An integration of multiple theoretical perspectives', *Academy of Management*, vol. 16, pp. 291–317.

Blackler, F. (1982) 'Organizational psychology' in Canter, S. and Canter, D. (eds) *Psychology in Practice*. Chichester: John Wiley.

Blackler, F. and Brown, C. (1986) 'Alternative models to guide the design and introduction of the new information technologies into work organizations', *Journal of Occupational Psychology*, vol. 59, pp. 287–314.

Blake, R.R. and Mouton, J.S. (1964) *The Managerial Grid*. Houston, TX: Gulf Publishing.

Blake, R.R. and Mouton, J.S. (1969) *Building a Dynamic Corporation Through Grid Organisation Development*. Reading, MA: Addison-Wesley.

Blake, R.R. and Mouton, J.S. (1976) *Organizational Change by Design*. Austin, TX: Scientific Methods.

Blau, G. (1993) 'Operationalizing direction and level of effort, and testing their relationships to individual job performance', *Organizational Behaviour and Human Decision Processes*, vol. 55, pp. 152–70.

Bloom, M. (1999) 'The performance effects of pay dispersion on individuals and organisations', *Academy of Management Journal*, vol. 42, pp. 25–40.

Blustein, D.L., Pauling, M.L., DeMania, M.E. and Faye, M. (1994) 'Relation between exploratory and choice factors and decisional progress', *Journal of Vocational Behavior*, vol. 44, pp. 75–90.

Bobko, P., Roth, P.L. and Potosky, D. (1999) 'Derivation and implications of a meta-analytic matrix incorporating cognitive ability, alternative predictors, and job performance', *Personnel Psychology*, vol. 52(3), pp. 561–89.

Bodenhausen, G.V. and Macrae, C.N. (1996) 'The self-regulation of intergroup perception: Mechanisms and consequences of stereotype suppression' in Macrae, C.N., Hewstone, M. and Stangor, C. (eds) *Foundations of Stereotypes and Stereotyping*. New York: Guildford Press.

Bolles, R.N. (2001) *What Color is your Parachute? 2002: A practical manual for job-hunters and career changers*. Berkeley, CA: Ten Speed Press.

Bontempo, R.N., Bottom, W.P. and Weber, E.U. (1997) 'Cross-cultural differences in risk perception: A model-based approach', *Risk Analysis*, vol. 17, pp. 479–88.

Boring, E.C. (1923) 'Intelligence as the tests test it', *New Republic*, vol. 35, pp. 35–7.

Bortner, R.W. (1969) 'A short rating scale as a potential measure of pattern A behaviour', *Journal of Chronic Diseases*, vol. 22, pp. 87–91.

Bosse, R., Aldwin, C., Levenson, M. and Workman-Daniels, K. (1991) 'How stressful is retirement? Findings from a normative aging study', *Journal of Gerontology*, vol. 46, pp. 9–14.

Bosveld, W., Koomen, W. and Voelaar, R. (1997) 'Constructing a social issue: Effects on attitudes and the false consensus effect', *British Journal of Social Psychology*, 36, pp. 263–72.

Bouchard, T.J. and McGue, M. (1990) 'Genetic and rearing environmental influences on adult personality: An analysis of adopted twins reared apart', *Journal of Personality*, vol. 58, pp. 263–92.

Boudreau, J.W. (1989) 'Selection utility analysis: A review and agenda for future research' in Smith, M. and Robertson, I.T. (eds) *Advances in Selection and Assessment*. Chichester: John Wiley.

Breckler, S.J. (1984) 'Empirical validation of affect, behavior and cognition as distinct attitude components', *Journal of Personality and Social Psychology*, vol. 47, pp. 1191–205.

Breland, K. and Breland, M. (1951) 'A field of applied animal psychology', *American Psychologist*, vol. 6, pp. 202–4.

Breslow, L. and Buell, P. (1960) 'Mortality from coronary heart disease and physical activity of work in California', *Journal of Chronic Diseases*, vol. 11, pp. 615–25.

Brett, J.M. and Stroh, L.K. (1997) 'Jumping ship: Who benefits from an external labour market career strategy?, *Journal of Applied Psychology*, vol. 82, pp. 331–41.

Brett, J.M., Stroh, L.K. and Reilly, A.H. (1992) 'Job transfer' in Cooper, C.L. and Robertson, I.T. (eds) *International Review of Industrial and Organizational Psychology*, vol. 7. Chichester: John Wiley.

Briner, R. and Reynolds, S. (1999) 'The costs, benefits, and limitations of organization level stress interventions', *Journal of Organizational Behavior*, vol. 20, pp. 647–64.

British Psychological Society (2000) *Code of Conduct, Ethical Principles and Guidelines*. Leicester: BPS. http://www.bps.org/documents/code.pdf

Brodbeck, F.C. *et al.* (2000) 'Cultural variation of leadership prototypes across 22 European countries', *Journal of Occupational and Organizational Psychology*, vol. 73, pp. 1–29.

Brotherton, C. (2003) 'Psychology and industrial relations' in Ackers, P. and Wilkinson, A. (eds) *Understanding Work and Employment*. Oxford: Oxford University Press.

Brown, A. (1995) *Organisational Culture*. London: Pitman.

Bryman, A. (1992) *Charisma and Leadership in Organizations*. London: Sage.

Bryman, A. (2001) *Social Research Methods*. Oxford: Oxford University Press.

Buchanan, D. and Boddy, D. (1992a) *The Expertise of the Change Agent*. London: Prentice Hall.

Buchanan, D. and Boddy, D. (1992b) *Take the Lead: Interpersonal skills for change agents*. London: Prentice Hall.

Buchanan, D.A. and Storey, J. (1997) 'Role-taking and role-switching in organizational change: The four pluralities' in McLoughlin, I. and Harris, M. (eds) *Innovation, Organizational Change and Technology*. London: International Thompson.

Bullock, R.J. and Batten, D. (1985) 'It's just a phase we're going through: A review and synthesis of OD phase analysis', *Group and Organization Studies*, vol. 10, December, pp. 383–412.

Burke, R.J. and McKeen, C.A. (1992) 'Social-sexual behavior at work: Experiences of managerial and professional women', *Women in Management Review*, vol. 2, pp. 22–30.

Burnes, B. (1989) *New Technology in Context*. Aldershot: Gower.

Burnes, B. (1996) 'No such thing as . . . a "One Best Way" to manage organizational change', *Management Decision*, vol. 34, pp. 11–18.

Burnes, B (1998) 'The planned approach to change: Come back Kurt Lewin – all is forgiven', paper presented to the Second Maintaining Organizational Effectiveness Conference, Edge Hill University College, Ormskirk, 17 June.

Burnes, B. (2000) *Managing Change: A strategic approach to organisational dynamics*, 3rd Edition. Harlow: FT/Prentice Hall.

Burns, J.M. (1978) *Leadership*. New York: Harper & Row.

Burt, C. (1940) *The Factors of Mind*. London: University of London Press.

Cacioppo, J.T. and Petty, R.E. (1979) 'Effects of message repetition and position on cognitive responses, recall, and persuasion', *Journal of Personality and Social Psychology*, vol. 37, pp. 97–109.

Cacioppo, J.T. and Petty, R.E. (1989) 'Effects of message repetition on argument processing, recall, and persuasion', *Basic and Applied Social Psychology*, vol. 10, pp. 3–12.

Cacioppo, J.T., Petty, R.E. and Green, T.R. (1989) 'From the tripartite to the homoeostasis model of attitudes' in Pratkanis, A.R., Breckler, S.J. and Greenwald, A.G. (eds) *Attitude Structure and Functions*. Hillsdale, NJ: Lawrence Erlbaum.

Campbell, D.T. and Stanley, J.C. (1963) *Experimental and Quasi-Experimental Designs for Research*. Chicago, IL: Rand McNally.

Campion, M.A. and McClelland, C.L. (1993) 'Follow-up and extension of the interdisciplinary costs and benefits of enlarged jobs', *Journal of Applied Psychology*, vol. 78, pp. 339–51.

Cannon, W.B. (1929) *Bodily Changes in Pain, Hunger, Fear and Rage*. New York: Appleton.

Cantalanello, R.F. and Kirkpatrick, D.L. (1968) 'Evaluating training programmes: The state of the art', *Training and Development Journal*, 9 May.

Cappelli, P. (1999) 'Career jobs *are* dead', *California Management Review*, vol. 42, pp. 146–67.

Carnall, C.A. (1990) *Managing Change in Organizations*. London: Prentice Hall.

Carnall, C.A. (1999) *Managing Change in Organizations*, 3rd edition. Harlow: FT/Prentice Hall.

Carnevale, P.J. and Pruitt, D.G. (1992) 'Negotiation and mediation', *Annual Review of Psychology*, vol. 43, pp. 531–82.

Carrick, P. and Williams, R. (1999) 'Development centres – a review of assumptions', *Human Resource Management Journal*, vol. 9, pp. 77–92.

Carson, K.P. and Gilliard, D.J. (1993) 'Construct validity of the Miner Sentence Completion Scale', *Journal of Occupational and Organizational Psychology*, vol. 66, pp. 171–5.

Cartwright, S. and Cooper, C.L. (1997) *Managing Workplace Stress*. London: Sage.

Cartwright, S. and Cooper C.L. (2001) *ASSET: An organizational stress screening tool*. Manchester: RCL Ltd.

Cascio, W. (2000) 'Managing a virtual workplace', *Academy of Management Executive*, vol. 14, pp. 81–90.

Cassell, C. (2000) 'The business case and the management of diversity' in Davidson, M.J. and Burke, R.J. (eds) *Women in Management*. London: Sage.

Cassidy, T. and Lynn, R. (1989) 'A multifactorial approach to achievement motivation: The development of a comprehensive measure', *Journal of Occupational Psychology*, vol. 62, pp. 301–12.

Catalyst (1996) *Women in Corporate Leadership: Progress and prospects*. New York: Catalyst.

Cattell, R.B. (1965) *The Scientific Analysis of Personality*. Harmondsworth: Penguin.

Cattell, R.B. (1987) *Intelligence: Its structure, growth and action*. New York: Elsevier Science.

Cattell, R.B. and Cattell, H.E.P. (1995) 'Personality structure and the new fifth edition of the 16PF,' *Educational and Psychological Measurement*, vol. 55, pp. 926–37.

Cattell, R.B., Eber, H.W. and Taksuoka, M.M. (1970) *Handbook for the Sixteen Personality Factor Questionnaire*. Windsor: National Foundation for Educational Research.

CBI (2001) *Understanding Absence*. London: CBI.

Central Statistical Office (1996) *Social Trends*, No. 26. London: HMSO.

Cervone, D. and Mischel, W. (eds) (2002) *Advances in Personality Science*. New York: Guilford Press.

Chaiken, S. (1987) 'The heuristic model of persuasion' in Zanna, M.P., Olson, J.M. and Herman, C.P. (eds) *Social Influence: The Ontario Symposium*. Hillsdale, NJ: Lawrence Erlbaum.

Chao, G.T., Walz, P.M. and Gardner, P.D. (1992) 'Formal and informal mentorships – a comparison on mentoring functions and contrast with nonmentored counterparts', *Personnel Psychology*, vol. 45(3), pp. 619–36.

Chao, G.T., O'Leary-Kelly, A.M., Wolf, S., Klein, H.J. and Gardner, P.D. (1994) 'Organizational socialization: Its content and consequences', *Journal of Applied Psychology*, vol. 79, pp. 730–43.

Chapman, M. (2000) ' "When the entrepreneur sneezes, the organization catches a cold": A practitioner's perspective on the state of the art in research on the entrepreneurial personality and the entrepreneurial process', *European Journal of Work and Organizational Psychology*, vol. 9, pp. 97–101.

Chase, B. and Karwowski, W. (2003) 'Advanced manufacturing technology' in Holman, D., Wall, T.D., Clegg, C.W., Sparrow, P. and Howard, A. (eds) *The New Workplace*. Chichester: John Wiley.

Chattopadhyay, A. and Alba, J.W. (1988) 'The situational importance of recall and inference in consumer decision making', *Journal of Consumer Research*, vol. 15, pp. 1–12.

Chen, C., Gustafson, D.H. and Lee, Y. (2002) 'The effect of a quantitative decision aid – analytic hierarchy process – on group polarization', *Group Decision and Negotiation*, vol. 11, pp. 329–44.

Chen, C.C., Yu, K.C. and Miner, J.B. (1997) 'Motivation to manage: A study of women in Chinese state-owned enterprises', *Journal of Applied Behavioural Science*, vol. 33, pp. 160–73.

Cherns, A.B. (1976) 'The principles of sociotechnical design', *Human Relations*, vol. 29, pp. 783–92.

Cherns, A.B. (1987) 'Principles of sociotechnical design revisited', *Human Relations*, vol. 40, pp. 153–62.

Child, J. (1972) 'Organizational structure, environment and performance: The role of strategic choice', *Sociology*, vol. 6 , pp. 1–22.

Child, J. (1984) *Organization*. Cambridge: Harper and Row.

Chokkar, J.S. and Wallin, J.A. (1984) 'A field study of the effect of feedback frequency on performance', *Journal of Applied Psychology*, vol. 69, pp. 524–30.

Church, A.H. (1997) 'Managerial self-awareness in high-performing individuals in organizations', *Journal of Applied Psychology*, vol. 82(2), pp. 281–92.

Cialdini, R.B. and Trost, M.R. (1998) 'Social influence: social norms, conformity, and compliance' in Gillbert, D.T, Fiske, S.T. and Lindzey, G. (eds) *The Handbook of Social Psychology*, vols 1 and 2, 4th edition. Boston: McGraw-Hill.

Clarke, A., Oswald, A. and Warr, P. (1996) 'Is job satisfaction U-shaped in age?', *Journal of Occupational and Organizational Psychology*, vol. 69, pp. 57–81.

Clarke, L. (1994) *The Essence of Change*. London: Prentice Hall.

Cleary, T.A. (1968) 'Test bias: Prediction of grades of negro and white students in integrated colleges', *Journal of Educational Measurement*, vol. 5, pp. 115–24.

Cleary, T.S. and Shapiro, S.I. (1996) 'Abraham Maslow and Asian psychology', *Psychologia*, vol. 39, pp. 213–22.

Clegg, C.W. (2003) 'e-Business: Future prospects' in Holman, D., Wall, T.D., Clegg, C.W., Sparrow, P. and Howard, A. (eds) *The New Workplace*. Chichester: John Wiley.

Clutterbuck, D. (2001) *Everyone Needs a Mentor*, 3rd edition. London: Chartered Institute of Personnel and Development.

Coch, L. and French, J.R.P. (1948) 'Overcoming resistance to change', *Human Relations*, vol. 1, pp. 512–32.

Coghlan, D. (1993) 'In defence of process consultation' in Mabey, C. and Mayon-White, B. (eds) *Managing Change*, 2nd edition. London: Open University/Paul Chapman.

Cohen, J. (1977) *Statistical Power Analysis for the Behavioral Sciences*. London: Academic Press.

Cohen, J., Cohen, P., West, S. and Aiken, L. (2003) *Applied Multiple Regression/Correlation Analysis for the Behavioral Sciences*, 3rd edition. Mahwah, NJ: Lawrence Erlbaum Associates.

Cohen, L. (2001) 'Careers: Individual, organisational and emerging perspectives' in Redman, T. and Wilkinson, A. (eds) *Human Resource Management: Theory and practice*. Harlow: Pearson Education.

Cokley, K., Dreher, G.F. and Stockdale, M.S. (2004) 'Towards the inclusiveness and career success of African Americans in the workplace' in Stockdale, M.S. and Crosby, F.J. (eds) *The Psychology and Management of Workplace Diversity*. Oxford: Blackwell.

Coleman, P.T. and Lim, Y.Y.J. (2001) 'A systematic approach to evaluating the effects of collaborative negotiation training on individuals and groups', *Negotiation Journal*, pp. 363–92.

Collins, D. (1998) *Organizational Change*. London: Routledge.

Colquitt, J.A., LePine, J.A. and Noe, R.A. (2000) 'Toward an integrative theory of training motivation: A meta-analytic path analysis of 20 years of research', *Journal of Applied Psychology*, vol. 85, pp. 678–707.

Conger, J.A. (1990) 'The dark side of leadership', *Organizational Dynamics*, Autumn, pp. 44–5.

Conger, J.A. and Kanungo, R.N. (1988) 'The empowerment process', *Academy of Management Review*, vol. 13, pp. 471–82.

Conger, J.A. and Kanungo, R.N. (1998) *Charismatic Leadership in Organizations*. London: Sage.

Conger, J.A., Kanungo, R.N. and Menon, S.T. (2000) 'Charismatic leadership and follower effects', *Journal of Organizational Behavior*, vol. 21(7), pp. 747–67.

Conn, S., and Rieke, M. (eds) (1994) *16PF-5. Technical manual*. Champaign, IL: Institute for Personality and Ability Testing

Conner, P.E. (1977) 'A critical enquiry into some assumptions and values characterizing OD', *Academy of Management Review*, vol. 2, pp. 635–44.

Cook, J.D., Hepworth, S.J., Wall, T.D. and Warr, P.B. (1981) *The Experience of Work*. London: Academic Press.

Cook, M. (1996) *Personnel Selection and Productivity*. Chichester: John Wiley.

Cook, T.D., Gruder, C.L., Hennigan, K.M. and Flay, B.R. (1979) 'History of the sleeper effect: Some logical pitfalls in accepting the null hypothesis', *Psychological Bulletin*, vol. 86, pp. 662–79.

Cook, T.D., Campbell, D.T. and Peracchio, L. (1990) 'Quasi experimentation' in Dunnette, M.D. and Hough, L.M. (eds) *Handbook of Industrial and Organizational Psychology*. Palo Alto, CA: Consulting Psychologists Press.

Coombs, R. and Hull, R. (1994) 'The best or the worst of both worlds: BPR, cost reduction, and the strategic management of IT', paper presented to the OASIG Seminar on Organisation Change through IT and BPR: Beyond the Hype, London, September.

Cooper, C.L. (1996) 'Working hours and health', *Work and Stress*, vol. 10(1), pp. 1–4.

Cooper C.L. (1997) 'Stress at work: how your job rates', *Sunday Times*.

Cooper, C.L. and Cartwright, S. (1994) 'Healthy mind; healthy organization – a proactive approach to occupational stress', *Human Relations*, vol. 47, pp. 455–71.

Cooper, C.L. and Lewis, S. (1993) *The Workplace Revolution: Managing today's dual career families*. London: Kogan Page.

Cooper, C.L. and Palmer, S. (2000) *Conquer Your Stress*. Wimbledon: CIPD.

Cooper, C.L. and Quick, J. (1999) *Stress and Strain*. Oxford: Health Press.

Cooper, C.L. and Sadri, G. (1991) 'The impact of stress counselling at work' in Perrewe, P.L. (ed.) *Handbook of Job Stress (Special Issue), Journal of Social Behavior and Personality*, vol. 6, pp. 411–23.

Cooper, C.L., Sloan, S. and Williams, S. (1987) *Occupational Stress Indicator*. Windsor: NFER/Nelson.

Cooper, C.L., Cooper, R.D. and Eaker, L.H. (1988a) *Living with Stress*. Harmondsworth: Penguin.

Cooper, C.L., Sloan, S. and Williams, S. (1988b) *Occupational Stress Indicator: The manual*. Windsor: NFER-Nelson.

Cooper, C.L., Makin, P. and Cox, C. (1993) 'Managing the boss', *Leadership and Organizational Development Journal*, vol. 19(5), pp. 28–32.

Cooper, C.L., Dewe, P. and O'Driscoll, M. (2001) *Organizational Stress: A review and critique of theory, research and application*. London: Sage.

Coopey, J. and Hartley, J. (1991) 'Reconsidering the case for organizational commitment', *Human Resource Management Journal*, vol. 1, pp. 18–32.

Cordery, J., Sevastos, P., Mueller, W. and Parker, S. (1993) 'Correlates of employee attitudes toward functional flexibility', *Human Relations*, vol. 46, pp. 705–23.

Corr, P.J. and Gray, J.A. (1996) 'Attributional style as a personality factor in insurance sales performance in the UK', *Journal of Occupational and Organizational Psychology*, vol. 69, pp. 83–7.

Costa, P.T. and McCrae, R.R. (1992) *The NEO PI-R Professional Manual*. Odessa, FL: Psychological Assessment Resources Inc.

Coulson-Thomas, C. and Coe, T. (1991) *The Flat Organization*. London: British Institute of Management.

Cowan, G. and Hodge, C. (1996) 'Judgements of hate speech: The effects of target group, publicness, and behavioural responses of the target', *Journal of Applied Social Psychology*, vol. 26, pp. 355–74.

Cox, T. (1978) *Stress*. London: Macmillan.

Cox, T. (1980) 'Repetitive work' in Cooper, C.L. and Payne, R. (eds) *Current Concerns in Occupational Stress*. Chichester: John Wiley.

Cronbach, L.J. (1967) 'How can instruction be adapted to individual differences?' in Gagné, R.M. (ed.) *Learning and Individual Differences*. Columbus, OH: Merrill.

Cropanzano, R., Byrne, Z.S., Bobocel, D.R. and Rupp, D.E., (2001) 'Moral virtues, fairness heuristics, social entities, and other denizens of organisational justice', *Journal of Vocational Behaviour*, vol. 58, pp. 164–209.

Crosby, P.B. (1979) *Quality is Free*. New York: McGraw-Hill.

Cross, W.E. Jr (1995) 'The psychology of nigrescence: Revising the Cross model' in Ponterotto, J.G., Casas, J.M., Suzuki, L.A. and Alexander, C.M. (eds) *Handbook of Multicultural Counseling*. Thousand Oaks, CA: Sage.

Crown, D.F. and Rose, J.G. (1995) 'Yours, mine, and ours: Facilitating group productivity through the integration of individual and group goals', *Organizational Behavior and Human Decision Process,* vol. 64, pp. 138–95.

Cruise O'Brien, R. and Voss, C. (1992) 'In search of quality', working paper. London: London Business School.

Cummings, T. and Cooper, C.L. (1979) 'A cybernetic framework for the study of occupational stress', *Human Relations*, vol. 32, pp. 395–419.

Cummings, T.G. and Huse, E.F. (1989) *Organization Development and Change*. St Paul, MN: West Publishing.

Cummings, T.G. and Worley, C.G. (1997) *Organization Development and Change*, 6th edition. Cincinnati, OH: South-Western College Publishing.

Dale, B.G. and Cooper, C.L. (1992) *Total Quality and Human Resources: An executive guide*. Oxford: Blackwell.

Dale, B.G., Cooper, C.L. and Wilkinson, A. (1998) *Managing Quality and Human Resources: A guide to continuous improvement*. Oxford: Blackwell.

Daly, J.P. and Geyer, P.D. (1994) 'The role of fairness in implementing large-scale change: Employee evaluations of process and outcome in seven facility relocations', *Journal of Organizational Behavior*, vol. 15, pp. 623–38.

Daniels, K. (2000) 'Job features and well-being' in Daniels, K., Lamond, D. and Standen, P. (eds) *Managing Telework: Perspectives from human resource management and work psychology*. London: Thompson Learning.

Davenport, T.H. (1993) *Process Innovation: Re-engineering work through IT*. Boston, MA: Harvard Business School Press.

Davidson, M.J. and Burke, R.J. (eds) (2000) *Women in Management: Current research issues*, vol. 2. London: Sage.

Davidson, M.J. and Cooper, C.L. (1992) *Shattering the Glass Ceiling: The woman manager*. London: Paul Chapman Publishing.

Davies, I.K. (1972) *The Management of Learning*. London: McGraw Hill.

Davis, J.H. (1992) 'Some compelling intuitions about group consensus decisions, theoretical and empirical research, and interpersonal aggregation phenomena: Selected examples, 1950–1990', *Organizational Behavior and Human Decision Processes*, vol. 52, pp. 3–38.

Davis, L.E. (1982) 'Organizational design', in Salvendy, G. (ed.) *Handbook of Industrial Engineering*. Chichester: John Wiley.

Davis, T.R. and Luthans, F. (1980) 'A social learning approach to organizational behavior', *Academy of Management Review*, vol. 5, pp. 281–90.

Dawis, R. and Lofquist, L.H. (1984) *A Psychological Theory of Work Adjustment*. Minneapolis, MN: University of Minnesota Press.

Dawson, P. (1994) *Organizational Change: A processual approach*. London: Paul Chapman Publishing.

Deal, T. and Kennedy, A. (1982) 'Culture: A new look through old lenses', *Journal of Applied Behavioral Science*, vol. 19, pp. 487–507.

Dean, J.W. Jr and Sharfman, M.P. (1996) 'Does decision process matter? A study of strategic decision-making effectiveness', *Academy of Management Journal*, vol. 39, pp. 368–96.

Deci, E.L. and Ryan, R.M. (1980) 'The empirical exploration of intrinsic motivational processes' in Berkowitz, L. (ed.) *Advances in Experimental Social Psychology*, vol. 13. New York: Academic Press.

Deci, E.L., Koestner, R. and Ryan, R.M. (1999) 'A meta-analytic review of experiments examining the effects of extrinsic rewards on intrinsic motivation', *Psychological Bulletin*, vol. 125, pp. 627–68.

DeFrank, R.S. and Cooper, C.L. (1987) 'Worksite stress management interventions: Their effectiveness and conceptualization', *Journal of Managerial Psychology*, vol. 2, pp. 4–10.

De Fruyt, F. and Mervielde, I. (1999) 'RIASEC types and big five traits as predictors of employment status and nature of employment', *Personnel Psychology*, vol. 52, pp. 701–27.

de Haas, M., Algeral, J.A., van Tuijl, H.F.J.M. and Meulman, J.J. (2000) 'Macro and micro goal setting: in search of coherence', *Applied Psychology – An International Review*, vol. 49(3), pp. 579–95.

Delbridge, R, Turnbull, P. and Wilkinson, B. (1992) 'Pushing back the frontiers: Management control and work intensification under JIT/TQM factory regimes', *New Technology, Work and Employment*, vol. 7, pp. 97–106.

Delgado, F. (2003) 'The fusing of sport and politics: Media construction of US versus Iran at France '98', *Journal of Sport and Social Issues*, vol. 27, pp. 293–307.

Deming, W.E. (1982) *Quality, Productivity and Competitive Position*. Boston, MA: MIT Press.

Demir, A., Ulusoy, M. and Ulusoy, M.F. (2003) 'Investigation of factors influencing burnout levels in professional and private lives of nurses', *International Journal of Nursing Studies*, vol. 40, pp. 807–27.

Den Hartog, D.N., Van Muijen, J.J. and Koopman, P.L. (1997) 'Transactional versus transformational leadership: An analysis of the MLQ', *Journal of Occupational and Organizational Psychology*, vol. 70, pp. 19–34.

Dess, G.G. and Picken, J.C. (2000) 'Changing roles: Leadership in the 21st century', *Organizational Dynamics*, vol. 28(3), pp. 18–34.

Deutsch, M. (2002) 'Social psychology's contributions to the study of conflict resolution', *Negotiation Journal*, pp. 307–20.

Devine, P.G. (1989) 'Stereotypes and prejudice: Their automatic and controlled components', *Journal of Personality and Social Psychology*, vol. 56, pp. 5–18.

De Witte, K. and van Muijen, J.J. (1999) 'Organizational culture: Critical questions for researchers and practitioners', *European Journal of Work and Organizational Psychology*, vol. 8, pp. 583–95.

Diamantopoulos, A. and Schlegelmilch, B. (1997) *Taking the Fear out of Data Analysis*. London: Dryden Press.

Dickson, M.W., Den Hartog, D.N. and Mitchelson, J.K. (2003) 'Research on leadership in a cross-cultural context: Making progress, and raising new questions', *Leadership Quarterly*, vol. 14(6), pp. 729–68.

Diefendorff, J.M, Hall, R.J., Lord, R.G. and Strean, M.L. (2000) 'Action-state orientation: Construct validity of a revised measure and its relationship to work-related variables', *Journal of Applied Psychology*, vol. 85, pp. 250–63.

Diehl, M. and Stroebe, W. (1987) 'Productivity loss in brainstorming groups: Toward the solution of a riddle', *Journal of Personality and Social Psychology*, vol. 53, pp. 497–509.

Digman, J.M. (1990) 'Personality structure: Emergence of the five-factor model', *Annual Review of Psychology*, vol. 41, pp. 417–40.

Digman, J.M. and Takemoto-Chock, N.K. (1981) 'Factors in the natural language of personality: Re-analysis and comparison of six major studies', *Multivariate Behavioral Research*, vol. 16, pp. 149–70.

Donnay, D.A.C. and Borgen, F.H. (1999) 'The incremental validity of vocational self-efficacy: An examination of interest, self-efficacy and occupation', *Journal of Counseling Psychology*, vol. 46(4), pp. 432–47.

Donovan, J.J. and Radosevich, D.J. (1998) 'The moderating role of goal commitment on the goal difficulty–performance relationship: A meta-analytic review and critical reanalysis', *Journal of Applied Psychology*, vol. 83, pp. 308–315.

Doogan, K. (2001) 'Insecurity and long-term employment', *Work Employment and Society*, vol. 15, pp. 419–41.

Dormann, C. and Zapf, D. (2001) 'Job satisfaction: A meta-analysis of stabilities', *Journal of Organizational Behaviour*, vol. 22, pp. 483–504.

Dornstein, M. (1988) 'Wage reference groups and their determinants: A study of blue-collar and white-collar employees in Israel', *Journal of Occupational Psychology*, vol. 61, pp. 221–35.

Drenth, P., Thierry, H., de Wolff, C.M. and de Wolff, C.J. (eds) (1998) *A Handbook of Work and Organizational Psychology*. Brighton: Psychology Press.

DTI (2001) UK Competitiveness Indicators. London: DTI Publications.

Duff, A.R., Robertson, I.T., Phillips, R.A. and Cooper, M.D. (1994) 'Improving safety by the modification of behaviour', *Construction Management and Economics*, vol. 12, pp. 67–78.

Dulewicz, V. (1989) 'Assessment centres as the route to competence', *Personnel Management*, November, pp. 56–9.

Dunham, R., Grube, J.A. and Castañeda, M.B. (1994) 'Organizational commitment: the utility of an integrative definition', *Journal of Applied Psychology*, vol. 79, pp. 370–80.

Dunphy, D. and Stace, D. (1992) *Under New Management: Australian organizations in transition*. Roseville, NSW, Australia: McGraw-Hill.

Dunphy, D. and Stace, D. (1993) 'The strategic management of corporate change', *Human Relations*, vol. 46(8), pp. 905–18.

Durham, C.C., Knight, D. and Locke, E.A. (1997) 'Effects of leader role, team-set goal difficulty, efficacy, and tactics on team effectiveness', *Organizational Behaviour and Human Decision Process,* vol. 72, pp. 203–31.

Durr, M. and Logan, J.R. (1997) 'Racial submarkets in government employment: African American managers in New York State', *Sociological Forum*, vol. 12, pp. 353–70.

Dweck, C.S. (1986) 'Motivational processes affecting learning', *American Psychologist*, vol. 41, pp. 1040–8.

Eagly, A.H. and Chaiken, S. (1975) 'An attribution analysis of the effect of communicator characteristics on opinion change: The case of communicator attractiveness', *Journal of Personality and Social Psychology*, vol. 33, pp. 136–44.

Eagly, A.H. and Chaiken, S. (1992) *The Psychology of Attitudes*. San Diego, CA: Harcourt Brace Johanovich.

Eagly, A.H., Wood, W. and Chaiken, S. (1978) 'Causal inferences about communicators and their effect on opinion change', *Journal of Personality and Social Psychology*, vol. 36, pp. 424–35.

Eagly, A.H., Makhijani, M.G. and Klonsky, B.G. (1992) 'Gender and the evaluation of leaders: A meta-analysis', *Psychological Bulletin*, vol. 111, pp. 3–22.

Eagly, A.H., Karau, S.J. and Makhijani, M.G. (1995) 'Gender and the effectiveness of leaders: A meta-analysis', *Psychological Bulletin*, vol. 117, pp. 125–45.

Earley, P.C. (1989) 'Social loafing and collectivism: A comparison of the United States and the People's Republic of China', *Administrative Science Quarterly*, vol. 34, pp. 565–81.

Earley, P.C., Connolly, T. and Ekegren, G. (1989) 'Goals, strategy development and task performance: Some limits on the efficacy of goal-setting', *Journal of Applied Psychology*, vol. 74, pp. 24–33.

Earnshaw, J. and Cooper, C.L. (2001) *Stress and Employer Liability*. London: CIPD Books.

Easterby-Smith, M., Burgoyne, J. and Araujo, L. (eds) (1999) *Organizational Learning and the Learning Organization: Developments in theory and practice*. London: Sage.

Easterby-Smith, M., Thorpe, R. and Lowe, A. (2002) *Management Research: An introduction*, 2nd edition. London: Sage.

Eby, L.T. and Russell, J.E.A. (2000) 'Predictors of employee willingness to relocate for the firm', *Journal of Vocational Behavior*, vol. 57, pp. 42–61.

Eby, L.T., Freeman, D.M., Rush, M.C. and Charles, L.E. (1999) 'Motivational bases of affective organizational commitment: A partial test of an integrative theoretical model', *Journal of Occupational and Organizational Psychology*, vol. 72, pp. 463–83.

Economist Intelligence Unit (1992) *Making Quality Work: Lessons from Europe's Leading Companies*. London: Economist Intelligence Unit.

Eden, M. and Chisholm, R.F. (1993) 'Emerging varieties of action research', *Human Relations*, vol. 46, pp. 121–42.

Eder, R.W. and Harris, M.M. (1999) *The Employment Interview Handbook*. London: Sage.

Edwardes, M. (1983) *Back from the Brink*. London: Collins.

Egan, G. (1998) *The Skilled Helper*, 6th edition. Pacific Grove, CA: Brooks/Cole.

Eiser, J.R. (1986) *Social Psychology: Attitudes, cognition and social behaviour*. Cambridge: Cambridge University Press.

Eiser, J.R. and van der Pligt, J. (1988) *Attitudes and Decisions*. London: Routledge.

Eldridge, J.E.T. and Crombie, A.D. (1974) *A Sociology of Organizations*. London: George Allen and Unwin.

Elkin, A.J. and Rosch, P.J. (1990) 'Promoting mental health at the workplace: The prevention side of stress management', *Occupational Medicine: State of the Art Review*, vol. 5, no. 4, pp. 739–54.

Elkins, T.J. and Phillips, J.S. (2000) 'Job context, selection decision outcome, and the perceived fairness of selection tests: biodata as an illustrative case', *Journal of Applied Psychology*, vol. 85(3), pp. 479–84.

Ellemers, N., Spears, R. and Doosji, B. (2002) 'Self and social identity', *Annual Review of Psychology*, vol. 53, pp. 161–86.

Ellis, C. and Sonnenfeld, J. (1994) 'Diverse approaches to managing diversity', *Human Resource Management*, vol. 33, pp. 79–109.

Ellison, R. (1995) 'Labour force projections for countries and regions in the United Kingdom 1995–2006', *Employment Gazette*, vol. 103, pp. 303–14.

Emmerling, R.J. and Goleman, D. (2003) 'Emotional intelligence: Issues and common misunderstandings', *The Consortium for Research on Emotional Intelligence in Organizations Issues in EI* (www.eiconsortium.org).

Erez, M. and Somech, A. (1996) 'Is group productivity loss the rule or the exception? Effects of culture and group-based motivation', *Academy of Management Journal*, vol. 39, pp. 1513–37.

Ettington, D.R. (1998) 'Successful career plateauing', *Journal of Vocational Behavior*, vol. 52, pp. 72–88.

European Commission (1998) *Status Report on European Telework*. Luxembourg: Office for Official Publications of the European Communities.

Ewen, R.B. (2003) *An Introduction to Theories of Personality*, 6th edition. Mahwah, NJ: Lawrence Erlbaum Associates.

Eysenck, H.J. (1967) *The Biological Basis of Personality*. Springfield, IL: Charles C. Thomas.

Eysenck, H.J. (1970) *The Structure of Human Personality*. London: Methuen.

Eysenck, H.J. (1981) 'General features of the model' in Eysenck, H.J. (ed.) *A Model for Personality*. New York: Springer-Verlag.

Eysenck, H.J. and Eysenck, M.J. (1985) *Personality and Individual Differences: A natural science approach*. New York: Plenum Press.

Eysenck, H.J. and Eysenck, S.B.G. (1964) *Manual of the Eysenck Personality Inventory*. London: University of London Press.

Eysenck, H.J. and Eysenck, S.B.G. (1975) *Manual of the Eysenck Personality Questionnaire*. Sevenoaks: Hodder and Stoughton.

Eysenck, H.J. and Eysenck, S.B.G. (1991) *Manual of the Eysenck Personality Scales*. London: Hodder and Stoughton.

Eysenck, H.J. and Kamin, L. (1981) *Intelligence: The battle for the mind*. London: Pan.

Eysenck, H.J. and Wilson, G.D. (1973) *The Experimental Study of Freudian Theories*. London: Methuen.

Ezzamel, M., Green, C., Lilley, S. and Willmott, H. (1994) 'Change management: Appendix 1 – A review and analysis of recent changes in UK management practices', Manchester: Financial Services Research Centre, UMIST.

Fagley, N.S. and Miller, P.M. (1987) 'The effects of decision framing on choice of risks vs. certain options', *Organizational Behavior and Human Decision Processes*, vol. 39, pp. 264–77.

Fahr, J.L., Dobbins, G.H. and Cheng, B.S. (1991) 'Cultural relativity in action: A comparison of self-ratings made by Chinese and US workers'. *Personnel Psychology*, vol. 44, pp. 129–44.

Farr, J.L., Hofman, D.A. and Ringenbach, K.L. (1993) 'Goal orientation and action control theory: Implications for industrial and organizational psychology' in Robertson, I.T. and Cooper, C.L. (eds) *International Review of Industrial and Organizational Psychology*, vol. 8. Chichester: John Wiley.

Feldman, D.C. (1994) 'The decision to retire early: A review and reconceptionization', *Academy of Management Review*, vol. 19, pp. 285–311.

Feldman, D.C. and Weitz, B.A. (1988) 'Career plateaux reconsidered', *Journal of Management*, vol. 14, pp. 69–80.

Feldman, S. (1991) 'Today's EAPs make the grade', *Personnel*, vol. 68, pp. 3–40.

Fiedler, F.E. (1967) *A Theory of Leadership Effectiveness*. New York: McGraw-Hill.

Fiedler, F.E. (1995) 'Cognitive resources and leadership performance', *Applied Psychology: An International Review*, vol. 44, pp. 5–28.

Fiedler, F.E. (1996) 'Research on leadership selection and training: One view of the future', *Administrative Science Quarterly*, vol. 41, pp. 241–50.

Fiedler, F.E. and Chemers, M.M. (1984) *Improving Leadership Effectiveness: The leader match concept*, 2nd edition. New York: John Wiley.

Fiedler, F.E. and Garcia, J.E. (1987) *New Approaches to Effective Leadership: Cognitive resources and organizational performance*. New York: John Wiley.

Fiedler, F.E., Murphy, S.E. and Gibson, F.W. (1992) 'Inaccurate reporting and inappropriate variables: A reply to Vecchio's (1990) examination of Cognitive Resource Theory', *Journal of Applied Psychology*, vol. 77, pp. 372–4.

Fiegenbaum, A. and Thomas, H. (1988) 'Attitudes toward risk and the risk return paradox: Prospect theory explanations', *Academy of Management Journal*, vol. 31, pp. 86–106.

Filby, I. and Willmott, H. (1988) 'Ideologies and contradictions in a public relations department', *Organization Studies*, vol. 9(3), pp. 335–51.

Filley, A.C., House, R.J. and Kerr, S. (1976) *Managerial Process and Organizational Behavior.* Glenview, IL: Scott, Foresman and Co.

Fine, S.A. and Wiley, W.W. (1974) 'An introduction to functional job analysis' in Fleishman, E.A. and Bass, A.R. (eds) *Studies in Personal and Industrial Psychology.* Homewood, IL: Dorsey Press.

Finegan, J.E. (2000) 'The impact of person and organizational values on organizational commitment,' *Journal of Occupational and Organizational Psychology*, vol. 73, pp. 149–69.

Fineman, S. (2003) *Understanding Emotion at Work.* London: Sage.

Finkelstein, S. (1992) 'Power in top management teams: Dimensions, measurement and validation', *Academy of Management Journal*, vol. 35, pp. 505–38.

Finstad, N. (1998) The rhetoric of organizational change, *Human Relations*, vol. 51, pp. 717–40.

Fisher, R., Ury, W. and Patton, B. (1991) *Getting to YES: Negotiating agreement without giving in*, 2nd edition. New York: Penguin Books.

Fisher, S.G., Hunter, T.A. and Macrosson, W.D.K. (1998) 'The distribution of Belbin team roles among UK managers', *Personnel Review*, vol. 29(2), pp. 124–36.

Fiske, A.P. and Tetlock, P.E. (1997) 'Taboo tradeoffs: Reactions to transactions that transgress the domains of relationships', *Political Psychology*, vol. 18, pp. 255–97.

Fitts, P.M. (1962) 'Factors in complex skill training' in Glaser, R. (ed.) *Training Research and Education.* New York: John Wiley.

Flanagan, J.C. (1954) 'The critical incident technique', *Psychological Bulletin*, vol. 51, pp. 327–58.

Fleishman, E.A. (1969) *Leadership Opinion Questionnaire Manual.* Henley-on-Thames: Science Research Associates.

Fletcher, C. (1998) 'Circular argument', *People Management*, October, pp. 46–9.

Fletcher, C. (2001) 'Performance appraisal and management: The developing research agenda', *Journal of Occupational and Organizational Psychology*, vol. 74, pp. 473–87.

Fletcher, C., Baldry, C. and Cunningham-Snell, N. (1998) 'The psychometric properties of 360 degree feedback', *International Journal of Selection & Assessment*, vol. 6, pp. 19–34.

Folger, R. and Cropanzano, R. (2001) 'Fairness theory: Justice as accountability' in Greenberg, J. and Cropanzano, R. (eds) *Advances in Organization Justice.* Stanford, CA: Stanford University Press.

Folger, R. and Konovsky, M.A. (1989) 'Effects of procedural and distributive justice on reactions to pay rise decisions', *Academy of Management Journal*, vol. 32, pp. 115–30.

Fondas, N. (1997) 'Feminization unveiled: Management qualities in contemporary writings', *Academy of Management Review*, vol. 22, pp. 257–82.

Forbes, D.P. and Milliken, F.J. (1999) 'Cognition and corporate governance: Understanding boards of directors as strategic decision-making groups', *Academy of Management Review*, vol. 24(3), pp. 489–505.

Forster, N. (1997) 'The persistent myth of high expatriate failure rates: A reappraisal', *International Journal of Human Resource Management*, vol. 8, pp. 414–33.

Fox, D.K., Hopkins, B.L. and Anger, W.K. (1987) 'The long-term effects of a token economy on safety performance in open-pit mining', *Journal of Applied Behavior Analysis*, vol. 20, pp. 215–24.

Franklin, B. (1997) *Newszak and News Media*. Arnold: London.

Fransella, F. and Bannister, D. (1977) *Manual for Repertory Grid Technique*. London: Academic Press.

French, J.R.P. and Caplan, R.D. (1972) 'Organizational stress and individual strain' in Marrow, A. (ed.) *The Failure of Success*. New York: AMACOM.

French, W.L. and Bell, C.H. (1973) *Organization Development*. Englewood Cliffs, NJ: Prentice Hall.

French, W.L. and Bell, C.H. (1984) *Organization Development*, 4th edition. Englewood Cliffs, NJ: Prentice Hall.

French, W.L. and Bell, C.H. (1995) *Organization Development*, 5th edition. Englewood Cliffs, NJ: Prentice Hall.

Frese, M. and Beimel, S. (2003) 'Action training for charismatic leadership: two evaluations of studies of a commercial training module on inspirational communication of a vision', *Personnel Psychology*, vol. 56, pp. 671–97.

Frese, M., Fay, D., Hilburger, T., Leng, K. and Tag, A. (1997) 'The concept of personal initiative: Operationalization, reliability and validity in two German samples', *Journal of Occupational and Organizational Psychology*, vol. 70, pp. 139–62.

Freud, S. (1960) *The Psychopathology of Everyday Life*. London: Hogarth (first published 1901).

Fried, Y. and Ferris, G.R. (1987) 'The validity of the job characteristics model: a review and meta-analysis', *Personnel Psychology*, vol. 40, pp. 287–322.

Friedman, R.A. and Krackhardt, D. (1997) 'Social capital and career mobility: A structural theory of lower returns to education for Asian employees', *Journal of Applied Behavioral Science*, vol. 33, pp. 316–34.

Frisch, D. and Clemen, R.T. (1994) 'Beyond expected utility: Rethinking behavioral decision research', *Psychological Bulletin*, vol. 116, pp. 46–54.

Frone, M.R. (2002) 'Work–family balance' in Quick, J.C. and Tetrick, L.E. (eds) *Handbook of Occupational Health Psychology*. Washington DC: American Psychology Association.

Fryer, D. (1998) 'Labour market disadvantage, deprivation and mental health' in Drenth, P. and Thierry, H. (eds) *Handbook of Work and Organizational Psychology*, vol. 2, pp. 215–27. Hove: Psychology Press/Erlbaum.

Furnham, A., Steele, H. and Pendleton, D. (1993) 'A psychometric assessment of the Belbin Team-Role Self-Perception Inventory', *Journal of Occupational and Organizational Psychology*, vol. 66, pp. 245–57.

Furnham, A., Kirkcaldy, B.D. and Lynn, R. (1994) 'National attitudes to competitiveness, money and work among young people: First, second and third world differences', *Human Relations*, vol. 47, no. 1, pp. 119–32.

Gagné, R.M. (1977) *The Conditions of Learning*, 3rd edition. New York: Rinehart and Winston.

Gallos, J.V. (1989) 'Exploring women's development: Implications for career theory, practice and research' in Arthur, M.B., Hall, D.T. and Lawrence, B.S. (eds) *Handbook of Career Theory*. Cambridge: Cambridge University Press.

Gardner, H. (1983) *Frames of mind: The theory of multiple intelligences*. New York: Basic Books.

Gardner, H. (1995) 'Reflections on multiple intelligences', *Phi Delta Kappan*, vol. 77, pp. 200–208.

Gardner, H. (2003) 'Higher education for the era of globalisation', *The Psychologist*, vol. 16, pp. 520–21.

Gardner, W.L. and Avolio, B.J. (1998) 'The charismatic relationship: A dramaturgical perspective', *Academy of Management Review*, vol. 23, pp. 32–58.

Garonzik, R., Brockner, J. and Siegel, P.A. (2000) 'Identifying international assignees at risk for premature departure: The interactive effect of outcome favourability and procedural fairness', *Journal of Applied Psychology*, vol. 85, pp. 13–20.

Garvin, D.A. (1993) 'Building a learning organization', *Harvard Business Review*, July/August, pp. 78–91.

Gastil, J. (1994) 'A definition and illustration of democratic leadership', *Human Relations*, vol. 47, pp. 953–75.

Gati, I., Saka, N. and Krausz, M. (2001) '"Should I use a computer-assisted career guidance system?" It depends on where your career decision-making difficulties lie', *British Journal of Guidance and Counselling*, vol. 29, pp. 301–21.

Gattiker, U. and Larwood, L. (1988) 'Predictors for managers' career mobility and satisfaction', *Human Relations*, vol. 41, pp. 569–91.

Gaugler, B., Rosenthal, D.B., Thornton, G.C. and Bentson, C. (1987) 'Meta-analysis of assessment center validity', *Journal of Applied Psychology*, vol. 72, pp. 493–511.

Geller, E.S. (2001) 'Sustaining participation in a safety improvement process: 10 relevant principles from behavioural science', *Professional Safety*, Vol. 46(9), pp. 24–9.

Geller, E.S., Davis, L. and Spicer, K. (1983) 'Industry-based incentives for promoting seat belt use: Differential impact on white-collar versus blue-collar employees', *Journal of Organizational Behavior Management*, vol. 5, pp. 17–29.

Gellerman, W., Frankel, M.S. and Ladenson, R.F. (1990) *Values and Ethics in Organizational and Human Systems Development: Responding to Dilemmas in Professional Life*. San Francisco, CA: Jossey-Bass.

Gemmill, G. and Oakley, J. (1992) 'Leadership: An alienating social myth?', *Human Relations*, vol. 45, pp. 113–29.

George, J.M. and Jones, G.R. (1997) 'Experiencing work: Values, attitudes and moods', *Human Relations*, vol. 50, pp. 393–416.

Geyer, A. and Steyrer, J.M. (1998) 'Transformational leadership and objective performance in banks', *Applied Psychology: An International Review*, vol. 47, pp. 397–420.

Gianakos, I. (1999) 'Patterns of career choice and career decision-making self-efficacy', *Journal of Vocational Behavior*, vol. 54, pp. 244–58.

Gibson, C.B. and Zellmer-Bruhn, M.E. (2002) 'Minding your metaphors: Applying the concept of teamwork metaphors to the management of teams in multicultural contexts', *Organizational Dynamics*, vol. 31, pp. 101–16.

Gilliland, S.W. (1993) 'The perceived fairness of selection systems – an organizational justice perspective', *Academy of Management Review*, vol. 18(4), pp. 694–734.

Gilliland, S.W. and Landis, R.S. (1992) 'Quality and quantity goals in a complex decision task: Strategies and outcomes', *Journal of Applied Psychology*, vol. 77, pp. 672–81.

Gioia, D.A. and Manz, C.C. (1985) 'Linking cognition and behavior: A script processing interpretation of vicarious learning', *Academy of Management Review*, vol. 10, pp. 527–39.

Gist, M.E. (1989) 'The influence of training methods on self-efficacy and idea generation among managers', *Personnel Psychology*, vol. 42, pp. 787–805.

Gittleman, M., Horrigan, M. and Joyce, M. (1998) '"Flexible" workplace practices: Evidence from a nationally representative survey', *Industrial and Labor Relations Review*, vol. 52(1), 99–115.

Glaser, B.G. and Strauss, A.L. (1967) *The Discovery of Grounded Theory*. Chicago, IL: Aldine.

Goffee, R. and Scase, R. (1992) 'Organizational change and the corporate career: The restructuring of managers' job aspirations', *Human Relations*, vol. 45, pp. 363–86.

Goffin, R.D. and Gellatly, I.R. (2001) 'A multi-rater assessment of organizational commitment: Are self-report measures biased?' *Journal of Organizational Behavior*, 22, pp. 437–51.

Goldstein, H.W., Yusko, K.P., Braverman, E.P., Smith, D.B. and Chung, B. (1998) 'The role of cognitive ability in the subgroup differences and incremental validity of assessment centre exercises', *Personnel Psychology*, vol. 51, pp. 357–74.

Goldstein, I.L. (1993) *Training in Organizations: Needs assessment, development and evaluation*. Pacific Grove, CA: Brooks/Cole.

Goleman, D. (1995) *Emotional Intelligence*. New York: Bantam Books.

Goleman, D. (1998) *Working with Emotional Intelligence*. New York: Bantam Books.

Goleman, D. (2001) 'An EI based theory of performance' in Cherniss, C. and Goleman, D. (eds) *The Emotionally Intelligent Workplace*. San Francisco, CA: Jossey-Bass Wiley.

Gottfredson, G. and Holland, J.L. (1996) *Dictionary of Holland Occupational Codes*, 3rd edition. Odessa, FL: Psychological Assessment Resources Inc.

Graves, L.M. and Powell, G.N. (1988) 'An investigation of sex discrimination in recruiters' evaluations of actual applicants', *Journal of Applied Psychology*, vol. 73, pp. 20–9.

Greenberg, H. (1980) *Coping with Job Stress*. Englewood Cliffs, NJ: Prentice Hall.

Greenberg, J. (2001) 'Setting the justice agenda: Seven unanswered questions about "What, Why and How"', *Journal of Vocational Behavior*, vol. 58, pp. 210–19.

Greenhaus, J.H. and Parasuraman, S. (1999) 'Research on work, family and gender: Current status and future directions' in Powell, G.N. (ed.) *Handbook of Gender and Work*. Thousand Oaks, C.A: Sage.

Greenhaus, J.H., Parasuraman, S. and Wormley, W.M. (1990) 'Effects of race on organizational experiences, job performance evaluations, and career outcomes', *Academy of Management Journal*, vol. 33, pp. 64–86.

Greenhaus, J.H., Callanan, G.A. and Godshalk, V. (2000) *Career Management*, 3rd edition. Orlando, FL: Dryden Press.

Greenleaf, R. (1983) *Servant Leadership: A journey into the nature of legitimate power and greatness*. Mahwah, NJ: Paulist Press.

Greenwald, A.G., McGhee, D.E. and Schwartz, J.L.K. (1998) 'Measuring individual differences in implicit cognition: The implicit association test', *Journal of Personality and Social Psychology*, vol. 74, pp. 1464–80.

Griffin, M.A., Patterson, M.G. and West, M.A. (2001) 'Job satisfaction and teamwork: The role of supervisor support', *Journal of Organizational Behavior*, vol. 22, pp. 537–50.

Griffin, R.W. (1991) 'Effects of work redesign on employee perceptions, attitudes and behaviours: A long-term investigation', *Academy of Management Journal*, vol. 34, pp. 425–35.

Griffin, R.W. and Bateman, T.S. (1986) 'Job satisfaction and organizational commitment' in Cooper, C.L. and Robertson, I.T. (eds) *International Review of Industrial and Organizational Psychology*, pp. 157–88. Chichester: John Wiley.

Grint, K. (1997) *Leadership: Classical, Contemporary and Critical Approaches*. Oxford: Oxford University Press.

Grinyer, P.H., Mayes, D.G. and McKiermon, P. (1988) *Sharpbenders: The secrets of unleashing corporate potential*. Oxford: Blackwell.

Gubrium, J. and Holstein, J. (1997) *The New Language of Qualitative Method*. Oxford: Oxford University Press.

Guest, D. (1998) 'Is the psychological contract worth taking seriously?', *Journal of Organizational Behavior,* vol. 19, pp. 649–64.

Guest, D.E. and Hoque, K. (1996) 'Human resource management and the new industrial relations' in Beardwell, I.J. (ed.) *Contemporary Industrial Relations*. Oxford: Oxford University Press.

Guilford, J.P. (1967) *The Nature of Human Intelligence*. New York: McGraw-Hill.

Gunz, H., Evans, M. and Jalland, R.M. (2000) 'Career boundaries in a boundaryless world' in Peiperl, M., Arthur, M.B., Goffee, R. and Morris, T. (eds) *Career Frontiers: New concepts in working lives*. Oxford: Oxford University Press.

Gutek, B. (1995) *The Dynamics of Service: Reflections on the Changing Nature of Customer/Provider Interactions*. San Francisco, CA: Jossey-Bass.

Guzzo, R.A. and Dickson, M.W. (1996) 'Teams in organizations: Recent research on performance and effectiveness', *Annual Review of Psychology*, vol. 47, pp. 307–38.

Guzzo, R.A., Jette, R.D. and Katzell, R.A. (1985) 'The effects of psychologically based intervention programmes on worker productivity: A meta-analysis', *Personnel Psychology*, vol. 38, pp. 275–91.

Hackman, J.R. (1990) *Groups that Work (and Those that Don't): Creating conditions for effective teamwork*. San Francisco, CA: Jossey-Bass.

Hackman, J.R. and Oldham, G.R. (1976) 'Motivation through the design of work: Test of a theory', *Organizational Behaviour and Human Performance*, vol. 16, pp. 250–79.

Hackman, J.R. and Oldham, G.R. (1980) *Work Redesign*. Reading, MA: Addison-Wesley.

Haddock, G. and Zanna, M.P. (2000) 'Cognition, affect, and the prediction of social attitudes' in Stroebe, W. and Hewstone, M. (eds) *European Review of Social Psychology*, vol. 10. Chichester: John Wiley.

Hakim, C. (2002) 'Lifestyle preferences as determinants of women's differentiated labour market careers', *Work and Occupations*, vol. 29, pp. 428–59.

Hale, A.R. and Glendon, A.I. (1987) *Individual Behavior in the Control of Danger*. Amsterdam: Elsevier.

Hall, D.T. (1986) 'Breaking career routines: Midcareer choice and identity development' in Hall, D.T. (ed.) *Career Development in Organizations*. London: Jossey-Bass.

Halvor Teigen, K. (1986) 'Old truths or fresh insights? A study of students' evaluations of proverbs', *British Journal of Social Psychology*, vol. 25, pp. 43–9.

Hammer, M. and Champy, J. (1993) *Re-engineering the Corporation*. London: Nicolas Brealey.

Hamner, W.C. (1974) 'Effects of bargaining strategy and pressure to reach agreement in a stalemated negotiation', *Journal of Personality and Social Psychology*, vol. 30, pp. 458–67.

Handy, C. (1979) *Gods of Management*. London: Pan.

Handy, C. (1986) *Understanding Organizations*. Harmondsworth: Penguin.

Handy, C. (1989) *The Age of Unreason*. London: Arrow.

Handy, C. (1994) *The Empty Raincoat*. London: Hutchinson.

Hanisch, K.A. (1994) 'Reasons people retire and their relations to attitudinal and behavioural correlates in retirement', *Journal of Vocational Behavior*, vol. 45, pp. 1–16.

Hanson, P. (1993) 'Made in Britain: The true state of manufacturing industry'. Paper presented at the Institution of Mechanical Engineers' Conference on Performance Measurement and Benchmarking, Birmingham, June.

Harley, B. (2001) 'Team membership and the experience of work in Britain: An analysis of the WERS98 data', *Work, Employment and Society* vol. 15(4), pp. 721–42.

Harmon, L.W., Hansen, J.C., Borgen, F.H. and Hammer, A.L. (1994) *Strong Interest Inventory: Applications and technical guide*. Stanford, CA: Stanford University Press.

Harris, C., Daniels, K. and Briner, R. (2003) 'A daily diary study of goals and affective well-being at work', *Journal of Occupational and Organizational Psychology*, vol. 76, pp. 401–10.

Harris, P.R. (1985) *Management in Transition*. San Francisco, CA: Jossey-Bass.

Harris-Bowlsbey, J. and Sampson, J.P. (2001) 'Computer-based career planning systems: Dreams and realities', *Career Development Quarterly*, vol. 49, pp. 250–60.

Harrison, R. (1972) 'How to describe your organization', *Harvard Business Review*, vol. 50, September–October.

Harrison, R. (1997) *Employee Development*. London: Chartered Institute of Personnel and Development.

Hart, P.M. and Cooper, C.L. (2001) 'Occupational stress: Toward a more integrated framework' in Anderson, N., Ones, D.S., Sinangil, H.K. and Viswesvaran, C. (eds) *Handbook of Work, Industrial and Organizational Psychology*, vol. 2. London: Sage.

Hartley, J.F. (1992) 'The psychology of employee relations' in Cooper, C.L. and Robertson, I.T. (eds) *International Review of Industrial and Organizational Psychology*, vol. 7. Chichester: John Wiley.

Hartshorn, D. (2000) 'Reinforcing the unsafe worker', *Occupational Hazards*, vol. 62(10), pp. 125–8.

Harvey, M. (1998) 'Dual-career couples during international relocation: The trailing spouse', *International Journal of Human Resource Management*, vol. 9, pp. 309–31.

Haslam, S.A., Powell, C. and Turner, J.C. (2000) 'Social identity, self-categorisation, and work motivation: Rethinking the contribution of the group to positive and sustainable organisational outcomes', *Applied Psychology: An International Review*, vol. 49, pp. 319–39.

Hass, R.G. (1975) 'Persuasion or moderation? Two experiments on anticipatory belief change', *Journal of Personality and Social Psychology*, vol. 31, pp. 1155–62.

Hassard, J. and Sharifi, S. (1989) 'Corporate culture and strategic change', *Journal of General Management*, vol. 15(2), pp. 4–19.

Hatch, M.J. (1997) *Organization Theory: Modern, symbolic and postmodern perspectives*. Oxford: Oxford University Press.

Hater, J. and Bass, B.M. (1988) 'Superiors' evaluations and subordinates' perceptions of transformational and transactional leadership', *Journal of Applied Psychology*, vol. 73, pp. 695–702.

Hay, D. and Oken, D. (1972) 'The psychological stresses of intensive care nursing', *Psychosomatic Medicine*, vol. 34, pp. 109–18.

Haynes, R.S., Pine, R.C. and Fitch, H.G. (1982) 'Reducing accident rates with organizational behavior modification', *Academy of Management Journal*, vol. 25, pp. 407–16.

Health and Safety Executive (1999). *Initial Advice Regarding Call Centre Working Practices.* Sheffield: HSE.

Heller, F. (1970) 'Group feed-back analysis as a change agent', *Human Relations*, vol. 23(4), pp. 319–33.

Heller, F. (1989) 'On humanising technology', *Applied Psychology: An International Review*, vol. 38, pp. 15–28.

Heller, F.A. and Misumi, J. (1987) 'Decision making' in Bass, B., Drenth, P. and Weissenberg, P. (eds) *Advances in Organizational Psychology*. London: Sage.

Heller, F.A., Drenth, P., Koopman, P. and Rus, V. (1988) *Decisions in Organizations: A three-country comparative study.* London: Sage.

Hellervik, L.W., Hazucha, F. and Schneider, R.J. (1992) 'Behavior change: Models, methods, and a review of evidence' in Dunnette, M.D. and Hough, L.M. (eds) *Handbook of Industrial and Organizational Psychology*, pp. 823–95. Palo Alto, CA: Consulting Psychologists Press.

Hendey, N. and Pascall, G. (2001) *Disability and Transition in Adulthood: Achieving independent living.* London: Pavilion Publishing.

Hendry, C. (1996) 'Understanding and creating whole organizational change through learning theory', *Human Relations*, vol. 48, pp. 621–41.

Hermelin, E. and Robertson, I.T. (2001) 'A critique and standardization of meta-analytic validity coefficients in personnel selection', *Journal of Occupational and Organizational Psychology*, vol. 74, pp. 153–77.

Herriot, P. (1989a) 'Attribution theory and interview decisions' in Eder, R.W. and Ferris, G.R. (eds) *The Employment Interview: Theory, research and practice*. London: Sage.

Herriot, P. (1989b) 'Selection as a social process' in Smith, M. and Robertson, I. (eds) *Advances in Selection and Assessment*. Chichester: John Wiley.

Herriot, P. and Pemberton, C. (1995) *New Deals*. Chichester: John Wiley.

Hersey, P. and Blanchard, K. (1982) *Management of Organizational Behavior*, 4th edition. Englewood Cliffs, NJ: Prentice Hall.

Herzberg, F. (1966) *Work and the Nature of Man*. Cleveland, OH: World Publishing.

Hewstone, M., Ruibin, M. and Willis, H. (2002) 'Intergroup bias', *Annual Review of Psychology*, vol. 53, pp. 575–604.

Highhouse, S. (1999) 'The brief history of personnel counseling in industrial–organizational psychology', *Journal of Vocational Behavior*, vol. 55, pp. 318–36.

Hill, G.W. (1982) 'Group versus individual performance: Are N+1 heads better than one?', *Psychological Bulletin*, vol. 91, pp. 517–39.

Hilton, J.L. and Von Hippel, W. (1996) 'Stereotypes', *Annual Review of Psychology*, vol. 47, pp. 237–71.

Hinkle, L.E. (1973) 'The concept of stress in the biological social sciences', *Stress Medicine*, vol. 1, pp. 31–48.

Hirsch, P.M. and Shanley, M. (1996) 'The rhetoric of boundaryless – or, how the newly empowered managerial class bought into its own marginalisation' in Arthur, M.B. and Rousseau, D.M. (eds) *The Boundaryless Career: A new employment principle for a new organisational era*. Oxford: Oxford University Press.

Hirsh, W. and Jackson, C. (1998) *Planning Your Own Career in a Week*, 2nd edition. Corby: Institute of Management.

Hirsh, W., Jackson, C. and Jackson, C. (1995) *Careers in Organizations: Issues for the future*, IES report 287. Brighton: Institute for Employment Studies.

Hodgkinson, G.P. (2003) 'The interface of cognitive and industrial, work and organizational psychology', *Journal of Occupational and Organizational Psychology*, vol. 76, pp. 1–25.

Hodgkinson, G.P., Bown, N.J., Maule, A.J., Glaister, K.W. and Pearman, A.D. (1999) 'Breaking the Frame: An analysis of strategic cognition and decision-making under uncertainty', *Strategic Management Journal*, vol. 20(10), pp. 977–85.

Hoel, H., Rayner, C. and Cooper, C.L. (1999) 'Workplace bullying' in Cooper, C.L. and Robertson, I.T. (eds) *International Review of Industrial and Organizational Psychology*, vol. 14. Chichester: John Wiley.

Hoffman, A.J. and Scott, L.D. (2003) 'Role stress and career satisfaction among registered nurses by work shift patterns', *Journal of Nursing Administration*, vol. 33, pp. 337–42.

Hoffman, L.R. and Maier, N.R.F. (1961) 'Quality and acceptance of problem solutions by members of homogeneous and heterogeneous groups', *Journal of Abnormal and Social Psychology*, vol. 62, pp. 401–7.

Hofstede, G (1980). *Culture's Consequences: International differences in work-related values.* London: Sage.

Hofstede, G. (1990) 'The cultural relativity of organizational practices and theories' in Wilson, D.C. and Rosenfeld, R.H. (eds) *Managing Organizations: Text, readings and cases.* London: McGraw-Hill.

Hofstede, G. (2001) *Culture's Consequences*, 2nd edition. London: Sage.

Hogan, P.M. (1983) 'A socioanalytic theory of personality' in Page, M.M. (ed.) *Nebraska Symposium on Motivation 1982. Personality: Current theory and research*, pp. 55–89. Lincoln, NE: Univ. of Nebraska Press.

Holland, J.L. (1997) *Making Vocational Choices: A theory of vocational personalities and work environment*, 3rd edition. Odessa, FL: Psychological Assessment Resources Inc.

Holland, J.L. (1998) *The Self-Directed Search*, 4th edition. Odessa: Psychological Assessment Resources Inc.

Hollenbeck, J.R., Williams, C.R. and Klein, H.J. (1989) 'An empirical examination of the antecedents of commitment to difficult goals', *Journal of Applied Psychology*, vol. 74, pp. 18–23.

Hollingshead, A.B. and McGrath, J.E. (1995) 'Computer-assisted groups: A critical review of the empirical research' in Guzzo, R.A. and Salas, E. (eds) *Team Effectiveness and Decision-making in Organizations.* San Francisco, CA: Jossey-Bass.

Holman, D. (2003) 'Call centres' in Holman, D., Wall, T.D., Clegg, C.W., Sparrow, P. and Howard, A. (eds) *The New Workplace.* Chichester: John Wiley.

Holman, D., Chissick, C. and Totterdell, P. (2002) 'The effects of performance monitoring and emotional labour on well-being in call centres', *Motivation and Emotion*, vol. 26, pp. 57–81.

Hom, P.W., Griffeth, R.W., Palich, L.E. and Bracker, J.S. (1999) 'Revisiting met expectations as a reason why realistic job previews work', *Personnel Psychology*, vol. 52, pp. 97–112.

Hopson, B. and Scally, M. (2000) *Build Your Own Rainbow: A workbook for career and life management.* London: Management Books.

Hough, L.M. (1992) 'The "Big Five" personality variables-construct, confusion: Description versus prediction', *Human Performance*, vol. 5, pp. 139–55.

Hough, L.M. and Furnham, A. (2003) 'Use of personality variables in work settings' in Borman, W.C., Ilgen, D.R., Klimoski, R. J. and Weiner, I.B. (eds) *Handbook of Psychology*, pp. 131–69. Hoboken, NJ: John Wiley.

Hough, L.M. and Ones, D.S. (2001) 'The structure, measurement, validity and use of personality variables in industrial, work, and organizational psychology' in Anderson, N., Ones, D.S., Sinangil, H.K. and Viswesvaran, C. (eds) *Handbook of Industrial, Work and Organizational Psychology*, vol. 1. London: Sage.

Hough, L.M. and Oswald, F.L. (2000) 'Personnel selection: Looking forward to the future – remembering the past', *Annual Review of Psychology*, vol. 51, pp. 631–64.

House, R.J. and Baetz, M.L. (1979) 'Leadership: Some empirical generalizations and new research directions' in Staw, B.M. (ed.) *Research in Organizational Behavior*, vol. 1. Greenwich, CT: JAI Press.

House, R.J., Spangler, W.D. and Woycke, J. (1991) 'Personality and charisma in the US presidency: A psychological theory of leader effectiveness', *Administrative Science Quarterly*, vol. 36, pp. 364–96.

Hovland, C. and Weiss, W. (1951) 'The influence of source credibility on communication effectiveness', *Public Opinion Quarterly*, vol. 15, pp. 635–50.

Hovland, C., Lumsdaine, A. and Sheffield, F. (1949) *Experiments on Mass Communication*. Princeton, NJ: Princeton University Press.

Howard, A. (1997) 'A reassessment of assessment centers: Challenges for the 21st century', *Journal of Social Behaviour and Personality*, vol. 12, pp. 13–52.

Howard, A. and Bray, D.W. (1988) *Managerial Lives in Transition*. New York: Guilford Press.

Huffcutt, A.I. and Roth, P.L. (1998) 'Racial group differences in employment interview evaluations', *Journal of Applied Psychology*, vol. 83, pp. 179–89.

Huffcutt, A.I., Conway, J.M., Roth, P.L. and Stone, N.J. (2001) 'Identification and meta–analytic assessment of psychological constructs measured in employment interviews', *Journal of Applied Psychology*, vol. 86, pp. 897–913.

Hughes, J.L. and McNamara, W.J. (1959) *Manual for the Revised Programmer Aptitude Test*. New York: Psychological Corporation.

Hull, C.L. (1952) *A Behavior System*. New Haven, CT: Yale University Press.

Hunt, R.G. (1989) 'On the metaphysics of choice, or when decisions aren't' in Cardy, R.L., Puffer, S.M. and Newman, J.M. (eds) *Information Processing and Decision-making in Organizations*. Greenwich, CT: JAI Press.

Hunter, J.E. and Schmidt, F.L. (1990) *Methods of Meta-analysis*. Newbury Park, CA: Sage.

Hurley, R.F., Church, A.H., Burke, W.W. and Van Eynde, D.F. (1992) 'Tension, change and values in OD', *OD Practitioner*, vol. 29, pp. 1–5.

Huseman, R.C., Hatfield, J.D. and Miles, E.W. (1987) 'A new perspective on equity theory: The equity sensitivity construct', *Academy of Management Review*, vol. 12, pp. 222–34.

Iaffaldano, M.T. and Muchinsky, P.M. (1985) 'Job satisfaction and job performance: A meta-analysis', *Psychological Bulletin*, vol. 97, pp. 251–73.

Ibarra, H. (1995) 'Race, opportunity, and diversity of social circles in managerial networks', *Academy of Management Journal*, vol. 18, pp. 673–703.

Igalens, J. and Roussel, P. (1999) 'A study of the relationships between compensation package, work motivation and job satisfaction', *Journal of Organizational Behavior*, vol. 20, pp. 1003–25.

Iles, P. and Mabey, C. (1993) 'Managerial career development programmes: Effectiveness, availability and acceptability', *British Journal of Management*, vol. 4, pp. 103–18.

Industrial Society (1997) *Culture Change: Managing best practice 35*. London: Industrial Society.

Inkson, K. (1995) 'Effects of changing economic conditions on managerial job changes and careers', *British Journal of Management*, vol. 6, pp. 183–94.

Institute of Management (1995) *Finding the Time: A survey of managers' attitudes to using and managing time*. London: Institute of Management.

International Labour Organisation (1998) *World of Work*, No. 23. Geneva, Switzerland: ILO.

Isabella, L.A. (1988) 'The effect of career stage on the meaning of key organizational events', *Journal of Organizational Behavior*, vol. 9, pp. 345–58.

Isen, A.M. (1993) 'Positive affect and decision making' in Lewis, M. and Haviland, J.M. (eds) *Handbook of Emotions*, pp. 261–77. New York: Guilford.

Isenberg, D.J. (1986) 'Group polarization, a critical review and meta-analysis', *Journal of Personality and Social Psychology*, vol. 50, pp. 1141–51.

Ivancevich, J.M. and Matteson, M.T. (1980) *Stress and Work*. Glenview, IL: Scott, Foresman and Co.

Ivancevich, J.M. and Matteson, M.T. (1988) 'Promoting the individual's health and well being' in Cooper, C.L. and Payne, R. (eds) *Causes, Coping and Consequences of Stress at Work*. Chichester: John Wiley.

Ivancevich, J.M., Matteson, M.T. and Richards, E.P. (1985) 'Who's liable for stress on the job?', *Harvard Business Review*, March/April.

Ivancevich, J.M., Matteson, M.T., Freedman, S.M. and Phillips, J.S. (1990) 'Worksite stress management interventions', *American Psychologist*, vol. 45, pp. 252–61.

Jackson, B.J. (2001) *Management Gurus and Management Fashions: A dramatistic enquiry*. London: Routledge.

Jackson, S.E., and Joshi, A. (2001) 'Research on domestic and international diversity in organizations: A merger that works?' in Anderson, N., Ones, D., Sinangil, H. and Viswesvaran, C. (eds) *Handbook of Industrial, Work and Organizational Psychology*, vol. 2. London: Sage.

Jackson, S.E., Brett, J.F., Sessa, V.I., Cooper, D.M., Julin, J.A. and Peyronnin, K. (1991) 'Some differences make a difference: Individual dissimilarity and group heterogeneity as correlates of recruitment, promotions, and turnover', *Journal of Applied Psychology*, vol. 76, pp. 675–89.

Jacoby, S.M. (1999) 'Are career jobs headed for extinction?', *California Management Review*, vol. 42, pp. 123–45.

Jahoda, M. (1979) 'The impact of unemployment in the 1930s and the 1970s', *Bulletin of the British Psychological Society*, vol. 32, pp. 309–14.

Janis, I.L. (1972) *Victims of Groupthink*. Boston, MA: Houghton Mifflin.

Janis, I.L. (1982a) *Groupthink*. Boston, MA: Houghton Mifflin.

Janis, I.L. (1982b) 'Counteracting the adverse effects of concurrence – seeking in policy planning groups: Theory and research perspectives' in Brandstatter, H., Davis, J.H. and Stocker-Kreichgauer, G. (eds) *Group Decision Making*. London: Academic Press.

Janis, I. and Feshbach, S. (1953) 'Effects of fear arousing communications', *Journal of Abnormal and Social Psychology*, vol. 48, pp. 78–92.

Janis, I.L. and Mann, L. (1977) *Decision-making: A psychological analysis of conflict, choice and commitment*. New York: Free Press.

Janz, J.T. (1989) 'The patterned behaviour description interview: The best prophet of the future is the past' in Eder, R.W. and Ferris, G.R. (eds) *The Employment Interview: Theory, research and practice*, pp. 158–68. London: Sage.

Jarvis, W.B.G. and Petty, R.E. (1996) 'The need to evaluate', *Journal of Personal and Social Psychology*, vol. 70, pp. 172–94.

Jehn, K.A., Northcraft, G.B. and Neale, M.A. (1999) 'Why differences make a difference: A field study of diversity, conflict, and performance of workgroups', *Administrative Science Quarterly*, vol. 44, pp. 741–63.

Jenkins, G.D., Mitra, A., Gupta, N. and Shaw, J.D. (1998) 'Are financial incentives related to performance? A meta-analytic review of empirical research', *Journal of Applied Psychology*, vol. 83, pp. 777–87.

Jenkinson, J.C. (1997) *Mainstream or Special? Educating students with disabilities*. London: Routledge.

Jensen, A.R. (1992) 'Commentary: Vehicles of g', *Psychological Science*, vol. 3, pp. 275–8.

Jepson, C. and Chaiken, S. (1990) 'Chronic issue-specific fear inhibits systematic processing of persuasive communications', *Journal of Social Behaviour and Personality*, vol. 5, pp. 61–84.

Johns, G. (1993) 'Constraints on the adoption of psychology-based personnel practices: Lessons from organizational innovation', *Personnel Psychology*, vol. 46, pp. 596–602.

Johns, G. (2001) 'In praise of context', *Journal of Organizational Behavior*, vol. 22, pp. 31–42.

Johnson, G. (1993) 'Processes of managing strategic change' in Mabey, C. and Mayon-White, B. (eds) *Managing Change,* 2nd edition. London: Open University/Paul Chapman Publishing.

Johnson, P. and Cassell, C. (2001) 'Epistemology and work psychology: New agendas', *Journal of Occupational and Organizational Psychology*, vol. 74, pp. 125–43.

Judd, C.M., McClelland, G.H. and Culhane, S.E. (1995) 'Data analysis: Continuing issues in the everyday analysis of psychological data', *Annual Review of Psychology*, vol. 46, pp. 433–65.

Judge, T.A. and Bono, J.E. (2000) 'Five-factor model of personality and transformational leadership', *Journal of Applied Psychology*, vol. 85(5), pp. 751–65.

Judge, T.A. and Hulin, C.L. (1993) 'Job satisfaction as a reflection of disposition: A multiple source causal analysis', *Organizational Behavior and Human Decision Processes*, vol. 56, pp. 388–421.

Judge, T.A., Cable, D.M., Boudreau, J.W. and Bretz, R.D. (1995) 'An empirical investigation of the predictors of career success', *Personnel Psychology*, vol. 48, pp. 485–519.

Judge, T.A., Thoreson, C.J., Bono, J.E. and Patton, G.K. (2001) 'The job satisfaction – job performance relationship: A qualitative and quantitative review', *Psychological Bulletin*, vol. 127, pp. 376–407.

Judiesch, M.K. and Lyness, K.S. (1999) 'Left behind? The impact of leaves of absence on managers' career success', *Academy of Management Journal*, vol. 42, pp. 641–51.

Jung, C.G. (1933) *Psychological Types*. New York: Harcourt, Brace and World.

Juran, J.M. (1988) *Quality Control Handbook*. New York: McGraw-Hill.

Kahneman, D. (1995) 'Varieties of counterfactual thinking' in Roese, N.J. and Olson, J.M. (eds) *What Might Have Been: The social psychology of counterfactual thinking*, pp. 375–96. Mahwah, NJ: Lawrence Erlbaum Associates.

Kahneman, D. and Tversky, A. (1979) 'Prospect theory: An analysis of decisions under risk', *Econometrica*, vol. 47, pp. 263–91.

Kahneman, D. and Tversky, A. (1981) 'The framing of decisions and the psychology of choice', *Science*, vol. 211, pp. 453–8.

Kahneman, D. and Tversky, A. (1984) 'Choices, values and frames', *American Psychologist*, vol. 39, pp. 341–50.

Kam, S., Hui, C. and Law, C. (1999) 'Organizational citizenship behaviour: Comparing perspectives of supervisors and subordinates across four international samples', *Journal of Applied Psychology*, vol. 84, pp. 594–601.

Kandola, B. and Fullerton, J. (1994) *Managing the Mosaic: Diversity in action*. London: Institute for Personnel and Development.

Kandola, R. (1995) 'Managing diversity: New broom or old hat?' in Cooper, C.L. and Robertson, I.T. (eds) *International Review of Industrial and Organizational Psychology*, vol. 10, pp. 131–67. Chichester: John Wiley.

Kanfer, R. (1992) 'Work motivation: New directions in theory and research' in Robertson, I.T. and Cooper, C.L. (eds) *International Review of Industrial and Organizational Psychology*, vol. 7. Chichester: John Wiley.

Kanfer, R. and Ackerman, P.L. (1989) 'Motivation and cognitive abilities: An integrative/aptitude–treatment interaction approach to skill acquisition', *Journal of Applied Psychology*, vol. 74, pp. 657–90.

Kanfer, R. and Ackerman, P.L. (2000) 'Individual differences in work motivation: Further explorations of a trait framework', *Applied Psychology: An International Review*, vol. 49, pp. 470–482.

Kanfer, R. and Ackerman, P.L. (2002) 'Non-ability influences on volition during skill training'. Paper presented as part of the symposium: New directions in research on motivational traits. Society for Industrial and Organizational Psychology 17th Annual Conference, Toronto.

Kanfer, R. and Heggestad, E.D. (1997) 'Motivational traits and skills: A person-centered approach to work motivation' in Cummings, L.L. and Staw, B.M. (eds) *Research in Organizational Behaviour*, vol. 19, pp. 1–56. Greenwich, C.T.: JAI Press.

Kanfer, R., Ackerman, P.L., Murtha, T.C. and Dugdale, B. (1994) 'Goal-setting, conditions of practice, and task performance: A resource allocation perspective', *Journal of Applied Psychology*, vol. 79, pp. 826–35.

Kanter, R.M. (1977) *Men and Women of the Corporation*. New York: Basic Books.

Kanter, R.M. (1989) *When Giants Learn to Dance: Mastering the challenges of strategy, management, and careers in the 1990s.* London: Unwin.

Kanter, R.M. (1997) *World Class: Thriving locally in the global economy.* New York: Simon & Schuster.

Kanter, R.M., Stein, B.A. and Jick, T.D. (1992) *The Challenge of Organizational Change: How companies experience it and leaders guide it.* New York: Free Press.

Karan, B.S. and Kopelman, R.E. (1987) 'The effects of objective feedback on vehicular and industrial accidents: a field experiment using outcome feedback', *Journal of Organizational Behavior Management*, vol. 8, pp. 45–56.

Karasek, R. (1989) 'Control in the workplace and its health related aspects' in Sauter, S.L., Hurrell, J.J. and Cooper, C.L. (eds) *Job Control and Worker Health.* Chichester: John Wiley.

Kazdin, A.E. (1980) *Behavior Modification in Applied Settings*, rev. edn. Homewood, IL: Dorsey Press.

Kearney, A.T. (1989) *Computer Integrated Manufacturing: Competitive advantage or technological dead end?* London: Kearney.

Kearney, A.T. (1992) *Total Quality: Time to take off the rose-tinted spectacles.* Kempston: IFS.

Keller, T. and Dansereau, F. (1995) 'Leadership and empowerment: A social exchange perspective', *Human Relations*, vol. 48, pp. 127–46.

Kelly, C. and Kelly, J.E. (1994) 'Who gets involved in collective action? Social psychological determinants of individual participation in trade unions', *Human Relations*, vol. 47, pp. 63–88.

Kelly, G.A. (1951) *The Psychology of Personal Constructs*, vols 1 and 2. New York: Norton.

Kelly, G.A. (1955) *The Psychology of Personal Constructs.* New York: Norton.

Kelly, J.E. (1993) 'Does job redesign theory explain job re-design outcomes?', *Human Relations*, vol. 45, pp. 753–74.

Kelly, J.E. (1998) *Rethinking Industrial Relations.* London: Routledge.

Kelly, J.E. and Kelly, C. (1991) '"Them and us": Social psychology and the "new employee relations"', *British Journal of Employee Relations*, vol. 29, pp. 25–48.

Kelly, M. and Cooper, C.L. (1981) 'Stress among blue collar workers', *Employee Relations*, vol. 3, pp. 6–9.

Kemp, N.J., Wall, T.D., Clegg, C.W. and Cordery, J.L. (1983) 'Autonomous work groups in a greenfield site: A comparative study', *Journal of Occupational Psychology*, vol. 56, pp. 271–88.

Kerr, N.L. and Bruun, S.E. (1983) 'Dispensability of member effort and group motivation losses: Free-rider effects', *Journal of Personality and Social Psychology*, vol. 44, pp. 78–94.

Kerr, S. and Jermier, J.M. (1978) 'Substitutes for leadership: Their meaning and measurement', *Organizational Behavior and Human Performance*, vol. 22, pp. 375–403.

Kiesler, C.A. (1971) *The Psychology of Commitment.* New York: Academic Press.

King, N. (1998) 'Template analysis' in Symon, G. and Cassell, C. (eds) *Qualitative Methods and Analysis in Organizational Research: A practical guide.* London: Sage.

King, N. (1992) 'Modelling the innovation process: An empirical comparison of approaches', *Journal of Occupational and Organizational Psychology*, vol. 65, pp. 89–100.

Kinicki, A.J., Prussia, G.E. and McKee Ryan, F.M. (2000) 'A panel study of coping with involuntary job loss', *Academy of Management Journal,* vol. 43, pp 90–100.

Kirkpatrick, D.L. (1967) 'Evaluation of training' in Craig, R.L. and Bittel, L.R. (eds) *Training and Development Handbook*. New York: McGraw-Hill.

Klein, K.J., Wesson, M.J., Hollenbeck, J.R. and Alge, B.J. (1999) 'Goal commitment and goal-setting process: Conceptual clarification and empirical synthesis', *Journal of Applied Psychology*, vol. 84, pp. 885–96.

Klemp, G.O. and McClelland, D.C. (1986) 'What characterizes intelligent functioning among senior managers' in Sternberg, R.J. and Wagner, R.K. (eds) *Practical Intelligence*. Cambridge: Cambridge University Press.

Klimoski, R.J. and Brickner, M. (1987) 'Why do assessment centers work? The puzzle of assessment center validity', *Personnel Psychology*, vol. 40, pp. 243–60.

Klimoski, R.J. and Donahue, L.M. (2001) 'Person perception in organizations: An overview of the field' in London, M. (ed.) *How People Evaluate Others in Organizations*, pp. 5–44. London: LEA.

Klimoski, R.J. and Inks, L. (1990) 'Accountability forces in performance appraisal', *Organizational Behavior and Human Decision Processes*, vol. 45, pp. 194–208.

Kline, P. (1999) *Handbook of Psychological Testing*. London: Sage Publications.

Kline, P. and Barrett, P. (1983) 'The factors in personality questionnaires among normal subjects', *Advances in Behavioral Research and Therapy*, vol. 5, pp. 141–202.

Kluger, A.N. and DeNisi, A. (1996) 'The effects of feedback interventions on performance: A historical review, a meta-analysis, and a preliminary feedback intervention theory', *Psychological Bulletin*, vol. 119, pp. 254–84.

Kluger, A. and Tikochinsky, J. (2001) 'The error of accepting the "theoretical" null hypothesis: The rise, fall and resurrection of commonsense hypotheses in psychology', *Psychological Bulletin*, vol. 127, pp. 408–23.

Komaki, J. and Jensen, M. (1986) 'Within group designs: An alternative to traditional control-group designs' in Cataldo, M.F. and Coates, T.J. (eds) *Health and Industry: A behavioral medicine perspective*. New York: John Wiley.

Komaki, J., Barwick, K. and Scott, L. (1978) 'A behavioural approach to occupational safety: Pinpointing and reinforcing safe performance in a food manufacturing plant', *Journal of Applied Psychology*, vol. 63, pp. 434–45.

Komaki, J.L., Collins, R.L. and Temlock, S. (1987) 'An alternative performance measurement approach: Applied operant measurement in the service sector', *Applied Psychology: An International Review*, vol. 38, pp. 71–86.

Komaki, J.L., Desseles, M.L. and Bownam, E.D. (1989) 'Definitely not a breeze: Extending an operant model to effective supervision to teams', *Journal of Applied Psychology*, vol. 74, pp. 522–9.

Kornhauser, A. (1965) *Mental Health of the Industrial Worker*. Chichester: John Wiley.

Kossek, E.E. and Ozeki, C. (1998) 'Work–family conflict policies, and the job–life satisfaction relationship: A review and directions for organizational behaviour–human resources research', *Journal of Applied Psychology*, vol. 83, pp. 139–49.

Kotter, J.P. (1996) *Leading Change*. Boston, MA: Harvard Business School Press.

Kraiger, K., Ford, J. and Salas, E. (1993) 'Application of cognitive skill based and affective theories of learning outcomes to new methods of training evaluation', *Journal of Applied Psychology*, vol. 78, pp. 311–28.

Kram, K.E. (1985) *Mentoring at Work: Developmental relationships in organizational life*. Glenview, IL: Scott Foresman.

Krech, D., Crutchfield, R.S. and Ballachey, E.L. (1962) *Individual in Society*. New York: McGraw-Hill.

Kristof, A.L. (1996) 'Person–organization fit: An integrative review of its conceptualisations, measurement, and implications', *Personnel Psychology*, vol. 49, pp. 1–48.

Krueger, J. (1991) 'Accentuation effects and illusory change in exemplar based category learning', *European Journal of Social Psychology*, vol. 21, pp. 37–48.

Krumboltz, J.D. and Worthington, R.L. (1999) 'The school-to-work transition from a learning theory perspective', *The Career Development Quarterly*, vol. 47, pp. 312–25.

Kuhl, J. (1992) 'A theory of self-regulation: Action versus state orientation, self-discrimination and some applications', *Applied Psychology: An International Review*, vol. 41, pp. 97–129.

Labour Force Survey (1998) *Quarterly Survey*, Spring. London: HMSO.

Labour Force Survey (2001) *Quarterly Survey*, Spring. London: HMSO.

Lamm, H. and Trommsdorf, G. (1973) 'Group versus individual performance on tasks requiring ideational proficiency (brainstorming)', *European Journal of Social Psychology*, vol. 3, pp. 361–87.

Lamond, D., Daniels, K. and Standen, P. (2003) 'Teleworking and virtual organisations: The human impact' in Holman, D., Wall, T.D., Clegg, C.W., Sparrow, P. and Howard, A. (eds) *The New Workplace*. Chichester: John Wiley.

Landy, F.J. (1985) *The Psychology of Work Behavior*, 3rd edition. Homewood, IL: Dorsey Press.

Landy, F.J. (1989) *Psychology of Work Behavior*, 4th edition. Homewood, IL: Brooks/Cole Publishing Co.

Lantz, A. (1998) 'Heavy users of electronic mail', *International Journal of Human Computer Interaction*, vol. 10, pp. 361–79.

Larson, C.E. and LaFasto, F.M.J. (1989) *Teamwork: What must go right/what can go wrong*. London: Sage.

Larwood, L. and Gutek, B.A. (1987) 'Working toward a theory of women's career development' in Gutek, B.A. and Larwood, L. (eds) *Women's Career Development*. Beverly Hills, CA: Sage.

Latane, B., Williams, K. and Harkins, S. (1979) 'Many hands make light the work: The causes and consequences of social loafing', *Journal of Personality and Social Psychology*, vol. 37, pp. 822–32.

Latham, G.P. and Locke, E.A. (1991) 'Self-regulation through goal-setting', *Organizational Behaviour and Human Decision Processes*, vol. 50, pp. 212–47.

Latham, G.P., Erez, M. and Locke, E.A. (1988) 'Resolving scientific disputes by the joint design of crucial experiments by the antagonists: Application to the Erez–Latham dispute regarding participation in goal setting', *Journal of Applied Psychology*, vol. 73, pp. 753–72.

Latham, G.P., Skarlicki, D., Irvine, D. and Siegal, J.P. (1993) 'The increasing importance of performance appraisals to employee effectiveness in organizational settings in North America' in Cooper, C.L. and Robertson, I.T. (eds) *International Review of Industrial and Organizational Psychology*, vol. 8. Chichester: John Wiley.

Lau, D.C. and Murnighan, J.K. (1998) 'Demographic diversity and faultlines: The compositional dynamics of organizational groups', *Academy of Management Review*, vol. 23, pp. 325–40.

Lavine, H. and Snyder, M. (1996) 'Cognitive processing and the functional matching effect in persuasion: the mediating role of subjective perceptions of message quality', *Journal of Experimental Social Psychology*, vol. 32, pp. 580–604.

Lawson, M.B. and Angle, H. (1994) 'When organizational relocation means family relocation: An emerging issue for strategic human resource management', *Human Resource Management*, vol. 33, pp. 33–54.

Lazarus, R.S. (1966) *Psychological Stress and Coping Process*. New York: McGraw-Hill.

Leclerc, G., Lefrançois, R., Dubé, M., Hébert, R., and Gaulin, P. (1998) 'The self-actualisation concept: A contest validation', *Journal of Social Behaviour and Personality*, vol. 13, pp. 69–84.

Lee, C., Ashford, S.J. and Jamieson, L.F. (1993) 'The effects of Type A behaviour dimensions and optimism on coping strategy, health and performance', *Journal of Organizational Behavior*, vol. 14, pp. 143–57.

Lee, K., Carswell, J.J. and Allen, N.J. (2000) 'A meta-analytic review of occupational commitment: Relations with person and work-related variables', *Journal of Applied Psychology*, vol. 85, pp. 799–811.

Lefkowitz, J. (1994) 'Sex-related differences in job attitudes and dispositional variables: Now you see them . . .', *Academy of Management Journal*, vol. 37, pp. 323–49.

Legge, K. (2003) 'Any nearer a "better" approach? A critical view' in Holman, D., Wall, T.D., Clegg, C.W., Sparrow, P. and Howard, A. (eds) *The New Workplace*. Chichester: John Wiley.

Lent, R.W., Brown, S.D. and Hackett, G. (1994) 'Toward a unifying social cognitive theory of career and academic interest, choice and performance', *Journal of Vocational Behavior*, vol. 45, pp. 79–122.

Leon, F.R. (1981) 'The role of positive and negative outcomes in the causation of motivational forces', *Journal of Applied Psychology*, vol. 66, pp. 45–53.

Leonard, N.H., Beauvois, L.L. and Scholl, R.W. (1999) 'Work motivation: The incorporation of self-concept-based processes', *Human Relations*, vol. 52, pp. 969–98.

Levinson, D.J. (1986) 'A conception of adult development', *American Psychologist*, vol. 41, pp. 3–13.

Levinson, D.J. with Darrow, C.N., Klein, E.B., Levinson, M.H. and McKee, B. (1978) *Seasons of a Man's Life*. New York: Knopf.

Lewicki, R.J., Weiss, S.E. and Lewin, D. (1992) 'Models of conflict, negotiation and third party intervention: A review and synthesis', *Journal of Organizational Behavior*, vol. 13, pp. 209–52.

Lewin, K. (1945) 'The Research Center for Group Dynamics at Massachusetts Institute of Technology', *Sociometry*, vol. 8, pp. 126–36.

Lewin, K. (1946) 'Action research and minority problems', *Journal of Social Issues*, vol. 2, pp. 34–6.

Lewin, K. (1958) 'Group decisions and social change' in Swanson, G.E., Newcomb, T.M. and Hartley, E.L. (eds) *Readings in Social Psychology*. New York: Holt, Rinehart and Winston.

Lewis, D.J. and Duncan, C.P. (1956) 'Effects of different percentages of money reward on extinction of a lever pulling response', *Journal of Experimental Psychology*, vol. 52, pp. 23–7.

Lewis, K.M. (2000) 'When leaders display emotion: How followers respond to negative emotional expression of male and female leaders', *Journal of Organizational Behavior*, vol. 21, pp. 221–34.

Licht, M.H. (1997) 'Multiple regression and correlation' in Grimm, L.G. and Yarnold, P.R. (eds) *Reading and Understanding Multivariate Statistics*. Washington DC: American Psychological Association.

Lievens, F. (2001) 'Assessors and use of assessment center dimensions: A fresh look at a troubling issue', *Journal of Organizational Behavior*, vol. 22(3), pp. 203–21.

Lievens, F. (2002) 'Trying to understand the different pieces of the construct validity puzzle of assessment centers: An examination of assessor and assessee effects', *Journal of Applied Psychology*, vol. 87, pp. 675–86.

Lievens, F. and Harris, M.M. (2003) 'Research on Internet recruitment and testing: Current status and future directions' in Cooper, C.L. and Robertson, I.T. (eds) *International Review of Industrial and Organizational Psychology*, vol. 18. Chicester: John Wiley.

Lievens, F. and Klimoski, R.J. (2001) 'Understanding the assessment centre process: Where are we now?' in Cooper, C.L. and Robertson, I.T. (eds) *International Review of Industrial and Organizational Psychology*, vol. 16, Chichester: Wiley.

Linehan, M. and Walsh, J. (2001) 'Key issues in the senior female international career move: A qualitative study in a European context', *British Journal of Management*, vol. 12, pp. 85–95.

Lippitt, R., Watson, J. and Westley, B. (1958) *The Dynamics of Planned Change*. New York: Harcourt, Brace and World.

Lobban, R.K., Husted, J. and Farewell, V.T. (1998) 'A comparison on the effect of job demand, decision latitude, role and supervisory style on self-reported job satisfaction', *Work and Stress*, vol. 12, pp. 337–50.

Locke, E.A. (1976) 'The nature and causes of job satisfaction' in Dunnette, M.D. (ed.) *Handbook of Industrial and Organizational Psychology*, pp. 1297–349. Chicago, IL: Rand McNally.

Locke, E.A. (1977) 'The myths of behavior modification in organizations', *Academy of Management Review*, vol. 4, pp. 543–53.

Locke, E.A. (1995) 'The micro-analysis of job satisfaction: Comments on Taber and Alliger', *Journal of Organizational Behavior*, vol. 16, pp. 123–5.

Locke, E.A. (2000) 'Motivation, cognition and action: An analysis of studies of task goals and knowledge', *Applied Psychology: An International Review*, vol. 49, pp. 408–29.

Locke, E.A. and Henne, D. (1986) 'Work motivation theories' in Cooper, C.L. and Robertson, I.T. (eds) *International Review of Industrial and Organizational Psychology*. Chichester: John Wiley.

Locke, E.A. and Latham, G.P. (1990) *A Theory of Goal-setting and Task Performance*. Englewood Cliffs, NJ: Prentice Hall.

Locke, E.A., Shaw, K.N., Saari, L.M. and Latham, G.P. (1981) 'Goal setting and task performance 1969–1980', *Psychological Bulletin*, vol. 90, pp. 125–52.

London, M. and Smither, J.W. (1995) 'Can multi-source feedback change perceptions of goal accomplishment, self-evaluations and performance related outcomes? Theory-based applications and directions for research', *Personnel Psychology*, vol. 48, pp. 803–39.

London, M. and Tornow, W.W. (1998) 'Introduction: 360-degree feedback – more than a tool!' in London, M. and Tornow, W.W. (eds) *Maximizing the Value of 360-degree Feedback*, pp. 1–8. Greensboro, NC: Center for Creative Leadership.

Lowe, K.B., Kroeck, K.G. and Sivasubramaniam, N. (1996) 'Effectiveness correlates of transformational and transactional leadership: A meta-analytic review of the MLQ literature', *Leadership Quarterly*, vol. 7, pp. 385–425.

Luthans, F. and Kreitner, R. (1975) *Organizational Behavior Modification*. Glenview, IL: Scott-Foresman.

Luthans, F. and Martinko, M. (1987) 'Behavioral approaches to organizations' in Cooper, C.L. and Robertson, I.T. (eds) *International Review of Industrial and Organizational Psychology*. Chichester: John Wiley.

Luthans, F., Paul, R. and Baker, D. (1981) 'An experimental analysis on salespersons' performance behaviours', *Journal of Applied Psychology*, vol. 66, pp. 314–23.

Lyness, K.S. and Thompson, D.E. (2000) 'Climbing the corporate ladder: Do female and male executives follow the same route?', *Journal of Applied Psychology*, vol. 85(1), pp. 86–101.

Mabe, P.A. and West, S.G. (1982) 'Validity of self-evaluation of ability: A review and meta-analysis', *Journal of Applied Psychology*, vol. 67, pp. 280–96.

Mabey, C. (1986) *Graduates into Industry*. Aldershot: Gower.

Mabey, C. and Mayon-White, B. (1993) *Managing Change*, 2nd edition. London: Open University/Paul Chapman Publishing.

Macy, B.A. and Izumi, H. (1993) 'Organizational change, design, and work innovations: A meta-analysis of 131 North American field studies 1961–1991' in Passmore, W. and Woodman, R. (eds) *Research in Organizational Change and Development*, vol. 7, pp. 235–313. Greenwich, CT: JAI Press.

Maczynski, J. (1997) 'A comparison of leadership style of Polish managers before and after market economy reforms', paper presented at the 'Eighth European Congress of Work and Organizational Psychology', Verona, April.

Maier, N.R.F. and Solem, A.R. (1952) 'The contribution of a discussion leader to the quality of group thinking: The effective use of minority opinions', *Human Relations*, vol. 5, pp. 277–88.

Makin, P.J. and Hoyle, D.J. (1993) 'The Premack principle: Professional engineers', *Leadership and Organization Development Journal*, vol. 14, pp. 16–21.

Makin, P., Cooper, C.L. and Cox, C. (1996) *Organizations and the Psychological Contract*. Leicester: British Psychological Society.

Malone, J.C. and Cruchon, N.M. (2001) 'Radical behaviorism and the rest of psychology: A review/précis of Skinner's *About Behaviorism*', *Behavior and Philosophy*, vol. 29, pp. 31–57.

Marrow, A.J. (1977) *The Practical Theorist: The life and work of Kurt Lewin*. New York: Teachers College Press.

Maslow, A.H. (1943) 'A theory of motivation', *Psychological Review*, vol. 50, pp. 370–96.

Maslow, A.H. (1954) *Motivation and Personality*. New York: Harper and Row.

Mathieu, J.E. and Zajac, D.M. (1990) 'A review and meta-analysis of the antecedents, correlates and consequences of organizational commitment', *Psychological Bulletin*, vol. 108, pp. 171–94.

Matthews, G. and Deary, I.J. (1998) *Personality traits*. New York: Cambridge University Press.

Matthews, G., Zeidner, M. and Roberts, R. (2003a) *Emotional Intelligence: Science and myth*. Cambridge, MA: MIT Press.

Matthews, G., Deary, I.J. and Whiteman, M.C. (2003b). *Personality Traits*, 2nd edition. Cambridge: Cambridge University Press.

Mau, W.C. (1999) 'Effects of computer-assisted career decision making on vocational identity and career exploratory behaviors', *Journal of Career Development*, vol. 25(4), pp. 261–74.

Mau, W.C. (2000) 'Cultural differences in career decision-making styles and self-efficacy', *Journal of Vocational Behavior*, vol. 57, pp. 365–78.

Maurer, S.D., Sue-Chan, C. and Latham, G.P. (1999) 'The situational interview' in Eder, R.W. and Harris, M.M. (eds) *The Employment Interview Handbook*, pp. 159–78. London: Sage.

Mayer, J.D. and Salovey, P. (1997) 'What is emotional intelligence?' in Salovey, P. and Sluyter, D.J. (eds) *Emotional Development and Emotional Intelligence: Educational implications*. New York: Basic Books.

Mayer, J.D., Caruso, D. and Salovey, P. (1999) 'Emotional intelligence meets traditional standards for an intelligence', *Intelligence*, vol. 27, pp. 267–98.

Mayer, J.D., Salovey, P. and Caruso, D.R. (2000) 'Emotional intelligence as zeitgeist, as personality, and as a mental ability' in Bar-On, R. and Parker, J.D.A. (eds) *Handbook of Emotional Intelligence*, pp. 92–117. San Francisco, CA: Jossey-Bass.

Mayer, J.D., Perkins, D., Caruso, D.R. and Salovey, P. (2001) 'Emotional intelligence and giftedness', *Roeper Review*, vol. 23(3), pp. 131–7.

Mayon-White, B. (1993) 'Problem-solving in small groups: Team members as agents of change' in Mabey, C. and Mayon-White, B. (eds) *Managing Change*, 2nd edition. London: Open University/Paul Chapman Publishing.

Maznevski, M.L. (1994) 'Understanding our differences: performance in decision-making groups with diverse members', *Human Relations*, vol. 47(5), pp. 531–52.

McCalman, J. and Paton, R.A. (1992) *Change Management: A guide to effective implementation*. London: Paul Chapman Publishing.

McCann, J.E. and Buckner, M. (1994) 'Redesigning work: Motivations, challenges and practices in 181 companies', *Human Resource Planning*, vol. 17(4), pp. 23–41.

McCarthy, A.M., Schoorman, F.D. and Cooper, A.C. (1993) 'Reinvestment decisions by entrepreneurs: Rational decision-making or escalation of commitment?', *Journal of Business Ventures*, vol. 8, pp. 9–24.

McClelland, D.C. (1961) *The Achieving Society*. Princeton, NJ: Van Nostrand.

McCormick, E.J., Jeanneret, P. and Meacham, R.C. (1972) 'A study of job characteristics and job dimensions as based on the position analysis questionnaires', *Journal of Applied Psychology*, vol. 36, pp. 347–68.

McCrae, R.R. and Costa, P.T. (1990) *Personality in Adulthood*. New York: Guilford Press.

McCrae, R.R. and Costa, P.T. (1997) 'Personality trait structure as a human universal', *American Psychologist*, vol. 52, pp. 509–16.

McFarlin, D.B. and Sweeney, P.D. (1992) 'Distributive and procedural justice as predictors of satisfaction with personal and organizational outcomes', *Academy of Management Journal*, vol. 35, pp. 626–37.

McGinnies, E. (1966) 'Studies in persuasion: Reactions of Japanese students to one sided and two sided communications', *Journal of Social Psychology*, vol. 70, pp. 62–74.

McGrath, J.E. (1984) *Groups: Interaction and performance*. Englewood Cliffs, NJ: Prentice Hall.

McGregor, D. (1960) *The Human Side of Enterprise*. New York: McGraw-Hill.

McGuire, W.J. and Papageorgis, D. (1961) 'The relative efficacy of various types of prior belief–defense in producing immunity against persuasion', *Journal of Abnormal and Social Psychology*, vol. 62, pp. 327–37.

McHugh, M.F. (1991) 'Disabled workers: Psychosocial issues' in Davidson, M.J. and Earnshaw, J. (eds) *Vulnerable Workers*. Chichester: John Wiley.

McKinlay, A. (2000) 'The bearable lightness of control' in Prichard, C., Hull, R., Chummer, M. and Willmott, H. (eds) *Managing Knowledge: Critical investigations of work and learning*. Basingstoke: Macmillan.

McKracken, J.K. (1986) 'Exploitation of FMS technology to achieve strategic objectives'. Paper presented to the 5th International Conference on Flexible Manufacturing Systems, Stratford-upon-Avon.

McLeod, P.L., Baron, R.S., Marti, M.W. and Yoon, K. (1997) 'The eyes have it: Minority influence in face-to-face and computer-mediated group discussion', *Journal of Applied Psychology*, vol. 82, pp. 706–18.

Meek, V.L. (1988) 'Organizational culture: Origins and weaknesses', *Organization Studies*, vol. 9(4), pp. 453–73.

Meindl, J.R. (1992) 'Reinventing leadership: A radical, social psychological approach' in Murnigham, K. (ed.) *Social Psychology in Organizations: Advances in theory and research*. Englewood Cliffs, NJ: Prentice Hall.

Meindl, J.R. (1995) 'The romance of leadership as a follower – centric theory: A social constructionist approach', *Leadership Quarterly*, vol. 6, pp. 329–41.

Meindl, J.R., Ehrlich, S.B. and Dukerich, J.M. (1985) 'The romance of leadership', *Administrative Science Quarterly*, vol. 30, pp. 78–102.

Melhuish, A. (1978) *Executive Health*. London: Business Books.

Mellers, B.A., Schwartz, A. and Cooke, A.D.J. (1998) 'Judgment and decision making', *Annual Review of Psychology*, vol. 49, pp. 447–77.

Mendenhall, M. and Stahl, G. (2000) 'Expatriate training and development: Where do we go from here?' *Human Resource Management*, vol. 39, pp. 251–65.

Mento, A.J., Steel, R.P. and Karren, R.J. (1987) 'A meta-analytic study of the effects of goal setting on task performance: 1966–1984', *Organizational Behavior and Human Decision Processes*, vol. 39, pp. 52–83.

Mento, A.J., Locke, E.A. and Klein, H.J. (1992) 'Relationship of goal level to valence and instrumentality', *Journal of Applied Psychology*, vol. 77, pp. 395–405.

Meyer, J. (2001) 'Action research' in Fulop, N., Allen, P., Clarke, A. and Black, N. (eds) *Studying the Organisation and Delivery of Health Services: Research methods*. London: Routledge.

Meyer, J.P. (1997) 'Organizational commitment' in Cooper, C.L. and Robertson, I.T. (eds) *International Review of Industrial and Organizational Psychology*, vol. 12. Chichester: John Wiley.

Meyer, J.P. and Gellatly, I.R. (1988) 'Perceived performance norm as a mediator in the effect of assigned goal on personal goal and task performance', *Journal of Applied Psychology*, vol. 73, pp. 410–20.

Meyer, J.P., Paunonen, S.V., Gellatly, I.R., Goffin, R.D. and Jackson, D.N. (1989) 'Organizational commitment and job performance: It's the nature of the commitment that counts', *Journal of Applied Psychology*, vol. 74, pp. 152–6.

Meyer, J.P., Allen, N.J. and Smith, C.A. (1993) 'Commitment to organizations and occupations: Extension and test of a three-component conceptualization', *Journal of Applied Psychology*, vol. 78, pp. 538–51.

Micceri, T. (1989) 'The unicorn, the normal curve, and other improbable creatures', *Psychological Bulletin*, vol. 105, pp. 156–66.

Mill, J. (1994) 'No pain, no gain', *Computing*, 3 February, pp. 26–27.

Millar, M.G. and Tesser, A. (1989) 'The effects of affective–cognitive consistency and thought on attitude–behavior relations', *Journal of Experimental Social Psychology*, vol. 25, pp. 189–202.

Miller, D. (1993) 'The architecture of simplicity', *Academy of Management Review*, vol. 18(1), pp. 116–38.

Miller, D. and Friesen, P.H. (1984) *Organizations: A quantum view*. Englewood Cliffs, NJ: Prentice Hall.

Miller, G.A. (1966) *Psychology: The science of mental life*. Harmondsworth: Penguin.

Millward, L. (2000) 'Focus groups' in Breakwell, G., Hammond, S. and Fife-Schaw, C. (eds) *Research Methods in Psychology*, 2nd edition. London: Sage.

Miner, J.B. (1964) *Scoring Guide for the Miner Sentence Completion Scale*. Atlanta, GA: Organizational Measurement Systems Press.

Miner, J.B. (2003) 'The rated importance, scientific validity, and practical usefulness of organizational behaviour theories: A quantitative review', *Academy of Management Learning and Education*, vol. 2, pp. 250–68.

Miner, J.B. and Smith, N.R. (1982) 'Decline and stabilization of managerial motivation over a 20-year period', *Journal of Applied Psychology*, vol. 67, pp. 297–305.

Miner, J.B., Chen, C.C. and Yu, K.C. (1991) 'Theory testing under adverse conditions: Motivation to manage in the People's Republic of China', *Journal of Applied Psychology*, vol. 76, pp. 343–49.

Mintzberg, H. (1983) *Power In and Around Organizations*. Englewood Cliffs, NJ: Prentice Hall.

Mintzberg, H. (1994) *The Rise and Fall of Strategic Planning*. London: Prentice Hall.

Mintzberg, H., Raisinghani, D. and Theoret, A. (1976) 'The structure of "unstructured" decision processes', *Administrative Science Quarterly*, vol. 21, pp. 246–75.

Mirvis, P.H. and Hall., D.T. (1994) 'Psychological success and the boundaryless career', *Journal of Organizational Behavior*, vol. 15(4), pp. 365–80.

Mischel, W. (1968) *Personality Assessment*. New York: John Wiley.

Mitchell, R.J. and Williamson, A.M. (2000) 'Evaluation of an 8 hour versus a 12 hour shift roster on employees at a power station', *Applied Ergonomics*, vol. 31, pp. 83–93.

Mohrman, S.A., Cohen, S.G. and Mohrman, A.M. Jr (1995) *Designing Team-based Organizations: New forms for knowledge work*. San Francisco, CA: Jossey Bass Wiley.

Moorman, R.H. (1991) 'Relationship between organizational justice and organizational citizenship behaviors – do fairness perceptions influence employee citizenship?', *Journal of Applied Psychology*, vol. 76(6), pp. 845–55.

Morgan, G. (1986) *Images of Organizations*. Beverly Hills, CA: Sage.

Morgan, G. (1997) *Images of Organization*, new edition. London: Sage.

Morgeson, F.P. and Campion, M.A. (2002) 'Minimizing trade-offs when redesigning work: Evidence from a longitudinal quasi-experiment', *Personnel Psychology*, vol. 55, pp. 589–612.

Morita, M. (2001) 'Have the seeds of Japanese teamworking taken root abroad?', *New Technology, Work and Employment*, vol. 16(3), pp. 178–90.

Morrison, E.W. (1993) 'Newcomer information-seeking: Exploring types, modes, sources and outcomes', *Academy of Management Journal*, vol. 38, pp. 557–89.

Mortimer, J.T. (2003) *Working and Growing up in America*, Cambridge, MA: Harvard University Press.

Moscovici, S. (1985) 'Social influence and conformity' in Lindzey, G. and Aronson, E. (eds) *The Handbook of Social Psychology*, 3rd edition. New York: Random House.

Moscovici, S. and Mugny, G. (1983) 'Minority influence' in Paulus, P.B. (ed.) *Basic Group Processes*. New York: Springer-Verlag.

Moser, K. and Schuler, H. (1989) 'The nature of psychological measurement' in Herriot, P. (ed.) *Assessment and Selection in Organizations*. Chichester: John Wiley.

Mowday, R., Steers, R. and Porter, L. (1979) 'The measurement of organizational commitment', *Journal of Vocational Behavior*, vol. 14, pp. 224–47.

Mowday, R.T. (1991) 'Equity theory predictions of behaviour in organisations' in Steers, R.M. and Porter, L.W. (eds) *Motivation and Work Behavior*, 5th edition, pp. 111–31. New York: McGraw-Hill.

Muchinsky, P.M. (1986) 'Personnel selection methods' in Cooper, C.L. and Robertson, I.T. (eds) *International Review of Industrial and Organizational Psychology*. Chichester: John Wiley.

Mulilis, J. and Lippa, R. (1990) 'Behavioral change in earthquake preparedness due to negative threat appeals: a test of protection motivation theory', *Journal of Applied Social Psychology*, vol. 20, pp. 619–38.

Mullen, B. and Copper, C. (1994) 'The relation between group cohesiveness and performance: An integration', *Psychological Bulletin*, vol. 115, pp. 210–27.

Murphy, G.C. and Athanasou, J.A. (1999) 'The effect of unemployment on mental health', *Journal of Occupational and Organizational Psychology*, vol. 72, pp. 83–99.

Murphy, K. and Cleveland, J. (1995) *Understanding Performance Appraisal: Social, organisational and goal-based perspectives*. London: Sage.

Murphy, L.R. (1988) 'Workplace interventions for stress reduction and prevention' in Cooper, C.L. and Payne, R. (eds) *Causes, Coping and Consequences of Stress at Work*. Chichester: John Wiley.

Murray, H.J. (1938) *Explorations in Personality*. Oxford: Oxford University Press.

Nadler, D.A. (1988) 'Concepts for the management of organizational change' in Tushman, M'L. and Moore, W.L. (eds) *Readings in the Management of Innovation*. New York: Ballinger.

Nadler, D.A. (1993) 'Concepts for the management of strategic change' in Mabey, C. and Mayon-White, B. (eds) *Managing Change*, 2nd edition. London: Open University/Paul Chapman Publishing.

Nagy, M.S. (2002) 'Using a single-item approach to measure facet job satisfaction', *Journal of Occupational and Organizational Psychology*, 75, pp. 77–86.

Nandram, S.S. and Klandermans, B. (1993) 'Stress experienced by active members of trade unions', *Journal of Organizational Behavior*, vol. 14, pp. 415–32.

Nathan, R. and Hill, L. (1992) *Career Counselling*. London: Sage.

Nelson, D.L. and Burke, R.J. (2000) 'Women, work stress and health' in Davidson, M.J. and Burke, R.J. (eds) *Women in Management*. London: Sage.

Nelson-Jones, R. (2000) *Introduction to Counselling Skills*. London: Sage.

Nemeth, C.J. (1986) 'Differential contributions of majority and minority influence', *Psychological Review*, vol. 93, pp. 23–32.

Nemetz, P.L. and Christensen, S.L. (1996) 'The challenge of cultural diversity: Harnessing adversity of views to understand multiculturalism', *Academy of Management Review*, vol. 21, pp. 434–62.

New, C. (1989) 'The challenge of transformation' in Burnes, B. and Weekes, B. (eds) *AMT: A strategy for success?* London: NEDO.

Ng, K.Y. and Van Dyne, L. (2001) 'Individualism–collectivism as a boundary condition for effectiveness of minority influence in decision making', *Organizational Behavior and Human Decision Processes*, vol. 84(2), pp. 198–225.

Nicholson, N. (1990) 'The transition cycle: Causes, outcomes, processes and forms' in Fisher, S. and Cooper, C.L. (eds) *On the Move: The psychology of change and transition*. Chichester: John Wiley.

Nicholson, N. and West, M.A. (1988) *Managerial Job Change: Men and women in transition*. Cambridge: Cambridge University Press.

NIOSH (1993) *A National Strategy for the Prevention of Psychological Disorders in the Workplace*. Cincinnati, OH: NIOSH.

Nisbett, R. and Wilson, T. (1977) 'Telling more than we know: Verbal reports on mental processes', *Psychological Review*, vol. 84, pp. 231–59.

Nonaka, I. (1988) 'Creating organizational order out of chaos: Self-renewal in Japanese firms', *Harvard Business Review*, November/December, pp. 96–104.

Nygren, T.E., Isen, A.M, Taylor, P.J. and Dulin, J. (1996) 'The influence of positive affect on the decision rule in risk situations: Focus on outcome (and especially avoidance of loss) rather than probability', *Organizational Behavior and Human Decision Processes*, vol. 66, pp. 59–72.

Nystrom, P.C. and Starbuck, W.H. (1984) 'To avoid crises, unlearn', *Organizational Dynamics*, vol. 12(4), pp. 53–65.

Nystedt, L., Sjöberg, A. and Hägglund, G. (1999) 'Discriminant validation of measures of organizational commitment, job involvement, and job satisfaction among Swedish army officers', *Scandinavian Journal of Psychology*, vol. 40, pp. 49–55.

O'Brien, R.M., Dickinson, A.M. and Rosow, M.P. (1982) *Industrial Behavior Modification*. New York: Pergamon Press.

OECD (1999) *Implementing the OECD Job Strategy: Assessing performance and policy*. Paris: OECD.

Offerrmann, L.R. and Gowing, M.K. (1990) 'Organizations of the future', *American Psychologist*, vol. 45, pp. 95–108.

Oliver, M. (1990) *The Politics of Disablement*. London: Macmillan.

Ones, D.S. and Viswesvaran, C. (1998) 'Gender, age, and race differences on overt integrity tests: results across four large-scale job applicant data sets', *Journal of Applied Psychology*, vol. 83(1), pp. 35–42.

Ones, D.S. and Viswesvaran, C. (2003) 'Job-specific applicant pools and national norms for personality scales: implications for range-restriction corrections in validation research', *Journal of Applied Psychology*, vol. 88(3), pp. 570–7.

O'Reilly, C. (1989) 'Corporations, culture and commitment', *California Management Review*, vol. 31, pp. 9–24.

O'Reilly, C.A. and Caldwell, D.F. (1985) 'The impact of normative social influence and cohesiveness on task perceptions and attitudes: A social information-processing approach', *Journal of Occupational Psychology*, vol. 58, pp. 193–206.

Organ, D.W. and Ryan, K. (1995) 'A meta-analytic review of attitudinal and dispositional predictors of organizational citizenship behavior', *Personnel Psychology*, vol. 48, pp. 775–802.

Osborn, A.F. (1957) *Applied Imagination*, rev. edition. New York: Scribner.

Papadakis, V.M. and Barwise, P. (2002) 'How much do CEOs and top management matter in strategic decision-making?', *British Journal of Management*, vol. 13(1), pp. 83–95.

Park, W. (2000) 'A comprehensive empirical investigation of the relationships among variables of the groupthink model', *Journal of Organizational Behavior*, vol. 21, pp. 873–87.

Parker, B. and Chusmir, L.H. (1991) 'Motivation needs and their relationship to life success', *Human Relations*, vol. 44, pp. 1301–12.

Parker, S.K. and Wall, T.D. (1998) *Job and Work Design*. San Francisco, CA: Sage.

Parker, S.K., Wall, T.D. and Cordery, J.L. (2001) 'Future work design research and practice: Towards an elaborated model of work design', *Journal of Occupational and Organizational Psychology*, vol. 74, pp. 413–40.

Parks, J.M. and Kidder, D.L. (1994) '"Till death us do part . . . ": Changing work relationships in the 1990s' in Cooper, C.L. and Rousseau, D.M. (eds) *Trends in Organizational Behaviour*, vol. 1, pp. 111–36. Chichester: John Wiley.

Parsons, F. (1909) *Choosing a Vocation*. Boston, MA: Houghton Mifflin.

Patrick, J. (1992) *Training: Research and practice*. London: Academic Press.

Patterson, F. (2001) 'Developments in work psychology: Emerging issues and future trends', *Journal of Occupational and Organizational Psychology*, vol. 74, part 4, pp. 381–90.

Patterson, F., Ferguson, E., Lane, P., Farrell, K., Martlew, J. and Wells, A. (2000) 'A competency model for general practice: implications for selection, training, and development', *British Journal of General Practice*, vol. 50(452), pp. 188–93.

Paulus, P.B. (2000) 'Groups, teams, and creativity: The creative potential of idea-generating groups', *Applied Psychology: An International Review*, vol. 49(2), pp. 237–62.

Pelled, L.H., Eisenhardt, K.M. and Xin, K.R. (1999) 'Exploring the black box: An analysis of work group diversity, conflict and performance', *Administrative Science Quarterly*, vol. 44, pp. 1–28.

Peluchette, J. (1993) 'Subjective career success: The influence of individual difference, family and organizational variables', *Journal of Vocational Behavior*, vol. 43, pp. 198–208.

Pendry, L.F. and Macrae, C.N. (1996) 'What the disinterested perceiver overlooks: Goal directed social observation', *Personality and Social Psychology Bulletin*, vol. 22, pp. 249–56.

Perlmutter, M. and Hall, E. (1992) *Adult Development and Aging*, 2nd edition. New York: John Wiley.

Pervin, L.A. (1980) *Personality: Theory, assessment and research*, 3rd edition. New York: John Wiley.

Pervin, L.A. (1989) 'Persons, situations, interactions: The history of a controversy and a discussion of situational models', *Academy of Management Review*, vol. 14, pp. 350–60.

Peters, L.H., Hartke, D.D. and Pohlmann, J.T. (1985) 'Fiedler's contingency theory of leadership: An application of the meta-analysis procedures of Schmidt and Hunter', *Psychological Bulletin*, vol. 97, pp. 274–85.

Peters, T. (1989) *Thriving on Chaos*. London: Pan.

Peters, T. (1993) *Liberation Management*. London: Pan.

Peters, T. (1995) *The Pursuit of WOW!* London: Macmillan.

Peters, T. (1997) *The Circle of Innovation: You can't shrink your way to greatness*. New York: Alfred A. Knopf.

Peters, T. and Waterman, R.H. (1982) *In Search of Excellence: Lessons from America's best-run companies*. London: Harper and Row.

Peterson, M.F., Smith, P.B. and Tayeb, M.H. (1993) 'Development and use of English versions of Japanese PM leadership measures in electronics plants', *Journal of Organizational Behavior*, vol. 14, pp. 251–67.

Pettigrew, A.M. (1987) 'Context and action in the transformation of the firm', *Journal of Management Sciences*, vol. 24(6), pp. 649–70.

Pettigrew, A.M. (1990a) 'Longitudinal field research on change: Theory and practice', *Organizational Science*, vol. 3, pp. 267–92.

Pettigrew, A.M. (1990b) 'Studying strategic choice and strategic change', *Organizational Studies*, vol. 11, pp. 6–11.

Pettigrew, A. and Whipp, R. (1993) 'Understanding the environment' in Mabey, C. and Mayon-White, B. (eds) *Managing Change*, 2nd edition. London: Open University/Paul Chapman Publishing.

Pettigrew, A.M., Ferlie, E. and McKee, L. (1992) *Shaping Strategic Change*. London: Sage.

Pettigrew, T.F. (1998) 'Intergroup contact theory', *Annual Review of Psychology*, vol. 49, pp. 65–85.

Petty, R.E. and Cacioppo, J.T. (1985) 'The elaboration likelihood model of persuasion' in Berkowitz, L. (ed.) *Advances in Experimental Social Psychology*, vol. 19. New York: Academic Press.

Petty, R.E. and Kronsnick, J.A. (1992) *Attitude Strength: Antecedents and consequences*. Hillsdale, NJ: Lawrence Erlbaum.

Pfau, M. (1997) 'The inoculation model of resistance to influence', *Programme Communication Sci.*, vol. 13, pp. 133–71.

Pfeffer, J. (1991) 'Organization theory and structural perspectives on management', *Journal of Management*, vol. 17, pp. 789–803.

Pfeffer, J. (1992) *Managing with Power: Politics and influence in organizations*. Boston, MA: Harvard Business School Press.

Phillips, S.D., Friedlander, M.L., Pazienza, N.L. and Kost, P.P. (1985) 'A factor analytic investigation of career decision-making styles', *Journal of Vocational Behavior*, vol. 26, pp. 106–15.

Pillai, R. and Meindl, J.R. (1991) 'The impact of a performance crisis on attributions of charismatic leadership: A preliminary study'. Paper presented at the Eastern Academy of Management, Hartford, CT.

Pincherle, A. (1972) 'Fitness for work', *Proceedings of the Royal Society of Medicine,* vol. 65, pp. 321–4.

Podsakoff, P.M., Ahearne, M. and MacKenzie, S.B. (1997) 'Organizational citizenship behaviour and the quantity and quality of work group performance', *Journal of Applied Psychology*, vol. 82, pp. 262–70.

Port, R. and Patterson, F. (2003) 'Maximising the benefits of psychometric testing in selection', *Selection Development Review*, Special issue, Test Users Conference, vol. 9(6), pp. 6–11.

Potter, J. (1997) 'Discourse analysis as a way of analysing naturally occurring talk' in Silverman, D. (ed.) *Qualitative Research: Theory, method and practice*. London: Sage.

Pratkanis, A.R. and Turner, M.E. (1994) 'Of what value is a job attitude? A socio-cognitive analysis', *Human Relations*, vol. 47, pp. 1545–76.

Prediger, D.J. and Vansickle, T.R. (1992) 'Locating occupations on Holland's hexagon: Beyond RIASEC', *Journal of Vocational Behavior*, vol. 40, pp. 111–28.

Premack, D. (1965) 'Reinforcement theory' in Levine, D. (ed.) *Nebraska Symposium on Motivation*, chapter 14. Lincoln, NE: University of Nebraska Press.

Price, R.E. and Patterson, F. (2003) 'Online application forms: psychological impact on applicants and implications for recruiters', *Selection and Development Review*, vol. 19(2), pp. 12–19.

Pritchard, R.D. (1969) 'Equity theory: A review and critique', *Organizational Behavior and Human Performance*, vol. 4, pp. 176–211.

Pritchard, R.D., Jones, S.D., Roth, P.L., Stuebing, K.K. and Ekeberg, S.E. (1988) 'Effects of group feedback, goal-setting and incentives on organizational productivity', *Journal of Applied Psychology*, vol. 73, pp. 337–58.

Procter, S. and Currie, G. (2002) 'How teamworking works in the Inland Revenue: Meaning operation and impact', *Personnel Review*, vol. 31(3), pp. 304–19.

Pruitt, D.G. (1981) *Negotiation Behavior*. New York: Academic Press.

Pruitt, D.G. and Rubin, J.Z. (1986) *Social Conflict: Escalation, stalemate and settlement*. New York: Random House.

Pruitt, D.G. and Syna, H. (1985) 'Mismatching the opponent's offers in negotiations', *Journal of Experimental Social Psychology*, vol. 21, pp. 103–13.

Ptacek, J.T., Smith, R.E. and Dodge, K.L. (1994) 'Gender differences in coping with stress: When stressor and appraisals do not differ', *Personality and Social Psychology Bulletin*, vol. 20, pp. 421–30.

Pugh, D. (1993) 'Understanding and managing organizational change' in Mabey, C. and Mayon-White, B. (eds) *Managing Change*, 2nd edition. London: Open University/Paul Chapman Publishing.

Quick, J.C. and Quick, J.D. (1984) *Organizational Stress and Preventive Management*. New York: McGraw-Hill.

Quinn, J.B. (1993) 'Managing strategic change' in Mabey, C. and Mayon-White, B. (eds) *Managing Change*, 2nd edition. London: Open University/Paul Chapman Publishing.

Quinn, R.E. and McGarth, M.R. (1985) 'The transformation of organizational cultures: A competing values perspective' in Frost, P.J., Moore, L.F., Louis, M.R., Lundberg C.C. and Martin, J. (eds) *Organizational Culture*. Newbury Park, CA: Sage.

Raley, A.B., Lucas, J.L. and Blazek, M.A. (2003) 'Representation of I-O psychology in introductory psychology textbooks', *The Industrial-Organizational Psychologist*, vol. 41, pp. 62–6.

Rauschenberger, J., Schmitt, N. and Hunter, J.E. (1980) 'A test of the need hierarchy concept by a Markov model of change in need strength', *Administrative Science Quarterly*, vol. 25, pp. 654–70.

Raven, J., Raven, J.C. and Court, J.H. (1996) *Raven's Progressive Matrices, Professional Manual*. Oxford: Oxford Psychologists Press.

Reardon, R.C. and Lenz, J.G. (1998) *The Self-directed Search and Related Holland Career Materials: A practitioner's guide*. Odessa, FL: Psychological Assessment Resources Inc.

Reday-Mulvey, G. and Taylor, P. (1996) 'Why working lives must be extended', *People Management*, 16 May, pp. 24–29.

Reddy, M. (1987) *The Managers' Guide to Counselling at Work*. Leicester: British Psychological Society.

Rees, D. and Porter, C. (2001) *The Skills of Management*. London: Thomson Learning.

Reichers, A.E. (1985) 'A review and re-conceptualization of organizational commitments', *Academy of Management Review*, vol. 10, pp. 465–76.

Reilly, R.R., Henry, S. and Smither, J.W. (1990) 'An examination of the effects of using behavior checklists on the construct validity of assessment center dimensions', *Personnel Psychology*, vol. 43, pp. 71–84.

Reynolds, S., Taylor, E. and Shapiro, D.A. (1993) 'Session impact in stress management training', *Journal of Occupational and Organizational Psychology*, vol. 66, pp. 99–113.

Richard, O.C. and Johnson, N.B. (1999) 'Making the connection between formal human resource diversity practices and organizational effectiveness: Behind management fashion', *Performance Improvement Quarterly*, vol. 12, pp. 77–96.

Rimm, D.C. and Masters, J.C. (1979) *Behavior Therapy: Techniques and empirical findings*, 2nd edition, chapter 14. New York: Academic Press.

Roberts, K.H. and Glick, W. (1981) 'The job characteristics approach to task design: A critical review', *Journal of Applied Psychology*, vol. 66, pp. 193–217.

Roberts, P. and Newton, P.M. (1987) 'Levinsonian studies of women's adult development', *Psychology and Ageing*, vol. 2, pp. 154–63.

Roberts, R.D., Zeidner, M. and Matthews, G. (2001) 'Does emotional intelligence meet traditional standards for an intelligence? Some new data and conclusions', *Emotions*, vol. 1, pp. 196–231.

Robertson, I.T. and Makin, P.J. (1986) 'Management selection in Britain: A survey and critique', *Journal of Occupational Psychology*, vol. 59, pp. 45–57.

Robertson, I.T. and Smith, M. (2001) 'Personnel selection', *Journal of Occupational and Organizational Psychology*, vol. 74, pp. 441–72.

Robertson, I.T., Gratton, L. and Sharpley, D. (1987) 'The psychometric properties and design of managerial assessment centres: Dimensions into exercises won't go', *Journal of Occupational Psychology*, vol. 60, pp. 187–95.

Robinson, S.L. and Morrison, E.W. (2000) 'The development of psychological contract breach and violation: A longitudinal study', *Journal of Organizational Behavior*, vol. 21, pp. 525–46.

Robinson, S.L. and Rousseau, D.M. (1994) 'Violating the psychological contract: Not the exception but the norm', *Journal of Organizational Behavior*, vol. 15, pp. 245–59.

Roethlisberger, F.J. and Dickson, W.J. (1939) *Management and the Worker*. New York: John Wiley.

Rogers, C.R. (1970) *On Becoming a Person*. Boston, MA: Houghton Mifflin.

Rogers, R.W. (1983) 'Cognitive and physiological processes in fear appeals and attitude change: A revised theory of protection motivation' in Cacioppo, J.T. and Petty, R.E. (eds) *Social Psychophysiology*. New York: Guilford.

Rogers, R.W. and Prentice-Dunn, S. (1997) 'Protection motivation theory' in Gochman, D. (ed.) *Handbook of Health Behavior Research*, vol 1, pp. 113–32. New York: Plenham.

Ronen, S. and Shenkar, O. (1985) 'Clustering countries on attitudinal dimensions: A review and synthesis', *Academy of Management Review*, vol. 10, pp. 435–54.

Rosenbaum, J.E. (1989) 'Organization career systems and employee misperceptions' in Arthur, M.B., Hall, D.T. and Lawrence, B.S. (1989) *Handbook of Career Theory*. Cambridge: Cambridge University Press.

Rosenfeld, P., Giacalone, R.A. and Riordan, C.A. (2002) *Impression Management: Building and enhancing reputations at work*. London: Thomson Learning.

Rosenman, R.H., Friedman, M. and Straus, R. (1964) 'A predictive study of CHD', *Journal of the Medical Association*, vol. 189, pp. 15–22.

Rosenthal, R. and DiMatteo, M.R. (2000) 'Meta analysis: Recent developments in quantitative methods for literature reviews', *Annual Review of Psychology*, vol. 52, pp. 59–82.

Rosenthal, R. and Rosnow, R.L. (1984) *Essentials of Behavioral Research, Methods and Data Analysis*. New York: McGraw-Hill.

Rousseau, D.M. (1995) *Psychological Contracts in Organizations*. London: Sage.

Rousseau, D.M. (1998) 'The "problem" of the psychological contract considered', *Journal of Organizational Behavior*, vol. 19, pp. 665–71.

Rousseau, D.M. (2001) 'Schema, promise and mutuality: The building blocks of the psychology contract', *Journal of Occupational and Organizational Psychology*, vol. 74, pp. 511–41.

Rowan, J. (1998) 'Maslow amended', *Journal of Humanistic Psychology*, vol. 28, pp. 81–92.

Rubin, I. (1967) 'Increasing self-acceptance: A means of reducing prejudice', *Journal of Personality and Social Psychology*, vol. 5, pp. 233–8.

Russek, H.I. and Zohman, B.L. (1958) 'Relative significance of heredity, diet and occupational stress in CHD of young adults', *American Journal of Medical Sciences*, vol. 235, pp. 266–75.

Russell, M.T. and Karol, D.L. (1994) *The UK Edition of the 16PF5: Administrator's Manual*. Windsor: National Foundation for Educational Research.

Ryan, A.M., Chan, D., Ployhart, R.E. and Slade, L.A. (1999) 'Employee attitude surveys in a multinational organization: Considering language and culture in assessing measurement equivalence', *Personnel Psychology*, vol. 52, pp. 37–58.

Ryan, T.A. (1970) *Intentional Behavior*. New York: Ronald Press.

Rynes, S.L., McNatt, D.B. and Bretz, R.D. (1999) 'Academic research inside organisations: Inputs, processes and outcomes', *Personnel Psychology*, vol. 52, pp. 869–98.

Saari, J. (1994) 'When does behaviour modification prevent accidents?', *Leadership and Organizational Development Journal*, vol. 15(5), pp. 11–15.

Saari, J. and Nasanen, M. (1989) 'The effect of positive feedback on industrial housekeeping and accidents; A long-term study at a shipyard', *International Journal of Industrial Ergonomics*, vol. 4, pp. 201–11.

Sackett, P.R. and Dreher, G.F. (1982) 'Constructs and assessment centre dimensions: Some troubling empirical findings', *Journal of Applied Psychology*, vol. 67, pp. 401–10.

Sackett, P.R. and Tuzinski, K.A. (2001) 'The role of dimensions and exercises in assessment centre judgements' in London, M. (ed.) *How People Evaluate Others in Organizations*, pp. 111–29. London: LEA.

Sagie, A., Elizur, D. and Yamauchi, A. (1996) 'The structure and strength of achievement motivation: A cross-cultural comparison', *Journal of Organizational Behavior*, vol. 17, pp. 431–44.

Saks, A.M. and Ashforth, B.E. (1999) 'Effects of individual differences and job search behaviors on the employment status of recent university graduates', *Journal of Vocational Behavior*, vol. 54, pp. 335–49.

Salancik, G.R. and Pfeffer, J. (1977) 'An examination of need satisfaction models of job attitudes', *Administrative Science Quarterly*, vol. 22, pp. 427–56.

Salancik, G.R. and Pfeffer, J.C. (1978) 'A social information processing approach to job attitudes and task design', *Administrative Science Quarterly*, vol. 23, pp. 224–53.

Salgado, J. (2003) 'FFM and non-FFM personality predictors of work performance', *Journal of Occupational and Organizational Psychology*, vol. 76, pp. 323–46.

Salgado, J.F., Viswesvaran, C. and Ones, D. (2001) 'Predictors used for personnel selection: An overview of constructs, methods, techniques' in Anderson, N., Ones, D.S., Sinangil, H.K. and Viswesvaran, C. (eds) *Handbook of Industrial, Work and Organizational Psychology*, pp. 165–200. London: Sage.

Salgado, J.F., Anderson, N., Moscoso, S., Bertua, C. and de Fruyt, F. (2003) 'International validity generalization of GMA and cognitive abilities: A European Community meta-analysis', *Personnel Psychology*, vol. 56., pp. 573–605.

Sampson, J.P.J. and Lumsden, J.A. (2000) 'Ethical issues in the design and use of internet-based career assessment', *Journal of Career Assessment*, vol. 8, pp. 21–35.

Sandberg, J. (2000) 'Understanding human competence at work: An interpretative approach', *Academy of Management Journal*, vol. 43, pp. 9–25.

Satterly, D.J. (1979) 'Covariation of cognitive styles, intelligence and achievement', *British Journal of Educational Psychology*, vol. 49, pp. 179–81.

Sauter, S., Hurrell, J.T. and Cooper, C.L. (1989) *Job Control and Worker Health*. Chichester: John Wiley.

Sawilowsky, S.S. and Blair, R.C. (1992) 'A more realistic look at the robustness and type II error properties of the *t*-test to departures from population normality', *Psychological Bulletin*, vol. 111, pp. 352–60.

Scandura, T.A. (1998) 'Dysfunctional mentoring relationships and outcomes', *Journal of Management*, vol. 24, pp. 449–67.

Scarbrough, H. (2003) 'Knowledge management' in Holman, D., Wall, T.D., Clegg, C.W., Sparrow, P. and Howard, A. (eds) *The New Workplace*. Chichester: John Wiley.

Schaubroeck, J. and Kuehn, K. (1992) 'Research design in industrial and organizational psychology' in Cooper, C.L. and Robertson, I.T. (eds) *International Review of Industrial and Organizational Psychology*, vol. 7. Chichester: John Wiley.

Schein, E.H. (1971) 'Occupational socialization in the professions: The case of the role innovator', *Journal of Psychiatric Research*, vol. 8, pp. 521–30.

Schein, E.H. (1978) *Career Dynamics: Matching individual and organizational needs*. Reading, MA: Addison-Wesley.

Schein, E.H. (1985) *Organizational Culture and Leadership: A dynamic view*. San Francisco, CA: Jossey-Bass.

Schein, E.H. (1988) *Organizational Psychology*, 3rd edition. Englewood Cliffs, NJ: Prentice Hall.

Schein, E.H. (1992) *Organizational Culture and Leadership*, 2nd edition. San Francisco, CA: Jossey-Bass.

Schein, E.H. (1993) *Career Anchors: Discovering your real values*, rev. edition. London: Pfeiffer & Co.

Schein, E.H. (1996) 'Career anchors revisited: implications for career development in the 21st century', *Academy of Management Executive*, vol. 10, pp. 80–88.

Schein, V.E. (1975) 'The relationship between sex role stereotypes and requisite management characteristics among female managers', *Journal of Applied Psychology*, vol. 60, pp. 340–44.

Schein, V. E., Mueller, R., Lituchy, T. and Liu, J. (1996) 'Think manager – think male: A global phenomenon?', *Journal of Organizational Behavior*, vol. 17, pp. 33–41.

Schmidt, F.L. and Hunter, J.E. (1998) 'The validity and utility of selection methods in personnel psychology: Practical and theoretical implications of 85 years of research findings', *Psychological Bulletin*, vol. 124, pp. 262–74.

Schmidt, F.L., Hunter, J.E., McKenzie, R.C. and Muldrow, T.W. (1979) 'Impact of valid selection procedures on workforce productivity', *Journal of Applied Psychology*, vol. 64, pp. 609–26.

Schmidt, F.L., Mack, M.J. and Hunter, J.E. (1984) 'Selection utility in the occupation of US Park Ranger for three modes of test use', *Journal of Applied Psychology*, vol. 69, pp. 490–97.

Schmitt, N. (1989) 'Fairness in employment selection' in Smith, J.M. and Robertson, I.T. (eds) *Advances in Selection and Assessment*. Chichester: John Wiley.

Schmitt, N. and Chan, D. (1998) *Personnel Selection: A theoretical approach*. Thousand Oaks, CA: Sage.

Schmitt, N. and Noe, R.A. (1986) 'Personnel selection and equal employment opportunity' in Cooper, C.L. and Robertson, I.T. (eds) *International Review of Industrial and Organizational Psychology*. Chichester: John Wiley.

Schneer, J.A. and Reitman, F. (1995) 'The impact of gender as managerial careers unfold', *Journal of Vocational Behavior*, vol. 47, pp. 290–315.

Schneider, B. (1987) 'The people make the place', *Personnel Psychology*, vol. 40, pp. 437–53.

Schneider, B., Ashworth, S.D., Higgs, A.C. and Carr, L. (1996) 'Design, validity and use of strategically focussed employee attitude surveys', *Personnel Psychology*, vol. 49, pp. 695–705.

Schneider, D.J. (1991) 'Social cognition', *Annual Review of Psychology*, vol. 42, pp. 527–61.

Schneider, S.C. and Dunbar, R.L.M. (1992) 'A psychoanalytic reading of hostile takeover events', *Academy of Management Review*, vol. 17, pp. 537–67.

Schrader, B.W. and Steiner, D.D. (1996) 'Common comparison standards: An approach to improving agreement between self and supervisory performance ratings', *Journal of Applied Psychology*, vol. 81(6), pp. 813–20.

Schönpflug, W. (1993) 'Applied psychology: Newcomer with a long tradition', *Applied Psychology: An International Review*, vol. 42, pp. 5–30.

Schriesheim, C.A., Tepper, B.J. and Tetrault, L.A. (1994) 'Least preferred coworker score, situational control, and leadership effectiveness: A meta-analysis of contingency model performance predictions', *Journal of Applied Psychology*, vol. 79, pp. 561–73.

Schultz, D.P. and Schultz, S.E. (2001) *Theories of Personality*, 7th edition. Belmont, CA: Wadsworth/Thomson Learning.

Schulz-Hardt, S., Jochims, M. and Frey, D. (2002) 'Productive conflict in group decision making: Genuine and contrived dissent as strategies to counteract biased information seeking', *Organizational Behavior and Human Decision Processes*, vol. 88, pp. 563–86.

Schurer Lambert, L., Edwards, J.R. and Cable, D.M. (2003) 'Breach and fulfillment of the psychological contract: A comparison of traditional and expanded views', *Personnel Psychology*, vol. 56, pp. 895–934.

Schwab, D.P., Olian-Gottlieb, J.D. and Heneman, H.G. (1979) 'Between subjects expectancy theory research: A statistical review of studies predicting effort and performance', *Psychological Bulletin*, vol. 86, pp. 139–47.

Scribner, S. (1986) 'Thinking in action: Some characteristics of practical thought' in Sternberg, R.J. and Wagner, R.K. (eds) *Practical Intelligence*. Cambridge: Cambridge University Press.

Secord, P.F. and Backman, C.W. (1969) *Social Psychology*. New York: McGraw-Hill.

Seibert, S.E., Kraimer, M.L. and Crant, J.M. (2001a) 'What do proactive people do? A longitudinal model linking proactive personality and career success', *Personnel Psychology*, vol. 54, pp. 845–74.

Seibert, S.E., Kraimer, M.L. and Liden, R.C. (2001b) 'A social capital theory of career success', *Academy of Management Journal*, vol. 44(2), p. 219–37.

Selmer, J. (2001) 'Expatriate selection: Back to basics?', *International Journal of Human Resource Management*, vol. 12, pp. 1219–33.

Selye, H. (1946) 'The General Adaptation Syndrome and the diseases of adaptation', *Journal of Clinical Endocrinology*, vol. 6, p. 117.

Selye, H. (1974) *Stress without Distress*. Philadelphia, PA: J.B. Lippincott.

Senger, J.M. (2002) 'Tales of the bazaar: Interest-based negotiation across cultures', *Negotiation Journal*, vol. 18, pp. 233–50.

Senior, B. (1997) *Organisational Change*. London: Pitman.

Senior, B. (2002) *Organisational Change,* 2nd edition. Harlow: FT/Prentice Hall.

Seymour, W.D. (1966) *Industrial Skills*. London: Pitman Publishing.

Shackleton, V. and Newell, S. (1997) 'International assessment and selection' in Anderson, N. and Herriot, P. (eds) *International Handbook of Selection and Assessment*. Chichester: Wiley.

Shah, S., Arnold, J. and Travers, C. (2004a) 'The mark of childhood on disabled professionals'. *Children and Society*.

Shah, S., Travers, C. and Arnold, J. (2004b) 'Disabled and successful: Education in the life stories of disabled high achievers', *Journal of Research in Special Educational Needs* (in press).

Sharf, R.F. (1992) *Applying Career Development Theory to Counseling*. Los Angeles, CA: Brooks/Cole.

Shaw, J.B. and Barrett-Power, E. (1998) 'The effects of diversity on small work group processes and performance', *Human Relations*, vol. 51(10), pp. 1307–25.

Shepherd, A. (1976) 'An improved tabular format for task analysis', *Journal of Occupational Psychology*, vol. 47, pp. 93–104.

Sherif, M. (1966) *Group Conflict and Co-operation*. London: Routledge and Kegan Paul.

Shimmin, S. and Wallis, D. (1994) *Fifty Years of Occupational Psychology in Britain*. Leicester: British Psychological Society.

Shippmann, J.S., Ash, R.A., Battista, M., Carr, L., Eyde, L.D., Hesketh, B., Kehoe, J., Pearlman, K., Prien, E.P. and Sanchez, J.I. (2000) 'The practice of competency modelling'. *Personnel Psychology*, vol. 53, pp. 703–40.

Shirom, A. and Mayer, A. (1993) 'Stress and strain among union lay officials and rank and file members', *Journal of Organizational Behavior*, vol. 14, pp. 401–14.

SHL (1984) *The Occupational Personality Questionnaires*. Thames Ditton: Saville and Holdsworth Ltd.

SHL (1990) *Occupational Personality Questionnaire Manual*. Thames Ditton: Saville and Holdsworth Ltd.

Short, J.E. and Venkatraman, N. (1992) 'Beyond business process redesign: Redefining Baxter's business network', *Sloan Management Review*, Fall, pp. 7–21.

Silverman, D. (2001) *Interpreting Qualitative Data*. London: Sage.

Silvester, J. (1996) 'Unfair discrimination in the selection interview: A case for more field research?', *Feminism and Psychology*, vol. 6, pp. 574–78.

Silvester, J. (2003) 'A natural selection', *People Management*, January. London: IPD.

Silvester, J. and Anderson, N.R. (2003) 'Technology and discourse: A comparison of face-to-face and telephone employment interviews'. Special Issue on Technology & Selection: *International Journal of Selection and Assessment*, vol. 11, pp. 206–14.

Silvester, J. and Chapman, A.J. (1996) 'Unfair discrimination in the selection interview: An attributional account', *International Journal of Selection and Assessment*, vol. 4, pp. 63–70.

Silvester, J. and Patterson, F. (2003) *Cognitive Predictors of Empathy in Trainee General Practitioners*. End of project report, Economic and Social Research Council (R000223765).

Silvester, J., Anderson, N.R. and Patterson, F. (1999) 'Organisational culture change: An inter-group attributional analysis', *Journal of Occupational and Organizational Psychology*, vol. 72, pp. 1–23.

Silvester, J., Anderson, N.R., Gibb, A., Haddleton, E. and Cunningham-Snell, N. (2000) 'A cross-modal comparison of the predictive validity of telephone and face-to-face selection interviews', *International Journal of Selection and Assessment*, vol. 8, pp. 16–21.

Silvester, J., Anderson-Gough, F.M., Anderson, N.R. and Mohammed, A.R. (2002) 'Locus of control, attributions and impression management in the selection interview', *Journal of Occupational and Organizational Psychology*, vol. 75, pp. 59–76.

Silvester, J., Patterson, F. and Ferguson, E. (2003) 'Comparing two attributional models of performance in retail sales: A field study', *Journal of Occupational and Organizational Psychology*, vol. 76, pp. 115–32.

Simonson, I. and Staw, B.M. (1992) 'De-escalation strategies: A comparison of techniques for reducing commitment to losing courses of action', *Journal of Applied Psychology*, vol. 77, pp. 419–26.

Singh, V. and Vinnicombe, S. (2000) 'What does "commitment" really mean?: Views of UK and Swedish engineering managers', *Personnel Review*, 29(1–2), pp. 228–54.

Skarlicki, D.P., Folger, R. and Tesluk, P. (1999) 'Personality as a moderator in the relationship between fairness and retaliation', *Academy of Management Journal*, vol. 42, pp. 100–108.

Skinner, B.F. (1948) *Walden Two*. New York: Macmillan.

Skinner, B.F. (1971) *Beyond Freedom and Dignity*. New York: Knopf.

Skinner, B.F. (1974) *About Behaviourism*. London: Cape.

Smith, C.M., Tindale, R.S. and Dugoni, B.L. (1996) 'Minority and majority influence in freely interacting groups: Qualitative versus quantitative differences', *British Journal of Social Psychology*, vol. 35, pp. 137–49.

Smith, J.M. and Robertson, I.T. (1993) *The Theory and Practice of Systematic Personnel Selection*. London: Macmillan.

Smith, M. and George, D. (1992) 'Selection methods' in Cooper, C.L. and Robertson, I.T. (eds) *International Review of Industrial and Organizational Psychology*, vol. 7. Chichester: John Wiley.

Smith, M., Beck, J., Cooper, C.L., Cox, C., Ottaway, D. and Talbot, R. (1982) *Introducing Organizational Behaviour*. London: Macmillan.

Smith, P. (1994) *The UK Standardization of the 16PF5: A supplement of norms and technical data*. Windsor: National Foundation for Educational Research.

Smith, P.B., Misumi, J., 'rayeb, M., Peterson, M. and Bond, M. (1989) 'On the generality of leadership style measures across cultures', *Journal of Occupational Psychology*, vol. 62, pp. 97–109.

Smith, P.B., Kruzella, P., Czegledi, R., Tsvetanova, S., Pop, D., Groblewska, B. and Halasova, D. (1997) 'Managerial leadership in Eastern Europe: From uniformity to diversity' in Pepermans, R., Buelens, A., Vinkenburg, C.J. and Jansen, P.G.W. (eds) *Managerial Behaviour and Practices: European Research Issues*. Leuven: Acco.

Smith, P.C. and Kendall, L.M. (1963) 'Retranslation of expectations: An approach to the construction of unambiguous anchors for rating scales', *Journal of Applied Psychology*, vol. 47, pp. 149–55.

Smith, P.C., Kendall, L.M. and Hulin, C.L. (1969) *The Measurement of Satisfaction in Work and Retirement*. Chicago, IL: Rand-McNally.

Smith, S. and Tranfield, D. (1987) 'The implementation and exploitation of advanced manufacturing technology: An outline methodology', Change Management Research Unit, Research Paper no. 2, Sheffield Business School.

Smither, J.W., Reilly, R.R. and Buda, R. (1988) 'Effect of prior performance information on ratings of present performance: Contrast versus assimilation revisited', *Journal of Applied Psychology*, vol. 73(3), pp. 487–96.

Smither, J.W., London, M., Vasilopoulos, M.L., Reilly, R.R., Millsap, R.E. and Salvemini, N. (1995) 'An examination of the effects of an upward feedback program over time', *Personnel Psychology*, vol. 48(1), pp. 1–34.

Snow, C., Miles, R. and Coleman, H. (1993) 'Managing 21st century network organizations' in Mabey, C. and Mayon-White, B. (eds) *Managing Change*. 2nd edition. London: Open University/Paul Chapman Publishing.

Sokol, M. and Louis, M.R. (1984) 'Career transitions and life event adaptation: Integrating alternative perspectives on role transition' in Allen, V.L. and Van de Vliert, E. (eds) *Role Transitions*. New York: Plenum Press.

Sorge, A. (1997) 'Organization behaviour' in Sorge, A. and Warner, M. (eds) *The IEBM Handbook of Organizational Behaviour*. London: International Thompson Business Press.

Sosik, J.J. and Godshalk, V.M. (2000) 'Leadership styles, mentoring functions received, and job-related stress: A conceptual model and preliminary study', *Journal of Organizational Behavior*, vol. 21, pp. 365–90.

Spangler, W.D. (1992) 'Validity of questionnaire and TAT measures of need for achievement: Two meta-analyses', *Psychological Bulletin*, vol. 112, pp. 140–54.

Sparks, K. and Cooper, C.L. (1999) 'Occupational differences in the work–strain relationship', *Journal of Occupational and Organizational Psychology*, vol. 72, pp. 219–29.

Sparks, K. Cooper, C.L., Fried, Y. and Shirom, A. (1997) 'The effects of hours of work on health', *Journal of Occupational and Organizational Psychology*, vol. 70, pp. 391–408.

Sparks, K., Faragher, B. and Cooper, C.L. (2001) 'Well-being and occupational health in the 21st century workplace', *Journal of Occupational and Organizational Psychology*, vol. 74, pp. 489–509.

Sparrow, P. (1999) 'Editorial', *Journal of Occupational and Organizational Psychology*, vol. 72, pp. 261–4.

Sparrow, P. (2003) 'The future of work?' in Holman, D., Wall, T.D., Clegg, C. W., Sparrow, P. and Howard, A. (eds) *The New Workplace* Chichester: John Wiley.

Spearman, C. (1927) *The Abilities of Man*. London: Macmillan.

Spears, L. (ed.) (1995) *Reflections on Leadership*. New York: John Wiley.

Spector, P.E. (2000) 'A control theory of the job stress process' in Cooper, C.L. (ed.) *Theories of Organizational Stress*. Oxford: Oxford University Press.

Spinelli, E. (1989) *The Interpreted World*. London: Sage.

Spokane, A.R., Meir, E.I. and Catalono, M., (2000) 'Person–environment congruence and Holland's theory: A review and reconsideration', *Journal of Vocational Behavior*, vol. 57, pp. 137–87.

Stace, D. and Dunphy, D. (2001) *Beyond the Boundaries: Leading and re-creating the successful enterprise*. Sydney: McGraw-Hill.

Stacey, R. (1993) *Strategic Management and Organisational Dynamics*. London: Pitman.

Stajkovic, A.D. and Luthans, F. (1997) 'A meta-analysis of the effects of organizational behaviour modification on task performance', *Academy of Management Journal*, vol. 40(5), pp. 1122–49.

Stajkovic, A.D. and Luthans, F. (2001) 'Differential effects of incentive motivations on work performance', *Academy of Management Journal*, vol. 44(3), pp. 580–90.

Stangor, C., Lynch, L., Duan, C. and Glass, B. (1992) 'Categorization of individuals on the basis of multiple social features', *Journal of Personality and Social Psychology*, vol. 62, pp. 207–18.

Staw, B.M. (1981) 'The escalation of commitment to a course of action', *Academy of Management Review*, vol. 6, pp. 577–87.

Staw, B.M., Bell, N.E. and Clausen, J.A. (1986) 'The dispositional approach to job attitudes: A lifetime longitudinal test', *Administrative Science Quarterly*, vol. 31, pp. 56–77.

Steijn, B. (2001) 'Work systems, quality of working life and attitudes of workers: An empirical study towards the effects of team and non-teamwork', *New Technology, Work and Employment*, vol. 16(3), pp. 191–203.

Sternberg, R.J. (1985) *Beyond IQ: A triarchic theory of human intelligence*. Cambridge: Cambridge University Press.

Sternberg, R.J. (1995) 'A triarchic view of "Cognitive resources and leadership performance"', *Applied Psychology: An International Review*, vol. 44, pp. 29–32.

Sternberg, R.J. and Wagner, R.K. (eds) (1986) *Practical Intelligence*. Cambridge: Cambridge University Press.

Sternberg, R.J. and colleagues (eds) (2000) *Practical Intelligence in Everyday Life*. Cambridge: Cambridge University Press.

Stevens, C.K. and Gist, M. (1997) 'Effects of self-efficacy and goal orientation training on negotiation skill maintenance: What are the mechanisms?', *Personnel Psychology*, vol. 50, pp. 955–78.

Stewart, L.D. and Perlow, R. (2001) 'Applicant race, job status, and racial attitude as predictors of employment discrimination', *Journal of Business and Psychology*, vol. 16, pp. 259–75.

Stickland, F. (1998) *The Dynamics of Change: Insights into organisational transition from the natural world*. London: Routledge.

Stogdill, R.M. (1974) *Handbook of Leadership: A survey of theory and research*. New York: Free Press.

Stokes, G.S. and Reddy, S. (1992) 'Use of background data in organizational decisions' in Cooper, C.L. and Robertson, I.T. (eds) *International Review of Industrial and Organizational Psychology*. Chichester: John Wiley.

Storey, J. (1992) *Developments in the Management of Human Resources*. Oxford: Blackwell.

Stroh, L.K., Brett, J.M. and Reilly, A.H. (1992) 'All the right stuff: A comparison of female and male managers' career progression', *Journal of Applied Psychology*, vol. 77, pp. 251–60.

Stumpf, C.A, Colarelli, S.M. and Hartman, K. (1983) 'Development of the Career Exploration Survey (CES)', *Journal of Vocational Behavior*, vol. 22, pp. 191–226.

Sturges, J. (1999) 'What it means to succeed: Personal conceptions of career success held by male and female managers at different ages', *British Journal of Management*, vol. 10, pp. 239–52.

Sturmey, P. (1998) 'History and contribution of organizational behavior management to services for persons with developmental disabilities', *Journal of Organizational Behavior Management*, Vol. 18(2–3), pp. 7–32.

Super, D.E. (1957) *The Psychology of Careers*. New York: Harper & Row.

Super, D.E. (1980) 'A life-span, life-space approach to career development', *Journal of Vocational Behavior*, vol. 13, pp. 282–98.

Super, D.E. (1990) 'A life-span, life-space approach to career development' in Brown, D. and Brooks, L. (eds) *Career Choice and Development*, 2nd edition. San Francisco, CA: Jossey-Bass.

Super, D.E. and Nevill, D.D. (1985) *The Salience Inventory*. Palo Alto, CA: Consulting Psychologists Press.

Super, D.E., Thompson, A.S. and Lindeman, R.H. (1985) *The Adult Career Concerns Inventory*. Palo Alto, CA: Consulting Psychologists Press.

Sutherland, V. and Cooper, C.L. (1987) *Man and Accidents Offshore*. London: Lloyd's.

Sutherland, V. and Cooper, C.L. (2000) *Strategic Stress Management*, London: Macmillan.

Symon, G. and Cassell, C. (eds) (1998) *Qualitative Methods and Analysis in Organizational Research: A practical guide*. London: Sage.

Taber, T.D. and Alliger, G.M. (1995) 'A task-level assessment of job satisfaction', *Journal of Organizational Behavior*, vol. 16, pp. 101–21.

Taguchi, G. (1986) *Introduction to Quality Engineering*. Dearborn, MI: Asian Production Organization.

Tajfel, H. (1972) *Differentiation between Social Groups: Studies in the social psychology of intergroup relations*. London: Academic Press.

Tajfel, H. and Turner, J. (1979) 'An integrative theory of intergroup conflict' in Austin, E.G. and Worchel, S. (eds) *The Social Psychology of Intergroup Relations*, pp. 33–48. Monterey, CA: Brooks-Cole.

Tan, C.A. and Salomone, P.R. (1994) 'Understanding career plateauing: Implications for counseling', *The Career Development Quarterly*, vol. 42, pp. 291–301.

Tannenbaum, P. (1956) 'Initial attitude toward source and concept as factors in attitude change through communication', *Public Opinion Quarterly*, vol. 20, pp. 413–26.

Tannenbaum, S.I. and Yukl, G.A. (1992) 'Training and development in work organisations', *Annual Review of Psychology*, vol. 43, pp. 399–441.

Tasto, D., Colligan, M., Skjei, E. and Polly, S. (1978) *Health Consequences of Shiftwork*. Washington, DC: NIOSH.

Taylor, J.C. (1979) 'Job design criteria twenty years later' in Davis, L.E. and Taylor, J.C. (eds) *Design of Jobs*, 2nd edition. Santa Monica, CA: Goodyear.

Taylor, M.S. and Ilgen, D.R. (1981) 'Sex discrimination against women in initial placement decisions: A laboratory investigation', *Academy of Management Journal*, vol. 24(4), pp. 859–65.

Taylor, K.M. and Betz, N.E. (1983) 'Applications of self-efficacy theory to the understanding and treatment of career indecision', *Journal of Vocational Behavior*, vol. 22, pp. 63–81.

Tesser, A. and Shaffer, D. (1990) 'Attitudes and attitude change' in Rosenzweig, M.R. and Porter, L.W. (eds) *Annual Review of Psychology*, vol. 41. Palo Alto, CA: Annual Reviews Inc.

Tetlock, P.E. (1992) 'The impact of accountability on judgment and choice: Toward a social contingency model', *Advances in Experimental Social Psychology*, vol. 25 pp. 331–76.

Tharenou, P., Latimer, S. and Conroy, D. (1994) 'How do you make it to the top? An examination of influences on women's and men's managerial advancement', *Academy of Management Journal*, vol. 37, pp. 899–931.

Thornton, G.C., Halenshead, J.D. and Larsh, S.L. (1997) 'Comparison of two measures of motivation to manage: Ethnic and gender differences', *Educational and Psychological Measurement*, vol. 57, pp. 241–53.

Thurstone, L.L. (1938) *Primary Mental Abilities*, Psychometric Monographs no. 1. Chicago, IL: University of Chicago Press.

Tjosvold, D., Wedley, W.C. and Field, R.H.G. (1986) 'Constructive controversy, the Vroom–Yetton model, and managerial decision-making', *Journal of Occupational Behaviour*, vol. 7, pp. 125–38.

Tokar, D.M. and Fischer, A.R. (1998) 'More on RIASEC and the five-factor model of personality: Direct assessment of Prediger's (1982) and Hogan's (1983) dimensions', *Journal of Vocational Behavior*, vol. 52, pp. 246–59.

Tokar, D.M. and Swanson, J.L. (1995) 'Evaluation of correspondence between Holland's vocational personality typology and the five-factor model of personality', *Journal of Vocational Behavior*, vol. 46, pp. 89–108.

Torrington, D.P. and Hall, L.A. (1991) *Personnel Management: A new approach*, 2nd edition. London: Prentice Hall.

Tourish, D. and Pinnington, A. (2002) 'Transformational leadership, corporate cultism and the spirituality paradigm: an unholy trinity in the workplace', *Human Relations*, vol. 55, pp. 147–72.

Tracey, J.B. and Hinkin, T.R. (1998) 'Transformational leadership or effective managerial practices', *Group and Organizational Management*, vol. 23, pp. 220–36.

Tracey, T.J. and Rounds, S.B. (1993) 'Evaluating Holland's and Gati's vocational-interest models: A structural meta-analysis', *Psychological Bulletin*, vol. 113, pp. 229–46.

Tracey, J.B., Tannenbaum, S.I. and Kavanaugh, M.J. (1995) 'Applying trained skills on the job: The importance of the work environment', *Journal of Applied Psychology*, vol. 80, pp. 239–52.

Tranberg, M., Slane, S. and Ekeberg, S.E. (1993) 'The relation between interest congruence and satisfaction: A meta-analysis', *Journal of Vocational Behavior*, vol. 42, pp. 253–64.

Travers, C. and Pemberton, C. (2000) 'Think career global, but act local: Understanding networking as a culturally differentiated career skill' in Davidson, M.J. and Burke, R.J. (eds) *Women in Management*. London: Sage.

Trist, E.L. and Bamforth, K.W. (1951) 'Some social and psychological consequences of the long-wall method of coal getting', *Human Relations*, vol. 4, pp. 3–38.

Trompenaars, F. (1993) *Riding the Waves of Culture*. London: Economist Books.

Trompenaars, F. and Hampden Turner, C. (1998) *Riding the Waves of Culture: Understanding cultural diversity in business*. London: McGraw-Hill.

Tubbs, M. (1994) 'Commitment and the role of ability in motivation: Comment on Wright, O'Leary-Kelly, Cortina, Klein and Hollenbeck (1994)', *Journal of Applied Psychology*, vol. 79, pp. 804–11.

Tuckman, B.W. (1965) 'Development sequence in small groups', *Psychological Review*, vol. 63, pp. 384–99.

Turner, A.N. and Lawrence, P.R. (1965) *Industrial Jobs and the Worker*. Cambridge, MA: Harvard University Press.

Turner, B. (1971) *Exploring the Industrial Subculture*. Macmillan: London.

Turner, J.C. (1991) *Social Influence*. Buckingham: Open University Press.

Turner, J.C. (1999) 'Some current themes in research on social identity and self-categorization theories' in Ellemers, N., Spears, R. and Doosje, B. (eds) *Social Identity: Context, commitment, content*, pp. 6–34. Oxford: Blackwell.

Turner, J.C. and Onorato, R. (1999) 'Social identity, personality and the self-concept: A self-categorization perspective' in Tyler, T.R., Kramer, R. and John, O. (eds) *The Psychology of the Social Self*. Hillsdale, NJ: Erlbaum.

Turnley, W.H. and Feldman, D.C. (1999) 'A discrepancy model of psychological contract violations', *Human Resource Management Review*, vol. 9, pp. 367–86.

Tversky, A. and Kahneman, D. (1974) 'Judgement under uncertainty: Heuristics and biases', *Science*, vol. 185, pp. 1124–31.

Tversky, A. and Kahneman, D. (1981) 'The framing of decisions and the psychology of choice', *Science*, vol. 211, pp. 453–58.

Tversky, A. and Kahneman, D. (1986) 'Rational choice and the framing of decisions', *Journal of Business*, vol. 59, pp. 251–78.

Ulrich, R., Strachnik, T. and Mabry, J. (eds) (1974) *Control of Human Behavior*. Glenview, IL: Scott-Foresman.

Valacich, J.S., Dennis, A.R. and Connolly, T. (1994) 'Idea generation in computer-based groups: A new ending to an old story', *Organizational Behavior and Human Decision Processes*, vol. 57, pp. 448–67.

Vandenberg, R.J., Richardson, H.A. and Eastman, L.J. (1999) 'The impact of high involvement work processes on organizational effectiveness: A second-order latent variable approach', *Group and Organization Management*, vol. 24(3), pp. 300–339.

Van de Vliert, E. and Prein, H.C.M. (1989) 'The difference in the meaning of forcing in the conflict management of actors and observers' in Rahim, M.A. (ed.) *Management Conflict: An interdisciplinary approach*. New York: Praeger.

Van Eerde, W. and Thierry, H. (1996) 'Vroom's expectancy models and work related criteria: A meta-analysis', *Journal of Applied Psychology*, vol. 81, pp. 575–86.

Van Harreveld, F., van der Plight, J., de Vries, N.K. and Andreas, S. (2000) 'The structure of attitudes: Attribute importance, accessibility, and judgement', *British Journal of Social Psychology*, vol. 39, pp. 363–80.

Van Hiel, A. and Mervielde, I. (2001) 'Preferences for behavioral style of minority and majority members who anticipate group interaction', *Social Behavior and Personality*, vol. 29(7), pp. 701–10.

Van Knippenberg, D. (2000) 'Work motivation and performance: A social identity perspective', *Applied Psychology: An International Review*, vol. 49, pp. 357–371.

Van Maanen, J. and Kunda, G. (1989) 'Real feelings: Emotional expression and organizational culture' in Staw, B. and Cummings, L. (eds) *Research in Organizational Behavior*, vol. 11, pp. 43–103. Greenwich, CT: JAI Press.

Van Maanen, J. and Schein, E.H. (1979) 'Toward a theory of organizational socialization' in Staw, B.M. (ed.) *Research in Organizational Behavior*, vol. 1. Greenwich, CT: JAI Press.

Van Rooy, D.L. and Viswesvaran, C. (in press) 'Emotional intelligence: a meta-analytic investigation of predictive validity and nomological net', *Journal of Vocational Behavior*.

Vecchio, R.P. (1987) 'Situational leadership theory: An examination of a prescriptive theory', *Journal of Applied Psychology*, vol. 72, pp. 444–51.

Vecchio, R.P. (1990) 'Theoretical and empirical examination of Cognitive Resource Theory', *Journal of Applied Psychology*, vol. 75, pp. 141–47.

Vecchio, R.P. (1992) 'Cognitive Resource Theory: Issues for specifying a test of the theory', *Journal of Applied Psychology*, vol. 77, pp. 375–76.

Veiga, J.F. (1983) 'Mobility influences during managerial career stages', *Academy of Management Journal*, vol. 26, pp. 64–85.

Verkuyten, M. (1998) 'Attitudes in public discourse: Speakers' own orientations', *Journal of Language and Social Psychology*, vol. 17(3), pp. 302–322.

Vernon, H.M. (1948) 'An autobiography', *Occupational Psychology*, vol. 23, pp. 73–82.

Vernon, P.E. (1956) *The Measurement of Abilities*. London: University of London Press.

Vernon, P.E. (1969) *Intelligence and Cultural Environment*, 2nd edition. London: Methuen.

Vince, R. (2002) 'The politics of imagined stability: A psychodynamic understanding of change at Hyder plc', *Human Relations*, vol. 55, pp. 1189–208.

Vinnicombe, S. (2000) 'The position of women in management in Europe' in Davidson, M.J. and Burke, R.J. (eds) *Women in Management*. London: Sage.

Vinnicombe, S. and Colwill, N.L. (1996) *The Essence of Women in Management*. Englewood Cliffs, NJ: Prentice Hall.

Viswesvaran, C. (2003) 'Introduction to special issue: Role of technology in shaping the future of staffing and assessment', *International Journal of Selection and Assessment*, vol. 11(2–3), pp. 107–12.

Viswesvaran, C. and Ones, D.S. (2000) 'Perspectives on models of job performance', *International Journal of Selection and Assessment*, vol. 8, pp. 216–25.

Vollrath, D.A., Sheppard, B.H., Hinsz, V.B. and Davis, J.H. (1989) 'Memory performance by decision-making groups and individuals', *Organizational Behavior and Human Decision Processes*, vol. 43, pp. 289–300.

Voss, C.A. (1985) 'Success and failure in advanced manufacturing technology', Warwick University working paper.

Vroom, V.H. (1964) *Work and Motivation*. Chichester: John Wiley.

Vroom, V.H. and Jago, A.G. (1988) *The New Leadership: Managing participation in organizations*. Englewood Cliffs, NJ: Prentice Hall.

Vroom, V.H. and Yetton, P.W. (1973) *Leadership and Decision Making*. Pittsburgh, PA: Pittsburgh Press.

Wagner, J.A. (1994) 'Participation's effects on performance and satisfaction: A reconsideration of research evidence', *Academy of Management Review*, vol. 19, pp. 312–30.

Wahba, M.A. and Bridwell, L.B. (1976) 'Maslow reconsidered: A review of research on the need hierarchy theory', *Organizational Behaviour and Human Performance*, vol. 15, pp. 212–40.

Waldman, D.A. and Yammarino, F.J. (1999) 'CEO charismatic leadership: Levels-of-management and levels-of-analysis effects', *Academy of Management Review*, vol. 24, pp. 266–85.

Walker, A. (1982) *Unqualified and Unemployed*. Basingstoke: Macmillan/National Children's Bureau.

Walker, A.G. and Smither, J.W. (1999) 'A five-year study of upward feedback: What managers do with their results matters', *Personnel Psychology*, vol. 52, pp. 393–23.

Walker, K.F. (1979) 'Psychology and employee relations: A general perspective' in Stephenson, G.M. and Brotherton, C.J. (eds) *Employee Relations: A social psychological approach*. Chichester: John Wiley.

Wall, T.D. (1982) 'Perspectives on job redesign' in Kelly, J.E. and Clegg, C.W. (eds) *Autonomy and Control in the Workplace*. London: Croom Helm.

Wall, T.D., Cardery, J.L. and Clegg, C.W. (2002) 'Empowerment, performance, and operational uncertainty: A theoretical integration', *Applied Psychology: An International Review*, vol. 51, pp. 146–69.

Wall, T.D., Clegg, C.W. and Kemp, N.J. (1987) *The Human Side of Advanced Manufacturing Technology*. Chichester: John Wiley.

Walsh, W.B. and Osipow, S.H. (eds) (1990) *Career Counseling*. Hillsdale, NJ: Lawrence Erlbaum.

Walton, R. and McKersie, R. (1965) *A Behavioral Theory of Labor Negotiations: An analysis of a social interaction system*. New York: McGraw-Hill.

Wanberg, C.R., Kammeyer-Mueller, J. and Shi, K. (2001) 'Job loss and the experience of unemployment: International research and perspectives' in Anderson, N., Ones, D.S., Sinangil, H.K. and Viswesvaran, C. (eds) *Handbook of Work, Industrial and Organizational Psychology*, vol. 2. London: Sage.

Wanous, J.P. (1989) 'Installing a realistic job preview: Ten tough choices', *Personnel Psychology*, vol. 42, pp. 117–33.

Wanous, J.P., Poland, T.D., Premack, S.L. and Davis, K.S. (1992) 'The effects of met expectations on newcomer attitudes and behaviors: A review and meta-analysis', *Journal of Applied Psychology*, vol. 77, pp. 288–97.

Wardwell, W., Hyman, I.M. and Bahnson, C.B. (1964) 'Stress and coronary disease in three field studies', *Journal of Chronic Disease*, vol. 17, pp. 73–4.

Warr, P.B. (1987) *Work, Unemployment and Mental Health*. Oxford: Oxford University Press.

Warr, P. and Bunce, D. (1995) 'Trainee characteristics and the outcome of open learning', *Personnel Psychology*, vol. 48, pp. 347–75.

Warr, P. and Wall, T. (1975) *Work and Well-Being*. Harmondsworth: Penguin.

Warr, P., Allen, C. and Birdi, K. (1999) 'Predicting three levels of training outcome', *Journal of Occupational and Organizational Psychology*, vol. 72, pp. 351–76.

Warr, P., Cook, J. and Wall, T. (1979) 'Scales for the measurement of some work attitudes and aspects of psychological well-being', *Journal of Occupational Psychology*, vol. 52, pp. 129–48.

Warshaw, L.J. (1979) *Managing Stress*. Reading, MA: Addison-Wesley.

Warwick, D.P. and Thompson, J.T. (1980) 'Still crazy after all these years', *Training and Development Journal*, vol. 34, pp. 16–22.

Wastell, D.G., White, P. and Kawalek, P. (1994) 'A methodology for business process redesign: Experience and issues', *Journal of Strategic Information Systems*, vol. 3(1), pp. 23–40.

Watson, T.J. (1997) *Sociology, Work and Industry*, 3rd edition. London: Routledge.

Webster, J. and Starbuck, W.H. (1988) 'Theory building in industrial and organisational psychology' in Cooper, C.L. and Robertson, I.T. (eds) *International Review of Industrial and Organizational Psychology*, vol. 3. Chichester: John Wiley.

Weick, K. (1996) 'Enactment and the boundaryless career: Organizing as we work' in Arthur, M.B. and Rousseau, D.E. (eds) *The Boundaryless Career*. Oxford: Oxford University Press.

Weirsma, U. and Latham, G.P. (1986) 'The practicality of behavioural expectation scales and trait scales', *Personnel Psychology*, vol. 39, pp. 619–28.

Werbel, J.D. (2000) 'Relationships among career exploration, job search intensity, and job search effectiveness in graduating college students', *Journal of Vocational Behavior*, vol. 57, pp. 379–94.

Werner, J.M. and Bolino, M.C. (1997) 'Explaining US courts of appeals decisions involving performance appraisal: Accuracy, fairness and validation', *Personnel Psychology*, vol. 50, pp. 1–24.

Wernimont, P.F. and Campbell, J.P. (1968) 'Signs, samples and criteria', *Journal of Applied Psychology*, vol. 52, pp. 372–76.

West, M.A. (1994) *Effective Teamwork*. Leicester: British Psychological Society.

West, M.A. (2001) 'The human team: Basic motivations and innovations' in Anderson, N. *et al.* (eds) *Handbook of Industrial Work and Organizational Psychology*, vol. 2. London: Sage.

West, M.A. (2002) 'Sparkling fountains or stagnant ponds: An integrative model of creativity and innovation implementation in work groups', *Applied Psychology: An International Review*, vol. 51(3), pp. 355–87.

Wexley, K.N. (1984) 'Personnel training', *Annual Review of Psychology*, vol. 35, pp. 519–51.

Wheatley, M. (1992) *The Future of Middle Management*. London: British Institute of Management.

White, B., Cox, C. and Cooper, C.L. (1992) *Women's Career Development: A study of high-flyers*. Oxford: Blackwell.

Whitley, W., Dougherty, T.W. and Dreher, G.F. (1991) 'Relationship of career mentoring and socioeconomic origin to managers' and professionals' early career progress', *Academy of Management Journal*, vol. 34, pp. 331–51.

Whittington, R. (1993) *What is Strategy and Does it Matter?* London: Routledge.

Whyte, G. (1989) 'Groupthink reconsidered', *Academy of Management Review*, vol. 14, pp. 40–56.

Whyte, G. (1993) 'Escalating commitment to individual and group decision making: A prospect theory approach', *Organizational Behavior and Human Decision Processes*, vol. 54, pp. 430–55.

Whyte, J. and Witcher, B. (1992) *The Adoption of Total Quality Management in Northern England*. Durham: Durham University Business School.

Wicker, A.W. (1969) 'Attitudes versus actions: The relationship of overt and behavioral responses to attitude objects', *Journal of Social Issues*, vol. 25, pp. 41–78.

Wilkinson, A. (1998) 'Empowerment theory and practice', *Personnel Review*, vol. 27, pp. 40–56.

Williams, K., Harkins, S. and Latane, B. (1981) 'Identifiability as a deterrent to social loafing: Two cheering experiments', *Journal of Personality and Social Psychology*, vol. 40, pp. 303–11.

Williams, M.L., Podsakoff, P.M., Todor, W.D., Huber, V.L., Howell, J.P. and Dorfman, P.W. (1988) 'A preliminary analysis of the construct validity of Kerr and Jermier's "substitutes for leadership" scales', *Journal of Occupational Psychology*, vol. 61, pp. 307–34.

Willmott, H. (1995) 'Strength is ignorance; slavery is freedom: Managing culture in modern organizations', *Journal of Management Studies*, vol. 30, pp. 511–12.

Wilson, D.C. (1992) *A Strategy of Change: Concepts and controversies in the management of change*. Routledge: London.

Wilson, L. (2000) 'Better methods, better results', *Occupational Health and Safety*, vol. 69(6), pp. 107–10.

Winefield, A.H. (1995) 'Unemployment: Its psychological costs' in Cooper, C.L. and Robertson, I.T. (eds) *International Review of Industrial and Organizational Psychology*, vol. 10, pp. 169–211. Chichester: Wiley.

Witcher, B. (1993) *The Adoption of Total Quality Management in Scotland*. Durham: Durham University Business School.

Wong, C.S., Hui, C. and Law, K.S. (1998) 'A longitudinal study of the job perception – job satisfaction relationship: A test of the three alternative specifications', *Journal of Occupational and Organizational Psychology*, 71(2), pp. 127–46.

Wood, W. (2000) 'Attitude change: Persuasion and social influence', *Annual Review of Psychology*, vol. 51, pp. 539–570.

Wood, W. and Kallgren, C.A. (1988) 'Communicator attributes and persuasion: Recipients' access to attitude-relevant information in memory', *Personality and Social Psychology Bulletin*, vol. 14, pp. 172–82.

Wood, W., Lundgren, S., Ouellette, J.A., Busceme, S. and Blackstone, T. (1994) 'Minority influence: A meta-analytic review of social influence processes', *Psychological Bulletin*, vol. 115, pp. 323–45.

Woodruffe, C. (1993) *Assessment Centres: Identifying and Developing Competence*, 2nd edition, London: Institute of Personnel and Development.

Wooford, J.C., Goodwin, V.L. and Premack, S. (1992) 'Meta-analysis of the antecedents of personal goal level and of the antecedents and consequences of goals commitment', *Journal of Management*, vol. 18, pp. 595–615.

Wooten, K.C. and White, L.P. (1999) 'Linking OD's philosophy with justice theory: Postmodern implications', *Journal of Organizational Change Management*, vol. 12, pp. 7–20.

Wright, P., Ferris, S.P., Hiller, J.S. and Kroll, M. (1995) 'Competitiveness through management of diversity: Effects on stock price evaluation', *Academy of Management Journal*, vol. 38(1), pp. 272–87.

Wright, P.M. and Dyer, L. (2001) *People in the e-Business: New challenges, new solutions*. Ithaca, NJ: Center for Advanced Human Resource Studies, Cornell University.

Wright, P.M., O'Leary-Kelly, A.M., Cortina, J.M., Klein, H.J. and Hollenbeck, J. (1994) 'On the meaning and measurement of goal commitment', *Journal of Applied Psychology*, vol. 79, pp. 795–803.

Wright, T.A. and Staw, B.M. (1999) 'Affect and favourable work outcomes: Two longitudinal tests of the happy-productive worker thesis', *Journal of Organizational Behavior*, vol. 20, pp. 1–23.

Yearta, S.K., Maithis, S. and Briner, R.B. (1995) 'An exploratory study of goal-setting in theory and practice: A motivational technique that works?', *Journal of Occupational and Organizational Psychology*, vol. 68, pp. 237–52.

Yost, E.B. and Corbishley, M.A. (1987) *Career Counseling*. London: Jossey-Bass.

Young, K. and Cooper, C.L. (1995) 'Occupational stress in the ambulance service: A diagnostic study', *Journal of Managerial Psychology*, vol. 10(3), pp. 29–36.

Yukl, G.A. (2001) *Leadership in Organizations*, 5th edition. Englewood Cliffs, NJ: Prentice Hall.

Zairi, M., Letza, S. and Oakland, J. (1994) 'Does TQM impact on bottom line results?', *TQM Magazine*, vol. 6(1), pp. 38–43.

Zeidner, M. and Endler, N.S. (1996) *Handbook of Coping: Theory, research, applications*. Oxford: John Wiley.

Zohar, D. and Fussfeld, N.A. (1981) 'A systems approach to organizational behaviour modification: Theoretical considerations and empirical evidence', *International Review of Applied Psychology*, vol. 30, pp. 491–505.

INDEX

Figures in **bold** indicate glossary entries